Crosswind Success Series:
CAPM® Exam Bootcamp Manual

Crosswind
Learning

www.crosswindpm.com

The link for your exam simulation application and supporting files is located at:
http://learn.crosswindpm.com

The following activation code can be used in the registration required to access the Exam Simulation Application and other Crosswind Online Content.

BCM60CAP12XHBY9U8E

If you purchased a copy of this book that didn't have an activation code, email your order information to info@crosswindpm.com

For technical support email info@crosswindpm.com and include the book name, version (**CAPM® Exam Bootcamp Manual v6.0**), activation code, and problem you are encountering.

Copyright Page

Crosswind Success Series: CAPM® Exam Bootcamp Manual

Tony Johnson. – v.6.0

Second printing
p.cm.
ISBN Thirteen Digit: 978-1-61908-162-8

Johnson, Tony 2. CAPM 3. CAPM Certification 4. Project Management I. Title

Thank you for choosing this book.

We hope your experience with it is as satisfying for you as it was for us to create.

-- Team Crosswind

Disclaimer

Every attempt has been made by the publisher and author to ensure that this book provides information that is accurate and can serve as a basis for the reader to pass the Certified Associate in Project Management (CAPM)® Examination. The publisher and author, however, accept no legal responsibility for the content therein. The opinions of the author in this book do not necessarily reflect that of the Project Management Institute, Inc.

Both the publisher and author of this book warn readers to use not just this book, but also the Project Management Institute, *A Guide to the Project Management Body of Knowledge, (PMBOK® Guide) - Sixth Edition*, Project Management Institute, Inc., 2017, in their attempts to pass the CAPM® Exam to become certified. The publisher and the author also acknowledge that the purchase of this book does not guarantee that the reader will pass the exam. Neither the author nor the publisher will be held liable for individuals who do not heed this warning.

This publication contains portions of material from the Project Management Institute, *A Guide to the Project Management Body of Knowledge, (PMBOK® Guide) - Sixth Edition*, Project Management Institute, Inc., 2017. This publication has been developed and reproduced with the permission of the Project Management Institute, Inc. Unauthorized reproduction of this material is strictly prohibited. This material is the copyrighted material of, and owned by, Crosswind Project Management, Inc., copyright 2018.

If you detect what you believe is an error in this book, please go to learn.crosswindpm.com for any errata that have been discovered. If you don't see the item under the question listed, email the page, section number, and details to info@crosswindpm.com.

Trademarks and Copyrights

Throughout this manual, we reference and recognize the following trademarks, service marks, and copyrights of the Project Management Institute, Inc.:

> Certified Associate in Project Management (CAPM)®
> Project Management Professional (PMP)®
> Project Management Institute, Inc. (PMI)®
> *PMBOK® Guide*
> *Standard for Program Management*
> *Standard for Portfolio Management*

Conventions

Throughout this manual, we post values and indicate special notations. Here are some of the conventions used in this manual: all monetary values are in U.S. dollars unless otherwise noted; and special notes and points are indicated in bold text.

Supplemental and Errata Updates

Visit learn.crosswindpm.com for updates on supplements and errata. This material includes content that supports the book with the most current information to prepare for the exam. Errata (errors) updates are also included. If you feel you have discovered an errata item not listed in the updates, please forward the information to info@crosswindpm.com.

Dedication

Our internal name for this product line is Mariana, after the Mariana Trench. The Mariana Trench is the deepest place on the planet, deeper than Mount Everest is tall. The name was selected because creating this product line would require me to look deep inside myself to create what I knew I had in me.

There were five people that were very important to the release of this book and are the past, present, and future of Crosswind. This book is dedicated to them.

Denise: You are the sun and the moon. You are not just our GM, but also our internal compass. We've worked together for more than a decade and have experienced the good, bad, sick, pretty, ugly, and more in the trenches of Crosswind. Your loyalty to me, to Crosswind, to our cause, and to those that put their trust in us, is unquestioned. I cannot thank you enough for being here with me through this and for being willing to experience the future at Crosswind as well. The Cowboys had Troy Aikman; Crosswind has you. Thank you from the deepest part of me for helping build the company I have envisioned since I was a kid in Kansas.

Lynda: We have averaged five books a year since we started together. You have made me better as a result of our time in the trenches. As the pressure mounts, we just push through and get it done. In the last few years your guidance and influence in business decisions has been immensely appreciated and respected as well. As I see your grandchildren grow up, I see the influence you have had and it reminds me that the world would be a far better place with more people like you in it. Thank you for everything.

Nicole Rose (Nikki): My first born, my heart, my little girl, my young lady. Our first book went to press two days before you were born. Since then it's been a crazy ride. What 13-year-old has a website with a shopping cart? What 13-year-old can quote all project management knowledge areas since she was four years old? What 13-year-old has known Cost of Goods Sold since she was eight years old? You have. Heart is hard to measure, but you have more of it than anyone I know. When you dedicate yourself to something, you not only do it, you own it. The next time we update this product line, you will be old enough to be involved. I so look forward to working with you when that time comes.

Jacob Duane (Jake): You are my hero. I see how you carry yourself; how you keep your sister in line and eliminate scope creep; and how you help me around the office running network cabling, hanging art, printing, and doing inventory, the majority of that since you were six. What nine-year-old boy can do communication channels and a forward backward pass on a dry erase board in front of a class? You can. Your heart is huge and caring. The more I see how you are growing up, the more I want to be like you. Like your sister, the next time we update this book you will be old enough to be involved. I know that working with you and your sister will be immeasurably rewarding.

Duane Johnson: You are not only my dad; you are my rock. Dad, thank you for everything. At the end of the day, my definition of integrity, responsibility, wisdom, and love is based on how you live your life. As I raise my kids, I ask myself WWDD: What would dad do? Thank you for setting the standard so high. I am better because of it and the kids will be as well.

Thanks

Team is a very important piece of the Crosswind culture. From our alumni network of evangelists to the Crosswind staff, to the team of people who contributed in various ways to what you are about to read in this book.

The following played a key role with their contributions:

Sergio, Analaura, Ramya, Bill - Thank you for helping build the foundation to help us become the success we are today.

Denise, Duane, Kendra, Kevin, Jessica, Joanna, Adrian, Greg, Lynda, and Bri - Thanks for focusing on product development and keeping things running each day as well. We aren't the same without you.

Ernie, Jim, Todd, Bob, Andy, Bill, and our extended review team - Thanks for your analysis, eyes, voices, and time.

Brian Salk - Thank you.

Tom - Your passion and growth of project management to make PM and our book all they can be.

The Houston PMI® Chapter - Your support is very appreciated!

The Dallas and Fort Worth PMI® Chapters - This is where it all started years ago and continues today!

The Crosswind Evangelist (Alumni) Network - For your never-ending desire to learn and keep me moving!

Gail and Stonebriar Lego - Thanks for keeping the brain sharp.

About Crosswind Learning

Crosswind started in 1998 to serve the needs of various technical customers in the Dallas/Fort Worth, Texas area. As the company evolved, it stepped into the education and training arena in the local junior colleges and began to grow its curriculum while helping make a difference in people's lives and careers.

As the dot com and telecom economies were at their peak, Crosswind was offering project management certification training to companies in the Dallas area, as well as the southern United States. All the while, the Crosswind Exam Success Series was being developed and fine-tuned.

Today, Crosswind Learning's product line contains some of the most integrated and effective products on the market for project management certification. They are currently used in numerous industries and in various universities, colleges, and project management chapters in at least 72 countries.

	Our Crosswind online applications allow you to study for your exams or maintain your credentials anywhere you have a modern Web browser and an Internet or Wi-Fi connection. Use your Mac, PC, Tablet, or other device to do exam prep or career development. For more information see our website at www.crosswindpm.com.
	Crosswind Success Series: Certification Study System includes a Bootcamp Manual, three Crosswind online audio products, a Crosswind online exam simulation application with over 5,000 questions and 100 exams, online Crosswind flashcards, seven placemats, four quick reference guides, a Tip of the Day subscription, and a carrying case.
	Visit www.crosswindpm.com to see the new products we have available for your project management exam needs including online Crosswind applications, PMTV™ online training, and online testing. It also includes information about pricing for chapters, colleges, and other quantity purchasers.
	Our Crosswind Success Series: Bootcamp Manual is the foundation of our product line. This book was designed to allow the future project manager to create a solid foundation for understanding the processes and to prepare for certification success. The book includes functional exercises, and over 330 test questions (additional questions are online). It covers all ten knowledge areas, five process groups, Framework, exam preparation strategies, "must-knows," and a link to a PDF file with step-by-step online application instructions for the exam.

	Our online Crosswind Success Series: Exam Simulation Application is unparalleled because it provides the ability to slice the questions by knowledge area or process group, to perform integrated testing with all the questions together, and to review your test output by knowledge area or process group. With over 5,000 questions, this application is the perfect complement to the Crosswind Success Series: Bootcamp Manual.
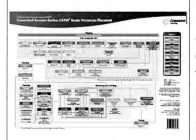	The Crosswind Success Series: Processes Placemat, Mind Maps Placemats, and Swim Lanes Placemat provide a detailed perspective of the information needed for the exam. Processes, inputs, tools & techniques outputs, plans, formulas, mind maps, process interaction, and other key pieces are all included. Seven double-sided, laminated 11" x 17" posters provide the key to exam success and a long-term quick reference for your use after you are certified. Also available as an online Crosswind application.
	The Crosswind Success Series PM Talks: An Audio Guide to the CAPM® Exam is ideal for that late night listening or carpool study time. Designed to complement the rest of the Crosswind Success Series, this audio presentation helps reinforce your development. Each product contains at least two hours of professionally recorded information that will help prepare you for the exam. Also available as an online Crosswind application.
	The Crosswind Success Series: Flashcards are a key tool for studying the 650+ terms, definitions, key inputs, key tools & techniques, key outputs, formulas, and variables. They help reinforce the learning and understanding of all 49 processes and their inputs, tools & techniques, and outputs. Also available as an online Crosswind application.

Please let us know about your success in achieving the Certified Associate in Project Management (CAPM)® certification. Email info@crosswindpm.com to tell us what we did that worked for you. Your feedback helps us evolve our products to make them some of the most advanced, cutting edge products on the market today.

PMTV™ Free Online Tip of the Day

PMTV's free online Tip of the Day, which provides review for the exam, is available. Visit www.crosswindpm.com to sign up for automated Tip of the Day updates. You will receive an email each day with an exam style question, term and definition, and the question, correct answer and explanation from the previous day's question.

About the Author

Tony Johnson, MBA, CCBA, CBAP, Project +, CSM, CSPO, CSP, PMI-SP, PMI-RMP, PMI-ACP, PMI-PBA, CAPM, PMP, PgMP, PfMP, has over 20 years experience as a project manager in industries such as telecommunications, finance, consulting, hardware and software development, education, and manufacturing.

He has multiple years of experience in training and curriculum development plus training in areas such as technology, manufacturing, Internet, electronic commerce, and project management. He has delivered over 9,000 hours of project management training in alignment with Project Management Institute, Inc. Standards.

He has contributed toward the three most recent releases for each of the PMI® Standards: specifically, the Project Management Institute, *A Guide to the Project Management Body of Knowledge, (PMBOK® Guide)* - Sixth Edition, Project Management Institute, Inc., 2017; the *Standard for Program Management;* and the *Standard for Portfolio Management.*

Former students come from companies such as:

AAFES	Accenture	ACS	Adea Solutions	Auto One
American Airlines	Anderson Consulting	AT&T	Avaya	Bank of America
Bank One	Bearing Point	Carreker	Ciber	Cisco
Cingular	Citi	CompUSA	Computer Associates	Crossmark
PMI® Dallas Chapter	Decision Consultants, Inc.	Department of Defense	Electronic Data Systems (EDS)	Excel Communications
Exe	Fujitsu	Harley-Davidson	Hewlett-Packard	Honeywell
IBM	Immedient	Intellimark-IT	Interstate Battery	JCPenney
Lucent	Genuity	KPMG	Macromedia	Match.com
MCI	Motorola	Nortel	Oracle	Perot Systems
PWC	Sabre	Southwest Airlines	Southwestern Bell Corporation	Technisource
Texas Instruments	Travelocity	Tyco	U.S. Air Force	Vartec
Verizon	U.S. Army	U.S. Navy	Walmart	Worldcom

Mr. Johnson is also an award-winning member of the Dallas PM chapter (one of the world's largest chapters with over 5,000 members, 67% of whom are certified), as well as a past member of the chapter's education committee. He has also been a key presenter at the chapter's meetings and exam prep forum.

Mr. Johnson has a bachelor's degree in Business Administration and Finance from Dallas Baptist University and an MBA in Operations and Strategic Management from Dallas Baptist University. He has taught at Southern Methodist University (SMU), as well as various colleges and universities in Dallas, Texas. He is the founder of Crosswind Learning (www.crosswindpm.com).

PMI, CAPM, and PMBOK are registered marks of the Project Management Institute, Inc.

viii © 2008-2018 Crosswind Learning, www.crosswindpm.com

Table of Contents

PMI, CAPM, and PMBOK are registered marks of the Project Management Institute, Inc.

x   © 2008-2018 Crosswind Learning, www.crosswindpm.com

PMI, CAPM, and PMBOK are registered marks of the Project Management Institute, Inc.

xii   © 2008-2018 Crosswind Learning, www.crosswindpm.com

Chapter 1

How to Attain Exam Success via the Crosswind Bootcamp Manual

This book is for anyone seeking an unconventional, yet solid, presentation of project management best practices, a book that maximizes learning and retention and leads to success in achieving the certification. Its driving objective is to provide content that benefits readers the most as they study for the certification.

Years ago, when I studied for my exam, I could not find many books on the topic. I didn't know many credential holders to help me measure how prepared I was after months of study. I remember studying, not feeling I knew enough, and continuing to study. I just couldn't find a product that provided a road map for success: one that would clarify when I was ready and contain supporting detail to help reinforce the material for the exam.

I also found that the preparation books that were available were not structured consistently and logically. They contained information not addressed by Project Management Institute, Inc. standards and did not include enough detail to help me truly understand why that information was pertinent.

I wanted a book that contained all the information I needed to know for the exam and I wanted that book to be organized logically and structured consistently. I wanted to be able to easily locate relevant terminology and formulas in the book. I also wanted to know everything I could about the questions that would be on the exam: the types of questions, how to decode situational questions, and, if the book contained practice tests, an explanation regarding the answers. That book is now available.

The *Crosswind Success Series: CAPM® Exam Bootcamp Manual* is one of the most comprehensive and detailed products on the market today for exam success.

This chapter provides directions for using the bootcamp manual to optimize your success with the exam.

1.1.   Overhead and Exam Environment

Sections 2.7, 2.8, and 2.9 describe the exam environment and explain how to prepare for the exam. Although this may sound elementary, if you don't know to prepare for a particular content area or if you show up at a test center without the required material, it will not seem so elementary after all.

1.2.   Questions

Sections 2.10 and 2.11 provide an overview of question characteristics and components. They also detail the seven question formats with a description and example of each format.

Question Format	Description
Question Characteristics and Components	Explains how to ignore disinformation (distracters) and focus on the actual point of the questions
Question Formats	Breaks down the seven basic formats of exam questions
Question Breakdown and Translation	Explains how to translate situational questions and break them down to their basic elements
	People often encounter obscure or unfamiliar topics on the exam. This manual explains how to eliminate distracters and clutter in the questions.

1.3.   Problem Solving for Situational Questions

Section 2.12 offers suggestions for addressing the challenging situational questions. There are certain rules that apply across all knowledge areas, which can be found in this manual.

1.4.   Methodology and Position Descriptions

Section 3.4 details the basic environment for the methodology by describing the process groups: initiation, planning, executing, monitoring and controlling, and closing. It also addresses various project related positions (e.g. project manager, stakeholder, and sponsor) and their roles during the project.

1.5.   Chapters

Chapters 3 through 14 address Framework, the ten knowledge areas, and Professional and Social Responsibility. In addition to sections that address chapter specific topics, most of these chapters contain the following:

Introduction	The Introduction contains an overview of chapter contents.
Tailoring and Trends	The Tailoring section presents information relevant to project tailoring for the specific knowledge area. The Trend section presents information relevant to current trends for the specific knowledge area.
Agile/Adaptive Environment	The Agile/Adaptive Environment section addresses the specific knowledge area in terms of an Agile or adaptive environment.

PMI, CAPM, and PMBOK are registered marks of the Project Management Institute, Inc.

2

© 2008-2018 Crosswind Learning, www.crosswindpm.com

Crosswind "Must Knows"	The Crosswind "Must Knows" section delineates information pertinent to the exam and can be used as a checklist.
	The check column ☑ is used to indicate a knowledge and understanding of the Must Know item.
	-- indicates an important point!
	There is plenty of white space for notes relevant to the "Must Know" or for other content in the book.
Data Flow Diagrams	Data Flow Diagrams precede process details and contain inputs, tools & techniques, and outputs for the knowledge area. The diagrams visually represent the process at a high-level and make excellent study aids.
Process Tables	The exam addresses 49 project management processes. For each knowledge area, the relevant processes are addressed in tables that summarize the process concept (process name and process group) and lists **key** inputs, tools & techniques, and outputs. The table describes the inputs needed to perform the process, the tools & techniques used to create the process outputs, and the expected outputs of the process.

Name (Process Group)		
Key Inputs	Project Scope Statement	The **project scope statement** defines the scope of the project.
Key Tools & Techniques	Decomposition	Scope decomposition breaks down project work into manageable pieces.
Key Outputs	Scope Baseline	The scope baseline provides details of the planned scope for the project.

	The Project Management Institute, *A Guide to the Project Management Body of Knowledge, (PMBOK® Guide)* - Sixth Edition, Project Management Institute, Inc., 2017 has over 1,000 inputs, tools & techniques, and outputs. The **key** inputs, tools & techniques, and outputs are described in the process tables.
Situational Question and Real World Application	The Situational Question and Real World Application elements: address problems that might arise if the process is ignored or only partially implemented, indicate the basis for a situational question, and/or indicate an application of the process in day-to-day project management.
Formulas and Variables	The Formulas and Variables section contains any formulas pertinent to the knowledge area and includes any variables that are part of the formulas. If a variable does not have to be calculated for the exam questions (i.e., the value is listed in the exam questions), the variable value is listed in the pertinent formula.
	If there are no formulas for the chapter, that fact is noted in this section.

Terminology	The terminology section lists terms you may be expected to know for the exam. Even though some terms may differ from those used at a specific organization, it is important to be familiar with the terms and their definitions as they appear in this section. Each term is listed in the most relevant chapter so that it only appears in one terminology list. A term may be included in the terminology section even though it does not appear elsewhere in the chapter.
Mind Maps	Each Mind Map is a powerful graphical tool for visualizing knowledge area processes. To use it effectively, start at the top, left-hand corner of the map proceeding downward, then move to the top, right-hand corner of the map proceeding downward. For each process, begin with the inputs, move to the tools & techniques, and end with the outputs. To access the mind maps, go to **http://learn.crosswindpm.com.**
Quick Test	The Quick Test section contains ten questions that require answers in a variety of formats other than multiple choice. Formats could be: short essay/list, fill in the blank, or circle the correct answer. To access the quick tests, go to **http://learn.crosswindpm.com.**
Other Exercises	The Other Exercises sections, included in select chapters, contain exercises that reinforce chapter-related calculations and concepts.
Chapter Practice Test	The Chapter Practice Test section contains 30 questions designed to replicate the question format used in the exam. The questions are based on information, terminology, calculations, concepts, and scenarios related to specific chapters and are designed to test project management knowledge and question format expertise. They are drawn from the Crosswind database, which contains over 5,000 questions.
Other Exercises Answers	Each Other Exercises Answers section contains each question from the Other Exercises section followed by its correct answer. For answers involving calculations, calculation details are included.
Chapter Practice Test Answers	The Chapter Practice Test Answers section contains each question from the chapter practice test followed by its correct answer, an explanation, and a reference. The explanation addresses the correct answer and the incorrect answers. The reference contains the relevant section numbers from the bootcamp manual and, if applicable, the Project Management Institute, *A Guide to the Project Management Body of Knowledge, (PMBOK® Guide) - Sixth Edition*, Project Management Institute, Inc., 2017. In addition to chapter content, this section is an excellent learning tool. It can be used to determine any topics that require additional study, including familiarity with the correct approach to interpreting specific question formats.

1.6. Pre and Post Test (Downloadable PDF)

A PDF of the 150-question integrated test that attempts to emulate the actual exam can be downloaded from **http://learn.crosswindpm.com**. It covers all ten knowledge areas, plus Framework and Professional and Social Responsibility. To emulate the exam, the questions are randomized by knowledge area instead of being organized by chapter.

1.7. Crosswind Online Content (Exam Simulation Application)

The bootcamp manual includes access to Crosswind online content, which contains a 150-question exam simulation application and ITTO exams.

Other support files, available for download include:

- Matching Processes in PDF format
- Excel workbook to breakdown your experience for the exam application
- Screen shots for the exam application in PDF format
- Mind Maps in PDF format
- Quick Tests in PDF format
- Network Diagram Exercises in PDF format
- Earned Value Exercises in PDF format
- Sample audio product in MP3 format
- Many other helpful tools

To maximize the benefit of the application, Crosswind suggests that you use **the activation code found in the first page of this manual and register immediately.**

If you have issues with activation, please email info@crosswindpm.com with your activation code and request activation support. Be certain to include your personal email address in the request. We suggest that you install the free update to the most current version of Internet Explorer or use the most current version of another popular, modern browser such as Firefox or Chrome.

If you do not receive an activation code, email info@crosswindpm.com. You may be asked to validate your manual purchase before a copy is delivered via email.

If you wish to purchase additional questions, visit www.crosswindpm.com and order Crosswind's online testing products. These products include over 5,000 questions, which can be sorted by knowledge area, process group, inputs/tools & techniques/outputs, terminology, and calculations.

Using for a Study Group or Training Company

If you are using our products for your study group or training company, thank you for choosing us. Depending on your experience level, schedule, and other factors, there are a variety of approaches you might utilize, but we suggest the following general principles:

- Use the table of contents as a road map for your studies
- After covering materials, be sure to review questions in the chapter
- When reviewing questions, focus on the reason you consider an answer to be the best answer and why the other answers aren't; such an approach doubly reinforces the material
- Follow the exercises in the book and online (including network diagram and earned value exercises)
- If you don't feel you understand a particular topic, try teaching it to your group; you'll be surprised at what you learn.

Slide Support

If you are a trainer, or represent a company, college, chapter of the Project Management Institute, Inc., or other organization using our products, we welcome you to contact us about group pricing and/or support material (including over 2,000 slides to help with your courses).

Trainer Registration

Crosswind frequently updates its training material. If you are a trainer, you are welcome to send an email to info@crosswindpm.com. Be certain to include your name, contact information, the Crosswind products you use, and where you use them. This provides Crosswind the details it needs to notify you of any new versions, errata, or information you can utilize to maximize your investment in Crosswind products.

Trainer Quick Reference (Downloadable)

If you are a trainer, please download the Trainer Quick Reference from http://learn.crosswindpm.com. This file provides information that can help minimize your ramp-up time as you use the Crosswind manual for training.

LinkedIn, Facebook, and Twitter

Please contact us using LinkedIn, Facebook, and/or Twitter for updates of our products, services, and other information. Look for Tony Johnson, PMP, or Crosswind Learning/Crosswind PM.

YouTube (PM Exam Guru)

The Crosswind YouTube channel has a variety of helpful videos available to aid in exam application assistance, exam readiness, and project management skill evolution. Most of the videos are short, information packed, and address common questions about popular exam and project management subjects. Be certain to visit often, because it's frequently updated!

PMI, CAPM, and PMBOK are registered marks of the Project Management Institute, Inc.

6   © 2008-2018 Crosswind Learning, www.crosswindpm.com

Chapter 2

Exam Registration and Environment

2.1. Registration Overview

To register for and take the exam, the applicant must meet certain criteria. These criteria take into account the applicant's experience, formal education, and hours of training. This chapter explains the criteria and attempts to eliminate any confusion about the process.

Because this book has been sent to press early in the exam transition stage, the Project Management Institute, Inc. could potentially update criteria. The Crosswind website at www.crosswindpm.com contains any updates to the criteria.

2.2. Qualifying for the Exam

The following two tables show the exam qualifications for the Certified Associate in Project Management (CAPM)® Certification or Project Management Professional (PMP)® Certification. A third table contains the description of each field.

Exam Qualifications for the Certified Associate in Project Management (CAPM)® Certification

Minimum Education and Hours of Experience Requirement	OR	Project Management Training Hours
High School Diploma (or equivalent) plus 1,500 hours of work on a project	OR	23 hours of formal project management training

Exam Qualifications for the Project Management Professional (PMP)® Certification

Minimum Education Requirement	Hours of Experience Needed	Required Experience Timeframe	Project Management Training Hours
Bachelor's Degree (or equivalent)	4,500 hours	3 years within the last 8 of submitting application	35 hours
High School Diploma (or equivalent)	7,500 hours	5 years within the last 8 of submitting application	35 hours

Certification Type	Certified Associate in Project Management (CAPM)® or Project Management Professional (PMP)®
Minimum Education Requirements	A completed bachelor's degree or high school diploma (or equivalent) *Those who attended college or university, but did not obtain a bachelor's degree, should follow the criteria associated with a high school diploma.*
Hours of Experience Needed	Minimum hours of project-related experience required to qualify for the exam *Note that hours spent working on multiple projects at one time may all be counted provided those hours were spent directing/leading project related tasks.*

PMI, CAPM, and PMBOK are registered marks of the Project Management Institute, Inc.

Certification Type	Certified Associate in Project Management (CAPM)® or Project Management Professional (PMP)®
Time Frame for the Experience	The years of project-related experience, within the last number of years specified, required to qualify for the exam *For example, four years of project-related experience within the last eight years meets the requirements for a bachelor's degree applicant, assuming the other exam qualifications are met.*
Project Management Training Hours	The actual hours of project management training needed to qualify *Successfully completing the Crosswind Exam Review bootcamp course, or other acceptable project management training, completes this requirement.*

2.3.   What Type of Experience Counts?

For those who have been involved in project management for a number of years, but haven't held the title of project manager the entire time, and those who have worked in project management, but have performed other functions (e.g. collecting requirements and validating scope), the type of experience that counts toward fulfilling the requirements may be of concern.

2.3.1.   How Much Does My Experience Count Toward Hours Needed?

The type of experience that counts toward fulfilling the requirements is dependent, not on a specific job title, but on the type of work done.

Activities in which the applicant has participated are the revised standard for the exam. If the applicant determined what needed to be done in a specific area of the project or helped lead a group of people to get the work done, that experience should be sufficient. Examples are determining the activities necessary to install and test system hardware in seven new satellite offices or leading the team in the creation of the work breakdown structure (WBS).

2.3.2.   Exam Application Experience and Deliverables

Applicants frequently ask for clarification about the exam application experience and description of deliverables.

Experience Verification

Experience verification is often misunderstood. Per the Project Management Institute, Inc., the applicant is notified instantly, or when scheduling the exam, if a prequalification application audit will be conducted. An applicant must submit contact information for those who can validate the experience in the audit form, typically the applicant's manager at that time. This enables the applicant to inform contacts that they must complete the documentation required in the event a prequalification audit is conducted. If the contact information is not available, the applicant should evaluate the PDF available at **http://learn.crosswindpm.com** and, if that document does not address the situation, the applicant should contact the Project Management Institute, Inc. directly.

PMI, CAPM, and PMBOK are registered marks of the Project Management Institute, Inc.

8   © 2008-2018 Crosswind Learning, www.crosswindpm.com

Description of Deliverables

The description of deliverables refers to project management deliverables, not necessarily to project deliverables. Items such as participating in the creation of the WBS or the Validate Scope effort are the type of deliverables that should be listed. A project deliverable, such as the coding that the software project accomplished or the electrical work for a shopping mall project, is typically not considered, but identifying the scope for the deliverables is.

2.4. Certified Associate in Project Management (CAPM)® Certification Experience Hours Spreadsheet (Downloadable)

It is recommended that applicants map out experience hours before filling in the experience section of the Certified Associate in Project Management (CAPM)® application.

The spreadsheet available for download at **http://learn.crosswindpm.com** can be used to track the requisite hours of experience in the format required by the Project Management Institute, Inc. The spreadsheet can accommodate as many as seven projects. In addition to documenting project hours, the spreadsheet is used to detail project-related contact information. That information will be useful if a prequalification application audit is conducted.

2.5. Certified Associate in Project Management (CAPM)® Online Application (Downloadable)

The Project Management Institute, Inc. has a revised application process for the exam. The step-by-step process can be downloaded from **http://learn.crosswindpm.com**. The current link for the exam application is also available at **http://learn.crosswindpm.com**.

Using the online application, rather than the paper application, can significantly reduce the time it takes to complete the Certified Associate in Project Management (CAPM)® application. Because the online registration does not require completion of the application in a single session, a partially completed application can be saved and accessed later.

The Project Management Institute, Inc. offers exam discounts to its members. To take advantage of the discount, the applicant must become a member before starting the application. Note that becoming a member of the Project Management Institute, Inc. (or any local chapter) is not required in order to take the exam.

2.6. Audit

As of this printing, the Project Management Institute, Inc. randomly audits 10% of online applications. There are **no triggers** for these audits; they are **truly random**. An applicant whose application is selected for audit will be notified instantly, or when scheduling an exam, by the Project Management Institute, Inc. The notification will contain hyperlinks for the experience validation documents that must be completed for the audit. The applicant must print those documents and present them to the individuals who can validate the work experience. These individuals are to complete the forms, seal them, and sign the seal as instructed. The applicant must also submit photocopies of any requested training certificates, diplomas, and/or transcripts. The Project Management Institute, Inc. typically completes its review in seven to ten days from receipt of the requested documentation.

2.7. Environment Overview

The best plan for exam success is to know the contents of this manual thoroughly and to be familiar with the environment in which the test will be given.

Crosswind devotes attention to the exam environment before the exam so that the environment does not become a distraction. The focus of the candidate should be entirely on the exam.

2.8. Preparing for Exam Day

There are a number of items the candidate must take to the exam center and a number of items Crosswind recommends.

Studying and Scheduling	**The exam should be scheduled for a time when the candidate is most alert.** The exam should not be scheduled following a day's work, unless there are no alternatives. The candidate should experience a good night's sleep the night before the exam and eat well a few days before the exam. The candidate should thoroughly review material pertinent to the exam the day before. This review can uncover any final subject areas that need last minute study. The candidate should also be able to recreate the tables, charts, and other items recommended for memorization by Crosswind: these are "musts" for exam success.
Practicing	Practice tests help the candidate become familiar with the exam environment and the question layout and timing. The candidate should focus on completion speed. On average, the candidate can take 72 seconds to answer each question. Setting a better pace than average allows the candidate to review selected questions, which can provide a distinct advantage. The tutorial can help the candidate better understand the options.
What to Take: Required	The following are required: • The eligibility letter with the authorization number on it • A photo ID and two other forms of ID (credit card, etc.) The names on the IDs and the letter must be identical. For example, Anthony on an ID and Tony on the letter could cause problems.
What to Take: Recommended	The candidate should dress in layers to accommodate temperature fluctuations in the test room. A t-shirt with a sweater is a good combination. The candidate may take food and drink to the test center, but they must be left in the provided locker since food and drink are not allowed in the test room. The candidate may take only the locker key and the provided pencils and paper into the test room.

2.9. About the Exam

Because this book has been sent to press early in the exam transition stage, the Project Management Institute, Inc. could potentially update alignment information. To ensure you are aware of updated alignment information, visit our website at www.crosswindpm.com.

2.9.1. Exam Questions

The exam consists of 150 questions, all of which should be answered. Only 135 are scored. The remaining questions, which are inserted randomly in the exam, are considered pre-test questions and are used to test the validity of future questions.

2.9.2. In and Out of Scope

Too many project managers think that 12 to 20 years of experience and reading the Project Management Institute, *A Guide to the Project Management Body of Knowledge, (PMBOK® Guide)* - Sixth Edition, Project Management Institute, Inc., 2017 a few times will provide the information they need to pass the exam. That is rarely (if ever) the case.

The exam tests the candidate's understanding of the *PMBOK® Guide* and the processes of the Project Management Institute, Inc. across all knowledge areas: both the processes used in the candidate's organization and the manner in which they are used are irrelevant to the test. Knowledge of the processes is particularly important when answering situational questions.

The exam also test's the candidate's knowledge of the terminology and any formulas listed in the knowledge area chapters plus Framework and Professional and Social Responsibility. Again, this knowledge is important when answering situational questions.

The exam tests the candidate's familiarity with the documents (e.g. the project charter, WBS, and schedule) advocated by the Project Management Institute, Inc. No matter how the documents are used by the candidate's organization, the exam questions must be interpreted and answered in alignment with the usage detailed by the Project Management Institute, Inc.

2.9.3. Exam "Theory Pills"™

A number of basic assumptions factor into how the exam addresses project management as opposed to how it is performed at the candidate's organization. To address this, Crosswind has prepared the following "Theory Pills" which present important information regarding the exam question.

- Engaging stakeholders and managing their expectations EARLY and OFTEN is of primary importance
- Historical information about existing projects can contribute to the corporate knowledge base, future estimating, and organizational process assets
- It is assumed that documentation exists to detail the project so that it could be recreated if necessary
- Meetings should be conducted in accordance with the meeting rules listed in this manual
- Risk must be considered when estimating time and cost
- Changes are subject to an official change control process with appropriate parties reviewing change requests for impact and approval
- The Project Management Institute, *A Guide to the Project Management Body of Knowledge, (PMBOK® Guide)* - Sixth Edition, Project Management Institute, Inc., 2017 processes must be used as they are described by the Project Management Institute, Inc. in the *PMBOK® Guide;* this manual describes the processes similarly
- The value of the WBS cannot be overemphasized; all planning is based on the WBS

- The project manager is responsible for delivering the project results within scope, on schedule, and on budget
- If one parameter of the triple constraint is modified, the others will likely change (e.g., if a schedule must be shortened, consideration should be given to revising or updating the project scope if the customer/sponsor decides to do so)
- The approach that the Project Management Institute, Inc. generally calls for requires a great deal of planning before actual execution of work; that is the only approach that should be considered when answering exam questions
- Unless otherwise stated, the exam questions assume that the organization performing the work is fairly mature regarding the application of project management methodology, processes, etc.
- The work of the project is built from the project management plan, which is what the team follows to complete the work of the project
- Issues should be corrected as soon as possible; letting them linger is more expensive and time consuming
- Ideally, influential stakeholders should be defined before the start of the project to ensure that they can provide input to the project management plan
- Assumptions cannot be made that the project or work is complete because the team believes it is complete; the project or work is only complete when the customer/sponsor formally accepts the project
- Roles and responsibilities as defined in the Crosswind manual are to be used when answering exam questions, regardless of how they are defined within the candidate's organization
- Any "analysis" or "technique" is always considered a tool/technique (regarding ITTOs)
- Any "update" is always considered an output (regarding ITTOs)
- Because reality is not often addressed in the questions, time and money are no object; unless limitations are specifically addressed in the exam question, time and money should be provided by the customer or project sponsor.

2.9.4. Brain Dump List

The brain dump, important information written down at the start of the exam, is key to exam success. The candidate should practice writing the brain dump before the exam to ensure it can be completed in fifteen minutes or less.

Although some candidates feel that using a brain dump indicates a lack of preparation, the reality is that the brain dump is an excellent way to organize key information, terms, and/or formulas for quick reference during the test.

Every brain dump is personal, but Crosswind feels that the items listed in the **Quick Reference Guide available at www.learn.crosswindpm.com** and the following table are an ideal basis for the brain dump:

Content	Location
EV formulas including those in the Crosswind table: • Cost Performance Index (CPI) • Cost Variance (CV) • Schedule Performance Index (SPI) • Schedule Variance (SV) • Estimate at Completion (EAC) • Estimate to Complete (ETC) • Variance at Completion (VAC) • Earned Value (EV) • Planned Value (PV) • Budget at Completion (BAC) • To-complete Performance Index (TCPI)	Cost Chapter
Percentages for 1, 2, 3, and 6 Sigma	Quality Chapter
Present and Future Value Formulas	Cost Chapter
Cost Estimate Funnel	Cost Chapter
Forward and Backward Pass Formulas	Schedule Chapter
Slack Formulas	Schedule Chapter
Organizational Structure Characteristics	Framework Chapter
Risk Response Strategies	Risk Chapter
Types of Power for the Project Manager	Resource Chapter
Conflict Resolution Types	Resource Chapter
Levels of Maslow's Hierarchy of Needs	Resource Chapter
Point of Total Assumption Formula and Variables	Procurement Chapter
List of Management Plans and Change Control Systems	Various Chapters

2.9.5. Black and White vs. Gray

When some candidates start studying for this exam, they find themselves frustrated, especially if they come from a technical environment. They are used to ABSOLUTE (black and white) terminology: terms such as ALWAYS, NEVER, and COMPLETELY.

While the exam employs ABSOLUTE terminology, it often employs QUALIFIED (gray) terminology: terms such as GENERALLY, SOMETIMES, MAY, SHOULD, and COULD.

The candidate must be very sensitive to the use of absolute or qualified terminology in the exam questions, because using a qualified term in place of an absolute term can significantly change the meaning of a question.

2.9.6. "The Wall"

"The wall" is the point where it becomes more difficult to think clearly through the questions and material. Most candidates hit "the wall" at some point during the exam.

To minimize the impact of "the wall," Crosswind recommends that candidates set milestones by mentally dividing the exam into percentages. Completion of the first 50 questions represents an exam that is 33% complete. Completion of the first 100 questions represents an exam that is 66% complete. After that, completion of the exam is within reach. Crosswind also recommends referencing the brain dump.

2.9.7. Time Management

Time management is a key area many candidates fail to consider as carefully as they should. The exam questions must be answered and the marked questions reviewed in the allocated time frame (four hours), so it's very important for the candidate to consider the average time that can be spent answering each question and reviewing the marked questions. The practice exams in the manual are ideal for establishing and, later, improving the candidate's speed.

Crosswind suggests that the candidate spends:

- The first fifteen minutes (or less) writing the brain dump
- The next two and a half hours answering all of the questions, marking those requiring later review
- The remaining time reviewing the marked questions

It is very important that all of the questions are answered during the first pass in case time runs out before all of the marked questions can be reviewed.

2.9.8. Marking Questions

The exam provides the option to mark questions for later review. Studies show that the initial response to a question is usually the right answer. The candidate should keep that study in mind during the review.

Crosswind suggests that the candidate limits marked questions to those with answers in which the candidate is not confident and questions with calculations (double checking math is recommended if there is time). Crosswind recommends limiting marked questions to fifteen or less. Typically, Crosswind classroom students who perform well on the exam mark between ten and fifteen questions.

2.9.9. Scoring

As of January 2008, the Project Management Institute, Inc. adopted industry best practices by issuing exam results of pass or fail and, in the five sub-domains, results of proficient, mildly proficient, or lacking proficiency. Crosswind suggests that the candidate's score for the exam simulation should be in the 80%+ range in order to provide room for error during the actual exam.

2.9.10. Changing the Test Date

In 2012, the Project Management Institute, Inc. instituted a policy of charging a $70 fee for changing the test date, provided the change occurs within 30 calendar days of the scheduled date. If the change is due to an emergency, the candidate should contact the Project Management Institute, Inc. to request a fee waiver.

2.9.11. New Score Report

By the time this manual goes to print, a new score report for the exam should be available. The previous report simply offered Pass or Fail for the exam and proficient, moderate, or below proficient for the five exam domains. The new report is expected to provide more information, including instructions for the candidate to access specific details about exam performance and, in the case the exam was not passed, the specific information areas that require additional study.

2.9.12. Surprise! It's Not Always Necessary to Schedule an Exam

A test center manager explained that the Project Management Institute, Inc. is a walk-in client, which means that the candidate can take the exam at a test center without scheduling the exam. To do so, the center requires the candidate to provide written evidence of approval to take the exam issued by the Project Management Institute, Inc.

If the candidate provides evidence of approval and if the center has the capacity (open seats) and sufficient time for the candidate to take the exam, the candidate can be seated. If the employee doing the check-in is unfamiliar with this policy, the test center manager should be contacted.

2.10. Exam Questions

2.10.1. Question Characteristics and Components

There are different characteristics and components that must be recognized when interpreting questions. Recognizing them in the questions, especially situational questions, allows the candidate to more easily interpret the question.

Question Characteristic or Component	Explanation
Distracter	Some questions contain information that has been inserted to distract the candidate from correctly interpreting the question. To correctly answer this type of question, the candidate must ignore the distracter. Note that Crosswind uses the term distracter to describe such information and also uses the term to describe potential answers that are not relevant.
Common Terminology	Some questions provide two potential answers that are similar and seem correct. In that case, the candidate must select the answer that corresponds to the terminology used by the Project Management Institute, Inc. For example, if two of the potential answers that seem correct are completion estimate and estimate at completion, the candidate should select estimate at completion as the best answer because it corresponds to the terminology used by the Project Management Institute, Inc.

Question Characteristic or Component	Explanation
Too Much Information (TMI)	Some questions, typically situational questions, contain too much information. For example, if a question lists a number of variables (e.g. schedule, cost, scope, and quality), the candidate should check each variable to determine which variables do not relate to the question, and interpret the questions considering only the remaining variables. The candidate could alternately determine which variables could indicate a potential issue (cost variable indicating that the project is over budget) and answer the question without considering the other variables.
Wrong Area, or Wrong Point in Time	Some questions have one or more answers that occur too early or too late in the process to be considered or that occur in a different knowledge area. Those answers may be eliminated from consideration. Other questions could ask the candidate to determine a process or activity sequence.

2.10.2. Question Formats

The exam uses a number of question formats. Some of the questions use multiple formats. Understanding the formats allows easier dissection of the questions and the potential answers. The most commonly used formats are:

- Select
- Select NOT/EXCEPT
- All (or a combination of) the answers
- Situational
- Chicken or the egg (sequence)
- None of the answers
- Calculation

Question Format	Description	Example
Select	The **select** format is the most straightforward question format. It simply asks the candidate to select the best answer. Note that it can also include other question formats, including the **Chicken or the Egg** format.	A milestone has what duration? A. One day B. Zero (no duration) (Correct) C. One hour D. Eight hours

PMI, CAPM, and PMBOK are registered marks of the Project Management Institute, Inc.

16   © 2008-2018 Crosswind Learning, www.crosswindpm.com

Question Format	Description	Example
Select NOT/EXCEPT	The **select NOT/EXCEPT** format requires the candidate to select the answer that does not apply. The key to answering this type of question is to determine which three answer selections have something in common and eliminate them from consideration.	All the following are areas of communications management except... A. Manage communications B. Monitor communications C. Perform quantitative risk analysis (Correct) D. Plan communications management
All (or a Combination of) the Answers	The **all (or a combination of) answers** format requires the candidate to determine if all - or a combination - of the answers are correct. The odds are in favor of "all the answers" being correct when two of the three potential answers are correct.	Which of the following are areas of risk management? A. Identify risks B. Perform quantitative risk analysis C. Plan risk responses D. All the answers (Correct)
Situational	This **situational** format is probably the most challenging. The exam may use this format in combination with other formats. This question format expects the candidate to draw on an understanding of the Project Management Institute, *A Guide to the Project Management Body of Knowledge (PMBOK® Guide)* - Sixth Edition, Project Management Institute, Inc. 2017 and personal project experience. It requires the candidate to have a thorough knowledge of the process tables in Chapters 4 through 13 of this manual, as well as a thorough knowledge of the roles defined in Chapter 3 of this manual.	You've taken over an existing project and discover that it has suffered major scope creep because the former project manager couldn't say "no" to the sponsor, and it lacked enough supporting documentation. What document do you first want to see (or create if it doesn't exist) about the project foundation? A. Risk list B. Project charter (Correct) C. Communications plan D. Budget

Question Format	Description	Example
Chicken or the Egg	The **chicken or the egg** format often presents two or more plausible potential answers. This question format requires the candidate to know the order in which process activities occur.	What comes before sequence activities? A. Estimate activity durations B. Estimate costs C. Define activities (Correct) D. Develop project management plan
None of the Answers	With the **none of the answers** format, all potential answers (other than "none of the above") are inapplicable to the question. This question format requires the candidate to evaluate each answer to determine its relevance to the cited knowledge area. If the relevant knowledge area for each answer lies outside the scope of the question, then the candidate should select "none of the answers."	What knowledge area is part of the triple constraint? A. Manage communications B. Procurement C. Professional and social responsibility D. None of the answers (Correct)
Calculation	The **calculation** format may include a **select, none of the answers**, or **not enough information** format. This question format typically requires the candidate to know the relevant formula. If the candidate does not know the formula, it may be possible for the candidate to determine the correct answer through reverse engineering (the question and/or potential answers could reference amounts that "add up" correctly). It is also possible that the question may not have sufficient data to complete the calculation (this may occur with future value or present value calculations); in that case it is important that the candidate knows all of the formula components.	What is the CPI for the following data? AC = $200, PV = $400, EV = $200, BAC = $1,000 A. $200 B. -$200 C. 1.0 (Correct) D. 0.5

2.11. Question Breakdown and Translation

The exam is known for its long, rambling situational questions. To minimize confusion, the candidate should be familiar with the following method.

- First, the candidate should focus on the last part of the question and determine what needs to be done, e.g. an estimate, an analysis, a straight forward selection
- Second, the candidate should read the entire question and eliminate any distracters (information that has no supporting evidence is a likely distracter)
- Third, the candidate should eliminate the two "worst" answers
- Finally, the candidate should determine the best answer

Sample Questions

Question #1

You are the project manager on an environmental excavating project. As you monitor progress, you determine that the activities are taking longer than estimated on the schedule because of holidays you failed to consider when creating the schedule. What is the best solution to fix this problem?

Breaking down the question	The first sentence establishes that you are the project manager. Unless something specific about the type of project comes up, that should be sufficient. Note that environmental excavating is a distracter. The second statement contains two items of value. The activities are taking longer than estimated, and the cause is failure to plan for holidays in the schedule. The final sentence is a request to determine the best way to fix this problem.
Translation (Plain English version)	You are a project manager. Your project is behind schedule because you didn't factor holidays into the schedule. What is the best solution to fix this problem?
Answer	Implement a schedule change control and re-baseline the schedule with the holidays factored in.

Question #2

You have taken over a project from another project manager who the sponsor felt was unsuccessful. The project represents a new type of work at your company. The cost is $50,000 over budget, and the former project manager did not view the schedule as a useful tool. Where should you place your initial focus?

Breaking down the question	The first sentence establishes that you are replacing an existing project manager. The sponsor issue is possibly a distracter. The second sentence is primarily a distracter but can help reinforce a later sentence. The third sentence establishes two facts. Fact one: the cost is $50K over budget, which is not helpful because you don't know if it's a $100K project or a $10M project (so you can't determine the importance of this fact). Fact two: the former project manager failed to use the schedule, which is definitely an issue in light of the project processes detailed by the Project Management Institute, Inc. The final sentence is a request to identify the most urgent area needing focus.
Translation (Plain English version)	You are the new project manager for an existing project. The project represents a new type of work at your company. Because you don't have a total budget value to tell you if the $50K over budget is a major or minor consideration, assume that is a distracter. There is either no schedule or one that is seriously deficient. Where should you place your initial focus?
Answer	You should first focus on reviewing, then readjusting/modifying, the existing schedule. If there is no existing schedule, you should first focus on creating a schedule.

Question #3

You are halfway through an Internet upgrade project. Presently, you know the following: Activity F has an early start of day seven and a late start of day 12. The cost performance index (CPI) is 0.92 and the schedule performance index is 0.87. The project has 18 stakeholders. Activity G requires a very experienced resource. What should you focus on first?

Breaking down the question	Try your hand at translating this question to see if you are starting to translate fluently.
Translation (Plain English version)	You are 50% done on a project. Because there is not enough information about the network diagram, Activity F appears to be a distracter. The spending efficiency is only getting $0.92 value for every dollar spent. The productivity is 87% of what is planned. The number of stakeholders and the resource issue on Activity G are distracters. Where should you place your initial focus?
Answer	The first area of focus should be the schedule, because the SPI is 0.87. After that, the focus should be the budget, because the CPI is 0.92.

PMI, CAPM, and PMBOK are registered marks of the Project Management Institute, Inc.

20 © 2008-2018 Crosswind Learning, www.crosswindpm.com

Question #4

You have been involved in the project as a project manager. After much analysis, arguing, and debate with the 17 stakeholders, the sponsor has made the decision to outsource a key piece of work on the project because of the risk associated with it. This is an example of what?

Breaking down the question	Try your hand at translating this question to see if you are starting to translate fluently.
Translation (Plain English version)	You are the project manager. It has been decided that a piece of the work will be outsourced. This is an example of what?
Answer	This is a situational terminology question. The decision to outsource a piece of work is based on a make-or-buy analysis.

2.12. Problem Solving on Situational Questions

Solving the problems posed by the situational questions is the most complicated exam challenge you will face.

Following are sample situational questions with the correct answers and the logic required to solve the problem.

Sample Situational Questions and Problem Solving Logic

1. You are the project manager on a project. It has been discovered that testing will begin a week late. Which is the best solution?

    (A) Perform analysis about the delay and if it indeed will not impact the scope, schedule, or cost of the project, approve it and keep the project running
    (B) Ask senior management to choose the solution
    (C) Ignore the testing issue because that part of the project hasn't come up yet
    (D) Ask the sponsor for an opinion about converging system testing and user acceptance testing

    Correct Answer: (A) Perform analysis about the delay and if it indeed will not impact the scope, time, or cost of the project, approve it and keep the project running

    Logic: When a problem arises and it doesn't violate the triple constraint, the project manager has the authority to approve a solution.

2. You are the manager of the project. It has been discovered that testing will begin a week late, causing the project finish date to slip a week. Which is the best solution?

    (A) Perform analysis about the week delay and if it will not impact the scope, schedule, or cost of the project, approve it and keep the project running
    (B) After analyzing the problem and potential solutions, alert senior management to the problem and potential solutions, and implement the solution they recommend
    (C) Ignore the testing issue; that part of the project hasn't come up yet
    (D) Ask the sponsor for an opinion about converging system testing and user acceptance testing

    Correct Answer: (B) After analyzing the problem and potential solutions, alert senior management to the problem and potential solutions, and implement the solution they recommend

    Logic: When a problem arises and it does violate the triple constraint, senior management or the sponsor must approve the solution. Typically, the project manager would not go to senior management or the sponsor for problem resolution without first having potential solutions to present.

3. You are a manager for a project awaiting some new positions to be filled. The schedule is already set to include the work of these new resources. The start date of these resources has passed without hearing back from the client on signing approval for these new resources. Who can best resolve this problem?

    (A) Senior management
    (B) Project manager
    (C) Sales executive
    (D) Program manager

    Correct Answer: (A) Senior management

    Logic: When the customer won't sign off or a similar situation arises, the key solution is to involve senior management. Your role is to inform the client that they must approve something. If they don't approve, you do not pursue the issue; instead, you involve senior management.

4. The project is not progressing well. It is behind schedule and over budget. The project manager has determined that the schedule was created without adequate team input and needs to be recreated. Reworking the schedule could effect the overall project finish date. Who can best address the schedule problem?

(A) The project manager because the project manager needs to put together a new schedule for approval by senior management
(B) Senior management because senior management needs to approve a violation of the triple constraint
(C) Functional manager because the functional manager is in control of the resources on the schedule
(D) Team member(s) because team members have input to the schedule

Correct Answer: (A) The project manager because the project manager needs to put together a new schedule for approval by senior management

Logic: Generally, the project manager does not go to senior management with a problem without first having potential solutions. (The previous rule was an exception.) Going to senior management without a solution is like screaming that the sky is falling. Remember, they hired you to get the work of the project complete, and you are to work through issues instead of running to senior management all the time.

5. The project is behind schedule because the key estimator wasn't available when the schedule was created. Senior management is aware of this and has allowed the project manager to re-baseline the schedule. What process will fix this problem?

(A) Develop schedule
(B) Sequence activities
(C) Work breakdown structure
(D) Control schedule

Correct Answer: (D) Control schedule

Logic: When asked what would fix a problem, examine the problem and select the answer that will resolve it.

6. The project is behind schedule as the key estimator wasn't available when the schedule was created. Senior management is aware of this and has allowed the project manager to re-baseline the schedule. In what process did this problem get created?

    (A) Develop schedule
    (B) Sequence activities
    (C) Work breakdown structure
    (D) Control schedule

    Correct Answer: (A) Develop schedule

    Logic: When asked when the problem was created, examine the answers and select the one that indicates the most likely point where the problem would have been created.

Chapter 3

Framework

Like all professional disciplines, project management is based on an evolving body of knowledge that encompasses practices generally accepted as good. The Project Management Institute, A Guide to the Project Management Body of Knowledge, (PMBOK® Guide) - Sixth Edition, Project Management Institute, Inc. 2017 contains a subset of that knowledge, including relevant terminology descriptions, organized by knowledge areas.

To attain the Certified Associate in Project Management (CAPM)® certification, the applicant must pass the exam; to pass the exam, the applicant must know the concepts, information, and terminology contained in the Project Management Institute, A Guide to the Project Management Body of Knowledge, (PMBOK® Guide) - Sixth Edition, Project Management Institute, Inc., 2017.

In this chapter, we discuss the following:

Disciplines

The Project and Its Relationships

Organizational Structures

Project Roles

Crosswind "Must Knows" for Framework

☐	Project management life cycle, project life cycle, and product life cycle
☐	Characteristics of a project and subproject
☐	Characteristics of programs and portfolios
☐	Characteristics and purpose of strategic planning
☐	Characteristics and benefits of a PMO (project management office)
☐	Triple constraint and how it functions
☐	How to align plan-do-check-act with the project management life cycle
☐	Phase to Phase Relationships and when to use sequential or overlapping phases
☐	Differences and characteristics of the personnel involved in project management
☐	Role of the project manager
☐	How the project manager performs integration
☐	Characteristics of a functional organization
☐	Characteristics of a projectized organization

☐ Characteristics of a matrix organization

☐ Characteristics of a composite organization

Although helpful, this list is not all-inclusive in regard to information needed for the exam. It is only suggested material that, if understood and memorized, may increase your exam score.

3.1. Overlap of Disciplines

To be successful, the project manager must know about project management, the project management system, the project management life cycle, the project life cycle, and the product life cycle. The project manager must also understand how those life cycles interact.

Project Management	Project management is the **application of information, skills, tools, and techniques to project activities in order to meet project needs.** It can include developing requirements, determining realistic goals, managing the triple constraint, and adapting the various plans to achieve project goals. Project management starts with selecting the processes associated with completing the work of the project and typically involves using an established methodology to align project and product requirements with the product specifications.
Project Management System	The project management system is a set of procedures, tools and techniques, processes, and methodologies used to manage projects. The system can be formal or informal and is typically supported by the project management plan during the execution of the project work.
Project Management Life Cycle (PMLC)	The project management life cycle includes the five process groups: initiating, planning, executing, monitoring and controlling, and closing. These process groups **can be applied to a project or to individual project phases.**
Project Life Cycle	The project life cycle includes the **project work processes.** For each phase, it describes the work being performed, who is performing the work, the deliverables, and the approval process. Examples of a work process are the building process for home construction and the development process for a computer program. The project life cycle typically coexists with the project management life cycle.
Product Life Cycle	The product life cycle **includes the product or service from concept to divestment (closure),** typically starting with a business plan, moving through the project that results in the product or service, then transitioning the product or service to operations, and ending with the retirement of the product or service.

Know the project management life cycle.

Know the project life cycle.

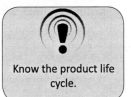
Know the product life cycle.

PMI, CAPM, and PMBOK are registered marks of the Project Management Institute, Inc.

26
© 2008-2018 Crosswind Learning, www.crosswindpm.com

Figure 3-1: Life Cycle Interaction demonstrates how the three life cycles interrelate. For the exam, it is important to know the characteristics and purpose of each type.

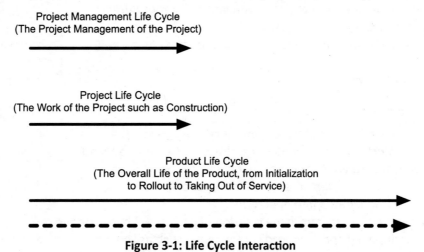

Figure 3-1: Life Cycle Interaction

It is also important that the project manager possesses technical knowledge relevant to the project, an understanding of the project environment, general management ability, and interpersonal (soft) skills.

The project environment includes **cultural, social, political, and international** variables.

General management ability includes having the ability to manage such areas as financing, purchasing (procurement), sales, law, manufacturing and logistics, health (safety), and information technology.

Interpersonal skills include communication, **influence**, leadership, motivation, **negotiation**, team building, decision-making, and political and cultural awareness.

The source for the above text is the Project Management Institute, *A Guide to the Project Management Body of Knowledge*, (*PMBOK® Guide*) – Sixth Edition, Project Management Institute Inc., 2017, Pages 98-104

3.2. Projects and Their Relationships

A project is a temporary initiative that creates business value. It has a **specific purpose**, creates **unique results**, drives **organizational change**, and has a **definite start and finish**.

It is initiated in response to:

- A stakeholder need or request
- A legal, regulatory, or social requirement
- A business or technological strategy
- A product, process, or service that needs to be created, enhanced, or corrected

A project is executed based on a progressively elaborated project management plan. **Progressive elaboration** is the refinement of the plan as new information relevant to the work of the project is discovered. This often involves multiple incremental changes.

Know the characteristics of a project.

A project may have subprojects, which are created when the project needs to be broken down into more manageable pieces. A common example of a **subproject** is the installation of a roof during a residential home construction project.

A project may be standalone or part of a program or portfolio.

Know the characteristics of a subproject.

3.2.1. Program

A project may be part of a program, since a **program encompasses projects** of similar work or correlated activities **managed in a coordinated way to attain benefits that could not be achieved separately**. The program might interact with operations if the program (and its projects) is integrated into operations.

An example of a program is the creation of computers based on the results of a number of projects that designed and produced components (such as the motherboard, disc drives, and other assemblies), and then assembled them to create the computers.

Know the characteristics of a program.

3.2.2. Portfolio

A project may be part of a portfolio, since a portfolio encompasses a group of projects (and/or) programs that have some degree of interactivity related to an overall strategic business goal.

Portfolio management focuses on doing the **right work**, while **project** management focuses on doing the **work right**.

Figure 3-2: Project, Program, Portfolio Interaction demonstrates how projects, programs, and portfolios interrelate with an organization's strategic planning.

Know the characteristics of a portfolio.

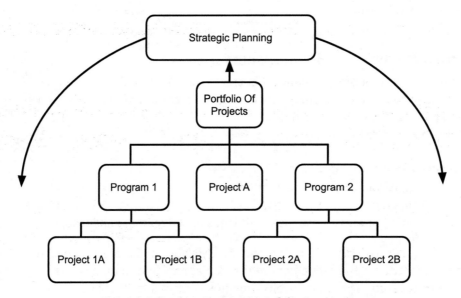

Figure 3-2: Project, Program, Portfolio Interaction

The source for the above figure is the Project Management Institute, *A Guide to the Project Management Body of Knowledge*, (*PMBOK® Guide*) – Sixth Edition, Project Management Institute Inc., 2017, Figure 1-3, Page 12

© 2008-2018 Crosswind Learning, www.crosswindpm.com

3.2.3. Strategic Planning

Strategic planning for the organization is the practice of defining its strategic goals (planned objectives) **three to five years** in the future, which it typically realizes through projects.

The Project Management Institute, Inc. has a tool and methodology approach, OPM3 (Organizational Project Management Maturity Model), for aligning an organization's goals and strategic planning with project management.

Know the characteristics and purpose of strategic planning.

3.2.4. Operations Management

Operations management consists of managing operational resources and the **day-to-day** activities of the organization. Operations managers must direct the planning, execution, and monitoring and controlling of the work.

Project management consists of managing project resources and the activities that make up the work of the project, which is a temporary initiative. Project managers must direct the planning, execution, and monitoring and controlling of the project work.

3.2.5. Project Management Office (PMO)

The Project Management Office (PMO) is a group that standardizes project governance and simplifies the sharing of resources, tools, techniques, and methodologies. The approach the PMO may take can be:

Know the characteristics and benefits of a PMO (Project Management Office).

- **Directive**
  PMO directly manages projects
- **Controlling**
  PMO provides support and requires compliance in the form of adoption of mandated project management frameworks, governance frameworks, and/or tools and documentation
- **Supportive**
  PMO provides project management templates, best practices, lessons learned, and access to other supportive information

The authority of the PMO depends on the organization.

The source for the above text is the Project Management Institute, *A Guide to the Project Management Body of Knowledge*, (*PMBOK® Guide*) – Sixth Edition, Project Management Institute Inc., 2017, Pages 98-104

3.3. Triple Constraint

One of the most basic foundations of traditional project management is the triple constraint: Scope, Schedule, and Cost.

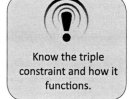

Know the triple constraint and how it functions.

Scope is the description, typically in the form of written requirements, of the expected product, service, or result of the project.

Schedule details the amount of time necessary to deliver the product, service, or result of the project. The schedule cannot be determined until scope is defined.

Cost is the amount of money needed to deliver the product, service, or result of the project. Cost cannot be determined until schedule is determined.

Unless otherwise stated, all three constraints are of equal importance. Achievement of the scope, schedule, and cost goals results in achieving quality.

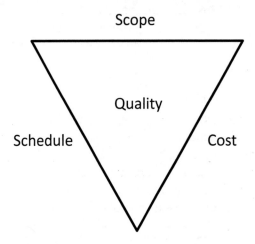

Figure 3-3: Triple Constraint

A more modern approach to the triple constraint is the enhanced triple constraint, which includes risk and resources. Risk and resources can have significant influence on a project and can influence the scope, schedule, cost, and quality goals of the project.

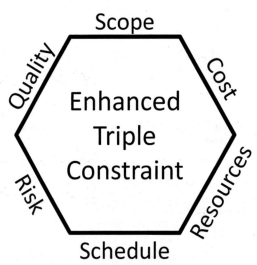

Figure 3-4: Enhanced Triple Constraint

The source for the above text is the Project Management Institute, *A Guide to the Project Management Body of Knowledge*, (*PMBOK® Guide*) – Sixth Edition, Project Management Institute Inc., 2017, Pages 98-104

3.4. Process Groups and Position Descriptions

3.4.1. Process Groups

There are five main process groups: initiating, planning, executing, monitoring and controlling, and closing.

For the exam, an understanding of each process group and the manner in which it interacts with the other process groups is important. It is also important to assume that all process groups, processes, and process interactions will be used unless otherwise stated, although in the working world, the project manager and project team often tailor their approach to a specific project.

The process groups are rarely executed in a linear manner. Moving from monitoring and controlling back to execution and/or planning is acceptable if relevant to the situation.

Reference Figure 3-5: Project Boundaries to understand how the processes interact in relation to boundaries.

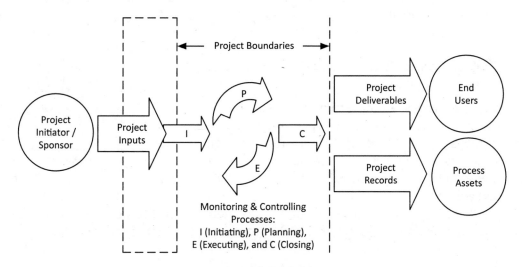

Figure 3-5: Project Boundaries
The source for the above figure is the Project Management Institute, *A Guide to the Project Management Body of Knowledge, (PMBOK® Guide) – Sixth Edition,* Project Management Institute Inc., 2017, Figure 2-1, Page 562

Initiating	During the initiating process group, the new project or new phase of an existing project is defined by obtaining authorization to begin the project or phase, the **project charter** and stakeholder register are created, and **stakeholder identification begins.** Typically, when a project moves beyond initiation, the project manager has been assigned, a sponsor is defined, and a high-level project scope statement, among other things, is put into place.
Planning	Because the success of the project is so dependent on planning, it is considered the **most important** of the process groups. The project manager creates the project management plan and the component management plans (Integration, Scope, Schedule, Cost, Quality, Resource, Communications, Risk, Procurement, and Stakeholder), then integrates the component plans into the **project management plan**. The project manager typically involves the team in planning.

Executing	During the executing process group, the actual **work of the project is performed** in accordance with the project management plan. This process group creates **work results**. Note that performing the work typically unearths unplanned events and unforecasted issues. The executing processes **create work results**.
Monitoring and Controlling	During the monitoring and controlling process group, the team checks for variances (monitoring) and adjusts the plan or output in light of the variances (controlling). This process group results in **preventative and corrective actions**. Note that any changes are subject to the change control process, which means that a change may only be implemented if it has received formal approval.
Closing	During the closing process group, the **project or phase is closed**. Assuming that the project or phase has been executed and is nearing completion, any procurements must be closed, and then the project or phase may be closed. Closing the project or phase involves archiving all project documentation and **transitioning** the **product, service, or result** of the project or phase to the customer.

3.4.2. Project Management Process Groups in the Plan-Do-Check-Act Format

The American Society for Quality (ASQ) defines the plan-do-check-act cycle as an approach to process development. While the project management process groups require a more sophisticated approach than the basic plan-do-check-act format, it can be used to illustrate how monitoring and controlling actually works with the other four process groups.

Know how to align the plan-do-check-act with the project management life cycle.

Reference Figure 3-6: Comparison of Plan-Do-Check-Act to PMLC for a depiction of the alignment of the plan-do-check-act format to the project management life cycle.

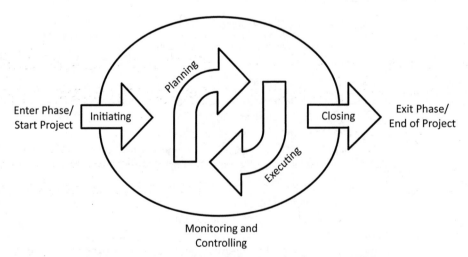

Figure 3-6: Comparison of Plan-Do-Check-Act to PMLC

PMI, CAPM, and PMBOK are registered marks of the Project Management Institute, Inc.

32   © 2008-2018 Crosswind Learning, www.crosswindpm.com

3.4.3. Phase to Phase Relationships

Phases in a multiple phase project are typically sequential, but there are instances when overlapping or concurrent (iterative) phases are more beneficial.

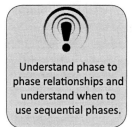

Understand phase to phase relationships and understand when to use sequential phases.

If the **phases** have a **sequential relationship,** a phase only begins after its predecessor phase has been completed. For example, phase two begins only after the completion of phase one.

Understand when to use sequential or overlapping phases.

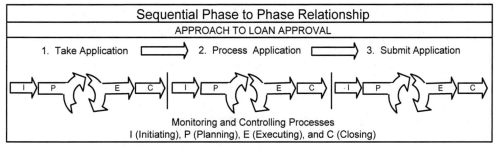

Figure 3-7: Sequential Phase to Phase Relationship
The source for the above figure is the Project Management Institute, *A Guide to the Project Management Body of Knowledge, (PMBOK® Guide) – Sixth Edition,* Project Management Institute Inc., 2017, Figure x3-3, Page 668

If the **phases** have an **overlapping relationship**, a phase can begin even if its predecessor phase has not been completed. For example, phase two can begin while phase one is still in process. An overlapping relationship is typically used if a compression technique, such as fast tracking, is applied. While the overall project could be completed sooner, overlapping phases may increase risk and rework may be required if a phase is started prior to obtaining accurate information from the prior phase.

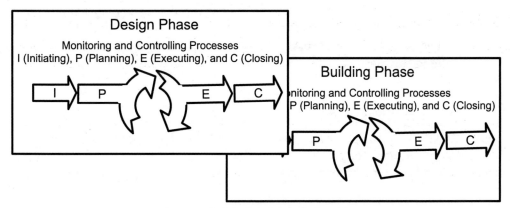

Figure 3-8: Overlapping Relationship
The source for the above figure is the Project Management Institute, *A Guide to the Project Management Body of Knowledge, (PMBOK® Guide) – Sixth Edition,* Project Management Institute Inc., 2017, Figure x3-3, Page 668

If the **phases** have an **iterative relationship, planning for the successor phase is conducted while work is being performed on the current phase.** This approach is typically used for a project characterized by uncertainty or a constantly evolving environment. Scope management is achieved through continuous incremental product delivery and continuous requirement prioritization.

3.4.4.   The relationship between Phases and Process Groups

A project phase is a piece of a multi-phase project and all five process groups are often applied to each project phase.

Note that the five process groups may have a sequential, overlapping, or iterative relationship. As an example, during the monitoring and control process group, a change impacting the project management plan is authorized through the change control process; a return to the planning process is required to revise the project management plan.

3.4.5.   Predictive Life Cycles

Projects with predictive life cycles use **waterfall or plan driven approaches** and the scope, schedule, and budget are established as early as possible in the project.

If the project has phases, it's common for them to have an overlapping relationship with the focus of each phase on specific tasks and processes that require the application of unique skill sets.

Changes are subject to the change control process and must be authorized before implementation.

The predictive life cycles approach is generally used when the work is well understood by the performing organization and the organization understands that the work must be completed for stakeholders to realize project value.

3.4.6.   Iterative or Incremental Life Cycles

Projects with an iterative or incremental life cycle also identify the project scope early in the project, but the schedule and budget are adjusted as the team learns more about the project work. Iteration durations and team members may change based on project need.

Since each iteration adds to the functionality of the project, an incremental evolution of project functionality occurs from one iteration to the next. A full project management life cycle with a focus on completed deliverables occurs at each iteration.

The iterative or incremental life cycle approach is typically used when the goal of the project is to minimize complexity or risk or when an incremental project delivery can be useful to some stakeholders.

3.4.7.   Adaptive Life Cycles

Projects with adaptive life cycles use an Agile method. Agile is generally considered to be a **change-driven approach** to project management, which is characterized by rapid iterations (**typically 2-4 weeks long** with fixed time and resources) and requires significant stakeholder/ customer involvement.

The initial iteration typically focuses on **vision** and creating a **master feature or backlog list**. As each iteration begins, an iteration backlog is created which lists the features to be completed during the iteration. At the end of the iteration, the features should be complete and ready for customer acceptance. The focus of projects with an adaptive life cycle is on delivering customer value with each iteration or release.

The adaptive life cycle approach is typically used in a rapidly changing project environment where the scope is difficult to identify or define in advance. It is also used when smaller increments of deliverables can add value to the stakeholder experience.

Examples of an adaptive approach include: **Agile, Scrum, Kanban**, and **Lean**.

3.4.8. Phase Gate

A phase gate is a review process undertaken to determine if a project is likely to succeed. At the end of a program or project phase, an authorized group reviews the work of the phase and either makes a decision to continue the project or stop future work on the initiative. The authorized group is typically a steering committee or independent party. As a result of the phase gate, a project considered unlikely to succeed is terminated early. A phase gate can be considered a "**kill point**."

3.4.9. Project Management Tailoring

Because of the uniqueness of each project, not every process, input, tool/technique, or output listed in the Project Management Institute, *A Guide to the Project Management Body of Knowledge, (PMBOK® Guide)* - Sixth Edition, Project Management Institute, Inc., 2017 is required for every project. Project management tailoring, or tailoring project management to the project, is the selection of the appropriate project management processes, inputs, tools/techniques, outputs, and project life cycle phases for the project after considering the required levels of governance and if the customer is internal or external.

The **project manager collaborates** with the project team, sponsor, and organizational management, as appropriate, to perform this activity.

One aspect that should be tailored is the competing constraints of scope, schedule, budget, resources, quality, and risk. Since the relative importance of these constraints can vary from project to project, the project manager must tailor the approach for their management based on the organizational culture, project environment, and other variables.

3.4.10. Project Management Methodology Tailoring

Most project managers apply a project management methodology to their work. Project management methodologies may be developed by experts in the organization, acquired from government agencies, obtained from a professional organization, or purchased from vendors.

Again, because of the uniqueness of each project, a methodology may require tailoring to ensure project success.

3.4.11. Position Descriptions

The following table briefly describes the key players and their responsibilities, roles, and interactions with other players.

Know the differences and characteristics of the various personnel involved in project management.

Portfolio Manager	The role of the portfolio manager is to **provide governance at a high level** for assigned programs and projects.
Portfolio Review Board	The role of the portfolio review board is to determine which projects should be pursued based on its **review of each project** in terms of its value, risks, ROI, and other designated attributes.
Program Manager	The role of the program manager is to **manage assigned projects in a manner that will provide enhanced benefits** and to provide support and guidance to the project managers.
Operations Management	The role of operations management (or business process management) is to manage an organization's day-to-day activities. In connection with project results that are transitioned to operations, operations management is responsible for incorporating those results into normal operations and providing ongoing support.
Sellers/Business Partners	Sellers are **external entities** that contract to provide components or services for the project. Sellers are also called vendors, contractors, and suppliers. Business partners are external entities that have a special relationship with the organization and provide it with a service, such as training or expertise.
Project Manager	Reference Section 3.5 of this manual for detailed information.
Project Management Team Member	A project management team member is **anyone on the team** who works on project management related items. Activities can include scheduling, cost budgeting, and change management.
Functional Manager	The functional manager is an operational position that **controls operational resources.** Because the functional manager often needs those resources for operational work, there can be **conflict with the project manager over operational resources** assigned to the project.
Influencer	An influencer is a **person or group indirectly related to a project. An influencer can have** a **negative or positive influence** on the project.

Project Coordinator	A project coordinator is put into place if the organizational structure doesn't support a full-scale project management environment or the project manager needs additional support. A project coordinator **acts as a communications link to senior management** and has some **limited decision-making abilities.**
Project Expediter	A project expediter is put into place if the organizational structure doesn't support a full-scale project management environment or the project manager needs additional support. A project expediter **acts as a communications link to senior management** and performs activities such as **verifying completion of assignments and checking on the status of an undertaking.** Typically, they **do not have decision-making abilities.**
Performing Organization	The performing organization is the **organization, a company within the organization, or a division** of the company that is **doing the work** of the project.
Sponsor	The sponsor is responsible for providing resources and support for the project. In certain organizations, the sponsor may secure financing for the project, create the project charter, be responsible for the success of the project, and/or sign off on project completion. Typically senior management **supports** the sponsor.
PMO (Project Management Office)	Reference Section 3.2.5 of this manual for detailed information.
Customer/User	A customer or user is the person or group that makes use of the work of the project. The customer is the owner of the project work and will pay for it. The user is the end person/group using the work.
Stakeholders	**Stakeholders can be members of the project team** or anyone actively involved in or impacted by (negatively or positively) the project. Examples are: • Consumers who depend on the project • Those who are employed as a result of project completion and deployment • Those whose job could be modified or eliminated by the completion of the project

Project Team Members	Team members are **those who actually do the work** that results in meeting the deliverables defined in the scope of the project. They perform activities delegated by the project manager, who assumes that they are competent to manage their own workload without the need for micromanagement. The primary difference between a team member and other stakeholders is that a team member **typically** bills their time as a cost to the project. Team members include analysts, programmers, technical writers, construction personnel, and testers. Team members also include those performing roles such as: • Project management staff • Supporting experts • Users or customers • Sellers/business partners The project team can be composed of: • Dedicated team members: those who only work on the project • Part-time team members: those who work on the project part-time • Virtual team members: those who work from diverse locations and time zones and interact via technology • Partnerships: joint ventures working together on the project
Senior Management	Senior management usually refers to management that **supports the sponsor, the project charter, and ultimately the project**. Some of the activities that senior management undertakes include: • Assisting with the **prioritization of items associated with other projects** • Coordinating with other groups or activities that can interfere with the project

PMI, CAPM, and PMBOK are registered marks of the Project Management Institute, Inc.

38 © 2008-2018 Crosswind Learning, www.crosswindpm.com

Senior Management (Cont.)

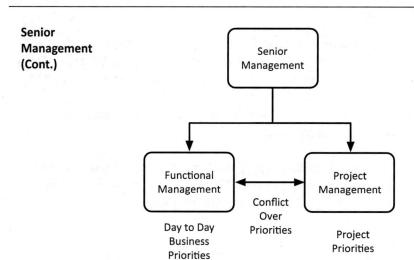

Figure 3-9: Senior Management Focus

3.5. The Role of the Project Manager

In their efforts to realize the goals of their projects, project managers have important roles in the leadership of their teams.

Know the role of the project manager.

Typically, project managers begin their roles at project initiation and continue them through project closure.

There are organizations that engage project managers in pre-initiation assessment and analysis. Pre-initiation assessment and analysis may include such activities as:

- Assisting with business analysis and business case development
- Working with executives and business leadership to flesh out ideas regarding
  - The enhancement of organizational performance
  - The promotion of strategic objectives
  - Meeting customer needs

There are also organizations that engage project managers in post-closure activities that are related to the realization of business benefits derived from the project.

While project managers are not expected to have the ability to perform all project roles, they should have technical knowledge and a thorough understanding of, and experience in, project management.

3.5.1. Sphere of Influence

The sphere of influence for project managers includes governance, the portfolio steering committee, the PMO, regulatory bodies, the project sponsor, end users, the project team, other project managers, program managers, resource managers, customers, shareholders, suppliers, and competitors.

Project managers perform a variety of roles within their sphere of influence and in accordance with their abilities. The roles mirror the value and contributions of project management.

Figure 3-10: Project Manager Interaction depicts the typical outlooks (in terms of a time range) of strategic, middle, and operations management. The project manager should consider these time ranges to ensure more meaningful interactions with the three management groups.

Figure 3-10: Project Manager Interaction

3.5.2. The Project

Project managers are assigned by the performing organization. They must lead the team responsible for realizing the goals of the project and satisfying stakeholder needs, set the direction of the project, and initiate the **vision of project success**. They must also work to **balance project constraints** against available resources and achieve consensus regarding project decisions and actions among sponsors, team members, and stakeholders with competing goals.

The most successful project managers are **excellent communicators** and have superb relationship skills. They exhibit the ability to communicate with a broad range of personalities and roles verbally, nonverbally, and in writing. Their written communications are succinct, relevant, and unambiguous. They develop, evolve, and follow the communication schedule predictably, communicating in alignment with the stakeholders' preferences and integrating feedback channels. Their relationship skills involve the nurturing and expansive networking of people within their sphere of influence: both formal (organizational reporting structures) and informal (individuals, including other project managers, subject matter experts, and important leaders).

3.5.3.   The Organization

A primary objective of project managers is to ensure that the needs of their projects are fulfilled.

Project managers should work toward establishing positive relationships with other project managers in the same organization. Such relationships can influence project success because projects led by other project managers may compete for the same resources, channels for the distribution or receipt of deliverables, prioritization for funding, and other considerations. They should also establish positive relationships with functional managers, program managers, portfolio managers, business analysts, and subject matter experts.

Project managers should also work to:

- Achieve and maintain a strong advocacy role in the organization
- Enhance the competence and capability of project management within the organization
- Demonstrate the merits of project management in the organization
- Promote the effectiveness of the PMO, if it exists in the organization

3.5.4.   The Industry

Project managers have an obligation to keep up with current industry trends and apply them as appropriate.

Current trends can include:

- Project management and quality management standards
- Technical support tools
- Product development
- New and changing markets
- Economic influences that impact the current project
- Influences that impact the project management discipline
- Strategies for sustainability

3.5.5.   Professional Discipline

Project managers have an obligation to continually transfer to others and integrate knowledge related to project management and other areas of expertise. The source of this knowledge can be continuing education and development in project management and other areas of expertise.

3.5.6. Project Manager Competencies

Project managers have an obligation to develop skill sets related to:

- Technical project management
  specifically, the knowledge, skills, and behaviors related to the project, program, and portfolio management domains
- Leadership
  specifically, the knowledge, skills, and behaviors required to lead and manage a team to assist the organization in the achievement of its business objectives
- Strategic and business management (business intelligence)
  specifically, the knowledge of and experience with the industry and organization

Figure 3-11:Talent Triangle

The source for the above figure is the Project Management Institute, *A Guide to the Project Management Body of Knowledge, (PMBOK® Guide) – Sixth Edition,* Project Management Institute Inc., 2017, Figure 3-2, Page 57

3.5.7. Levels of Skill Capability

Project managers have an obligation to develop competencies in the skills needed for the project. All project managers should maintain a current inventory of their competence levels for each requisite skill.

Skill levels begin with **unconsciously incompetent**, then move though **consciously incompetent**, **consciously competent**, and **unconsciously competent**, to **chosen conscious competence**.

PMI, CAPM, and PMBOK are registered marks of the Project Management Institute, Inc.

42   © 2008-2018 Crosswind Learning, www.crosswindpm.com

3.5.8. Technical Project Management

Project managers have an obligation to develop technical project management skills, which are the skills required to productively use project management knowledge to deliver the desired outcomes for the pertinent project or program.

Technical skills include:

- The effective use of the applicable knowledge area processes
- Expert judgment
- Expertise (including utilizing the expertise of others) in applicable areas
- The ability to tailor both traditional and adaptive tools, techniques, and methods for a specific project
- Thorough planning
- Effective prioritization
- A focus on important technical project elements, such as critical factors to achieve success for a specific project and the availability of applicable documents (financial reports, issue logs, and the schedule among others)
- Expert management of project elements such as resources, risks, the schedule, and the budget

3.5.9. Strategic and Business Management

To remain viable in today's business environment, project managers should develop applicable strategic and business management skills, such as:

- Expertise in negotiation
- A basic understanding of the pertinent industry and products
- Business (domain) knowledge essential to the project
- The ability to discern the organization at a high level
- Sufficient organizational knowledge to explain the organization's strategy, mission, goals and objectives, products and services, operations, markets and market conditions, and competition
- The ability to apply organizational knowledge to the project to ensure alignment with strategy, mission, goals and objectives, priorities, tactics, and deliverables
- The ability to implement decisions supportive of strategic alignment and innovation
- A working knowledge of functional disciplines such as marketing, finance, and operations
- The ability to determine the manner in which business and strategic factors affect the project - factors include such things as financial implications (including performing cost/benefit analysis), risks, and issues
- The ability to develop an appropriate delivery strategy based on the insights of the sponsor, team, and subject matter experts

Project managers should diligently apply business knowledge in order to make sound decisions and recommendations, working continuously with the sponsor to ensure the alignment of business and project strategies.

3.5.10. Leadership Skills

To remain viable in today's business environment, project managers should develop the skills that guide, inspire, and direct a team. They should also apply these skills when interfacing with anyone within their sphere of influence.

Leadership skills include resilience, **critical thinking**, **negotiation**, **communicating effectively**, problem solving, and **interpersonal (soft) skills**. Interpersonal skills include listening, social awareness, cultural awareness, and the ability to communicate clearly, motivate others, and effectively negotiate.

3.5.11. Leadership vs. Management

Project managers should have the ability to apply either leadership or management to a situation as appropriate.

Leadership versus Management	
Leadership	**Management**
Guides, influences, and collaborates using relational power	Directs using positional power
Develops	Maintains
Innovates	Administrates
Focuses on relationships	Focuses on systems and structure
Inspires trust	Relies on control
Focuses on a long-range vision	Focuses on near-term goals
Asks what and why	Asks how and when
Focuses on the horizon	Focuses on the bottom line
Challenges the status quo	Accepts the status quo
Does the right things	Does things right
Focuses on vision, alignment, motivation, and inspiration	Focuses on operational issues and problem solving

3.5.12. Personality

Personality is characterized by differences in thinking, feeling, and behaving. Effective project managers possess some level of ability with the personality attributes listed below.

Personality Attributes	
Authentic	Shows open concern, accepts others for who they are
Courteous	Has the ability to behave appropriately and politely
Creative	Has the ability to think abstractly, see things differently, innovate
Cultural	Is sensitive to the values, norms, and beliefs of other cultures
Emotional	Has the ability to perceive, interpret, and manage emotions
Intellectual	Is able to learn, understand, and/or solve problems in multiple aptitudes
Managerial	Has experience and aptitude in management practices
Political	Is motivated to accomplish things through the exercise of power
Service-oriented	Has a willingness and ability to serve others (generally, a pleasant, knowledgeable individual with good communication skills)

3.6. Project Manager Performing Integration

Project managers have two roles in connection with the performance of project integration.

Know how the project manager performs integration.

They ensure the alignment of project objectives and results with those of the business area, program, and portfolio after working with the sponsor to understand strategic objectives. This allows them to contribute to the integration of the strategy.

They assume responsibility for persuading everyone on the team to work toward attaining project objectives and focus on project-level essentials. This is accomplished by integrating processes, knowledge, and people.

3.6.1. Process Level

At the process level, project managers determine how often and when to apply the processes selected during project tailoring.

3.6.2. Cognitive Level

At the cognitive level, project managers determine the methodology that will be used to manage the project. They are expected to exercise proficiency in all knowledge areas and apply experience, leadership, and technical and business management skills to the project. The successful achievement of project objectives and results is predicated on the ability of project managers to integrate the processes in the knowledge areas.

3.6.3. Context Level

At the context level, project managers need to be aware of and understand new technologies and considerations (social networks, virtual teams, multicultural considerations, and new values) when managing integration.

3.7. Organizational Cultures, Communications, and Structures

A critical aspect of project success is the project manager's ability to align the project with the organizational structure in which it exists. Most project environments have some common components such as values, norms, expectations, policies, procedures, established authority relationships, governance, and work hours.

For the exam, it is important to know the six main organizational types and their characteristics. The six main organizational types are:

Figure 3-12: Organizational Types and Resource Control depicts the six organizational types and indicates the controller of resources.

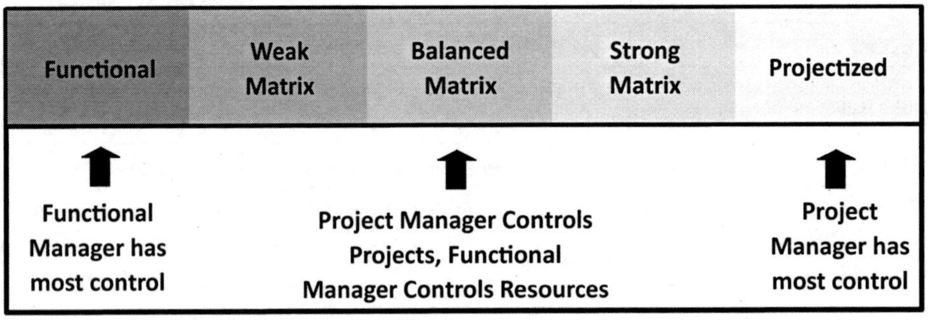

Functional	Weak Matrix	Balanced Matrix	Strong Matrix	Projectized
↑		↑		↑
Functional Manager has most control		Project Manager Controls Projects, Functional Manager Controls Resources		Project Manager has most control

Figure 3-12: Organizational Types and Resource Control
The source for the above figure is the Project Management Institute, *A Guide to the Project Management Body of Knowledge, (PMBOK® Guide) – Sixth Edition*, Project Management Institute Inc., 2017, Figure 3-10, Page 46

3.7.1. Organizational Cultures and Styles

Organizations consist of people, companies, divisions, and departments, as applicable, which focus on accomplishing business and project goals. An organization develops its culture (or style) over time based on those within the organization and their experiences. This culture can influence project environments, which can ultimately affect project success.

To be effective, the project manager should be aware of the most influential decision makers in the project environment and be sensitive to the primary culture if working on a geographically diverse project.

Organizational culture can manifest itself as:

- Values, beliefs, and expectations
- Policies, processes, methods, and procedures
- Motivation, reward, and compensation systems
- Risk tolerance (seeker, neutral, avoidance)
- Views on leadership, structure, and authority
- Work ethic, hours, and approach to work

3.7.2. Organizational Communications

As organizations and projects become more global, communication and culture play a greater role in project success. The project manager must be able to utilize various tools to communicate with stakeholders throughout the organization, regardless of physical location. Communication tools include computer networks, social networking, websites, email, conference calls, and video conferencing.

3.7.3. Functional Organization

The functional organization structure is the established, most commonly used structure in business today. It focuses on **operations where people of a similar skill set are grouped together and managed by someone with that same skill set**.

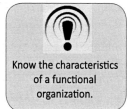

Know the characteristics of a functional organization.

This structure is sometimes called a silo organizational structure because the members of the individual groups (or silos) typically work among themselves more than with the other groups. That makes managing resources, in relation to project management activities, rather difficult because there is little incentive for the resources temporarily assigned to the project to focus on the project rather than on operational responsibilities and activities.

The characteristics of functional organizations include:

- A primary focus on operations and daily repetitive activities
- A secondary focus on projects
- A primary interest in full-time operations personnel
- A secondary interest in full-time project personnel

Figure 3-13: Functional Organization Chart illustrates the typical reporting structure of a functional organization.

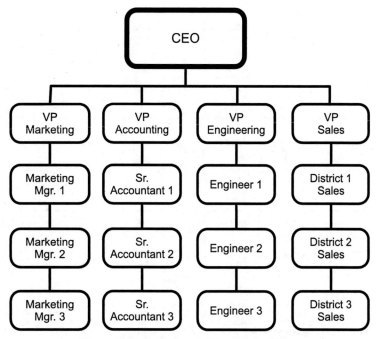

Figure 3-13: Functional Organization Chart
The source for the above figure is the Project Management Institute, *A Guide to the Project Management Body of Knowledge*, (*PMBOK® Guide*) – Sixth Edition, Project Management Institute Inc., 2017, Figure 3-10, Page 46

Project Manager Authority	Resources Available for Project Work	Who Controls Project Spending	Person's Role as a PM	PM Support Staff
Little or None	Little or None	Functional Manager	Part-time	Part-time

3.7.4. Projectized Organization

Know the characteristics of a projectized organization.

The projectized organization is a modern structure that has eliminated the silos of specialization that characterize a functional organization. Although this structure has silos, the primary focus is on the project (or operations by project). **This greatly increases the project team's ability to optimize its chances of success.**

The major drawback of this structure is that, upon project completion, there might not be positions available for all team members. In a matrix or functional environment, team members simply return to their operational positions.

The characteristics of projectized organizations include a team focus on the project work and teams consisting of mixed skills because the focus is on the project rather than a department.

Figure 3-14: Projectized Organization Chart illustrates the typical reporting structure of a projectized organization.

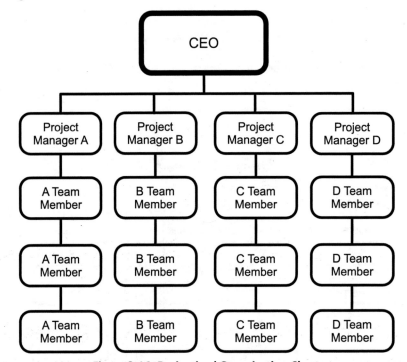

Figure 3-14: Projectized Organization Chart

The source for the above figure is the Project Management Institute, *A Guide to the Project Management Body of Knowledge*, (*PMBOK® Guide*) – Sixth Edition, Project Management Institute Inc., 2017, Figure 4-11, Page 47

Project Manager Authority	Resources Available for Project Work	Who Controls Project Spending	Person's Role as a PM	Project Management Support Staff
High to Almost Total	High to Almost Total	Project Manager	Full-time	Full-time

PMI, CAPM, and PMBOK are registered marks of the Project Management Institute, Inc.

48   © 2008-2018 Crosswind Learning, www.crosswindpm.com

3.7.5. Matrix Organization

A matrix organization accommodates established functional organization structures while being flexible enough to implement projects. The organization retains its functional foundation and uses cross-functional teams, bringing resources from various silos together to work on a project.

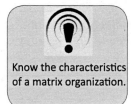

Know the characteristics of a matrix organization.

The primary drawback of a matrix organization is that a team member may report to more than one manager, which may result in conflicting priorities.

Matrix Organization Types	
Weak Matrix	The weak matrix organization is similar to a functional organization, but makes some accommodations for projects.
Balanced Matrix	The balanced matrix organization represents the middle ground between a strong matrix organization and a weak matrix organization. The **functional manager controls resources** and the **project manager delivers the results of the projects**.
Strong Matrix	The strong matrix organization is almost "projectized," but its roots are still functional. It usually has a project management function or group that provides a solid foundation for project management in the organization.

The characteristics of a matrix organization includes:

- A dual focus on operations and projects (as they transition from weak to strong, the project focus increases)
- Dual managers (a functional manager and project manager) for employees
- Resources that focus on dual priorities (projects and operations)

Figure 3-15: Matrix Organization Chart illustrates the typical reporting structure of a matrix organization.

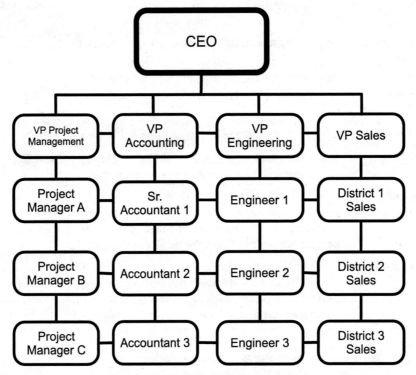

Figure 3-15: Matrix Organization Chart

The source for the above figure is the Project Management Institute, *A Guide to the Project Management Body of Knowledge, (PMBOK® Guide) – Sixth Edition,* Project Management Institute Inc., 2017, Figure 3-12, Page 48

Matrix	Project Manager Authority	Resources Available for Project Work	Who Controls Project Spending	Person's Role as a PM	PM Support Staff
Weak	Limited	Limited	Functional Manager	Part-time	Part-time
Balanced	Low to Moderate	Low to Moderate	Mixed	**Full-time**	**Part-time**
Strong	Moderate to High	Moderate to High	Project Manager	Full-time	Full-time

3.7.6. Composite Organization

A composite organization is a **hybrid** structure that can have characteristics of a matrix, projectized, and functional environment.

Know the characteristics of a composite organization.

Composite characteristics include the following:

- A flexible configuration for performing projects in a company
- Project management or leadership which can vary from organization to organization

Figure 3-16: Composite Organization Chart illustrates the typical reporting structure of a composite organization.

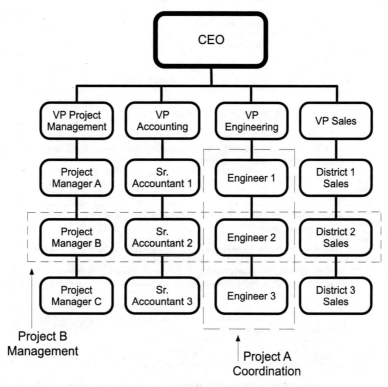

Figure 3-16: Composite Organization Chart

The source for the above figure is the Project Management Institute, *A Guide to the Project Management Body of Knowledge*, (*PMBOK® Guide*) – Sixth Edition, Project Management Institute Inc., 2017, Figure 3-13, Page 49

3.8. Framework Formulas and Variables

There are no formulas related to framework.

3.9. Framework Terminology

Term	Description
Adaptive Life Cycle	The progression of project phases characterized by a willingness to embrace change and involving significant stakeholder interaction with a focus on the incremental release of work, typically every two to four weeks; uses fixed time and resources; also called agile
Application Area	A category of projects that have common components, often categorized as technology projects, customer projects, or industry projects
Closing Process Group	The group of activities associated with concluding the project or phase
Closing Processes	Activities during which formal acceptance and completion procedures are attained from either a phase or the project itself
Customer	The internal or external individual(s) or entity(ies) that pay(s) to obtain a project product, service, or result
Enterprise	A company, business, or other formal structure that encompasses a business function
Execute	Perform the tasks of the project management plan, create the project deliverables, and generate work performance information
Executing Process Group	The processes performed to achieve the work detailed in the project management plan in order to meet the requirements delineated in the project specifications per the work identified in the project management plan
Functional Manager	A manager of any unit that creates a product or executes a service; also known as a line manager
Functional Organization	An entity that is arranged by department or purpose and focuses on operational work rather than project work
Goods	Products that have been created and are available for purchase
Incremental Life Cycle	The progression of project phases characterized by an early determination of scope, the adjustment of time and cost estimates as the team learns more about the product, and an increase in functionality resulting from incremental delivery
Influencer	A person or organization that is not necessarily directly related to the project but can influence the project in either a good or bad way
Initiating Process Group	The processes associated with the inauguration of a new project or phase; typically involves obtaining approval and identifying project stakeholders
Initiator	An organization or individual authorized and capable of starting a project
Input	Any internal or external item that is required before a process can continue; it can also be an output from a predecessor process
Iterative Life Cycle	The progression of project phases characterized by the development of scope details one iteration at a time, the adjustment of time and cost estimates as the team learns more about the product, and an increase in functionality resulting from iterative development
Management by Projects	Performing day-to-day operations by a project management approach
Material	Any materials used on a project; examples include equipment, tools, machinery, and supplies
Matrix Diagrams	A quality management tool that analyzes data by showing relationships between the data
Matrix Organization	An organizational framework that mandates the sharing of responsibility for the assignment of resources and priorities between the project manager and the functional manager

PMI, CAPM, and PMBOK are registered marks of the Project Management Institute, Inc.

52

© 2008-2018 Crosswind Learning, www.crosswindpm.com

Term	Description
Methodology	A body of rules, practices, processes, and techniques employed within a field
Monitor	Accrue project data for comparison to project plans, produce performance measures, and report project information
Monitor and Control Project Work	The process of monitoring, evaluating, and governing performance progress as detailed in accordance with the project management plan
Monitoring and Controlling Process Group	The processes required to monitor, evaluate, and govern performance progress in accordance with the project management plan and to effect and record any necessary modification of the project management plan
Operations	The day-to-day repeatable activities that a company performs
Organizational Learning	The study of the manner in which knowledge is elaborated by individuals, groups, and organizations
Output	A product, service, or result created by a process; could also be an input to another process
Performing Organization	An organizational framework whose employees are primarily involved in doing the work of the project or program
Phase Gate	A review which is conducted at the end of a phase to decide if the project should continue to the next phase, if the project should continue to the next phase with modification, or if the project or program should be terminated
Planning Process Group	The processes required to create the management and other planning documents that comprise the project management plan
Policy	A course of action adopted by an organization to facilitate operational and project work
Portfolio	The projects, programs, and other work that comprise the portfolio and are managed in a coordinated manner to accomplish strategic goals
Portfolio Management	The coordinated management of the projects, programs, and other work that comprise the portfolio for the purpose of accomplishing strategic goals
Practice	A professional or management activity that feeds the execution of a process that may use one or more tools or techniques
Predictive Life Cycle	A life cycle type that determines project scope, schedule, and cost during the early phases of the life cycle
Process	An ordered series of activities executed to create a product, result, service, or output
Program	A group of related projects, subprograms, and program activities administered in a coordinated manner in order to realize benefits that would not be available if administered separately
Program Management	The exercise of knowledge, expertise, tools and techniques to meet program requirements and to realize the benefits and control only available when the component projects are administered under the program
Progressive Elaboration	The iterative process of increasing the level of detail in accordance with the increase in information discovery and estimation accuracy
Project	A temporary undertaking to produce a unique product, service, or result
Project Governance	The alignment of project goals with the strategy established by the organization, the project sponsor, and team; must fit within the organizational governance, but is separate from that organizational governance
Project Initiation	The process that can result in project authorization
Project Life Cycle	The phases, from initiation through closure, of a project associated with the work of the project, as opposed to being associated with its project management

Term	Description
Project Management	The exercise of knowledge, expertise, and the tools & techniques to meet project requirements
Project Management Body of Knowledge	The total knowledge contained within the project management profession including its practices, both customary and groundbreaking, whether published or non-published
Project Management Knowledge Area	A recognized project management area that is qualified by its component practices, processes, inputs, outputs, tools and techniques and is delineated by its knowledge requisites
Project Management Office (PMO)	An organization area responsible for standardizing governance processes for projects and for making available resources, methodologies, and tools and techniques
Project Management Process Group	The aggregation of the processes, along with their inputs, tools and techniques, and outputs that make up project management including initiating, planning, executing, monitoring and controlling, and closing
Project Management System	An organized approach to project management that can include processes, procedures, tools, techniques, methodologies, and resources; can be used by the project manager or organization
Project Management Team	The individuals on the project team who perform project management activities
Project Manager (PM)	The person authorized by the performing organization to direct the team accountable for realizing project objectives
Project Phase	An aggregation of logically related activities that results in the completion of a deliverable or deliverables
Project-based Organizations (PBO)	An organizational framework that is structured to conduct most of its activities as project work rather than functional work
Projectized Organization	An organizational framework that provides the project manager with the authority to establish priorities, assign resources, and direct the work of the project team
Regulation	A requirement of local, state, or federal government that can mandate product, process, or service characteristics including any applicable administrative provisions
Service	Work performed without resulting in a physical product
Sponsor	The person or group responsible for providing resources and reinforcement for the project and for enabling the project to realize its objectives
Standard	An established norm or requirement
Subphase	A division of a phase of a project
Subproject	A portion of the overall project that is established when the project is subdivided into components that are more easily managed
Tailoring	The determination of the conglomeration of processes, inputs, tools, techniques, outputs, and life cycle phases appropriate to the management of a project
Technique	A procedure, that may employ one or more tools, exercised by a resource to complete project activities
Templates	A partially completed instrument that provides the desired format for the assemblage, ordering, and presentation of data and information
Tight Matrix	A phrase that describes a war room or close environment for the team; can also be used as a distracter answer on organizational-related questions
Tool	A device used during the performance of an activity to produce a result or product; templates, software programs, and models are all tools
Virtual Team	A group of people with similar goals who form a team but spend little (if any) time together
War Room	A room, shared by project personnel, that can be used for planning and meeting, and to display charts, graphs, and various other project information

The source for the above definitions is the Glossary of the Project Management Institute, *A Guide to the Project Management Body of Knowledge, (PMBOK® Guide) – Sixth Edition*, Project Management Institute Inc., 2017

3.10. Framework Tests and Exercises

3.10.1. Framework Practice Test

Answers are in section 3.11.1.

1. What is an organization that controls project managers, documentation, and policies called?

    (A) Project management office
    (B) Tight matrix
    (C) Functional
    (D) Projectized

2. You are brought into a planning meeting by senior management at your company. They inform you that you have been selected to be the project manager for a new project that will help the company create a new product line to be introduced about four years from now. This project is the result of what type of planning?

    (A) Portfolio planning
    (B) Program planning
    (C) Strategic planning
    (D) Product life cycle planning

3. All the following are examples of projects interacting with operations except...

    (A) Upgrading a factory line with new computer components
    (B) Initiating the Go-live phase of a project
    (C) Increasing output to meet unusually high customer demand
    (D) Closing a large sales office

4. Which of the following is an example of an enterprise environmental factor?

    (A) Project life cycle documentation
    (B) Stakeholder risk tolerance
    (C) Standard performance measurement criteria
    (D) Financial, change, and risk control procedures

5. Which of the following is the prioritized order of the project constraints?

    (A) Schedule, risk, cost
    (B) Quality, schedule, cost
    (C) Scope, schedule, budget
    (D) They are all of equal importance unless otherwise stated

6.   Which of the following is an example of a standard?

(A) Data transfer rate for Thunderbolt 3.0 connections
(B) The number of slides in your last presentation
(C) The shade of paint selected to paint your office
(D) The average speed that someone drives to work

7.   On a large medical billing system project, the team is large and communication has been quite a challenge to control. The project expediter has been used to help with this problem. What is one of the main differences between the project expediter and the project coordinator?

(A) The project expediter is another title for the project manager
(B) The project expediter is another title for project coordinator
(C) The project expediter typically has no decision-making ability
(D) The project expediter has decision-making ability

8.   What is the main role of functional managers related to projects?

(A) To provide subject matter experts (SMEs) or services
(B) To manage the project when the project manager isn't available
(C) To deliver the results of the project
(D) To manage the project managers

9.   Which of the following is not an example of organizational culture and style?

(A) Accepting the majority of change requests the customer submits
(B) Working long hours, taking work home, and working weekends
(C) Empowering local managers to make most significant decisions
(D) Focusing most product development on a specific market segment

10.   Which process updates progress and manages changes to the schedule baseline?

(A) Control schedule
(B) Develop schedule management plan
(C) Direct and manage project work
(D) Create project management plan

11.   Which of the following uses cross-functional work teams?

(A) A data warehouse practice
(B) An offshore company
(C) A project that utilizes all groups across a company
(D) Union-approved workplaces

12. Which of the following is the most important job for the project manager?

(A) Controlling stakeholders
(B) Controlling unnecessary change
(C) Creating the project management plan
(D) Exceeding customer expectations

13. What is the typical role of senior management on a project?

(A) Support the project
(B) Pay for it
(C) Support the project and resolve resource and other conflicts
(D) Resolve resource and other conflicts

14. A new project has just completed the initiating process group. The planning process group is getting ready to begin. Which process has just been accomplished, and which process is getting ready to start?

(A) Develop project management plan and direct and manage project work
(B) Identify stakeholders and develop project management plan
(C) Develop project management plan and manage project knowledge
(D) Develop project charter and direct and manage project execution

15. Which of the following stakeholders typically "owns" the work of the project when the project is complete?

(A) Stockholders
(B) The project manager
(C) Functional manager
(D) Operations management

16. What is the difference between a project management life cycle and a project life cycle?

(A) They are the same
(B) The project management life cycle is the project management piece of the project and the project life cycle is the process of completing the work of the project
(C) The project management life cycle is done in the project and the project life cycle is done after the project is complete
(D) The project management life cycle is the process of completing the work of the project and the project life cycle is the project management piece of the project

17. The functional manager is planning the billing system replacement project with the newest project manager at the company. In discussing this project, the functional manager focuses on the cost associated with running the system after it is created and the number of years the system will last before it must be replaced. What best describes what the functional manager is focusing on?

    (A) Project life cycle
    (B) Product life cycle
    (C) Project management life cycle
    (D) Program management life cycle

18. What is the ideal project manager function regarding project changes?

    (A) To delay changes so the project can be completed
    (B) To control unnecessary change
    (C) To prevent the change control board from seeing any more change than it needs to see
    (D) To expedite all change requests to the change control board

19. What is created in the initiating process group?

    (A) Project charter and requirements documentation
    (B) Project scope statement and various management plans
    (C) Project charter and project knowledge
    (D) Project charter and stakeholder register

20. A business analyst has a career path that has been very important to her throughout the ten years of her career. She is put on a very important project with a strong matrix organizational structure. Which of the following is likely viewed as the most serious drawback of being on the project?

    (A) Being away from the group might make career advancement in the department more difficult
    (B) Working with people who have similar skills
    (C) Working long hours because the project is a high priority
    (D) Not being able to take the BAP Certification test because she will be so busy

21. Which of the following is the definition of program management?

    (A) Managing related or similar projects in a coordinated way
    (B) The process of computer program management
    (C) Managing a television program
    (D) Done for a purpose

22. Who is accountable for creating and executing the project management plan?

    (A) The team
    (B) The company that was awarded the outsourcing contract
    (C) The project manager and the project management team
    (D) The project manager

23. What are the five process groups used in the Project Management Institute, Inc. approach to project management?

    (A) Initiating, planning, executing, monitoring and controlling, closing
    (B) Initiating, planning, executing, testing, sign off
    (C) Requirements, system development, testing, UAT, sign off
    (D) Initiating, planning, executing, testing, closure

24. Which of the following is an advantage of a projectized organization?

    (A) Business unit competency
    (B) Optimization for a single focus on the project
    (C) Having to get approval from functional management
    (D) A place to go when the project is complete

25. What is the name of the comprehensive document created during the planning process group?

    (A) Project charter
    (B) Project scope statement
    (C) Project management plan
    (D) A signed contract

26. Which of the following best describes a stakeholder on a project?

    (A) A team member
    (B) The project manager
    (C) Someone who works in an area impacted by the work of the project
    (D) All the answers

27. The data warehouse project is about halfway complete at a major retail client. Your company is doing the implementation and has 12 team members in various locations across three different buildings. Communication and team building has been a real challenge. Which of the following would fix or improve this problem?

    (A) Changing the organization to a functional structure
    (B) Colocation
    (C) Replacing the project manager
    (D) Hiring project coordinators

28. The project management life cycle is similar to which of the following?

    (A) Project life cycle
    (B) SDLC
    (C) Plan-do-check-act
    (D) Use case analysis

29. Which of the following is not a regulation?

    (A) The building code for a city
    (B) The documented way to dispose of old computers
    (C) The average speed on a street in a day
    (D) The zoning for an area

30. Which of the following is an advantage of a functional organization?

    (A) Having a home to go to when the project is complete
    (B) Not having a home when the project is complete
    (C) Having more than one project to work on
    (D) Having more than one boss

3.11. Framework Answers for Tests and Exercises

3.11.1. Framework Practice Test Answers

We recommend that you download answer sheets from the Crosswind website, so you can practice the test as many times as you like.

1. What is an organization that controls project managers, documentation, and policies called?

   Correct Answer: (A) Project management office
   Explanation: The project management office (PMO) can control project managers, documentation and policies or anything else needed within reason for the management of projects within an organization. [Crosswind Manual 3.2.5; *PMBOK® Guide* 2.4.4.3]

2. You are brought into a planning meeting by senior management at your company. They inform you that you have been selected to be the project manager for a new project that will help the company create a new product line to be introduced about four years from now. This project is the result of what type of planning?

   Correct Answer: (C) Strategic planning
   Explanation: Strategic planning is typically done three to five years in advance. It is very common for projects to be driven by strategic initiatives at a company. Product life cycle involves the entire cycle from "cradle-to-grave" for a product. The other answers are distracters. [Crosswind Manual 3.2.3; *PMBOK® Guide* 1.2.3.1]

3. All the following are examples of projects interacting with operations except...

   Correct Answer: (C) Increasing output to meet unusually high customer demand
   Explanation: Accommodating high demand still falls under the realm of operations. Anticipating and scheduling daily, monthly, seasonal, or cyclical fluctuations are common duties for "operational" individuals. All other answers involve a project impacting the day-to-day operations in some significant way. [Crosswind Manual 3.2; *PMBOK® Guide* 1.2.1]

4. Which of the following is an example of an enterprise environmental factor?

   Correct Answer: (B) Stakeholder risk tolerance
   Explanation: All incorrect answers are examples of organizational process assets. [Crosswind Manual 4.1.2; *PMBOK® Guide* 2.2]

5. Which of the following is the prioritized order of the project constraints?

   Correct Answer: (D) They are all of equal importance unless otherwise stated
   Explanation: The constraint of project management states that scope, quality, schedule, budget, resources, and risks are all equal unless otherwise defined as such. [Crosswind Manual 3.3; No *PMBOK® Guide* Reference]

6. Which of the following is an example of a standard?

Correct Answer: (A) Data transfer rate for Thunderbolt 3.0 connections
Explanation: A standard is a measurement for something that is consistent and generally accepted. In this case, the data transfer rate for Thunderbolt 3.0 connections is the only "standard" listed in the answers. [Crosswind Manual 3.9; No *PMBOK® Guide* Reference]

7. On a large medical billing system project, the team is large and communication has been quite a challenge to control. The project expediter has been used to help with this problem. What is one of the main differences between the project expediter and the project coordinator?

Correct Answer: (C) The project expediter typically has no decision-making ability
Explanation: The project expediter and the project coordinator have similar responsibilities with the difference being that the project coordinator has some decision-making ability. [Crosswind Manual 3.4.11; No *PMBOK® Guide* Reference]

8. What is the main role of functional managers related to projects?

Correct Answer: (A) To provide subject matter experts (SMEs) or services
Explanation: Functional managers like human resources managers or accounting managers have a permanent staff and a clear directive to manage all tasks within their domain. Related to projects, however, they may provide SMEs or services to support projects. Project managers do not always report to functional managers. The functional manager runs a department or area of business, not the project manager. To incorporate the project deliverables into normal operations is the role of operations management. [Crosswind Manual 3.4.11; No *PMBOK® Guide* Reference]

9. Which of the following is not an example of organizational culture and style?

Correct Answer: (D) Focusing most product development on a specific market segment
Explanation: Focusing on a particular market is more a strategic business decision than a cultural aspect. All other answers are examples of the pervasive aspects of organizational culture. [Crosswind Manual 3.7; No *PMBOK® Guide* Reference]

10. Which process updates progress and manages changes to the schedule baseline?

Correct Answer: (A) Control schedule
Explanation: This is the basic definition of Control Schedule. There is no process called develop schedule management plan, though the schedule management plan (a document) would give guidance on the basic tools and techniques of HOW to update progress and manage changes through the Control Schedule process. Note the verb tense: "Which process **updates** progress and **manages**." This implies doing it, not planning it, making Control Schedule the correct answer. [Crosswind Manual 6.6; *PMBOK® Guide* 6.6]

11. Which of the following uses cross-functional work teams?

Correct Answer: (C) A project that utilizes all groups across a company
Explanation: A project that utilizes all groups across a company utilizes cross-functional teams to take advantage of the knowledge and skills available. A data warehouse practice is likely a projectized organization. An offshore company is too vague an answer. Union-approved workplaces is a distracter. [Crosswind Manual 3.7.5; No *PMBOK® Guide* Reference]

12. Which of the following is the most important job for the project manager?

Correct Answer: (B) Controlling unnecessary change
Explanation: Controlling unnecessary change is one of the biggest challenges for project managers. If they don't do this well, the project can go out of control. Creating the project management plan is a good answer, but if changes are out of control, the best plan won't do any good. Exceeding customer expectations is unnecessary and could likely result in gold plating, which isn't good. Controlling stakeholders is a distracter. The expectations of stakeholders are to be managed, not controlled. [Crosswind Manual 3.5; No *PMBOK® Guide* Reference]

13. What is the typical role of senior management on a project?

Correct Answer: (C) Support the project and resolve resource and other conflicts
Explanation: Senior management outranks the project manager. They support the project by helping resolve resource issues and other conflicts. The sponsor pays for the project. [Crosswind Manual 3.4.11; No *PMBOK® Guide* Reference]

14. A new project has just completed the initiating process group. The planning process group is getting ready to begin. Which process has just been accomplished, and which process is getting ready to start?

Correct Answer: (B) Identify stakeholders and develop project management plan
Explanation: The initiating process group ends with the Identify Stakeholders process, and the planning process group begins with Develop Project Management Plan. [Crosswind Manual 1.2.4.5; *PMBOK® Guide* 3.4.1]

15. Which of the following stakeholders typically "owns" the work of the project when the project is complete?

Correct Answer: (D) Operations management
Explanation: Notice the word "typically". Virtually anyone could own the work, depending on the nature of the project and the product. However, operations management accepts the product from project management, and then operations management incorporates the product or service into normal operations, as well maintains the product or service. [Crosswind Manual 3.4.11; No *PMBOK® Guide* Reference]

16. What is the difference between a project management life cycle and a project life cycle?

Correct Answer: (B) The project management life cycle is the project management piece of the project and the project life cycle is the process of completing the work of the project.
Explanation: The project management life cycle (PMLC) is the project management methodology used on a project. The project life cycle applies to whatever is being built. It can be the software approach for a software project or a building approach for construction. [Crosswind Manual 3.1; *PMBOK® Guide* Table 1-3]

17. The functional manager is planning the billing system replacement project with the newest project manager at the company. In discussing this project, the functional manager focuses on the cost associated with running the system after it is created and the number of years the system will last before it must be replaced. What best describes what the functional manager is focusing on?

Correct Answer: (B) Product life cycle
Explanation: The product life cycle focuses on the overall ownership cost of the product of the project, not just the project cost to create the product. The project life cycle involves the processes used to create the product of the project such as the steps to build a house or a computer system. The project management life cycle is the project management approach to the project. Program management life cycle is a distracter. [Crosswind Manual 3.1; *PMBOK® Guide* 1.2.4.1]

18. What is the ideal project manager function regarding project changes?

Correct Answer: (B) To control unnecessary change
Explanation: The main job of a project manager, other than managing the project itself, is to control unnecessary changes that can derail the project. Delaying changes and protecting the change control board from changes are both unprofessional. Expediting changes to the CCB is not a bad answer but not the best because it doesn't help in controlling unnecessary change. [Crosswind Manual 3.5; No *PMBOK® Guide* Reference]

19. What is created in the initiating process group?

Correct Answer: (D) Project charter and stakeholder register
Explanation: Answer D contains all documents created during the initiating process group. All others are created during the planning process group. [Crosswind Manual 3.4.1; *PMBOK® Guide* Part 2, 2.1, 2.2]

20. A business analyst has a career path that has been very important to her throughout the ten years of her career. She is put on a very important project with a strong matrix organizational structure. Which of the following is likely viewed as the most serious drawback of being on the project?

Correct Answer: (A) Being away from the group might make career advancement in the department more difficult
Explanation: Being away from the normal group and not being able to be as easily promoted is the best answer. Being in a strong matrix environment feels fairly similar to being in a projectized organization where skill set specialty in groups does not have as high a priority. The other answers are distracters. [Crosswind Manual 3.5; No *PMBOK® Guide* Reference]

21. Which of the following is the definition of program management?

Correct Answer: (A) Managing related or similar projects in a coordinated way
Explanation: Program management utilizes a coordinated management of related projects. Done for a purpose is a characteristic of a project. The other answers are distracters. [Crosswind Manual 3.2.1; *PMBOK® Guide* 1.2.3.2]

22. Who is accountable for creating and executing the project management plan?

Correct Answer: (D) The project manager
Explanation: The project manager is ultimately responsible for creating the project management plan. This creation typically comes with the help of the project management team. The project manager is responsible for execution of the plan and the team members are responsible for the plan's activities. The outsourcing answer is a distracter. [Crosswind Manual 3.5; *PMBOK® Guide* 3.1]

23. What are the five process groups used in the Project Management Institute, Inc. approach to project management?

Correct Answer: (A) Initiating, planning, executing, monitoring and controlling, closing
Explanation: Per the *PMBOK® Guide*, the process groups that make up the PMI® methodology or "project management life cycle" are initiating, planning, executing, monitoring and controlling, and closing. [Crosswind Manual 3.4.1; *PMBOK® Guide* Table 1-4]

24. Which of the following is an advantage of a projectized organization?

Correct Answer: (B) Optimization for a single focus on the project
Explanation: Optimization for a single focus on the project means that the team can focus on what the work of the project is and usually only that. The other answers are associated with functional organizations. [Crosswind Manual 3.7.4; No *PMBOK® Guide* Reference]

25. What is the name of the comprehensive document created during the planning process group?

Correct Answer: (C) Project management plan
Explanation: The main output of the planning process group is the project management plan. The project charter comes from Initiation. The project scope statement is created during the planning process group, but it's far less comprehensive than the project management plan. A signed contract is a distracter. [Crosswind Manual 3.4.1; *PMBOK® Guide* 1.2.4.5]

26. Which of the following best describes a stakeholder on a project?

(A) A team member
(B) The project manager
(C) Someone who works in an area impacted by the work of the project

Correct Answer: (D) All the answers
Explanation: The stakeholder can be anyone impacted by the project. A stakeholder could be the sponsor, senior management, project manager, functional manager, team member, or end user. [Crosswind Manual 3.4.11; *PMBOK® Guide* 13.1]

27. The data warehouse project is about halfway complete at a major retail client. Your company is doing the implementation and has 12 team members in various locations across three different buildings. Communication and team building has been a real challenge. Which of the following would fix or improve this problem?

Correct Answer: (B) Colocation
Explanation: Colocation is the process of putting personnel closer together or in the same room to help with team building and project communication. [Crosswind Manual 3.9; No *PMBOK® Guide* Reference]

28. The project management life cycle is similar to which of the following?

Correct Answer: (C) Plan-do-check-act
Explanation: Plan-do-check-act is defined by the American Society for Quality as an approach to process development. It can show how the project management life cycle components co-exist or overlap. The project life cycle builds the work of the project. SDLC and use case analysis are software development approaches. [Crosswind Manual 3.4.2; *PMBOK® Guide* Chapter 8 Intro]

29. Which of the following is not a regulation?

Correct Answer: (C) The average speed on a street in a day
Explanation: The average speed on a street in a day is simply a value. It's not a regulation, which the other answers are. The other answers have defined criteria that they must meet to be acceptable. [Crosswind Manual 3.9; No *PMBOK® Guide* Reference]

30. Which of the following is an advantage of a functional organization?

Correct Answer: (A) Having a home to go to when the project is complete
Explanation: Having a home when the project is complete is a key advantage of a functional organization. Having more than one boss and more than one project could be characteristics of a matrix organization. [Crosswind Manual 3.7.3; No *PMBOK® Guide* Reference]

Chapter 4

Project Integration Management

While the other nine knowledge areas may be managed, in whole or in part, by specialists, Project Integration Management is the sole purview of the project manager. Accountability for this knowledge area cannot be transferred or delegated.

The goals of Project Integration Management are to:

- Make certain that the due dates of the benefits management plan, the product life cycle, and the project result, service, or product are in alignment
- Deliver a project management plan that will result in the achievement of project objectives
- Make certain that appropriate knowledge is generated and utilized both in and out of the project as necessary
- Manage activities delineated in the project management plan, in terms of both performance and change
- Quantify and monitor project progress, taking appropriate steps to ensure project objectives will be met
- Collecting and analyzing data in connection with results achieved, then communicating the information to appropriate stakeholders
- Completing all the project work and formally closing each phase, each contract, and the project as a whole

The sophistication of the approach needed to successfully perform Project Integration Management is directly related to the complexity of the project and the diversity of stakeholder expectations.

Trends
The five most notable trends are:

- The use of automated tools
  Project managers are experiencing the need to integrate increased amounts of data and information necessitating the use of a project management information system (PMIS) and automated tools for the collection, analysis, and use of the information.
- The use of visual management tools
  Project teams, especially those involved in adaptive or hybrid projects, are using visual management tools (e.g. deliverables for current sprint) in place of written plans and other items to document critical project factors. Visual management tools make critical project factors visible to the entire team.

- Project knowledge management
  To insure that project knowledge is not lost when the work force is becoming more dispersed and transitory, project managers are putting in place a stringent process for knowledge identification throughout the project and transference of that knowledge to the appropriate parties.
- Project boundary expansion
  Project managers are more frequently assuming a collaborative or management role in the initiation and finalization of the project, activities that were controlled by management and the project office. Project managers are also more frequently involved in a more exhaustive effort to identify and engage stakeholders, including the management of interfaces with senior management and operations.
- Hybrid methodologies
  The project team is adopting many practices from an adaptive environment, including Agile practices, the application of business analysis techniques to requirements management, the application of change management techniques to the transition of project outputs to the organization, and the applications of tools that identify complex project elements.

Tailoring

Project tailoring, the manner in which processes of a knowledge area are exercised, is employed to address the distinctive nature of each project. Successful project tailoring is predicated on a careful consideration of:

- The approaches employed for life cycle, development, and management
- Knowledge management
- Change
- Governance
- Lessons learned
- Benefits

Agile/Adaptive Environment

Agile, and other iterative project approaches, encourage a reliance on team members as local domain experts for integration management. During project integration management, the team members determine the manner in which project plans and components are integrated.

The project manager is responsible for building a collaborative decision making environment and ensuring that the team can respond to change.

Note that teams with an extended skill base are generally more effective at collaboration than those whose members have a narrower skill base.

The source for the above text is the Project Management Institute, *A Guide to the Project Management Body of Knowledge*, (PMBOK® Guide) – Sixth Edition, Project Management Institute Inc., 2017, Pages 72-76

PMI, CAPM, and PMBOK are registered marks of the Project Management Institute, Inc.

68   © 2008-2018 Crosswind Learning, www.crosswindpm.com

In this chapter, we discuss the following:

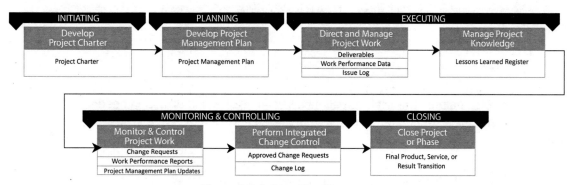

Figure 4-1: Integration Processes

The source for the above figure is the Project Management Institute, *A Guide to the Project Management Body of Knowledge, (PMBOK® Guide) – Sixth Edition*, Project Management Institute Inc., 2017, Figure 4-1, Page 73

☑ **Crosswind "Must Knows" for Project Integration Management**

	Key Inputs, Tools & Techniques, and Outputs for Develop Project Charter
	Key Inputs, Tools & Techniques, and Outputs for Develop Project Management Plan
	Key Inputs, Tools & Techniques, and Outputs for Direct and Manage Project Work
	Key Inputs, Tools & Techniques, and Outputs for Manage Project Knowledge
	Key Inputs, Tools & Techniques, and Outputs for Monitor and Control Project Work
	Key Inputs, Tools & Techniques, and Outputs for Perform Integrated Change Control
	Key Inputs, Tools & Techniques, and Outputs for Close Project or Phase
	General attributes of organizational process assets
	General attributes of enterprise environmental factors
	Characteristics of the project charter, how it is used, who creates it, and how project management uses it
	Characteristics of project selection techniques and their importance
	Characteristics and components of a project management plan
	What assumptions and constraints are as they relate to a project
	Characteristics and importance of a baseline
	Characteristics of a Project Management Information System
	Characteristics of a work authorization system
	Differences between requested changes and approved changes
	Characteristics of a change control system

Chapter 4
Integration

	Characteristics of a configuration management system
	Important considerations of closing a project such as product verification, lessons learned, updating of records, reporting, archiving, and formal acceptance of components
	The definition and importance of lessons learned
	How to close a project and the documentation required to do so

Although helpful, this list is not all-inclusive in regard to information needed for the exam. It is only suggested material that, if understood and memorized, may increase your exam score.

4.1. Project Influence

The environments in which a project resides and operates may exert an influence, favorable or unfavorable, on the project.

The two major sources of influence are organization process assets (OPAs) and enterprise environmental factors (EEFs).

4.1.1. Organizational Process Assets

Organizational process assets can be inputs to many processes and can include information systems, company policies and procedures, process definitions, templates, criteria to complete (close) projects, organization communication needs, issue management, financial infrastructure, change control processes, risk management, and work authorization.

Know the general attributes of organizational process assets.

A corporate knowledge base can also be broadened by expanding the organizational process assets to include: process data, project files and records, lessons learned, historical information, configuration management data, databases, and financial data.

4.1.2. Enterprise Environmental Factors

Enterprise environmental factors can also be inputs to many processes and can include government regulations, market conditions, organizational structure and culture, business infrastructure systems, government standards, personnel policies, the business market, stakeholder tolerance for risk, and PMIS (Project Management Information Systems).

Know the general attributes of enterprise environmental factors.

Because these factors have the potential to influence project success, it is important that they are identified and considered during project planning.

4.2. Project Management Plan Updates

The project management plan is a **living, breathing document**. As the project evolves, the project management plan is updated to accommodate the modification or clarification of any planning process. The plan is also updated to accommodate any adjustments resulting from a monitoring and/or controlling process.

4.3. Project Documents Updates

Note that updates and clarifications to project documents do not always warrant comparable changes to the project management plan. For example, clarifying the scope statement or moving money from one cost center to another does not require an update to the project management plan.

4.4. Project Business Documents

The project manager is responsible for ensuring that the project management approach aligns with the intent of the project's business documents, specifically the business case and the business management plan. The business documents are interdependent and are developed and maintained iteratively throughout the project's life cycle.

The project manager is also responsible for providing recommendations and oversight to keep the success measures for the project management plan, business case, and benefits management plan in alignment with one another and with the goals and objectives of the organization.

The project manager is responsible for tailoring the project documents

4.4.1. Business Case

The business case, which usually describes the business need and contains a cost-benefit analysis, is used to justify the creation of the project and is the basis for the project charter.

At the end of the project, the business case can be used to measure project success in terms of achieving project objectives.

4.4.2. Benefits Management Plan

The benefits management plan describes the alignment of the project with organizational business goals, the targeted benefits, and the manner in which the benefits are transitioned and measured.

The benefits management plan and the project management plan include a description of business value and the metrics that will be used to measure business value. Business value can be used to measure project success.

4.4.3. Success Measures

Traditionally, project success was measured by the project adhering to the schedule, cost, and scope parameters. Today, project success is often dependent on other factors.

The project manager and stakeholders must agree on, and then document, the factors that define project success, the approach to measuring success, and the factors that will impact success.

Note that success may be further defined by criteria linked to organizational strategy and the delivery of business results.

Project objectives may include:

- Completion of the benefits management plan
- Meeting agreed-upon financial measures defined in the business case
- Meeting non-financial objectives defined in the business case
- Moving the organization from it's current state to a desired future state
- Fulfilling contract terms and conditions
- Meeting organizational strategy, goals, and objectives
- Achieving stakeholder satisfaction
- Achieving acceptable customer/end-user adoption
- Integrating project deliverables into operations
- Achieving the agreed-upon quality of delivery
- Meeting governance criteria
- Achieving other agreed-upon criteria

Project success increases if business alignment is constant because the project will align with the organization's strategic direction.

4.5. Project Information

Project evolution results in project information evolution. Project information can include work performance data, work performance information, and work performance reports.

Figure 4-2: Project Information Evolution illustrates the evolution of information throughout the project:

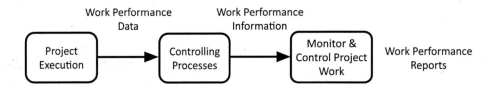

Figure 4-2: Project Information Evolution

4.5.1. Work Performance Data

Work performance data is raw data generated as a result of project work. Examples include **start** and **finish dates**, **completion percent for activities**, **number of defects**, and **number of change requests**.

Work performance data is analyzed and then converted to project information.

4.5.2. Work Performance Information

Work performance information is generally created as a result of the monitoring and/or controlling processes. Once analyzed, the analysis results are presented as a representation of the state of the project in areas such as the **state of deliverables**, the **status of change requests**, and **forecasts** related to schedule and cost. Such information is the basis of reports used to fulfill stakeholder communication requirements.

4.5.3. Work Performance Reports

Work performance reports are physical or electronic depictions of work performance information in the form of project documents that help stakeholders make decisions. Examples include **status and progress reports**, **memos**, **recommendations**, and **updates**.

The source for the above text is the Project Management Institute, *A Guide to the Project Management Body of Knowledge*, (*PMBOK® Guide*) – Sixth Edition, Project Management Institute Inc., 2017, Pages 76-78

4.6. Develop Project Charter (Initiating Process Group)

Develop Project Charter is the process which creates the document which formally authorizes the project or project phases and authorizes the project manager to use organizational resources for project activities.

The charter aligns the project with organizational objectives, creates a formal record of the project, and is evidence of organizational commitment to the project.

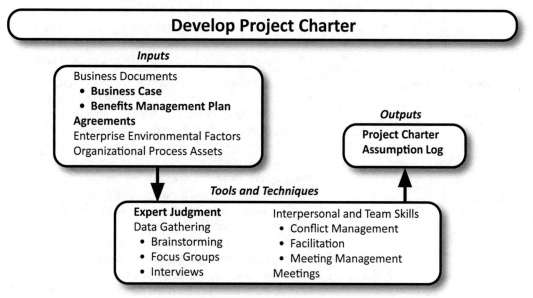

Know the Key Inputs, Tools & Techniques, and Outputs for Develop Project Charter.

Primary items are bolded and elaborated on in the content that follows.

Bullet indicate subsets of the preceding item.

Figure 4-3: Develop Project Charter Data Flow Diagram

The source for the above figure is the Project Management Institute, *A Guide to the Project Management Body of Knowledge*, (*PMBOK® Guide*) – Sixth Edition, Project Management Institute Inc., 2017, Figure 4-2, Page 77

Develop Project Charter (Initiating)		
Key Inputs	Business Case	A business case, which usually describes the business need and contains a cost-benefit analysis, is used to justify the creation of the project and is the basis for the project charter. Note that the project manager is not responsible for updating or modifying the business case since it is a business document.

- Sponsor is always internal
  * If the project is external, then you have an internal sponsor that's representing the external customer

Gather this info from Sponsor

When you join as PM, these docs will help you get up to speed

EEFs: Regs.

OPAs: Templates,

Develop Project Charter (Continued)		
Key Inputs (Cont.)	Benefits Management Plan	The benefits management plan describes the alignment of the project with organizational business goals, the targeted benefits, and the manner in which the benefits are transitioned and measured. Note that the project manager is not responsible for updating or modifying the benefits management plan since it is a business document.
	Agreements	Agreements define project intentions and can be written (such as letters of agreements, contracts, memorandum of understanding, service level agreements, and email) or verbal. For work to be performed by an external source, a contract between buyer and seller is typically used.
Key Tools & Techniques	Expert Judgment	Expert judgment is judgment based on expertise acquired in a specific area. It is often more significant and accurate than the best modeling tools available and can be provided by stakeholders, company personnel external to the project, professional organizations or groups, and consultants. It is important to consider expertise related to industry-related technical details, management of benefits, organizational strategy, risks, time, and budget.
Key Outputs	Project Charter	The project charter is the document that provides authorization for the existence of the project and gives the project manager the power to use organizational resources to execute the project. The project charter typically lists the key deliverables, the milestones, and the roles and responsibilities of each person involved in the project. Note that the high level assumptions and constraints listed in the business case are often included in the charter. As an example, the statement "there will be a robust market for the product created as a result of this project once it is available to the public" is an assumption. A constraint is a restrictive or limiting factor. As an example, the operations manager insistence that a key subject matter expert must dedicate at least six hours a day to operations is a constraint on the project.

Develop Project Charter (Continued)		
Key Outputs	Assumption Log	The assumption log is a document that lists the assumptions and constraints identified during the creation of the project charter. An assumption is an idea or statement taken to be true. An example of an assumption is the statement "there will be a robust market for the product created as a result of this project once it is available to the public." Examples of constraints are the project completion deadline, the budget threshold, or the limit on the number of employees that can be dedicated to the project. It's important to identify assumptions and constraints as early as possible and monitor them as the project evolves.

Situational Question and Real World Application

Failure to effectively perform the Develop Project Charter process can result in a project that does not exist.

4.6.1. Project Charter

The project charter, which authorizes the existence of the project, is typically created after an initiative goes through preliminary planning or a feasibility study.

Typically, the project charter includes:

Know what a project charter is, how it is used, who creates it, and how a project manager uses it.

- Project justification and purpose
- Success criteria
- High-level scope (requirements) of the project
- Any constraints and assumptions
- Time and cost goals
- Authority level of the project manager
- Stakeholder definition and level of influence
- Organizational information
- Project approval requirements

It may be created by anyone with the authority to create a charter, even the project manager, but it must be signed by someone, typically senior management or the sponsor, who can invest authority for the project.

4.6.2. Kickoff Meeting

A kickoff meeting is generally the official start to a project. It can be held at the beginning of planning or executing, depending on priority and approach.

If held at the start of planning, the meeting can be used to set expectations of what project planning will include and create when complete.

If held at the start of execution, the meeting can be used to set expectations and communicate details of the project management plan to the team members so they understand their roles and know the expected results, product, or service of the project.

Kickoff meeting attendees may vary, but should include anyone with a key role in the project.

4.6.3. Project Selection

An organization can determine the projects it will pursue based on a variety of factors. A project is typically created to solve a problem, to take advantage of an opportunity, or to fulfill a business requirement. Other factors that can result in the creation of a project can include a response to a market demand, a technological advance, a customer request, or a legal requirement.

Be familiar with project selection techniques and their importance.

Mathematical Models	There are various mathematical models that can be used for project selection. They include the following: • Constrained optimization • Linear programming • Non-linear programming • Dynamic analysis • Integer programming • Complex calculation • Algorithms (multi-objective programming) This approach ultimately comes down to trying to forecast as many variables as possible and predict the outcome via mathematical analysis.
Benefit Measurement Model	This could also be considered a scoring model. This model takes the following into consideration: • Comparative approach • Scoring models • Benefit contribution • Economic model

Typically, selected projects relate to the strategic goals of the organization and corresponding financial performance.

For the exam, accounting skills are unnecessary. The following table contains a guide for project selection based on the method used. Details are in the Cost chapter.

Financial Metrics Table			
Project Selection Tool	**Also Known As**	**Option to Select**	**Example**
Return on Investment	ROI	The Biggest Number or Percentage	$50,000 or 7%
Internal Rate of Return	IRR	The Biggest Percentage	15.50%
Net Present Value	NPV	The Biggest Number (Years are already factored in)	$47,500
Benefit Cost Ratio	BCR	The Biggest Ratio	3.5:1
Opportunity Cost	--	The Amounts That Are Not Selected	Project A ($7,000) over Project B ($5,000)
Payback Period	--	The Shortest Duration	7 months

The source for the above text is the Project Management Institute, *A Guide to the Project Management Body of Knowledge*, (*PMBOK® Guide*) – Sixth Edition, Project Management Institute Inc., 2017, Pages 78-83

4.7. Develop Project Management Plan (Planning Process Group)

The Develop Project Management Plan process defines, prepares, and coordinates all plan components and consolidates them into an integrated project management plan. The project management plan can include (but is not limited to) the management plans for scope, schedule, cost, quality, resource, communication, risk, procurement, and stakeholder.

Know the Key Inputs, Tools & Techniques, and Outputs for Develop Project Management Plan.

The project management plan defines the project work, the manner in which it will be performed, and the manner in which it is monitored and controlled.

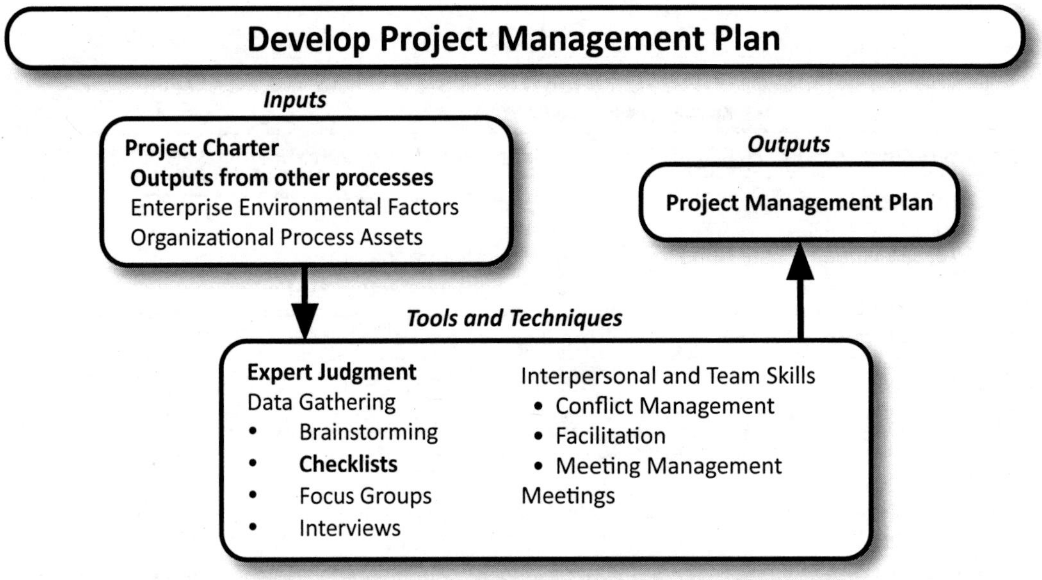

Develop Project Management Plan

Inputs

Project Charter
Outputs from other processes
Enterprise Environmental Factors
Organizational Process Assets

Outputs

Project Management Plan

Tools and Techniques

Expert Judgment
Data Gathering
- Brainstorming
- **Checklists**
- Focus Groups
- Interviews

Interpersonal and Team Skills
- Conflict Management
- Facilitation
- Meeting Management
Meetings

Figure 4-4: Develop Project Management Plan Data Flow Diagram
The source for the above figure is the Project Management Institute, *A Guide to the Project Management Body of Knowledge*, (*PMBOK® Guide*) – Sixth Edition, Project Management Institute Inc., 2017, Figure 4-4, Page 83

Develop Project Management Plan (Planning)		
Key Inputs	Project Charter	The project charter serves as the foundation of project planning and should contain sufficient high-level information to initiate the project management plan components.
	Outputs from Other Processes	The outputs (baselines and component plans) from the various project management process groups are integrated to comprise the project management plan. Any changes to the documents typically require an update to the project management plan.
Key Tools & Techniques	Expert Judgment	Expert judgment is judgment based on expertise acquired in a specific area. It is important to consider expertise related to adapting the project management process to accommodate the needs of the project; identifying the resources, skill levels, and tools and techniques to be used to successfully execute the project; determining the level of configuration management appropriate to the project and the documents subject to formal change control; prioritizing project work with consideration of resource allocation; and establishing those managerial and technical details that will be included in the project management plan.

Develop Project Management Plan (Continued)		
Key Tools & Techniques (Cont.)	Checklists	Checklists are utilized to ensure that appropriate procedures are followed during the creation of the project management plan. They are also utilized to confirm that the plan contains all necessary information. Standardized checklists developed by the organization or the industry are often used.
Key Outputs	Project Management Plan	The project management plan integrates subsidiary plans (those representing the knowledge areas identified by the Project Management Institute, Inc.), baselines from the planning processes, the project life cycle, the development approach, and management reviews. Supporting detail is included to validate the information contained.

Situational Question and Real World Application

It is very important that the project management plan addresses the knowledge areas.

Scope Management: If you fail to effectively address scope management, your client may start requesting additional items that could impact project goals. There is no control loop for scope.

Schedule Management: If you fail to effectively address schedule management, the schedule could slip rapidly or you may be unable to determine any variances between planned time and actual time.

Cost Management: If you fail to effectively address cost management, you may be unable to determine variances between planned cost and actual cost.

Quality Management: If you fail to effectively address quality management, you may be unable to obtain sign off on completed work products due to the lack of clearly defined standards of acceptable completion criteria. This could result in cost and schedule overruns.

Resource Management: If you fail to effectively address resource management, you may be unable to place the right resources on the project at the right time.

Communications Management: If you fail to effectively address communications management, you may be unable to work effectively with stakeholders and the team, which could result in strained stakeholder expectations or activity completion issues.

Risk Management: If you fail to effectively address risk management, the project could encounter unforeseen (and thus, unplanned) risk events that could damage or potentially destroy the project.

Procurement Management: If you fail to effectively address procurement management, your failure to engage outside vendors successfully could result in scope and completion issues.

Stakeholder Management: If you fail to effectively address stakeholder management, your failure to engage stakeholders could result in stakeholder engagement and expectation issues.

4.7.1. Project Management Plan

The project management plan is a cumulative document that **contains all of the documents used in the management approach to the project**.

It describes the steps associated with executing, monitoring and controlling, and closing the project and can be at a summary or detailed level.

Generally, the plan includes the processes associated with the definition, integration, and coordination of the various documents in the following table.

Once the project is baselined, the plan should only be updated to reflect changes authorized through the formal change control process.

The documents contained can differ from project to project. In general, the following management plans and documents are included in the project management plan.

Know the characteristics and components of a project management plan.

Management Plans in the Project Management Plan Document	
Requirements Management Plan	Scope Management Plan
Schedule Management Plan	Cost Management Plan
Quality Management Plan	Process Improvement Plan
Communications Management Plan	Resource Management Plan
Procurement Management Plan	Risk Management Plan
Change Management Plan	Stakeholder Management Plan
Configuration Management Plan	

Also for Consideration in the Project Management Plan Document or Project Documents			
Milestone List	Milestone Schedule	Resource List and Calendar	(Project) Organizational Chart
Requirements	Requirements Traceability Matrix	Project Scope Statement	Work Breakdown Structure
Scope Baseline	Schedule Baseline	Cost Baseline	Quality Baseline
Risk Breakdown Structure	Risk Register	Change Control Systems	Stakeholder Register

4.7.2. Assumptions

During planning, it is necessary to make assumptions regarding scheduling, budgeting, and any other aspect of the project that is not yet known.

Lessons learned is valuable in helping to create valid assumptions.

As the project evolves, assumptions decrease.

Know assumptions as they relate to a project.

PMI, CAPM, and PMBOK are registered marks of the Project Management Institute, Inc.

80 © 2008-2018 Crosswind Learning, www.crosswindpm.com

4.7.3. Constraints

Constraints are factors that limit project options, and can include such items as the number of people, the amount of time, or the amount of money available to complete the work of the project.

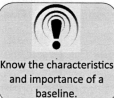

Know constraints as they relate to a project.

4.7.4. Baseline

The baseline is the approved version of a work product. The baseline value is the value against which the work results (sometimes called actuals) are compared. There can be a baseline value for any item on the project that will be measured. **Scope, schedule, cost, and quality** are typically baselined.

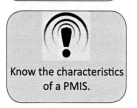

Know the characteristics and importance of a baseline.

4.7.5. Project Management Information System (PMIS)

The project management information system is used for communication and information distribution on the project. It is not necessarily a high tech system, but is often a mixture of technical and non-technical tools.

Know the characteristics of a PMIS.

The source for the above text is the Project Management Institute, *A Guide to the Project Management Body of Knowledge*, (PMBOK® Guide) – Sixth Edition, Project Management Institute Inc., 2017, Pages 83-89

4.8. Direct and Manage Project Work (Executing Process Group)

The Direct and Manage Project work process consists of leading and performing project work in accordance with the project management plan, as well as implementing authorized changes.

The project manager, with the project team, directs the performance of the work, manages the technical and organizational interfaces in the project, and implements authorized changes.

During this process, resources are allocated as available, their work is managed, and any changes that arise from the analysis of work performance data and work performance information are put into place.

Note that work performance data is an input into the monitoring and controlling process group and can be used as feedback for lessons learned.

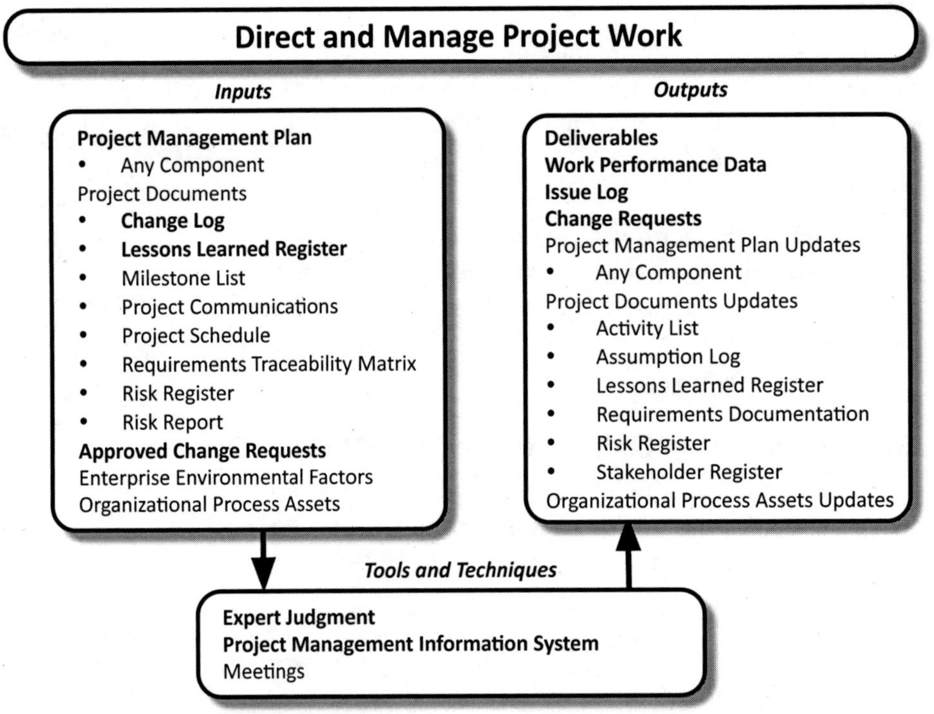

Direct and Manage Project Work

Inputs

Project Management Plan
- Any Component

Project Documents
- **Change Log**
- **Lessons Learned Register**
- Milestone List
- Project Communications
- Project Schedule
- Requirements Traceability Matrix
- Risk Register
- Risk Report

Approved Change Requests

Enterprise Environmental Factors

Organizational Process Assets

Outputs

Deliverables
Work Performance Data
Issue Log
Change Requests
Project Management Plan Updates
- Any Component

Project Documents Updates
- Activity List
- Assumption Log
- Lessons Learned Register
- Requirements Documentation
- Risk Register
- Stakeholder Register

Organizational Process Assets Updates

Tools and Techniques

Expert Judgment
Project Management Information System
Meetings

Figure 4-5: Direct and Manage Project Work Data Flow Diagram
The source for the above figure is the Project Management Institute, *A Guide to the Project Management Body of Knowledge*, (*PMBOK® Guide*) – Sixth Edition, Project Management Institute Inc., 2017, Figure 4-6, Page 91

Direct and Manage Project Work (Executing)		
Key Inputs	Project Management Plan	The project management plan integrates subsidiary plans (those representing the knowledge areas identified by the Project Management Institute, Inc.), baselines from the planning processes, the project life cycle, the development approach, and management reviews. Supporting detail is included to validate the information contained.
	Change Log	The change log is key to the execution of the project management plan. The log allows the team to ensure that it has the most current information on the state of project change requests.
	Lessons Learned Register	The lessons learned register is a document the team can reference to discover the challenges, problems, and successes of the project (what worked and didn't work) so the team can establish guidelines, continuously improve its performance, and evolve as a team.

Direct and Manage Project Work (Continued)		
Key Inputs (Cont.)	Approved Change Requests	Approved change requests are requests for modification of the project that have been approved by authorized personnel during the formal change control process. The changes can expand or contract the scope of the project and modify policies, procedures, the project management plan, budgets, and schedules.
Key Tools & Techniques	Expert Judgment	Expert judgment is judgment based on expertise acquired in a specific area. It is important to consider expertise related to organizational governance, industry-related technical details, legal and procurement matters, management of cost and budget, and legislative and regulatory directives.
	Project Management Information System	The project management information system (PMIS) is part of the enterprise environmental factors. It is the portal to automated tools, a system that gathers and distributes information, a configuration management system, and/or interfaces to online automated systems that are used to direct and manage project work.
Key Outputs	Deliverables	Deliverables represent the completion of predefined pieces of the work. They are distinctive and demonstrable products, results, or services. Upon completion of a deliverable, change control should be applied.
	Work Performance Data	Work performance data represents the raw metrics and observations identified during the performance of project work activities. The data is passed to controlling processes for analysis.
	Issue Log	The issue log is used to record and track any project challenges that cannot be immediately resolved. The project team uses the log to ensure issues are resolved during the execution of the project management plan. Updates occur during activities performed while monitoring and controlling the project.
	Change Requests	Change requests are requests for modification that have not been formally approved through the change control process. Modifications can be requested from inside or outside the project and may include: corrective action, preventative action, defect repair, updates to documentation, or updates to information.

4.8.1. Work Authorization System

A work authorization system is a formal or informal system used in project management to ensure that work is done as planned. It ensures that the right work is done, in the right order, at the right time, and by the right people. The system can help control cost.

If work is not done in the sequence as planned, sequence deviation can potentially cause issues that result in rework.

A work authorization system can also be used to minimize or eliminate gold plating. Discussed in the Quality chapter, gold plating involves providing more than was promised or committed. Part of the problem associated with the lack of a work authorization system and/or using gold plating is that the work that isn't part of the project can keep resources from completing legitimate project work or lead to rework if defects result.

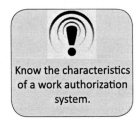

Know the characteristics of a work authorization system.

4.8.2. The Project Manager's Role in Integration

Project managers are responsible for the planning and completion of the project management plan and for project integration. Project managers must be sensitive to the project's needs, especially at **key interface points** on the project.

The source for the above text is the Project Management Institute, *A Guide to the Project Management Body of Knowledge, (PMBOK® Guide)* – Sixth Edition, Project Management Institute Inc., 2017, Pages 90-97

4.9. Manage Project Knowledge   *New Process for 6th Edition*

The Manage Project Knowledge process entails creating new knowledge from existing knowledge in order to achieve project objectives and add to organizational learning.

Existing knowledge is used to improve project outcomes and new knowledge (obtained as a result of the project) is used to support operations as well as future projects and phases.

Know the Key Inputs, Tools & Techniques, and Outputs for Manage Project Knowledge.

Knowledge is either explicit (can be easily expressed using words, pictures, and/or numbers) or tacit (can be difficult to express, such as insights, beliefs, or experiences). Both explicit and tacit learning must be managed.

Managing knowledge is very complex because explicit knowledge lacks context, so it is open to interpretation, and tacit knowledge includes context, but is difficult to express. Another hurdle to knowledge management is that people are not always motivated to share their knowledge. This hurdle can be overcome by creating an atmosphere of trust.

From an organizational perspective, the objective of project knowledge management is to ensure that the skills, expertise, and experience of the project team and knowledgeable stakeholders are utilized before, during, and after the project.

PMI, CAPM, and PMBOK are registered marks of the Project Management Institute, Inc.

84   © 2008-2018 Crosswind Learning, www.crosswindpm.com

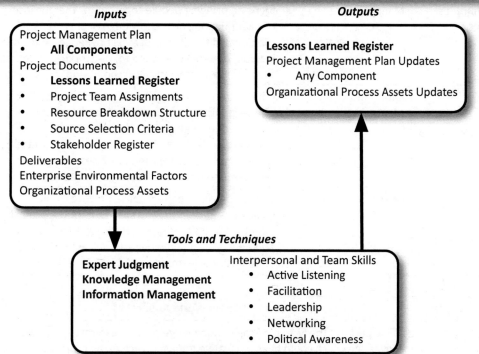

Manage Project Knowledge

Inputs

Project Management Plan
- **All Components**

Project Documents
- **Lessons Learned Register**
- Project Team Assignments
- Resource Breakdown Structure
- Source Selection Criteria
- Stakeholder Register

Deliverables
Enterprise Environmental Factors
Organizational Process Assets

Outputs

Lessons Learned Register
Project Management Plan Updates
- Any Component

Organizational Process Assets Updates

Tools and Techniques

Expert Judgment
Knowledge Management
Information Management

Interpersonal and Team Skills
- Active Listening
- Facilitation
- Leadership
- Networking
- Political Awareness

Figure 4-6: Manage Project Knowledge Data Flow Diagram

The source for the above figure is the Project Management Institute, *A Guide to the Project Management Body of Knowledge*, (*PMBOK® Guide*) – Sixth Edition, Project Management Institute Inc., 2017, Figure 4-8, Page 98

Manage Project Knowledge (Executing)		
Key Inputs	All Components of Project Management Plan	All components of the project management plan contribute to project management knowledge. Components can include, but are not limited to, the work breakdown structure, the subsidiary plans (representing the knowledge areas identified by the Project Management Institute, Inc.), baselines from the planning processes, the project life cycle, the development approach, management reviews, and the lessons learned register.
	Lessons Learned Register	The lessons learned register is a record of the challenges, problems, and successes of the project (what worked and didn't). The register contains detailed and important project knowledge.
Key Tools & Techniques	Expert Judgment	Expert judgment is judgment based on expertise acquired in a specific area. It is important to consider expertise related to information management, knowledge management, organizational learning, knowledge obtained from other projects, and tools for the management of information.

Manage Project Knowledge (Continued)		
Key Tools & Techniques (Cont.)	Knowledge Management	Knowledge management tools and techniques focus on bringing people together for the purpose of disseminating new knowledge or sharing tacit (personal, difficult to express) knowledge. Tools can include, but are not limited to, networking, meetings, focus groups, seminars, workshops, and conferences.
	Information Management	Information management tools and techniques focus on the creation and dissemination of explicit (easily expressed through pictures, words, or numbers) knowledge. Tools can include, but are not limited to, lessons learned registers, web searches, library services, and document management systems.
Key Outputs	Lessons Learned Register	The lessons learned register is a record of the challenges, problems, and successes of the project (what worked and didn't). It is used to track existing and new project knowledge as well as contribute to organizational learning.

Situational Question and Real World Application

Failure to effectively perform the Manage Project Knowledge process can result in a failure to create new knowledge which could have a negative impact on achieving project objectives and adding to organizational learning.

4.9.1. Lessons Learned Register

The lessons learned register records what worked and what didn't work in relation to the project. The register is also used to monitor existing project knowledge and new project knowledge and to contribute to organizational learning.

The source for the above text is the Project Management Institute, *A Guide to the Project Management Body of Knowledge*, (PMBOK® Guide) – Sixth Edition, Project Management Institute Inc., 2017, Pages 98-104

4.10. Monitor and Control Project Work (Monitoring and Controlling Process Group)

Know the Key Inputs, Tools & Techniques, and Outputs for Monitor and Control Project Work.

The Monitor and Control Project Work process involves tracking, reviewing, and reporting project progress (through initiating, planning, executing, and closing) in order to achieve project objectives as described in the project management plan.

The process provides stakeholders with an insight into the current state of the project, the information to understand actions taken to address performance issues, and (based on forecasts) the information to determine the future state of the project.

Monitoring is performed throughout the project and encompasses activities related to **gathering, quantifying, and distributing performance information**, as well as analyzing metrics and trends in order to execute process improvements.

Controlling encompasses activities related to determining preventative or corrective actions and following up to determine that those actions resolved the issue.

The process is concerned with:

- The comparison of actual performance against the project management plan
- Assessing performance to determine if preventative or correction action is warranted, then recommending the appropriate action
- Checking the status of individual project risks
- Maintaining an accurate information base regarding the project's products
- Providing information for status reporting, progress metrics, and forecasting
- Providing forecasts to update current budget and schedule information
- Monitoring the implementation of authorized changes
- Providing status and progress information to program management if the project is part of a program
- Ensuring the project stays in alignment with business needs

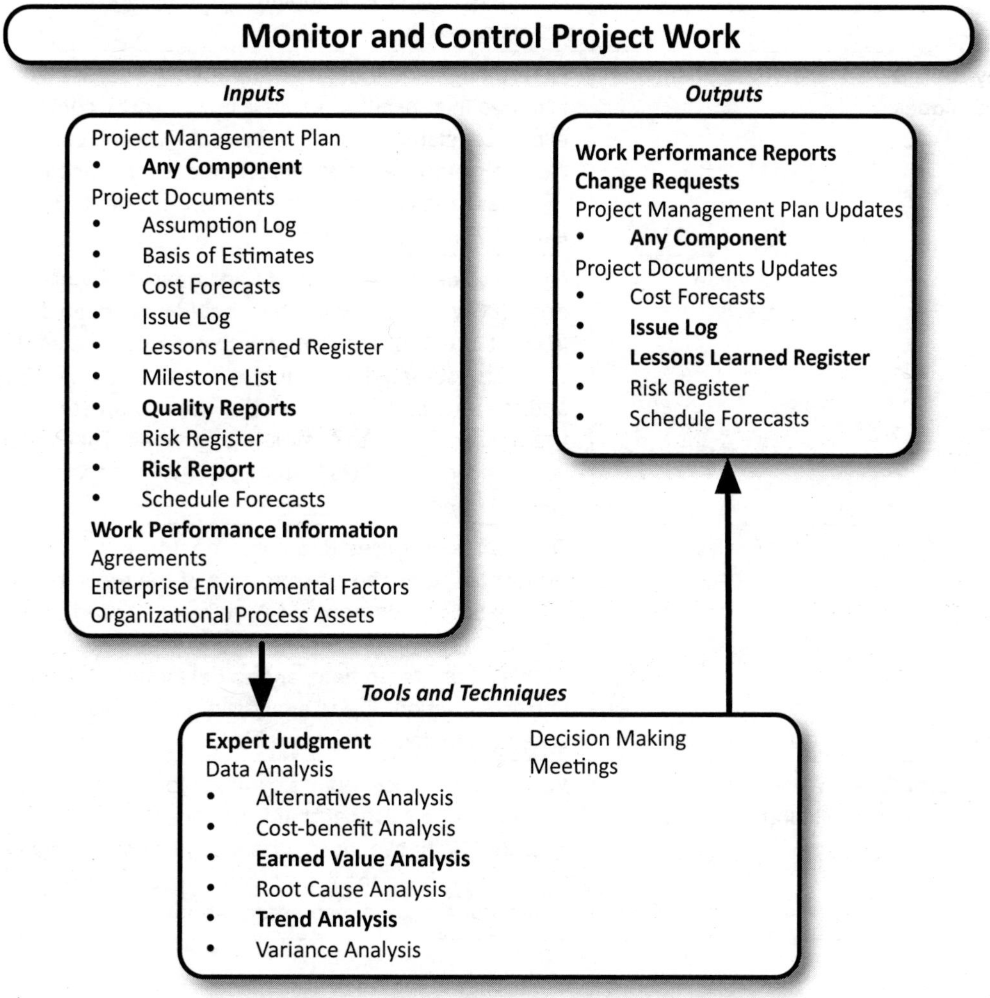

Monitor and Control Project Work

Inputs

Project Management Plan
- **Any Component**

Project Documents
- Assumption Log
- Basis of Estimates
- Cost Forecasts
- Issue Log
- Lessons Learned Register
- Milestone List
- **Quality Reports**
- Risk Register
- **Risk Report**
- Schedule Forecasts

Work Performance Information
Agreements
Enterprise Environmental Factors
Organizational Process Assets

Outputs

Work Performance Reports
Change Requests
Project Management Plan Updates
- **Any Component**

Project Documents Updates
- Cost Forecasts
- **Issue Log**
- **Lessons Learned Register**
- Risk Register
- Schedule Forecasts

Tools and Techniques

Expert Judgment
Data Analysis
- Alternatives Analysis
- Cost-benefit Analysis
- **Earned Value Analysis**
- Root Cause Analysis
- **Trend Analysis**
- Variance Analysis

Decision Making
Meetings

Figure 4-7: Monitor and Control Project Work Data Flow Diagram
The source for the above figure is the Project Management Institute, *A Guide to the Project Management Body of Knowledge*, (*PMBOK® Guide*) – Sixth Edition, Project Management Institute Inc., 2017, Figure 4-10, Page 105

Monitor and Control Project Work (Monitoring and Controlling)		
Key Inputs	Any Component of the Project Management Plan	Any component of the project management plan can serve as a baseline to evaluate the state of the project. For example, the schedule, budget, and other documents describe which project activities and events should occur and detail when they should occur.
	Quality Reports	Quality reports provide key stakeholders with information about quality management issues, recommendations for improvements and corrective actions, and a recap of quality-related findings.
	Risk Report	The risk report lists project risks and provides details about specific risks.
	Work Performance Information	Work performance information is performance data gathered from control processes and subsequently evaluated in comparison with the components of the project management plan and other applicable artifacts.
Key Tools & Techniques	Expert Judgment	Expert judgment is judgment based on expertise acquired in a specific area. It is important to consider expertise related to management of risks and contracts, trend diagnosis, estimation techniques for schedule and cost, data analysis, industry technical information, and earned value management
	Earned Value Analysis	Earned value analysis is used to compare the work done (BCWP) to the work that should have been done (BCWS), the costs associated with work completed to the costs estimated to complete that work (ACWP), and the time associated with the work completed to the time projected to complete that work. The earned value analysis provides a numerical evaluation of the state of the project.
	Trend Analysis	Trend analysis is used to project the future state of the project based on the present state of the project, in other words, to determine future results based on past results. The analysis can be used to predict issues, such as slippages in time, and to determine and effect corrective action. Trend analysis typically relates to the schedule, budget, or deliverables.
Key Outputs	Work Performance Reports	Work performance reports contain work performance information in a format that is designed to promote decisions, initiative, or cognizance. Work performance reports may be in the form of status reports, memos, notes, updates, and recommendations.

PMI, CAPM, and PMBOK are registered marks of the Project Management Institute, Inc.

88 © 2008-2018 Crosswind Learning, www.crosswindpm.com

Monitor and Control Project Work (Continued)		
Key Outputs (Cont.)	Change Requests	Change requests are requests for modification that have not been formally approved through the change control process. Modifications can be requested from inside or outside the project and may include: corrective action, preventative action, defect repair, or updates to documentation or information.
	Any Component of the Project Management Plan	Changes to the project management plan are subject to the change control process. Authorized changes are used to update the plan so that it reflects the current approach to, and state of, the project.
	Issue Log	The issue log is used to record and track any project challenges that cannot be immediately resolved. As new issues are identified and existing issues addressed, the issue log is updated.
	Lessons Learned Register	The lessons learned register is a document the team can reference to discover the challenges, problems, and successes of the project. As new lessons learned are identified, or existing issues refined, the lessons learned register is updated.

Situational Question and Real World Application

Failure to effectively perform the Monitor and Control Project Work process can result in reactive, rather than proactive, project management.

The source for the above text is the Project Management Institute, *A Guide to the Project Management Body of Knowledge*, (*PMBOK® Guide*) – Sixth Edition, Project Management Institute Inc., 2017, Pages 105-112

4.11. Perform Integrated Change Control (Monitoring and Controlling Process Group)

Know the Key Inputs, Tools & Techniques, and Outputs for Perform Integrated Change Control.

The Perform Integrated Change Control process entails the review of all change requests; the approval, rejection, modification, or suspension of each request; the management of approved changes; and the communication of the decisions. Even if a change control board (CCB) evaluates changes as part of the configuration control and change control procedures, the process is the responsibility of the project manager. Change requests can be made by any stakeholder and can occur at anytime throughout the life of the project. Before baselines are established, changes are not required to be subject to the change control process.

Because proposed changes are reviewed from an integration perspective (considering all impacted knowledge areas), overall project risk is addressed.

Approved change requests can necessitate new or revised activity sequencing, cost estimates, resource requirements, schedule adjustments, and/or risk response alternatives analysis. In turn, changes to the project management and other project documents may be indicated.

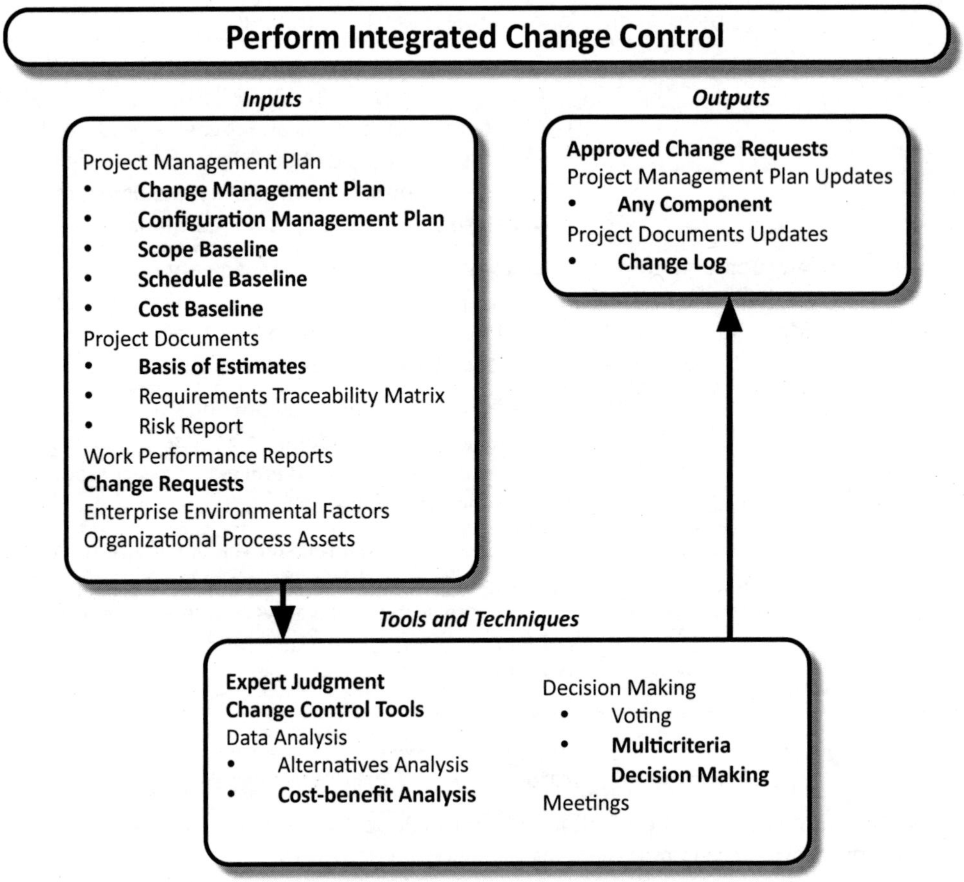

Perform Integrated Change Control

Inputs

Project Management Plan
- **Change Management Plan**
- **Configuration Management Plan**
- **Scope Baseline**
- **Schedule Baseline**
- **Cost Baseline**

Project Documents
- **Basis of Estimates**
- Requirements Traceability Matrix
- Risk Report

Work Performance Reports

Change Requests

Enterprise Environmental Factors

Organizational Process Assets

Outputs

Approved Change Requests

Project Management Plan Updates
- **Any Component**

Project Documents Updates
- **Change Log**

Tools and Techniques

Expert Judgment

Change Control Tools

Data Analysis
- Alternatives Analysis
- **Cost-benefit Analysis**

Decision Making
- Voting
- **Multicriteria Decision Making**

Meetings

Figure 4-8: Perform Integrated Change Control Data Flow Diagram

The source for the above figure is the Project Management Institute, *A Guide to the Project Management Body of Knowledge*, (*PMBOK® Guide*) – Sixth Edition, Project Management Institute Inc., 2017, Figure 4-12, Page 113

Perform Integrated Change Control (Monitoring and Controlling)		
Key Inputs	Change Management Plan	The change management plan provides direction for administering the change control process and formalizes the change control board.
	Configuration Management Plan	The configuration management plan provides direction for administering the configuration process by detailing the technical specifications of all applicable processes and deliverables.

Perform Integrated Change Control (Continued)		
Key Inputs (Cont.)	Scope Baseline	The scope baseline is the authorized version of project scope. It contains the project scope statement, the work breakdown statement (WBS), the work package, one or more planning packages, and the WBS dictionary. It describes the work the project is trying to complete. The scope baseline is subject to change management and is a component of the project management plan.
	Schedule Baseline	The schedule baseline is the authorized version of the schedule model. It lists connected activities with planned dates such as the planned start date and finish date for each activity, durations, milestones, and resources. Because it contains the start and finish dates of activities, it is referenced before approval of a change that is impacted by these dates. The schedule baseline is subject to change management and is a component of the project management plan.
	Cost Baseline	The cost baseline is the approved version of the time-phased budget, exclusive of management reserves. It contains a summation of the authorized budget for scheduled activities, which is used to compare the baseline to actual results, and cost estimates for activities and their contingency reserves collected into work package costs, which are further collected into control accounts. The cost baseline is subject to change management and is a component of the project management plan.
	Basis of Estimates	The basis of estimates supports how the duration estimate was established and describes how the basis of estimates was evolved, the project, assumptions and constraints considered, the level of confidence in the estimate, and the range of possible estimates (using the format plus or minus the appropriate percentage).
	Change Requests	Change requests are requests for modification that have not been formally approved through the change control process. Modifications can be requested from inside or outside the project and may include: corrective action, preventative action, defect repair, or updates to documentation or information.
Key Tools & Techniques	Expert Judgment	Expert judgment is judgment based on expertise acquired in a specific area. It is important to consider expertise related to regulatory and legislative directives, legal, procurement, management of risks, configuration management, and industry-related technical details.

	Perform Integrated Change Control (Continued)	
Key Tools & Techniques (Cont.)	Change Control Tools	Change control tools are tools that facilitate the determination, documentation, and acceptance, denial, deferment or modification of change requests. They should support configuration management activities, specifically configuration item identification, configuration item status accounting, configuration item verification and audit, modification identification, documentation of modifications, analysis and approval of modifications, and implementation of modifications.
	Cost-benefit Analysis	The change control board may perform a cost-benefit analysis for a change request. The analysis involves comparing the cost of the proposed change to its benefit.
	Multicriterua Decision Making	Decision making techniques are utilized to determine whether to accept, defer, deny, or modify a change request. Techniques include voting or a multicriteria decision making. Voting by **unanimity**, **majority**, **plurality,** or **autocracy** are acceptable voting types. Multicriteria decision making involves the use of a decision matrix. There can be a number of factors that go into the overall decision including, but not limited to, schedule, budget, quality, and team capacity.
Key Outputs	Approved Change Requests	Approved change requests are requests for modification that have been approved by authorized personnel during the formal change control process. The changes can expand or contract the scope of the project and modify policies, procedures, the project management plan, budgets, and schedules. Any change to the status of a change request must be updated in the change request log.
	Any Component of the Project Management Plan	The project management plan is a living, breathing document. Changes to the plan are subject to the change control process. Authorized changes are used to update the plan so that it reflects the current approach to, and state of, the project. All updates to the plan should be executed accordingly.
	Change Log	The change log allows the team to ensure it has the most current information on the state of project change requests.

Failure to effectively execute the Perform Integrated Change Control process can result in undocumented or unapproved changes that are required to achieve project objectives. It can also result in a failure to address all areas of impact.

4.11.1. Change Requests vs. Approved Changes

A change request is simply a request for change made by a project stakeholder. In situational exam questions, a requested change isn't considered approved unless so stated.

An approved change is a request for change that has been approved through the formal change control process.

Know the difference between change requests and approved changes.

4.11.2. Change Control System

A change control system is used to assess the impact and consequences of requested changes on the project. An overall change control system considers the impact the requested change will have on all knowledge areas. For example, if a scope change is requested, it is likely to impact both schedule (schedule management plan) and cost (cost management plan), in addition to scope.

Know the characteristics of a change control system.

4.11.3. Change Control Board (CCB)

A change control board is typically used on larger projects, which often involve multiple departments or divisions of the organization. If multiple departments or divisions of the organization are involved, board members should include representatives of those departments or divisions.

The function of the board is to review (and approve, suspend, modify, or reject) changes on the project as they relate to the various areas of the represented business. Each change control board should establish rules and guidelines that are aligned with the needs of the organization and the project.

4.11.4. Configuration Management

Configuration management is the process used to control product features and details through change control. It standardizes the change process associated with the project baseline. To ensure that the project conforms to requirements and creates only what it's intended to create, it defines and locks down details associated with the project scope.

The goals of a configuration management system are:

- To develop a consistent process for the evaluation of changes
- To create an environment in which the decision to approve, suspend, modify, or reject a change request is based on it's overall project impact
- To establish standards so the decision to approve, suspend, modify, or reject a change request can be clearly communicated in a timely manner to the appropriate stakeholders

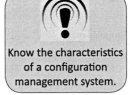

Know the characteristics of a configuration management system.

Configuration management activities include, but are not limited to:

- Configuration identification to establish the baseline and validate (verify) status
  Configuration identification is the basis for defining and verifying product configuration, labeling products, managing change, and maintaining accountability
- Configuration status accounting to provide documentation, storage, and access to project product data
  Configuration status accounting is the recording and reporting of data about the configuration item including item identification, proposed change status, and implementation status of approved changes
- Configuration verification and audits to provide verification of the project's results
  Performance of configuration verification and audits ensures that the functional requirements defined in the configuration documentation have been met, that the composition of a project's configuration items is correct, and that corresponding changes have been registered, assessed, approved, tracked, and correctly implemented.

The source for the above text is the Project Management Institute, *A Guide to the Project Management Body of Knowledge*, (*PMBOK® Guide*) – Sixth Edition, Project Management Institute Inc., 2017, Pages 113-119

4.12. Close Project or Phase (Closing Process Group)

The Close Project or Phase process involves the completion of activities across all process groups for the project, phase, or contract.

Once completed, the related project, phase, or contract information must be archived and all organizational resources released. The process is performed once or at predefined points in the project.

Activities necessary for administrative closure include, but are not limited to:

Know the Key Inputs, Tools & Techniques, and Outputs for Close Project or Phase.

- Activities required to meet completion criteria
  Ensuring that all documents have been updated, any outstanding issues have been resolved, and all costs have been charged to the project; confirming the delivery and formal acceptance of deliverables by the customer/sponsor; closing project accounts; releasing and/or reassigning human resources; reallocate physical resources
- Activities required to complete any outstanding contractual agreements
  Confirming that the work has been formally accepted; finalizing open claims; updating records; archiving appropriate information

- Activities required to gather records, audit project success or failure, manage the sharing or transfer of project knowledge, determine lessons learned, and archive project information
- Activities required to transfer the results of the project to the next phase, production, or operations
- Activities required to gather suggestions for updating/improving organizational policies and procedures and send them to the appropriate organizational unit

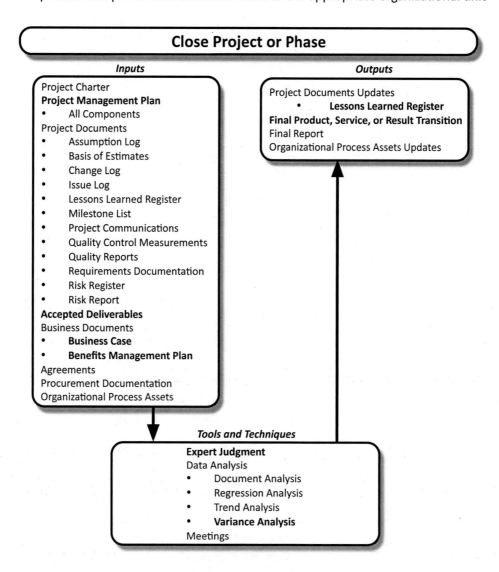

Figure 4-9: Close Project or Phase Data Flow Diagram
The source for the above figure is the Project Management Institute, *A Guide to the Project Management Body of Knowledge*, (*PMBOK® Guide*) – Sixth Edition, Project Management Institute Inc., 2017, Figure 4-14, Page 120

Close Project or Phase (Closing)		
Key Inputs	Project Management Plan	The project management plan integrates subsidiary plans (those representing the knowledge areas identified by the Project Management Institute, Inc.), baselines from the planning processes, the project life cycle, the development approach, and management reviews. Supporting detail is included to validate that the project is ready for completion.
	Accepted Deliverables	Accepted deliverables are deliverables that have fulfilled the acceptance standards and have been approved and signed off by authorized personnel. They may include work performance documents, authorized product specifications, and delivery receipts.
	Business Case	The business case, which usually describes the business need and contains a cost-benefit analysis, is used to justify the creation of the project and is the basis for the project charter. The business case is referenced to ensure that the approved deliverables align with the proposed project results.
	Benefits Management Plan	The benefits management plan describes the alignment of the project with organizational business goals, the targeted benefits, and the manner in which the benefits are transitioned and measured.
Key Tools & Techniques	Expert Judgment	Expert judgment is judgment based on expertise acquired in a specific area. It is important to consider expertise related to audit policy and procedure, management control, regulatory and legislative directives, legal, and procurement.
	Variance Analysis	Variance analysis is used to compare the proposed project results to the actual project results.
Key Outputs	Lessons Learned Register	The lessons learned repository is a record of the challenges, problems, and successes of the project (what worked and didn't). The repository contains detailed and important project knowledge. It is updated to reflect new knowledge that can be helpful for the next phase of the project, or the next project in the organization.
	Final Product, Service, or Result Transition	The final product, service, or result transition refers to the delivery or availability of the product, service, or result to a different group or organization for operation, maintenance, and support. The final product, service, or result is the main work or purpose of the project.

PMI, CAPM, and PMBOK are registered marks of the Project Management Institute, Inc.

96   © 2008-2018 Crosswind Learning, www.crosswindpm.com

> **Situational Question and Real World Application**
>
> Failure to effectively execute the Close Project or Phase process can result in the inappropriate closing of the project and inadequate/incomplete lessons learned, project archives, records, and storage. This can lead to a failure to obtain formal acceptance without extensive rework.

4.12.1. Project Files and the Contract File

Project files are created throughout the project, then organized and archived during the closing of the project. **Project files** are any project documents that record what occurred, what decisions were made, and what changes were approved. **Financial records and legal documents** are examples of project files.

The contract file is created during Conduct Procurements and Control Procurements. It contains documentation associated with the **contract**, **approved contract changes, and formal acceptance.**

Know important project closing considerations such as product verification, lessons learned, updating of records, reporting, archiving, and formal acceptance of components.

4.12.2. Closing the Project

Close Project or Phase typically occurs when the customer or sponsor formally accepts the product, service, or result of the project. After the project is closed, any additional work is warranty work or new work.

4.12.3. Lessons Learned

Lessons learned (the challenges, issues, and successes of the project) are entered in the lessons learned register, which can be updated throughout the project and during the Close Project or Phase.

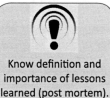

Know definition and importance of lessons learned (post mortem).

Lessons Learned at the End of the Phase or Project

During the Close Project or Phase process, feedback is solicited regarding what worked and didn't work on the project, as well as what could have been done to maximize the positive and minimize or eliminate the negative. This information is then recorded and tabulated.

There are several methods used to solicit feedback:

- A meeting or open discussion may be conducted
- A questionnaire may be distributed for completion
  Anonymous completion is often an option to ensure that team members express their opinions honestly and completely without fear of negative consequences.
- A combination of a meeting/open discussion and a questionnaire
  The combination often results in broader and more detailed feedback.

4.12.4. Control Procurements and Close Project or Phase

From a process standpoint, the Control Procurements process should occur before the Close Project or Phase Process, but there are situations where that sequence does not work due to the impact that timing and resource usage has on the closing of the contract and on the closing of the project or phase.

Understand how to close a project and know the documentation required to do so.

Figure 4-10: Control Procurements and Close Project or Phase Interaction shows the ideal sequence.

Note that the Project Management Institute, Inc. states that not all process interactions are shown in Project Management Institute, *A Guide to the Project Management Body of Knowledge, (PMBOK® Guide) - Sixth Edition*, Project Management Institute, Inc., 2017.

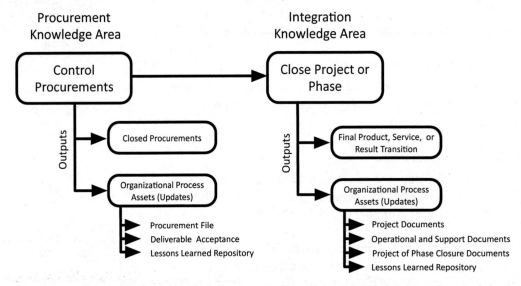

Figure 4-10: Control Procurements and Close Project or Phase Interaction

Sequence for Closure

The sequence of closing activities for the project is:

1. Close out any contracts with outside vendors.
2. Deliver any required reports associated with closure (organizational process assets updates).
3. Complete any Close Project or Phase activities.
4. Gather and record lessons learned.
5. Complete the archives of any project files (organizational process assets updates).
6. Release resources for other projects

Note that variations can occur from organization to organization.

The source for the above text is the Project Management Institute, *A Guide to the Project Management Body of Knowledge, (PMBOK® Guide) – Sixth Edition*, Project Management Institute Inc., 2017, Pages 120-127

4.13. Project Integration Management Formulas and Variables

There are no formulas for this chapter. See the Cost chapter for earned value management formulas.

4.14. Project Integration Management Terminology

Term	Description
Approved Change Request	A modification request that has been authorized as a result of undergoing the integrated change control process
Approved Change Requests Review	Audit of the implementation of approved modifications to ensure they function as intended
Assumption	A premise considered to be true without benefit of proof
Assumptions Analysis	The evaluation of project assumptions used to determine the risks that could be incurred as a result of the inexact, fragmentary, or unpredictable nature of the assumptions
Baseline	The agreed upon level of work (or other variable) used as a basis for comparison; once established, any changes must be authorized through formal change control procedures
Benefits Management Plan	A component of the project management plan that details the manner in which the benefits provided by a project or program are created, maximized, and sustained
Business Case	A document that attempts to prove the economic feasibility of a business idea, such as a product or service, to justify the project
Business Value	An abstraction that includes tangible and intangible elements associated with project, program, and portfolio management that maximize the value to the organization
Change	A modification to any deliverable, project management plan component, or project document subject to the formal change control process
Change Control	The process of determining, documenting, reviewing, and then approving or rejecting any proposed modifications to project documentation, deliverables, or baselines
Change Control Board (CCB)	The group accountable for considering, appraising, and making decisions about (approval, postponement, or rejection) proposed project changes and for documenting and communicating those decisions
Change Control System	The procedures that govern modifications to project documents, deliverables, and baselines
Change Control Tools	Tools associated with modification and configuration management
Change Log	A list of proposed project modifications and their associated details including description, date, requester, and status
Change Management Plan	A plan that defines the project change management process
Change Request	A formal solicitation for a project modification that relates to the approach to, or outcome of, the project
Close Project or Phase	The process of completing each activity across all process groups in order to finalize a project or phase
Configuration Management	A process which verifies that the products of the project are complete and accurate
Configuration Management System	A subsystem within the project management system that is comprised of documented procedures that delineate the method by which the attributes of a product, result, service, or component of a project are determined; attribute changes are controlled via authorization rules and a tracking system; conformance requirements can be corroborated through audit
Constraint	An internal or external limitation of the project

Term	Description
Corrective Action	An action to bring project work performance into alignment with the project management plan
Data	Discrete, unordered, unprocessed metrics or raw observations.
Data Analysis Techniques	Techniques used to order, assess, and evaluate data and information
Data Gathering Techniques	Techniques utilized to amass data and information from diverse sources
Data Representation Techniques	Approaches, especially the creation of graphical representations, utilized to communicate data and information
Deliverable	Any product, result, or service that must be generated to complete a process, phase, or project
Develop Project Charter	The process of evolving the document that authorizes the project and authorizes the project manager to employ organizational resources to do the work of the project
Develop Project Management Plan	The process of specifying, creating or adapting, reconciling, and integrating applicable management and other planning documents into one comprehensive document
Development Approach	The method (predictive, iterative, incremental, agile, or hybrid) utilized during the project life cycle to produce and elaborate the product, service, or result of the project
Direct and Manage Project Work	The process of administering the execution of the project management plan
Enterprise Environmental Factors	Internal and external variables, not under the control of the project team, that impact the project
Expert Judgment	The opinion of an authority on a project-related subject
Explicit Knowledge	Knowledge that can be classified utilizing such symbols as words, numerals, and images
Formal Acceptance	Attaining signature for a piece of the project or the complete project, where the signature represents completion or closure of the project or that piece of the project
Historical Information	Documented data from prior projects consulted as a learning tool
Information	Ordered data that has been processed to be meaningful, significant, and utilitarian in specific contexts
Information Management System	A system that collects, stores, and distributes data to project stakeholders; data format may be physical or electronic
Initiation	Commitment from the sponsor and organization to start a project or to continue it to the next phase
Knowledge	The composite of experience, values and beliefs, contextual information, intuition, and insight that people employ in an attempt to make sense of new experiences and information
Lessons Learned	The knowledge of what worked and what didn't work during a project
Lessons Learned Register	A project document utilized to record knowledge gained, both positive and negative, during the project; the information contained in register can be used in the current project and entered into the lessons learned repository for use with future projects
Lessons Learned Repository	A container, typically electronic, for storing historical information about lessons learned during the performance of project work
Manage Project Knowledge	The process of utilizing existing knowledge and producing new knowledge to achieve a project's goals and contribute to organizational knowledge
Market Research	The process of gathering information about customers or markets
Objective	A goal that the project is expected to accomplish; the goal could be related to a strategic position, purpose, result, service, or product

Term	Description
Organizational Process Assets	The process-related assets of the performing organization including, but not limited to, procedures, processes, policies, knowledge bases, templates, documentation, and plans
Payback Period	The amount of time needed to recover the investment in the project
Perform Integrated Change Control	The process of determining, recording, and approving or rejecting changes to project documentation, deliverables, or baselines
Project Archives	A set of records that correctly describe and document the history of the project
Project Charter	An instrument issued by the project sponsor or initiator that approves the existence of the project and authorizes the project manager to assign resources held by the organization to project activities
Project Integration Management	The processes and activities required to determine, depict, conjoin, unify, and reconcile project management processes and activities
Project Management Information System (PMIS)	A system, either manual or automated, comprised of the tools and techniques used to amass, incorporate, and disseminate the results of project management processes in order to reinforce all facets of the project
Project Management Plan	The cumulative document, containing all management plans and other planning documents, that serves as the blueprint for realizing the objectives of the project
Requested Change	A formal request for change that is submitted to the integrated change control process
Result	The consequence of completing a series of activities or processes; examples include outcomes and documents
Return on Investment (ROI)	The amount of income from an investment; income divided by the investment
Sponsoring Organization	The entity that has the responsibility of providing the project's sponsor and acting as a conduit for project funding or other project resources
Strategic Planning	Long-term planning by a company (usually three to five years in the future)
System	An integrated set of pieces used to achieve a specific project goal; could be an actual process or management process, or some mix of both approaches
Technical Performance Measurement	A measurement approach that compares what was technically created in the project to what the project management plan shows should have been created
Update	A modification to any deliverable, project management plan component, or project document that has not been subjected to the formal change control process
Weighted Scoring Model	A project selection technique based on criteria that have been weighted in terms of importance; selection criteria is determined and assigned a relative percentage, each project receives a total score based on the weighted value of its criteria, and the project with the highest score is selected
Work Authorization	The authorization to begin work on an activity, work package, or control account at the correct time, by the correct entity, and in the correct progression
Work Authorization System	A subsystem within the project management system that is comprised of documented procedures that delineate the method by which project work is authorized so that it will be done at the correct time, by the correct entity, and in the correct progression
Work Performance Data	Measurements or statistics related to the execution of project work
Work Performance Information	The evaluation and integration of project execution statistics and measurements gathered from control processes

The source for the above definitions is the Glossary of the Project Management Institute,
A Guide to the Project Management Body of Knowledge, (*PMBOK® Guide*) – Sixth Edition, Project Management Institute Inc., 2017

4.15. Project Integration Management Tests and Exercises

4.15.1. Project Integration Management Practice Test

Answers are in section 4.16.1.

1. Which of the following is the least desirable reason to pursue a project?

   (A) To increase market penetration for the top two customers by 13%
   (B) To increase employee satisfaction by 6%
   (C) To provide regulatory compliance
   (D) To ensure that all technology in place at key branches is less than three years old

2. Sign-off has just occurred on the project charter. There are items in the project charter that mandate a specific vendor and describe the maximum amount of physical and computer storage space available to the team. These are examples of what?

   (A) Assumptions that impact the project
   (B) Constraints that impact the project
   (C) Risks of the project
   (D) Activity resource requirements

3. The project to create a new drill type for an oil exploration initiation has been in progress for twelve months. Of the following, what best describes when it closes?

   (A) When the validate scope process is completed for the project
   (B) When the project is canceled
   (C) When the project funds are depleted
   (D) All of the answers

4. The new system integration project impacts all the departments in the company, directly or indirectly. Which of the following is the best description of tools used for the project's communications?

   (A) Communications management plan (CMP)
   (B) Communications model media (CMM)
   (C) Information distribution planning (IDP)
   (D) Project management information system (PMIS)

5. Which of the following best describes configuration management?

   (A) Procedures used to document and control product or service characteristics
   (B) System used to store versions of software code
   (C) System used to store versions of project documentation
   (D) Interface of an automated project management system created to set up project variables

6. All the following are typically components of the project management plan except...

    (A) The schedule management plan
    (B) The knowledge management plan
    (C) The risk management plan
    (D) The requirements management plan

7. You are assigned to a new data warehouse system project and notice the project charter lists four business units as sponsors. The data warehouse system has been discussed at your organization for some time, but it's everyone's first exposure to implementing such a system. Which of the following could present the biggest challenge to implementing this project?

    (A) Conflicting goals of the sponsors
    (B) The implementation team
    (C) The work breakdown structure (WBS)
    (D) The perform integrated change control process

8. The team has completed the planning process group and received approval from the sponsor and senior management to move to the executing process group. During the executing processes, the team will compare their work to...

    (A) The project actuals
    (B) The project baseline
    (C) The stakeholder expectations
    (D) The project variance

9. The team has just completed the process of evaluating how the project went. The team members analyzed what worked well and what didn't. They evaluated the planning and executing. They documented how the sponsor and senior management supported the project. What process did they perform?

    (A) Compiling lessons learned
    (B) Closing the project or phase
    (C) Directing and managing project work
    (D) Monitoring and controlling the project

10. The project manager for the electric engine improvement project has implemented a work authorization system. What is the main benefit of utilizing a work authorization system?

    (A) To show what work is to be done during the project
    (B) To show who is responsible for what work
    (C) To control gold plating
    (D) To serve as a time-tracking system

11. Neal the project manager has started the planning for the frontiers project. Neal and his team are focusing on assumptions that the planning is based on. The assumptions are key as much of the planning revolves around them. Which of the following best describes the earliest that the assumptions will potentially be identified?

(A) With change requests as needed
(B) The project management plan
(C) The charter
(D) The assumptions log

12. Project management roles not only describe project participation levels of various personnel, they also indicate responsibility. Which of the following is the most accurate in terms of its description?

(A) Senior management has ultimate control over project personnel
(B) Project management reports directly to the CEO
(C) Functional management manages the functionality of the project
(D) The sponsor pays for the project and could own the work of the project when it is complete

13. When is a project complete?

(A) When the budgeted funds are spent
(B) When formal acceptance has been obtained from the customer
(C) When the work is done
(D) When the customer is satisfied

14. The company is implementing an enterprise reporting system. This system will integrate a number of business units. This project is something that is new at the company. They realize they will learn a great deal as they adjust while going through the project. Which process best fits tracking their knowledge related to the project?

(A) Perform integrated change control
(B) Manage project issues
(C) Manage project knowledge
(D) Manage communications

15. As a best practice, who should create the project management plan?

(A) Project manager alone
(B) Project manager and the project management team
(C) The project manager, the project management team, and the owner of the project
(D) The project owner alone

16. Sam is creating the project management plan for the Infinity tour project. He is having a discussion with Sarah about the project management plan. They are having a disagreement about the plan and can't come to a common understanding. Which of the following best describes the project management plan?

(A) The project management plan can change whenever the team feels it's necessary
(B) The project management plan is a static picture of what the project is to accomplish and should not change
(C) The project management plan is a living document that evolves as the project evolves
(D) Change should only occur when there is no schedule or budget impact

17. The project will be starting the executing process group next week. The project sponsor and project manager have a meeting scheduled with the team and the business units that are impacted by the project. They explain what is expected to occur on the project and how each of the people can help contribute to the success of the project. What is this event called?

(A) Kickoff meeting to officially start the project
(B) An integral part of the team building effort
(C) Perform quality assurance and validate scope
(D) Project management plan development

18. Of the following, which is not an acceptable method of project creation?

(A) The project manager creates the project charter and has someone with the appropriate authority sign it
(B) Senior management creates the project charter and signs it
(C) The sponsor creates the project charter and signs it
(D) A project charter is taken from a similar project and reused

19. During the monitor and control project work process, the project manager is placing a great deal of reliance on expert judgment. Do you think this reliance is well founded?

(A) No, if expert judgment is so important there wouldn't be such a market for modeling tools
(B) Not to such an extent, because modeling tools are more effective
(C) Yes, although modeling tools are effective, expert judgment is often more significant and more accurate than those tools
(D) Not to such an extent, because expert judgment functions only as a check against the results of modeling tools

20. The project manager and her team have worked diligently to complete the project scope on time and within budget. They are in the process of creating the project files. Of the following, which is the best and most complete definition of project files?

(A) Project documents that record what occurred during the project and what changes were approved
(B) Project documents that record what occurred during the project, what changes were approved, and what decisions were made
(C) Project documents that record what occurred during the project, basic project statistics (scope, time, and cost), and what changes were approved
(D) Project documents that record what occurred during the project, what changes were approved, basic project statistics (scope, time, and cost), and what decisions were made

21. The team has just completed the work on a project that contracted with a number of vendors. A contract file was created during the procurement process. What items must be contained in this file?

(A) For each contract, the bidding documentation, the contract, the approved changes, and the formal acceptance
(B) For each contract, the contract, the approved changes, and the formal acceptance
(C) For each contract, the bidding documentation, the amended contract, and the formal acceptance
(D) For each contract, the amended contract and the formal acceptance

22. The company is implementing an enterprise reporting system. This system will integrate a number of business units. This project is something that is new at the company. They realize they will learn a great deal as they adjust while going through the project. They are doing the process called manage project knowledge. What will they create as a result of this process?

(A) Lessons learned register
(B) Project knowledge
(C) Deliverables
(D) Manage communications

23. The healthcare project is in the planning stage and the project manager and his team are making decisions about the project management information system (PMIS). In discussing the system they feel will work best, which of the following statements is the project manager most likely to make?

   (A) It is vital that the system accommodates our need to update payroll for the project management team
   (B) It is vital that the system accommodates our need to update the chart of accounts for procurement items
   (C) It is vital that the system accommodates our need to access functional management records to identify expert judgment candidates
   (D) It is vital that the system accommodates our need to send the right information to the right people in a timely and appropriate manner

24. The project manager and his team are in the planning stage of the retooling project and they are making assumptions for scheduling and budgeting. Of the following, what is the most likely source for the assumptions they will make?

   (A) Pertinent human resource and procurement records
   (B) Lessons learned from prior projects
   (C) Resource list and chart of accounts
   (D) Expert judgment and functional management input

25. During the monitor and control project work process for the Meaningful Curriculum project, the project manager and his team are considering performance information. Of the following, which best describes what they will do with this information?

   (A) Document and track the information
   (B) Collect, measure, and interpret the information
   (C) Determine who will have access to the information
   (D) All of the answers

26. The company is determining which proposed projects it should pursue during a severe economic downturn. Of the following, which is the most likely project it will approve?

   (A) A project that is proposed in response to a technological advance
   (B) A project that is proposed in response to a legal requirement
   (C) A project that is proposed in response to a business opportunity
   (D) A project that is proposed in response to a business problem

27. The project manager and his team have just started the perform integrated change control process for a high profile project. They are carefully considering all the inputs to make certain that the process is conducted successfully. Which of the following is not an input to this process?

   (A) Work performance reports
   (B) Change control meetings
   (C) Change requests
   (D) The project management plan

28. The project to setup the recording studio has just been completed. The customer contacts the project manager and complains that the Realtor next door is making noise that is being picked up when recording. The project manager investigates why this is occurring and discovers that the wall insulation was not put in after wiring and plumbing but before the sheetrock/wallboard, per the plan. What most likely caused this problem?

   (A) A change request wasn't approved
   (B) Scope creep
   (C) The work authorization system wasn't followed and the wallboard was installed before it should have been
   (D) The plan wasn't detailed enough

29. You are the project manager for a highway construction project. You have just finished integrating the various management plans into a complete document. What process will you perform next?

   (A) Develop project management plan
   (B) Manage project knowledge
   (C) Direct and manage project work
   (D) Develop project charter

30. At the weekly infrastructure project staff meeting, the customer informs the project team that, due to a change in market conditions, he must request a significant change to the product that will be created as a result of the project. The project is 85% complete. What should the project manager do in this case?

   (A) Advise the customer that the project is too close to completion to integrate the change
   (B) Evaluate the impact the requested change will have on the project and advise the customer of the impact and his options
   (C) Ignore the customer in the hope that he will not pursue the request
   (D) Create a new project to accommodate the requested change and release the project as-is to the market

4.16. Project Integration Management Answers for Tests and Exercises

4.16.1. Project Integration Management Practice Test Answers

We recommend that you download answer sheets from the Crosswind website, so you can practice the test as many times as you like.

1. Which of the following is the least desirable reason to pursue a project?

   Correct Answer: (D) To ensure that all technology in place at key branches is less than three years old
   Explanation: Without additional information, there is no indication that technology in place is unreliable or insufficient for the task. All other answers are desirable, including employee satisfaction. As a general rule, satisfied employees are more productive and less likely to seek other employment opportunities. [Crosswind Manual 4.6.3; PMBOK® Guide 1.2.6.4]

2. Sign-off has just occurred on the project charter. There are items in the project charter that mandate a specific vendor and describe the maximum amount of physical and computer storage space available to the team. These are examples of what?

   Correct Answer: (B) Constraints that impact the project
   Explanation: Constraints are variables that limit the team's options. They typically deal with resources, time, or money. Assumptions are educated guesses made on the project about items that are not known. Risks deal with varying degrees of unknowns that may generate risks. Activity resource requirements are generated later in the planning process group. [Crosswind Manual 4.7.3; PMBOK® Guide 1.2.4.7]

3. The project to create a new drill type for an oil exploration initiation has been in progress for twelve months. Of the following, what best describes when it closes?

   (A) When the validate scope process is completed for the project
   (B) When the project is canceled
   (C) When the project funds are depleted

   Correct Answer: (D) All of the answers
   Explanation: Whenever a project ends, it should be formally closed. This closure allows the team and organization to learn what worked and what didn't on the project and to formally close out the initiative. When a project completes the Validate Scope process, the deliverables of the project are formally accepted and thus, the project is complete. When a project is canceled or when it runs out of money the administrative activities associated with closure of the project are conducted. [Crosswind Manual 4.12; PMBOK® Guide 4.5]

4. The new system integration project impacts all the departments in the company, directly or indirectly. Which of the following is the best description of tools used for the project's communications?

Correct Answer: (D) Project management information system (PMIS)
Explanation: The project management information system (PMIS) is a system that stores and distributes project information. It can be a manual or a high tech system. The other answers are distracters. [Crosswind Manual 4.7.5; *PMBOK® Guide* 4.3.2.2]

5. Which of the following best describes configuration management?

Correct Answer: (A) Procedures used to document and control product or service characteristics
Explanation: Configuration management ensures that the project is building what it should build. It utilizes a very thorough and detailed change control process to ensure that project results conform to requirements and exhibit Fitness for Use. [Crosswind Manual 4.11.4; *PMBOK® Guide* 4.7]

6. All the following are typically components of the project management plan except...

Correct Answer: (B) The knowledge management plan
Explanation: The knowledge management plan is a distracter. Manage project knowledge actually is an executing process resulting in a lessons learned register. The other items are typically in the project management plan. [Crosswind Manual 4.7.1; *PMBOK® Guide* 1.2.4.7]

7. You are assigned to a new data warehouse system project and notice the project charter lists four business units as sponsors. The data warehouse system has been discussed at your organization for some time, but it's everyone's first exposure to implementing such a system. Which of the following could present the biggest challenge to implementing this project?

Correct Answer: (A) Conflicting goals of the sponsors
Explanation: Conflicting sponsor goals can significantly impact the project because any attempt to build what works for all sponsors could radically alter the plan. The creation of the WBS is a challenge as well, but not the best answer. The other answers are distracters. [Crosswind Manual 13.1.1; No *PMBOK® Guide* Reference]

8. The team has completed the planning process group and received approval from the sponsor and senior management to move to the executing process group. During the executing processes, the team will compare their work to...

Correct Answer: (B) The project baseline
Explanation: The baseline is the estimate for the project. It can be for the scope, schedule, and cost of the project. The actuals are the scope, schedule, and cost data for the project at a certain point in time. The variance is the difference between the baseline and actual. Stakeholder expectations is a distracter. [Crosswind Manual 4.7.4; *PMBOK® Guide* 4.3.2.1]

9.   The team has just completed the process of evaluating how the project went. The team members analyzed what worked well and what didn't. They evaluated the planning and executing. They documented how the sponsor and senior management supported the project. What process did they perform?

Correct Answer: (B) Closing the project or phase
Explanation: They completed closing the project or phase, which is in the closing process group. The activities described in the question are lessons learned. Controlling and executing have already occurred. [Crosswind Manual 4.12; *PMBOK® Guide* 4.5]

10. The project manager for the electric engine improvement project has implemented a work authorization system. What is the main benefit of utilizing a work authorization system?

Correct Answer: (C) To control gold plating
Explanation: The question focuses on the benefit, as opposed to the purpose, of a work authorization system. The Work Authorization System sanctions or releases certain work to be done at a certain time in a certain order by a particular organization. The primary benefit of the system is to minimize gold plating on a project, which can occur if this control mechanism is not in place. The work breakdown structure (WBS) shows what work is to be done on the project. The responsibility assignment matrix (RAM) shows who is responsible for what work. To serve as a time-tracking system is a distracter. [Crosswind Manual 4.8.1; *PMBOK® Guide* 4.1.3.1]

11. Neal the project manager has started the planning for the frontiers project. Neal and his team are focusing on assumptions that the planning is based on. The assumptions are key as much of the planning revolves around them. Which of the following best describes the earliest that the assumptions will potentially be identified?

Correct Answer: (C) The charter
Explanation: Assumptions are identified as early as possible in the project That means the charter is the best answer. The other answers are applicable as needed because the assumptions will be updated as the project evolves. Planning is established based on the assumptions and as the assumptions evolve, the planning and changes evolve. [Crosswind Manual 4.6; *PMBOK® Guide* 4.1.1.1]

12. Project management roles not only describe the project participation levels of various personnel, they also indicate responsibility. Which of the following is the most accurate in terms of its description?

Correct Answer: (D) The sponsor pays for the project and could own the work of the project when it is complete
Explanation: Typically, the sponsor's responsibility is to pay for the project, own it when it is complete, and provide support as the champion if escalation is necessary. Senior management is responsible for a number of areas on a project. Its main responsibility is to help support the project and resolve resource conflicts as they occur. Remember, unless otherwise stated, for situational questions assume that you are in a balanced matrix environment. This environment has functional managers controlling resources. The project manager's responsibility is to drive the completion of the work of the project. [Crosswind Manual 3.4.11; No *PMBOK® Guide* reference]

13. When is a project complete?

   Correct Answer: (B) When formal acceptance has been obtained from the customer
   Explanation: Only when formal acceptance has been obtained from the customer, can the project be considered complete. When the budgeted funds are spent simply means that the project is out of money. When the work is done does not mean that the customer agrees that the work is done. When the customer is satisfied is only relevant when the customer formally accepts the project. [Crosswind Manual 4.12; *PMBOK® Guide* 4.5]

14. The company is implementing an enterprise reporting system. This system will integrate a number of business units. This project is something that is new at the company. They realize they will learn a great deal as they adjust while going through the project. Which process best fits tracking their knowledge related to the project?

   Correct Answer: (C) Manage project knowledge
   Explanation: Manage project knowledge results in the creation of the lessons learned register and the best fit for the question. Perform integrated change control references change management. Managing project issues is a distracter and not a process. Manage communications might be used to share the information learned, but it's not as good an answer as manage project knowledge. [Crosswind Manual 4.9; *PMBOK® Guide* 4.2]

15. As a best practice, who should create the project management plan?

   Correct Answer: (B) The project manager and the project management team
   Explanation: The project manager and team should create the project management plan and the estimates that feed into it. They are the people doing the work, so they should have the opportunity to estimate and plan it. The other answers are distracters. [Crosswind Manual 4.7; *PMBOK® Guide* 1.2.4.7]

16. Sam is creating the project management plan for the Infinity tour project. He is having a discussion with Sarah about the project management plan. They are having a disagreement about the plan and can't come to a common understanding. Which of the following best describes the project management plan?

   Correct Answer: (C) The project management plan is a living document that evolves as the project evolves
   Explanation: The project management plan is a living document that will evolve as the project evolves. Changes can occur, but will only be implemented when approved. Changes can be implemented when approved even if there is schedule, budget or other area impacted, if the change is approved. Just because the team wants a change doesn't mean it happens. It has to be approved first. [Crosswind Manual 4.7; *PMBOK® Guide* 1.2.4.7]

17. The project will be starting the executing process group next week. The project sponsor and project manager have a meeting scheduled with the team and the business units that are impacted by the project. They explain what is expected to occur on the project and how each of the people can help contribute to the success of the project. What is this event called?

Correct Answer: (A) Kickoff meeting to officially start the project
Explanation: The kickoff meeting is what is commonly used on a project to formally start the project and it can occur at the beginning of planning or executing depending on priority or approach. It allows the sponsor to set expectations, and the team to learn about details of the plan. Team building occurs in the executing process group, but it's not as definitive an answer as kickoff meeting. Project management plan development produces a project management plan. Perform Quality Assurance and Validate Scope are distracters. [Crosswind Manual 4.6.2; *PMBOK® Guide* 1.2.6.2]

18. Of the following, which is not an acceptable method of project creation?

Correct Answer: (D) A project charter is taken from a similar project and reused
Explanation: Using a project charter from a previous project does not create a new project, since every project is unique. If that charter were appropriately modified and re-authorized, that could work, but that is not included in the answer. To create a project, the project charter must be created by anyone authorized to do so, even the project manager, but it must be signed by someone who can provide the project manager with the authority to manage the project, typically the sponsor or senior management. [Crosswind Manual 4.6; *PMBOK® Guide* 4.1.1.1]

19. During the monitor and control project work process, the project manager is placing a great deal of reliance on expert judgment. Do you think this reliance is well founded?

Correct Answer: (C) Yes, although modeling tools are effective, expert judgment is often more significant and more accurate than those tools
Explanation: Although modeling tools are effective, expert judgment can be more significant and more accurate than those tools. The other answers are distracters. [Crosswind Manual 4.10; *PMBOK® Guide* 4.3]

20. The project manager and her team have worked diligently to complete the project scope on time and within budget. They are in the process of creating the project files. Of the following, which is the best and most complete definition of project files?

Correct Answer: (B) Project documents that record what occurred during the project, what changes were approved, and what decisions were made
Explanation: Project files are project documents that record what occurred during the project, what changes were approved, and what decisions were made. Financial records and legal documents are included in these files. [Crosswind Manual 4.14.1; No *PMBOK® Guide* Reference]

21. The team has just completed the work on a project that contracted with a number of vendors. A contract file was created during the procurement process. What items must be contained in this file?

Correct Answer: (B) For each contract, the contract, the approved changes, and the formal acceptance

Explanation: For each contract, the contract itself, the approved changes, and the formal acceptance must be contained in the contract file. The other answers are distracters. [Crosswind Manual 4.14.1; No *PMBOK® Guide* Reference]

22. The company is implementing an enterprise reporting system. This system will integrate a number of business units. This project is something that is new at the company. They realize they will learn a great deal as they adjust while going through the project. They are doing the process called manage project knowledge. What will they create as a result of this process?

Correct Answer: (A) Lessons learned register

Explanation: The manage project knowledge process creates the lessons learned register. Deliverables are created in the prior process, direct and manage project work. Project knowledge is a general item that occurs from doing the project, but not the specific answer. Manage communications occurs as the project occurs, but is a bit of a generic answer here. [Crosswind Manual 4.9.1; *PMBOK® Guide* 4.2.3.1]

23. The healthcare project is in the planning stage and the project manager and his team are making decisions about the project management information system (PMIS). In discussing the system they feel will work best, which of the following statements is the project manager most likely to make?

Correct Answer: (D) It is vital that the system accommodates our need to send the right information to the right people in a timely and appropriate manner

Explanation: The purpose of the project management information system (PMIS) is communication and information distribution. It is often a combination of technical and non-technical tools used by various project participants to communicate and distribute project related information. The other answers reference systems or information that would not be directly accessible to the project management team. [Crosswind Manual 4.9.5; *PMBOK® Guide* 4.3.2.2]

24. The project manager and his team are in the planning stage of the retooling project and they are making assumptions for scheduling and budgeting. Of the following, what is the most likely source for the assumptions they will make?

Correct Answer: (B) Lessons learned from prior projects

Explanation: Lessons learned is a source often used for making assumptions about any facet of a project. The other answers are distracters. [Crosswind Manual 4.12.3; *PMBOK® Guide* 4.7.3.4]

PMI, CAPM, and PMBOK are registered marks of the Project Management Institute, Inc.

114   © 2008-2018 Crosswind Learning, www.crosswindpm.com

25. During the monitor and control project work process for the Meaningful Curriculum project, the project manager and his team are considering performance information. Of the following, which best describes what they will do with this information?

    Correct Answer: (B) Collect, measure, and interpret the information
    Explanation: During the Monitor and Control Project Work process, performance information is collected, measured, and interpreted. The other answers are distracters. [Crosswind Manual 4.10; PMBOK® Guide 4.3]

26. The company is determining which proposed projects it should pursue during a severe economic downturn. Of the following, which is the most likely project it will approve?

    Correct Answer: (B) A project that is proposed in response to a legal requirement
    Explanation: A project that is proposed in response to a legal requirement is the most likely to be approved because non-compliance can be very costly. There is insufficient information to determine if there is any likelihood that a project proposed in response to a business opportunity, business problem, or technological advance would take precedence. [Crosswind Manual 4.6.3; PMBOK® Guide 1.2.6.4]

27. The project manager and his team have just started the perform integrated change control process for a high profile project. They are carefully considering all the inputs to make certain that the process is conducted successfully. Which of the following is not an input to this process?

    Correct Answer: (B) Change control meetings
    Explanation: Change control meetings is a tool and technique of the Perform Integrated Change Control process. All others are inputs. [Crosswind Manual 4.11; PMBOK® Guide 4.4]

28. The project to setup the recording studio has just been completed. The customer contacts the project manager and complains that the Realtor next door is making noise that is being picked up when recording. The project manager investigates why this is occurring and discovers that the wall insulation was not put in after wiring and plumbing but before the sheetrock/wallboard, per the plan. What most likely caused this problem?

    Correct Answer: (C) The work authorization system wasn't followed and the wallboard was installed before it should have been
    Explanation: The work authorization system appears to have not been followed correctly. This would ensure conditions were such that the next step could be done because all previous steps were correct. A change that wasn't approved or scope creep wouldn't fit because the wall insulation was part of the plan. The plan wasn't detailed enough is a distracter. [Crosswind Manual 4.8.1; PMBOK® Guide 4.13.1]

29. You are the project manager for a highway construction project. You have just finished integrating the various management plans into a complete document. What process will you perform next?

Correct Answer: (C) Direct and manage project work

Explanation: The Direct and Manage Project Work process occurs after the Develop Project Management Plan process. The key output of the Develop Project Management Plan process is the Project Management Plan, which integrates all the project's management plans. The Manage Project Knowledge process follows the Direct and Manage Project Work process. The key output is the lessons learned register. [Crosswind Manual 4.8; *PMBOK® Guide* 4.1]

30. At the weekly infrastructure project staff meeting, the customer informs the project team that, due to a change in market conditions, he must request a significant change to the product that will be created as a result of the project. The project is 85% complete. What should the project manager do in this case?

Correct Answer: (B) Evaluate the impact the requested change will have on the project and advise the customer of the impact and his options

Explanation: The project manager needs to evaluate the impact the requested change will have on the project and advise the customer of the impact and his options. Advising the customer that the project is too close to completion to integrate the change isn't within the purview of the project manager; neither is the creation of a new project to accommodate the requested change. Ignoring the customer in the hope that he will not pursue the request is professionally irresponsible. [Crosswind Manual 13.1.2; No *PMBOK® Guide* Reference]

Chapter 5

Project Scope Management

Project Scope Management requires that the scope management processes are executed in a timely and effective manner so they result in **complete requirements documentation, the project scope statement, the scope management plan, and the work breakdown structure (WBS).**

Scope can relate to both:

- **Product scope**
  Product scope is associated with what is created as a result of the project and is weighed against the product requirements.
- **Project scope**
  Project scope is associated with the work required to create the project results and is weighed against the scope management plan.

Trends

Requirements management has always been a challenge for project management and the challenge has become more complex with the expansion of global and virtual project environments and the evolution of business analysis and Agile.

It's important to remember that all projects start with a business need, whether that need can be satisfied through a standalone project or a project under the umbrella of a program or a portfolio.

Business analysis activities are utilized to:

- Determine the business need
- Suggest solutions
- Elicit, record, and administer stakeholder requirements

Tailoring

Project tailoring, the manner in which the processes of a knowledge area are exercised, is employed to address the distinctive nature of each project. Successful project tailoring is predicated on a careful consideration of:

- Knowledge and requirements management systems
- Guidelines, policies, and procedures related to validation and control
- Development approaches
- Stability of requirements
- Guidelines, policies, and procedures related to governance

Agile/Adaptive Environment

For high-risk projects, as well as projects with emerging requirements or a high degree of uncertainty, consider an approach that employs Agile methods. Instead of defining scope and locking down requirements at the outset of the project, Agile methods focus on delivering value **early and often**. Agilists often construct a prototype, improving it as their knowledge grows, in order to refine the project scope and requirements.

The source for the above text is the Project Management Institute, *A Guide to the Project Management Body of Knowledge*, (PMBOK® Guide) – Sixth Edition, Project Management Institute Inc., 2017, Page 128-132

In this chapter, we discuss the following:

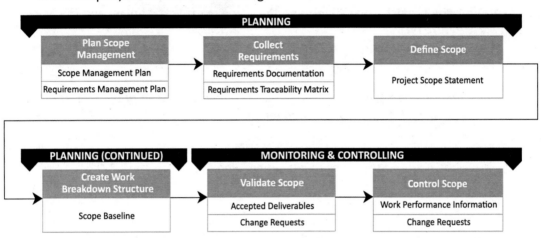

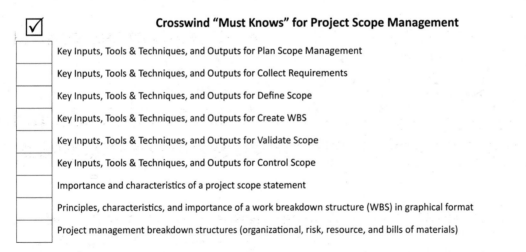

Figure 5-1: Scope Processes

The source for the above figure is the Project Management Institute, *A Guide to the Project Management Body of Knowledge*, (PMBOK® Guide) – Sixth Edition, Project Management Institute Inc., 2017, Figure 5.1, Page 129

☑ Crosswind "Must Knows" for Project Scope Management

☐	Key Inputs, Tools & Techniques, and Outputs for Plan Scope Management
☐	Key Inputs, Tools & Techniques, and Outputs for Collect Requirements
☐	Key Inputs, Tools & Techniques, and Outputs for Define Scope
☐	Key Inputs, Tools & Techniques, and Outputs for Create WBS
☐	Key Inputs, Tools & Techniques, and Outputs for Validate Scope
☐	Key Inputs, Tools & Techniques, and Outputs for Control Scope
☐	Importance and characteristics of a project scope statement
☐	Principles, characteristics, and importance of a work breakdown structure (WBS) in graphical format
☐	Project management breakdown structures (organizational, risk, resource, and bills of materials)

Although helpful, this list is not all-inclusive in regard to information needed for the exam. It is only suggested material that, if understood and memorized, may increase your exam score.

PMI, CAPM, and PMBOK are registered marks of the Project Management Institute, Inc.

118   © 2008-2018 Crosswind Learning, www.crosswindpm.com

5.1. Plan Scope Management (Planning Process Group)

Know the Key Inputs, Tools & Techniques, and Outputs for Plan Scope Management.

During Plan Scope Management, the scope management plan and the requirements management plan are created.

The scope management plan contributes to the management and definition of the project by defining how the scope of the project will be managed, including the creation of the requirements, scope statement, work breakdown structure (WBS), and WBS dictionary, as well as the validation and control of the project scope.

The requirements management plan is a component of the project management plan that details the evaluation, documentation, and administration of project requirements.

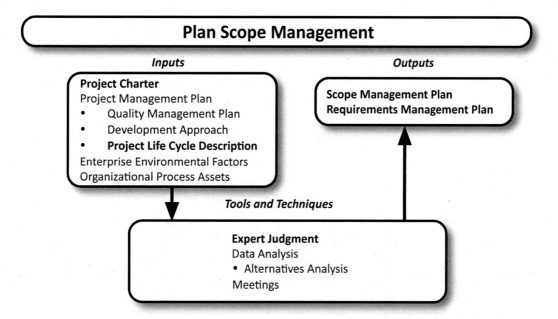

Figure 5-2: Plan Scope Management Data Flow Diagram

The source for the above figure is the Project Management Institute, *A Guide to the Project Management Body of Knowledge*, (*PMBOK® Guide*) – Sixth Edition, Project Management Institute Inc., 2017, Figure 5.2, Page 133

Plan Scope Management (Planning)		
Key Inputs	Project Charter	The project charter is the document that provides authorization for the existence of the project and gives the project manager the power to use organizational resources to execute the project. The project charter typically lists the key deliverables, the milestones, and the roles and responsibilities of each person involved in the project. Note that the project charter delineates the purpose of the project, high-level project description, requirements, assumptions, and constraints. The project charter is used to plan the scope management processes.

Plan Scope Management (Continued)		
Key Inputs (Cont.)	Project Life Cycle Description	The project life cycle description delineates the phases of the project and which development approach (waterfall, agile, adaptive, iterative, or hybrid) will be utilized.
Key Tools and Techniques	Expert Judgment	Expert judgment is judgment based on expertise acquired in a specific area. It is important to consider expertise related to knowledge of the industry or area of application and experience with previous projects similar to the current project.
Key Outputs	Scope Management Plan	The scope management plan is a component of the project management plan that details the delineation, evolution, monitoring, controlling, and validation of scope. It includes the methods for creating the project scope statement, authorizing and maintaining the WBS, authorizing formal acceptance of deliverables, and controlling change requests related to the scope statement, WBS, and requirements.
	Requirements Management Plan	The requirements management plan is a component of the project management plan that details the evaluation, documentation, and administration of project requirements. It includes the methods for designing, monitoring, and reporting requirement activities and configuration activities; prioritizing requirements; determining requirement metrics; and capturing attributes for the requirement traceability matrix.

Situational Question and Real World Application
Failure to effectively execute the Plan Scope Management process can result in scope creep. Scope creep can occur when the scope is not adequately defined and locked down, since the product owner has carte blanche to request changes regardless of impact to the project schedule, project budget, and/or project resources. The scope management plan is the key document referenced to promote scope containment.

5.1.1.   Scope Management Plan

The scope management plan helps the project manager and the team establish the rules for managing scope.

The plan may include the methods that will be used to:

- Create a scope statement
- Create a work breakdown structure
- Validate project deliverables
- Address scope change requests

5.1.2. Requirements Management Plan

The requirements management plan helps the project manager and team analyze, document, and manage the project requirements.

The plan may include:

- The methods that will be used to manage requirements
- The methods that will be used to create requirements
- The methods that will be used to plan, track, and report requirement activities
- The methods that will be used to perform configuration management activities (notably how to initiate changes to the product, service, or result, how to analyze the impact of the changes, and how to change approval authorization)
- The methods that will be used to prioritize requirements
- The methods that will be used to determine product metrics and usage rationale
- The traceability structure that will be used to show what requirement attributes will be included in the requirement traceability matrix
- The methods that will be used to create the traceability matrix, specifically the requirement attributes that will be included in the matrix and the other project documents to which the requirements will be traced

The source for the above text is the Project Management Institute, *A Guide to the Project Management Body of Knowledge*, (*PMBOK® Guide*) – Sixth Edition, Project Management Institute Inc., 2017, Pages 132-136

5.2. Collect Requirements (Planning Process Group)

Know the Key Inputs, Tools & Techniques, and Outputs for Collect Requirements.

During Collect Requirements, project requirements are created based on an analysis of project stakeholder needs. The focus should be on appropriately defining the measurable needs of the sponsor, customer, and applicable stakeholders. Those needs, in the form of requirements, feed the WBS and ultimately the quality, schedule, and cost estimates for the project.

The process begins with an analysis of the project charter and stakeholder register. The business case, regulatory documents, use cases, and lessons learned register might also be referenced.

The main documents created during this process include the **requirements documentation and the requirements traceability matrix.**

The project requirements, at this point, serve as a basis for all planning as they define what the customer needs, and expects, the project result(s) to do.

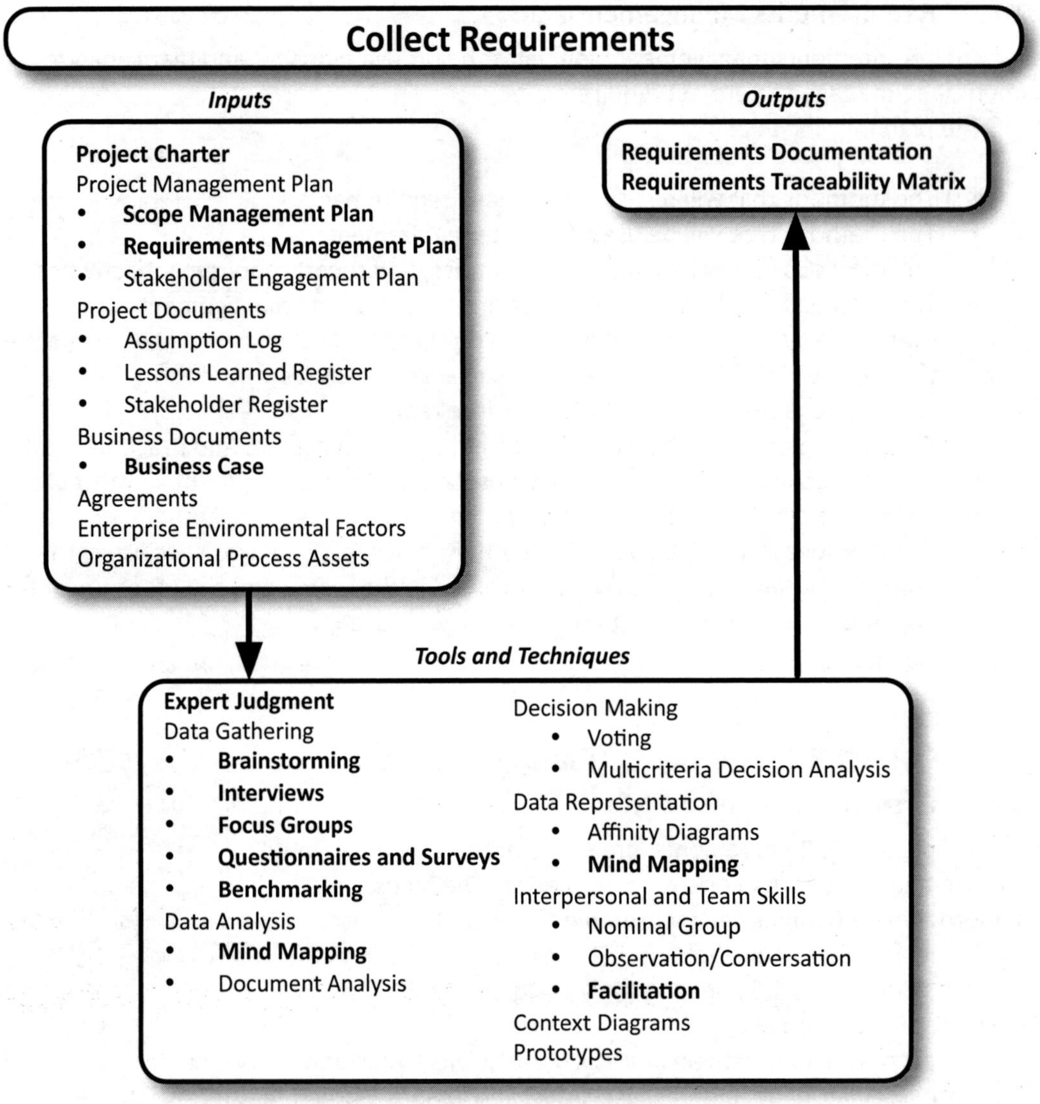

Collect Requirements

Inputs

Project Charter
Project Management Plan
- **Scope Management Plan**
- **Requirements Management Plan**
- Stakeholder Engagement Plan

Project Documents
- Assumption Log
- Lessons Learned Register
- Stakeholder Register

Business Documents
- **Business Case**

Agreements
Enterprise Environmental Factors
Organizational Process Assets

Outputs

Requirements Documentation
Requirements Traceability Matrix

Tools and Techniques

Expert Judgment
Data Gathering
- **Brainstorming**
- **Interviews**
- **Focus Groups**
- **Questionnaires and Surveys**
- **Benchmarking**

Data Analysis
- **Mind Mapping**
- Document Analysis

Decision Making
- Voting
- Multicriteria Decision Analysis

Data Representation
- Affinity Diagrams
- **Mind Mapping**

Interpersonal and Team Skills
- Nominal Group
- Observation/Conversation
- **Facilitation**

Context Diagrams
Prototypes

Figure 5-3: Collect Requirements Data Flow Diagram
The source for the above figure is the Project Management Institute, *A Guide to the Project Management Body of Knowledge*, (*PMBOK® Guide*) – Sixth Edition, Project Management Institute Inc., 2017, Figure 5.4, Page 136

Collect Requirements (Planning)		
Key Inputs	Project Charter	The project charter is the document that provides authorization for the existence of the project and gives the project manager the power to use organizational resources to execute the project. The project charter typically lists the key deliverables, the milestones, and the roles and responsibilities of each person involved in the project. Note that the project charter delineates the purpose of the project, high-level project description, requirements, assumptions, and constraints. The high-level requirements are the basis for creating detailed requirements.

Collect Requirements (Continued)		
Key Inputs (Cont.)	Scope Management Plan	The scope management plan is a component of the project management plan that details the delineation, evolution, monitoring, controlling, and validation of scope. The plan is referenced to identify project requirements.
	Requirements Management Plan	The requirements management plan is a component of the project management plan that details the methods for gathering, evaluating, and documenting project requirements.
	Business Case	The business case, which usually describes the business need and contains a cost-benefit analysis, is used to justify the creation of the project and is the basis for the project charter. The business case is referenced to ensure that the requirements align with the business needs.
Key Tools and Techniques	Expert Judgment	Expert judgment is judgment based on expertise acquired in a specific area. It is important to consider expertise related to business evaluation, requirements elicitation, requirements evaluation, requirements documentation, diagramming, facilitation, and management of disagreement.
	Brainstorming	Brainstorming is a technique used to amass a number of ideas in a brief period, specifically ideas related to the project and its requirements.
	Interviews	Interviews are direct elicitations of information and can be formal or informal. Typically, the interviewer asks questions of the interviewees and records the responses. The responses lead to the determination and delineation of the features and functions of what the project will create.
	Focus Groups	Focus groups are interactive discussions conducted by an experienced moderator with specific stakeholders and subject matter experts to determine their expectations and attitudes about what the project will create.
	Questionnaires and Surveys	Questionnaires and surveys are sets of composed questions used to obtain information from a large group of correspondents in order to determine that the elicited requirements are complete and accurate.
	Benchmarking	Benchmarking is used to compare an organization's practices to those of corresponding organizations in order to identify best practices, ideas for improvement, and performance metrics.
	Mind Mapping	Mind mapping integrates ideas into a single map that highlights similarities and differences and can be used to inspire new ideas.

Collect Requirements (Continued)		
Key Tools and Techniques (Cont.)	Facilitation	Facilitation is the ability to direct a group event to achieve a successful conclusion, specifically the delineation of product requirements by stakeholders. The facilitator ensures attendee participation, consideration and mutual understanding of all contributions, appropriate action for any agreements, and acceptance of results in accordance with the agreed upon decision process.
Key Outputs	Requirements Documentation	Requirements documentation delineates how requirements fulfill the business needs of the project. Before baselining requirements, they must be **measurable, testable, traceable, complete, consistent, and acceptable** to appropriate stakeholders. Requirements may be categorized as **business** requirements, **solution** requirements (both **functional** and **non-functional**), **transition** requirements, **project** requirements, and **quality** requirements. Once categorized, requirements can be refined as they are evolved.
	Requirements Traceability Matrix	The requirements traceability matrix is a grid used to align requirements to the deliverables that satisfy them to ensure the requirement adds value. The matrix allows the requirements to be monitored throughout the project life cycle and provides a framework for managing scope changes. At a minimum, requirements can be traced to business needs, project aims, project scope and WBS deliverables, product design and development, testing, and high-level requirements. Requirements attributes can be recorded in the matrix to delineate important information about the requirement, such as a unique identifier, the version, the priority, the current status and status date, a description, the reason for inclusion, the owner, the source, and fulfillment of stakeholder satisfaction.

Situational Question and Real World Application

Failure to effectively execute the Collect Requirements process can result in incomplete or incorrect requirements. Since project requirements are the basis for all planning, there can be a failure in planning and that can result in consequences that range from budget issues to project failure.

5.2.1. Evolution of Requirements

The evolution of requirements starts with **business requirements**, which are created in alignment with enterprise goals.

Stakeholder requirements are created next. Stakeholder requirements focus on stakeholder needs as they align with the business goals and serve as a bridge between business requirements and solution requirements.

PMI, CAPM, and PMBOK are registered marks of the Project Management Institute, Inc.

124 © 2008-2018 Crosswind Learning, www.crosswindpm.com

Solution requirements are then created to ensure that the business need is met. Solution requirements can include functional and non-functional requirements.

Transition requirements are created last and focus on the activities needed to implement the new solution.

5.2.2.   Requirements Traceability Matrix

The requirements traceability matrix associates requirements with their origins and traces them throughout the project life cycle.

It associates requirements with their business and project objective(s) and traces:

- Requirements to project scope/WBS deliverables, to product design and development, and to test strategy and scenarios
- High-level requirements to detailed requirements

It also traces requirement attributes. Attributes typically traced in the matrix are: description, unique identifier, owner, source, version, priority, status, completion date, acceptance criteria, and inclusion rationale.

Requirements	Subsystems				Layers					Tiers			
	Administration	Scheduling	Accounting	Printing	Presentation	User Interface	Business Logic	Services	Data Access	Client	Web	Application	Data
SR 1.1	X	X	X	X		X	X	X	X		X	X	X
SR 1.2		X	X	X	X	X	X	X	X	X	X	X	X
SR 1.3		X	X	X	X				X	X	X	X	
SR 1.4	X	X	X	X		X	X	X	X	X	X	X	X
SR 2	X	X	X	X	X	X	X	X		X	X	X	X
SR 3	X	X	X	X		X	X		X	X	X	X	X
SR 4		X	X	X	X	X	X	X	X	X	X	X	X
SR 5	X	X	X			X	X	X		X	X	X	X

Figure 5-4: Requirements Traceability Matrix
The source for the above figure is the Project Management Institute, *A Guide to the Project Management Body of Knowledge*, (*PMBOK® Guide*) – Sixth Edition, Project Management Institute Inc., 2017, Figure 5.7, Page 149

Upon project completion, the matrix is used to determine that each requirement was successfully delivered.

The source for the above text is the Project Management Institute, *A Guide to the Project Management Body of Knowledge*, (*PMBOK® Guide*) – Sixth Edition, Project Management Institute Inc., 2017, Pages 136-147

5.3.   Define Scope (Planning Process Group)

During Define Scope, a written project scope statement is created. The scope statement is used for decision-making throughout the project. It typically includes:

Know the Key Inputs, Tools & Techniques, and Outputs for Define Scope.

- What is included in the project
- What is involved in the creation of the project
- What the project is expected to do upon completion

To eliminate confusion, **the project scope statement often states exclusions** to the project.

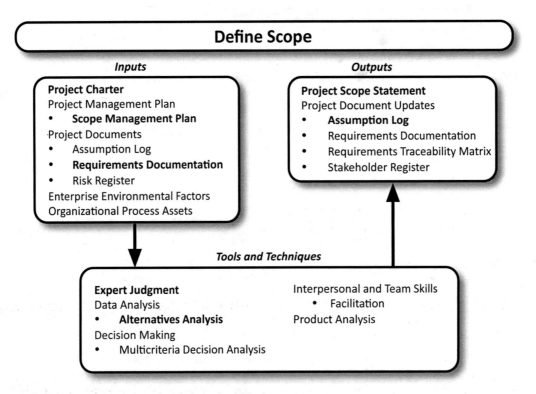

Figure 5-5: Define Scope Data Flow Diagram
The source for the above figure is the Project Management Institute, *A Guide to the Project Management Body of Knowledge*, (*PMBOK® Guide*) – Sixth Edition, Project Management Institute Inc., 2017, Figure 5.8, Page 147

Define Scope (Planning)		
Key Inputs	Project Charter	The project charter is the document that provides authorization for the existence of the project and gives the project manager the power to use organizational resources to execute the project. The project charter typically lists the key deliverables, the milestones, and the roles and responsibilities of each person involved in the project. It also delineates the purpose of the project, a high-level project description, project characteristics, and approval requirements.

Define Scope (Continued)		
Key Inputs (Cont.)	Scope Management Plan	The scope management plan is a component of the project management plan that details the delineation, evolution, monitoring, controlling, and validation of scope. It includes the methods for creating the project scope statement, authorizing and maintaining the WBS, authorizing formal acceptance of deliverables, and controlling change requests related to the scope statement.
	Requirements Documentation	Requirements documentation delineates the requirements that will be included in the scope.
Key Tools and Techniques	Expert Judgment	Expert judgment is judgment based on expertise acquired in a specific area. It is often **more significant and accurate than the best modeling tools** available and can be provided by stakeholders, company personnel external to the project, professional organizations or groups, and consultants. It is important to consider expertise related to awareness of proficiency with comparable projects.
	Alternatives Analysis	Alternatives analysis is used to identify approaches to the execution and performance of the project requirements and objectives listed in the project charter. It can include **brainstorming** and **lateral thinking**. Lateral thinking is a set of techniques (such as free association) used to stimulate creative thinking.
Key Outputs	Project Scope Statement	The project scope statement defines the project by describing its scope, detailed deliverables and the process to create those deliverables, product acceptance criteria, exclusions, assumptions, and constraints. The statement provides all stakeholders with a common understanding of the scope of the project and enable the project team to effectively engage in detailed planning, guides the team's work during execution, and defines if change requests or additional work is within the scope of the project. The detailed scope statement includes a product scope description, a description of all deliverables, acceptance criteria for the deliverables, and exclusions. The **scope statement differs from the project charter** in that the **charter is high-level** and the **scope statement is detailed**.

Define Scope (Continued)		
Key Outputs (Cont.)	Assumption Log	The assumption log is a document that lists the assumptions and constraints identified during the creation of the project charter. An assumption is an idea or statement taken to be true. An example of an assumption is the statement "there will be a robust market for the product created as a result of this project once it is available to the public." Examples of constraints are the project completion deadline, the budget threshold, or the limit on the number of employees that can be dedicated to the project. It's important to identify assumptions and constraints as early as possible and to update them as the project evolves.

Situational Question and Real World Application

Failure to effectively perform the Define Scope process can result in a discovery of requirements not determined during planning, which can lead to a variance in scope, schedule, or budget.

5.3.1. Project Scope Statement

The project scope statement is a document that develops and helps attain buy-in on a common interpretation of the project scope. It can describe **what is, as well as what is not, included in the project**.

It typically includes the following:

Know the importance and characteristics of a project scope statement.

- Product scope description (progressively elaborated)
- Product acceptance criteria
- Project deliverables
- Project exclusions
- Project constraints & assumptions

The source for the above text is the Project Management Institute, *A Guide to the Project Management Body of Knowledge*, (PMBOK® Guide) – Sixth Edition, Project Management Institute Inc., 2017, Pages 147-152

5.4. Create WBS (Planning Process Group)

During Create WBS, the major deliverables are divided into smaller components that can be easily estimated (schedule and cost), managed, and controlled. These components are ultimately rolled into the work breakdown structure (WBS).

Know the Key Inputs, Tools & Techniques, and Outputs for Create WBS.

Rolling wave planning can be used when information about the project is sparse, thereby resulting in a failure to appropriately decompose for a deliverable or subproject until future project information is known later in the project.

The lowest level of the WBS is the work package. Any subsequent decomposition generally results in the creation of activity lists.

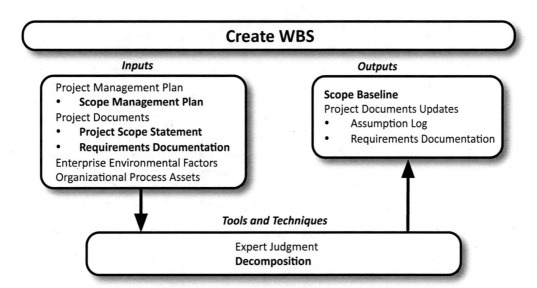

Create WBS

Inputs	Outputs

Inputs

Project Management Plan
- **Scope Management Plan**

Project Documents
- **Project Scope Statement**
- **Requirements Documentation**

Enterprise Environmental Factors
Organizational Process Assets

Outputs

Scope Baseline
Project Documents Updates
- Assumption Log
- Requirements Documentation

Tools and Techniques

Expert Judgment
Decomposition

Figure 5-6: Create WBS Data Flow Diagram

The source for the above figure is the Project Management Institute, *A Guide to the Project Management Body of Knowledge*, (*PMBOK® Guide*) – Sixth Edition, Project Management Institute Inc., 2017, Figure 5.10, Page 153

Create WBS (Planning)		
Key Inputs	Scope Management Plan	The scope management plan is a component of the project management plan that details the delineation, evolution, monitoring, controlling, and validation of scope. It includes the methods for creating the project scope statement, authorizing and maintaining the WBS, authorizing formal acceptance of deliverables, and controlling change requests related to the scope statement. Note that the plan also delineates the manner in which the WBS will be created from the project scope statement.
	Project Scope Statement	The project scope statement defines the project by describing its scope, detailed deliverables and the process to create those deliverables, product acceptance criteria, exclusions, assumptions, and constraints. The statement provides all stakeholders with a common understanding of the scope of the project and enables the project team to effectively engage in detailed planning, guides the team's work during execution, and defines if change requests or additional work is within the scope of the project. The detailed scope statement includes a product scope description, a description of all deliverables, acceptance criteria for the deliverables, and exclusions. The scope statement differs from the project charter in that the charter is high-level and the scope statement is detailed.

Create WBS (Continued)		
Key Inputs (Cont.)	Requirements Documentation	Requirements documentation delineates the requirements that will be included in the scope and the manner in which the particular requirements meet the business needs of the project.
Key Tools and Techniques	Decomposition	Decomposition breaks down the project scope and deliverables into manageable components. The work breakdown structure decomposes the work into work packages, the smallest components that can be managed and estimated in terms of schedule and budget. Decomposition generally involves determining and evaluating the deliverables and related work, constructing and organizing the WBS, decomposing upper-level components by subdividing the work for each deliverable into its most basic components, creating and assigning identification codes to WBS components, and verifying that the decomposition of deliverables has been done appropriately.
Key Outputs	Scope Baseline	The scope baseline is the authorized version of the **scope statement**, **WBS** (to the level of work package with individual identification codes), and **WBS dictionary**. The scope baseline is subject to change control. Note that each work package is a part of a control account, a management control item where scope, budget, and schedule are combined and compared to measure performance.

Situational Question and Real World Application

Failure to effectively perform the Create WBS process can result in the discovery of required items that were not considered during initial planning, therefore not addressed in the work breakdown structure (WBS). This can result in scope, schedule, or cost variance.

5.4.1. Work Breakdown Structure (WBS)

The work breakdown structure (WBS) is one of the most important documents created during the project planning process. The main output of the Create WBS process is decomposition of the project scope statement and the project scope. Generally **created by the project manager and the team** doing the work, the WBS describes the work breakdown and restricts its content to listing **only the project work**. It also helps the team's buy-in to the project by allowing its input.

Know the principles, characteristics, and importance of a work breakdown structure (WBS) in graphical format.

To create the WBS, the main pieces of the project work must be defined and then decomposed to an appropriate level of detail so that each activity is definable, trackable, and manageable. When completed, the **WBS should encompass all of the work of the project**.

Generally, a heuristic (rule of thumb) is used to determine how the **work is broken down and the level of decomposition required for the work packages**. Work packages can be loosely considered deliverables because their completion should result in project completion.

Once the WBS is created, a number of key items can be started including the activity list, the schedule, the budget, any resources to be assigned, and risk planning. If time and attention is not properly allocated to the WBS, the project may have challenges or even fail.

Figure 5-7: WBS Process Components illustrates the components of the WBS: **control accounts, planning packages, and work packages (the lowest level of the WBS)**. Dashed lines define the boundary of WBS decomposition from the most detailed output through the least detailed output. Note that the milestones and activities lists, which align with the WBS, are created during the Define Activities process in the Project Schedule Management chapter.

Control accounts are specific points in the work breakdown structure (WBS) where the project scope, budget, actual cost, and schedule are combined and then compared to measure performance metrics. This allows tracking progress at appropriate levels of detail throughout the work breakdown structure (WBS). Reference the Project Schedule Management chapter for details.

In some situations, the work of a project cannot be fully decomposed since it is not fully defined. Such situations occur in **Agile or adaptive** environments where the **rolling wave** planning approach is used.

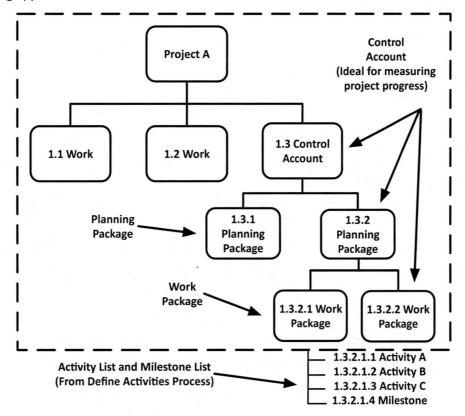

Figure 5-7: WBS Process Components

5.4.2. 100% Rule

The 100% rule states that 100% of the work of a project (or program) needs to be represented in the WBS. For example, if there are testing activities and/or administrative work associated with the project, the 100% rule would require **inclusion** of all testing and administrative work in the WBS. Failure to consider this will undoubtedly result in incorrect schedule, budget, and resource estimates, which will ultimately impact the budget and schedule.

5.4.3. WBS Numbering

Work breakdown structure numbering is applied to indicate where work fits in the project. The numbering system is often similar to that used in this manual. The high level control account is assigned a number comparable to a chapter number (e.g. 5.0), a control account at the planning package level is assigned a number comparable to a major element of the chapter (e.g. 5.1), and a control account at the work package level is assigned a number comparable to a subordinate element (e.g. 5.1.1).

5.4.4. WBS Dictionary

The WBS dictionary provides supporting detail that is typically not practical to apply to the graphical format of the WBS (work breakdown structure). It can include the following items:

WBS Dictionary Components		
Code of account identifier	Description of work	Responsible organization
List of scheduled milestones	Associated schedule activities	Resources required
Cost estimates	Quality requirements	Acceptance criteria
Technical references	Contract information	

It's not unexpected that some additional schedule, cost, and resource related planning processes (other than Create WBS) are started before the WBS dictionary can be completed.

5.4.5. Various Breakdown Structures

There are numerous breakdown structures in project management. It's important that you know the differences.
The breakdown structures are:

Know the project management breakdown structures.

- **Organizational breakdown structure (OBS)** - The OBS, also known as an organizational chart, shows how the project organization is structured to accomplish project activities (reference the Project Resource Management chapter)
- **Risk breakdown structure (RBS)** – The RBS depicts the risks that can potentially occur during the project, broken down by risk category (reference the Project Risk Management chapter)
- **Resource breakdown structure (RBS)** – The RBS depicts the type of resources used during the project (reference the Project Schedule Management chapter)
- **Bill of materials (BOM)** – The BOM includes the components, sub-assemblies, and assemblies used to build a product or service

The source for the above text is the Project Management Institute, *A Guide to the Project Management Body of Knowledge*, (PMBOK® Guide) – Sixth Edition, Project Management Institute Inc., 2017, Pages 152-158

5.5. Validate Scope (Monitoring and Controlling Process Group)

The main goal of Validate Scope is to **secure sign-off (formal acceptance)** of the project scope at logical intervals during the process (each milestone, each deliverable, or each phase depending upon the nature of the project) and/or when the entire work of the project is completed. Think of Validate Scope as accepting deliverables and remember the phrase, **"validate early and validate often."**

Know the Key Inputs, Tools & Techniques, and Outputs for Validate Scope.

For a predictive project, such as a **traditional project,** Validate Scope is executed with **each deliverable** or phase review. For an **adaptive project**, such as an Agile project, Validate Scope is repeated for **each iteration**.

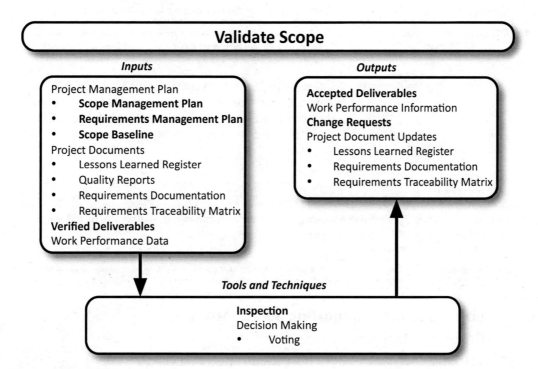

Figure 5-8: Validate Scope Data Flow Diagram
The source for the above figure is the Project Management Institute, *A Guide to the Project Management Body of Knowledge*, (*PMBOK® Guide*) – Sixth Edition, Project Management Institute Inc., 2017, Figure 5.15, Page 160

Validate Scope (Monitoring and Controlling)		
Key Inputs	Scope Management Plan	The scope management plan is a component of the project management plan that details the delineation, evolution, monitoring, controlling, and validation of scope.
	Requirements Management Plan	The requirements management plan is a component of the project management plan that details the validation of project requirements.

Validate Scope (Continued)		
Key Inputs (Cont.)	Scope Baseline	The scope baseline is the authorized version of the scope statement, WBS (to the level of work package with individual identification codes), and WBS dictionary. The scope baseline is subject to change control and is compared to actual results to ascertain if any changes, corrective actions, or precautionary actions are required.
	Verified Deliverables	Verified deliverables are deliverables that have been concluded and checked for accuracy through the quality control process.
Tools and Techniques	Inspection	An inspection is performed to measure, examine, and validate that the work and deliverables fulfill requirements and product acceptance criteria as documented.
Key Outputs	Accepted Deliverables	Accepted deliverables are deliverables that have fulfilled acceptance criteria and have received formal sign-off from the sponsor or customer.
	Change Requests	Change requests are requests for modification that have not yet been approved through the formal change control process. A deliverable that has failed to fulfill its acceptance criteria may require a change request to meet those criteria.

Situational Question and Real World Application
Failure to effectively perform the Validate Scope process can result in difficulty or failure to obtain formal sign-off for deliverables or the project.

The source for the above text is the Project Management Institute, *A Guide to the Project Management Body of Knowledge*, (*PMBOK® Guide*) – Sixth Edition, Project Management Institute Inc., 2017, Pages 158-163

5.6. Control Scope (Monitoring and Controlling Process Group)

Know the Key Inputs, Tools & Techniques, and Outputs for Control Scope.

Control Scope addresses, through the Perform Integrated Change Control process, scope change requests and recommended remedial/corrective actions. The process also addresses the management of approved changes.

For a predictive project, such as a traditional project, Control Scope is executed on an ongoing basis. For an adaptive project, such as an Agile project, Control Scope is repeated for each iteration.

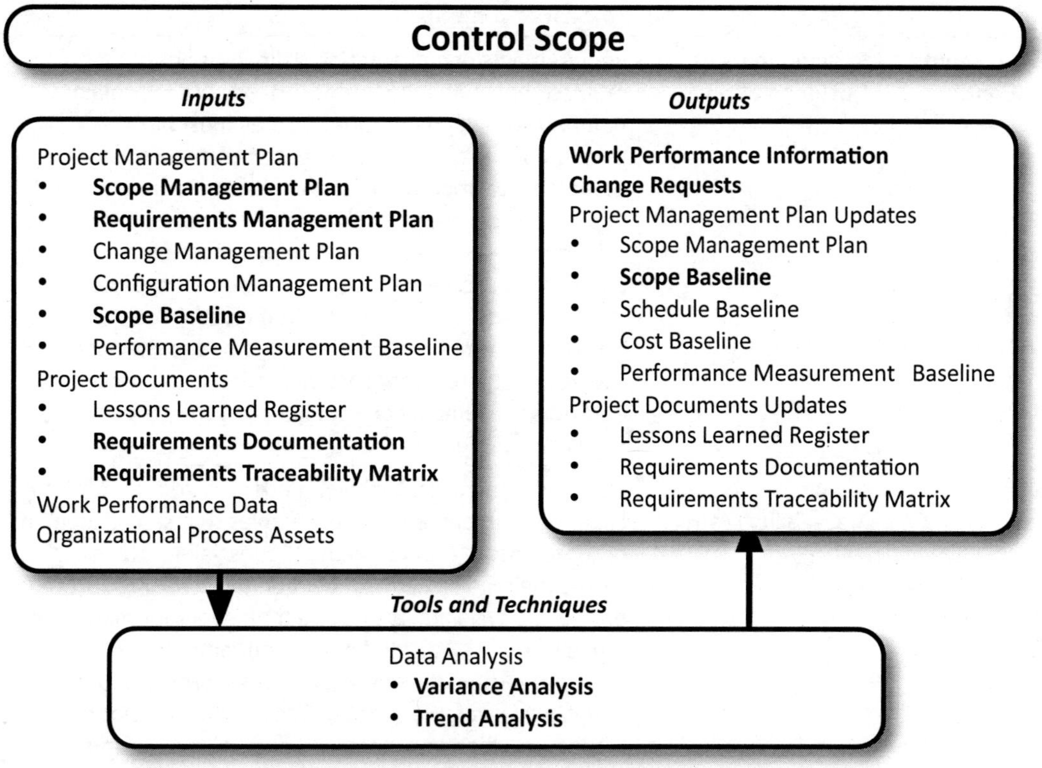

Control Scope

Inputs	Outputs
Project Management Plan • **Scope Management Plan** • **Requirements Management Plan** • Change Management Plan • Configuration Management Plan • **Scope Baseline** • Performance Measurement Baseline Project Documents • Lessons Learned Register • **Requirements Documentation** • **Requirements Traceability Matrix** Work Performance Data Organizational Process Assets	**Work Performance Information** **Change Requests** Project Management Plan Updates • Scope Management Plan • **Scope Baseline** • Schedule Baseline • Cost Baseline • Performance Measurement Baseline Project Documents Updates • Lessons Learned Register • Requirements Documentation • Requirements Traceability Matrix

Tools and Techniques

Data Analysis
• **Variance Analysis**
• **Trend Analysis**

Figure 5-9: Control Scope Data Flow Diagram

The source for the above figure is the Project Management Institute, *A Guide to the Project Management Body of Knowledge*, (*PMBOK® Guide*) – Sixth Edition, Project Management Institute Inc., 2017, Figure 5.17, Page 165

Control Scope (Monitoring and Controlling)		
Key Inputs	Scope Management Plan	The scope management plan is a component of the project management plan that details the delineation, evolution, monitoring, controlling, and validation of scope.
	Requirements Management Plan	The requirements management plan is a component of the project management plan that details the validation of project requirements.
	Scope Baseline	The scope baseline is the authorized version of the scope statement, WBS (to the level of work package with individual identification codes), and WBS dictionary. The scope baseline is subject to change control and is compared to actual results to ascertain if any changes, corrective actions, or precautionary actions are required.

Control Scope (Continued)		
Key Inputs (Cont.)	Requirements Documentation	Requirements documentation delineates how requirements fulfill the business needs of the project. Before baselining requirements, they must be measurable, testable, traceable, complete, consistent, and acceptable to appropriate stakeholders. Requirements may be categorized as business requirements, stakeholder requirements, solution requirements (both functional and non-functional), transition requirements, project requirements, and quality requirements. Once categorized, requirements can be refined as they are evolved. Requirements documentation is referenced to determine the impact of any change to the scope of the project or product.
	Requirements Traceability Matrix	The requirements traceability matrix is a grid used to align requirements to the deliverables that satisfy them in order to ensure the requirement adds value. The matrix allows the requirements to be monitored throughout the project life cycle and provides a framework for managing scope changes. At a minimum, requirements can be traced to business needs, project aims, project scope and WBS deliverables, product design and development, testing, and high-level requirements. Requirements attributes can be recorded in the matrix to delineate important information about the requirement, such as a unique identifier, the version, the priority, the current status and status date, a description, the reason for inclusion, the owner, the source, and fulfillment of stakeholder satisfaction. The requirements traceability matrix is referenced to determine the impact of any change to the scope baseline of the project objectives.
Tools and Techniques	Variance Analysis	Variance analysis is used to compare the baseline to the actual results and to ascertain if any variance is within acceptable thresholds or if any changes, corrective actions, or precautionary actions are required.
	Trend Analysis	Trend analysis is used to project the future state of the project based on the present state of the project, in other words, to determine future results based on past results. The analysis can be used to ascertain the reason for, and degree of any variance relative to the scope baseline to effect a decision regarding, the need for corrective or precautionary action.

PMI, CAPM, and PMBOK are registered marks of the Project Management Institute, Inc.

136

		Control Scope (Continued)
Key Outputs	Work Performance Information	Work performance information includes supplemental and contextualized information regarding the performance of the project scope in comparison to the scope baseline. The information can contain important facets of scope control such as scope variances and their causes, how those variances impact cost and schedule, and a prognosis for future scope performance.
	Change Requests	Change requests are requests for modification that have not yet been approved through the formal change control process. Evaluation of project performance may engender a change request to the cost and schedule baselines as well as other components of the project management plan.
	Scope Baseline	The scope baseline is the authorized version of the scope statement, WBS (to the level of work package with individual identification codes), and WBS dictionary. The scope baseline is subject to change control and is compared to actual results to ascertain if any changes, corrective actions, or precautionary actions are required.

Situational Question and Real World Application

Failure to effectively perform the Control Scope process can result in the team working on an unapproved change request.   If the request is later rejected or modified, additional work will result. The additional work may lead to cost or schedule variances.

The source for the above text is the Project Management Institute, *A Guide to the Project Management Body of Knowledge*, (*PMBOK® Guide*) – Sixth Edition, Project Management Institute Inc., 2017, Pages 163-167

5.7.   Project Scope Management Formulas and Variables

There are no formulas for this chapter.

5.8.   Project Scope Management Terminology

Term	Description
Acceptance	The process of formally receiving the work of the project, which should be complete and fulfill the objectives of the project
Acceptance Criteria	The contingencies that must be satisfied prior to acceptance of work
Accepted Deliverables	Products, results or capabilities that have been accepted by the customer as meeting requirements
Affinity Diagram	A tool used to gather ideas and organize them into groupings so they can be reviewed and analyzed; typically used for ideas generated from brainstorming sessions
Alternative Analysis	A technique used to evaluate project execution approaches
Alternatives Generation	A technique used to create as many project execution approaches as possible
Analogy Approach	A methodology for establishing values for the current project based on those from a previous project with similar characteristics; values obtained from this method include activity duration, required resources, and estimated costs
Brainstorming	A creative technique used to gather a large amount of information from team members and/or subject matter experts; applicable to ideas, risk identification, and solutions
Collect Requirements	The process of arranging for, determining, and documenting the needs of the stakeholders to align with project objectives
Context Diagrams	A graphical representation of the scope of a business system that includes processes, equipment, and computer systems and indicates the manner in which people and other systems interact with the business system
Control Scope	The process of observing project status and scope in order to administer scope baseline revisions
Create WBS	The process of breaking down the work of the project into minimal components for more effective management
Decomposition	The process of breaking down the work of the project into smaller, more controllable components
Define Scope	The process of developing the project scope statement, the document that details the expected results of the project
Delphi Technique	A technique used to gain concurrence from a group of experts about a specific issue; the technique is effected by using a questionnaire to solicit ideas from the experts, having the ideas summarized, having the experts add comments to the summaries, and repeating the process until a consensus is reached
Diagramming Technique	A method that indicates the logical links between data
Facilitated Workshop	A focused session involving cross-functional stakeholders and a designated leader that is conducted to achieve a specific goal, such as the creation of project requirements
Focus Group	A focused session involving prequalified stakeholders, subject matter experts (SMEs), and a designated leader that is conducted to determine expectations and views regarding a potential product, service, or result
Group Creativity Technique	A focused session involving stakeholders and a designated leader that is conducted to develop ideas

Term	Description
Group Decision-Making Technique	A focused session involving stakeholders and a designated leader that is conducted to review decision methods available for use with specific activities such as generating, classifying, and prioritizing requirements
Interviews	A focused session involving individual stakeholders and a designated leader that is conducted to elicit specific information
Management by Objectives (MBO)	An administration method that aligns, or realigns, projects to strategic objectives
Mind-mapping	A technique used to integrate ideas created through individual brainstorming sessions into a single map in order to highlight similarities and differences in understanding and generate new ideas
Nominal Group Technique	A technique, effected by a voting process, that is used to prioritize ideas by utility for further brainstorming
Plan Scope Management	The process of creating a document that designates how the project scope will be defined, validated, and controlled; the document may also offer guidance for requirements and include the scope statement, the work breakdown structure (WBS), and the scope baseline
Planning Package	A WBS component that has no detailed scheduled activities even though it is known to have work content
Plurality	The votes of the largest block in a group when a majority is not required, typically used to denote agreement with a decision
Product	An output of the project that is quantifiable and can be described as material and goods
Product Analysis	An approach used to convert a business-defined product into project deliverables; typically involves asking business representatives questions about the intended uses and characteristics of the product
Product Life Cycle	The phases of product development, typically defined as conception through delivery, expansion, maturity, and disengagement
Product Scope	The features and functions of a project's product, service, or result
Product Scope Description	The documented depiction of the features and functions of a project's product, service, or result
Project Scope	The work executed to deliver a product, service, or result that satisfies the specified features and functions
Project Scope Management	The processes required to ensure that all the work needed to complete the project, and only that work, is included in the project
Project Scope Statement	The document that describes the major deliverables, assumptions, constraints, and scope of the project
Prototype	A working model of the product created to obtain detailed stakeholder feedback
Questionnaires	Written surveys designed to quickly gather information from a large number of respondents
Requirement	A condition or capability that must be made available through a product, service, or result in order to fulfill a contract or formal specification
Requirements Documentation	A document that describes requirements for creating a product or a feature of the product
Requirements Management Plan	The document, part of the project or program management plan, used to describe the evaluation, recording, and administration of project requirements
Requirements Traceability Matrix	A graphical representation that illustrates the relationships between the origins of the product requirements to the deliverables that fulfill the requirements
Scope	The products, services, and results expected to be provided by the project

Term	Description
Scope Baseline	The authorized scope statement, WBS, and WBS dictionary that contain only those modifications authorized through a formal change control process; used as a basis for comparison
Scope Change	A change to the product or product scope accompanied by the appropriate modifications to the budget or schedule
Scope Creep	A change to the product or product scope not accompanied by the appropriate modifications to the budget or schedule
Scope Management Plan	The document, part of the project or program management plan, used to define the manner in which the project scope will be delineated, elaborated, monitored, controlled, and authenticated
Statement of Work (SOW)	A detailed description of the products, services, or results expected from a project or other initiative
Unanimity	A decision with which all group members concurred
User	The person, division, or company that will be the user or owner of the product when the project is complete
Validate Scope	The process in which the customer or sponsor reviews and accepts project deliverables as being complete and correct in accordance with the requirements
Validation	The process of determining that the results of the project are in compliance with requirements imposed by the customer and appropriate stakeholders and typically involving acceptance by them
WBS Dictionary	A document that itemizes deliverable, activity, and scheduling information for each WBS component
Work Breakdown Structure (WBS)	A decomposition of the work of the project
Work Breakdown Structure Component	Any unit of work defined in the WBS
Work Package	The smallest level of WBS work for which cost and time can be assessed and administered

The source for the above definitions is the Glossary of the Project Management Institute,
A Guide to the Project Management Body of Knowledge, (PMBOK® Guide) – Sixth Edition, Project Management Institute Inc., 2017

PMI, CAPM, and PMBOK are registered marks of the Project Management Institute, Inc.

140   © 2008-2018 Crosswind Learning, www.crosswindpm.com

5.9. Project Scope Management Tests and Exercises

5.9.1. Project Scope Management Practice Test

Answers are in section 5.10.1.

1. What is the most significant benefit of having the project management team's assistance in creating the work breakdown structure?

    (A) It establishes the project manager's authority
    (B) It helps generate a more accurate budget
    (C) It helps attain buy-in from the team doing the work
    (D) It helps generate a more accurate schedule

2. The approval of the project charter has been delayed for weeks due to market fluctuation. Upon approval, you are assigned as the project manager and senior management wants you to begin the planning process group immediately. When will you schedule validate scope?

    (A) At the end of every phase on the project
    (B) After the sponsor defines what they want the project to create
    (C) When the project management plan is awaiting sign-off
    (D) When the work of the project is done

3. During what processes is work decomposition performed?

    (A) Create WBS and define activities
    (B) Define scope and create WBS
    (C) Define activities and control schedule
    (D) Create WBS and control scope

4. The company is designing touchscreen displays for use on mobile workstation tablets. A requirements traceability matrix is being utilized. Of the following, which is the best description of how the project manager will use the matrix?

    (A) To trace requirements to business and project objectives
    (B) To trace requirements to project scope/WBS deliverables, to product design and development, and to test strategy and scenarios
    (C) To trace high-level requirements to detailed requirements
    (D) All of the answers

5.   Which of the following is a heuristic for WBS decomposition?

(A) Breaking down work until it is done by a single resource
(B) Using an organizational structure appearance
(C) Creating a WBS in which the summary activities are equal to the detail underneath
(D) Breaking work down to a realistic level (work packages being the lowest level)

6.   The project manager is working with the customer to gain formal acceptance of the project deliverables. The customer is saying that three of the deliverables are not meeting project goals and are unusable in their present form. The team discovers this was caused by an inconsistency between the requirements, scope statement and WBS. Which process will the team use to align these documents?

(A) Analyze scope
(B) Gather requirements
(C) Control scope
(D) Validate scope

7.   During the create WBS process for the financial reporting improvement project, as planning evolves, the team could create all the following except…

(A) Bill of materials
(B) Communication breakdown structure
(C) Risk breakdown structure
(D) Resource breakdown structure

8.   Due to the complexity of the project to design touchscreen displays for use on mobile workstation tablets, a number of breakdown structures will be used. Of the following breakdown structures and descriptions, which is correct?

(A) Organizational breakdown structure, which graphically illustrates how project management is structured to accomplish project activities
(B) Risk breakdown structure, which lists risks that are grouped by probability of occurrence and listed by severity of impact
(C) Resource breakdown structure, which graphically illustrates the availability of resources
(D) Bill of materials, which lists the components, assemblies, and sub-assemblies used to build the product

9.   As the project manager establishes the scope baseline, which of the following best describes what she will create or reference?

(A) Requirements, scope statement, and WBS
(B) WBS and WBS dictionary
(C) Scope statement, WBS, and WBS dictionary
(D) Requirements, scope statement, and WBS dictionary

10. The project to consolidate the accounting departments of two recently merged hospitals is extremely complex. The project manager and his team are keenly aware of the importance of properly decomposing the work of the project. If they decompose the work beyond work packages, what is the likely result?

    (A) The application of rolling wave planning
    (B) The creation of activity lists
    (C) A variance in the scope definition
    (D) The creation of the WBS dictionary

11. The WBS has been created for the textbook selection project and the team is creating the WBS dictionary. How will they go about this?

    (A) By documenting the work packages and listing the organizations responsible for completion of the work
    (B) By documenting the work packages, documenting the control accounts, and listing the organizations responsible for completion of the work
    (C) By documenting the work packages, documenting test criteria and test cases, documenting the control accounts, and listing the organizations responsible for completion of the work
    (D) By documenting the work packages, documenting the scope baseline, and listing the organizations responsible for completion of the work

12. The medical billing system project has entered closure. As the project manager and the team prepare for closure, they are told that validate scope will be very important to the success of the project. Of the following, which best describes the importance of validate scope?

    (A) Validate scope should have been done earlier in the project and since it wasn't done then, it's important to complete it before the project is complete
    (B) Validate scope authenticates that the sponsor signed the project scope statement at the beginning of planning
    (C) Validate scope is the process of comparing what the project created to the project scope statement, product description, and anything else that helps ensure that the results of the project will function as intended
    (D) Validate scope is used to confirm that the project team understands the scope of the project

13. The project team is creating the WBS for their stadium restoration project. Which of the following best describes the layers that would likely be included?

    (A) Control accounts, planning packages, work packages
    (B) Control accounts, planning packages, work packages, activity lists
    (C) Activity packages, planning packages, work packages
    (D) Control accounts, planning packages, work packages, milestone packages

14. The project manager is working with the business analyst to create requirements for the upgrade to the security platform of the company website. Which of the following best describes the order in which the processes will be created?

(A) Business requirements, solution requirements, stakeholder requirements, transition requirements
(B) Stakeholder requirements, business requirements, solution requirements, transition requirements
(C) Business requirements, stakeholder requirements, solution requirements, transition requirements
(D) Transition requirements, business requirements, stakeholder requirements, solution requirements

15. Which of the following describes a work breakdown structure (WBS)?

(A) The work should be decomposed to a realistic level of detail
(B) If the work is not listed in the WBS, it is not in the project
(C) The accumulation of the work in the WBS should be equal to the work of the project
(D) All of the answers

16. The project manager wants to better control her project. She is using decomposition after attending a project management class. Of the following breakdown structures and descriptions, which is correct?

(A) Organizational breakdown structure, which graphically illustrates how project management is structured to accomplish project activities
(B) Risk breakdown structure, which lists potential risks broken down by risk category
(C) Resource breakdown structure, which graphically illustrates the availability of resources
(D) Bill of materials, which lists the cost of the components, assemblies, and sub-assemblies used to build the product

17. All the following are true about a work breakdown structure (WBS) except...

(A) The project management team and the project manager should be involved in creating it
(B) It will resemble an organizational chart in appearance when complete
(C) Activity sequencing of WBS components requires parallel or concurrent dependencies
(D) It is a decomposition of the work of the project

18. The project manager is in the process of creating the scope statement. There are a number of items that can exist both in the requirements and scope statement. Which of the following items are most likely to be only in the scope statement?

(A) The systems involved in the project
(B) Items to be excluded from the project
(C) Items that are required for the project
(D) The areas of the company impacted by the project

19. Which of the following requirement types can contain both functional and non-functional requirements?

(A) Stakeholder requirements
(B) Solution requirements
(C) Transition requirements
(D) Business requirements

20. Project A is two months long, has three stakeholders, and has completed the planning process group. Project B is 12 months long, has 10 stakeholders, and is in the monitoring and controlling process group. Project C is 12 months long, has three stakeholders, and is in the planning process group. Which project is most likely to experience scope creep?

(A) Project A
(B) Project B
(C) Project C
(D) Not enough information

21. The project to create a new database system is approximately halfway complete when a senior manager says that a major change needs to occur with the scope of the project or the system will not function in his department when it's rolled out. He further explains this change is going to delay the anticipated finish date of the project. After he explains the details of the proposed change in scope, what do you do first?

(A) Let him know what the delay to the project will be
(B) Implement change control to incorporate the new work
(C) Tell him "no" because it will change the finish date of the project
(D) Meet with the team to determine the impact

22. Which of the following is the tool or technique the project manager will use in the process of creating a WBS?

(A) Work packages
(B) Decomposition
(C) Stakeholder management
(D) WBS dictionary

23. A project manager is beginning the collect requirements process. Which of the following is the most important activity he should perform?

   (A) Create a list of preferred vendors for outsourcing
   (B) Create the work breakdown structure (WBS)
   (C) Create the project scope statement in sufficient detail to enable further planning
   (D) Verify that all key stakeholders have provided their input

24. The validate scope process has been started at the end of phase 3 of the project. The main deliverable was sent to the customer. Three weeks have passed and the customer acts as if the deliverable was never received. Which of the following is the best action to take?

   (A) Stop work on the project until the customer acknowledges and approves the deliverable
   (B) Ask the sponsor for assistance
   (C) Document the issue in the issue log
   (D) Ask the customer's supervisor why the deliverable has not been acknowledged

25. Of the following breakdown structures and descriptions, which is correct?

   (A) Organizational breakdown structure, which graphically illustrates how the project organization is structured to accomplish project activities
   (B) Risk breakdown structure, which lists risks grouped by probability of occurrence and listed by severity of impact
   (C) Resource breakdown structure, which graphically illustrates the availability of resources
   (D) Bill of materials, which lists the cost of the components, assemblies, and sub-assemblies used to build the product

26. Which of the following tools and techniques are not used by the project manager during the process of creating a scope statement?

   (A) Product analysis
   (B) Expert judgment
   (C) Facilitation
   (D) Requirements documentation

27. Dirk, the project manager, is leading the team during the execution of the project management plan. His testing manager, Sarah, has just completed deliverable testing, which resulted in deliverables that met all requirements. What have Dirk and Sarah created and what is the next process the deliverables will undergo?

   (A) Quality Audits and Control Quality
   (B) Control Quality and Change Requests
   (C) Validate Scope and Close Project or Phase
   (D) Verified Deliverables and Validate Scope

28. The product owner is working with the development team to finalize items in the current iteration. The product owner has just changed priority on a few items in the backlog. The approach being used is most likely?

(A) Change driven
(B) Plan driven
(C) Gantt Chart
(D) Program Management

29. Which of the following are created as a result of validating project scope?

(A) Accepted deliverables
(B) Change requests
(C) Approved change requests
(D) Accepted deliverables and change requests

30. The retail ERP project is the largest the company has done in its history. There are a number of pieces of work the team has decomposed via a breakdown structure to better control the project. Of the following breakdown structures and descriptions, which is correct?

(A) Organizational breakdown structure, which graphically illustrates how project management is structured to accomplish project activities
(B) Risk breakdown structure, which lists risks grouped by probability of occurrence and listed by severity of impact
(C) Resource breakdown structure, which shows the type of resources used on the project
(D) Bill of materials, which lists the cost of components, assemblies, and sub-assemblies used to build the product

5.10.   Project Scope Management Answers for Tests and Exercises

5.10.1.   Project Scope Management Practice Test Answers

We recommend that you download answer sheets from the Crosswind website, so you can practice the test as many times as you like.

1.   What is the most significant benefit of having the project management team's assistance in creating the work breakdown structure?

Correct Answer: (C) It helps attain buy-in from the team doing the work
Explanation: Having the project team assist in the creation of the WBS has a number of positive benefits. The most positive benefit is obtaining buy-in from the people doing the work. Though the WBS is reviewed later in the planning process group to create the budget and schedule, it is the team's buy-in (and experience) that drives the accuracy of all future documents. As a minor point, schedule and budget are equally important, and thus neither answer by itself could be the "best" answer. Authority comes from the project charter. [Crosswind Manual 5.4; *PMBOK® Guide* 5.4]

2.   The approval of the project charter has been delayed for weeks due to market fluctuation. Upon approval, you are assigned as the project manager and senior management wants you to begin the planning process group immediately. When will you schedule validate scope?

Correct Answer: (A) At the end of every phase on the project
Explanation: It is better to schedule scope validation more frequently on a project instead of simply waiting until the end. Such validation makes it possible to detect issues early in the project, facilitating adjustment of work as the project evolves. Scheduling the process after the sponsors define what they want the project to create is too early in the project to do scope validation. [Crosswind Manual 5.5; *PMBOK® Guide* 5.5]

3.   During what processes is work decomposition performed?

Correct Answer: (A) Creating the WBS and define activities
Explanation: The work of the project is decomposed in the Create WBS process to establish work packages and in the Define Activities process (Schedule knowledge area) to create activity lists. No other process involves the systematic break down of work elements. [Crosswind Manual 5.4; *PMBOK® Guide* 5.4]

PMI, CAPM, and PMBOK are registered marks of the Project Management Institute, Inc.

148   © 2008-2018 Crosswind Learning, www.crosswindpm.com

4.   The company is designing touchscreen displays for use on mobile workstation tablets. A requirements traceability matrix is being utilized. Of the following, which is the best description of how the project manager will use the matrix?

(A) To trace requirements to business and project objectives
(B) To trace requirements to project scope/WBS deliverables, to product design and development, and to test strategy and scenarios
(C) To trace high-level requirements to detailed requirements

Correct Answer: (D) All of the answers
Explanation: A requirements traceability matrix is used to trace requirements to business and project objectives; trace requirements to project scope/WBS deliverables, to product design and development, and to test strategy and scenarios; and trace high-level requirements to detailed requirements. [Crosswind Manual 5.2.2; *PMBOK® Guide* 5.2.3.2]

5.   Which of the following is a heuristic for WBS decomposition?

Correct Answer: (D) Breaking work down to a realistic level (work packages being the lowest level)
Explanation: A general rule of thumb is to break down the work of the project into work packages. Breaking work packages or activities down to a single resource assigned is not always practical. Creating a WBS where the summary activities are equal to the detail underneath is a characteristic of a WBS. Using an organizational structure appearance is a distracter. [Crosswind Manual 5.4; *PMBOK® Guide* 5.4]

6.   The project manager is working with the customer to gain formal acceptance of the project deliverables. The customer is saying that three of the deliverables are not meeting project goals and are unusable in their present form. The team discovers this was caused by an inconsistency between the requirements, scope statement and WBS. Which process will the team use to align these documents?

Correct Answer: (C) Control scope
Explanation: Control Scope is used to review, then approve or reject, project scope change requests. A change request would be created to align the inconsistencies with the requirements, scope statement, and WBS. Analyze Scope and Gather Requirements are distracters. Validate Scope determines that project deliverables have fulfilled acceptance criteria and have received formal sign-off from the authorized party or parties. [Crosswind Manual 5.6; *PMBOK® Guide* 5.6]

7.   During the create WBS process for the financial reporting improvement project, as planning evolves, the team could create all the following except...

Correct Answer: (B) Communication breakdown structure
Explanation: The communication breakdown structure is a distracter in that it does not exist. The bill of materials lists all of the components, assemblies, and sub-assemblies used to build a product. The risk breakdown structure depicts potential project risks by risk category. The resource breakdown structure depicts the type of resources utilized during the project. [Crosswind Manual 5.4.5; *PMBOK® Guide* 9.1.2.2]

8. Due to the complexity of the project to design touchscreen displays for use on mobile workstation tablets, a number of breakdown structures will be used. Of the following breakdown structures and descriptions, which is correct?

Correct Answer: (D) Bill of materials, which lists the components, assemblies, and sub-assemblies used to build the product
Explanation: The bill of materials lists the components, assemblies, and sub-assemblies used to build the product or service of the project. The organizational breakdown structure shows how the project organization is structured to accomplish project activities. The risk breakdown structure shows the risks that can potentially occur on a project, broken down by risk category. The resource breakdown structure shows the type of resources used on a project. [Crosswind Manual 5.4.5; PMBOK® Guide 9.1.2.2]

9. As the project manager establishes the scope baseline, which of the following best describes what she will create or reference?

Correct Answer: (C) Scope statement, WBS, and WBS dictionary
Explanation: The scope baseline consists of the scope statement, WBS, and WBS dictionary. [Crosswind Manual 5.4; PMBOK® Guide 5.4]

10. The project to consolidate the accounting departments of two recently merged hospitals is extremely complex. The project manager and his team are keenly aware of the importance of properly decomposing the work of the project. If they decompose the work beyond work packages, what is the likely result?

Correct Answer: (B) The creation of activity lists
Explanation: If they decompose the work beyond work packages, the creation of activity lists is the likely result. This occurs in the Define Activities process in the Schedule knowledge area. [Crosswind Manual 6.2; PMBOK® Guide 6.2]

11. The WBS has been created for the textbook selection project and the team is creating the WBS dictionary. How will they go about this?

Correct Answer: (C) By documenting the work packages, documenting test criteria and test cases, documenting the control accounts, and listing the organizations responsible for completion of the work
Explanation: The team will create the WBS dictionary by documenting the work packages, documenting test criteria and test cases, documenting the control accounts, and listing the organizations responsible for completion of the work. [Crosswind Manual 5.4.4; PMBOK® Guide 5.4.3.1]

12. The medical billing system project has entered closure. As the project manager and the team prepare for closure, they are told that validate scope will be very important to the success of the project. Of the following, which best describes the importance of validate scope?

Correct Answer: (C) Validate scope is the process of comparing what the project created to the project scope statement, product description, and anything else that helps ensure that the results of the project will function as intended
Explanation: Validate Scope is used to compare the work the project created to that which was planned to build, and to ensure that the results of the project will function as intended. It can include using the project management plan, requirements documentation, and validated deliverables. If the validation process is satisfactory, the work of the project is typically viewed as acceptable. [Crosswind Manual 5.5; *PMBOK® Guide* 5.5]

13. The project team is creating the WBS for their stadium restoration project. Which of the following best describes the layers that would likely be included?

Correct Answer: (A) Control accounts, planning packages, work packages
Explanation: The three layers that would likely be included in various levels of decomposition are the control account, planning package, and work package. The activity list and milestone list are created in the Define Activity process. The activity package and milestone package are distracters (they do not exist). [Crosswind Manual 5.4.1; *PMBOK® Guide* 5.4.3.1]

14. The project manager is working with the business analyst to create requirements for the upgrade to the security platform of the company website. Which of the following best describes the order in which the processes will be created?

Correct Answer: (C) Business requirements, stakeholder requirements, solution requirements, transition requirements
Explanation: The order in which requirements are created is: business requirements, stakeholder requirements, solution requirements, and then transition requirements. Business requirements define business needs; stakeholder requirements align with specific stakeholder needs; solution requirements are created from the stakeholder requirements; and transition requirements are established to move to the new product, service, or result from the project to a business environment. [Crosswind Manual 5.2.1 *PMBOK® Guide* 5.2.3.1]

15. Which of the following describes a work breakdown structure (WBS)?

(A) The work should be decomposed to a realistic level of detail
(B) If the work is not listed in the WBS, it is not in the project
(C) The accumulation of the work in the WBS should be equal to the work of the project

Correct Answer: (D) All of the answers
Explanation: A WBS includes all the work in the project. If it is not listed in the WBS, it's not part of the project. A WBS should be decomposed to a realistic level of detail. Not breaking it down sufficiently opens the way for work to slip through the cracks. Breaking it down into too much detail can result in micro-management. The work listed in the WBS should exactly correspond to the work that is in the project. [Crosswind Manual 5.4; *PMBOK® Guide* 5.4]

16. The project manager wants to better control her project. She is using decomposition after attending a project management class. Of the following breakdown structures and descriptions, which is correct?

Correct Answer: (B) Risk breakdown structure, which lists potential risks broken down by risk category

Explanation: The risk breakdown structure shows the risks that can potentially occur on a project, broken down by risk category. The organizational breakdown structure shows how the project organization is structured to accomplish project activities. The resource breakdown structure shows the type of resources used on a project. The bill of materials lists the components, assemblies, and sub-assemblies used to build the product or service of the project. [Crosswind Manual 5.4.5; *PMBOK® Guide* 9.1.2,2]

17. All the following are true about a work breakdown structure (WBS) except…

Correct Answer: (C) Activity sequencing of WBS components requires parallel or concurrent dependencies

Explanation: Answer C is a distracter because it makes no logical sense. The other answers are characteristics of a work breakdown structure (WBS). [Crosswind Manual 5.4; *PMBOK® Guide* 5.4]

18. The project manager is in the process of creating the scope statement. There are a number of items that can exist both in the requirements and scope statement. Which of the following items are most likely to be only in the scope statement?

Correct Answer: (B) Items to be excluded from the project

Explanation: There can be some overlap between requirements and the scope statement. The scope statement is typically a summary of intent: what the project will do, include, and exclude. The requirements typically references what the project needs, should do, and should accomplish, with a focus on systems and areas of the company. [Crosswind Manual 5.3.1; *PMBOK® Guide* 5.3.3.1]

19. Which of the following requirement types can contain both functional and non-functional requirements?

Correct Answer: (B) Solution requirements

Explanation: Solution requirements can be both functional and non-functional. The other requirements (business, stakeholder, and transition) do not differentiate between functional and non-functional. [Crosswind 5.2.1; *PMBOK® Guide* 5.2.3.1]

20. Project A is two months long, has three stakeholders, and has completed the planning process group. Project B is 12 months long, has 10 stakeholders, and is in the monitoring and controlling process group. Project C is 12 months long, has three stakeholders, and is in the planning process group. Which project is most likely to experience scope creep?

Correct Answer: (B) Project B

Explanation: Project B is tied for the longest project but has the most stakeholders. The longer the project and the greater the number of stakeholders involved, the more an environment is prone to scope creep. The process group is a distracter. [Crosswind Manual 13.1; *PMBOK® Guide* Chapter 13 Introduction]

21. The project to create a new database system is approximately halfway complete when a senior manager says that a major change needs to occur with the scope of the project or the system will not function in his department when it's rolled out. He further explains this change is going to delay the anticipated finish date of the project. After he explains the details of the proposed change in scope, what do you do first?

Correct Answer: (D) Meet with the team to determine the impact
Explanation: Meet with the team to determine the impact to the project plus discovery of any solutions and any violation of the finish date that was defined in the project charter. Then pass solution options to senior management and the sponsor so they can select the best one. You should never tell a senior manager or sponsor "no." Instead, you should let them know the options and impact associated with the request. You cannot explain a project delay until the team helps determine what the project impacts are. Change control of this size is not likely to be implemented by a project manager, but more likely by the senior management or sponsor. [Crosswind Manual 13.1.2; No *PMBOK® Guide* Reference]

22. Which of the following is the tool or technique the project manager will use in the process of creating a WBS?

Correct Answer: (B) Decomposition
Explanation: The tool or technique used during the Create WBS process is decomposition. Work packages are the lowest level of decomposition within the WBS. The WBS dictionary is one of the outputs of the Create WBS process since it is part of the scope baseline. Stakeholder management is a distracter. [Crosswind Manual 5.4; *PMBOK® Guide* 5.4]

23. A project manager is beginning the collect requirements process. Which of the following is the most important activity he should perform?

Correct Answer: (D) Verify that all key stakeholders have provided their input
Explanation: Verifying that all key stakeholders have provided their input is the most important item. If this doesn't occur, the project could be delayed or derailed. The WBS isn't addressed in the Plan Scope process. Creating the project scope statement in sufficient detail is valid, but still less important than having the right requirements from the right stakeholders. The other answers are distracters. [Crosswind Manual 5.2; *PMBOK® Guide* 5.2]

24. The validate scope process has been started at the end of phase 3 of the project. The main deliverable was sent to the customer. Three weeks have passed and the customer acts as if the deliverable was never received. Which of the following is the best action to take?

Correct Answer: (B) Ask the sponsor for assistance
Explanation: If the customer is not responding and the project manager has already communicated with him, then the sponsor is the role that should provide assistance, particularly since this is an escalation issue. Stopping work and asking the customer's supervisor is unprofessional. Documenting the issue and doing nothing else is inappropriate because a project manager should be proactive in addressing problems. [Crosswind Manual 13.1.2; No *PMBOK® Guide* Reference]

25. Of the following breakdown structures and descriptions, which is correct?

Correct Answer: (A) Organizational breakdown structure, which graphically illustrates how the project organization is structured to accomplish project activities

Explanation: The organizational breakdown structure shows how the project organization is structured to accomplish project activities. The risk breakdown structure shows the risks that can potentially occur on a project, broken down by risk category. The resource breakdown structure shows the type of resources used on a project. The bill of materials lists the components, assemblies, and sub-assemblies used to build the product or service of the project. [Crosswind Manual 5.4.5; *PMBOK® Guide* 9.1.2.2]

26. Which of the following tools and techniques are not used by the project manager during the process of creating a scope statement?

Correct Answer: (D) Requirements documentation

Explanation: The tools and techniques used during the Define Scope process are expert judgment, product analysis, decision making, alternatives analysis, multicriteria decision analysis, interpersonal and team skills, and facilitation. [Crosswind Manual 5.3; *PMBOK® Guide* 5.3]

27. Dirk, the project manager, is leading the team during the execution of the project management plan. His testing manager, Sarah, has just completed deliverable testing, which resulted in deliverables that met all requirements. What have Dirk and Sarah created and what is the next process the deliverables will undergo?

Correct Answer: (D) Verified deliverables and validate scope

Explanation: The question references both the Control Quality process, which creates verified deliverables, and the Validate Scope process, which occurs later and results in customer acceptance of those deliverables. Quality audits occur during the Manage Quality process. The Close Project or Phase results in the transition of the project outcome. Verified Deliverables is not a project management process. [Crosswind 5.5 and 8.10; *PMBOK® Guide* 5.5 and 8.3]

28. The product owner is working with the development team to finalize items in the current iteration. The product owner has just changed priority on a few items in the backlog. The approach being used is most likely?

Correct Answer: (A) Change driven

Explanation: A product owner working within an iteration with a backlog is a change driven approach such as agile, scrum or Kanban. Plan driven is a more traditional project management approach. A Gantt chart is typically used more in plan driven approaches. Program management is for initiatives that consist of multiple projects. [Crosswind 3.4.7, *PMBOK® Guide* Chapter 5 Intro]

29. Which of the following are created as a result of validating project scope?

Correct Answer: (D) Accepted deliverables and change requests

Explanation: The outputs of Validate Scope are accepted deliverables and change requests. [Crosswind Manual 5.5; *PMBOK® Guide* 5.5]

PMI, CAPM, and PMBOK are registered marks of the Project Management Institute, Inc.

154 © 2008-2018 Crosswind Learning, www.crosswindpm.com

30. The retail ERP project is the largest the company has done in its history. There are a number of pieces of work the team has decomposed via a breakdown structure to better control the project. Of the following breakdown structures and descriptions, which is correct?

Correct Answer: (C) Resource breakdown structure, which shows the type of resources used on the project

Explanation: The resource breakdown structure shows the type of resources used on a project. The organizational breakdown structure shows how the project organization is structured to accomplish project activities. The risk breakdown structure shows the risks that can potentially occur on a project, broken down by risk category. The bill of materials lists the components, assemblies, and sub-assemblies used to build the product or service of the project. [Crosswind Manual 5.4.5; *PMBOK® Guide* 9.1.2.2]

PMI, CAPM, and PMBOK are registered marks of the Project Management Institute, Inc.

156   © 2008-2018 Crosswind Learning, www.crosswindpm.com

Chapter 6

Project Schedule Management

The intended result of Project Schedule Management is a schedule and a schedule management plan that details the timing and the manner in which project products, services, and results are delivered in accordance with the project scope. The plan is an important reference for communication and management of stakeholder expectations and is the foundation for performance reporting.

Once a scheduling method has been selected, pertinent information (activities, planned dates, durations, resources, dependencies, constraints, and milestones) is entered into the scheduling tool to create a scheduling model. The scheduling model becomes the project schedule once dates are assigned and the team is ready to execute the project. In practice, both the schedule model and the schedule are typically referred to as the schedule.

For small projects, defining activities, sequencing activities, estimating activity durations, and developing the schedule model can be viewed as a single process since these can be performed by a single person relatively quickly. For larger projects, these processes are distinct since the tools and techniques vary with each process.

The detailed project schedule should be flexible throughout the project, whenever feasible, because adjustments will undoubtedly be made as project knowledge evolves, non-value-added activities are decreased, and risk is better understood.

For the exam, Crosswind recommends a thorough examination of each process with an emphasis on the tools and techniques, as well as the impact that the outputs of one process has on its subsequent process.

Trends

The two most notable trends currently impacting scheduling are:

- Iterative scheduling with a backlog: a type of rolling wave planning used in adaptive project management (such as Agile) to deliver incremental value to the customer during an iteration (usually a 2-4 week period)
  The schedule is based on project requirements that are documented with user stories. User stories are prioritized and clarified to define the requirements for product features that are developed within a defined work period (a time-boxed period). The backlog is the list of features that have yet to be developed during the current increment.
- On-demand scheduling: an approach typically used in a Kanban system to limit the team's work in progress in order to balance demand against throughput
  The schedule is subject to the availability of resources: work is pulled from a backlog or work queue based on the theory of constraints and pull-based scheduling concepts used in lean manufacturing.

The role of the project manager remains the same whether the project management approach is predictive or hybrid (an approach using predictive and adaptive methods). Success, however, is dependent upon the project manager's mastery of process tools and techniques and an understanding of how the adaptive practices impact the management of the project.

Tailoring

Project tailoring, the manner in which processes of a knowledge area are exercised, is employed to address the distinctive nature of each project. Successful project tailoring is predicated on a careful consideration of:

- The life cycle approach employed
- The availability of resources
- The complexity of the project (including such elements as technological uncertainty, progress tracking, and product novelty) and its impact on the desired level of control
- Technological support

Agile/Adaptive Environment

Agile methods employ short cycles (typically two to four periods) to perform the work, review the results, and, if necessary, adapt. Such cycles support rapid feedback on the scheduling methods (typically based on iterative scheduling or on-demand, pull based scheduling).

The source for the above text is the Project Management Institute, *A Guide to the Project Management Body of Knowledge*, (*PMBOK® Guide*) – Sixth Edition, Project Management Institute Inc., 2017, Pages 168-173

In this chapter, we discuss the following:

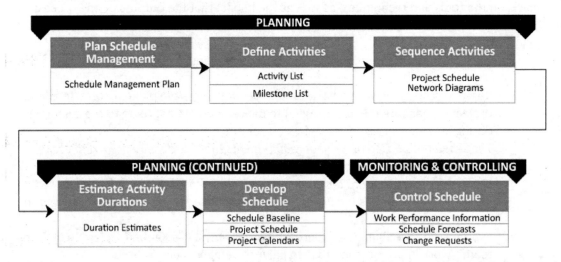

Figure 6-1: Schedule Processes
The source for the above figure is the Project Management Institute, *A Guide to the Project Management Body of Knowledge*, (*PMBOK® Guide*) – Sixth Edition, Project Management Institute Inc., 2017, Figure 6-1, Page 169

☑	**Crosswind "Must Knows" For Project Schedule Management**
	Key Inputs, Tools & Techniques, and Outputs for Plan Schedule Management
	Key Inputs, Tools & Techniques, and Outputs for Define Activities
	Key Inputs, Tools & Techniques, and Outputs for Sequence Activities
	Key Inputs, Tools & Techniques, and Outputs for Estimate Activity Durations
	Key Inputs, Tools & Techniques, and Outputs for Develop Schedule
	Key Inputs, Tools & Techniques, and Outputs for Control Schedule
	Concepts of rolling wave planning, control accounts, and planning packages
	Characteristics of the four dependencies (mandatory, discretionary, internal, and external)
	Principles of a network diagram, how to draw a diagram based on a word problem, and how to analyze a diagram from a pop-up screen using either the precedence diagramming method (PDM) or arrow diagramming method (ADM)
	Differences between the precedence diagramming method (PDM) and the arrow diagramming method (ADM)
	Concepts of the GERT (Graphical Evaluation Review Technique) diagramming method
	Four predecessor types (finish-to-start, finish-to-finish, start-to-start, and start-to-finish)
	Definitions of lead and lag
	Characteristics of the estimating methods: analogous, bottom-up, parametric, and computerized
	Concepts of the PERT estimating method and that PERT stands for Program Evaluation Review Technique
	How to recognize a critical path and why it is important
	Characteristics of free slack (free float), total slack (total float), and project slack (project float)
	Concepts of CPM (critical path method) estimation
	How to do a forward pass and a backward pass substitution technique on a network diagram
	Characteristics and benefits of "crashing" and "fast tracking"
	Characteristics of a logic bar chart (Gantt chart)
	Characteristics of a milestone schedule including its zero duration
	Characteristics of a summary schedule

Chapter 6 Schedule

Although helpful, this list is not all-inclusive in regard to information needed for the exam. It is only suggested material that, if understood and memorized, may increase your exam score.

6.1. Plan Schedule Management (Planning Process Group)

The plan schedule management process is used to create the schedule management plan, which can be formal or informal and provides guidance for creating an appropriately detailed schedule, **establishing control thresholds**, and **updating/modifying the schedule as necessary**. The schedule management plan is part of the project management plan.

Know the Key Inputs, Tools & Techniques, and Outputs for Plan Schedule Management.

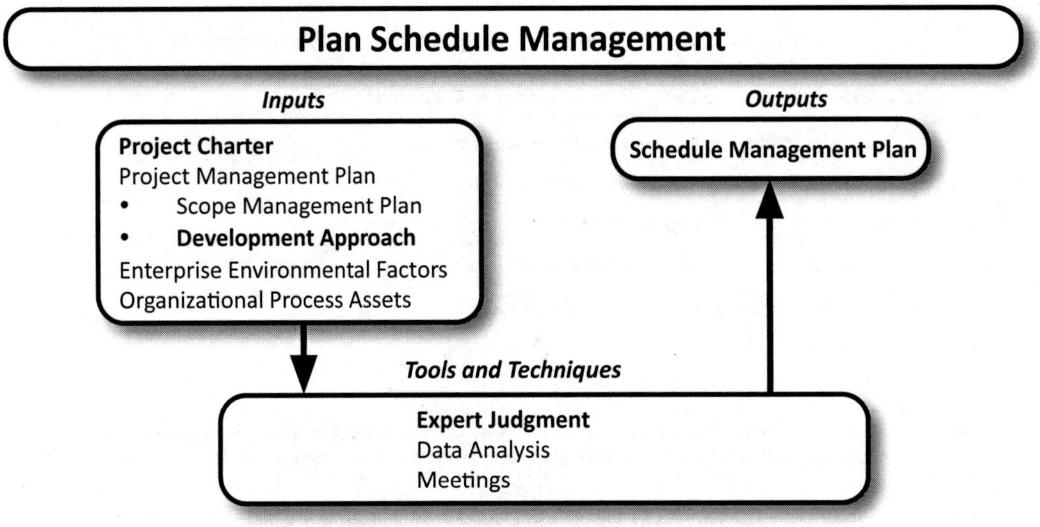

Plan Schedule Management

Inputs

Project Charter
Project Management Plan
- Scope Management Plan
- **Development Approach**
Enterprise Environmental Factors
Organizational Process Assets

Outputs

Schedule Management Plan

Tools and Techniques

Expert Judgment
Data Analysis
Meetings

Figure 6-2: Plan Schedule Management Data Flow Diagram
The source for the above figure is the Project Management Institute, *A Guide to the Project Management Body of Knowledge*, (*PMBOK® Guide*) – Sixth Edition, Project Management Institute Inc., 2017, Figure 6-3, Page 174

Plan Schedule Management (Planning)		
Key Inputs	Project Charter	The project charter is the document that provides authorization for the existence of the project and gives the project manager the power to use organizational resources to execute the project. The project charter typically lists the key deliverables, the milestones, and the roles and responsibilities of each person involved in the project. Note that the project charter delineates the purpose of the project, high-level project description, requirements, assumptions, and constraints. The project charter delineates the summary milestone schedule that impacts the schedule management processes.
	Development Approach	The development approach delineates the method (iterative, agile, waterfall, or hybrid) used for scheduling, the techniques and tools used for estimation and scheduling, and the techniques used for controlling the schedule.
Key Tools & Techniques	Expert Judgment	Expert judgment is judgment based on expertise acquired in a specific area. It is important to consider expertise related to schedule evolution, scheduling methods (predictive or adaptive life cycle), the industry that will utilize the product, service or result of the project, and scheduling software.

Plan Schedule Management (Continued)		
Key Outputs	Schedule Management Plan	The schedule management plan is a component of the project management plan that details the delineation, evolution, monitoring, and control of the schedule. It includes the methods for evolving and maintaining the project schedule model, controlling the duration of releases and iterations, determining degrees of accuracy and metric units, using the WBS as the framework for the schedule management plan, establishing variance thresholds, and determining performance measurement rules.

Situational Question and Real World Application

Failure to effectively perform the Plan Schedule Management process can lead to the creation and modification of a schedule without controls or guidance and inconsistency would likely define the project. If program/portfolio management is also performed, the inconsistency would impact the relationship between the project and other projects or programs.

6.1.1. Schedule Management Plan

The schedule management plan establishes:

- The project schedule model development and maintenance practices
- The level of accuracy that will be required for activity duration estimates
- The units of measure (time and quantity) that will be used for each resource
- Organizational procedures links based on the WBS
- Control thresholds for monitoring schedule performance

Using the schedule management plan, the project manager and team can then:

- Decompose work packages (deliverables) into activities and milestones
- Establish the network diagram
- Determine the durations for the activities
- Integrate all activity components into a schedule
- Manage schedule changes and updates

The source for the above text is the Project Management Institute, *A Guide to the Project Management Body of Knowledge*, (PMBOK® Guide) – Sixth Edition, Project Management Institute Inc., 2017, Pages 173-177

6.2. Define Activities (Planning Process Group)

Define Activities is the process of determining and listing the activities required to create the deliverables of the project.

Note that the list is created without regard to necessary resources, start dates, or completion dates.

Know the Key Inputs, Tools & Techniques, and Outputs for Define Activities.

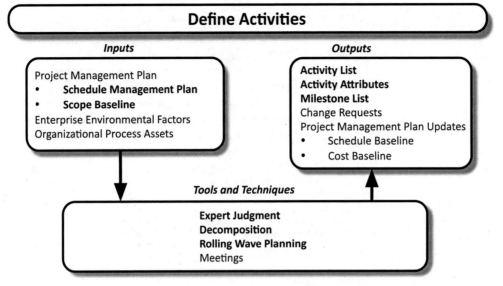

Figure 6-3: Define Activities Data Flow Diagram

The source for the above figure is the Project Management Institute, *A Guide to the Project Management Body of Knowledge*, (*PMBOK® Guide*) – Sixth Edition, Project Management Institute Inc., 2017, Figure 6-5, Page 178

Define Activities (Planning)		
Key Inputs	Schedule Management Plan	The schedule management plan is a component of the project management plan that details the delineation, evolution, monitoring, and control of the schedule. It delineates the manner in which reserves are to be used and the schedule is to be controlled. The plan also establishes the frequency of updates to the schedule.
	Scope Baseline	The scope baseline is the authorized version of the scope statement, WBS (to the level of work package with individual identification codes) and WBS dictionary. The scope baseline is expressly considered while delineating activities.
Key Tools & Techniques	Expert Judgment	Expert judgment is judgment based on expertise acquired in a specific area. It is important to consider expertise related to knowledge of the industry or area of application and experience with previous projects similar to the current project.

PMI, CAPM, and PMBOK are registered marks of the Project Management Institute, Inc.

162   © 2008-2018 Crosswind Learning, www.crosswindpm.com

Define Activities (Continued)		
Key Tools & Techniques (Cont.)	Decomposition	Decomposition breaks down the project scope and deliverables into manageable components. The work breakdown structure decomposes the work into work packages, the smallest components that can be managed and estimated in terms of schedule and budget. Decomposition generally involves determining and evaluating the deliverables and related work, constructing and organizing the WBS, decomposing upper-level components by subdividing the work for each deliverable into its most basic components, creating and assigning identification codes to WBS components, verifying that the decomposition of deliverables has been done appropriately.
	Rolling Wave Planning	Rolling wave planning is an iterative technique where upcoming work is carefully itemized and future work is generalized. It is a form of progressive elaboration used with work packages, planning packages, and release planning.
Key Outputs	Activity List	The activity list enumerates each schedule activity stipulated for the project, including its identifier and scope description sufficiently detailed to ensure an understanding of the work by each team member. It is a component of the schedule, but NOT of the WBS. A rule of thumb is to break down the activity list to the point where the activities are **4-80 hours in duration**. Project managers commonly call activities "tasks," but the term "activities" is generally more appropriate according to Project Management Institute, Inc. standards. If rolling wave planning or agile is used, the list must be reviewed regularly and updated as necessary.
	Activity Attributes	Activity attributes clarify an activity by identifying multiple components related to the activity. The components evolve during the project: during the initial stage, they include a singular activity identifier, a WBS identifier, and an activity label; when completed they typically include a description of the activity, predecessor and successor activities, logical relationships, leads and lags, resource needs, constraints, assumptions, and exact dates. They are used to evolve the schedule and clarify reporting.
	Milestone List	The milestone list enumerates the most consequential points or events in the project and indicates if the milestone is required or optional. A milestone has a duration of zero.

Rolling Wave Planning	Rolling wave planning is a **concept that utilizes the progressive elaboration concept in planning**. It defines a low level of detail on the WBS for the immediate work being accomplished while the work to be done in the future is only at a high level of decomposition in the WBS until it is soon-to-be-started.
Control Accounts	Control accounts are **specific points in the work breakdown structure (WBS) where the project scope, budget, actual cost, and schedule are combined** in order to establish performance measurements. This allows tracking progress at appropriate levels of detail throughout the work breakdown structure (WBS). See Figure 5-7: WBS Process Components.
Planning Package	The planning package is a **piece of the work breakdown structure (WBS) above the work package**. It is used to plan work that has been scoped but lacks sufficient work package level details. See Figure 5-7: WBS Process Components.

Know the concepts of rolling wave planning, control accounts, and planning packages.

The source for the above text is the Project Management Institute, *A Guide to the Project Management Body of Knowledge*, (PMBOK® Guide) – Sixth Edition, Project Management Institute Inc., 2017, Pages 177-181

6.3. Sequence Activities (Planning Process Group)

During Sequence Activities, the focus is on the order of the activities: **the arrangement of activities in the most efficient and effective order.**

Know the Key Inputs, Tools & Techniques, and Outputs for Sequence Activities.

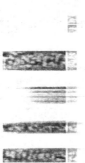

PMI, CAPM, and PMBOK are registered marks of the Project Management Institute, Inc.

164   © 2008-2018 Crosswind Learning, www.crosswindpm.com

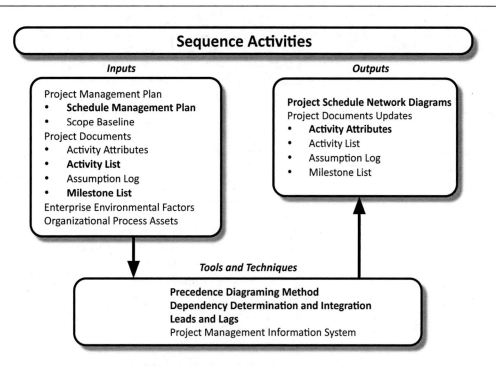

Figure 6-4: Sequence Activities Data Flow Diagram
The source for the above figure is the Project Management Institute, *A Guide to the Project Management Body of Knowledge*, (*PMBOK® Guide*) – Sixth Edition,
Project Management Institute Inc., 2017, Figure 6-7, Page 181

Sequence Activities (Planning)		
Key Inputs	Schedule Management Plan	The schedule management plan is a component of the project management plan that details the delineation, evolution, monitoring, and control of the schedule, including the degree of expected accuracy. It delineates scheduling methodology, wave duration for rolling wave planning, and the degree of detail required for work management.
	Activity List	The activity list enumerates the schedule activities stipulated for sequencing. Sequencing can be influenced by dependencies and other constraints. Note that the activity list is a component of the schedule, but NOT of the WBS. A rule of thumb is to break down the activity list to the point where the activities are **4-80 hours in duration**. Project managers commonly call activities "tasks," but according to Project Management Institute, Inc. standards, the term "activities" is generally more appropriate. If rolling wave planning or agile is used the list must be reviewed regularly and updated as necessary.

		Sequence Activities (Continued)
Key Inputs (Cont.)	Milestone List	The milestone list enumerates the most consequential points or events in the project and indicates if the milestone is required or optional. **A milestone has a duration of zero**. If the milestone has been assigned a specific date, it typically impacts the manner in which activities are scheduled.
Key Tools & Techniques	Precedence Diagramming Method	The precedence diagramming method (PDM) is a schedule model construction technique used to show the sequence of activity performance. It represents activities as nodes graphically linked by one or more logical relationships, such as finish-to-start (FS), finish-to-finish (FF) start-to-start (SS) and start-to-finish (SF). Note that two activities can have two or more concurrent logical relationships. Multiple relationships are discouraged, so the relationship with the highest impact is generally represented. Closed loops are also discouraged.
	Dependency Determination and Integration	Dependencies can be mandatory or discretionary and internal or external; that is, a dependency could be mandatory and internal, mandatory and external, discretionary and internal, or discretionary and external. A mandatory dependency is required contractually, legally, or inherently (based on the nature of the work, such as a physical limitation on a construction project). A discretionary (soft logic) dependency is typically based on best practices. An external dependency describes a relationship between a project activity and a non-project activity. An internal dependency describes a relationship between a project activity and another project activity.
	Leads and Lags	A lead is the amount of time that a successor activity will be started before a predecessor activity is completed. A lag is the amount of time that a successor activity will be delayed after the predecessor activity is completed.
Key Outputs	Project Schedule Network Diagrams	Project schedule network diagrams illustrate the dependencies (logical relationships) between project schedule activities. They can be high-level or detailed and include a summary narrative delineating the basic approach to activity sequencing and detailing unusual sequences. Activities with multiple predecessor or successor activities should note a path convergence (predecessor activities), since these have greater risk.

PMI, CAPM, and PMBOK are registered marks of the Project Management Institute, Inc.

166   © 2008-2018 Crosswind Learning, www.crosswindpm.com

Sequence Activities (Continued)		
Key Outputs (Cont.)	Activity Attributes	Activity attributes clarify an activity by identifying multiple components related to the activity. The components evolve during the project: during the initial stage, they include a singular activity identifier, a WBS identifier, and an activity label; when completed they typically include a description of the activity, predecessor and successor activities, logical relationships, leads and lags, resource needs, constraints, assumptions, and exact dates. They are used to evolve the schedule and clarify reporting.

Situational Question and Real World Application
Failure to effectively perform the Sequence Activities process can generate a variety of issues, such as the inability to start work because predecessor activities have not been completed or performing work that doesn't make logical sense in relation to the overall output of the project.

6.3.1. Dependencies

During the creation of the project schedule, dependencies must be considered. They may be flexible, causing no real impact, or inflexible, providing no options except work-arounds.

Know the characteristics of the four dependencies.

Type	Definition	Example
Mandatory (Hard Logic)	A dependency that **must** be completed before subsequent items can start	You must have the roof on before you can begin to apply shingles to it.
Discretionary (Soft Logic)	A dependency that **should** be completed but is not absolutely required to be completed before subsequent items can start	You prefer to, but do not absolutely have to, finish system testing before beginning user acceptance testing.
Internal	A mandatory or discretionary dependency that originates from **within the project or company**	You have to wait for the power supply to complete the testing of the computer you are designing.
External	A mandatory or discretionary dependency that originates from an entity **external** to the project team or organization	The city inspector must approve any construction before issuing a certificate of occupancy so the tenant can move in.

6.3.2. Network Diagram

The network diagram is a schematic of project activities. It shows how the various activities are connected as a result of Sequence Activities. This diagram provides a visual representation of the project work flow. It is also a **tool that can be used to evaluate schedule compression techniques** such as **crashing** and **fast tracking.**

Know the principles of a network diagram, how to draw a diagram based on a word problem, and how to analyze a diagram from a pop-up screen as either precedence diagramming method (PDM) or arrow diagramming method (ADM).

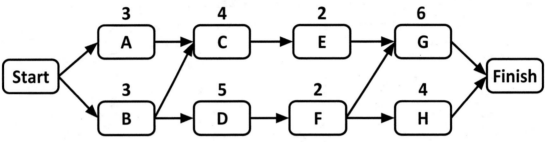

Figure 6-5: Network Diagram Sample

The source for the above figure is the Project Management Institute, *A Guide to the Project Management Body of Knowledge*, (*PMBOK® Guide*) – Sixth Edition, Project Management Institute Inc., 2017, Figure 6-11, Page 178

6.3.3. Diagramming Types

The main differences between the diagramming methods are delineated in the following table, which should be memorized for the exam.

Know the differences between PDM and ADM.

Full Name	Acronym	Predecessor Types	Special Diagram Types and Characteristics	Application	Graphic Appearance
Precedence Diagramming Method Activity-on-node	PDM AON	Finish-to-start Start-to-start Finish-to-finish Start-to-finish	No dummies allowed	Most modern project scheduling software	Figure 6-6
Arrow Diagramming Method Activity-on-arrow Activity-on-line	ADM AOA AOL	Finish-to-start	Dummies allowed	Outdated manually drawn mostly	Figure 6-7

PMI, CAPM, and PMBOK are registered marks of the Project Management Institute, Inc.

168   © 2008-2018 Crosswind Learning, www.crosswindpm.com

The **precedence diagramming method (PDM)** is typically used with modern project management scheduling software. This method depicts each activity in a box (node) and connects the activities by arrows. It is sometimes called activity-on-node (AON).

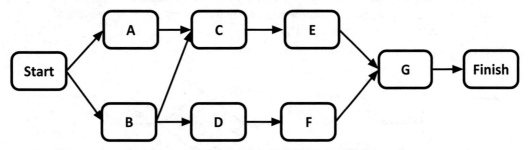

Figure 6-6: Precedence Diagramming Method Sample

The source for the above figure is the Project Management Institute, *A Guide to the Project Management Body of Knowledge*, (*PMBOK® Guide*) – Sixth Edition, Project Management Institute Inc., 2017, Figure 6-11, Page 178

The **arrow diagramming method (ADM)** is typically used for manual drawing. This method depicts each activity on an arrow or line, and activities are connected by a circle or box and is sometimes called activity-on-arrow (AOA).

A dummy may also be used with ADM. A dummy is a dashed line that connects two activities where a relationship exists, but is not directly connected. **The dummy is not an activity and has a zero duration.** The dummy "H" has been added to Figure 6-7: Arrow Diagramming Method Sample to show the dependency between activities B and C.

Activities may also be depicted in another format resulting in a diagram with an appearance closer to the PDM diagram. This format represents activities as "Start-A," "A-C," and "H-Finish."

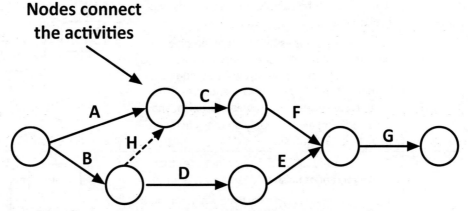

Figure 6-7: Arrow Diagramming Method Sample

GERT (Graphical Evaluation Review Technique)

GERT is a diagramming technique that uses **feedback loops** or multiple passes through a diagram as iterations are completed.

A practical use of GERT is software testing where multiple passes usually have to be made through the routine until testing is complete.

In the exam, GERT is typically only the correct answer if the question references a technique with a feedback loop.

Know the concepts of the GERT diagramming method.
Know that GERT stands for Graphical Evaluation Review Technique.

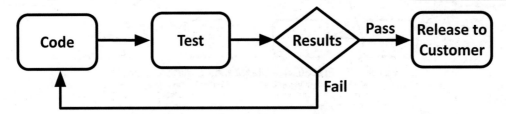

Figure 6-8: GERT Diagramming Sample

6.3.4. Predecessors

During the creation of the project schedule, predecessors are used to establish the sequencing of activities.

The following table delineates the characteristics of the four predecessor types.

Know the four predecessor types.

Predecessor		Diagram
Finish-to-start (FS)	The finish-to-start predecessor indicates that Activity A must be completed before Activity B begins. This predecessor is usually the default type for most modern project scheduling software and is usable in the activity-on-arrow (AOA) and activity-on-node (AON) diagramming techniques. The other types (start-to-start, finish-to-finish, and start-to-finish) are used only on the activity-on-node (AON) diagram.	
Finish-to-finish (FF)	The finish-to-finish predecessor indicates that Activity B cannot finish until Activity A is finished. This predecessor is typically used when multiple activities must finish at the same time.	

	Predecessor	Diagram
Start-to-start (SS)	The start-to-start predecessor indicates that Activity B can start when Activity A starts. This predecessor is used when multiple activities can start simultaneously.	A ← → B
Start-to-finish (SF)	The start-to-finish predecessor indicates that Activity A must start before Activity B finishes. The start-to-finish predecessor is typically used in situations where a new system must start before an existing system is shut down (finished). Start-to-finish is considered unusual because it is so seldom used.	A ← → B

6.3.5. Lead and Lag

A lead is the time period in which an activity can be started before its predecessor has been completed.

Figure 6-9 represents a two-day lead before completing installation of the electric outlets and starting the installation of the cabinets.

Know the definitions for leads and lags.

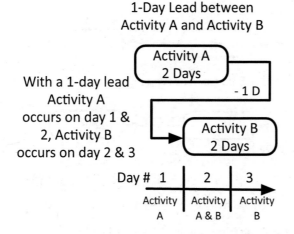

1-Day Lead between
Activity A and Activity B

With a 1-day lead Activity A occurs on day 1 & 2, Activity B occurs on day 2 & 3

Figure 6-9: Lead

The source for the above figure is the Project Management Institute, *A Guide to the Project Management Body of Knowledge*, (*PMBOK® Guide*) – Sixth Edition, Project Management Institute Inc., 2017, Figure 6-10, Page 186

A lag is a delay between activities. Figure 6-10 represents a two-day lag between completing the wall texture and painting the walls.

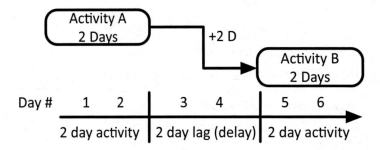

2-Day Lag between
Activity A and Activity B

Figure 6-10: Lag
The source for the above figure is the Project Management Institute, *A Guide to the Project Management Body of Knowledge*, (*PMBOK® Guide*) – Sixth Edition, Project Management Institute Inc., 2017, Figure 6-10, Page 186

Figure 6-11 represents both a lead of five days and a lag of two days.

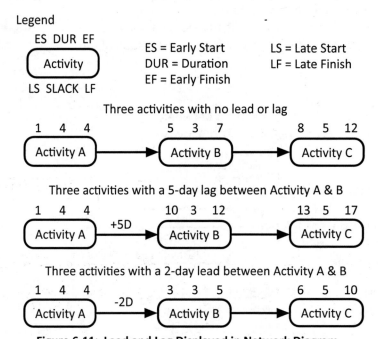

Figure 6-11: Lead and Lag Displayed in Network Diagram
The source for the above figure is the Project Management Institute, *A Guide to the Project Management Body of Knowledge*, (*PMBOK® Guide*) – Sixth Edition, Project Management Institute Inc., 2017, Figure 6-10, Page 186

Section 6.5.9 references how to apply the early start (ES) and early finish (EF) dates to the activities.

The source for the above text is the Project Management Institute, *A Guide to the Project Management Body of Knowledge*, (*PMBOK® Guide*) – Sixth Edition, Project Management Institute Inc., 2017, Pages 181-188

6.4. Estimate Activity Durations (Planning Process Group)

During the Estimate Activity Durations process, the number of workdays (or hours) to complete each activity is estimated.

That estimation then rolls up to create summary (high-level) estimates.

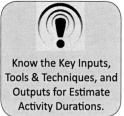

Know the Key Inputs, Tools & Techniques, and Outputs for Estimate Activity Durations.

Estimate Activity Durations

Inputs

Project Management Plan
- **Schedule Management Plan**
- Scope Baseline

Project Documents
- Activity Attributes
- **Activity List**
- **Assumption Log**
- **Lessons Learned Register**
- Milestone List
- Project Team Assignments
- Resource Breakdown Structure
- Resource Calendars
- Resource Requirements
- Risk Register

Enterprise Environmental Factors
Organizational Process Assets

Outputs

Duration Estimates
Basis of Estimates
Project Documents Updates
- **Activity Attributes**
- Assumption Log
- Lessons Learned Register

Tools and Techniques

Expert Judgment
Analogous Estimating
Parametric Estimating
Three-point Estimating
Bottom-up Estimating

Data Analysis
- Alternatives Analysis
- **Reserve Analysis**

Decision Making
Meetings

Figure 6-12: Estimate Activity Durations Data Flow Diagram

The source for the above figure is the Project Management Institute, *A Guide to the Project Management Body of Knowledge*, (*PMBOK® Guide*) – Sixth Edition, Project Management Institute Inc., 2017, Figure 6-12, Page 189

Estimate Activity Durations (Planning)		
Key Inputs	Schedule Management Plan	The schedule management plan is a component of the project management plan that details the delineation, evolution, monitoring, and control of the schedule. It delineates scheduling methodology, as well as the degree of expected accuracy needed to estimate the duration of the scheduled activities.

Chapter 6
Schedule

Estimate Activity Durations (Continued)		
Key Inputs (Cont.)	Activity List	The activity list enumerates the schedule activities stipulated for sequencing. Sequencing can be influenced by dependencies and other constraints. Activity attributes may delineate successor or predecessor, lead, lag, and logical associations that may influence the estimation of durations. Note that the activity list is a component of the schedule, but NOT of the WBS. A rule of thumb is to break down the activity list to the point where the activities are **4-80** hours in duration. Project managers commonly call activities "tasks," but according to Project Management Institute, Inc. standards, the term "activities" is generally more appropriate. If rolling wave planning or agile is used the list must be reviewed regularly and updated as necessary.
	Assumption Log	The assumption log is a document that lists the assumptions and constraints identified during the creation of the project charter. An assumption is an idea or statement taken to be true. An example of an assumption is the statement "there will be a robust market for the product created as a result of this project once it is available to the public" is an assumption. Examples of constraints are the project completion deadline, the budget threshold, or the limit on the number of employees that can be dedicated to the project. It's important to identify assumptions and constraints as early as possible and to update them as the project evolves. Due to the risks inherent in assumptions and constraints, they may impact the project schedule.
	Lessons Learned Register	The lessons learned register is a record of the challenges, problems, and successes of the project (what worked and didn't). The register contains detailed and important project knowledge. It is updated to reflect new knowledge and can be helpful to increase the degree of accuracy for duration and work estimates.
Key Tools & Techniques	Expert Judgment	Expert judgment is judgment based on expertise acquired in a specific area. It is important to consider expertise related to the evolution, administration, and control of the schedule, estimation techniques, and knowledge of the industry or area of application and experience with previous projects similar to the current project.

PMI, CAPM, and PMBOK are registered marks of the Project Management Institute, Inc.

174
© 2008-2018 Crosswind Learning, www.crosswindpm.com

Estimate Activity Durations (Continued)		
Key Tools & Techniques (Cont.)	Analogous Estimating	Analogous estimating is a high-level estimation technique based on historical duration or cost data from a similar activity or project. The technique adjusts for known variances in complexity from the current activity or project under consideration and the historical activity or project. While this technique costs less and is not as time consuming as more detailed techniques, it is typically not as accurate.
	Parametric Estimating	Parametric estimating is an estimation technique in which an algorithm is used to calculate duration or cost based on historical duration or cost data and other variables from a similar activity or project. The quantitative technique uses a mathematical relationship between historical data and other variables. The accuracy of this technique is dependent on the underlying model.
	Three-point Estimating	Three-point estimating is an estimation technique in which the range for activity duration is averaged based on pessimistic, optimistic, and realistic (most likely) estimates. The **triangular distribution** formula is often used if the historical data is insufficient and the **beta distribution** formula is often used when the historical data is sufficient. Three-point estimating, unlike PERT estimating, does not apply a weighted average.
	Bottom-up Estimating	Bottom-up estimating is an estimation technique in which duration or cost is determined by rolling up estimates of each WBS component of the item being estimated.
	Reserve Analysis	Reserve analysis is used to determine the amount of contingency and management reserves required for the project. By analyzing the known unknowns (identified risks, typically with mitigation plans), contingency reserves can be determined to account for schedule uncertainties. Management reserves are budget reserves set aside to account for unknown unknowns (unforeseen work within the scope of the project).
Key Outputs	Duration Estimates	Duration estimates are quantitative estimates of activity durations in which lags are not considered. They are often expressed as a range of time or a probability of reaching a specific duration.

Estimate Activity Durations (Continued)		
Key Outputs (Cont.)	Basis of Estimates	The basis of estimates for duration includes documentation that delineates the manner in which the estimates were determined, lists all assumptions and constraints, identifies the range of estimates used and the degree of certainty associated with those estimates, and details individual project risks that impacted those estimates.
	Activity Attributes	Activity attributes clarify an activity by identifying multiple components related to the activity. The components evolve during the project: during the initial stage, they include a singular activity identifier, a WBS identifier, and an activity label; when completed they typically include a description of the activity, predecessor and successor activities, logical relationships, leads and lags, resource needs, constraints, assumptions, and exact dates. They are used to evolve the schedule and clarify reporting.

Situational Question and Real World Application
Failure to effectively perform the Estimate Activity Durations process can result in the failure to properly estimate activities, which often results in schedule and cost overruns. If inaccurate estimates cause time slippage, the cost component of the triple constraint is often impacted.

6.4.1. Estimating Methods

It is very important to understand and recognize the estimating methods used in situational examples:

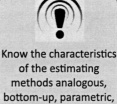

Know the characteristics of the estimating methods analogous, bottom-up, parametric, and computerized.

- Analogous
- Bottom-up
- Parametric
- Computerized (Monte Carlo)

Method	Description	Example
Analogous (Sometimes called Top-Down)	This estimate is usually a total time or cost estimate that has no significant detail. The main advantage of this estimate is that it can be created **quickly**; the disadvantage is that it **lacks detail** or individual piece estimates. Typically, it is called an **analogous method** when the estimate is based on the time or cost of a **similar project**.	An executive or a subject matter expert (SME) creates a high-level estimate **based on experience or past project history.**

PMI, CAPM, and PMBOK are registered marks of the Project Management Institute, Inc.

176   © 2008-2018 Crosswind Learning, www.crosswindpm.com

Method	Description	Example
Bottom-up	Compared to the analogous estimate, the main advantage of the bottom-up method is **detail and accuracy**. The disadvantage is that it **can take significant time to create** and the team may pad the estimate to compensate for unknowns.	The project manager and the team work together to create a complete estimate from the bottom (activity level) up and roll it up to the total estimate.
Parametric	Based on an **existing parameter**, this method is usually created by industry standards or experience. The advantage is that it **can be done quickly** and is usually **accurate**.	A house builder quotes the cost of a house at $150.00 per square foot. A carpet installer quotes $5.00 per square yard for installation.
Computerized/ Monte Carlo	Monte Carlo is a **computerized tool that simulates project outcome** to determine factors such as **time** or **cost** or number of needed **resources**. The main advantages are the accuracy of estimates and the "what-if" analysis that can be performed. The main disadvantages are the ramp-up time and cost associated with setting up of the tool.	Variables could include the overall time and cost estimates, as well as the confidence levels of the estimates. Variables could also include the number of people needed to achieve project goals.

PERT (*Program Evaluation Review Technique*)

The Program Evaluation Review Technique (PERT) is a weighted averaging approach that uses three estimates per activity: pessimistic, optimistic, and most likely (realistic).

The theory is that using a pessimistic, optimistic, and most likely (realistic) approach yields a more accurate result.

Note that the PERT formula can be used to calculate time or cost.

Know the concepts of the PERT estimating method. Know that PERT stands for Program Evaluation Review Technique.

The formula for PERT is:

$$\frac{(O + P + (4 \times M))}{6} \quad \text{or} \quad t_E = \frac{t_O + 4t_M + t_P}{6}$$

In the first formula, O is Optimistic, P is Pessimistic, and M is Most Likely (R,Realistic, could be substituted for M). In the second formula, t is Time, E is Estimated, O is Optimistic, M is Most Likely, and P is Pessimistic.

6.4.2. Parkinson's Law

According to Parkinson's Law, work expands to consume the time scheduled for its completion. This observation of economics was made by C. Northcote Parkinson based on his experience in the British Civil Service. He noted that as the British Empire shrank in size and significance, the colonial office staff actually increased.

Parkinson's Law can be applied to:

- Generalized situations
  The demand upon a resource expands to match the supply of the resource.
- Computer storage
  Data expands to fill the space available.
- Financial situations
  Expenses rise to meet income.

6.4.3. Schedule Processes

Figure 6-13: Overview of Schedule Processes illustrates the processes and primary artifacts of the Project Schedule Management knowledge area.

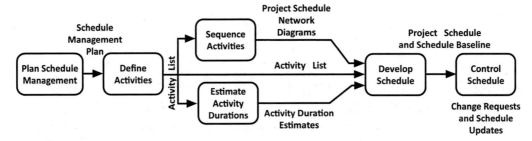

Figure 6-13: Overview of Schedule Processes

The source for the above figure is the Project Management Institute, *A Guide to the Project Management Body of Knowledge, (PMBOK® Guide) – Sixth Edition,* Project Management Institute Inc., 2017, Figure 6-1, Page 169

The processes in sections 6.1, 6.2, 6.3, and 6.4 lead to the development of the project schedule and establishment of the schedule baseline.

The source for the above text is the Project Management Institute, *A Guide to the Project Management Body of Knowledge, (PMBOK® Guide) – Sixth Edition,* Project Management Institute Inc., 2017, Pages 188-197

6.5. Develop Schedule (Planning Process Group)

During the Develop Schedule process, the creation of activity lists, the sequencing of activities, and the estimation of activity durations all come together to create the project schedule.

Note that on smaller projects, Define Activities, Sequence Activities, Estimate Activity Resources (EAD), and Develop Schedule may occur as a single overall process.

Know the Develop Schedule concepts. Know the Key Inputs, Tools & Techniques, and Outputs for Develop Schedule.

PMI, CAPM, and PMBOK are registered marks of the Project Management Institute, Inc.

178   © 2008-2018 Crosswind Learning, www.crosswindpm.com

Develop Schedule

Inputs	Outputs
Project Management Plan	**Schedule Baseline**
• **Schedule Management Plan**	**Project Schedule**
• Scope Baseline	Schedule Data
Project Documents	**Project Calendars**
• **Activity Attributes**	Change Requests
• **Activity List**	Project Management Plan Updates
• Assumption Log	• Schedule Management Plan
• Basis of Estimates	• Cost Baseline
• **Duration Estimates**	Project Documents Updates
• Lessons Learned Register	• Activity Attributes
• **Milestone List**	• Assumption Log
• **Project Schedule Network Diagrams**	• Duration Estimates
• **Project Team Assignments**	• Lessons Learned Register
• **Resource Calendars**	• Resource Requirements
• **Resource Requirements**	• Risk Register
• **Risk Register**	
Agreements	
Enterprise Environmental Factors	
Organizational Process Assets	

Tools and Techniques

Schedule Network Analysis	**Leads and Lags**
Critical Path Method	**Schedule Compression**
Resource Optimization	Project Management Information System
Data Analysis	**Agile Release Planning**
• What-If Scenario	
• Simulation	

Figure 6-14: Develop Schedule Data Flow Diagram

The source for the above figure is the Project Management Institute, *A Guide to the Project Management Body of Knowledge*, (*PMBOK® Guide*) – Sixth Edition, Project Management Institute Inc., 2017, Figure 6-14, Page 198

Develop Schedule (Planning)		
Key Inputs	Schedule Management Plan	The schedule management plan is a component of the project management plan that details the delineation, evolution, monitoring, and control of the schedule. It delineates scheduling methodology, the degree of expected accuracy needed to estimate the duration of the scheduled activities, the mechanism used to produce the schedule, and the manner in which the schedule will be calculated.

Develop Schedule (Continued)		
Key Inputs (Cont.)	Activity Attributes	Activity attributes clarify an activity by identifying multiple components related to the activity. The components evolve during the project: during the initial stage, they include a singular activity identifier, a WBS identifier, and an activity label; when completed they typically include a description of the activity, predecessor and successor activities, logical relationships, leads and lags, resource needs, constraints, assumptions, and exact dates. They are used to create the schedule model.
	Activity List	The activity list enumerates the activities included in the schedule model.
	Duration Estimates	Duration estimates are quantitative estimates of activity durations in which lags are not considered. They are often expressed as a range of time or a probability of reaching a specific duration.
	Milestone List	The milestone list enumerates the most consequential points or events in the project and indicates if the milestone is required or optional. A milestone has a duration of zero. If the milestone has been assigned a specific date, it typically impacts the manner in which activities are scheduled.
	Project Schedule Network Diagrams	Project schedule network diagrams illustrate the dependencies (logical relationships) between project schedule activities. They can be high-level or detailed and include a summary narrative delineating the basic approach to activity sequencing and detailing unusual sequences. Activities with multiple predecessor or successor activities should note a path convergence (predecessor activities), since these have greater risk.
	Project Team Assignments	Project team assignments delineate the resources that are assigned to an individual activity.
	Resource Calendars	Resource calendars delineate project resource accessibility
	Resource Requirements	Resource requirements delineate the classes and numbers of resources that are needed for individual activities utilized in the schedule model. Note that resources are not limited to people, but include items such as equipment and office space.

Develop Schedule (Continued)		
Key Inputs (Cont.)	Risk Register	The risk register delineates all identified risks that impact the schedule model and their characteristics. The information is used to establish schedule reserves.
	Agreements	Agreements, sometimes referenced as contracts, may impact the schedule as the vendors delineate how they will perform the work detailed in the agreement.
Key Tools & Techniques	Schedule Network Analysis	Schedule network analysis is the designation used to describe the techniques utilized to create the schedule model. The analysis typically includes critical path analysis, modeling techniques, and techniques to increase the effectiveness of resources. It may also include, among other pertinent analysis techniques, a network review to determine any risks that might engender schedule slippage and an analysis regarding the efficacy of aggregating schedule reserves to offset schedule slippage.
	Critical Path Method	The critical path method is a schedule network analysis technique that establishes the amount of flexibility (slack) on network paths (the sequence of activities) within the schedule model. The critical path is the longest path through the project and represents the minimum project duration. The method uses forward and backward pass approaches to calculate the early start, early finish, late start, and late finish dates of each activity to establish slack for each activity. It is typically used with Precedence Diagram Method sequencing.
	Resource Optimization	Resource optimization uses techniques, such as resource leveling and resource smoothing, to adjust the schedule to accommodate resource availability. Resource leveling is accomplished by adjusting start and finish dates to offset resource demand with resource supply. Resource smoothing is accomplished by using an activity's float to offset resource demand with resource supply. These techniques can also be used to schedule a consistent level of hours (usually either daily or weekly) for project resources.
	Leads and Lags	A lead is the amount of time that a successor activity will be started before a predecessor activity is completed. A lag is the amount of time that a successor activity will be delayed after the predecessor activity is completed.

Develop Schedule (Continued)		
Key Tools & Techniques	Schedule Compression	Schedule compression is utilized to decrease the duration of the project schedule without decreasing its scope. Techniques include crashing, decreasing the schedule duration by increasing resources for activities on the critical path, and fast tracking, decreasing the schedule duration by performing activities or phases at the same time, instead of in sequence, for at least a part of their duration.
	Agile Release Planning	Agile release planning creates a high-level timeline of the release schedule for the next three to six months in accordance with the product roadmap. The number of iterations or sprints in the release is determined during planning so decisions can be made regarding the extent of product development and the length of time required to release the product. The customer typically finds the timeline more understandable than the project schedule since it exhibits the features that will be functional as a result of each iteration.
Key Outputs	Schedule Baseline	The schedule baseline is the authorized version of the schedule model. It contains baseline start and baseline finish dates, is subject to change control, and is used as the basis of comparison to actual results.
	Project Schedule	The project schedule is the product of a schedule model containing linked activities and their planned dates, durations, milestones, and resources. It is usually formatted as a bar chart, milestone chart, or project schedule network diagram, although tabular formatting may occur. Until resources have been allocated and start and finish dates substantiated, the project schedule is preliminary. A master schedule or milestone schedule is a summary form of the project schedule.
	Project Calendars	A project calendar is created to depict working days and shifts for scheduled activities based on resource availability. To determine the project schedule, more than one calendar might be used to accommodate different work periods for particular activities.

Situational Question and Real World Application
Failure to effectively perform the Develop Schedule process can result in not knowing when activities should occur. If resources are not addressed appropriately, misallocation of resources can result. If duration estimates are significantly out of alignment, problems associated with schedule slippage can occur.

6.5.1. Schedule Examples

There are a variety of schedule formats. The most common formats are activity lists, bar charts, and network diagrams.

Activity lists contain all required schedule activities for the project, an identifier for each activity, and a rather detailed scope of work description for each activity. **Bar charts** are an easy to read representation of schedule activities (bars) and denote the start date, end date, and duration of each activity. **Network diagrams** are visual representations of network logic and scheduling. Typically, the diagrams contain date information for critical path activities and are formatted as activity-on-node or logic bar chart.

6.5.2. Schedule Baseline

A schedule baseline is a specific version of the project schedule that is selected and approved by the project management team as the baseline and includes baseline start and finish dates.

6.5.3. Critical Path Method (CPM)

The critical path method utilizes a forward pass to establish the earliest start (ES) and finish (EF) dates for activities and a backward pass to establish the latest start (LS) and finish (LF) date for activities.

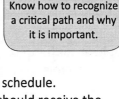

Know how to recognize a critical path and why it is important.

Determining this information for each path and activity allows the calculation of the critical path and the amount of slack (float) on each activity as well. Any activity on the critical path typically has zero slack (float), but there can be negative slack (float) if the project is behind schedule.

In most cases, the activities on the critical path are the ones that should receive the most focus and attention from the project manager.

6.5.4. Slack (Also Known as Float)

Slack (float) is the amount of time that an activity can slip or be delayed without delaying the finish date of the project (or activity or published project completion date). Typically, slack (float) is calculated using a forward and backward pass.

If an activity has no slack (float), it is on the critical path; therefore, if it slips, it pushes out the finish date.

Negative or positive slack (float) can also exist, extending or contracting the actual finish date of the project. For example, if a project finishes two weeks early, there are two weeks of positive slack (float). If the project finishes two weeks late (without approval of a new date), there are two weeks of negative slack (float).

Know the characteristics of free slack (free float), total slack (total float), and project slack (project float).

Slack (Float) Type	Description
Free Slack	Free slack (float) involves determining the latest that an activity can start without delaying the activities that follow it.
Total Slack	Total slack (float) is the latest an activity can start without delaying the project finish date.
Project Slack	Project slack (float) is the amount of time something can be delayed without delaying the published finish date. Most scheduling software will calculate these dates for you.

The concepts needed for the exam, which focus on total slack (float), follow.

6.5.5. Critical Path

The critical path is the **longest path on the project network diagram.** It typically has no slack (float), yet the duration can change as the project evolves. The greatest project risk normally occurs on the critical path.

Know the concepts of CPM (critical path method) estimation.

The project end date can be delayed if an activity on the critical path has a problem. The increase or slippage of an activity on the critical path can cause the overall finish date to slip.

A project has **negative slack (float) if it is behind schedule and a new finish date has not been authorized.**

A project can have multiple critical paths, but that would increase the risk of schedule slippage.

6.5.6. How to Calculate the Critical Path

The following table represents a data table typically found on the exam. It is used to create a network diagram and then determine the critical path.

Activity	Preceding Activities	Duration in Days
A	Start	4
B	Start	5
C	A	4
D	B	2
E	C, D	6
F	D	1
G	E, F	5

When the project starts, Activity A (4 days) and B (5 days) can begin. When Activity A is done, Activity C (4 days) can begin. When Activity B is done, Activity D (2 days) can begin. Activities C and D must finish before Activity E (6 days) can begin. Activity F (1 day) can begin when Activity D is complete. Activity G can begin when Activities E and F are complete. When Activity G (5 days) is complete, the project is complete.

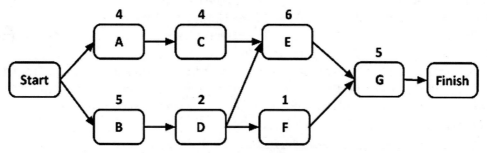

Figure 6-15: Network Diagram for Critical Path Analysis (A)
The source for the above figure is the Project Management Institute, *A Guide to the Project Management Body of Knowledge, (PMBOK® Guide) – Sixth Edition*,
Project Management Institute Inc., 2017, Figure 6-11, Page 187

Paths: ACEG = 19   BDEG =18   BDFG = 13

The critical path is the path that is the longest. That is path ACEG with a total of 19 days.

Note the following for the exam:

- For word problems related to network diagrams, draw the network diagram and then double check connections, activity labels, and activity durations
- List all paths and calculate the duration of each path using the top to bottom approach (list the paths as they start at the top of the diagram and work toward those on the bottom so you don't miss anything)
- Determine the critical path by selecting the longest (duration) path

6.5.7.   Forward and Backward Pass Calculation

A forward and backward pass calculation is a standard calculation used to determine the critical path of the network diagram, the amount of slack (float) for each activity, and the amount of total slack (float).

- Slack (float) defines the amount of time an activity can slip before delaying the next activity
- Total slack (float) defines the amount of time an activity can slip before it delays the project finish date.

Mnemonics (memory tools) for the steps needed to perform a forward pass and a backward pass are **FIB** and **BDS**.

- **FIB** is the mnemonic for **Forward: Increment** (one day to another between activities) and choose the **Bigger** of all Early Finish (EF) dates feeding into an Early Start (ES) for the next activity
- **BDS** is the mnemonic for **Backward: Decrement** (one day to another between activities) and choose the **Smaller** of all Late Starts (LS)) feeding into the Late Finish (LF) of the next activity

The **forward pass** starts at the start (left) of the network diagram and works through to the finish establishing the Early Start (ES) and Early Finish (EF) of the activities.

The **backward pass** starts at the finish and works backward to the left of the diagram establishing the Late Finish (LF) and Late Start (LS) of the activities.

Note that there are two approaches to a forward/backward pass: counting from day zero or counting from day one. Crosswind uses the day one approach, but either approach will work, so Crosswind has created a downloadable file that recreates sections 6.5.7 through 6.5.9 using the day zero approach. That file is located at http://www.crosswindpm.com/download/crosswindpmpday0.pdf.

Forward Pass Purpose	Provides the early start (ES) and early finish (EF) dates of each activity on the network diagram
Forward Pass Formula	ES + Duration - 1 = EF
Assumptions	A day starts at 8:00 a.m. and finishes at 5:00 p.m.
Starting Point	At the left of the network diagram, typically the start activity
Variables	**Early start (ES)** - The earliest an activity can start based on network diagram logic
	Early finish (EF) - The earliest an activity can finish based on network diagram logic
	Duration - The length of an activity
	Convergence - Where the output of more than one activity is a predecessor to an activity on the network diagram

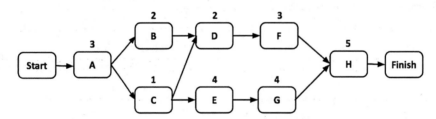

Figure 6-16: Network Diagram for Critical Path Analysis

The source for the above figure is the Project Management Institute, *A Guide to the Project Management Body of Knowledge, (PMBOK® Guide) – Sixth Edition,* Project Management Institute Inc., 2017, Figure 6-16, Page 203

Instructions for the Performance of a Forward Pass

Read the section below at least once, then perform the following steps referencing figure 6-16: Network Diagram for Critical Path Analysis.

1. Set the early start (ES) of Activity A to one (the first day of the project).
2. Apply the forward pass formula (EF = ES + Duration - 1) to the network diagram activity-by-activity from start to finish. As you move from one activity to another, increment the early finish (EF) of the current activity by one to give you the early start (ES) of the next activity. For example, Activity A has an early finish (EF) of 3; the early start (ES) of the following activity is 4.
   If you encounter a convergence (reference step 3), return to the beginning of the diagram and continue this step for all activities leading into the convergence.
3. Wherever you encounter a convergence, select the larger of the early finish (EF) values and continue applying the forward pass formula from start to finish on the network diagram.
4. Perform steps 2 and 3 until you have applied the forward pass formula to all activities. The forward pass is complete at this point. The network diagram should also be complete.

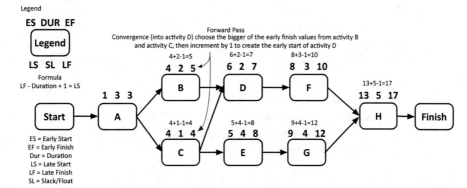

Figure 6-17: Forward Pass Calculation Description
The source for the above figure is the Project Management Institute, *A Guide to the Project Management Body of Knowledge*, (*PMBOK® Guide*) – Sixth Edition, Project Management Institute Inc., 2017, Figure 6-16, Page 203

Note that the calculations are not part of a typical diagram but are shown for clarification.

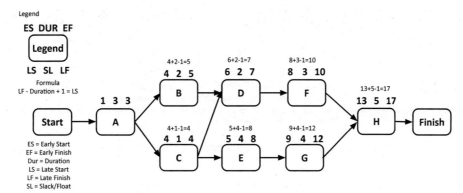

Figure 6-18: Forward Pass
The source for the above figure is the Project Management Institute, *A Guide to the Project Management Body of Knowledge*, (*PMBOK® Guide*) – Sixth Edition, Project Management Institute Inc., 2017, Figure 6-16, Page 203

Backward Pass Purpose	Provides the late start (LS) and late finish (LF) dates of each of the activities on the network diagram
Backward Pass Formula	LF - Duration + 1 = LS
Variables	**Late start (LS)** - The latest an activity can start based on the network diagram logic
	Late finish (LF) - The latest an activity can finish based on the network diagram logic
	Duration - The length of an activity
	Burst – Where an activity has multiple outputs that are predecessors to more than one activity
Assumptions	A day starts at 8:00 a.m. and finishes at 5:00 p.m.
Starting Point	At the right of the network diagram, typically the finish or end activity

Instructions for the Performance of a Backward Pass

1. The late finish (LF) is the same as the early finish (EF) on the last activity (also, the duration of the critical path). If the network diagram ends with multiple activities, the Late Finish (LF) for all is the greatest Early Finish (EF).

2. Apply the backward pass formula (LF - Duration + 1 = LS) from the finish (right) to the start (left) of the network diagram. As you move from one activity to another, decrease the late start (LS) by one to give you the late finish (LF) of the next activity. For example, Activity H has a late start (LS) of 13; the activity that precedes it has a late finish (LF) of 12.

   If you encounter a burst (see Backward Pass Calculation Description in this step), return to the finish (right) of the diagram and continue this step for all activities leading (from the right to the left) into the burst.

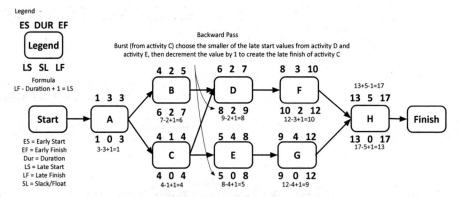

Figure 6-19: Backward Pass Calculation Description

The source for the above figure is the Project Management Institute, *A Guide to the Project Management Body of Knowledge*, (*PMBOK® Guide*) – Sixth Edition, Project Management Institute Inc., 2017, Figure 6-16, Page 203

3. At any burst on the network diagram, select the smaller of the late start (LS) values.

4. Perform steps 2 and 3 until all activities are done. At this point, the network diagram should resemble Figure 6-20: Backward Pass.

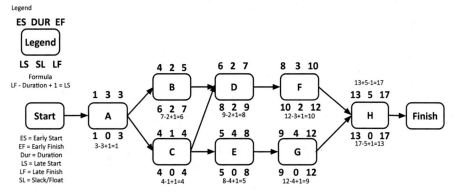

Figure 6-20: Backward Pass

The source for the above figure is the Project Management Institute, *A Guide to the Project Management Body of Knowledge, (PMBOK® Guide)* – Sixth Edition, Project Management Institute Inc., 2017, Figure 6-16, Page 203

Critical Path: The critical path is the longest path in the network diagram. Any activities on the critical path have an early start and late start that are the same value, as well as an early finish and late finish that are the same value. They have zero slack (float), meaning that if any of the activities slip, the overall project finish date slips as well.

6.5.8. Instructions for the Performance of a Forward and Backward Pass Substitute Technique

To calculate the slack (float) of a path (or activity), without having to do the traditional forward/backward pass approach, do the following:

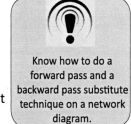

Know how to do a forward pass and a backward pass substitute technique on a network diagram.

1. Add the durations of all paths and list them in the format "path name and total duration."
2. List each activity (A =, B=, etc.) to later list the slack of each activity after the equal sign.
3. Identify the critical path of the network diagram. This is the path with the longest duration.
4. Put 0 (zero) for slack (float) for each activity on the critical path.
5. On the next longest path, subtract that overall duration from the critical path duration (for example, 1-day difference).
6. Any activity from that path that does not already have a slack (float) number on it, put the difference (for example, 1 day) from step four as slack (float) for those activities.
7. Repeat steps five and six until all activities have slack (float) numbers.

If the path under review is not at the end of the diagram, you can still use this method. Other methods show subtracting all the activities one by one until you have the slack (float) value you are calculating for. You need to do that method only if you must calculate an early start or early finish of an activity. The next paragraph covers calculation of the early/late start and finishes.

6.5.9. Network Diagram Analysis

The Network Diagram (Figure 6-21: Network Diagram Analysis) contains the arrows and formulas necessary for the calculation of duration or slack (float). The relevant formulas are listed in the diagram and the diagram arrows point in the starting direction. Note that if an activity is on the critical path, the slack (float) is zero.

Instructions for Using the Alternative Method to Calculate the Slack (Float) of an Activity

Use the formula LF - EF (late finish - early finish) or LS - ES (late start - early start) to calculate the slack (float) of an activity by using the date provided in the exercise. If the difference is zero, the activity is on the critical path. If the value is negative, the activity has negative slack (float); if the value is positive, the activity has positive slack (float).

Network Diagram Analysis

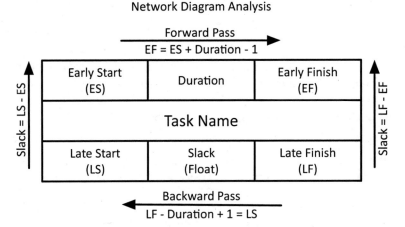

Figure 6-21: Network Diagram Analysis
The source for the above figure is the Project Management Institute, *A Guide to the Project Management Body of Knowledge*, (*PMBOK® Guide*) – Sixth Edition, Project Management Institute Inc., 2017, Figure 6-16, Page 203

6.5.10. Schedule Compression Techniques

If it is necessary to compress the schedule (usually to achieve a more aggressive time goal), the two main techniques are **crashing** and **fast tracking**. Schedule compression may employ either or both techniques.

Crashing is the application of additional resources (human) to the critical path items, excluding any resequencing activities.

Fast tracking is the analysis of the network diagram and activity sequencing to determine the sequencing adjustments that will accelerate the completion of work. Fast tracking does include the risk exposure associated with the resequencing.

Instructions for Fast Tracking

Figure 6-22: Network Diagram Pre-fast Tracking has two paths: the first path is A, B, D, E, F with a total duration of 13 and the second path is A, C, D, E, F with a total duration of 12.   Path A, B, D, E, F is the critical path because it is the longer of the two paths.

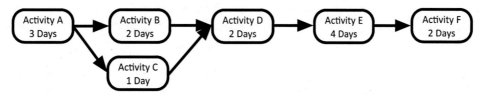

Figure 6-22: Network Diagram Pre-fast Tracking

The source for the above figure is the Project Management Institute, *A Guide to the Project Management Body of Knowledge*, (*PMBOK® Guide*) – Sixth Edition, Project Management Institute Inc., 2017, Figure 6-19, Page 207

To compress the overall duration using the fast tracking technique, resequence the diagram in Figure 6-23: Network Diagram Post-fast Tracking. Path A, B, D, F has a total duration of 9. Path A, B, E, F has a total duration of 11 and path A, C, D, F has a total duration of 8. Path A, B, E, F is the critical path because it is the longest of the three paths. Fast tracking has reduced the critical path from 13 (the original sequencing) to 11 (the revised sequencing).

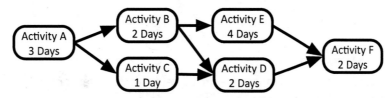

Figure 6-23: Network Diagram Post-fast Tracking

The source for the above figure is the Project Management Institute, *A Guide to the Project Management Body of Knowledge*, (*PMBOK® Guide*) – Sixth Edition, Project Management Institute Inc., 2017, Figure 6-19, Page 207

Characteristics of both are listed in the following table.

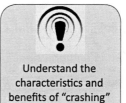

Understand the characteristics and benefits of "crashing" and "fast tracking."

Technique	Characteristics			
	Key	**Cost**	**Quality**	**Additional**
Crashing	**Putting more resources** on critical path activities	Usually increases cost	Minimal risk exposure (Compared to fast tracking)	Requires more people than originally planned.
Fast Tracking	**Doing activities in parallel** that are normally in sequence	Flexible, but may increase cost from potential rework	Additional risk exposure due to possible rework	Can require additional communication to coordinate activities

6.5.11.   Resource Leveling

As the schedule is created, resources are assigned often resulting in a pattern of peaks and valleys as depicted in Figure 6-24: Resource Allocation (Pre-leveling). These peaks and valleys represent resources that can be applied for 12 hours one day but only four hours the next. It is possible to considerably soften the peaks and valleys, reference Figure 6-25: Resource Allocation (Post-leveling), by applying resource leveling. Note that applying resource leveling to the schedule often results in an overall finish date later than originally scheduled.

Resource leveling and schedule compression techniques are typically used together in several iterations to attain an optimal balance between delivery deadlines and resource utilization.

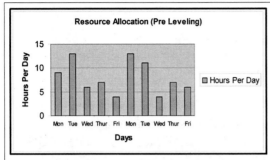

Figure 6-24: Resource Allocation (Pre-leveling)

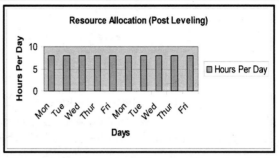

Figure 6-25: Resource Allocation (Post-leveling)

The source for the above figures is the Project Management Institute, *A Guide to the Project Management Body of Knowledge*, (*PMBOK® Guide*) – Sixth Edition, Project Management Institute Inc., 2017, Figure 6-17, Page 204

6.5.12. Resource Smoothing

Resource smoothing is similar to resource leveling in that it also removes peaks and valleys. The difference is that the focus of resource smoothing is on predefined resource limits (for example, resource A is limited to working six hours daily) **rather than merely preventing over-allocation** of resources.

6.5.13. Logic Bar Chart

A logic bar chart, sometimes called a Gantt chart, is a common chart **used to track the day-to-day details of the project.** It contains a table of information (usually activities, dates, resources, etc.) on the left and horizontal bars showing when those activities occur on the right. It may also have vertical lines that connect the horizontal bars, which are typically used to indicate a project phase. Although the logic bar chart depicts sequencing, the network diagram is the preferred tool for viewing the sequence of activities.

Know the characteristics of a logic bar chart.

WBS #	Activity (Task)	Days	Timeline				
			Jan	Feb	Mar	Apr	May
1.1	CRM Application Development Starts	0	◇				
1.1.1	Module A	40	▨▨				
1.1.1.1	Requirements A	20	▨				
1.1.1.2	Code A	20	▨				
1.1.1.3	Test A	20		▨			
1.1.2	Module B	40		▨▨			
1.1.2.1	Requirements B	20		▨			
1.1.2.2	Code B	20		▨			
1.1.2.3	Test B	20			▨		
1.1.3	Module C	40			▨▨		
1.1.3.1	Requirements C	20			▨		
1.1.3.2	Code C	20			▨		
1.1.3.3	Test C	20				▨	
1.2	Deployment	20					▨
1.2.1	Production Cut Over	20					▨

Figure 6-26: Logic Bar Chart Sample

The source for the above figure is the Project Management Institute, *A Guide to the Project Management Body of Knowledge*, (*PMBOK® Guide*) – Sixth Edition, Project Management Institute Inc., 2017, Figure 6-21, Page 210

6.5.14. Milestone Schedule

The milestone schedule is **typically used in executive reporting**, and each milestone has a **zero (0) duration.** It lacks detail, generally listing only the main project milestones as diamonds instead of Gantt bars. Like the logic bar chart, the milestone schedule does not require lines connecting the milestone diamonds.

Executives usually don't require much detail, so the milestone schedule fits their needs. Because project teams require more detail, they typically use Gantt charts.

Know the characteristics of a milestone schedule. A common misunderstanding about a milestone is the duration. This is something you should know for the exam. A milestone has 0 (zero) duration.

Milestone Schedule

WBS #	Activity (Task)	Days	Timeline				
			Jan	Feb	Mar	Apr	May
1.1	CRM Application Development Starts	0	◇				
1.1.1	Module A	0		◇			
1.1.2	Module B	0			◇		
1.1.3	Module C	0				◇	
1.2	Deployment	0					◇
1.2.1	Production Cut Over	0					◇

Figure 6-27: Milestone Schedule Sample

The source for the above figure is the Project Management Institute, *A Guide to the Project Management Body of Knowledge*, (*PMBOK® Guide*) – Sixth Edition, Project Management Institute Inc., 2017, Figure 6-21, Page 210

6.5.15. Summary Schedule

The summary schedule shows an aggregate or rolled up view of the various activities at a summary level. It gives senior management, the project management team, and team members a picture of how long the summary level work packages will take, and in what sequence they will occur.

WBS #	Activity (Task)	Days	Timeline				
			Jan	Feb	Mar	Apr	May
1.1	CRM Application Development Starts	100					
1.1.1	Module A	40					
1.1.2	Module B	40					
1.1.3	Module C	40					
1.2	Deployment	20					
1.2.1	Production Cut Over	20					

Figure 6-28: Summary Schedule Sample

The source for the above figure is the Project Management Institute, *A Guide to the Project Management Body of Knowledge*, (*PMBOK® Guide*) – Sixth Edition, Project Management Institute Inc., 2017, Figure 6-21, Page 210

6.5.16. Hammock Activity

A hammock activity is a summary activity that encompasses all of the tasks or activities underneath it. The summary or hammock activity starts at the earliest start date of the activities encompassed and finishes at the latest finish date of the activities encompassed. For example in Figure 6-28, Module A, Module B, and Module C are part of the hammock activity CRM Application Development Starts. The hammock activity is scheduled to start in January and end before May.

6.5.17. Agile Release Planning

The coach/facilitator facilitates the release planning meeting. The team and the product owner/customer attend this meeting. The team selects the user stories/requirements to be included in the release based primarily on product owner/customer prioritization. The team typically places the user stories/requirements, listed on sticky notes, on a white board. The team then divides the release, or designated unit of calendar time, into iterations. It is very important that all team members, even those that are not co-located, participate in this meeting.

The source for the above text is the Project Management Institute, *A Guide to the Project Management Body of Knowledge*, (*PMBOK® Guide*) – Sixth Edition, Project Management Institute Inc., 2017, Pages 197-212

6.6. Control Schedule (Monitoring and Controlling Process Group)

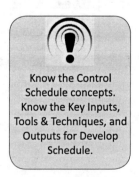

During the Control Schedule process, changes to the schedule are managed and controlled.

PMI, CAPM, and PMBOK are registered marks of the Project Management Institute, Inc.

194

© 2008-2018 Crosswind Learning, www.crosswindpm.com

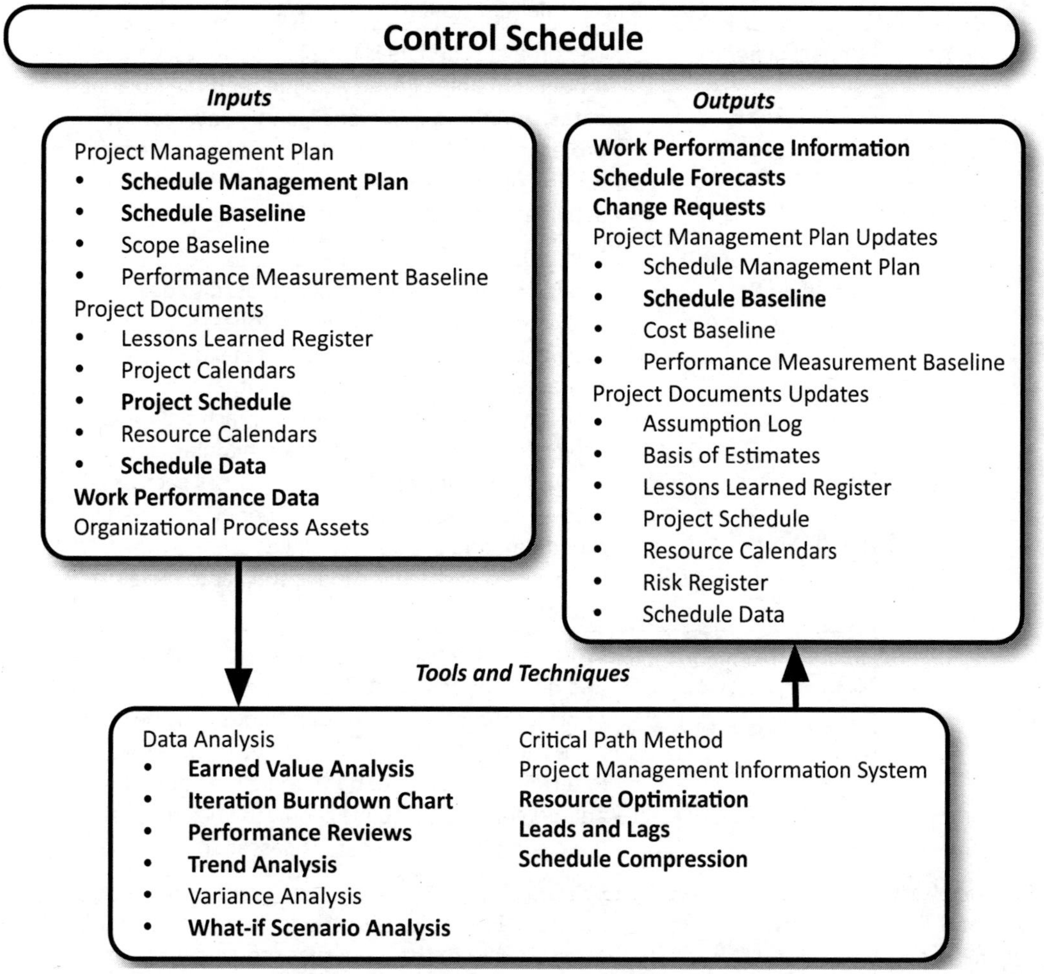

Control Schedule

Inputs

Project Management Plan
- **Schedule Management Plan**
- **Schedule Baseline**
- Scope Baseline
- Performance Measurement Baseline

Project Documents
- Lessons Learned Register
- Project Calendars
- **Project Schedule**
- Resource Calendars
- **Schedule Data**

Work Performance Data

Organizational Process Assets

Outputs

Work Performance Information

Schedule Forecasts

Change Requests

Project Management Plan Updates
- Schedule Management Plan
- **Schedule Baseline**
- Cost Baseline
- Performance Measurement Baseline

Project Documents Updates
- Assumption Log
- Basis of Estimates
- Lessons Learned Register
- Project Schedule
- Resource Calendars
- Risk Register
- Schedule Data

Tools and Techniques

Data Analysis
- **Earned Value Analysis**
- **Iteration Burndown Chart**
- **Performance Reviews**
- **Trend Analysis**
- Variance Analysis
- **What-if Scenario Analysis**

Critical Path Method
Project Management Information System
Resource Optimization
Leads and Lags
Schedule Compression

Figure 6-29: Control Schedule Data Flow Diagram
The source for the above figure is the Project Management Institute, *A Guide to the Project Management Body of Knowledge*, (PMBOK® Guide) – Sixth Edition, Project Management Institute Inc., 2017, Figure 6-22, Page 214

Control Schedule (Monitoring and Controlling)		
Key Inputs	Schedule Management Plan	The schedule management plan is a component of the project management plan that details the delineation, evolution, monitoring, and control of the schedule. It delineates the manner in which reserves are to be used and the schedule is to be controlled. The plan also establishes the frequency of updates to the schedule.
	Schedule Baseline	The schedule baseline is compared to actual results to discover any variances. The proper course of action is then determined based on those variances.

Control Schedule (Continued)		
Key Inputs	Project Schedule	The project schedule is the product of a schedule model containing linked activities and their planned dates, durations, milestones, and resources. The project schedule always refers to the most recent version of the schedule with documented updates, activities that have been completed, and activities that have started.
	Schedule Data	Schedule data is the information used to delineate and control the schedule. Milestones, activities, activity attributes, assumptions, constraints are contained in the schedule data. Other information may include, but is not limited to, cash-flow projections, order and delivery schedules, and resource histograms. Supporting detail such as resource requirements by time period, alternative schedules, and applied schedule reserves may also be included. Schedule data is subject to review and update during this process.
	Work Performance Data	Work performance data represents the raw metrics and observations identified during the performance of project work activities. It includes activities that have started; the progression of those activities in terms of duration to date, remaining duration, and percentage complete; and activities that have been completed. The data is passed to controlling processes for analysis.
Key Tools & Techniques	Earned Value Analysis	Earned value analysis is used to compare the work done (BCWP) to the work that should have been done (BCWS), this provides the state of the schedule. Comparing the work done (BCWP) to the actual costs associated with work completed (ACWP), provides the state of the budget. The earned value analysis provides a numerical evaluation of the state of the project. Schedule performance measurements, such as schedule variance (SV) and schedule performance index (SPI), are used to determine the significance of variance from the original schedule baseline. Cost performance measurements, such as cost variance (CV) and cost performance index (CPI), are used to determine the performance efficiency and variance of the budget.

PMI, CAPM, and PMBOK are registered marks of the Project Management Institute, Inc.

196   © 2008-2018 Crosswind Learning, www.crosswindpm.com

Control Schedule (Continued)		
Key Tools & Techniques (Cont.)	Iteration Burndown Chart	The iteration burndown chart depicts remaining work from the iteration backlog. An ideal burndown (the burndown established during iteration planning) is used as the basis for comparison and analysis. Using a forecast trend line, the variance at iteration completion can be determined so that the proper course of action can be taken.
	Performance Reviews	Performance reviews compare, measure, and analyze schedule performance against the schedule baseline. Items considered include the remaining duration of work, the start and finish dates of an activity, and completion percentage.
	Trend Analysis	Trend analysis is used to project the future state of project performance based on the present state of project performance, in other words, to determine if performance is improving or declining. The analysis can be used to predict issues, such as slippages in time, to determine and effect corrective action.
	What-if Scenario Analysis	What-if scenario analysis is the assessment of scenarios so that their effect on project goals can be predicted. A schedule network analysis is performed utilizing the schedule to determine the consequence of a scenario. The result of the analysis is useful in evaluating project success under different conditions and to determine schedule reserves and response plans to address risk.
	Resource Optimization	Resource optimization techniques, such as resource leveling and resource smoothing, are used to adjust the schedule to accommodate resource availability. Resource leveling is accomplished by adjusting start and finish dates to offset resource demand with resource supply. Resource smoothing is accomplished by using an activity's float to offset resource demand with resource supply. These techniques can also be used to schedule a consistent level of hours (usually either daily or weekly) for project resources.
	Leads and Lags	A lead is the amount of time that a successor activity will be started before a predecessor activity is completed. A lag is the amount of time that a successor activity will be delayed after the predecessor activity is completed.

Control Schedule (Continued)		
Key Tools & Techniques (Cont.)	Schedule Compression	Schedule compression techniques are utilized to align activities that have slipped into alignment with the plan. Techniques include crashing, decreasing the schedule duration by increasing resources for activities on the critical path, and fast tracking, decreasing the schedule duration by performing activities or phases at the same time, instead of in sequence for at least a part of their duration.
Key Outputs	Work Performance Information	Work performance information represents the raw metrics and observations identified during the performance of project work activities. It includes activities that have started; the progression of those activities in terms of duration to date, remaining duration, and percentage complete; and activities that have been completed. The information is analyzed against the schedule baseline. Start date, finish date, and duration variances can be determined at the work package or control account level. If earned value management is applied to the information, the schedule variance (SV) and schedule performance index (SPI) are documented in work performance reporting.
	Schedule Forecasts	Schedule forecasts are utilized to predict the occurrence of future events or contingencies based on current knowledge. They are updated and reissued in accordance with work performance information during project execution.
	Change Requests	Change requests are requests for modification that have not been formally approved through the change control process. Changes to the baseline, scope baseline, or other components of the project management plan may be requested as the result of schedule variance analysis, progress report scrutiny, enacted performance measures, and alterations to the project schedule or scope.
	Schedule Baseline	The schedule baseline is updated in response to approved change requests related to project scope, activity resources, or activity duration estimates. It is also updated to reflect changes that occurred due to the application of schedule compression techniques or performance issues.

Situational Question and Real World Application

Failure to effectively perform the Control Schedule process can result in the existence of multiple schedule versions, all different and all "official," and the communication of outdated schedule information.

PMI, CAPM, and PMBOK are registered marks of the Project Management Institute, Inc.

198 © 2008-2018 Crosswind Learning, www.crosswindpm.com

6.6.1. Iteration Burndown Chart

The iteration burndown chart depicts remaining work from the iteration backlog. An ideal burndown (the burndown established during iteration planning) is used as the basis for comparison and analysis.

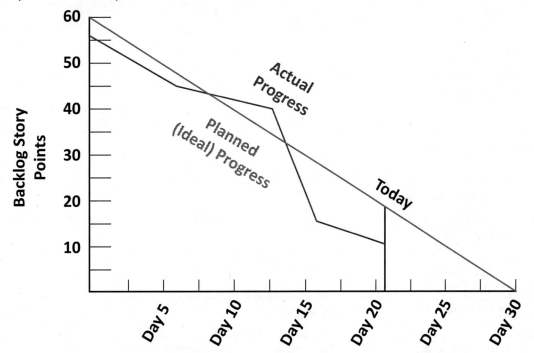

Figure 6-30: Iteration Burndown Chart

The source for the above figure is the Project Management Institute, *A Guide to the Project Management Body of Knowledge*, (*PMBOK® Guide*) – Sixth Edition, Project Management Institute Inc., 2017, Figure 6-24, Page 217

Using a forecast trend line, the variance at iteration completion can be determined so that the proper course of action can be taken.

The source for the above text is the Project Management Institute, *A Guide to the Project Management Body of Knowledge*, (*PMBOK® Guide*) – Sixth Edition, Project Management Institute Inc., 2017, Pages 197-212

6.7. Project Schedule Management Formulas and Variables

Description	Formula	Variable (Component)	Example
Standard deviation is the measurement of variation within a distribution	$(P - O) / 6$	Standard Deviation	$(20 - 4) / 6 = 2.67$
The **variance** is a measure of how spread out a distribution is.	$((P - O) / 6)^2$	Variance	$((20 - 4) / 6)^2 = 7.11$
Weighted Averaging (PERT) represents an estimation technique used to calculate duration estimates. **This is used in a beta distribution.**	$(P + O + (4 \times M)) / 6$ Or $t_E = (t_O + 4t_M + t_P) / 6$	PERT	$(20 + 4 + (4 \times 14)) / 6 = 13.33$
Simple Averaging (three-point estimate). **This is used in a triangular distribution.**	$(P + O + M) / 3$	Three-Point Estimate	$(20 + 4 + 14) / 3 = 12.67$
Pessimistic estimate is a worse case estimate.	Provided on exam	P	$P = 10$
Optimistic estimate is a best-case estimate.	Provided on exam	O	$O = 4$
Most likely (or realistic) estimate	Provided on exam	M (also could be R, "realistic")	$M = 6$
Slack represents the amount of time (typically days) an activity can be delayed without causing impact.	Slack = LS - ES or LF - EF	Slack (Also called Float)	$6 - 4 = 2$ or $18 - 10 = 8$
Forward pass formula	EF = ES + Duration - 1	EF	$6 + 2 - 1 = 7$ or $EF = 10$
Early Start is the earliest an activity can start	Provided on exam	ES	$ES = 4$
Late Finish is the latest an activity can finish without causing impact	Provided on exam	LF	$LF = 18$
Backward pass formula	LS = LF - Duration + 1	LS	$10 - 5 + 1 = 6$ or $LS = 6$

6.8. Project Schedule Management Terminology

Term	Description
Activity	A unique, scheduled segment of project work that typically has an associated cost, duration, and resources; sometimes called a task
Activity Attributes	The characteristics of an activity that include activity codes, predecessor activities, successor activities, logical relationships, leads and lags, resource requirements, imposed dates, constraints, and assumptions
Activity Duration	The span of time, expressed as calendar units, between a scheduled activity's start and finish
Activity Duration Estimate	The projected duration of an activity
Activity Identifier	A unique number or code used to identify an activity that is used to eliminate confusion with a similarly named activity
Activity List	A listing of scheduled activities, with such details of a description, identifier, and scope of work, used to ensure that team members comprehend the work that will be performed during the project
Activity Network Diagrams	A graphical representation of the interconnectivity of project activities
Activity Resource Requirements	The determination of required resources for each work package and work period that are derived from the determination of required resources for each activity within the work package
Actual Duration	The amount of elapsed time between the start and finish of an activity
Adjusting Leads and Lags	A technique used to align project activities with their scheduled target dates
Analogous Estimating	An estimation technique that relies on data (time, cost, resources needed) from a similar activity or project
Applying Leads and Lags	A technique used to adjust time between activities by applying a lag (lengthening the time) or applying a lead (shortening the time)
Activity-on-arrow (AOA)	A network diagramming method in which activities are represented by arrows and connected at nodes to show their sequences; also known as ADM (arrow diagramming method)
Activity-on-node (AON)	A network diagramming method in which activities are represented by boxes or circles and connected via arrows; also known as PDM (precedence diagramming method)
Backward Pass	A network diagramming method that calculates the late start (LS) and late finish (LF) dates of each activity by working backward through the schedule from the project completion date
Bar Chart	A graphical representation of schedule-related information; typically, schedule activities or work breakdown structure components are displayed vertically on the far left of the chart, dates are displayed horizontally across the top of the chart, and activity durations are displayed as date-placed horizontal bars; also see Gantt chart
BIPERT (Bilogic Extension of the Network Diagram)	A model for parallel programs that depicts ingoing (inclusive) and outgoing (exclusive) links
Bottom-Up Estimating	An estimating technique in which individual estimates are rolled up to create a summary estimate for the project
Buffer	Reserves used to alleviate risks that could negatively impact the budget or schedule
Burst	The separation (or divergence) of activities on a network diagram from a central node
Calendar Unit	The smallest time unit used in project schedules; it could be minutes, hours, shifts, days, weeks, months, quarters

Term	Description
Control Schedule	The process of observing project status in order to revise progress and administer schedule baseline revisions
Crashing	A compression technique to shorten the duration of the schedule, typically by adding additional resources to critical path activities
Critical Chain Method	A technique applied to the schedule so the project team can ascertain the amount of float needed to offset uncertainties or limited resources that appertain to a schedule path
Critical Path	The progression of activities that comprise the longest path through the project; used to ascertain the project duration
Critical Path Activity	An activity on the critical path of a project schedule
Critical Path Method	A technique used to assess minimum project duration and ascertain any schedule adaptability that appertains to logical network paths
Data Date	The point in time when the project data is recorded or monitored
Define Activities	The process of determining specific activities that must be executed in order to create project deliverables
Dependency	The relationship between two activities or between an activity and a milestone, also known as a logical relationship
Dependency Determination	The assignment of logical relationships between activities; logical relationships are designated as mandatory or discretionary and internal or external
Develop Schedule	The process of evaluating the progression and duration of activities, the demands on resources, and the limitations imposed on the schedule to create the model for the project schedule
Discrete Effort	Work that can be directly tied to the completion of WBS components or deliverables; the work must be measurable
Discretionary Dependency	An activity that the project manager (or other decision-maker) arbitrarily chooses to designate as a dependency; for example, making the reservation of a hotel room dependent on the purchase of a plane ticket; also known as soft logic
Dummy Activities	A zero duration activity used in the arrow diagramming method (ADM) to show a logical relationship; represented graphically with an arrow having a dashed line
Duration (DU or DUR)	The time, exclusive of holidays or other days in which business is not conducted and typically measured in workdays or workweeks, required to complete a specific activity or WBS component
Early Finish Date (EF)	The earliest possible date for an activity to be completed based upon the schedule network logic
Early Start Date (ES)	The earliest possible date for an activity to be started based upon the schedule network logic
Effort	The amount of labor (typically measured in hours, days, or weeks) required to complete an activity or WBS component
Estimate	An approximation of an outcome, based on experience or calculation, that is typically applied to cost, effort, or duration and usually contains a modifier (e.g. preliminary) and an accuracy indication (e.g. ±%)
Estimate Activity Durations	The process of approximating the number of work periods required to complete activities in consideration of available resources
Estimate Activity Resources	The process of approximating the amount of people and equipment needed to perform each activity
External Dependency	A relationship between project activities and non-project activities

PMI, CAPM, and PMBOK are registered marks of the Project Management Institute, Inc.

202   © 2008-2018 Crosswind Learning, www.crosswindpm.com

Term	Description
Fast Tracking	A schedule compression technique that results in adjustments to the schedule and is used to perform sequenced activities in parallel as applicable
Finish Date	A point in time related to the completion of a schedule activity and typically qualified as actual, planned, estimated, scheduled, early, late, baseline, target, or current
Finish-to-finish (FF)	A dependency that requires the completion of a predecessor activity prior to the completion of the successor activity
Finish-to-start (FS)	A dependency that requires the completion of a predecessor activity prior to the start of the successor activity
Float	The amount of time an activity can be delayed without delaying successor activities or the project completion date
Forward Pass	A network diagramming method that calculates the early start (ES) and early finish (EF) dates of each activity by working forward through the schedule from the project inception date or a specific point in time
Free Float	The amount of time an activity can be delayed without violating any schedule limitation and without delaying the early start date of successor activities
Gantt Chart	A graphical representation that registers activities on the vertical axis and depicts the activity durations, based on their start and finish dates, on the horizontal axis; also known as a bar chart
Hammock Activity	A group of related activities reported as a single activity, sometimes called a summary activity
Imposed Date	A fixed date exacted on a scheduled activity or milestone, usually formulated as "not to start before" and "not to finish after"
Independent Estimates	The use of estimates created by an independent person or group to support internal project estimates
Lag	The amount of time, predicated on the start or finish of a predecessor activity, a successor activity must be delayed
Late Finish Date (LF)	The latest possible date for an activity to be completed based upon the schedule network logic, the project finish date, and schedule limitations
Late Start Date (LS)	The latest possible date for an activity to be started based upon the schedule network logic, the project finish date, and schedule limitations
Lead	The amount of time, predicated on the start or finish of a predecessor activity, a successor activity can be moved up
Level of Effort (LOE)	An activity that doesn't produce an end product, but is required to support work-related activities or the project and involves a consistent rate of work over time; for example, liaising with the customer or performing administrative duties
Logical Relationship	A connection between two activities, or between an activity and a milestone
Mandatory Dependency	A relationship that is necessitated by virtue of a contractual requirement or the work itself
Master Schedule	A summary timetable that includes significant deliverables, key WBS components, and key milestones
Merge	A coming together (convergence) of activities on a network diagram
Milestone	A meaningful project event typically preceded by a series of activities that lead to its completion
Milestone List	A list of significant events in the project that may be designated as mandatory or optional
Milestone Schedule	A summary timetable that itemizes key milestones
Most Likely Duration	The most probable, or realistic, estimate of elapsed time for an activity based on data from previous projects or expert judgment

Term	Description
Near-critical Activity	Any schedule network diagram activity that is close to zero slack
Network Diagram	A schematic of logical relationships that make up the flow of activities on the project; always drawn from left to right
Network Logic	The assemblage of activity dependencies that constitutes the project schedule network diagram
Network Path	An uninterrupted series of activities depicted in a schedule network diagram and connected by dependencies
Node	A point in a schedule network that is the juncture of some or all dependency lines
Optimistic Duration	The shortest estimate of elapsed time or lowest cost for an activity based on data from previous projects or expert judgment
Parametric Estimating	A technique, effected by a calculation that employs an algorithm, used to determine cost or duration
Path Convergence	A node on a network diagram that indicates the merger of parallel paths; distinguished by an activity with multiple predecessors
Path Divergence	A dependency between a schedule activity and its multiple successors; sometimes called a burst
Percent Complete	The completed work estimate of an activity or WBS component expressed as a percentage
PERT Weighted Average	An estimating technique used to take the pessimistic, optimistic, and realistic (most likely) estimates to achieve a cumulative estimate
Pessimistic Duration	The longest estimate of elapsed time for an activity based on data from previous projects or expert judgment; typically used in three-point or parametric estimates
Plan Schedule Management	The process of creating policies, procedures, and documentation for the planning, executing, and controlling of the project schedule and related documents
Precedence Diagramming Method (PDM)	A technique used to create a schedule model in which activities are represented by nodes and graphically linked by one or more logical relationships in order to display the sequence in which the activities are to be performed
Precedence Relationship	A dependency in the precedence diagramming method; also known as a logical relationship
Predecessor Activity	An activity that logically precedes a successor activity
Program Evaluation and Review Technique (PERT)	An estimation technique, used when individual estimates are questionable, that involves applying a weighted average of optimistic, pessimistic, and most likely estimates
Project Calendar	A calendar that indicates working days and shifts available for project activities
Project Network Diagram	A view of the logical relationship (sequencing) of project activities
Project Schedule	The document, an output of the schedule model, that depicts linked activities with their estimated dates, durations, milestones, and resources
Project Schedule Management	Project schedule management encompasses the processes required to manage the timely conclusion of the project
Project Schedule Network Diagram	A graphical representation of the logical relationships that exist among activities in the project schedule
Resource Breakdown Structure	A representation of resources ranked by category and type

Term	Description
Resource Histogram	A bar chart depicting the amount of time a resource is scheduled to work over a specified number time periods; resource availability and number of resources used may be considered for the purpose of comparison or contrast
Resource Leveling	A technique in which resource constraints dictate start and finish date adjustments in order to balance the demand for resources with the resources available
Resource Optimization Techniques	An approach to resource allocation that adjusts schedule start and finish dates to ensure that resource assignments do not exceed predefined capacity limits resource availability and number of resources used may be considered for the purpose of comparison or contrast
Resource Smoothing	An approach to resource allocation that more uniformly allocates a resource over time; used in cases where resource assignments exceed predefined capacity limits
Rolling Wave Planning	An iterative planning technique that involves detailed planning for near-term work and higher level planning for future work
Schedule Baseline	The authorized version of the schedule model that is used as the basis for comparison and can only be modified through a formal change control procedure
Schedule Compression	Any technique, such as crashing or fast tracking, used to shorten the duration of the schedule while maintaining the project scope
Schedule Data	Information associated with the management of a project schedule
Schedule Forecasts	Estimates, based on current project information, that are associated with future schedule events
Schedule Management Plan	The document, part of the project or program management plan, that authenticates standards and activities used to produce, track, and administer the schedule
Schedule Milestone	A major event in the project schedule; typically involves the start or completion of a major component of the project
Schedule Model	A model which includes activity durations and dependencies, used to produce the project schedule
Schedule Network Analysis	A technique used to determine late start (LS), late finish (LF), early start (ES), and early finish (EF) dates for incomplete schedule activities
Schedule Network Templates	A set of activities and relationships from past projects that meet current project needs
Scheduled Finish Date	The planned finish date for an activity, work package, or other piece of the schedule
Scheduled Start Date	The planned start date for an activity, work package, or other piece of the schedule
Scheduling Tool	A tool that accelerates scheduling by automatically producing activity start and finish dates based on the entry of activities, relationships, resources, and durations
Sequence Activities	The process of determining and recording dependencies between project activities
Start Date	The date work begins on an activity; can include qualifiers such as actual, planned, estimated, scheduled, early, late, target, baseline, and current
Start-to-finish (SF)	A dependency that requires the start of a predecessor activity prior to the completion of the successor activity
Start-to-start (SS)	A dependency that requires the start of a predecessor activity prior to the start of the successor activity
Sub-network	A section of the project schedule diagram, typically a work package or subproject, that is frequently used to depict a proposed schedule condition
Successor Activity	An activity that logically follows its predecessor activity

Term	Description
Summary Activity	An array of related schedule activities aggregated and displayed as a single activity
Target Completion Date (TC)	A requested project completion date that can be a constraint for the project
Target Finish Date (TF)	The date that the project (or activity) is anticipated to be completed
Target Schedule	A preliminary schedule that can be used during initial stages of planning; could differ from the baseline schedule at the conclusion of planning
Target Start Date (TS)	The planned start date of the project or activity
Task	An activity to be completed on the project
Three-Point Estimate	A technique used to evaluate the cost or duration of an activity by averaging the optimistic, pessimistic, and most likely estimates
Time-scaled Schedule Network Diagram	A graphical representation of the project schedule that displays relative to its duration; may include bar charts showing network logic (sequence)
Top-Down Estimating	An estimating technique in which the project manager estimates the cost or duration of the project based on the cost or duration of a previous project that is very similar to the current project
Total Slack (Total Float)	The amount of time an activity can slip (be delayed) from its early start date without delaying the overall finish date

The source for the above definitions is the Glossary of the Project Management Institute,
A Guide to the Project Management Body of Knowledge, (*PMBOK® Guide*) – Sixth Edition, Project Management Institute Inc., 2017

6.9. Project Schedule Management Tests and Exercises

6.9.1. Project Schedule Management Network Diagramming Exercise

Answers are in section 6.10.1. Additional exercises are available at learn.crosswindpm.com.

Exercise - Project A – Moving across the country

Activity A: Get bids on moving company
Activity B: Choose a moving company
Activity C: Go through belongings and decide what to keep and what to sell/give away (This will help ensure that you select a moving company capable of the scope of the job.)
Activity D: Prepare for and do a yard sale for unwanted items
Activity E: Give away unwanted items not sold in yard sale
Activity F: Inventory remaining items
Activity G: Pack remaining items
Activity H: Move

Activity	Preceding Activities	Duration in days
A	Start	9
B	A, C	3
C	Start	13
D	C	9
E	D	2
F	E	10
G	F	11
H	B, G	3

1. Which path is the critical path and what is its duration?

2. What is the slack (float) for Activity B?

3. Which path has the longest (most) slack (float)?

4. What is the slack (float) of the path in question 3?

5. If Activity B slips from three days to six days, what is the critical path?

6. With the duration adjustment in question 5, what is the new slack (float) of Activity B?

6.9.2. Project Schedule Management Practice Test

Answers are in section 6.10.2.

1. Calculate the variance for the following: Pessimistic = 12, Optimistic = 2, Realistic = 5.

    (A) 5
    (B) 2.79
    (C) 5.67
    (D) Not enough information

2. Task C on the project has an ES of day three, an EF of day seven and an LS of day seven. Which of the following best describes this task?

    (A) It has slack (float) of zero days
    (B) It is behind schedule
    (C) It has slack (float) of four days and duration of five days
    (D) It has slack (float) of zero days and duration of four days

3. Which of the following is an example of a lag?

    (A) The latest a new system can be ordered from the manufacturer without delaying the project
    (B) The critical path
    (C) A delay after the sheetrock (wallboard) is done in a house to allow it to dry before continuing work in that area
    (D) The earliest a new system can be ordered from the manufacturer

4. Which of the following best describes the critical path slack (float)?

    (A) It can be the shortest duration on the project
    (B) It can be a positive number or zero
    (C) It can be a negative number or zero
    (D) It can be a positive number, negative number, or zero

5. The project manager is considering resource leveling the schedule to get the project back on track within resource constraints. Which of the following is most likely the project manager's primary concern?

    (A) Tasks could be done in parallel instead of the way intended
    (B) The project team might not be able to assign resources to activities
    (C) The finish date could be pushed out further
    (D) Resources working a more consistent number of hours each day

Chapter 6
Schedule

6. Of the following differences between the activity-on-node diagramming method and the activity-on-arrow diagramming method, which is the most accurate?

(A) The activity-on-arrow method is more modern than the activity-on-node method
(B) The activity-on-arrow method may only have one predecessor type and the activity-on-node method may have four predecessor types
(C) The activity-on-arrow method is a precedence diagramming method and the activity-on-node method is not
(D) The activity-on-arrow method is always used with project scheduling software and the activity-on-node method is manual

7. Sam is a new project manager. He has been assigned to a new website creation project. He is reviewing the schedule with the team. He comes upon a hammock activity in the schedule. Which of the following best describes a hammock activity?

(A) A summary activity with each task listed above it
(B) A summary activity with each task listed beneath it and the details of each task indented beneath that task
(C) An executive activity report
(D) A dummy used in the activity on arrow (AOA) diagrams

8. To improve efficiencies for the technical infrastructure project, the project manager has decided to apply resource leveling while building the schedule. Of the following, which is the best description of what he'll be doing?

(A) Reviewing the logic bar chart to determine the optimal assignment of resources
(B) Obtaining an optimal balance between delivery deadlines and resource utilization
(C) Reviewing a resource allocation chart for peaks and valleys and making adjustments to create a level use of resources
(D) Tracking the day-to-day details of the project so he can reassign resources as needed

9. Of the following, which best describes a milestone schedule?

(A) A high-level schedule that typically accompanies schedule variance reports
(B) A high-level schedule typically prepared for executives
(C) A high-level schedule typically used to determine the critical path
(D) A high-level schedule typically used in daily briefings with the project team

10. Of the following statements about the critical path, which is accurate?

(A) There can only be one critical path per project
(B) If ahead of schedule, a project can have negative slack (float)
(C) The least project risk occurs on the critical path
(D) The critical path is the longest path on the project network diagram

11. The e-commerce project is six weeks behind schedule with five team members working on it. Three of these team members are working on the critical path-related items. What is the slack (float) of the critical path?

(A) Negative six weeks
(B) 30
(C) 0 (Zero)
(D) Not enough information

12. What are the Schedule knowledge area processes?

(A) Plan schedule management, define activities, sequence activities, estimate activity resources, estimate activity durations, create baseline schedule, and control schedule
(B) Plan schedule management, create WBS, define activities, sequence activities, estimate activity durations, develop schedule, and control schedule
(C) Plan schedule management, define activities, create network diagram, estimate activity durations, develop schedule, and control schedule
(D) Plan schedule management, define activities, sequence activities, estimate activity durations, develop schedule, and control schedule

13. Which of the following duration estimate types is most likely to be used where there is minimal information known about the project?

(A) Bottom-up
(B) Parametric
(C) Top-down
(D) Three-point

14. You are the project manager on a defense project and are creating a network diagram. Activity A (3 days) and Activity B (6 days) can start immediately. Activity C (2 days) can start after Activity A is complete. Activity D (1 day) and Activity F (2 days) can start after Activity B is complete. Activity E (4 days) can start after Activity C and Activity D are complete. Activity G (5 days) can start after Activity D and Activity F are complete. When Activity E and Activity G are complete, the project is done. What is the critical path?

    (A) BDE
    (B) ACE
    (C) BFG
    (D) BDG

15. Using the information in question 14, what is the slack (float) of Activity D?

    (A) Two days
    (B) One day
    (C) Four days
    (D) Not enough information

16. Using the information in question 14, if Activity D increases from one to three days, what is the critical path, and what is the length?

    (A) BDE, 13 days
    (B) ACE, 14 days
    (C) BFG, 13 days
    (D) BDG, 14 days

17. Sam, the project manager, is attending project management training at his company. Sam and the trainer are talking about new trends in scheduling and project management. Which of the following best describes what they are most likely discussing?

    (A) On-demand scheduling and critical path scheduling
    (B) Waterfall and Gantt chart scheduling
    (C) Iterative and waterfall scheduling
    (D) Iterative and on-demand scheduling

18. Of the following, which best describes the logic bar chart?

    (A) The ideal tool to view activity sequencing
    (B) A chart that represents high-level activities and their durations
    (C) A chart used to track day-to-day activities
    (D) A chart that represents the logical sequence of high-level activities

19. In defining a milestone, which of the following is most correct?

(A) It defines the phase of a project
(B) It has a duration of no more than one day
(C) It has a duration of zero (0)
(D) It has value in the project charter but not in the plan

20. The project manager and his team have created the schedule for the hospital wireless network upgrade project. They have identified an area in the schedule that requires a five-day delay for certification of the security of the wireless network (after the network is turned on and before the hospital can use the network). Which of the following best describes the five-day delay?

(A) A lag from one activity to another
(B) A lead from one activity to another
(C) The float of the activity
(D) A need to level resources

21. What will the project manager create as a result of the develop schedule process?

(A) Project schedule
(B) Schedule baseline
(C) Schedule baseline and project schedule
(D) Schedule dictionary

22. The construction project is underway after encountering some initial schedule delays associated with the weather. As the team is working on the job site, the city building inspector shows up and asks for their building permit for the next phase. The project manager discovers it wasn't applied for. The city inspector explains it will take a week to process the application after the application is submitted. This is an example of what?

(A) A city employee not wanting to do his job
(B) Discretionary dependency
(C) External mandatory dependency
(D) Mandatory dependency

23. You are estimating the duration of the project and you do not have much information about the overall estimate. Which of the following estimating techniques will you most likely use?

(A) Analogous
(B) Bottom-up
(C) Three-point
(D) Top-down

24. You and a fellow project manager are having a discussion about his project. He says its network diagram has two paths that have the maximum duration of 32 units. He also says there is no critical path because the longest paths are the same length and there can only be one critical path. Which of the following is a true statement?

(A) You can have more than one critical path, but they are the longest paths on the project, and having more than one critical path increases your project risk
(B) The critical path is the shortest path on the project
(C) You can have more than one critical path, but they are the longest paths on the project, and having more than one critical path decreases your project risk
(D) You can have more than one critical path, but they are the shortest paths not the longest

25. You are estimating project duration. You don't have a lot of time to go into detail, so you estimate based on a past project that was similar to the current project. Which of the following estimating techniques is most likely used?

(A) Analogous
(B) Bottom-up
(C) Three-point
(D) Top-down

26. Float is calculated by which of the following?

(A) Late finish - early finish (LF - EF)
(B) Late start - early start (LS - ES)
(C) Late finish - late start (LF - LS)
(D) A and B

27. The project manager is creating an estimate for building a company WAN (wide area network). It is something that is new to the project manager and his team. They decide to create a bottom-up estimate. All the following are advantages of this type of estimate except...

(A) It provides supporting detail of the estimate
(B) It provides team buy-in when they help create it
(C) It takes a great amount of time to create
(D) There is a greater degree of accuracy because of the detail at which it was created

28. The project team is working together on detailed planning. They have had some issues coming to the same opinion, so they are creating a project schedule network diagram. What will this show the team?

(A) The sequencing of the activities on the project
(B) The decomposition of the work of the project
(C) The schedule
(D) The duration estimate of the project

29. The project manager and team have created the schedule for the hospital wireless network upgrade project. The schedule includes a five-day delay for network approval before the hospital can use the upgraded network. This causes the finish date of the project to slip by five days. Which of the following best describes the delay?

(A) A lag from one activity to another
(B) A schedule delay of an item on the critical path
(C) The float of the activity
(D) A need to level resources

30. The project manager is creating an estimate for a data warehouse. This is something he is quite experienced at. The client needs the estimate quickly. Which of the following types of estimates is he likely to provide?

(A) Analogous
(B) Gut feel
(C) Bottom-up
(D) Parametric

6.10. Project Schedule Management Answers for Tests and Exercises

6.10.1. Project Schedule Management Network Diagramming Exercise Answers

Exercise - Project A – Moving across the country - Answers

Activity A: Get bids on moving company
Activity B: Choose a moving company
Activity C: Go through belongings and decide what to keep and what to sell/give away (This will help ensure that you select a moving company capable of the scope of the job)
Activity D: Prepare for and do a yard sale for unwanted items
Activity E: Give away unwanted items not sold in yard sale
Activity F: Inventory remaining items
Activity G: Pack remaining items
Activity H: Move

Activity	Preceding Activities	Duration in days
A	Start	9
B	A, C	3
C	Start	13
D	C	9
E	D	2
F	E	10
G	F	11
H	B, G	3

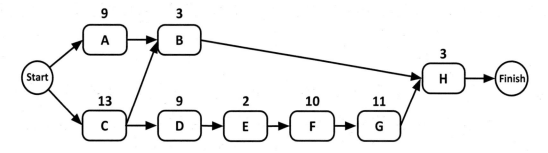

1. Which path is the critical path and what is its duration?

   The paths on the network diagram are as follows.
   A + B + H   9 + 3 + 3 = 15
   C + B + H   13 + 3 + 3 = 19
   C + D + E + F + G + H   13 + 9 + 2 + 10 + 11 + 3 = 48

   The critical path is the longest path; thus, C + D + E + F + G + H is the critical path, and the duration is 48.

2. What is the slack (float) for Activity B?

   Calculate the slack (float) for Activity B by taking the critical path length and subtracting the duration of the longest path that has Activity B in it. This path is C + B + H and the slack (float) for Activity B is 48 - 19 = 29.

3. Which path has the longest (most) slack (float)?

   The shortest path is subtracted from the critical path duration. That is 48 - 15 = 33 which is path A + B + H.

4. What is the slack (float) of the path in question 3?

   The shortest path is subtracted from the critical path duration. That is 48 - 15 = 33.

5. If Activity B slips from three days to six days, what is the critical path?

   Increasing Activity B from three to six days doesn't change the critical path because there are more than three days of slack (float) between every path with B on it. The critical path is still C + D + E + F + G + H for a total of 48.

6. With the duration adjustment in question 5, what is the new slack (float) of Activity B?

   The new slack (float) for Activity B is 26 days. Calculate it by taking the critical path (48 days) and subtracting from it the revised path of C + B + H (22 days), 48 - 22 = 26.

6.10.2. Project Schedule Management Practice Test Answers

We recommend that you download answer sheets from the Crosswind website, so you can practice the test as many times as you like.

1. Calculate the variance for the following: Pessimistic = 12, Optimistic = 2, Realistic = 5.

   Correct Answer: (B) 2.79
   Explanation: The formula for variance is ((Pessimistic - Optimistic) divided by 6)^2 or ((P - O) / 6)^2. The answer is 2.79. [Crosswind Manual 6.8; No *PMBOK® Guide* Reference]

2. Task C on the project has an ES of day three, an EF of day seven and an LS of day seven. Which of the following best describes this task?

   Correct Answer: (C) It has slack (float) of four days and duration of five days
   Explanation: The task has a slack (float) of four days and a duration of five days. The slack (float) is calculated by subtracting the ES of day three from the LS of day seven for a slack (float) of four days. To calculate the duration, do not subtract the early start day from the early finish day. Count the early start day, the early finish day, and each day in between: in this case, count day three, day four, day five, day six, and day seven for a duration of five days. [Crosswind Manual 6.5.9; *PMBOK® Guide* 6.5.2.2]

3. Which of the following is an example of a lag?

   Correct Answer: (C) A delay after the sheetrock (wallboard) is done in a house to allow it to dry before continuing work in that area
   Explanation: A delay after the sheetrock is done to allow it to dry before continuing work in that area is an example of a lag. The delay is not part of either activity but occurs between the activities. The other answers are distracters. [Crosswind Manual 6.3.5; *PMBOK® Guide* 6.3.2.3]

4. Which of the following best describes the critical path slack (float)?

   Correct Answer: (D) It can be a positive number, negative number, or zero
   Slack = total Float
   Explanation: The critical path slack (float) can be any number. Technically the slack (float) of the critical path is zero, but if you are ahead of schedule it is a positive number and if you are behind schedule, it is a negative number. It is actually the longest path on the project, not the shortest. [Crosswind Manual 6.5.4; *PMBOK® Guide* 6.5.2.2]

5. The project manager is considering resource leveling the schedule to get the project back on track within resource constraints. Which of the following is most likely the project manager's primary concern?

   Correct Answer: (C) The finish date could be pushed out further
   Explanation: The item of most concern to the project manager is pushing out the finish date of the project as a result of resource leveling. Resources working a more consistent number of hours each day is a characteristic of resource leveling, but it isn't typically a concern. Doing tasks in parallel relates to fast tracking a schedule. Not being able to assign resources to activities would relate to crashing a schedule. [Crosswind Manual 6.5.11; *PMBOK® Guide* 6.5.2.2]

6.   Of the following differences between the activity-on-node diagramming method and the activity-on-arrow diagramming method, which is the most accurate?

Correct Answer: (B) The activity-on-arrow method may only have one predecessor type and the activity-on-node method may have four predecessor types
Explanation: The activity-on-node method is a precedence diagramming method that may have four predecessor types, is typically used with modern project scheduling software, depicts the activities in boxes connected by arrows, and does not allow dummy activities. The other answers incorrectly attributed modernity, precedence diagramming, and use with project scheduling software to the activity-on-arrow method. [Crosswind Manual 6.3.3; *PMBOK® Guide* 6.3.2.1]

7.   Sam is a new project manager. He has been assigned to a new website creation project. He is reviewing the schedule with the team. He comes upon a hammock activity in the schedule. Which of the following best describes a hammock activity?

Correct Answer: (B) A summary activity with each task listed beneath it and the details of each task indented beneath that task
Explanation: The hammock activity is a summary activity with each task beneath it and the details of each task indented beneath that task. The earliest start (ES) date of the tasks comprising the activity is the start date of the hammock and the last date of the tasks comprising the activity is the final date of the hammock. It can be used for executive reporting, but that isn't the main purpose and there are better tools for that such as a milestone schedule. The AOA answer is a distracter. [Crosswind Manual 6.5.15; *PMBOK® Guide* 6.5.3.2]

8.   To improve efficiencies for the technical infrastructure project, the project manager has decided to apply resource leveling while building the schedule. Of the following, which is the best description of what he'll be doing?

Correct Answer: (C) Reviewing a resource allocation chart for peaks and valleys and making adjustments to create a level use of resources
Explanation: Resource leveling consists of reviewing a resource allocation chart for peaks and valleys and making adjustments to create a level use of resources. Applying resource leveling and schedule compression helps the PM obtain an optimal balance between delivery deadlines and resource utilization. The other answers are distracters. [Crosswind Manual 6.5.11; *PMBOK® Guide* 6.5.2.3]

9.   Of the following, which best describes a milestone schedule?

Correct Answer: (B) A high-level schedule typically prepared for executives
Explanation: A milestone schedule is high-level schedule typically prepared for executives. The milestone schedule records a 0 duration for each milestone. [Crosswind Manual 6.6.14; *PMBOK® Guide* 6.5.3.2]

10.   Of the following statements about the critical path, which is accurate?

Correct Answer: (D) The critical path is the longest path on the project network diagram
Explanation: The critical path is the longest path on the project network diagram. There can be multiple critical paths. If the project is behind schedule, there can be negative slack (float). The greatest project risk occurs along the critical path. [Crosswind Manual 6.5.5; *PMBOK® Guide* 6.5.2.2]

11. The e-commerce project is six weeks behind schedule with five team members working on it. Three of these team members are working on the critical path-related items. What is the slack (float) of the critical path?

Correct Answer: (A) Negative six weeks
Explanation: Technically, a critical path has a slack (float) of zero. If the project is truly behind schedule, and the baseline date is still being used as the reference, the project could actually have negative slack (float) on the critical path. In this case, the negative slack (float) is six weeks. [Crosswind Manual 6.5.4; *PMBOK® Guide* 6.5.2.2]

12. What are the Schedule knowledge area processes?

Correct Answer: (D) Plan schedule management, define activities, sequence activities, estimate activity durations, develop schedule, and control schedule
Explanation: The Schedule processes are Plan Schedule Management, Define Activities, Sequence Activities, Estimate Activity Durations, Develop Schedule, and Control Schedule. [Crosswind Manual Chapter 6 Introduction; *PMBOK® Guide* Chapter 6 Introduction]

13. Which of the following duration estimate types is most likely to be used where there is minimal information known about the project?

Correct Answer: (C) Top-down
Explanation: The top-down estimate, sometimes called an analogous estimate, is an estimate used when there is not a lot of detail. The estimate is based upon overall project characteristics and can be applied when you have past experience in the area. The parametric estimate is used when parameters and quantity are used. For example $2 a square foot for carpet. The three-point estimate is based upon best case, worse case, and realistic estimates. [Crosswind Manual 6.4.1; *PMBOK® Guide* 6.4.2]

14. You are the project manager on a defense project and are creating a network diagram. Activity A (3 days) and Activity B (6 days) can start immediately. Activity C (2 days) can start after Activity A is complete. Activity D (1 day) and Activity F (2 days) can start after Activity B is complete. Activity E (4 days) can start after Activity C and Activity D are complete. Activity G (5 days) can start after Activity D and Activity F are complete. When Activity E and Activity G are complete, the project is done. What is the critical path?

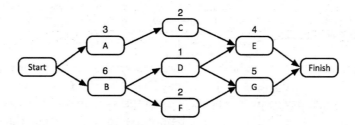

Correct Answer: (C) BFG
Explanation: The critical path is the longest path in the diagram. Of the four paths, BFG is the longest at 13 days. ACE is nine days long. BDE is 11 days. BDG is 12 days. [Crosswind Manual 6.5.8; *PMBOK® Guide* 6.5.2.2]

15. Using the information in question 14, what is the slack (float) of Activity D?

Correct Answer: (B) One day
Explanation: The longest path with Activity D on it is path BDG with a duration of 12 days. The critical path of BFG is 13 days. Subtracting the length of BDG from the critical path (13-12) shows a difference of one day. This is the slack (float) of Activity D. [Crosswind Manual 6.5.8; *PMBOK® Guide* 6.5.2.2]

16. Using the information in question 14, if Activity D increases from one to three days, what is the critical path, and what is the length?

Correct Answer: (D) BDG, 14 days
Explanation: By increasing Activity D from one day to three days the path BDG increases to fourteen days. This is the longest of the paths on the network diagram. [Crosswind Manual 6.5.8; *PMBOK® Guide* 6.5.2.2]

17. Sam, the project manager, is attending project management training at his company. Sam and the trainer are talking about new trends in scheduling and project management. Which of the following best describes what they are most likely discussing?

Correct Answer: (D) Iterative and on-demand scheduling
Explanation: The two most notable trends currently impacting scheduling are iterative scheduling and on-demand scheduling. Iterative scheduling is a type of adaptive project management used to deliver incremental value to the customer during an iteration. On-demand scheduling is an approach, typically used in a Kanban system, used to limit the team's work in progress in order to balance demand against throughput. [Crosswind Manual Chapter 6 Introduction; *PMBOK® Guide* Chapter 6 Trends and Emerging Practices]

18. Of the following, which best describes the logic bar chart?

Correct Answer: (C) A chart used to track day-to-day activities
Explanation: A logic bar chart, sometimes called a Gantt chart, is a common chart used to track the day-to-day details of the project. [Crosswind Chapter 6.5.13; *PMBOK® Guide* 6.5.3.2]

19. In defining a milestone, which of the following is correct?

Correct Answer: (C) It has a duration of zero (0)
Explanation: The milestone has a duration of zero. The milestone is typically used to define the completion of a series of activities. The other answers are distracters. [Crosswind Manual 6.5.14; *PMBOK® Guide* 6.5.3.2]

20. The project manager and his team have created the schedule for the hospital wireless network upgrade project. They have identified an area in the schedule that requires a five-day delay for certification of the security of the wireless network (after the network is turned on and before the hospital can use the network). Which of the following best describes the five-day delay?

Correct Answer: (A) A lag from one activity to another
Explanation: The five-day delay is a requirement. That makes it a lag. A lead is the amount of time a successor activity can be started before its predecessor is complete. Float is also known as slack, but is not applicable in this case. A need to level resources is a distracter. [Crosswind Manual 6.3.5; *PMBOK® Guide* 6.3.2.3]

21. What will the project manager create as a result of the develop schedule process?

Correct Answer: (C) Schedule baseline and project schedule
Explanation: The outputs of the Develop Schedule process are the schedule baseline and the project schedule. Schedule dictionary is a distracter. [Crosswind Manual 6.5; *PMBOK® Guide* 6.5]

22. The construction project is underway after encountering some initial schedule delays associated with the weather. As the team is working on the job site, the city building inspector shows up and asks for their building permit for the next phase. The project manager discovers it wasn't applied for. The city inspector explains it will take a week to process the application after the application is submitted. This is an example of what?

Correct Answer: (C) External mandatory dependency
Explanation: The external mandatory dependency is a required dependency that is outside the organization's control that is required. The building inspector fits this criterion. The mandatory dependency is required and internal to the project. The discretionary dependency is at the option of the project manager and team. The city employee answer is a distracter. [Crosswind Manual 6.3.1; *PMBOK® Guide* 6.3.2.2]

23. You are estimating the duration of the project and you do not have much information about the overall estimate. Which of the following estimating techniques will you most likely use?

Correct Answer: (D) Top-down
Explanation: Answering this question may be difficult since analogous and top-down are very close in meaning. Generally analogous and top-down are thought of as the same. They differ when the top-down estimate doesn't have a lot of detail. The analogous estimate is used when the estimate is based on something you or the company has done before. [Crosswind Manual 6.4.1; *PMBOK® Guide* 6.4.2]

24. You and a fellow project manager are having a discussion about his project. He says the network diagram has two paths that have the maximum duration of 32 units. He also says there is no critical path because the longest paths are the same length and there can only be one critical path. Which of the following is a true statement?

Correct Answer: (A) You can have more than one critical path, but they are the longest paths on the project, and having more than one critical path increases your project risk
Explanation: The critical path is the longest path on the project. If you have more than one path of identical length, you have multiple critical paths. The more of them you have, the riskier the project is. [Crosswind Manual 6.5.5; *PMBOK® Guide* 6.5.2.2]

25. You are estimating project duration. You don't have a lot of time to go into detail, so you estimate based on a past project that was similar to the current project. Which of the following estimating techniques is most likely used?

Correct Answer: (A) Analogous
Explanation: Answering this question may be difficult since analogous and top-down are very close in meaning. Generally analogous and top-down are thought of as the same. They differ when the analogous estimate is used when the estimate is based on something you or the company has done before. The top-down estimate doesn't have a lot of detail. [Crosswind Manual 6.4.1; *PMBOK® Guide* 6.4.2]

26. Float is calculated by which of the following?

(A) Late finish - early finish (LF - EF)
(B) Late start - early start (LS - ES)

Correct Answer: (D) A and B
Explanation: Float is calculated by subtracting either the late finish (LF) from the early finish (EF) or the late start (LS) from the early start (ES). [Crosswind Manual 6.5.9; *PMBOK® Guide* 6.5.2.2]

27. The project manager is creating an estimate for building a company WAN (wide area network). It is something that is new to the project manager and his team. They decide to create a bottom-up estimate. All the following are advantages of this type of estimate except…

Correct Answer: (C) It takes a great amount of time to create
Explanation: All the answers are characteristic of the bottom-up estimate. Taking a great amount of time to create is not an advantage of the estimate. [Crosswind Manual 6.4.1; *PMBOK® Guide* 6.4.2]

28. The project team is working together on detailed planning. They have had some issues coming to the same opinion, so they are creating a project schedule network diagram. What will this show the team?

Correct Answer: (A) The sequencing of the activities on the project
Explanation: The project schedule network diagram shows the sequencing of the activities on the project. The work breakdown structure (WBS) shows the decomposition of the work of the project. The duration estimate of the project comes from the schedule. [Crosswind Manual 6.3.2; *PMBOK® Guide* 6.3.3.1]

29. The project manager and team have created the schedule for the hospital wireless network upgrade project. The schedule includes a five-day delay for network approval before the hospital can use the upgraded network. This causes the finish date of the project to slip by five days. Which of the following best describes the delay?

Correct Answer: (A) A lag from one activity to another
Explanation: Float is also known as slack and in this case it's negative since the schedule finish is delayed by five days. The planned delay is a lag. A lead is the amount of time a successor activity can be shortened based on its predecessor. A need to level resources is a distracter. [Crosswind Manual 6.3.5; *PMBOK® Guide* 6.3.2.3]

PMI, CAPM, and PMBOK are registered marks of the Project Management Institute, Inc.

222 © 2008-2018 Crosswind Learning, www.crosswindpm.com

30. The project manager is creating an estimate for a data warehouse. This is something he is quite experienced at. The client needs the estimate quickly. Which of the following types of estimates is he likely to provide?

Correct Answer: (A) Analogous

Explanation: The analogous estimate is also considered a form of a top-down estimate, can be quickly created because it is based on expert knowledge of an area from previous projects. Parametric is an estimating technique that uses parameters, such as so much time per unit. A bottom-up estimate is created by the team and can take time to create because of the details. Gut feel is a distracter. [Crosswind Manual 6.4.1; *PMBOK® Guide* 6.4.2]

PMI, CAPM, and PMBOK are registered marks of the Project Management Institute, Inc.

224 © 2008-2018 Crosswind Learning, www.crosswindpm.com

Chapter 7

Project Cost Management

Project Cost Management primarily entails the management of costs related to those resources required to complete the work of the project.

A strong secondary consideration is the impact that project decisions could have on the entire product life cycle, specifically the operational costs of the product. For instance, if a decision is made to decrease the time spent on testing, it is likely that support and maintenance costs will increase.

It is important to be aware that project costs may be measured differently, and at different times, by different stakeholders. For instance, acquisition cost may be measured at the time the decision is made, at the time the order is placed, at the time the item is received, or at the time the cost is actually incurred.

Successful performance on the Project Cost Management section of the test requires:

- A familiarity with the basic financial terms and concepts listed in sections 7.1 through 7.9
- A solid understanding of earned value analysis through the utilization of memorization tools and the information in section 7.14
- A knowledge of the basic calculations listed in sections 7.14 and 7.15
- An adherence to the three rules applicable to algebraic formulas
    Rule 1: First, perform any calculations inside parentheses
    Rule 2: Next, perform all multiplications and divisions, working from left to right
    Rule 3: Finally, perform all additions and subtractions, working from left to right

Tailoring

Project tailoring, the manner in which processes of a knowledge area are exercised, is employed to address the distinctive nature of each project. Successful project tailoring is predicated on a careful consideration of:

- Knowledge management
- Estimating and budgeting
- Earned value management
- Use of the Agile approach
- Governance

Agile/Adaptive Environment

Agile methods are typically applied to projects with high degrees of uncertainty and these may not benefit from detailed cost calculations. Instead, estimation methods are utilized to create high-level forecasts of project resource costs.

For projects with high degrees of uncertainty and firm budgets, scope and schedule are typically adjusted rather than cost.

The source for the above text is the Project Management Institute, *A Guide to the Project Management Body of Knowledge*, (*PMBOK® Guide*) – Sixth Edition, Project Management Institute Inc., 2017, Pages 221-224

In this chapter, we discuss the following:

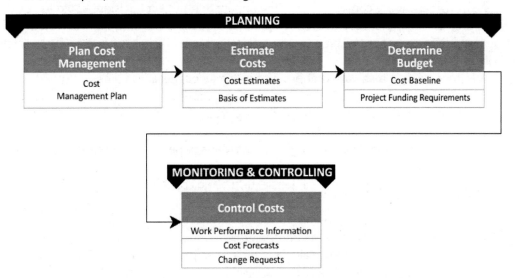

Figure 7-1: Cost Processes

The source for the above figure is the Project Management Institute, *A Guide to the Project Management Body of Knowledge*, (*PMBOK® Guide*) – Sixth Edition, Project Management Institute Inc., 2017, Figure 7-1, Page 222

☑	Crosswind "Must Knows" for Project Cost Management
	Key Inputs, Tools & Techniques, and Outputs for Plan Cost Management
	Key Inputs, Tools & Techniques, and Outputs for Estimate Costs
	Key Inputs, Tools & Techniques, and Outputs for Determine Budget
	Key Inputs, Tools & Techniques, and Outputs for Control Costs
	How to recognize the types of cost and how to differentiate between variable direct, variable indirect, fixed direct, and fixed indirect
	How to recognize cost-based selection techniques: return on investment (ROI), internal rate of return (IRR), net present value (NPV), benefit cost ratio (BCR), opportunity cost, and payback period
	What return on investment (ROI) represents and how it is used in project selection
	What internal rate of return (IRR) represents and how it is used in project selection
	What net present value (NPV) represents and how it is used in project selection
	What benefit cost ratio (BCR) represents and how it is used in project selection
	The principles of opportunity cost

	The principles of the payback period
	The principles of sunk cost
	The characteristics of standard depreciation and accelerated depreciation
	The principles of life cycle costing
	The characteristics and formulas related to earned value management (EVM), cost variance (CV), cost performance index (CPI), to-complete performance index (TCPI), schedule variance (SV), and schedule performance index (SPI)
	Earned value management triangle
	Earned value forecast table
	TCPI - CPI Similarities

Although helpful, this list is not all-inclusive in regard to information needed for the exam. It is only suggested material that, if understood and memorized, may increase your exam score.

7.1. Types of Cost

There are four types of cost on a project: direct, indirect, fixed, and variable. They may be combined by mixing direct or indirect with fixed or variable (e.g. fixed direct cost).

A direct cost is a cost that relates directly to the project. An indirect cost is a cost that does not relate directly to the project.

A fixed cost is a cost that can be consistently forecasted independent of project activity. A variable cost is a cost that changes based on project activity.

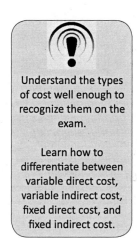

Understand the types of cost well enough to recognize them on the exam.

Learn how to differentiate between variable direct cost, variable indirect cost, fixed direct cost, and fixed indirect cost.

Type	Definition
Direct Cost	Direct cost is cost that is directly attributable to the project and is *incurred **as a result of project work.** An example is the salaries of coders on a software project.
Indirect Cost	Indirect cost is cost that is not directly attributable to the project, but often allocated to the project. Such a cost could be security for the building where the work of the project is performed.
Fixed Cost	Fixed cost is cost that is **consistent throughout the project life cycle regardless of project activity. The leasing of office space for a software project is a fixed cost.**
Variable Cost	Variable cost is cost that **fluctuates with project activity.** The cost of tile for a project to build twenty designer homes fluctuates depending on the materials selected by the homebuyers.

7.2. Cost-based Project Selection Techniques

There are many project selection techniques that can be utilized to ensure that the organization makes prudent selection decisions.

While these techniques are financial, there is no need to take accounting courses or perform a multitude of calculations for the exam.

Recognize the cost-based selection techniques, know what they represent, and know which project to select if given a choice of multiple projects with the particular type of data.

Project Selection Technique Name	Also Known As	Option to elect	Example
Return on Investment	ROI	Largest number or percentage	$50,000 or 7%
Internal Rate of Return	IRR	Largest percentage	15.50%
Net Present Value	NPV	Largest number (years are already factored in)	$47,500
Benefit Cost Ratio	BCR	Largest ratio	3.5:1
Opportunity Cost	---	The value of the opportunity not selected	If Project A ($57,000) is selected rather than Project B ($55,000), the opportunity cost is $55,000
Payback Period	---	Shortest duration	Seven months

(handwritten note, left margin:) The only one → that will need to be calculated

The following table provides shortcuts for memorization and understanding.

Technique	Discussion
Return on Investment (ROI)	Return on investment (ROI) may be calculated using a variety of formulas. In the case of ROI and project selection, typically, select the project with the **largest ROI (number** or **percentage)**.

Know what ROI represents and how it is used in project selection.

PMI, CAPM, and PMBOK are registered marks of the Project Management Institute, Inc.

228 © 2008-2018 Crosswind Learning, www.crosswindpm.com

Technique	Discussion
Internal Rate of Return (IRR)	Often used in capital budgeting, the interest rate makes the **net present value of all cash flow equal to zero**. In the case of IRR and project selection, **select the project with the highest IRR**.
Net Present Value (NPV)	Net present value, used in capital budgeting, is calculated by subtracting the present value of cash inflows from the present value of cash outflows. NPV **compares the value of a dollar today versus the value of that same dollar in the future, after taking inflation and discount rate into account.** Although it's unlikely the exam will ask you to calculate this value, you should know how to select a project based on NPV. For example, if Project A has an NPV of $150,000 and six months and Project B has an NPV of $295,000 and one year, select Project B because it has **the larger NPV AND** the **years are already factored into the dollar amount.** Generally, NPV represents income and expenses over time. If the expenses include capital acquisitions, capital **COULD** be included in NPV functionality.
Benefit Cost Ratio (BCR)	Benefit cost ratio is an analysis technique that compares the **benefit** to the **cost** of the initiative. If the BCR is 3.65:1, the benefits of the project outweigh the costs 3.65 to 1. If a related exam question includes a reference to profit, profit is a distracter. **The benefit, cost, and ratio are the main components.** For example, if a project has a BCR of less than one (0.75:1), each dollar invested only results in a value (benefit) of 75 cents and you would not approve that project. Note that projects that are necessary (e.g. due to regulatory compliance) would be approved despite such a BCR. **Be prepared to calculate a BCR.** Divide revenue by cost and apply the quotient to 1. For example: $200,000 in revenue and $50,000 in cost have a BCR of 4:1.

Know what IRR represents and how it is used in project selection.

Know what net present value (NPV) represents and how it is used in project selection.

Understand and know how to calculate the benefit cost ratio (BCR).

Chapter 7
Cost

Technique	Discussion
Opportunity Cost	**Opportunity cost is the cost of taking one opportunity over another.** It is the cost of the opportunity that is not selected (the opportunity left on the table). For example, if a person accepts a $75,000 a year job in lieu of a $60,000 a year job, the opportunity cost of taking the $75,000 job is $60,000.
Payback Period	Payback period is the **amount of time needed to earn back the original investment.** If the payback period is the priority, select the project with the **shortest payback period**.

Know the principles of opportunity cost.

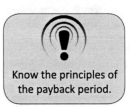

Know the principles of the payback period.

7.3. Future Value (FV)

Future value is the value of something at a specific point in the future.

The certification candidate should focus on understanding the concept of future value, rather than the calculation. As an example: to produce the desired amount in the future, would the future value of the money at a certain interest rate require more or less money than the current amount? It's reasonable to expect a question with an incomplete formula (missing one or more components). In that case, "not enough information" is the best answer.

The future value formula shown below has four variables, with PV representing the present value, r representing the interest rate, n representing the number of periods, and FV representing the future value.

$$FV = PV \times (1 + r)^n \qquad \text{For Example, } \$1,000 \times (1 + 0.08)^3 = \$1,259.71$$

7.4. Present Value (PV)

Present value is the amount that must be invested today to realize an expected value in the future.

The candidate should focus on understanding the concept of present value, rather than the calculation. It's reasonable to expect a question with an incomplete formula (missing one or more components). In that case, "not enough information" is the best answer.

The present value formula, shown below, has four variables with PV representing the present value, r representing the interest rate, n representing the number of periods, and FV representing the future value.

$$PV = \frac{FV}{(1+r)^n} \qquad \text{For Example, } \$1984.58 = \frac{\$2500}{(1+0.08)^3}$$

PMI, CAPM, and PMBOK are registered marks of the Project Management Institute, Inc.

230 © 2008-2018 Crosswind Learning, www.crosswindpm.com

NOTE: The Project Management Institute, Inc. uses PV to represent both present value and planned value. Present value is used to measure an investment; planned value is used with earned value management to measure the amount of work that should have been done at a specific point of time on the project.

7.5.   Sunk Cost

Sunk cost represents the cost that has already been spent on a project.

Sunk cost is not considered when making future project decisions. For example: if a project has a budget of $175,000 and has already spent $200,000, the $200,000 is not a consideration in deciding if the project should be continued.

Know the principles of sunk cost.

7.6.   Depreciation

Depreciation is the process of devaluing a capital asset in the tax system. Capital assets are those that are purchased and depreciated over time. Examples of capital assets include office equipment, vehicles, and technology infrastructure. When using depreciation over a period of time (schedule), an asset's worth decreases until it has no value or a predefined value at the end of its depreciation schedule. Generally, calculating depreciation is complicated, involving tables, formulas, and more.

Know what standard depreciation and accelerated depreciation are.

Although the exam does not involve any complex calculations related to depreciation, it is important that the candidate understands standard depreciation and accelerated depreciation and knows how to calculate a basic depreciation situation.

7.6.1.   Standard Depreciation (Straight Line Depreciation)

Standard depreciation is a simple calculation. To calculate standard depreciation for the exam, the candidate must know:

- The initial value or purchase price of the item being depreciated
- The scrap value of the item being depreciated
- The depreciation timeframe

One example is a $5,000 video editing system that has a five-year depreciation schedule with a scrap value of $0. To determine the annual depreciation, the value of the item being depreciated must be divided by the number of years it will depreciate: $5,000 / 5 = $1,000 annual depreciation.

Another example is a $10,000 copier that has a four-year depreciation schedule with a scrap value of $2,000. Since the full initial value or purchase price will not be depreciated, the amount that will be depreciated must be established: $10,000 - $2,000 = $8,000. Then the amount being depreciated must be divided by the number of years it will depreciate: $8,000 / 4 = $2,000 annual depreciation.

7.6.2. Accelerated Depreciation

Accelerated depreciation is a little more complex and generally requires tables of data to calculate.

The candidate needs to know that there are two main types of accelerated depreciation:

- Sum of the year's digits
- Double declining balance (DDB)

Accelerated depreciation does what its name implies; it **depreciates faster than standard depreciation.**

7.7. Life Cycle Costing (Total Cost of Ownership)

Know the principles of life cycle costing.

Life cycle costing (sometimes called Total Cost of Ownership or TCO) is the process of examining all costs associated with a project plus the product's operational costs (operational costs are costs associated with production, maintenance, and support of the product once the project is closed).

It is very important to consider the total cost of ownership when developing a project strategy. To decrease operational costs and/or extend the life of the product, it may be necessary to increase project costs.

As an example, the project was created to produce an electric automobile. A necessary component cannot be produced in-house. One vendor charges $50,000 to create a prototype of the component, and then charges $2,000 per component. Another vendor does not charge for the prototype, but charges $4,000 per component. The vendor with the higher upfront cost, but lower unit cost, is actually the more responsible choice because the organization will recognize a cost savings if at least 26 components will be produced.

	25 Devices	30 Devices
Vendor A	25 x $2,000 + $50,000 = $100,000	30 x $2,000 + $50,000 = $110,000
Vendor B	25 x $4,000 = $100,000	30 x $4,000 = $120,000

7.8. Fixed Formula Progress Reporting (Earned Value Rules)

Fixed formula progress reporting (sometimes called earned value rules) is a technique that creates a consistent status report for project activities. Instead of having a "gut feel" for the percentage of completion from each person on a project, this type of reporting is essentially binary. The project planning process defines the split of the percentages (for example, 25%/75% or 50%/50%). This process works as follows: when an activity starts, it receives the initial percentage (for example, 25%). It receives the remaining percentage (for example, 75%) only when the activity is complete, thereby reporting 100% completion of the activity. Then, as the summary activities are rolled up to create cumulative percentages, they are based on the (as an example) 0%, 25%, or 100% status of each activity.

This formula can be used for earned value management (EVM) or other less evolved means of capturing the schedule status. Typically, it is used on shorter duration activities or those generally **not exceeding two reporting periods.**

7.9. Weighted Milestone

The weighted milestone approach is utilized for activities that typically are **longer than two reporting periods**.

For the weighted milestone approach, the work is divided into multiple milestones with a measurable output for each section of work and fixed formula progress reporting is applied to each milestone.

7.10. Plan Cost Management (Planning Process Group)

The Plan Cost Management process is used to create the cost management plan.

The cost management plan can be formal or relaxed and provides guidance for selecting the methods that will be used to establish and modify cost estimates, budget, performance baseline, and control thresholds. It also establishes the appropriate degree of detail that will be applied to the budget. The cost management plan is part of the project management plan.

Know the Key Inputs, Tools & Techniques, and Outputs for Plan Cost Management.

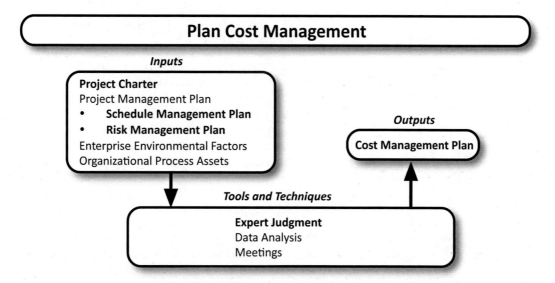

Figure 7-2: Plan Cost Management Data Flow Diagram

The source for the above figure is the Project Management Institute, *A Guide to the Project Management Body of Knowledge*, (*PMBOK® Guide*) – Sixth Edition, Project Management Institute Inc., 2017, Figure 7-2, Page 224

Plan Cost Management (Planning)		
Key Inputs	Project Charter	The project charter is the document that provides authorization for the existence of the project and gives the project manager the power to use organizational resources to execute the project. The project charter typically lists the key deliverables, the milestones, and the roles and responsibilities of each person involved in the project. It details preapproved resources used to elaborate detailed project costs and defines project approval requirements impacting cost administration. Note that the high level assumptions and constraints listed in the business case are often included in the charter. An assumption is an idea or statement taken to be true even though it is not known to be true. As an example, the statement "there will be a robust market for the product created as a result of this project once it is available to the public" is an assumption. A constraint is a restrictive or limiting factor. As an example, the operations manager insistence that a key subject matter expert must dedicate at least six hours a day to operations is a constraint on the project.
	Schedule Management Plan	The schedule management plan is a component of the project management plan that details the delineation, evolution, monitoring, and control of the schedule. It documents the standards and processes that will evolve, monitor, and control the schedule. It also delineates scheduling methodology, the degree of expected accuracy needed to estimate the duration of the scheduled activities, the mechanism used to produce the schedule, and the manner in which the schedule will be calculated.
	Risk Management Plan	The risk management plan is a component of the project management plan that details the manner in which risk management activities are configured and implemented. Typically it addresses risk strategy, risk methodology, roles and responsibilities, financing, timing, and classification. It documents processes and controls that influence the estimation and administration of cost.

Plan Cost Management (Continued)		
Key Tools & Techniques	Expert Judgment	Expert judgment is judgment based on expertise acquired in a specific area. It is often more significant and accurate than the best modeling tools available and can be provided by stakeholders, company personnel external to the project, professional organizations or groups, and consultants. It is important to consider expertise related to authoritative information in cost estimation and financial administration, earned value management, and similar projects.
Key Outputs	Cost Management Plan	The cost management plan is a component of the project management plan that details the manner in which project costs are planned, configured, and controlled. It documents the processes and tools that will used to manage project costs. Typically, it addresses metrics, the establishment of earned value management techniques, the junctures in the work breakdown structure (WBS) used to measure control accounts, acceptable cost performance variances, reporting configurations, satisfactory levels of accuracy (range) and precision (rounding), and the unique codes that associate the control accounts to the organization's accounting system.

Situational Question and Real World Application
Failure to effectively perform the Plan Cost Management process can result in the project manager spending money without established controls or guidance, leading to inconsistency. Additionally, the project would likely fail to align with other projects at the company, which is critical to effective program and portfolio management.

7.10.1. Cost Management Plan

The cost management plan helps the project manager and team do the following:

- Establish the cost of activities and work packages on the project
- Establish the cost accounts and the procedures necessary to use the chart of accounts with the WBS and schedule
- Establish policies associated with updating the budget and distribution of the budget through the work of the project
- Update actual costs and adjust the cost baseline
- Establish the policies and procedures for changes to cost

The cost management plan can be used to establish:

- Level of accuracy
- Units of measure
- Organizational procedures links, which includes control account (CA) links to the project WBS and company accounting system
- Control thresholds
- Reporting of cost performance

The source for the above text is the Project Management Institute, *A Guide to the Project Management Body of Knowledge*, (*PMBOK® Guide*) – Sixth Edition, Project Management Institute Inc., 2017, Pages 224-228

7.11. Estimate Costs (Planning Process Group)

The Estimate Costs process is vital because the accuracy of cost estimates directly impacts the likelihood that a project does not exceed its budget. The focus is on establishing the costs of either the work packages or the activities in order to establish the total project cost.

Know the Key Inputs, Tools & Techniques, and Outputs for Estimate Costs.

There are a number of cost estimating methods that can be used to establish activity cost estimates:

- Analogous (comparison to a previous, similar project)
- Parametric (parameters for building the estimate)
- Bottom-up (estimates of individual items that are added together to establish a total cost estimate)
- Computerized tools

Depending on what is known about the scope of the project, the choice of method can be influenced by schedule, resources, and risk.

PMI, CAPM, and PMBOK are registered marks of the Project Management Institute, Inc.

236   © 2008-2018 Crosswind Learning, www.crosswindpm.com

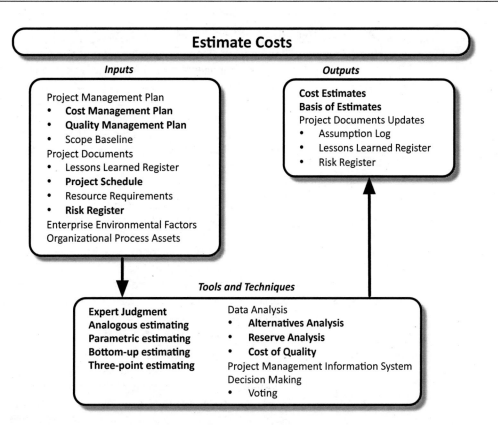

Estimate Costs

Inputs

Project Management Plan
- **Cost Management Plan**
- **Quality Management Plan**
- Scope Baseline

Project Documents
- Lessons Learned Register
- **Project Schedule**
- Resource Requirements
- **Risk Register**

Enterprise Environmental Factors
Organizational Process Assets

Outputs

Cost Estimates
Basis of Estimates
Project Documents Updates
- Assumption Log
- Lessons Learned Register
- Risk Register

Tools and Techniques

Expert Judgment
Analogous estimating
Parametric estimating
Bottom-up estimating
Three-point estimating

Data Analysis
- **Alternatives Analysis**
- **Reserve Analysis**
- **Cost of Quality**

Project Management Information System
Decision Making
- Voting

Figure 7-3: Estimate Costs Data Flow Diagram

The source for the above figure is the Project Management Institute, *A Guide to the Project Management Body of Knowledge*, (*PMBOK® Guide*) – Sixth Edition, Project Management Institute Inc., 2017, Figure 7-2, Page 224

Estimate Costs (Planning)		
Key Inputs	Cost Management Plan	The cost management plan is a component of the project management plan that details the manner in which project costs are planned, configured, and controlled. It documents the processes and tools that will used to manage project costs. Typically, it addresses metrics, the establishment of earned value management techniques, the junctures in the work breakdown structure (WBS) used to measure control accounts, acceptable cost performance variances, reporting configurations, satisfactory levels of accuracy (range) and precision (rounding), and the unique codes that associate the control accounts to the organization's accounting system.

Estimate Costs (Continued)		
Key Inputs (Cont.)	Quality Management Plan	The quality management plan is a component of the project management plan that details the manner in which the policies, methods, and criteria of the organization are executed. It details activities and necessary resources to accomplish quality goals. Typically the plan addresses quality criteria, roles and responsibilities, tools, objectives, and procedures (including those for continuous improvement). It also identifies the processes and deliverables subject to quality review.
	Project Schedule	The project schedule is the product of a schedule model containing linked activities and their planned dates, durations, milestones, and resources. Duration estimates impact cost estimates when resources fluctuate seasonally and are changed based on unit of time. Useful data can be obtained from the schedule in cases where the cost of financing, such as interest charges, is included in the project.
	Risk Register	The risk register documents identified project risks. The volume of documentation varies in accordance with the size and complexity of the project. Typically the risk register includes the list of risks sufficiently described to ensure clear-cut understanding, the risk owner for each risk, and the response(s) for each risk.
Key Tools & Techniques	Expert Judgment	Expert judgment is judgment based on expertise acquired in a specific area. It is often more significant and accurate than the best modeling tools available and can be provided by stakeholders, organizational personnel external to the project, professional organizations or groups, and consultants. It is important to consider expertise related to authoritative information in cost estimation and financial administration, earned value management, and similar projects.
	Analogous Estimating	Analogous estimating is a high-level estimation technique based on historical duration or cost data from a similar activity or project. The technique adjusts for known variances in complexity from the current activity or project under consideration and the historical activity or project. Analogous estimating is typically used to estimate a value or values in projects where there is a limited amount of detailed data. It can be used to estimate the entire project or a portion of the project. While this technique costs less and is not as time consuming as more detailed techniques, it is typically not as accurate.

Estimate Costs (Continued)		
Key Tools & Techniques (Cont.)	Parametric Estimating	Parametric estimating is an estimation technique in which an algorithm is used to calculate duration or cost based on historical duration or cost data and other variables from a similar activity or project. The quantitative technique uses a mathematical relationship between historical data and other variables. Parametric estimating can be used to estimate the entire project or a portion of the project. The accuracy of this technique is dependent on the underlying model.
	Bottom-up Estimating	Bottom-up estimating is an estimation technique in which duration or cost is determined by rolling up estimates of each WBS component of the item being estimated. The size and complexity of the item being estimated impacts the cost and accuracy of the estimation.
	Three-point Estimating	Three-point estimating is an estimation technique in which the range for activity duration is averaged based on pessimistic, optimistic, and realistic (most likely) estimates. The triangular distribution formula is often used if the historical data is insufficient and the beta distribution formula is often used when the historical data is sufficient. **Three-point estimating, unlike PERT estimating, does not apply a weighted average.**
	Alternatives Analysis	Alternatives analysis is a technique utilized to assess the most appropriate options to execute the work of the project. Some examples are renting a resource rather than purchasing it, purchasing off the shelf software rather than programming an application in-house, and utilizing a vendor to perform new equipment installation instead of in-house technicians.
	Reserve Analysis	Reserve analysis is used to determine the amount of contingency and management reserves required for the project. By analyzing the known unknowns (identified risks, typically with mitigation plans), contingency reserves can be determined to account for budget uncertainties and are included in the cost baseline and project funding requirements. Management reserves are budget reserves set aside to account for unknown unknowns (unforeseen work within the scope of the project). They are part of the overall project budget and are considered in the funding requirements. Funds in the management reserve are not included in the cost baseline until they are used for unforeseen work.

Estimate Costs (Continued)		
Key Tools & Techniques (Cont.)	Cost of Quality	The cost of quality (COQ) considers **preventative costs** (costs associated with preventing unsatisfactory quality), **appraisal costs** (costs associated with evaluation and testing), and/or **failure costs** (costs associated with failure to meet stakeholder expectations) that relate to the result of the project (products, deliverables, and services). The cost of prevention and appraisal should be compared to the cost of failure in order to achieve the optimal balance. Models demonstrate that investing in additional prevention/appraisal is not cost effective.
Key Outputs	Cost Estimates	Cost estimates include quantitative estimates of work completion costs, contingency reserves for identified risks, and management reserves for unidentified work. The estimates consider all resources involved including direct labor, equipment, material, facilities, exchange rates, information technology, financing costs, inflation allowance, and/or a cost contingency reserve.
	Basis of Estimates	The basis of estimates for costs includes documentation that delineates the manner in which the estimates were determined, lists all assumptions and constraints, identifies the range of estimates used and the degree of certainty associated with those estimates, and details individual project risks that impacted those estimates.

[handwritten note in left margin: look at PMBOK pg. 283 Cost of quality table - cost of conformance - cost of non-conformance]

Situational Question and Real World Application
Failure to effectively perform the Estimate Costs process can result in project termination if there is a funding shortfall or if a subsequent cost analysis shows that the project is operating with an unacceptable profit margin. Alternatively, the project could be subject to delays due to uncertainty about obtaining funding for the resources necessary to complete the project in a timely fashion.

7.12. Cost Range

Cost range tolerance varies from company to company. A key principle in any environment is that the less that is known (earlier in the project), the wider the tolerance of the cost range should be (compared to when more is known later in the project when the range is minimized).

To align with the new project management standards, the candidate must know that, during **initiation, a tolerance range for a rough order of magnitude (ROM) estimate could be -25% to +75%**, and as the project work evolves into **execution, the tolerance could narrow to -5% to +10%.**

PMI, CAPM, and PMBOK are registered marks of the Project Management Institute, Inc.

240 © 2008-2018 Crosswind Learning, www.crosswindpm.com

Figure 7-4: Cost Funnel depicts a "rough order of magnitude estimate" and a "**definitive** estimate," sometimes referenced as a "**control** estimate."

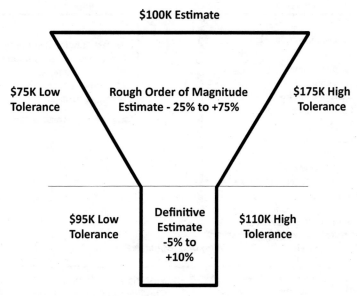

$100K Estimate

| $75K Low Tolerance | Rough Order of Magnitude Estimate - 25% to +75% | $175K High Tolerance |

| $95K Low Tolerance | Definitive Estimate -5% to +10% | $110K High Tolerance |

Figure 7-4: Cost Funnel

The rough order of magnitude estimate occurs at the start, or the top of, the project. It has the widest tolerance. The final definitive (or control) estimate occurs at the end, or the bottom, of the project. It has the least tolerance.

If a project has a $100,000 estimate (assuming it didn't change as it went through the estimating process), the rough order of magnitude tolerance is $75,000 to $175,000. The definitive (or control) estimate tolerance is $95,000 to $110,000.

The source for the above text is the Project Management Institute, *A Guide to the Project Management Body of Knowledge*, (PMBOK® Guide) – Sixth Edition, Project Management Institute Inc., 2017, Pages 228-235

7.13. Determine Budget (Planning Process Group)

During the Determine Budget process, the primary activity is rolling up the cost estimates for the activities or work packages to create a total project budget amount that will serve as the cost baseline.

Know the Key Inputs, Tools & Techniques, and Outputs for Determine Budget.

A detailed estimate of the project cost, as well as its individual pieces, is the result of this process.

The cost baseline created at this point should include a time-based approach to determine project cost needs as time passes. It establishes the basis for measuring, monitoring, and controlling project cost.

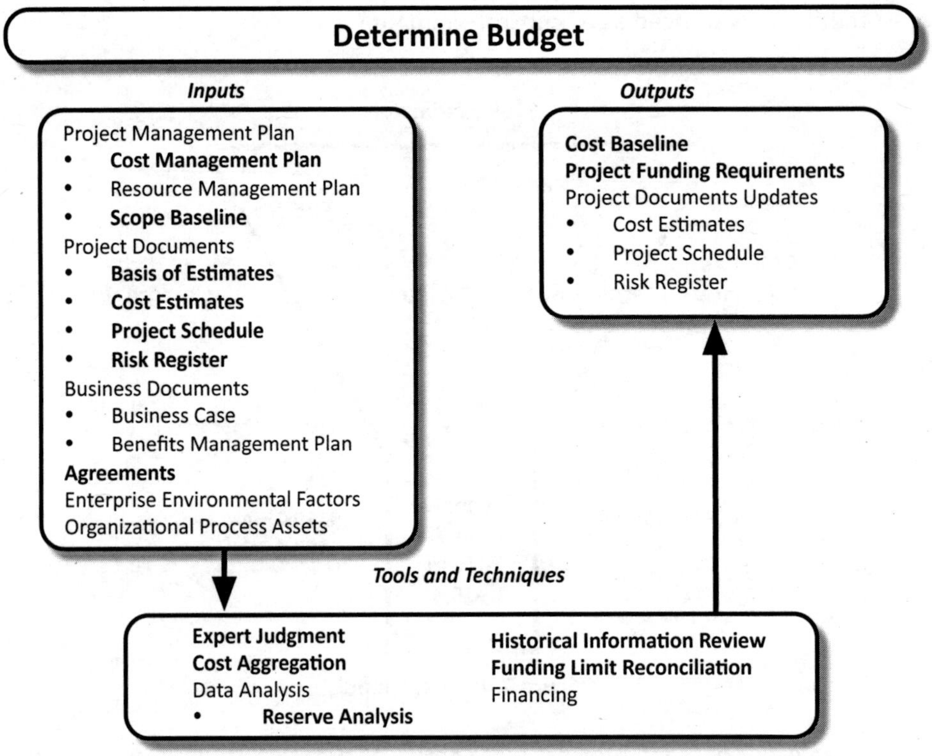

Determine Budget

Inputs

Project Management Plan
- **Cost Management Plan**
- Resource Management Plan
- **Scope Baseline**

Project Documents
- **Basis of Estimates**
- **Cost Estimates**
- **Project Schedule**
- **Risk Register**

Business Documents
- Business Case
- Benefits Management Plan

Agreements
Enterprise Environmental Factors
Organizational Process Assets

Outputs

Cost Baseline
Project Funding Requirements
Project Documents Updates
- Cost Estimates
- Project Schedule
- Risk Register

Tools and Techniques

Expert Judgment
Cost Aggregation
Data Analysis
- **Reserve Analysis**

Historical Information Review
Funding Limit Reconciliation
Financing

Figure 7-5: Determine Budget Data Flow Diagram

The source for the above figure is the Project Management Institute, *A Guide to the Project Management Body of Knowledge*, (*PMBOK® Guide*) – Sixth Edition, Project Management Institute Inc., 2017, Figure 7-6, Page 236

Determine Budget (Planning)		
Key Inputs	Cost Management Plan	The cost management plan is a component of the project management plan that details the manner in which project costs are planned, configured, controlled, and structured into the budget. It documents the processes and tools that will used to manage project costs. Typically, it addresses metrics, the establishment of earned value management techniques, the junctures in the work breakdown structure (WBS) used to measure control accounts, acceptable cost performance variances, reporting configurations, satisfactory levels of accuracy (range) and precision (rounding), and the unique codes that associate the control accounts to the organization's accounting system.

PMI, CAPM, and PMBOK are registered marks of the Project Management Institute, Inc.

242

© 2008-2018 Crosswind Learning, www.crosswindpm.com

		Determine Budget (Continued)
Key Inputs (Cont.)	Scope Baseline	The scope baseline is the authorized version of project scope. It contains the project scope statement, the work breakdown structure (WBS), the work package, one or more planning packages, and the WBS dictionary. It describes the work the project is trying to complete. The baseline is subject to change management and is a component of the project management plan.
	Basis of Estimates	The basis of estimates for costs includes documentation that delineates the manner in which the estimates were determined, lists all assumptions (including those associated with the inclusion or exclusion of indirect costs in the budget) and constraints, identifies the range of estimates used and the degree of certainty associated with those estimates, and details individual project risks that impacted those estimates.
	Cost Estimates	Cost estimates include quantitative estimates of work completion costs, contingency reserves for identified risks, and management reserves for unidentified work. The estimates consider all resources involved including direct labor, equipment, material, facilities, exchange rates, information technology, financing costs, inflation allowance, and/or a cost contingency reserve. Note that estimates for each activity in a work package are totaled to determine the cost estimate for the work package.
	Project Schedule	The project schedule is the product of a schedule model containing linked activities and their planned dates, durations, milestones, and resources. The schedule data can be used to determine costs that will be incurred during a specific calendar period.
	Risk Register	The risk register documents identified project risks. The volume of documentation varies in accordance with the size and complexity of the project. Typically the risk register includes the list of risks sufficiently described to ensure clear-cut understanding, the risk owner for each risk, and the response(s) for each risk. The register, along with any updates, should be considered to determine the total costs related to risk responses.

Determine Budget (Continued)		
Key Inputs (Cont.)	Agreements	Agreements define project intentions and can be written (such as letters of agreements, contracts, memorandum of understanding, service level agreements, and email) or verbal. For work to be performed by an external source, a contract between buyer and seller is typically used. The related costs are determined for aggregation into the budget.
Key Tools & Techniques	Expert Judgment	Expert judgment is judgment based on expertise acquired in a specific area. It is often more significant and accurate than the best modeling tools available and can be provided by stakeholders, organizational personnel external to the project, professional organizations or groups, and consultants. It is important to consider expertise related to financing principals, funding requirements, funding sources, and similar projects.
	Cost Aggregation	Cost aggregation is the process of collecting individual cost estimates into a whole. Specifically, cost estimates are aggregated by work packages, then into higher components (typically monitored by control accounts) of the work breakdown structure (WBS), and then for the entire project.
	Reserve Analysis	Reserve analysis is used to determine the amount of contingency and management reserves required for the project. By analyzing the known unknowns (identified risks, typically with mitigation plans), contingency reserves can be determined to account for budget uncertainties and are included in the cost baseline and project funding requirements. Management reserves are budget reserves set aside to account for unknown unknowns (unforeseen work within the scope of the project). They are part of the overall project budget and are considered in the funding requirements. Funds in the management reserve are not included in the cost baseline until they are used for unforeseen work.
	Historical Information Review	Review of historical information can be used to develop parametric or analogous estimates. Historical information may include project characteristics to evolve mathematical models to forecast total project costs. The models may be simple or complex with varied cost and accuracy. The most reliable models depend on the accuracy of the historical data, easily quantifiable parameters, and scalable (applicable to any project size or phase) models.

PMI, CAPM, and PMBOK are registered marks of the Project Management Institute, Inc.

244 © 2008-2018 Crosswind Learning, www.crosswindpm.com

Determine Budget (Continued)		
Key Tools & Techniques (Cont.)	Funding Limit Reconciliation	Funding limit reconciliation consists of accommodating the expenditure of funds to established funding limits for a specific period of time. Any variances between expenditures and funding limits can result in rescheduling work. To prevent this, any date constraints for work should be included in the work schedule.
Key Outputs	Cost Baseline	The cost baseline is the authorized version of the time-phased budget for the project, excluding management reserves, and is subject to change control. It is evolved from a summation of approved budgets for specific schedule activities. Cost estimates are aggregated by work packages, then into higher components of the work breakdown structure (WBS), and then for the entire project. Because the cost estimates included in the cost baseline are linked to schedule activities, a time-phased view of the cost baseline is enabled. It is usually depicted as an S-curve. If the project uses earned value management (EVM), the cost baseline is known as the performance measurement baseline. The budget consists of the cost baseline plus the management reserves.
	Project Funding Requirements	Project funding requirements, both total and periodic, are extrapolated from the cost baseline (forecasted costs plus expected liabilities). Funding sources may also be documented. Total funds required are determined by adding the funds included in the cost baseline to the management reserves.

Situational Question and Real World Application

Failure to effectively execute the Determine Budget process is likely to result in cost overruns. An alternate possibility is that the project could be delayed due to a lack of funds needed to acquire equipment or materials necessary for the project.

7.13.1.   Chart of Accounts

A chart of accounts is a list of accounts used by the organization's accounting and/or project management system to establish and track budgets associated with work packages, projects, and other efforts that require defining a cost baseline and tracking actual cost against it. The Determine Budget process uses the chart of accounts to show where funds are allocated for the estimated work.

7.13.2. Code of Accounts

A code of accounts is a numbering system that is applied to identify individual pieces of work in the work breakdown structure.

For example, 2.3.2.5.17.4 could represent a piece of work six layers deep in a WBS.

The source for the above text is the Project Management Institute, *A Guide to the Project Management Body of Knowledge*, (*PMBOK® Guide*) – Sixth Edition, Project Management Institute Inc., 2017, Pages 235-242

7.14. Control Costs (Monitoring and Controlling Process Group)

Control Costs focuses on how to control any project budget changes and can involve influencing and managing changes related to cost, managing cost levels compared to the baseline, analyzing and managing cost variance, documenting cost records, and communicating with stakeholders regarding cost issues. Tools used during Control Costs typically include a cost change control system, earned value management (EVM), and computerized tools.

Know the Key Inputs, Tools & Techniques, and Outputs for Control Costs.

Control Costs

Inputs

Project Management Plan
- **Cost Management Plan**
- **Cost Baseline**
- Performance Measurement Baseline

Project Documents
- Lessons Learned Register

Project Funding Requirements
Work Performance Data
Organizational Process Assets

Outputs

Work Performance Information
Cost Forecasts
Change Requests
Project Management Plan Updates
- Cost Management Plan
- **Cost Baseline**
- Performance Measurement Baseline

Project Document Updates
- Assumption Log
- Basis of Estimates
- Cost Estimates
- Lessons Learned Register
- Risk Register

Tools and Techniques

Expert Judgement
Data Analysis
- **Earned Value Analysis**
- **Variance Analysis**
- **Trend Analysis**
- **Reserve Analysis**

To-complete Performance Index
Project Management Information System

Figure 7-6: Control Costs Data Flow Diagram

The source for the above figure is the Project Management Institute, *A Guide to the Project Management Body of Knowledge*, (*PMBOK® Guide*) – Sixth Edition, Project Management Institute Inc., 2017, Figure 7-10, Page 242

Control Costs (Monitoring and Controlling)		
Key Inputs	Cost Management Plan	The cost management plan is a component of the project management plan that details the manner in which project costs are planned, configured, and controlled. It documents the processes and tools that will be used to manage project costs. Typically, it addresses metrics, the establishment of earned value management techniques, the junctures in the work breakdown structure (WBS) used to measure control accounts, acceptable cost performance variances, reporting configurations, satisfactory levels of accuracy (range) and precision (rounding), and the unique codes that associate the control accounts to the organization's accounting system.
	Cost Baseline	The cost baseline is the authorized version of the time-phased budget for the project, excluding management reserves, and is subject to change control. It is compared to actual results to determine the necessity of a modification, corrective measure, or preventative measure. It is evolved from a summation of approved budgets for specific schedule activities. Cost estimates are aggregated by work packages, then into higher components of the work breakdown structure (WBS), and then for the entire project. Because the cost estimates included in the cost baseline are linked to schedule activities, a time-phased view of the cost baseline is enabled. It is usually depicted as an S-curve. If the project uses earned value management (EVM), the cost baseline is known as the **performance measurement baseline**. The budget consists of the cost baseline plus the management reserves.
	Project Funding Requirements	Project funding requirements, both total and periodic, are extrapolated from the cost baseline (forecasted costs plus expected liabilities). Funding sources may also be documented. Total funds required are determined by adding the funds included in the cost baseline to the management reserves.
	Work Performance Data	Work performance data represents the raw metrics and observations identified during the performance of project work activities. It includes facts related to project status, specifically costs that have been sanctioned, incurred, billed, and paid.

Control Costs (Continued)		
Key Tools & Techniques	Earned Value Analysis	Earned value analysis (EVA) is used to compare the performance management baseline to the actual schedule and cost performance. Earned value management (EVM) integrates the scope baseline with the cost baseline and schedule baseline to produce the performance measurement baseline. It also evolves and observes planned value (PV), earned value (EV), and actual cost (AC) for each work package and control account. PV, sometimes known as the performance measurement baseline, is the authorized budget for scheduled work. EV is a metric describing work performed in terms of the authorized budget for that work. To measure work in progress, progress measurement criteria for each WBS component should be determined. The EV for a component cannot be greater than its PV. EV is checked incrementally to determine current status and cumulatively to determine long-term performance trends. AC is the cost incurred for work performed on an activity over a specific period of time: the total cost of the work defined by the EV. The earned value analysis provides a numerical evaluation of the state of the project. Cost performance measurements are used to determine the significance of variance from the original cost baseline. Cost variance (CV) is the difference between earned value and actual value. At the end of the project, it is the difference between budget at completion (BAC) and the actual amount spent.
	Variance Analysis	Variance analysis is used to **compare the proposed project results to the actual project results**. Cost variance (CV) is the difference between earned value and actual value. At the end of the project, it is the difference between budget at completion (BAC) and the actual amount spent.
	Trend Analysis	Trend analysis is used to project the future state of the project based on the present state of the project, in other words, to determine future results based on past results. The analysis can be used to predict issues, such as cost variances, to determine and effect corrective action. Trend analysis typically relates to the schedule, budget, or deliverables.

Control Costs (Continued)		
Key Tools & Techniques (Cont.)	Reserve Analysis	Reserve analysis is used to determine the status of contingency and management reserves for the project. Contingency reserves account for budget uncertainties and are included in the cost baseline and project funding requirements. Management reserves are budget reserves set aside to account for unknown unknowns (unforeseen work within the scope of the project). They are part of the overall project budget and are considered in the funding requirements. Funds in the management reserve are not included in the cost baseline until they are used for unforeseen work.
	To-complete Performance Index	The to-complete performance index (TCPI) measures the cost performance required to meet a defined management objective with the remaining resources. It is expressed as the ratio of the remaining work to the remaining budget and is calculated as budget at completion (BAC) minus earned value (EV) divided by the budget at completion (BAC) minus the actual cost (AC): $TCPI = (BAC - EV) / (BAC - AC)$.
Key Outputs	Work Performance Information	Work performance information includes supplemental and contextualized information regarding the performance of the project scope in comparison to the scope baseline. The information can contain important facets of scope control such as scope variances and their causes, how those variances impact cost and schedule, and a prognosis for future scope performance. The information is used to check the EVM components: planned value (PV), earned value (EV), and actual costs (AC). It is also utilized to depict trends graphically and to forecast a range of alternative project results.

Control Costs (Continued)		
Key Outputs (Cont.)	Cost Forecasts	Cost forecasts, such as estimate at completion (EAC) and a bottom-up EAC, are documented and conveyed to stakeholders.
	Change Requests	Change requests are requests for modification that have not been formally approved through the change control process. Modifications to the cost baseline may be requested based on analysis or severe changes to the scope, resources, or cost estimates.
	Cost Baseline	The cost baseline is the authorized version of the time-phased budget for the project, excluding management reserves, and is subject to change control. It is evolved from a summation of approved budgets for specific schedule activities. Cost estimates are aggregated by work packages, then into higher components of the work breakdown structure (WBS), and then for the entire project. Because the cost estimates included in the cost baseline are linked to schedule activities, a time-phased view of the cost baseline is enabled. It is usually depicted as an S-curve. If the project uses earned value management (EVM), the cost baseline is known as the performance measurement baseline. Changes to the scope, resources, or cost estimates, if severe, can result in a revised cost baseline.

Situational Question and Real World Application
Failure to effectively Control Costs could result in delays that arise from efforts to determine the most effective approach for the elimination of cost overruns.

7.14.1. Earned Value Management (EVM)

Earned value management (EVM) is a technique for measuring the progress of a project by looking at its scope, schedule, and cost in an integrated manner. If the initial focus is on the relationships between the components, rather than on the formulas, determining earned value is not complicated.

Know the characteristics and formulas related to earned value management (EVM), cost variance (CV), cost performance index (CPI), to-complete performance index (TCPI), schedule variance (SV), and schedule performance index (SPI).

To understand EVM and Cost Analysis, the components and formulas should be considered within the context of a home building project.

To determine earned value and perform cost and schedule analysis, the total project value and, at a distinct point in time, the completion percentage, the amount of work that should have been completed, and the amount that has been spent must be known.

The value of the project is $100,000 (BAC) as of the end of today (a specific point in time):

- The house is 40% completed, thus $40,000 of work has been done
- The amount of work that should have been completed is $60,000
- The amount that has been spent is $80,000

Determining Earned Value		
Component	**Definition**	**Calculation/Amount**
Budget at Completion (BAC) *aka Performance Baseline*	The amount the project is expected to cost	Total the costs of each project activity without regard to completion status: $100,000
Planned Value (PV) *aka Budgeted Cost of Work Scheduled (BCWS)*	The value of the work that should have been completed at a specific point in time, **excluding any work started ahead of schedule**	Total the value of each project activity scheduled for completion at a specific point in time: $60,000
Actual Cost (AC) *aka Actual Cost of Work Performed (ACWP)*	The cost of the work that has been completed at a specific point in time, **including any work started ahead of schedule**	Total all the project costs at a specific point in time: $80,000
Earned Value (EV) *aka Budgeted Cost of Work Performed (BCWP)*	A measurement of the project's progress and the basis for cost analysis, **including any work started ahead of schedule**	BAC or PV multiplied by percentage complete (**40%**): $40,000

Schedule analysis is comparing the amount of work completed versus the amount of work that should have been done. Using planned value (PV) and earned value (EV), the SPI and SV can be determined.

Handwritten left margin note: *Constantly calculating these to track progress and cost*

Performing Schedule Analysis		
Index/Variance	Formula/Result	Result Interpretation
Schedule Performance Index (SPI)	EV / PV $40,000 / $60,000 = **.67** Be able to calculate EV or PV if given SPI and EV or PV. For example: PV x SPI = EV or EV / SPI = PV	An efficiency indicator that denotes the amount of work done at a single point in time. If the result is **1.0**, the amount of work done on the project at a single point in time is **on track**. If the result is **greater than 1.0**, the amount of work done on the project at a single point in time is **better than expected**. If the result is **less than 1.0**, the amount of work done on the project at a single point in time is **less than expected**. In this case, the result is .67; therefore only *67% of the work scheduled to be done has been done.*
Schedule Variance (SV)	EV - PV $40,000 - $60,000 = **-$20,000** Be able to calculate EV or PV if given SV and EV or PV. For example: PV + SV = EV or EV − SV = PV	A variance indicator that denotes the difference between the value of the work completed and the value of the work that should have been completed. If the result is **0**, the project is **on track**. If the result is **greater than 0**, the project is **ahead of schedule**. If the result is **less than 0**, the project is **behind schedule**. In this case, the result is less than 0; therefore **the project is behind schedule by $20,000.**

Cost analysis, at its most basic, is determining progress in terms of the amount of work completed (EV) versus what was paid to complete the work (AC). Using budget at completion, planned value, actual cost, and earned value, the CPI, CV, and TCPI can be determined.

Performing Cost Analysis		
Index/Variance	Formula/Result	Result Interpretation
Cost Performance Index (CPI)	EV / AC $40,000 / $80,000 = **.5** Be able to calculate EV or AC if given CPI and EV or AC. For example: AC x CPI = EV or EV / CPI = AC	An efficiency indicator that denotes the return on each dollar spent at a single point in time. If the result is **1.0**, the return on the project at a single point in time is **on track**. If the result is **greater than 1.0**, the return on the project at a single point in time is **under budget**. If the result is **less than 1.0**, the return on the project at a single point in time is **over budget**. A CPI of .5 means that **50 cents of project work is completed for every dollar spent**.
Cost Variance (CV)	EV-AC $40,000 - $80,000 = **-$40,000** Be able to calculate EV or AC if given CV and EV or AC. For example: AC + CV = EV or EV – CV = AC	A variance indicator that denotes the difference between the value of the work completed and the cost of the work completed. If the result is **0**, the project is **on track.** If the result is **greater than 0**, the project is **under budget.** If the result is **less than 0**, the project is **over budget.** In this case, the result is less than 0; therefore **the project is over budget by $40,000.**

(handwritten, left margin, rotated) Constantly calculating these to track progress and cost

(handwritten, below table) – Index is a percentage and variance is a dollar amount

7.14.2. Calculating the Basics of Earned Value Management (EVM)

Figure 7-7: Earned Value Management Triangle shows the relationship of earned value concepts.

Memorize the earned value management triangle.

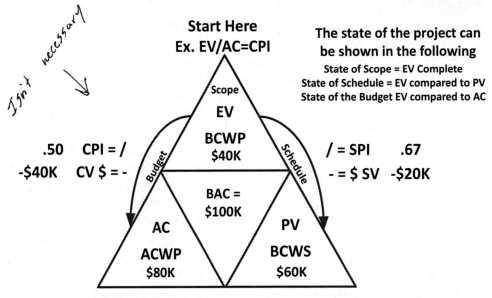

Figure 7-7: Earned Value Management Triangle

The earned value management triangle is ideal to memorize because it depicts the calculation of (cost or schedule) variances or performance indices. To interpret the graphic, start with EV and follow the arrows. For example EV divided ($\div$) by PV equals SPI or EV minus AC equals CV.

The following table contains keys to memorizing the earned value management triangle.

Performance Indices (CPI, SPI)	Variances (CV, SV)
Listed first (vertically)	Listed last (vertically)
Calculated by division	Calculated by subtraction
If less than one (<1), project is behind schedule or over budget	If negative, project is behind schedule or over budget
If greater than one (>1), project is ahead of schedule or under budget	If positive, project is ahead of schedule or under budget

NOTE: The AC (ACWP), EV (BCWP), and PV (BCWS) are listed alphabetically (horizontally). Although the values for actual cost (AC), earned value (EV), and planned value (PV) are generally provided, you may have to calculate them. The details that follow describe how to calculate planned value (PV), actual cost (AC) and earned value (EV) at the activity level.

Planned Value (PV or BCWS)	Determine the date or "complete through" level. **Add the planned values of activities that should have occurred as of the date or "complete through" level.** Do not add the planned value of activities that have started ahead of schedule. For example, today is June 6th, and there are two activities that should not start until June 8th but have already started. If an activity should be partially complete at the point you are measuring, the percent (%) complete will have to be provided or assumed. For example, a four-day activity is generally considered to be 50% done two days into the work.				
Actual Cost (AC or ACWP)	Add all "actual costs" related to the project. In the case of an activity, add the cost regardless of its completion status (1% to 100%), even if the activity was started ahead of schedule.				
Earned Value (EV or BCWP)	1. List the planned value (PV) of all the following types of activities: • The activities that should have started and haven't started yet • The activities that should have started and have actually started • The activities that shouldn't have started, but have (ahead of schedule) 2. Determine the % complete of each activity listed in step 1. 3. Multiply planned value (PV) by the % complete for each activity, giving the earned value of an individual activity. 4. **Add all the earned value measurements** (calculated in step 3) from each activity to get the total earned value for the project or situation.				

Activity Name	Planned Day	Actual Cost ($)	Earned Value ($)†	% Complete	Planned Value ($)
		(AC)	(EV)		(PV)
Activity A	Day 1	$300	$300	100%	$300
Activity B	Day 2	$200	$150	100%	$150
Activity C	Day 2	$150	$100	100%	$100
Activity D	Day 3	$225	$200	100%	$200
Activity E	Day 3	$100	$100	100%	$100
Activity F	Day 3	$300	$150	60%	$250
Activity G	Day 4	$140*	$130*	65%	$200
Activity H	Day 4	$100*	$80*	20%	$400
Activity I	Day 5	$0	$0	0%	$300
Activity J	Day 5	$0	$0	0%	$200

(The bolded line between Activities F and G represents the measuring point for the analysis.)

† PV x % complete

*These activities started ahead of schedule and their progress must be included.

PMI, CAPM, and PMBOK are registered marks of the Project Management Institute, Inc.

© 2008-2018 Crosswind Learning, www.crosswindpm.com   255

Using the previous table, perform earned value analysis as of the end of day three (the horizontal line in the previous table indicates that the information above the line represents days one, two, and three).

Budget at Completion (BAC)	BAC is calculated by totaling the planned values for all the project activities. The total budget at completion is **$2,200**.
Planned Value (PV)	Planned value is calculated by **adding up the planned value for each activity through day three. The total is $1,100.** This value represents the planned value or the value of the work that should be completed through day three. Note that, even though some work is ahead of schedule, only the work that should have been done through day three is considered.
Actual Cost (AC)	Actual cost is calculated by totaling the amounts spent through day three. **All costs**, even for work that was started ahead of schedule, must be considered. The actual cost is $1,515.
Earned Value (EV)	The earned value (EV) for an activity is calculated by multiplying its planned value (**regardless if it should have started yet or not**) by the percentage complete (%). The earned value for the project is calculated by totaling the earned values for each activity (**regardless if it should have started yet or not**). The earned value (EV) for the project, which is equal to the budgeted cost of work performed (BCWP), is $1,210.
Interpretation	**Through day three**, $1,100 worth of work should have been done and Activities A through F should have been completed. In actuality, $1,515 has been spent, but the earned value for the project (the value of the work completed) is only $1,210.

Based on the above table, the project metrics are:

CPI:	0.8	=	$1,210 / $1,515	CV:	-$305	=	$1,210 - $1,515
SPI:	1.1	=	$1,210 / $1,100	SV:	$110	=	$1,210 - $1,100

The CPI indicates that the project realizes $.80 in value for every dollar spent. The CV indicates the project is presently $305 over budget. The SPI indicates that the project is progressing at 110% of the rate planned and the SV indicates that the project has accomplished $110 more in work than was scheduled. The project is ahead of schedule but over budget.

Based on the forecasting table in section 7.14.3, the project metrics are:

EAC:	$2,750	=	$2,200 / .8	VAC:	-$550	=	$2,200 - $2,750
ETC:	$1,235	=	$2,750 - $1,515			

The EAC indicates that the project is expected to cost $2,750 at the current rate of spending and progress. The ETC indicates that the remaining amount to complete the project is expected to cost $1,235. The VAC indicates that, based on current spending, the project is expected to be $550 over budget when complete.

PMI, CAPM, and PMBOK are registered marks of the Project Management Institute, Inc.

7.14.3. Forecasts

Forecasts are estimates or predictions of the future state of the project based on past performance and expected future performance. The forecasts in the following table are based on the EVM table in section 7.14.2.

Cost Forecast	Description	Formula*
Estimate at Completion (EAC)	The estimate at completion (EAC) represents the current, projected final cost based on the current spending efficiency (CPI). If the CPI is greater than one (>1), the number will be less than the BAC; therefore, the project will likely finish under budget. If the CPI is less than one (<1), the number will be greater than the BAC; therefore, the project will likely finish over budget. If the CPI equals 1, the number will be equal to the BAC; therefore, the project will likely finish on budget. **EAC:** $200,000; therefore, the project is on pace to come in over the BAC of $100,000.	EAC = BAC / CPI Or $100,000 / .5 = $200,000
Estimate to Complete (ETC)	The estimate to complete (ETC) represents the amount needed to finish the project based on the current spending efficiency of the project. This figure is the EAC without the actual cost to date. **ETC:** $120,000; therefore, the project is on pace to exceed the BAC amount after factoring in what has already been spent.	ETC = EAC - AC Or $200,000 - $80,000 = $120,000
Variance at Completion (VAC)	The variance at completion (VAC) is the difference between the budget at completion (BAC) and the estimate at completion (EAC). This difference indicates the amount the completed project is expected to be over or under budget. **VAC:** -$100,000; therefore, the project is on pace to be completed over budget based on its current spending efficiency.	VAC = BAC - EAC Or $100,000 - $200,000 = -$100,000

Cost Forecast	Description	Formula*
To-complete Performance Index (TCPI)	The to-complete performance index (TCPI) is an efficiency indicator that denotes the efficiency needed from the remaining resources to meet the cost goals of the project and finish the project on budget.	TCPI = (BAC -EV) / (BAC - AC) Or ($100k - $40k) / ($100k - $80k) = 3.0

(handwritten margin note: Should be doing this on a weekly basis)

(handwritten in table cell: TCPI = (BAC - EV)/(EAC - AC))

* Variations of these formulas are listed in the Cost Formulas and Variables section. It is important to be become familiar with all the Estimate At Completion (EAC) formulas and related situations.

Figure 7-8: Earned Value Forecast Table, is formatted as a tic-tac-toe grid and contains the formulas for EAC, ETC, and VAC. Note that connecting the instances of EAC results in a diagonal line.
This table can be used as a quick reference for the exam.

Know the earned value forecast table.

Earned Value Forecast Table

EAC $200K	BAC $100K	CPI .5
ETC $120K	EAC $200K	AC $80K
VAC -$100K	BAC $100K	EAC $200K

Figure 7-8: Earned Value Forecast Table

Figure 7-9: TCPI - CPI Similarities , illustrates the similarities of the to-complete performance index and the cost performance index.

Know the TCPI-CPI Similarities.

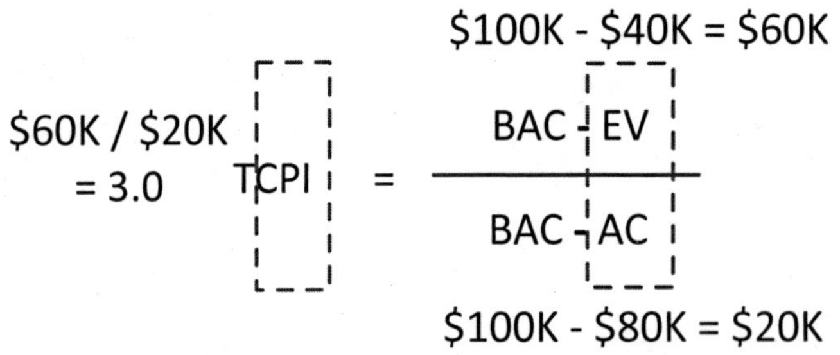

$$\text{TCPI} = \frac{\text{BAC} - \text{EV}}{\text{BAC} - \text{AC}}$$

$100K - $40K = $60K (BAC - EV)

$60K / $20K = 3.0

$100K - $80K = $20K (BAC - AC)

Figure 7-9: TCPI - CPI Similarities

7.14.4. Calculating the Basics of Earned Value Management (EVM) at the Project Level

The sunroom project detailed in the table below illustrates Earned Value Management at the project level. The sunroom is projected to be complete in five days at a cost of $2,000 per day. At the end of day three, the project is 40% complete and $5,000 has been spent.

Variable	Formula/Description	Value
Actual Cost (AC)	Sum of Actual Costs	$5,000
Earned Value (EV)	% Complete of Project	$4,000
Planned Value (PV)	Value of Scheduled Work	$6,000
Budget at Completion (BAC)	Total Budget	$10,000
Cost Performance Index (CPI)	EV/AC	0.8
Cost Variance (CV)	EV-AC	-$1,000
Schedule Performance Index (SPI)	EV/PV	0.667
Schedule Variance (SV)	EV-PV	-$2,000
Estimate at Completion (EAC)	BAC/CPI	$12,500
Estimate to Complete (ETC)	EAC-AC	$7,500
Variance at Completion (VAC)	BAC-EAC	-$2,500
To-Complete Performance Index (TCPI)	Rem. Wk./Rem. $	1.2

Chapter 7
Cost

7.14.5. S Curve

An S Curve is a graphical representation of earned value management. The classic S Curve shows the interaction between scope, cost, and time over the life of the project.

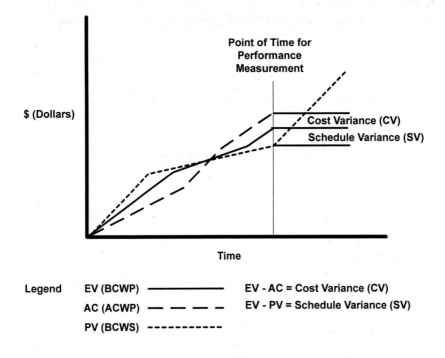

Figure 7-10: S Curve

The source for the above figure is the Project Management Institute, *A Guide to the Project Management Body of Knowledge*, (*PMBOK® Guide*) – Sixth Edition, Project Management Institute Inc., 2017, Figure 7-9, Page 246

Figure 7-10: S Curve illustrates that the project, at a specific point in time, is over budget (the cost variance indicates more was spent on the work than budgeted) and ahead of schedule (the schedule variance indicates more work was completed than scheduled). The closely dotted line represents planned value (PV). The uninterrupted line represents earned value (EV). The widely dotted line represents actual costs (AC).

One of the most common misunderstandings in performance reporting is that schedule, cost, and progress are directly related: for example, people commonly assume that a twelve month project that started on January 1st should be 50% complete on July 1st (halfway through the duration). The direct relationship only occurs if time is utilized and costs are paid at a consistent rate calculated to reach 100% of cost or schedule at the completion of the project.

It's important to remember that each project will have its own unique S Curve based on the amount of work expected to be accomplished over time. In a perfect world, an S-Curve would have three lines (AC, EV and PV) and they would all be on top of each other. This would mean everything went as planned on the project. Since this rarely occurs, three separate lines are typical.

The source for the above text is the Project Management Institute, *A Guide to the Project Management Body of Knowledge*, (*PMBOK® Guide*) – Sixth Edition, Project Management Institute Inc., 2017, Pages 242-253

PMI, CAPM, and PMBOK are registered marks of the Project Management Institute, Inc.

260   © 2008-2018 Crosswind Learning, www.crosswindpm.com

7.15. Project Cost Management Formulas and Variables

Description	Formula	Variable (Component)	Example
Actual Cost (AC) represents the current amount actually spent on the project to date or during a particular time period.	The addition of actual expenses to date or during a particular time period	AC (ACWP) = actual cost (actual cost of work performed)	AC = $5,000
Earned Value (EV) represents the current amount of work (product) completed to date or during a particular time period, regardless of cost or time.	The percent complete of each activity multiplied by the planned value (PV) of the activity to date or during a particular time period	EV (BCWP) = earned value (budgeted cost of work performed)	EV = $ 4,500 or EV = $4,500 = $9,000 x 50% Complete
Planned Value (PV) represents the current amount that should have been spent on the project to date or during a particular time period.	The addition of all work that should have been completed to date or during a particular time period	PV (BCWS) = planned value (budgeted cost of work scheduled)	PV = $ 5,500
Budget at Completion (BAC) represents the total budget projected for the project. Also, it is the **sum of all planned value (PV)**.	The total amount originally (or in accordance with an approved revision) expected to be spent on the project	BAC = budget at completion	BAC = $10,000
Cost Performance Index (CPI) represents the current efficiency of spending on the project. Less than 1.0 is not good, greater than 1.0 is good, and 1.0 is on track.	CPI = EV / AC	CPI = cost performance index	CPI = 1.0 (on track: $1.00 spent, $1.00 value) CPI = 0.8 (over budget: $1.00 spent, $.80 value) CPI = 1.2 (under budget: $1.00 spent, $1.20 value)
Cost Variance (CV) represents the difference between what has been accomplished and what has been spent.	CV = EV - AC	CV = Cost Variance	CV = -$500 (spent more than allocated) CV = 0 (spent as planned) CV = $500 (spent less than allocated)

Description	Formula	Variable (Component)	Example
Schedule Performance Index (SPI) represents the current efficiency of progress on the project. Less than 1.0 is not good; greater than 1.0 is good; 1.0 is on track.	SPI = EV / PV	SPI = schedule performance index	SPI = 1.0 (On track and progressing as it should) SPI = 0.8 (Behind schedule, only progressing at 80% of what was planned) SPI = 1.2 (Ahead of schedule, progressing at 120% of what was planned)
Schedule Variance (SV) represents the difference between what has been accomplished and what should have been accomplished.	SV = EV - PV	SV = schedule variance	SV = -$500 (took more time than allocated) SV = 0 (time as planned) SV = $500 (took less time than allocated)
To-complete Performance Index (TCPI) represents the efficiency needed from the remaining resources to meet the cost goals of the project.	TCPI = (BAC-EV) / (BAC-AC) or (BAC-EV) / (EAC-AC)	TCPI = to-complete performance index	TCPI = 1.25 = ($1,000 - $500) / ($1,000 - $600) BAC or EAC = $1,000 EV = $500 AC = $600
Estimate at Completion (EAC) represents the current total project cost based on the current efficiency (CPI) of project spending.	EAC = BAC / CPI Or EAC = BAC / Cumulative CPI	EAC = estimate at completion	EAC = $50,000 EAC greater than BAC (over budget) EAC less than BAC (under budget)
EAC using a new estimate, represents the actual cost (AC) to date plus a new ETC.	EAC = AC + ETC	EAC = estimate at completion	EAC = $50,000 = $2,000 + $48,000
EAC using the remaining budget represents the budget needed to complete the remaining work plus the actual cost (AC). The budget needed to complete the remaining work is the budget at completion (BAC) minus the earned value (EV).	EAC = AC + BAC-EV	EAC = estimate at completion	EAC = $51,000 = $7,000 + ($50,000 - $6,000) AC = $7,000 BAC = $50,000 EV= $6,000

Description	Formula	Variable (Component)	Example
EAC using CPI also represents the budget needed to complete the remaining work plus the actual cost (AC). However, the budget required to complete the remaining work is adjusted by a performance factor, very often CPI.	$EAC = AC + \dfrac{BAC - EV}{CPI \times SPI}$	EAC = estimate at completion	EAC = $43,477 = $7,000 + ($50,000 - $8,000) / (1.14 x 1.01) AC = $7,000 BAC = $50,000 EV = $8,000 CPI = 1.14 SPI = 1.01
Estimate to Complete (ETC) represents the current total project cost REMAINING to be spent, based on the current efficiency (CPI) of project spending.	ETC = EAC - AC	ETC = estimate to complete	ETC = $40,000
Variance at Completion (VAC) represents the difference between the BAC and EAC.	VAC = BAC - EAC	VAC = variance at completion	VAC = $32,500
Present Value (PV) shows the amount of money needed now at the interest rate (r) for a desired future outcome (FV) over a number of periods (n).	$PV = \dfrac{FV}{(1+r)^n}$	(PV) present value	PV = $463.19 if FV = $1,000, r = 8%, n = 10
Future Value (FV) shows the amount of money needed in the future at the set interest rate (r) for an amount of money (PV) now over a number of periods (n).	$FV = PV \times (1+r)^n$	(FV) future value	FV = $215.89 if PV = $100, r = 8%, n = 10
The **interest rate** of an investment in a project	Provided on the exam	r (interest rate)	r = 8% = 0.08
The **number of periods of time** (months, years, etc.) of investment in a project	Provided on the exam	n (number of periods)	n = 5 years

Description	Formula	Variable (Component)	Example
PERT, while technically a type of three-point estimate, can be used with beta distributions	$c_E = \dfrac{c_O + 4c_M + c_P}{6}$	PERT	$13.33 = ((20 + (4 \times 14) + 4)) / 6$
Pessimistic Cost (c_P) estimate is a worst-case estimate.	Provided on exam	c_P	$c_P = 4$
Optimistic Cost (c_O) estimate is a best-case estimate.	Provided on exam	c_O	$c_O = 20$
Most likely (c_M), or **realistic** (c_R) estimate	Provided on exam	c_M (also could be c_R, "realistic")	$c_M = 14$

7.16. Project Cost Management Terminology

Term	Description
Activity Cost Estimate	The projected cost of completing an activity
Actual Cost (AC)	The total cost accrued for an activity over a designated time period; also known as the actual cost of work performed (ACWP)
Basis of Estimates	Supporting details associated with an estimate, typically time or cost, that may include assumptions, constraints, level of detail, ranges, and confidence levels
Budget	The total estimate for the project, or any activity, that has been approved
Budget at Completion (BAC)	The total project budget derived from incorporating all items from the project's individual budgets; also called the sum of all planned value (PV)
Budgetary Estimate	An estimate used to put money into a company's (or project's) budget
Chart of Accounts	A structure used to monitor project cost that usually aligns with a company's accounting system and WBS of the project or program
Code of Accounts	The numbering system used to distinguish constituents of the WBS
Control Account	A specific point in the work breakdown structure (WBS) where the project scope, budget, actual cost, and schedule are combined and then compared to earned value in order to establish performance metrics
Control Costs	The process of observing project status in order to revise project costs and administer cost baseline revisions
Cost Aggregation	Adding together the work package cost estimates for high-level WBS components, including control accounts, for the purpose of establishing the value of the total project or the control account work
Cost Baseline	The authorized project budget version, exclusive of management reserves, that requires a formal control process to effect changes and is used as the basis of comparison to actual costs
Cost Management Plan	The document, part of the project or program management plan, used to describe the framing, forming, observation, and control of project costs
Cost of Quality	The total cost of achieving or failing to achieve desired quality: specifically the costs of achievement are those associated with planning, controlling, and assuring quality and the costs of failure are those associated with reworking, warranty, waste, and negative reputation
Cost Performance Index (CPI)	The ratio indicating the cost efficiency of resources, calculated by dividing earned value (EV) by actual cost (AC): a CPI of 1.0 indicates the project is proceeding as planned financially; a CPI greater than 1.0 more indicates the project is proceeding better than planned financially; and a CPI less than 1.0 indicates the project is not proceeding as well as planned financially
Cost Variance (CV)	The deficit or surplus of the budget at any specific point in time, calculated by subtracting the actual cost (AC) from the earned value (EV): a value of 0 indicates the project is on budget, a value greater than 0 indicates the project is under budget, and a value less than 0 indicates the project is over budget
Cost-benefit Analysis	A financial analysis method that compares the potential revenue derived from an opportunity to the cost of that opportunity
Definitive Estimate	A cost estimate that provides an accurate estimate of the project cost; the final cost estimate used before implementation; typically the estimate has a tolerance range of -10% to +10%

Term	Description
Determine Budget	The process of totaling the evaluations of individual activities to arrive at an authorized cost baseline
Direct Cost	Cost that is directly applicable to the project; examples include the cost of a test computer for software being created by the project, the cost of IC chips, or the costs of project labor
Earned Value (EV)	The value of the work that has been completed as of a specific point in time calculated by multiplying the completion percent of activity by its planned value, then adding the results; also known as the budgeted cost of work performed (BCWP)
Earned Value Management	A technique, effected by considering actual cost (AC), time (PV), and what has been accomplished (EV), that is used to determine project progress and performance
Earned Value Technique (EVT)	The technique associated with measuring the amount of completion of a work breakdown structure component, control account or project
Estimate at Completion (EAC)	The expected cost of performing all of the work in the project calculated by adding the actual cost (AC) to the estimate to complete (ETC)
Estimate Costs	The process of approximating the monetary resources required to complete the work of the project
Estimate to Complete (ETC)	The expected monetary resources required to complete the remaining work of the project; calculated by subtracting actual cost (AC) from the estimate at completion (EAC)
Fixed Formula Method	A progress reporting approach, typically applied when an activity is two reporting periods or less in duration, that assigns a percentage to an activity at its start and the remaining percentage at its completion so that the percentage at completion equals 100%; for example, if an activity is assigned 30% at its start, 70% will be added at its completion resulting in a completion percentage of 100%
Funding Limit Reconciliation	The process of comparing planned project expenses to any limitations or constraints in project funding
Indirect Cost	Cost that is not directly accrued on the project (for example, electricity, taxes, rent)
Internal Rate of Return (IRR)	A project comparison value; represents the discounted rate that zeros out the net present value (NPV)
Learning Curve Theory	A theory which states that the more of something that is produced, the lower the unit cost of it becomes due to an improvement in efficiency
Life Cycle Costing	Consideration of not just project cost, but total ownership (operations and support) cost of the item created by the project
Net Present Value (NPV)	A value used in capital budgeting, in which the present value of cash inflow is subtracted from the present value of cash outflows; compares the value of a dollar today versus the value of that same dollar in the future, after taking inflation and return into account
Opportunity Cost	The amount associated with bypassing one opportunity in favor of another; as an example, if the pursuit of project B with a value of $75K is elected over the pursuit of project A with a value of $50K, $50k value of project A will not be realized
Parametric Modeling	Application of a mathematical model used to estimate project components (time, cost, scope) by having other variables entered into the application
Performance Measurement Baseline (PMB)	The comparison of project execution to the approved and integrated scope, schedule, and budget (exclusive of management reserves, but inclusive of contingency reserves) for the purpose of gauging and administering performance
Plan Cost Management	The process of establishing policies, procedures, and documentation for the planning, execution, and monitoring and controlling of cost-related project items

Term	Description
Planned Value (PV)	The total value of the work scheduled as of a certain point in time; also known as the budgeted cost of work scheduled (BCWS)
Profit	Money made after expenses have been subtracted from revenue
Profit Margin	Ratio between revenues and profit on a project, product, or initiative
Project Cost Management	The processes required to estimate, budget, disburse, administer, and regulate costs in order to complete the project within the approved budget
Project Funding Requirements	The forecast of project costs based on the cost baseline for the total project plus any anticipated liabilities; the forecast can be applied to specific time periods rather than to the project as a whole
Rough Order of Magnitude (ROM) Estimate	A cost estimate, performed early in the project, of the completion cost of the project; the tolerance range is -25% to +75%.
S Curve	Graphic representation of costs, work, and other quantities over time so that the planned value, earned value, and actual cost of the work can be seen
Schedule Performance Index (SPI)	A measure of project schedule efficiency calculated by dividing the earned value (EV) by the planned value (PV): a value of 1.0 indicates the work is being performed as expected, a value greater than 1.0 means the work is being performed ahead of schedule, and a value of less than 1.0 means the work is being performed behind schedule
Schedule Variance (SV)	A determination of schedule performance calculated by subtracting the planned value (PV) from the earned value (EV): if the result is zero, the project is performing as expected; if the result is positive, the project is ahead of schedule; if the result is negative, the project is behind schedule
Sunk Cost	Money that has already been spent on a project; should not be considered when selecting or evaluating a project
Tangible Cost/ Benefit	Easily measurable cost or benefit of a project; measured in dollars
To-complete Performance Index (TCPI)	The ratio that represents the cost performance required to complete the work of the project given the remaining resources; calculated by dividing the remaining project work by the remaining budget (BAC - EV / BAC - AC)
Variance At Completion (VAC)	The projected amount the project will be over or under budget based on the difference between the budget at completion (BAC) and the estimate at completion (EAC)
Weighted Milestone Method	An approach to the earned value method in which an activity with a duration exceeding two reporting periods is broken down into smaller activities with durations limited to two reporting periods or less

The source for the above definitions is the Glossary of the Project Management Institute,
A Guide to the Project Management Body of Knowledge, (PMBOK® Guide) – Sixth Edition, Project Management Institute Inc., 2017

7.17. Project Cost Management Tests and Exercises

7.17.1. Situational Earned Value Exercises

Answers are in section 7.18.1.

Earned Value Exercise #1

You are managing a project to build a product. The project has seven activities, each with a finish-to-start relationship. Below is project baseline information indicating the planned schedule and budgeted cost of each activity. **Calculate anything with a dollar value to the nearest cent (for example, $456.32) and anything else to three digits (for example, 1.024).** Recommendation: Use a basic calculator or your calculations could have rounding variance. **Product Release 1.0 row is a summary activity reflecting the contents below it.**

Planned

Activity Name	% Complete	Baseline Duration	Baseline Start	Baseline Finish	Baseline Cost
Product Release 1.0	**0%**	**240 days**	**01/06/xx**	**12/05/xx**	**$295,000.00**
Requirements	0%	30 days	01/06/xx	02/14/xx	$30,000.00
Design	0%	60 days	02/17/xx	05/09/xx	$70,000.00
Proof of Concept	0%	30 days	05/12/xx	06/20/xx	$45,000.00
Build Product	0%	45 days	06/23/xx	08/22/xx	$60,000.00
Test Product	0%	45 days	08/25/xx	10/24/xx	$60,000.00
Deploy Product	0%	30 days	10/27/xx	12/05/xx	$30,000.00
Product Release Complete	0%	0 days	12/05/xx	12/05/xx	$0.00

The project is currently in the middle of the execution phase and the date is **June 20th**. The information in the chart below provides the schedule and cost information to date.

Actual

Activity Name	% Complete	Actual Duration	Actual Start	Actual Finish	Actual Cost
Product Release 1.0	**47.63%**	**122 days**	**01/06/xx**	**NA**	**$147,000.00**
Requirements	100%	35 days	01/06/xx	02/21/xx	$32,000.00
Design	100%	60 days	02/24/xx	05/16/xx	$70,000.00
Proof of Concept	90%	27 days	05/19/xx	NA	$45,000.00
Build Product	0%	0 days	NA	NA	$0.00
Test Product	0%	0 days	NA	NA	$0.00
Deploy Product	0%	0 days	NA	NA	$0.00
Product Release Complete	0%	0 days	NA	NA	$0.00

PMI, CAPM, and PMBOK are registered marks of the Project Management Institute, Inc.

268 © 2008-2018 Crosswind Learning, www.crosswindpm.com

Using the calculations from the data tables, provide a status report on the project by answering the following questions. Calculate to the nearest cent for dollars and three significant digits for everything else.

1. What measurement is used to determine whether the project is ahead of schedule, behind schedule, or on time, and how much is the amount?

2. What measurement is used to determine the rate of the project's progress according to plan and what is its value?

3. Based on these schedule measurements, is the project on schedule, behind schedule, or on time?

4. At what percentage rate is the project progressing compared to its planned baseline rate of progression?

5. What measurement is used to determine whether the project is over budget, under budget, or if it is breaking even, and how much is the difference?

6. What measurement is used to determine the spending efficiency of the project, and what is its value?

7. Based on these measurements, is the project over budget, under budget, or breaking even?

8. Currently, the project is making how many cents for every dollar spent?

9. Based on the current status and performance of the project, how much do you estimate the project will cost at completion? On what measurement do you base this estimate?

10. How much money must be spent from this point forward to complete the project? What calculations have you made to support this figure?

11. Will the project be over budget, under budget, or right on target at completion? What information do you have to support this estimate?

PMI, CAPM, and PMBOK are registered marks of the Project Management Institute, Inc.
© 2008-2018 Crosswind Learning, www.crosswindpm.com

7.17.2. Project Cost Management Practice Test

Answers are in section 7.18.2.

1. Activity A is worth $200, is 100% complete, should have been done on day one, and actually cost $200. Activity B is worth $75, is 90% complete, should have been done on day two, and actually cost $120 so far. Activity C is worth $200, is 75% complete and should have been done on day three, and has cost $175 so far. The total budget is $1,000. What is the planned value as of day two?

    (A) $275.00
    (B) -$417.50
    (C) $495.00
    (D) -$275.00

2. The project team is developing rules for reporting updates on the project. The majority of the activities are greater than two reporting periods long. Which format is best to use in this case?

    (A) Fixed formula progress reporting
    (B) Weighted milestone
    (C) Earned value
    (D) Forecast reporting

3. Project A has an NPV of $150K over three years. Project B has an NPV of $330K over six years. Project C has an NPV of $170K over six years. Which of the following do you select?

    (A) Project A
    (B) Project B
    (C) Project C
    (D) Project A and C

4. You are having a home theater room added to your house. The project should take five days and cost $1,500 per day to complete. After three days, the project is 30% complete and $5,000 has been spent. What is the CPI?

    (A) 0.45
    (B) 0.50
    (C) 0.40
    (D) 1.00

5. You are having a home theater room added to your house. The project should take five days and cost $1,500 per day to complete. After three days, the project is 30% complete and $5,000 has been spent. What is the total value of the project?

(A) $7,500
(B) $2,250
(C) $5,000
(D) $10,000

6. You are having a home theater room added to your house. The project should take five days and cost $1,500 per day to complete. After three days, the project is 30% complete and $5,000 has been spent. What is the EV?

(A) $7,500
(B) $2,250
(C) $5,000
(D) $10,000

7. Company-wide server upgrades are an example of what type of project cost?

(A) Variable indirect
(B) Variable
(C) Fixed
(D) Fixed direct

8. The project team is planning an upgrade to a client's website and infrastructure. During planning, the team discovers the need for a data communications line to connect to the servers. What type of cost is this?

(A) Direct
(B) Indirect
(C) Variable
(D) Indirect fixed

9. The infrastructure project is behind schedule and over budget. So far, $3M has been spent on the project. The sponsor is considering if it should allow the project to continue. What should he consider the $3M that has been spent so far?

(A) The amount for phase one
(B) Sunk cost
(C) The budgeted cost of work performed
(D) Opportunity cost

10. The highway project is in the middle of planning when the project manager presents a status reporting method to the team. The team members haven't heard of this method before. It's called earned value. To attain buy-in from the team, the project manager begins to explain what earned value status reporting can do for the project, explaining that it will measure which of the following?

(A) Schedule and cost
(B) Scope, schedule, and cost
(C) Scope and cost
(D) Scope and schedule

11. You are having a home theater room added to your house. The project should take five days and cost $1,500 per day to complete. After three days, the project is 30% complete and $5,000 has been spent. What is the amount of work that should have been done so far?

(A) $7,500
(B) $2,250
(C) $5,000
(D) $4,500

12. Project A has an NPV of $275K over 2.5 years. Project B has an IRR of 3.2%. Project C has a BCR of 0.89:1. Project D has four people on it and is encountering scope creep. Which of the following projects stand the greatest chance of getting canceled?

(A) Project A
(B) Project B
(C) Project C
(D) Project D

13. The BCR project comparison function utilizes what variable(s)?

(A) Revenue and cost
(B) Revenue and profit
(C) Benefit and profit
(D) Profit margin

14. The project planning process group is progressing. The team has involved the accounting department to set up a system of codes that the accounting department will use to track work on the project. This is known as what?

(A) Accounting codes
(B) WBS numbering
(C) Determine budget
(D) Chart of accounts

15. The project management team has performed earned value analysis on its project and discovered that the project is behind schedule and over budget. The SPI is 0.82 and the CPI is 0.73. The team is trying to determine how efficient it needs to be with the remaining resources to complete the project on budget. Which of the following is the team trying to calculate?

(A) Cost variance
(B) Cost performance index
(C) Estimate to complete
(D) To-complete performance index

16. What is the range of a rough order of magnitude (ROM) estimate?

(A) -10% to +10%
(B) -5% to +10%
(C) -25% to +75%
(D) -300% to +75%

17. The project is using a new server that cost $25,000. The project manager is told to set up depreciation for the server over a five-year schedule, with the server having a value of $0 at the end of five years. Standard depreciation will be used in the calculation. What is the amount per year the server will depreciate?

(A) $5,000
(B) $10,000
(C) $2,500
(D) Not enough information

18. You are having a home theater room added to your house. The project should take five days and cost $1,500 per day to complete. After three days, the project is 30% complete and $5,000 has been spent. What is the ETC?

(A) $11,666.67
(B) $16,666.67
(C) $5,000
(D) $0

19. Which of the following shows the remaining amount to be spent on the project based on current spending efficiency?

(A) Cost variance
(B) Estimate to complete
(C) Estimate at completion
(D) Budget remaining

20. Which of the following shows the rate at which the project is progressing compared to what was planned?

(A) Schedule variance
(B) Gantt chart
(C) Variance report
(D) Schedule performance index

21. Which process aggregates estimated costs from the individual work packages or activities to create a summary and detailed breakdown of project costs?

(A) Control costs
(B) Estimate costs
(C) Determine budget
(D) Earned value management

22. The project team is planning an upgrade to a client's website and infrastructure. During planning, the team members are confronted with the cost options for a data communications line to connect to the servers. They consider the cost of purchasing the communication line for the time they need to develop the project. After that, the customer takes over the purchase of the line. They are also considering a long-term commitment that the customer can make with the communication line provider, which provides a less costly solution over the use of the system. What type of analysis is the team considering?

(A) Life cycle costing
(B) Make-or-buy analysis
(C) Fixed cost
(D) Procurement planning

23. You are having a home theater room added to your house. The project should take five days and cost $1,500 per day to complete. After three days, the project is 30% complete and $5,000 has been spent. What do you expect the project to cost at completion based on the current performance?

(A) $11,666.67
(B) $16,666.67
(C) $5,000
(D) $0

24. The planning process group is progressing. The team has involved a number of expert opinions in trying to approximate the costs needed to complete project activities. This process is known as?

(A) Determine budget
(B) Control costs
(C) Analogous estimating
(D) Estimate costs

25. Which of the following is an example of fixed formula status reporting?

(A) Getting status updates from the project team
(B) PV multiplied by % complete
(C) The project manager updating the status reports quantitatively
(D) 30%/70% rule

26. The project is using some application and database servers in the development environment. The finance department explains that the servers will be depreciated using the double declining balance (DDB) format. This is an example of what?

(A) Fixed cost
(B) Fixed direct cost
(C) Accelerated depreciation
(D) Standard depreciation

27. The project team is developing rules for reporting updates on the project. The majority of their activities are less than two reporting periods long. Which format is best to use in this case?

(A) Fixed formula progress reporting
(B) Weighted milestone
(C) Earned value
(D) Forecast reporting

28. You have $1,000 today and can earn 8%. In future years, how much money will this be worth?

(A) $1,175
(B) $883
(C) $1,202
(D) Not enough information

29. You are having a home theater room added to your house. The project should take five days and cost $1,500 per day to complete. After three days, the project is 30% complete and $5,000 has been spent. What is the SPI?

(A) 0.45
(B) 0.50
(C) 0.40
(D) 1.00

30. Which of the following metrics tells you if you are ahead of schedule?

(A) Schedule performance index (SPI)
(B) Cost performance index (CPI)
(C) Cost variance (CV)
(D) Budget at completion (BAC)

7.18. Project Cost Management Answers for Tests and Exercises

7.18.1. Situational Earned Value Exercise Answers

Earned Value Exercise #1 Answers

You are managing a project to build a product. The project has seven activities, each with a finish-to-start relationship. Below is project baseline information indicating the planned schedule and budgeted cost of each activity. **Calculate anything with a dollar value to the nearest cent (for example, $456.32) and anything else to three digits (for example, 1.024).** Recommendation: Use a basic calculator or your calculations could have rounding variance. **Product Release 1.0 row is a summary activity reflecting the contents below it.**

Planned

Activity Name	% Complete	Baseline Duration	Baseline Start	Baseline Finish	Baseline Cost
Product Release 1.0	**0%**	**240 days**	**01/06/xx**	**12/05/xx**	**$295,000.00**
Requirements	0%	30 days	01/06/xx	02/14/xx	$30,000.00
Design	0%	60 days	02/17/xx	05/09/xx	$70,000.00
Proof of Concept	0%	30 days	05/12/xx	06/20/xx	$45,000.00
Build Product	0%	45 days	06/23/xx	08/22/xx	$60,000.00
Test Product	0%	45 days	08/25/xx	10/24/xx	$60,000.00
Deploy Product	0%	30 days	10/27/xx	12/05/xx	$30,000.00
Product Release Complete	0%	0 days	12/05/xx	12/05/xx	$0.00

The project is currently in the middle of the execution phase and the date is June 20th. The information in the chart below provides the schedule and cost information to date.

Actual

Activity Name	% Complete	Actual Duration	Actual Start	Actual Finish	Actual Cost
Product Release 1.0	**47.63%**	**122 days**	**01/06/xx**	**NA**	**$147,000.00**
Requirements	100%	35 days	01/06/xx	02/21/xx	$32,000.00
Design	100%	60 days	02/24/xx	05/16/xx	$70,000.00
Proof of Concept	90%	27 days	05/19/xx	NA	$45,000.00
Build Product	0%	0 days	NA	NA	$0.00
Test Product	0%	0 days	NA	NA	$0.00
Deploy Product	0%	0 days	NA	NA	$0.00
Product Release Complete	0%	0 days	NA	NA	$0.00

PMI, CAPM, and PMBOK are registered marks of the Project Management Institute, Inc.

Earned Value Exercise #1 Status Report Answers

1. What measurement is used to determine whether the project is ahead of schedule, behind schedule, or on time, and how much is the amount?

    SV – schedule variance

    First, you must determine the value of the following:
    AC = $147,000 (actual cost to date)
    PV = $145,000 (what was the planned value of the work to date)
    EV = $140,500 (what is the value of the work done to date)
    $30,000 + $70,000 + (90% of $45,000 = $40,500) = $140,500

    SV = EV – PV   **SV = $140,500 – $145,000 = -$4,500**

2. What measurement is used to determine the rate of the project's progress according to plan and what is its value?

    SPI – schedule performance index
    SPI = EV / PV   **SPI = $140,500 / $145,000 = 0.969**

3. Based on these schedule measurements, is the project on schedule, behind schedule, or on time?

    The project is behind schedule.

4. At what percentage rate is the project progressing compared to its planned baseline rate of progression?

    The project is progressing at 96.9% of the rate of the original plan.

5. What measurement is used to determine whether the project is over budget, under budget, or if it is breaking even, and how much is the difference?

    CV – cost variance
    AC = $147,000 (actual cost to date)
    PV = $145,000 (what was the planned value of the work to date)
    EV = $140,500 (what is the value of the work done to date)
    $30,000 + $70,000 + (90% of $45,000 = $40,500) = $140,500
    CV = EV – AC   **CV = $140,500 – $147,000 = -$6,500**

6. What measurement is used to determine the spending efficiency of the project and what is its value?

    CPI – cost performance index
    CPI = EV / AC   **CPI = $140,500 / $147,000 = 0.956**

7. Based on these measurements, is the project over budget, under budget, or breaking even?

The project is over budget.

8. Currently, the project is making how many cents for every dollar spent?

The project is making 96 cents on every dollar it spends.

9. Based on the current status and performance of the project, how much do you estimate the project will cost at completion? On what measurement do you base this estimate?

The estimate at completion (EAC) is the value that tells what the project is expected to cost at the end, based on the project spending efficiency. This estimate is calculated in a variety of ways. Use BAC / CPI to calculate EAC. The BAC (budget at completion) is $295,000 and the CPI (cost performance index) is 0.956. This gives an EAC of $308,577.40.

10. How much money must be spent from this point forward to complete the project? What calculations have you made to support this figure?

This is the ETC (estimate to complete). Calculate it by subtracting AC (actual cost) from the EAC (estimate at completion). $308,577.40 - $147,000 = $161,577.40

11. Will the project be over budget, under budget, or right on target at completion? What information do you have to support this estimate?

Based on the estimate at completion, the project will be over budget.

The budget at completion (BAC) is $295,000 and the estimate at completion (EAC) is $308,577.40.

The variance at completion (VAC) is BAC - EAC and in this project is $13,577.40 over budget.

7.18.2.   Project Cost Management Practice Test Answers

We recommend that you download answer sheets from the Crosswind website, so you can practice the test as many times as you like.

1.   Activity A is worth $200, is 100% complete, should have been done on day one, and actually cost $200. Activity B is worth $75, is 90% complete, should have been done on day two, and actually cost $120 so far. Activity C is worth $200, is 75% complete and should have been done on day three, and has cost $175 so far. The total budget is $1,000. What is the planned value as of day two?

Correct Answer: (A) $275.00
Explanation: The planned value as of day two is $275.00 Obtain this value by adding the planned value (PV) of Activity A ($200) and B ($75), which should have been done as of day two on the project. [Crosswind Manual 7.14.1; *PMBOK® Guide* 7.4.2.2]

2.   The project team is developing rules for reporting updates on the project. The majority of the activities are greater than two reporting periods long. Which format is best to use in this case?

Correct Answer: (B) Weighted milestone
Explanation: The weighted milestone approach is ideal when an activity is over two reporting periods in length. Fixed formula uses a partial credit approach such as 50/50 and is ideal when an activity is short, such as two or less reporting periods long. Earned value shows the status of the scope, schedule, and cost of the project. Forecast reporting focuses on what is getting ready to be done on the project. [Crosswind Manual 7.9; *PMBOK® Guide* Glossary]

3.   Project A has an NPV of $150K over three years. Project B has an NPV of $330K over six years. Project C has an NPV of $170K over six years. Which of the following do you select?

Correct Answer: (B) Project B
Explanation: Project B is the most attractive project because it has the highest dollar amount. The years listed with the NPV are distracters because they are already factored into the dollar amount of the project. Project A and C are of less value than Project B. [Crosswind Manual 7.2; No *PMBOK® Guide* Reference]

4.   You are having a home theater room added to your house. The project should take five days and cost $1,500 per day to complete. After three days, the project is 30% complete and $5,000 has been spent. What is the CPI?

Correct Answer: (A) 0.45
Explanation: The formula for calculating the CPI (cost performance index) is CPI = EV / AC. In this instance three steps are required. First, determine the BAC (budget at completion), which is the sum of all PV (planned value): $1,500 per day cost multiplied by five days equals a BAC of $7,500. Second, calculate the EV (earned value) by multiplying the BAC by the percentage complete: $7,500 BAC multiplied by 30% complete equals an EV of $2,250. Third, calculate the CPI by dividing the EV by the AC (actual cost): $2,250 EV divided by $5,000 AC equals a CPI of 0.45. Note that planned value is defined as the work that should have been completed to date or during a particular time period (in this case, through day five of the project since the percentage complete relates to the overall project.) [Crosswind Manual 7.14.1; *PMBOK® Guide* 7.4.2.2]

5. You are having a home theater room added to your house. The project should take five days and cost $1,500 per day to complete. After three days, the project is 30% complete and $5,000 has been spent. What is the total value of the project?

Correct Answer: (A) $7,500
Explanation: The total value of the project is the equivalent of the project budget or the BAC (budget at completion). To determine the BAC multiply the cost per day times the number of days the project is scheduled to take: $1,500 per day cost multiplied by five days equals a BAC of $7,500. [Crosswind Manual 7.14.1; *PMBOK® Guide* 7.4.2.2]

6. You are having a home theater room added to your house. The project should take five days and cost $1,500 per day to complete. After three days, the project is 30% complete and $5,000 has been spent. What is the EV?

Correct Answer: (B) $2,250
Explanation: The formula for calculating the EV (earned value) is EV equals percentage complete of each activity (or in this case the entire project) multiplied by BAC (budget at completion). In this instance, two steps are required. First, determine the BAC for the project: $1,500 per day cost multiplied by five days equals a BAC of $7,500. Second, calculate the EV by multiplying the BAC by the percentage complete: $7,500 BAC multiplied by 30% complete equals an EV of $2,250. Note that planned value is defined as the work that should have been completed to date or during a particular time period. In this case, the time period is defined as "through day five of the project," since the percentage complete relates to the overall project. [Crosswind Manual 7.14.1; *PMBOK® Guide* 7.4.2.2]

7. Company-wide server upgrades are an example of what type of project cost?

Correct Answer: (A) Variable indirect
Explanation: This type of cost typically increases for every server and is not likely associated with a specific project. Therefore, variable indirect is the best description. Variable is not the best answer. Fixed and fixed direct cost descriptions don't fit this type of cost except in one instance: If the question had limited the server upgrades to a fixed license fee for a web server used in a web project, the answer would have been (C) Fixed. [Crosswind Manual 7.1; No *PMBOK® Guide* Reference]

8. The project team is planning an upgrade to a client's website and infrastructure. During planning, the team members discover the need for a data communications line to connect to the servers. What type of cost is this?

Correct Answer: (A) Direct
Explanation: The data communication line is a direct cost. It is something purchased directly for the project. It is not an indirect or variable cost. [Crosswind Manual 7.1; No *PMBOK® Guide* Reference]

9. The infrastructure project is behind schedule and over budget. So far, $3M has been spent on the project. The sponsor is considering if it should allow the project to continue. What should he consider the $3M that has been spent so far?

Correct Answer: (B) Sunk cost
Explanation: Sunk cost is one that has already been spent on the project. It shouldn't be taken into consideration when determining whether to continue on the project. There is nothing in the situation about phasing the project. The budgeted cost of work performed is the earned value (EV). Opportunity cost doesn't apply here. [Crosswind Manual 7.5; No *PMBOK® Guide* Reference]

10. The highway project is in the middle of planning when the project manager presents a status reporting method to the team. The team members haven't heard of this method before. It's called earned value. To attain buy-in from the team, the project manager begins to explain what earned value status reporting can do for the project, explaining that it will measure which of the following?

Correct Answer: (B) Scope, schedule, and cost
Explanation: Earned value deals with scope, schedule, and cost. Actual cost (AC) shows cost. Planned value (PV) shows the state of the schedule. Earned value (EV) shows scope. The formulas that work with these three variables show how the three are interacting together. [Crosswind Manual 7.14.1; *PMBOK® Guide* 7.4.2.2]

11. You are having a home theater room added to your house. The project should take five days and cost $1,500 per day to complete. After three days, the project is 30% complete and $5,000 has been spent. What is the amount of work that should have been done so far?

Correct Answer: (D) $4,500
Explanation: To determine the PV (planned value) for the days already worked, multiply the cost per day by the number of days worked: $1,500 multiplied by three days equals $4,500. Note that planned value is defined as the work that should have been completed either to date or during a particular time period (in this case, to date through day three). [Crosswind Manual 7.14.1; *PMBOK® Guide* 7.4.2.2]

12. Project A has an NPV of $275K over 2.5 years. Project B has an IRR of 3.2%. Project C has a BCR of 0.89:1. Project D has four people on it and is encountering scope creep. Which of the following projects stand the greatest chance of getting canceled?

Correct Answer: (C) Project C
Explanation: Project C has a negative BCR because it is creating less revenue than the cost. Project A and B have positive financials. Project D appears to have some issues, but we don't know enough about it to determine anything else. [Crosswind Manual 7.2; No *PMBOK® Guide* Reference]

13. The BCR project comparison function utilizes what variable(s)?

Correct Answer: (A) Revenue and cost
Explanation: The BCR is the benefit cost ratio. It considers the benefit (or revenue) and cost of an initiative. It doesn't factor in profit or profit margin. [Crosswind Manual 7.2; No *PMBOK® Guide* Reference]

14. The project planning process group is progressing. The team has involved the accounting department to set up a system of codes that the accounting department will use to track work on the project. This is known as what?

Correct Answer: (D) Chart of accounts
Explanation: The chart of accounts sets up codes that will be used to track project cost. The other answers are distracters. [Crosswind Manual 7.13.1; No *PMBOK® Guide* Reference]

15. The project management team has performed earned value analysis on its project and discovered that the project is behind schedule and over budget. The SPI is 0.82 and the CPI is 0.73. The team is trying to determine how efficient it needs to be with the remaining resources to complete the project on budget. Which of the following is the team trying to calculate?

Correct Answer: (D) To-complete performance index
Explanation: The to-complete performance index (TCPI) shows the efficiency needed of the remaining resources to come in on budget. Cost variance (CV) shows the difference between work done and what was paid for it. Cost performance index (CPI) shows the ratio between the work done and what was paid for it. The estimate to complete (ETC) shows the amount remaining to be spent based on the current spending efficiency (CPI). [Crosswind Manual 7.14.1; *PMBOK® Guide* 7.4.2.2]

16. What is the range of a rough order of magnitude (ROM) estimate?

Correct Answer: (C) -25% to +75%
Explanation: The range of a rough order of magnitude (ROM) estimate is -25% to +75%. The other answers are distracters. [Crosswind Manual 7.12; *PMBOK® Guide* 7.2]

17. The project is using a new server that cost $25,000. The project manager is told to set up depreciation for the server over a five-year schedule, with the server having a value of $0 at the end of five years. Standard depreciation will be used in the calculation. What is the amount per year the server will depreciate?

Correct Answer: (A) $5,000
Explanation: To calculate this value, determine a few values first. What is the value of the asset at the end of the schedule? What is the amount of the asset to begin with? What is the number of years of the depreciation schedule? First, subtract the ending value of the asset from the beginning value of the asset ($25K - $0 = $25K). The $25K is then divided by the years (5) of the depreciation schedule. This calculation results in $5K per year of depreciation. [Crosswind Manual 7.6.1; No *PMBOK® Guide* Reference]

18. You are having a home theater room added to your house. The project should take five days and cost $1,500 per day to complete. After three days, the project is 30% complete and $5,000 has been spent. What is the ETC?

Correct Answer: (A) $11,666.67
Explanation: The formula for calculating the ETC (estimate to complete) is ETC = EAC – AC. In this instance five steps are required. First, determine the BAC (budget at completion) by multiplying the cost per day by the number of days it will take to complete the project: $1,500 x 5 = a BAC of $7,500. Second, calculate the EV (earned value) by multiplying the BAC by the percentage complete: $7,500 BAC x 30% complete = an EV of $2,250. Third, calculate the CPI (cost performance index) by dividing the EV by the AC (actual cost): $2,250 EV divided by $5,000 AC = a CPI of .45. Fourth, calculate the EAC (estimate at completion) by dividing the BAC by the CPI: $7,500 / .45 = $16,666.67. Fifth, subtract the AC from the EAC: $16,666.67 - $5,000 = $11,666.67. [Crosswind Manual 7.14.1; *PMBOK® Guide* 7.4.2.2]

19. Which of the following shows the remaining amount to be spent on the project based on current spending efficiency?

Correct Answer: (B) Estimate to complete
Explanation: Estimate to complete (ETC) shows the remaining amount to be spent on a project based on spending efficiency. This value is the difference between actual cost (AC) and estimate at completion (EAC). Estimate at completion (EAC) is a forecast of total project cost, based on spending efficiency. Cost variance (CV) is the difference between the amount of work done and what was paid for it. Budget remaining is a distracter. [Crosswind Manual 7.14.1; *PMBOK® Guide* 7.4.2.2]

20. Which of the following shows the rate at which the project is progressing compared to what was planned?

Correct Answer: (D) Schedule performance index
Explanation: The schedule performance index (SPI) shows the rate at which the schedule is progressing. The SPI is established by showing the ratio between work done, also known as earned value (EV) and work scheduled, also known as planned value (PV). The schedule variance (SV) is the difference between work done, also known as earned value (EV) and work scheduled, also known as planned value (PV). The Gantt chart shows the schedule of the project. A variance report shows the difference between two items being measured. [Crosswind Manual 7.14.1; *PMBOK® Guide* 7.4.2.2]

21. Which process aggregates estimated costs from the individual work packages or activities to create a summary and detailed breakdown of project costs?

Correct Answer: (C) Determine budget
Explanation: Determine Budget applies costs from the individual work packages or activities to establish an authorized cost baseline. This could be at a summary or detailed level depending on the needs of the project at the time. Estimate Costs approximates the costs needed to complete project activities. Control Costs manages the cost of the project. Earned value management is a distracter. [Crosswind Manual 7.13; *PMBOK® Guide* 7.3]

22. The project team is planning an upgrade to a client's website and infrastructure. During planning, the team members are confronted with the cost options for a data communications line to connect to the servers. They consider the cost of purchasing the communication line for the time they need to develop the project. After that, the customer takes over the purchase of the line. They are also considering a long-term commitment that the customer can make with the communication line provider, which provides a less costly solution over the use of the system. What type of analysis is the team considering?

Correct Answer: (A) Life cycle costing
Explanation: Life cycle costing looks at the long-term cost of something, instead of simply what it costs to create it. This can increase project cost but in the long run save the owner of the system money. The other answers are distracters. [Crosswind Manual 7.7; No *PMBOK® Guide* Reference]

23. You are having a home theater room added to your house. The project should take five days and cost $1,500 per day to complete. After three days, the project is 30% complete and $5,000 has been spent. What do you expect the project to cost at completion based on the current performance?

Correct Answer: (B) $16,666.67
Explanation: The formula for calculating the EAC (estimate at completion) is EAC = BAC / CPI. In this instance four steps are required. First, determine the BAC (budget at completion) by multiplying the cost per day by the number of days it will take to complete the project: $1,500 x 5 = $7,500. Second, calculate the EV (earned value) by multiplying the BAC by the percentage complete: $7,500 x 30% = $2,250. Third, calculate the CPI (cost performance index) by dividing the EV by the AC (actual cost): $2,250 / $5,000 AC = .45. Fourth, calculate the EAC by dividing the BAC by the CPI: $7,500 / .45 = $16,666.67. [Crosswind Manual 7.14.1; *PMBOK® Guide* 7.4.2.2]

24. The planning process group is progressing. The team has involved a number of expert opinions in trying to approximate the costs needed to complete project activities. This process is known as?

Correct Answer: (D) Estimate costs
Explanation: Estimate Costs obtains an approximation of the resource costs for activities or work packages. Determine Budget sums the costs to the individual work packages or activities to establish an authorized cost baseline. Control Costs manages the cost of the project. Analogous estimating is a distracter. [Crosswind Manual 7.11; *PMBOK® Guide* 7.2]

25. Which of the following is an example of fixed formula status reporting?

Correct Answer: (D) 30%/70% rule
Explanation: The 30%/70% rule is an example of fixed formula progress reporting. It means that when the activity starts, it is given a 30% complete status and will not receive the remaining 70% until it is fully complete. PV x percentage complete of each activity is the formula for earned value. The other answers are distracters. [Crosswind Manual 7.8; No *PMBOK® Guide* Reference]

26. The project is using some application and database servers in the development environment. The finance department explains that the servers will be depreciated using the double declining balance (DDB) format. This is an example of what?

Correct Answer: (C) Accelerated depreciation
Explanation: Double declining balance and sum of the digits are both examples of accelerated depreciation. DDB is not standard depreciation. The other answers are distracters. [Crosswind Manual 7.6.2; No *PMBOK® Guide* Reference]

27. The project team is developing rules for reporting updates on the project. The majority of their activities are less than two reporting periods long. Which format is best to use in this case?

Correct Answer: (A) Fixed formula progress reporting
Explanation: Fixed formula uses a partial credit approach such as 50/50 and is ideal when an activity is short, such as two or less reporting periods long. The weighted milestone approach is ideal when an activity is over two reporting periods in length. Earned value shows the status of the scope, schedule, and cost of the project. Forecast reporting focuses on what is getting ready to be done on the project. [Crosswind Manual 7.8; No *PMBOK® Guide* Reference]

28. You have $1,000 today and can earn 8%. In future years, how much money will this be worth?

Correct Answer: (D) Not enough information
Explanation: To calculate future value (FV), you need to have a present value (PV), an interest rate, and the time period involved. Therefore, without a time period in the question there is not enough information to answer the question. [Crosswind Manual 7.3, 7.4; No *PMBOK® Guide* Reference]

29. You are having a home theater room added to your house. The project should take five days and cost $1,500 per day to complete. After three days, the project is 30% complete and $5,000 has been spent. What is the SPI?

Correct Answer: (B) 0.50
Explanation: The formula for calculating the SPI (schedule performance index) is SPI = EV / PV. In this instance three steps are required. First, determine the PV (planned value): $1,500 per day cost multiplied by three days equals a PV of $4,500. Second, calculate the EV (earned value) by multiplying the BAC (budget at completion), since the percentage complete refers to the entire project, by the percentage complete: $7,500 x 30% = $2,250. Third, calculate the SPI by dividing the EV by the PV: $2,250 / $4,500 = 0.5. Note that planned value is defined as the work that should have been completed to date or during a particular time period (in this case, through day three of the project). [Crosswind Manual 7.14.1; *PMBOK® Guide* 7.4.2.2]

30. Which of the following metrics tell you if you are ahead of schedule?

Correct Answer: (A) Schedule performance index (SPI)
Explanation: The schedule performance index (SPI) tells you if you are ahead of, on, or behind schedule. An index less than 1.0 means you are having schedule problems. An index of 1.0 means you are doing exactly as planned on the schedule. An index greater than 1.0 means you are progressing faster than planned. The cost performance index (CPI) shows the spending efficiency of the project. The budget at completion (BAC) is the overall budget estimate for the project. The cost variance (CV) shows the amount that the project is over or under budget. [Crosswind Manual 7.14.1; *PMBOK® Guide* 7.4.2.2]

Chapter 8

Project Quality Management

Project Quality Management entails meeting the stakeholders objectives by assimilating the organization's quality policy into the planning, management, and control of the project and project quality requirements. The specific approaches, tools, and techniques used are dependent on the type of deliverables the project will produce.

Project Quality Management also reinforces a continuous quality improvement culture.

The goal of the quality processes is to align them with the International Organization for Standardization (ISO). They should align with concepts created by Deming, Juran, and Crosby, as well as TQM (Total Quality Management), Six Sigma, FMEA (Failure Mode and Effect Analysis), VOC (Voice of the Customer), Continuous Improvement, and COQ (Cost of Quality).

Figure 8-1: Quality Management Process Interaction shows the three quality processes.

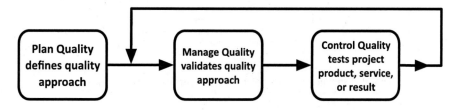

Figure 8-1: Quality Management Process Interaction
The source for the above figure is the Project Management Institute, *A Guide to the Project Management Body of Knowledge*, (*PMBOK® Guide*) – Sixth Edition, Project Management Institute Inc., 2017, Figure 8.1, Page 255

A memory tool for Quality is **PMC** (**P**lan Quality, **M**anage Quality, **C**ontrol Quality).

Trends
Selected quality approaches should reduce variances and produce results that meet requirements. They should emphasize customer satisfaction, continuous improvement, management responsibility, and, if applicable, a mutually beneficial relationship with suppliers.

Tailoring
Project tailoring, the manner in which processes of a knowledge area are exercised, is employed to address the distinctive nature of each project. Successful project tailoring is predicated on a careful consideration of:

- Policy compliance and auditing
- Standards and regulatory compliance
- Continuous improvement
- Stakeholder engagement

Agile/Adaptive Environment

Agile methods employ frequent quality and review events that occur throughout the project. Recurring retrospectives are used to examine the proficiency of the quality processes. If any issue is discovered, an analysis of the root cause is undertaken and new approaches may be employed on a trial basis. The new approaches are then evaluated during subsequent retrospectives. The goal of employing frequent quality and review events is to discover inconsistencies and issues early on, when the cost of change is less expensive.

The source for the above text is the Project Management Institute, *A Guide to the Project Management Body of Knowledge*, (*PMBOK® Guide*) – Sixth Edition, Project Management Institute Inc., 2017, Pages 254-259

In this chapter, we discuss the following:

Figure 8-2: Quality Processes

The source for the above figure is the Project Management Institute, *A Guide to the Project Management Body of Knowledge*, (*PMBOK® Guide*) – Sixth Edition, Project Management Institute Inc., 2017, Figure 8.2, Page 256

	Crosswind "Must Knows" for Project Quality Management
	Key Inputs, Tools & Techniques, and Outputs for Plan Quality Management
	Key Inputs, Tools & Techniques, and Outputs for Manage Quality
	Key Inputs, Tools & Techniques, and Outputs for Control Quality
	Definition of quality
	Definition of Total Quality Management
	Continuous improvement concepts
	Definition of gold plating
	Differences between grade and quality, and how to apply them
	Differences between precision and accuracy
	Differences between prevention and inspection
	Cost of conformance and nonconformance
	Definition and application of Design of Experiments (DOE)
	Basics of Just-in-Time (JIT) inventory and that the amount of inventory needed is 0%
	The percentages of 1, 2, 3 and 6 sigma
	Basics of probabilities and concept that the sum of all possible probabilities must equal 1.0 (100%)
	The more recognizable proprietary quality management methodologies and when to apply them
	At what point the worker, the project manager, and senior management are all responsible for quality

Chapter 8 Quality

	Principles of measuring a sample vs. the entire population
	Variables and attributes
	Statistical independence and mutual exclusivity
	Characteristics of a Pareto diagram
	Characteristics of a scatter diagram
	Principles and components of a control (run) chart including the upper and lower control limits, upper and lower specification limits, and the mean
	The characteristics of a cause-and-effect (Ishikawa/fishbone) diagram and the environment in which it is used

Although helpful, this list is not all-inclusive in regard to information needed for the exam. It is only suggested material that, if understood and memorized, may increase your exam score.

8.1. Definition of Quality

Project Management Institute, Inc. defines quality **as the degree to which a set of inherent characteristics fulfill requirements**. It's key to understand that stated (or implied) needs are used to generate project requirements. Generating the requirements is typically accomplished via stakeholder management by using key (influential) stakeholder wants, needs, and expectations to generate those requirements during the processes associated with project scope.

Learn the definition of quality.

Crosswind also recommends familiarity with an older definition of quality: conformance to requirements and Fitness for Use.

8.2. Project Management and Quality Management

Project management and quality management should complement each other as they work together. Both focus on items such as customer satisfaction, management responsibility, continuous improvement, and prevention over inspection.

8.3. Total Quality Management (TQM)

Total Quality Management is a quality management philosophy conceived by **Dr. Deming** that approaches quality management proactively and applies statistical analysis as the basis for documenting improvement.

Know the definition of Total Quality Management.

The philosophy espouses planning quality and testing throughout development rather than relying on inspections after completion of the work. Testing throughout development provides an immediate feedback loop so that process problems are likely to be detected early on, when less time and money are required to correct the problems.

W. Edwards Deming's 14 principles of management are considered the foundational basis for Total Quality Management. While knowing all 14 principals is not necessary for the exam, familiarity with the following points is important:

- Be proactive, not reactive
- Utilize leadership and accountability
- Measure improvement throughout the process, striving for continuous improvement
  Continuous process improvement is key to TQM.

8.4. Zero Defects

Zero Defects is a concept created by **Philip Crosby**. Its goal is to meet quality requirements the first time and every time. It emphasizes prevention over inspection (prevent problems rather than discover them during inspections that occur at the end of the process when correction is costlier in terms of time and cost).

8.5. Fitness for Use

The **Fitness for Use** concept was created by **Joseph Juran** with the primary goal of determining and satisfying the **real needs of the customer and stakeholders**.

Pareto Chart
80% / 20% rule

8.6. Continuous Improvement (Kaizen)

Continuous Improvement takes a **proactive approach to development with the emphasis on making improvements throughout a process**. An example of process improvement is using automated shipping software instead of performing all shipping activities manually. This approach improves the shipping process by reducing the potential for error.

Understand Continuous Improvement concepts.

Unless there is a major environmental change, major process improvements are likely to occur at the beginning of an initiative with minor improvements occurring later.

Popular process improvement approaches include **Malcolm Baldrige**, **Organizational Project Management Maturity Model (OPM3)**, and **Capability Maturity Model Integration (CMMI)**.

8.7. Gold Plating

Gold plating is the practice of providing more than what the customer requested. This practice is unacceptable and professionally irresponsible. The project team is obligated to provide the product, service, or result that corresponds exactly to customer requirements.

Understand what gold plating means.

An example of gold plating is including functionality in a software application that is not included in the finalized customer requirements.

8.8. Plan Quality Management (Planning Process Group)

Planning quality management consists of determining and designing the standards, policies, and procedures for the project. It requires giving careful consideration to the rules that will define quality and establishing the procedures that will be used to ensure that the product, service, or result of the project fulfills expected requirements and meets the project's quality standards.

Know the Key Inputs, Tools & Techniques, and Outputs for Plan Quality Management.

Plan Quality Management

Inputs

Project charter
Project management plan
- **Requirements Management Plan**
- **Risk Management Plan**
- Stakeholder Engagement Plan
- **Scope Baseline**
Project documents
- Assumption Log
- **Requirements Documentation**
- **Requirements Traceability Matrix**
- **Risk Register**
- **Stakeholder Register**
Enterprise Environmental Factors
Organizational Process Assets

Outputs

Quality Management Plan
Quality Metrics
Project Management Plan Updates
- Risk Management Plan
- Scope Baseline
Project Documents Updates
- Lessons Learned Register
- Requirements Traceability Matrix
- Risk Register
- Stakeholder Register

Tools and Techniques

Expert Judgment
Data Gathering
- **Benchmarking**
- Brainstorming
- Interviews
Data Analysis
- **Cost-benefit Analysis**
- **Cost of Quality**

Decision Making
- Multicriteria Decision Analysis
Data Representation
- **Flowcharts**
- Logical Data Model
- Matrix Diagrams
- Mind Mapping
Test and inspection planning
Meetings

Figure 8-3: Plan Quality Management Data Flow Diagram
The source for the above figure is the Project Management Institute, *A Guide to the Project Management Body of Knowledge*, (*PMBOK® Guide*) – Sixth Edition, Project Management Institute Inc., 2017, Figure 8.3, Page 260

Chapter 8
Quality

Plan Quality Management (Planning)		
Key Inputs	Requirements Management Plan	The requirements management plan is a component of the project management plan that details the evaluation, documentation, and administration of project requirements. It includes the methods for designing, monitoring, and reporting requirement activities and configuration activities; prioritizing requirements; determining requirement metrics; and capturing attributes for the requirements traceability matrix. It also includes the requirements for project approval, measurable project goals, and related success criteria that impact the quality management of the project.
	Risk Management Plan	The risk management plan is a component of the project management plan that details the manner in which risk management activities are configured and implemented. Typically it addresses risk strategy, risk methodology, roles and responsibilities, financing, timing, and classification. It documents processes and controls that influence the estimation and administration of cost. The risk management plan and the quality management plan are considered together to ensure product and project success.
	Scope Baseline	The scope baseline is the authorized version of project scope. It contains the project scope statement, the work breakdown statement (WBS), the work package, one or more planning packages, and the WBS dictionary. It describes the work the project is trying to complete. The baseline is subject to change management and is a component of the project management plan. The WBS and the scope statement (specially the deliverables, constraints, and assumption) are referenced in order to establish appropriate quality standards and goals.
	Requirements Documentation	Requirements documentation delineates how requirements fulfill the business needs of the project. In order to baseline requirements, they must be measurable, testable, traceable, complete, consistent, and acceptable to appropriate stakeholders. Requirements may be categorized as **business requirements**, **stakeholder requirements**, s**olution requirements** (both **functional** and **non-functional**), **transition requirements**, **project requirements**, and **quality requirements**. Once categorized, requirements can be refined as they evolve. Requirements related to quality are used to establish the manner in which project quality control is executed.

Plan Quality Management (Continued)		
Key Inputs (Cont.)	Requirements Traceability Matrix	To ensure that requirements add value, the requirements traceability matrix is a grid used to align requirements to the deliverables that satisfy them. The matrix allows the requirements to be monitored throughout the project life cycle and provides a framework for managing scope changes. At a minimum, requirements can be traced to business needs, project aims, project scope and WBS deliverables, product design and development, testing, and high-level requirements. The matrix associates product requirements with deliverables in an effort to insure that each requirement is tested and that the tested requirements increase overall project quality.
	Risk Register	The risk register lists all identified risks, along with the owner of and potential response(s) to each risk. The register may also contain, for each risk, a short title, category, status, source(s), impact(s), trigger(s), WBS reference for affected activities, and timing data. Additionally, the register lists details regarding threats and opportunities that could impact quality, especially in areas that coincide with the needs and expectations of the customer and sponsor.
	Stakeholder Register	The stakeholder register delineates stakeholder information that includes, but is not limited to, identification data (name, position, location, contact information, and project role), assessment information (important requirements, expectations, and level of influence), and classification (internal or external, influence, or other classification model). The register is used to determine which stakeholders have an interest in or influence on quality, especially in areas that coincide with the needs and expectations of the customer and sponsor.
Key Tools & Techniques	Expert Judgment	Expert judgment is judgment based on expertise acquired in a specific area. It is often more significant and accurate than the best modeling tools available and can be provided by stakeholders, organizational personnel external to the project, professional organizations or groups, and consultants. It is important to consider expertise related to quality assurance, control, metrics, improvements and systems.

Plan Quality Management (Continued)		
Key Tools & Techniques (Cont.)	Benchmarking	Benchmarking is used to compare an organization's practices to those of corresponding organizations in order to identify best practices, ideas for improvement, and performance metrics. Benchmarking may involve projects inside or outside of the organization and from inside or outside the same application area.
	Cost-benefit Analysis	Cost-benefit analysis is a tool used to determine the most cost effective course of action by establishing and assessing the positives and negatives of those considered. If the planned quality activities are the most cost effective, quality requirements will be met and the project is likely to experience less rework, higher productivity, increased stakeholder satisfaction, and increased profitability.
	Cost of Quality	The cost of quality (COQ) considers **preventative costs** (costs associated with preventing unsatisfactory quality), **appraisal costs** (costs associated with evaluation and testing), and/or **failure costs** (costs associated with failure to meet the stakeholders' expectations) that relate to the result of the project (products, deliverables, and services). The cost of prevention and appraisal should be compared to the cost of failure in order to achieve the optimal balance. Models demonstrate that there is an optimal quality cost for a project.
	Flowcharts	Flowcharts graphically display the progression of activities (and their branching potential) for a process that converts one or more inputs into one or more outputs. They display the activities, decision points, branching loops, parallel paths, and order of processing, Flowcharts may be useful in determining the cost of quality for a process.
	Test and Inspection Planning	Test and inspection planning occurs during planning. The project manager and project team establish the manner in which the product, deliverable, or service will be tested or inspected in order to meet stakeholders' needs or expectations, correspond with the appropriate industry (e.g. strength tests for construction projects), and satisfy performance and reliability goals.

Plan Quality Management (Continued)		
Key Outputs	Quality Management Plan	The quality management plan is a component of the project management plan that details the manner in which the policies, methods, and criteria of the organization are executed. It details activities and necessary resources to accomplish quality goals. Typically the plan addresses quality criteria, roles and responsibilities, tools, objectives, control and quality management activities, and procedures (including those for continuous improvement). It also identifies the processes and deliverables subject to quality review.
	Quality Metrics	Quality metrics delineate the manner in which the Control Quality process verifies compliance with a project or product through its defined attributes. Quality metrics include cost performance, failure rate, defect frequency, maintainability, test coverage, and reliability among others.

Situational Question and Real World Application

Failure to effectively perform the Plan Quality Management process often produces project results that are out of alignment with the project scope statement. If the quality management plan does not reference the acceptance criteria included in the scope baseline, there can be no effective verification of acceptability or determination of the specific areas of unacceptability.

8.8.1.   Quality Management Plan

The purpose of the quality management plan is to assist the project team in:

- Establishing the definition of quality for the project and its work (quality baseline)
- Establishing checklists to ensure processes are followed
- Defining all process steps
- Validating that established quality processes are effective
- Testing throughout development
- Formatting project/process data for communication to project stakeholders
- Responding effectively to any changes in the project's quality standards and processes

---

8.8.2. Grade vs. Quality

It is very important to understand the difference between grade and quality: while **grade** refers to the **characteristics of the product,** **quality** refers to the **stability or predictability of the product.**

A high-grade product is a product with high functionality (for instance, an automatic nail gun that can be used with 10 kinds of nails and can apply various levels of pressure, essentially meeting any type of nailing need). A low-grade product is a product with minimum functionality (for instance, an inexpensive nail gun that can only apply one level of pressure).

A high-quality product is designed and constructed for dependability and efficiency. It functions in accordance with customer requirements, is reasonably sturdy, and, if necessary, has clear and effective instructions. Any product that does not do this is lacking in quality.

Understand the differences between grade and quality and how to apply them.

8.8.3. Accuracy vs. Precision

It is also important to understand the difference between accuracy and precision.

Accuracy refers to the **alignment of a value with its target value.** For example, if the targeted output of a process is 300 milliliters, accuracy is determined by calculating how close the actual output is to the 300 milliliters target.

Precision refers to the **consistency of the output**. If a process has a targeted output of 300 milliliters, precision is determined by calculating the percentage of tests with an output of 300 milliliters in relation to the total number of tests.

Understand the differences between precision and accuracy.

8.8.4. Prevention vs. Inspection

Prevention, a proactive approach to quality, entails **eliminating defects and potential defects** from the process.

Inspection, a reactive approach to quality, entails discovering **errors or defects after the work is complete.**

8.8.5. Attribute Sampling vs. Variable Sampling

Attribute sampling entails **checking that the actual result conforms** to the expected result.

Variable sampling entails **rating the result on a continuous scale that determines the degree of conformity** to the expected result.

8.8.6. Tolerances vs. Control Limits

Tolerances are a **specified range of acceptable results.**

Control limits are **identified boundaries of common variation in a statistically stable process** or process performances.

Understand the differences between prevention and inspection.

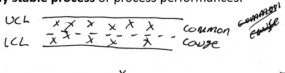

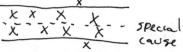

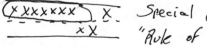

PMI, CAPM, and PMBOK are registered marks of the Project Management Institute, Inc.

296   © 2008-2018 Crosswind Learning, www.crosswindpm.com

8.8.7. Cost of Quality

PMBOK pg. 283

The cost of quality is equal to the **cost of conformance or the cost of nonconformance**.

Conformance to quality is a proactive approach that typically requires paying for quality upfront by investing in initiatives that plan quality into the work. Examples of proactive investments are additional planning, testing throughout development (adjusting processes as needed to improve quality), and providing quality training to the team.   Conformance to quality typically has a positive effect on team morale, customer perception, and product cost.

Conformance:

Nonconformance:

Nonconformance to quality is a reactive approach that typically requires paying for quality after the work is complete by investing in rework. Examples of reactive investments are the costs associated with rework in terms of salaries and materials. Nonconformance typically has a negative impact on team morale, customer perception, and product cost in the form of excessive inventory, waste, and warranty support.

Understand the cost of conformance and nonconformance.

Cost of Conformance and Cost of Nonconformance		
Cost Item	**Conformance (Prevention)**	**Nonconformance (Inspection)**
Proactive analysis of process improvement	X	
Company training relating to quality and continuous improvement	X	
Excess inventory	X	
Reduced warranty support	X	
Excessive inventory		X
Throwing away defective products		X
Warranty support		X
Reacting to problems after they occur		X

8.8.8. Design of Experiments

Design of Experiments (DOE) is a statistical process used to determine the factors that can influence variables associated with a process or product. DOE should be applied during the Plan Quality Management process to determine the overall impact on the cost of quality based on testing types and number. It is useful when optimizing products or processes.

Know the definition and application of Design of Experiments (DOE).

8.8.9.   Just-in-Time (JIT)

Just-in-Time (JIT) is an inventory management process that results in little to no inventory, other than what is required to fulfill existing orders. Ideally, **zero inventory** is stocked and supplies arrive only when needed for product fulfillment. JIT reduces overall costs by lowering or eliminating the costs associated with unnecessary inventory.

Know the basics of Just-in-Time (JIT) inventory and that the amount of inventory needed is 0%.

8.8.10.   Normal Distribution

Normal distribution is typically depicted as a bell shaped curve that represents a typical outcome from project activity with no abnormalities, that is a curve with an equal mean, medium, and mode. A variance in the bell shape (the curve is tighter or the "hill" is steeper) is still normal; the data is just much closer in the measurement. Other examples of distribution formats include **beta** and **triangular** distributions.

8.8.11.   Sigma (σ)

Sigma (σ), also known as standard deviation, is often used as a quality measure. The formula for standard deviation is (P - O) / 6 where P represents Pessimistic and **O** represents Optimistic.

Memorize the percentages of 1, 2, 3, and 6 sigma.

It is not necessary to become a statistician to understand the concept of sigma in relation to quality. Instead, apply the concept of **"Realistics®."** Realistics® was developed by Crosswind as a sensible way to approach sigma. While Six Sigma expresses sigma as +/- (for example 68.26% is +/- 1 sigma), Realistics would express 68.26% as 1 sigma.

The following diagram represents **68.26% as 1 sigma,** which is the typical quality standard used in the workplace. To meet the quality standard when producing 100 units, 68.26 or more units must work and 31.74 units or less (100% of 100 - 68.26% of 100) may fail. That failure rate leads to rework/waste costs.

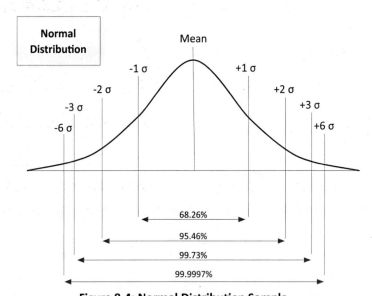

Figure 8-4: Normal Distribution Sample

The source for the above figure is the Project Management Institute, *A Guide to the Project Management Body of Knowledge*, (*PMBOK® Guide*) – Sixth Edition, Project Management Institute Inc., 2017, Figure 8.4, Page 260

PMI, CAPM, and PMBOK are registered marks of the Project Management Institute, Inc.

298   © 2008-2018 Crosswind Learning, www.crosswindpm.com

By increasing the standard to **2 sigma** (**95.46%**), the quantity of expected passing measurement or product must be increased to 95.46 units out of 100 units (no more than 4.54 units can fail). While this decreases the cost of rework and waste, costs associated with achieving the standard (quality training and other proactive activities) must be considered. The precision used to calculate these values will result in slightly different answers (e.g., 68.26%, 68.27%, 68.28% etc.). Note that the exam might use percentages that vary slightly (68.2%, 95.0%, 99.7%, 99.999%) .

8.8.12. Probabilities

A probability is the likelihood that something will occur. It can be expressed in a percentage (1%, 75%, 100%) or as a decimal (0.01, 0.75, 1.0). For the exam, it is key to understand that the sum of all probabilities equals 100% or 1.0.

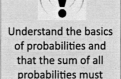

Understand the basics of probabilities and that the sum of all probabilities must equal 1.0 (100%).

8.8.13. Proprietary Quality Management Methodologies

There are many proprietary quality management methodologies. Among the more recognizable are:

- CMMI
- Six Sigma
- Lean Six Sigma
- Quality Function Deployment

Understand the more recognizable proprietary quality management methodologies and know when to apply them.

8.8.14. Six Sigma

Six Sigma is a modern quality philosophy made popular by Motorola and other companies in the late 80s. It involves setting a very high standard of 6 sigma for the products or processes that the company produces. In essence, this philosophy states that at least **99.9997%** of everything created, or processes executed, are virtually error-free.

8.8.15. ISO 9000 (International Organization for Standardization)

The International Organization for Standardization (ISO) standard is associated with companies that wish to document and adhere to their processes. While quality improvement is not always a result of this standard, the repeatability associated with it typically shows a positive benefit. A company can also use this standard as a requirement for its partners to ensure they have defined repeatable processes.

Generally ISO involves:

- Documenting what is done
- Doing what is documented
- Documenting any variance (from the normal processes)

8.8.16. Quality Responsibility

It is very important to know the level of responsibility for quality by role.

This knowledge:

- May be required to correctly answer some question on the exam
- May insure that project quality will not slip as a result of a misunderstanding regarding which role is responsible for quality

The following table details three roles, their levels of responsibility, and an example.

Role	Level of Responsibility	Example
Team member or worker	Responsible for the quality of their own work	The electrician is accountable for doing satisfactory work on the job.
Project Manager	Responsible for the quality standards on the project	The project manager is responsible for the quality of the networking project.
Senior/Executive Management	Responsible for the quality standards at the organization	The CEO and senior management are responsible for quality at the organization.

Know at what point the worker, the project manager, and senior management are responsible for quality.

8.9. Manage Quality (Executing Process Group)

Manage Quality is the process of executing the project quality management plan and verifying/validating that the quality standards defined for the project will meet the desired standards. This process **validates the quality process, not the product,** by taking a random sampling of items created in order to verify a desired level of acceptability.

During Manage Quality, the quality management plan is executed.

For the situational questions on the exam, the Project Management Institute, Inc. assumes that the environment has a quality assurance initiative and a quality assurance/audit system in place.

Know the Key Inputs, Tools & Techniques, and Outputs for Manage Quality.

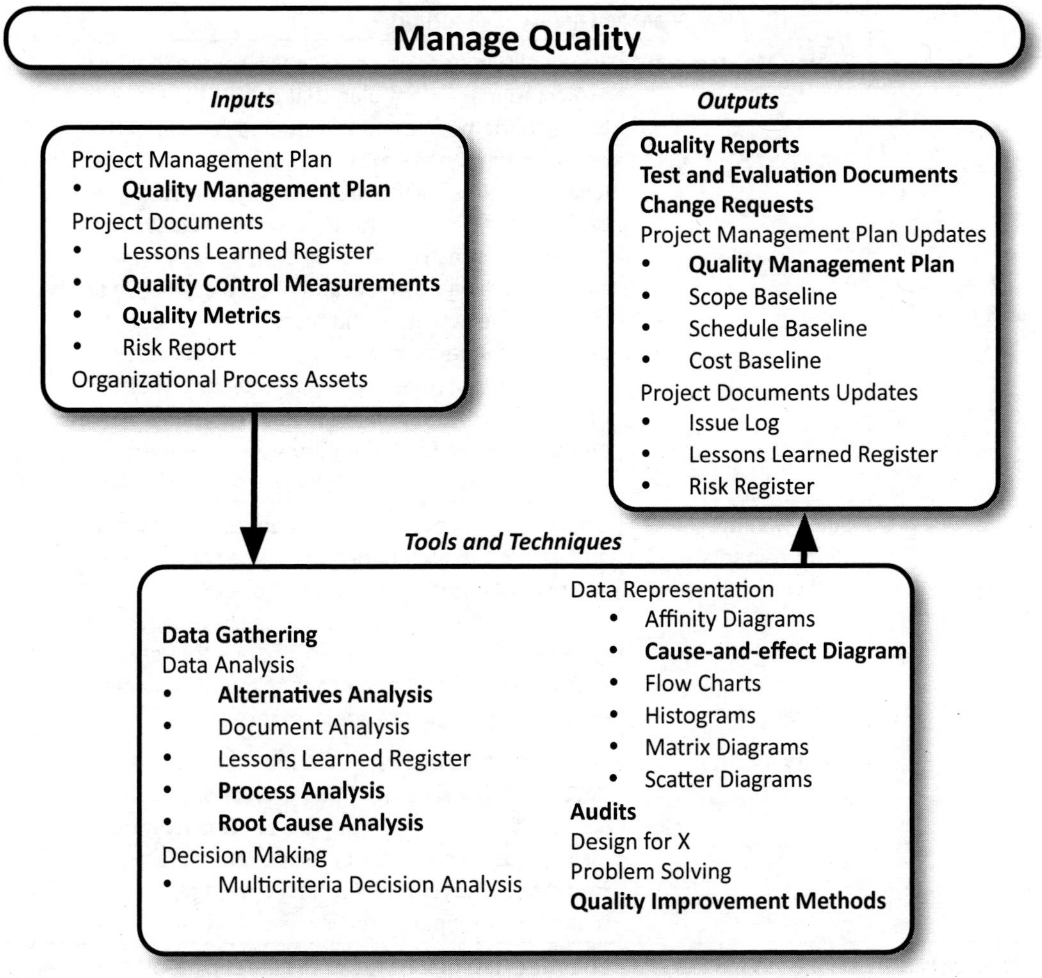

Manage Quality

Inputs

Project Management Plan
- **Quality Management Plan**

Project Documents
- Lessons Learned Register
- **Quality Control Measurements**
- **Quality Metrics**
- Risk Report

Organizational Process Assets

Outputs

Quality Reports
Test and Evaluation Documents
Change Requests
Project Management Plan Updates
- **Quality Management Plan**
- Scope Baseline
- Schedule Baseline
- Cost Baseline

Project Documents Updates
- Issue Log
- Lessons Learned Register
- Risk Register

Tools and Techniques

Data Gathering
Data Analysis
- **Alternatives Analysis**
- Document Analysis
- Lessons Learned Register
- **Process Analysis**
- **Root Cause Analysis**

Decision Making
- Multicriteria Decision Analysis

Data Representation
- Affinity Diagrams
- **Cause-and-effect Diagram**
- Flow Charts
- Histograms
- Matrix Diagrams
- Scatter Diagrams

Audits
Design for X
Problem Solving
Quality Improvement Methods

Figure 8-5: Manage Quality Data Flow Diagram
The source for the above figure is the Project Management Institute, *A Guide to the Project Management Body of Knowledge*, (*PMBOK® Guide*) – Sixth Edition, Project Management Institute Inc., 2017, Figure 8.7, Page 269

Manage Quality (Executing)		
Key Inputs	Quality Management Plan	The quality management plan is a component of the project management plan that details the manner in which the policies, methods, and criteria of the organization are executed. It delineates the expected level of quality for the project and product, details the manner in which this level will be achieved, and provides instructions for the disposition of nonconforming products and related corrective action. It details the activities and resources necessary to accomplish quality goals. Typically it addresses quality criteria, roles and responsibilities, tools, objectives, control and quality management activities, and procedures (including those for continuous improvement).
	Quality Control Measurements	Quality control measurements are utilized to analyze and assess the quality of a process or deliverable against organizational standards or defined requirements. Quality control measurements can also be utilized to compare processes that create measurements and assess actual measurements to establish their level of conformance.
	Quality Metrics	Quality metrics delineate the manner in which the determination is made that a project or product conforms to its defined attributes. Quality metrics include cost performance, failure rate, defect frequency, maintainability, test coverage, and reliability among others.
Key Tools & Techniques	Data Gathering	Checklists are one of the data gathering tools that may be utilized. Using checklists ensures that appropriate procedures are followed. Checklists should integrate acceptance criteria from the scope baseline. Standardized checklists developed by the organization or the industry are often used.
	Alternatives Analysis	Alternatives analysis is a technique utilized to assess the most appropriate quality options or approaches.
	Process Analysis	Process analysis is used to determine process improvement opportunities by examining the issues, constraints, and non-value-added activities that occur during a process.
	Root Cause Analysis	Root cause analysis (RCA) is used to ascertain the underlying cause of a variance, defect, or risk. It is an analytical technique that may also be used to ascertain the root causes of an issue in order to resolve that issue.

Manage Quality (Continued)		
Key Tools & Techniques (Cont.)	Cause-and-effect Diagram	Cause-and-effect diagrams, also known as fishbone, Ishikawa, or why-why diagrams), are used to decompose the identified causes of a problem statement into separate branches in order to determine the root cause of a problem.
	Audits	A quality audit is a separate, configured technique that is performed randomly or in conformity with a set schedule. It is conducted to establish the compliance of project activities against organizational and project policies, processes, and procedures. A team external to the project or organization typically performs the quality audit in order to determine good and best practices; to determine any shortcomings or instances of non-conformity; to share good practices from similar projects; to propose positive help in the improvement of processes that will increase the team's effectiveness; and to emphasize audit contributions in the organizational lessons learned repository. Correction of discovered deficiencies typically decreases the overall cost of quality and increases customer product acceptance.
	Quality Improvement Methods	Quality improvement methods are quality improvement tools, such as plan-do-check-act and Six Sigma, utilized to assess improvement opportunities. Improvement opportunities can arise as a result of quality audits, quality control processes, or problem solving.
Key Outputs	Quality Reports	Quality reports, which can be presented in graphical, numeric, or qualitative form, can be used as the basis for the performance of corrective action(s) in order to meet project quality expectations. Information included in the reports can include any quality issues promoted by the team, corrective action recommendations, and improvements to a process, project, or product.
	Test and Evaluation Documents	Test and evaluation documents are used to assess the realization of quality goals. The documents can be generated based on industry needs and organizational templates. Dedicated checklists and a detailed requirements traceability matrix can be included in the documentation.
	Change Requests	Change requests are requests for modification that have not been formally approved through the change control process.

Manage Quality (Continued)		
Key Outputs (Cont.)	Quality Management Plan	The quality management plan is a component of the project management plan that details the manner in which the policies, methods, and criteria of the organization are executed. It delineates the expected level of quality for the project and product, details the manner in which this level will be achieved, and provides instructions for the disposition of nonconforming products and related corrective action. It details the activities and resources necessary to accomplish quality goals and typically addresses quality criteria, roles and responsibilities, tools, objectives, control and quality management activities, and procedures (including those for continuous improvement).

Situational Question and Real World Application

Failure to effectively Manage Quality could produce a project result that was not functional because the specifications were inaccurate.

8.9.1. Audits

Audits are structured, independent processes conducted to establish that project activities comply with organizational and project policies, processes, and procedures.

Quality audits are typically conducted by a team external to the project or organization in order to:

- Determine good and best practices
- Determine any shortcomings or instances of non-conformity
- Share good practices from similar projects
- Propose positive help in the improvement of processes in order to increase the team's effectiveness
- Emphasize audit contributions in the organizational lessons learned repository

Correction of discovered deficiencies typically decreases the cost of quality and increases customer product acceptance.

8.9.2. Design for X

Design for X (DfX) is a set of technical guidelines that may be used while designing a product in order to ensure the maximum functionality of the product. The X in DfX can be applied to specific aspects of product development such as reliability, cost, service, safety, and quality.

Applying DfX may result in:

- Cost reduction
- Superior performance
- Quality advances
- Customer satisfaction

8.9.3. Quality Reports

Quality reports, which are typically used to meet quality expectations for the project, can be qualitative, numerical, or graphic.

The information contained in the reports may include:

- Quality management issues escalated by the team
- Recommendations for corrective actions
- Recommendations for the improvement of processes, the product, and the project
- Summary of findings from the Control Quality process

8.9.4. Test and Evaluation Documents

Test and evaluation documents, typically based on organizational templates and industry needs, are used to assess if quality expectations are met.

Note that dedicated checklists and detailed requirements traceability matrices may be incorporated into test and evaluation documents.

The source for the above text is the Project Management Institute, *A Guide to the Project Management Body of Knowledge*, (PMBOK® Guide) – Sixth Edition, Project Management Institute Inc., 2017, Pages 268-276

8.10. Control Quality (Monitoring and Controlling Process Group)

Know the Key Inputs, Tools & Techniques, and Outputs for Control Quality.

Control Quality is the process area in which the **product, or the output of the process, is measured against the specifications.**

During Control Quality, project results are measured against the approved standard.

There are a number of tools/techniques and outputs that are key to Control Quality, but their usefulness depends on the type of work being done.

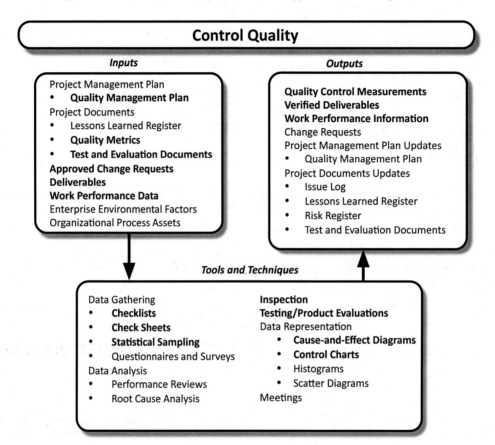

Figure 8-6: Control Quality Data Flow Diagram

The source for the above figure is the Project Management Institute, *A Guide to the Project Management Body of Knowledge*, (*PMBOK® Guide*) – Sixth Edition, Project Management Institute Inc., 2017, Figure 8.10, Page 277

Chapter 8 Quality

Control Quality (Monitoring and Controlling)		
Key Inputs	Quality Management Plan	The quality management plan is a component of the project management plan that details the manner in which the policies, methods, and criteria of the organization are executed. It delineates the expected level of quality for the project and product, details the manner in which this level will be achieved, and provides instructions for the disposition of nonconforming products and related corrective action. The plan details activities and necessary resources to accomplish quality goals. Typically it addresses quality criteria, roles and responsibilities, tools, objectives, control and quality management activities, and procedures (including those for continuous improvement). Note that modification of the agreed-upon approach may be required due to actual results.
	Quality Metrics	Quality metrics delineate the manner in which the determination is made that a project or product conforms to its defined attributes. Quality metrics include cost performance, failure rate, defect frequency, maintainability, test coverage, and reliability among other metrics.
	Test and Evaluation Documents	Test and evaluation documents are used to assess the realization of quality goals. The documents can be generated based on industry needs and organizational templates. Dedicated checklists and a detailed requirements traceability matrix can be included in the documentation.
	Approved Change Requests	Approved change requests are requests for modification that have been approved by authorized personnel during the formal change control process. The changes can expand or contract the scope of the project and modify policies, procedures, the project management plan, budgets, and schedules. Approved change requests include such items as correction of defects, revised approaches to the work of the project, and revised schedules. An approved change implementation should be verified, its completeness confirmed, retested, and then certified for correctness. Any change to the status of a change request must be updated in the change request log.
	Deliverables	Deliverables are singular and verifiable products, results, or capabilities that result in a verifiable deliverable required by the project.

Control Quality (Continued)		
Key Inputs (Cont.)	Work Performance Data	Work performance data represents the raw metrics and observations identified during the performance of project work activities. It contains information about product status, including observations, quality metrics, technical performance measurements, and quality-related schedule performance and cost performance data.
Key Tools & Techniques	Checklists	Checklists are utilized to ensure that quality activities are managed in a structural manner. Standardized checklists developed by the organization or the industry are often used.
	Check Sheets	Check sheets, also known as tally sheets, are utilized to organize facts in a manner that will make data regarding a potential quality problem easier to collect. A check sheet used to gather attributes data while performing an inspection is very effective for identifying the frequency with which defects occur.
	Statistical Sampling	Statistical sampling selects a portion of a defined population, such as 100 of the 2000 product population, for examination. Controls are measured and quality is authenticated against the sampling. Sampling frequency and extent are typically resolved during planning.
	Inspection	An inspection is used to analyze the item under review in order to identify any nonconformance to the quality standards for the item or to verify defect corrections. Inspection results typically include metrics.
	Testing/Product Evaluations	Testing/product evaluations are used to identify errors, defects, bugs, and nonconformance issues in the product or service as documented in the requirements. The quality management plan dictates the type, frequency, and limits of the testing in accordance with the nature, schedule, and budget of the project.
	Cause-and-effect Diagrams	Cause-and-effect diagrams, also known as a fishbone, Ishikawa, or why-why diagrams, are used to decompose the identified causes of a problem statement into separate branches in order to determine the root cause of a problem. They are also used to forecast possible effects of quality defects and inaccuracies.

PMI, CAPM, and PMBOK are registered marks of the Project Management Institute, Inc.

308 © 2008-2018 Crosswind Learning, www.crosswindpm.com

Control Quality (Continued)		
Key Tools & Techniques (Cont.)	Control Charts	Control charts are utilized to decide if a process is stable or performs predictably. Upper and lower specification limits are applied in accordance with the requirements of the agreement. Control charts can be used to determine the points at which action should be taken to avert performance that falls outside control limits.
Key Outputs	Quality Control Measurements	Quality control measurements are results of activities performed during the Control Quality process. They are acquired and recorded in the format set forth in the quality management plan.
	Verified Deliverables	Verified deliverables are deliverables that have been subjected to the Control Quality process, but not yet formally accepted. They are subject to customer acceptance as a result of the Validate Scope process.
	Work Performance Information	Work performance information is performance data gathered from control processes and subsequently evaluated in comparison with the components of the project management plan and other applicable artifacts. It includes information about the fulfillment of the project requirements, reasons for any rejections, required rework, list of verified deliverables, suggested corrective actions, metrics status, and required adaptation of processes.

Situational Question and Real World Application
Failure to effectively perform Control Quality or to fully implement Control Quality can result in excessive rework of the product being created and/or product returns by the customer.

8.10.1. Testing

Control Quality **tests the process output.** There are many items to consider when testing. Typically, these items are addressed in Plan Quality Management, but applied in Control Quality.

8.10.2. Sample Testing vs. Population Testing

It is very important to establish the optimal rate of testing for the project to avoid both over-testing, which may result in increased cost, and under-testing, which may result in decreased quality.

There are two types of testing: **population testing** and **sample testing**.

Population testing tests every item created (for example, every airplane built). It is used if the confidence level needs to be 100%, such as with an election or with medical manufacturing.

Sample testing tests a predetermined percentage of every item created. The optimum percentage ensures the discovery of defects, while keeping testing costs to a reasonable level. The percentage may start with an educated guess (one of every ten items), then evolve to a more reasonable percentage if the Manage Quality process indicates that the percentage is too low (little or no failures) or too high (some failures, but not enough to justify the costs of additional testing). Obviously, the higher the percentage tested, the higher the confidence level.

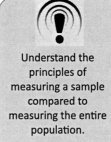

Understand the principles of measuring a sample compared to measuring the entire population.

8.10.3. Variable Sampling

A variable is a generic characteristic, such as capacity or height, measured during the Control Quality process.

8.10.4. Attribute Sampling

An attribute is a **specific measurement that is typically recorded.** For example, **square feet, inches, or meters.**

A variable must be defined **before** an attribute can be defined.

Know what variables and attributes are as they relate to quality.

8.10.5. Statistical Independence

Statistical independence is the state in which the **outcomes** of processes **are separate from one another.** As an example, buying a lottery ticket last week doesn't increase the odds of winning the lottery this week.

Understand statistical independence and mutual exclusivity.

8.10.6. Mutual Exclusivity

Mutual exclusivity is a principal that states that selecting an attribute for a single instance excludes all other attribute choices. For instance, if the capacity of the elevator is 500 pounds, the capacity of that same elevator cannot also be 100 pounds.

8.10.7. Heuristic

An heuristic is an aid to problem solving or learning that may not be perfect, but will serve to meet immediate goals.

For example, to quickly determine if $100 is sufficient to pay for five items, round and approximate to the nearest $10 increment. Instead of trying to add $12.13, $19.99, $5.76, $3.47, and $10.42, add $10, $20, $10, $10, and $10. Without rounding and approximation, the answer is $51.77. With rounding and approximation, the answer is $60.00.

8.10.8. Special Causes vs. Common Causes

Special causes, sometimes called **unusual events**, are activities or results that typically do not occur during a process. **Common causes**, sometimes called **random causes** or **normal process variations**, are variations that can occur within a process or random events.

8.10.9. Rolled Throughput Yield (RTY)

Rolled Throughput Yield (RTY) is a term used in Six Sigma to describe the probability that a unit can pass through a process without defects. It is the product of the first pass yields (Y) at each step:

$$RTY = Y_1 \times Y_2 \times Y_3 \times .. Y_n$$

In the following example, there are three stages to the process performed on 100 units. In stage one, the 100 units have 10 defects resulting in a 90% (0.9) RTY. In stage two, the remaining 90 units have 18 defects, resulting in an 80% (0.8) RTY. In stage three, the remaining 72 units have seven defects, resulting in a 90% (0.9) RTY. The cumulative affect of the three stages (0.9 x 0.8 x 0.9) is 0.648.

Process Stage	Units	Defects	RTY
1	100	10	0.9
2	90	18	0.8
3	72	7	0.9
Results	65	35	0.648

8.11. The Basic Tools of Quality

The basic quality tools are used to resolve quality issues. They include check sheets and checklists, flowcharts, histograms, Pareto diagrams, scatter diagrams, control (run) charts, cause-and-effect diagrams, and the Five WHYs.

8.11.1. Check Sheets and Checklists

Check sheets are tools used to capture and categorize quantitative or qualitative data.
Check sheets can be used for tracking such items as instances of process failure in specific areas over a specific period of time. The example in Figure 8-7: Check Sheet depicts the daily calls received by a business.

Reason	Mon	Tues	Wed	Thurs	Fri
Wrong Number	3	5	2	1	3
Info Request	12	10	12	13	16
Sales Order	15	15	20	18	13
Boss	4	4	4	5	8
Total	34	34	38	37	40

Figure 8-7: Check Sheet
The source for the above figure is the Project Management Institute, *A Guide to the Project Management Body of Knowledge*, (*PMBOK® Guide*) – Sixth Edition, Project Management Institute Inc., 2017, Figure 8.12, Page 280

Checklists are tools used to ensure that all process steps have been completed as planned. The use of checklists can improve quality and eliminate defects.

8.11.2. Flowcharts

Flowcharting is a technique used in Plan Quality Management to map the flow of a process or a technique. Flowcharting can improve quality by increasing the stability and repeatability of a process.

The flowchart (sometimes called a process flow) is a good tool for defining, in proper order, the steps that need to be completed to achieve a particular goal or output. There are a variety of flowchart formats including the **SIPOC (Supplier, Inputs, Process, Outputs, Customers} model.**

The following image depicts a generic flowchart.

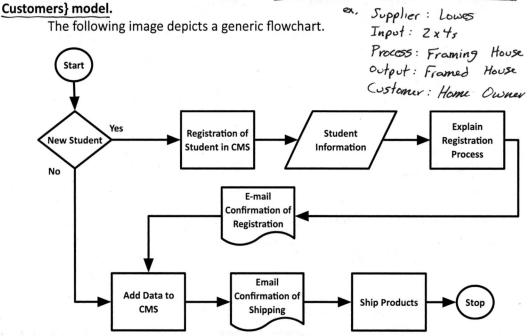

ex. Supplier: Lowes
Input: 2 x 4s
Process: Framing House
Output: Framed House
Customer: Home Owner

Figure 8-8: Flowchart Sample

The source for the above figure is the Project Management Institute, *A Guide to the Project Management Body of Knowledge*, (*PMBOK® Guide*) – Sixth Edition, Project Management Institute Inc., 2017, Figure 8.6, Page 266

PMI, CAPM, and PMBOK are registered marks of the Project Management Institute, Inc.

312   © 2008-2018 Crosswind Learning, www.crosswindpm.com

8.11.3. Histogram

A histogram is a bar chart that indicates the occurrence of a variable. The columns represent a characteristic and the height of the bar in each column represents the frequency of that characteristic's occurrence. Figure 8-9: Histogram Sample shows defects by count, not severity.

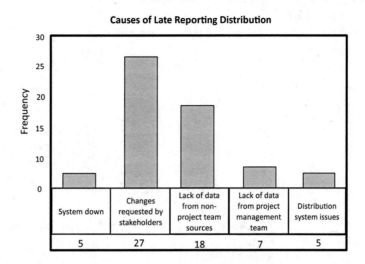

Figure 8-9: Histogram Sample

8.11.4. Pareto Diagram

The Pareto diagram is **a cumulative histogram that can be used to determine the most common issues/defects ordered by the frequency of their occurrence. This diagram also depicts a cumulative percentage of issues/defects.**

The Pareto diagram typically reflects the 80/20 rule, which states that, as a general rule, 80% of the problems arise from 20% of the issues/defects.

Know the characteristics of a Pareto diagram.

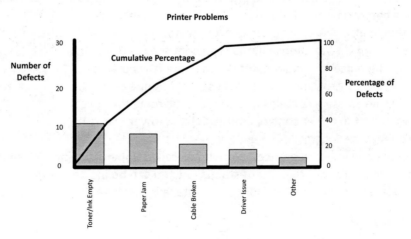

Figure 8-10: Pareto Diagram Sample

8.11.5. Scatter Diagram

The scatter diagram **shows a pattern between two variables associated with a process.**

The purpose of the diagram is to **show any correlation** that might exist between the variables.

The closer the output represents a diagonal line, the more dependent the variables are.

The less the output resembles a diagonal line, the more independent the variables are.

Know the characteristics of a scatter diagram.

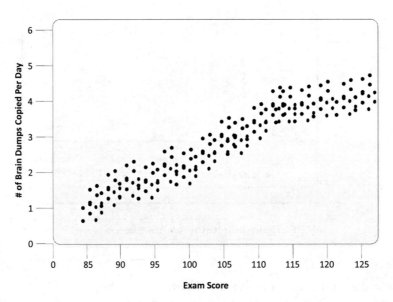

Figure 8-11: Scatter Diagram Sample

8.11.6. Control Chart

A control chart (a form of run chart) depicts the **process output over time.** It can be used to track technical performance, schedule performance, or cost performance. The primary difference between a run chart and a control chart is that the control chart has defined control and specification limits, whereas the **run chart may not**.

The **upper and lower control limits** represent the control points of the process. The process is under control if the data falls between the lower and upper control limits. This applies in all but one case: the Seven Run Rule (the Glossary contains information regarding the Seven Run Rule). **Typically, the upper control limit (UCL) and lower control limit (LCL) are set at +/- 3 sigma.**

Learn the principles and components of a control (run) chart, including the upper and lower control limits, upper and lower specification limits, and the mean.

The upper and lower **tolerances,** sometimes called **upper (USL) and lower (LSL) specification (spec) limits, are customer established and can be inside or outside the control limits**. The process outcome is acceptable if the data falls between the lower and upper tolerance limits.

To understand control chart terminology, consider a road. The **mean** is the middle of the road, the **control limits** are the stripes on the outer edge of the road, and the **tolerance limits** are the actual edges of the road.

Figure 8-12 Control (Run) Chart Sample, shows a control chart with limits, tolerances, and the mean. The mean, located in the middle of the chart, represents the target measurement.

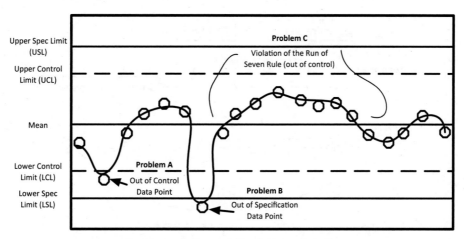

Figure 8-12: Control (Run) Chart Sample

8.11.7. Cause-and-effect (Ishikawa, Why-Why, or Fishbone) Diagram (Fish shape optional)

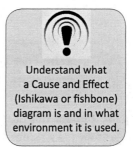

Understand what a Cause and Effect (Ishikawa or fishbone) diagram is and in what environment it is used.

A cause-and-effect (Ishikawa, Why-Why, or fishbone) diagram is a tool used during initialization to **evaluate what could potentially cause defects** in a project or process.

After the project has started, it can be used to **review symptoms and determine the real problem (continue to ask questions until the root cause is determined).**

Creating this diagram follows the same logic as decomposing work.

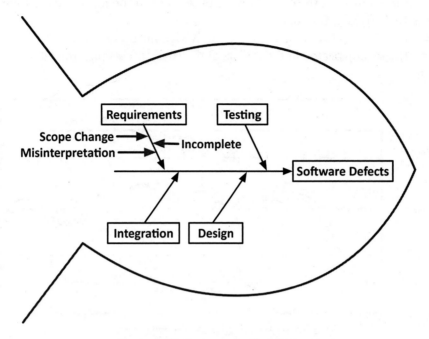

Figure 8-13: Cause-and-effect Diagram
The source for the above figure is the Project Management Institute, *A Guide to the Project Management Body of Knowledge*, (*PMBOK® Guide*) – Sixth Edition, Project Management Institute Inc., 2017, Figure 8.9, Page 274

8.11.8. The Five WHYs

The Five WHYs is a technique used to determine the root cause of a quality defect. When a quality defect is discovered, ask "Why?" No matter what the answer is, ask "Why?" again. **Repeat this as needed until you discover the defect's root cause**, rather than uncovering a symptom. Typically, five Whys are needed to determine the root cause.

The source for the above text is the Project Management Institute, *A Guide to the Project Management Body of Knowledge*, (*PMBOK® Guide*) – Sixth Edition, Project Management Institute Inc., 2017, Pages 276-284

8.12. Project Quality Management Formulas and Variables

Description	Formula	Variable (Component)	Example
Standard Deviation shows how far the measurement is from the mean (average).	St Dev = (P - O) / 6	P = Pessimistic Estimate O = Optimistic Estimate	(120 - 60) / 6 = 10
Sigma (These values represent the pure math value, without factoring in process variance, which can be up to 1.5 sigma.)	N/A	1 sigma = **68.26%** 2 sigma = **95.46%** 3 sigma = **99.73%** 6 sigma = **99.9999998%** or **99.9997%** Memorize the values in bold for 1, 2, 3, and 6!	1 sigma = 68.26% 2 sigma = 95.46% 3 sigma = 99.73% 6 sigma = 99.9999998%
Upper Specification Limit is the maximum value used to determine if a process is within specification.	Data Provided	USL	USL = 10
Upper Control Limit is the maximum value used to determine if a process is within control.	Data Provided	UCL	UCL = 8
Lower Control Limit is the minimum value used to determine if a process is within control.	Data Provided	LCL	LCL = 4
Lower Specification Limit is the minimum value used to determine if a process is within specification.	Data Provided	LSL	LSL = 2
Mean is the average value of measurement.	Data Provided	Mean	Mean = 6
RTY - Rolled throughput yield is the probability or likelihood, measured in percentage, of a unit going through a process with no defects.	$RTY = Y_1 \times Y_2 \times Y_3 \times .. Y_n$	RTY	0.648 = .9 x .8 x .9

8.13. Project Quality Management Terminology

Term	Description
Accuracy	The degree of correctness within a quality system
Attribute Sampling	A testing approach that involves noting the presence or lack of a characteristic (attribute) in each unit being tested and then deciding if the entire sample will be accepted, rejected, or require re-testing after the addition of additional units
Audit	A review of the quality system to determine that it is capable of ensuring quality project results
Benchmarking	The comparison of enterprise standards and practices to those used in similar organizations for the purpose of determining best practices and/or improvements and establishing a basis for performance measurements
Cause-and-effect Diagram	A decomposition approach used to identify the root cause of a problem; also known as a fishbone or Ishikawa diagram
Central Tendency	A property of the central limit theorem, which states that data tends to group around a central location; typically utilizes three measurements: the mean, the median, and the mode
Checklist Analysis	An evaluation of project checklists to determine their effectiveness
Check Sheets	Tools that can be used to capture and categorize data
Common Cause	A predictable source of variation in a system
Compliance	Conformance to a rule, standard, law, or requirement
Conformance	Within the quality management system, the delivery of a product or result that falls within the acceptable tolerance levels of quality requirements
Conformance to Requirement	The point where the project and product meet the standards of the written specifications defined at project inception (or modified through change control)
Conformance Work	Endeavors, typically related to prevention and inspection, that compensate for issues preventing organizations from achieving planned results
Control Chart	A graphic representation of process data over time that is set against documented control limits and has a center line (mean) to assist in identifying trends
Control Limits	The area comprised of three standard deviations that occur on either side of the mean of normal data distribution on a control chart
Control Quality	The process of testing a project's product, service, or result and then issuing an approval or recommendation for change
Cost of Nonconformance	Cost associated with not meeting quality expectations of the project or product
Criteria	Standards applied to a product, service, result, or process in order to make a decision or render a judgment about that product, service, result or process
Customer Satisfaction	Meeting or exceeding customer expectations as a result of evaluation within the quality system
Defect	A fault or inadequacy in a project component that must be corrected or replaced before project requirements or specifications can be met
Defect Repair	The correction of a fault or inadequacy in a project component
Design of Experiments	A statistical process used to determine the factors that may impact specific product or process variables
Documentation Reviews	The process of ensuring the accuracy and completeness of project exhibits

PMI, CAPM, and PMBOK are registered marks of the Project Management Institute, Inc.

318 © 2008-2018 Crosswind Learning, www.crosswindpm.com

Term	Description
Failure Mode and Effect Analysis (FMEA)	An analytical process that examines all possible failure points, individually or in conjunction with others, to ascertain the impact on the product or system
Features	The characteristics that the user desires built into a product
Fitness for Use	A product that can be used as it was intended when designed
Flowchart	A graphical representation, including inputs, actions, and outputs, of one or more of the system processes
Flowcharting (Technique)	A decomposition approach to breaking a system or process into block steps that can be repeated by following the diagram
Grade	A ranking to classify products that have different functions or features
Guideline	An official recommendation that describes the policies, standards, or processes related to the completion or a process or activity
Histogram	A graphical representation, in the format of bar chart, that depicts the central tendency, dispersal, and shape of a statistical distribution
Influence Diagram	A graphical representation of relationship between variables and outcomes including situations with causal influence and event time sequences
Inspection	The evaluation of an activity, product, result, service, or component to determine that it meets the desired standards for use and conforms to requirements
Interrelationship Diagrams	A graphical representation of the cause-and-effect relationships of the variables of creative problem solving
ISO 9000	Developed by the International Organization for Standardization (ISO) as a means to plan, control, and document processes, and overall improve quality
Kaizen	A technique that takes a proactive stance to process development, one that makes improvements throughout a process as time evolves
Manage Quality	The process of converting the quality management plan into executable activities that integrate the organization's quality policies into the project
Mean	The average value in a measurement of a population
Nonconformance Work	The work associated with correcting errors, including those that arise from a failure to adhere to the policies, standards, rules, and regulations that impact the project
Normal Distribution	A bell-shaped curve that is in sync with the mean of the population
Pareto Analysis	A technique used to identify instances of frequently recurring issues that impact a system, project, or process
Pareto Diagram	A bar chart, ordered by occurrence frequency, depicting the number of outcomes for each identified cause
Performance	The level of success at which a product performs its intended use
Plan Quality Management	The process of identifying quality requirements and standards for the project and deliverables as well as documenting compliance with the project's quality approach and requirements
Population	The entire group of similar criteria (Ex: All Americans, all owners of a particular product)
Precision	The accuracy of the measurements used by the quality management system
Prevention Cost	Cost of planning and executing a project within an acceptable range of error (or error free)
Preventive Action	An activity performed to evade an event that would negatively impact project performance

Term	Description
Prioritization Matrices	A quality management tool used to identify issues and potential alternatives related to the establishment of implementation priorities
Procedure	A method executed to achieve a suitable performance or result
Process Adjustments	Adjustments made to modify the output of a process to achieve a better degree of quality
Process Analysis	The evaluation of a process with the goal of identifying potential improvements
Process Decision Program Charts (PDPC)	A graphical representation used to develop contingency plans based on possible failure points in the main plan
Project Quality Management	The processes defined and activities performed by the organization to identify quality related policies, aims, and responsibilities in order to ensure that the project meets its objectives
Quality	The degree to which a group of fundamental characteristics satisfies requirements
Quality Assurance	The repetitive examination of quality requirements and quality control measurements to effect the use of requisite quality control standards and operational definitions
Quality Audits	A formal, independent process that assesses whether project activities are in compliance with organizational and project policies, processes, and procedures
Quality Checklists	A tool used to verify that project work and deliverables have been completed in accordance with project requirements
Quality Control Measurements	The documented outcome of quality control functions
Quality Management and Control Tools	Mechanisms used to ensure quality products and processes, often more efficiently and at a lower cost
Quality Management Plan	The document, part of the project or program management plan, used to describe the execution of the organization's quality policies
Quality Management System	The system within a company that provides policies, processes, and resources to implement the project's quality management plan; that the quality management plan typically aligns with the company's quality system
Quality Metrics	The description of a project or product attribute and the measurements that must be applied to the attribute within the quality control process; examples of metrics include failure rate, defect frequency, cost control, reliability, and availability
Quality Policy	The organizational policies crafted to achieve quality goals
Quality Report	A project document that addresses quality management issues, recommendations for corrective actions, and a recap of findings from quality control activities; the report may include advice related to the improvement of process, project, and product
Quality Requirement	Condition designed to ensure that a deliverable conforms to its intended use
Regression Analysis	An analytical technique that examines a series of input variables in relation to their corresponding output results for the purpose of establishing a mathematical or statistical relationship
Reliability	The likelihood of a product or service to function as planned
Rework	Action taken to bring any component that is flawed or out of conformance into compliance with specifications or requirements
Sample	A part of the population used for a measurement (instead of the entire population)
Scatter Diagram	A graphical representation that shows the relationship between two variables by putting one on the x axis, the other on the y axis, and analyzing the intersecting points; typically used to determine root causes or the presence of a cause-and-effect relationship

Term	Description
Seven Basic Quality Tools	A group of devices used by quality management for quality planning and for monitoring and controlling
Seven Run Rule	A rule that states if seven consecutive data points are on one side of the mean (above or below) or increasing/decreasing, then the process is out of control and should be investigated
Sigma	A measurement of acceptability of a product or process
Special Cause	A non-random or intermittent variable in a system
Specification	An instrument that effectively defines the requirements, design, characteristics, and other attributes of a system, component, product, result or service and typically provides for procedures to determine that the provisions of the instrument have been met
Specification Limits	The area on either side of the mean of data distribution on a control chart
Standard Deviation	The measurement of variation within a distribution
Statistical Sampling	The selection of a part of a population for examination rather than using the entire population
Test and Evaluation Documents	Project Documents that delineate the activities used to determine if the product satisfies the quality objectives described in the quality management plan
Tolerance	The measure of acceptable variation
Tree Diagram	A graphical representation that uses decomposition to organize data into parent and child relationships
Value Engineering	An approach to efficiently and effectively execute the project to decrease life cycle costs and time, increase profits and market share, improve quality and use of resources, and competently resolve issues and problems
Variation	The difference between the baseline project management plan and actual project data at a specific point in time
Verification	The process, typically internal, of determining that the results of the project are in compliance with appropriate specifications, requirements, regulatory requirements, and imposed conditions
Verified Deliverables	Completed project deliverables that have been reviewed and confirmed for correctness through the Control Quality Process
Voice of the Customer (VOC)	The translation of customer requirements into requisite technical requirements in a manner that ensures the results of the project will meet the requirements of the customer

The source for the above definitions is the Glossary of the Project Management Institute,
A Guide to the Project Management Body of Knowledge, (PMBOK® Guide) – Sixth Edition, Project Management Institute Inc., 2017

Chapter 8
Quality

8.14. Project Quality Management Tests and Exercises

8.14.1. Project Quality Management Practice Test

Answers are in section 8.15.1.

1. The project manager has concerns about the software developer's project work in terms of quality and has spoken to the developer about this on several occasions. This involvement derives from the relationship between project management and quality management that should complement each other. What specifically is the relationship between the two?

   (A) Both focus on management responsibility, fulfillment of requirements, continuous improvement, prevention over inspection, and product excellence
   (B) Both focus on management responsibility, continuous improvement, prevention over inspection, and customer satisfaction
   (C) Both focus on management responsibility, fulfillment of requirements, continuous improvement, prevention over inspection, and customer satisfaction
   (D) Both focus on management responsibility, continuous improvement, prevention over inspection, and product excellence

2. The project manager of a natural gas discovery software development project is known for his adherence to Deming's Total Quality Management philosophy. Which of the following approaches to quality can the project team expect him to utilize?

   (A) Be proactive, not reactive
   (B) Utilize leadership and accountability
   (C) Constant improvement
   (D) All the answers

3. The project manager and his team are using an Ishikawa or fishbone diagram as part of the quality component for the coal extraction project. Of the following, which best describes the reason they are utilizing this diagram?

   (A) To assess the defects which are creating quality issues
   (B) To evaluate project activities that have the potential to create defects
   (C) To review symptoms to determine the source of the defects
   (D) B and C

4. The project management team is analyzing defects and trying to isolate the cause of a problem on the project. They have isolated two variables via the data that is available. They suspect the problem is compounded by the impact of one variable on another. They want to see if there is a relationship between the two variables. Which of the following will help them verify this relationship and why?

(A) Run chart because the closer the lower control limit is to +/- 3 sigma, the more dependent the variables are
(B) Pareto diagram because the closer the percentages are on the separate problems, the more dependent the variables are
(C) Control chart because the closer the upper control limit is to +/- 3 sigma, the more dependent the variables are
(D) Scatter diagram because the closer the output resembles a diagonal line, the more dependent the variables are

5. You are defining the quality standards for the project to create a new microchip that has the capacity to contain more instructions than any prior chip. You have defined which variables are to be measured. You have also determined what attributes are important to you. Although the product is not expensive, it is expected to bring a steady income stream to the company because it is integral to the production of animatronic toys and robots that are tremendously popular. Which testing method will you use and why?

(A) Population testing because the product is so crucial to the company's success
(B) Sample testing because the cost of population testing is prohibitive
(C) Sample testing because the product is so crucial to the company's success
(D) Population testing because the cost of population testing is prohibitive

6. You are the project manager on a project that will improve the manufacturing process at your company. Quality has been a big issue because there has been an excessive amount spent on inventory with a lot of waste in the building process and return of product after it has been sold. Presently, the company has a 1 sigma quality standard with its manufacturing process. There is a general belief that there are process issues behind this problem. Which of the following options appears to make the most sense in terms of making the process more consistent?

(A) Watching for violations of the seven run rule
(B) Making a greater use of checklists
(C) Increasing the quality standard to a sigma level greater than 1
(D) Utilizing a fishbone diagram

7. The project team is ordering a server after discovering that it was missed in the original scope discovery of the project. There is an urgency to have it delivered quickly to minimize schedule slippage, but the project team does not want to spend money from dwindling reserves to pay for the additional shipping charges. Which of the following is the most accurate description of this situation?

(A) There is an attribute issue since fast shipping and low cost shipping are both characteristics associated with shipping
(B) There is a budget issue since there isn't extra money for shipping
(C) There is a mutual exclusivity issue since shipping fast and low cost do not correlate to each other
(D) There is a time issue since the server needs to arrive quickly

8. The finance department is building a call center for its new auto finance division. The project manager and his team completed a model project management plan. What component of the plan will they most likely reference during the project's control quality process?

(A) Detailed process improvement plan
(B) Clearly defined standards of acceptable completion criteria
(C) Complete testing matrix developed for auto loan call centers
(D) Acceptable quality management methodology specifics

9. The project is going through the manage quality process. Which of the following is a key tool that will be utilized in this process?

(A) Cost-benefit analysis, which is used to analyze how to minimize rework due to lack of quality and how to maximize satisfaction and productivity
(B) Quality audits, which help verify process and output compliance
(C) Quality analysis, which is used to optimize project execution and achieve high process quality
(D) Quality management plan, which provides acceptable quality management methodology information

10. You are performing the plan quality management process on a project. The sponsor puts into the project charter that the quality standard wanted on the project is +/- 2 sigma. This translates to what percentage?

(A) 68.26%
(B) 95.46%
(C) 50%
(D) 99.73%

11. There is a variance in the manufacturing process that is causing concern among the team. Some results have been above the specification limits, and some within the control tolerances. You want to learn more about the output of the process over the last month. Which of the following items is the most useful for this purpose?

(A) Run chart because it indicates output over time and provides the opportunity to determine trends and variances
(B) Pareto diagram because the closer the percentages are on the separate problems, the easier it is to determine trends and variances
(C) Control chart because it indicates output and highlights trends and variances
(D) Scatter diagram because the closer the output resembles a diagonal line, the more obvious trends and variances

12. You are the project manager on a project that will improve the manufacturing process at your company that has a 1 sigma quality standard with its manufacturing process. Quality has been a major issue because there has been an excessive amount spent on inventory with a lot of waste in the building process and product returns. There is talk of utilizing quality tools at the company to help minimize these problems. Which of the following options looks like the best example of a quality tool for problem isolation?

(A) Utilizing a fishbone diagram
(B) Watching for violations of the seven run rule
(C) Increasing the quality to a sigma level greater than 1
(D) Making a greater use of checklists

13. The sum of all probabilities equals what?

(A) 100
(B) 1.0
(C) 1.0 or 100%
(D) 100%

14. The project manager of the On-line Loan Application Interface project instructs his team to ensure that the manage quality process is performed thoroughly. What is involved in this process?

(A) Auditing the quality processes to ensure that appropriate standards are used
(B) Identifying quality requirements for the project and product, and auditing them appropriately
(C) Implementing predefined and validated methodologies to record the results of quality activities
(D) Evaluating proposed quality initiatives considering factors such as expected customer satisfaction, the cost of conformance, and the cost of nonconformance

15. The project is going through the control quality process. Which of the following is a key tool that will be utilized in this process and why?

    (A) Flowcharting shows what areas are causing the most issues and point to what needs it most on the project
    (B) A cause-and-effect diagram (also known as Ishikawa and fishbone) helps to isolate any potential problems that relate to quality on a project
    (C) The control chart helps to verify that the process is followed accurately
    (D) A Pareto chart shows output over time so monitoring for variance and trends can be completed

16. The project to improve the insurance section of the customer service division is very complex in terms of updating organizational process assets. Which of the following best describes the appropriate time to update these assets?

    (A) Updates should occur during the manage quality process
    (B) Updates should occur as validation data is available from the manage quality process
    (C) Updates should occur as validation data is available from the plan quality management process
    (D) Updates should occur during the control quality process

17. While establishing an overall picture of process output over time, the team plots a chart based on the data available. The plotted chart has seven consecutive data points on one side of the mean. What can be determined from the plotted chart?

    (A) The control limits are too tight
    (B) The control limits are acceptable
    (C) The control limits are too loose
    (D) A seven run rule violation has occurred

18. Of the following, which is the best description of the relationship between quality control measurements and the manage quality process?

    (A) They are an output of the manage quality process
    (B) They can be fed into the manage quality process to validate the efficiency and cost effectiveness of control quality
    (C) They are an output of the control quality process
    (D) Both A and C

19. The company is implementing a stricter and more proactive quality standard for projects in an attempt to improve the quality culture. Once implemented, which of the following impacts on the product support department is most likely to occur?

    (A) Increased warranty support
    (B) Decreased warranty support
    (C) Increased inventory requirements
    (D) Decreased inventory requirements

20. The computer manufacturer is putting a policy in place to use Just-in-Time manufacturing. It feels this policy will help minimize excess inventory cost and improve efficiency. The amount of inventory needed for this type of process is what?

(A) There is insufficient information to determine the answer
(B) 27% (3 sigma) or .0003% (6 sigma)
(C) Zero plus predefined organizational buffer
(D) Ideally, zero with supplies obtained only when the product is being built

21. To counteract a perception in the marketplace that RM Manufacturing designs products with defects, the company hires a new project manager to head the key design project in its new initiative. The project manager's commitment to quality has earned her industry-wide respect. One of the techniques she utilizes to ensure quality results is flowcharting. Of the following, which is the best description of this technique and in what process is it typically used?

(A) A technique used during the plan quality management process to define the components of a process and the order in which they should be performed
(B) A technique used during the control quality process to determine variance and trends
(C) A technique used during the control quality process to define the components of a process and the order in which they should be performed
(D) A technique used during the plan quality management process to determine variance and trends

22. Crews Manufacturing is known for producing products with consistently high quality. The project manager prefers prevention over inspection for design projects. Which of the following is the best description of this approach to quality?

(A) A proactive approach to increase the stability and repeatability of a process
(B) A reactive approach to eliminate defects and potential defects from the process
(C) A reactive approach to increase the stability and repeatability of a process
(D) A proactive approach to eliminate defects and potential defects from the process

23. The project team is about to begin testing the engine it is creating. The project manager and his team have decided to use sample testing rather than population testing. Of the following reasons, which is not valid in regard to sample testing?

(A) Sample testing is less expensive
(B) Sample testing is less destructive
(C) Sample testing is more thorough
(D) Sample testing is quicker

24. The company that won the procurement contract is providing additional functionality and reporting in an effort to win more business from the customer. Which of the following best describes this situation?

(A) The company is gold plating, which is a good practice because it increases the prospect of being awarded future contracts with that customer
(B) The company is gold plating, which is not a good practice because it creates unreasonable expectations on the part of the customer
(C) The company is gold plating, which is a good practice because it exceeds the standard of delivering the exact product, service, or result that is finalized in the project charter
(D) The company is gold plating, which is not a good practice because it violates the standard of delivering the exact product, service, or result that is finalized in the project charter

25. You are the project manager on a project that will improve the manufacturing process at your company, which has a 1 sigma quality standard with its manufacturing process. Quality has been a major issue because there has been an excessive amount spent on inventory with a lot of waste in the building process and product returns. Which of the following is the best approach to increasing the quality standard?

(A) Watching for violations of the seven run rule
(B) Making a greater use of checklists
(C) Changing the quality to a sigma level greater than 1
(D) Utilizing a fishbone diagram

26. In testing, special cause variations should be eliminated in a timely manner. How should common cause variations be addressed?

(A) Common cause variations should be ignored
(B) Common cause variations should be addressed through long-term process improvements
(C) Common cause variations should also be eliminated in a timely manner
(D) Common cause variations should be addressed before special cause variations

27. The company is in the testing phase of its project. It is tracking defects discovered by customers who are testing the project. Given the nature of a new project, a variety of defects are being discovered. Organizing and prioritizing the defects is becoming a challenge. What tool helps organize this type of information and why?

(A) The Pareto diagram is a cumulative history of issues prioritized by frequency
(B) The flowchart is a cumulative history of issues prioritized by impact on the project
(C) A run chart is a cumulative history of issues prioritized by frequency
(D) A scatter diagram is a cumulative history of issues prioritized by impact on the project

28. In preparing his team for the quality improvement initiative, the project manager is holding a quality meeting. He intends to open the meeting with a brief slide show. Slide one contains the definition of quality by the Project Management Institute, Inc. Which of the following definitions corresponds to the one used by the Project Management Institute, Inc.?

(A) Meeting the customers needs
(B) Conformance to use and fitness of requirements
(C) The degree to which a set of inherent characteristics fulfill requirements
(D) Conformance to the requirements in the project charter

29. The company has established a control chart that has an upper control limit of five and a lower control limit of two. The customer, however, does not require such a high standard. What is the upper specification limit?

(A) Greater than two and less than five
(B) Greater than five
(C) Between five and two
(D) None of the answers

30. In preparing his team for the quality improvement initiative, the project manager is holding a quality meeting. He intends to open the meeting with a brief slide show, which will include highlighting several quality concepts. Before he discusses the concepts, he asks the team to match the concept with its creator. Which of the following contains the correct matches?

(A) TQM and Joseph Juran, Fitness for Use and W. Edwards Deming, Zero Defects and Philip Crosby
(B) TQM and W. Edwards Deming, Fitness for Use and Joseph Juran, Zero Defects and Philip Crosby
(C) TQM and W. Edwards Deming, Fitness for Use and Philip Crosby, Zero Defects and Joseph Juran
(D) TQM and Philip Crosby, Fitness for Use and W. Edwards Deming, Zero Defects and Joseph Juran

8.15. Project Quality Management Answers for Tests and Exercises

8.15.1. Project Quality Management Practice Test Answers

We recommend that you download answer sheets from the Crosswind website, so you can practice the test as many times as you like.

1. The project manager has concerns about the software developer's project work in terms of quality and has spoken to the developer about this on several occasions. This involvement derives from the relationship between project management and quality management that should complement each other. What specifically is the relationship between the two?

   Correct Answer: (B) Both focus on management responsibility, continuous improvement, prevention over inspection, and customer satisfaction
   Explanation: The relationship between project management and quality management is that both focus on management responsibility, continuous improvement, prevention over inspection, and customer satisfaction. [Crosswind Manual 8.2; No *PMBOK® Guide* Reference]

2. The project manager of a natural gas discovery software development project is known for his adherence to Deming's Total Quality Management philosophy. Which of the following approaches to quality can the project team expect him to utilize?

   (A) Be proactive, not reactive
   (B) Utilize leadership and accountability
   (C) Constant improvement

   Correct Answer: (D) All the answers
   Explanation: Deming's Total Quality Management philosophy advocates an approach to quality that is proactive, that utilizes leadership and accountability, and that promotes continuous improvement. [Crosswind Manual 8.3; *PMBOK® Guide* Chapter 8 Introduction]

3. The project manager and his team are using an Ishikawa or fishbone diagram as part of the quality component for the coal extraction project. Of the following, which best describes the reason they are utilizing this diagram?

   (B) To evaluate project activities that have the potential to create defects
   (C) To review symptoms to determine the source of the defects

   Correct Answer: (D) B and C
   Explanation: Ishikawa diagrams are utilized in the Plan Quality Management process to evaluate project activities that have the potential to create defects. Ishikawa diagrams are utilized after the planning process to review symptoms in an effort to determine the source of the defects. The other answers are distracters. [Crosswind Manual 8.11.7; *PMBOK® Guide* 8.2.3.5]

4. The project management team is analyzing defects and trying to isolate the cause of a problem on the project. They have isolated two variables via the data that is available. They suspect the problem is compounded by the impact of one variable on another. They want to see if there is a relationship between the two variables. Which of the following will help them verify this relationship and why?

Correct Answer: (D) Scatter diagram because the closer the output resembles a diagonal line, the more dependent the variables are
Explanation: The scatter diagram shows a relationship (or lack of a relationship) between two variables. The run chart (sometimes called a control chart) shows output over time. The Pareto diagram shows defect by quantity. [Crosswind Manual 8.11.5; PMBOK® Guide 8.3.2.6]

5. You are defining the quality standards for the project to create a new microchip that has the capacity to contain more instructions than any prior chip. You have defined which variables are to be measured. You have also determined what attributes are important to you. Although the product is not expensive, it is expected to bring a steady income stream to the company because it is integral to the production of animatronic toys and robots that are tremendously popular. Which testing method will you use and why?

Correct Answer: (B) Sample testing because the cost of population testing is prohibitive
Explanation: Sample testing tests a percentage of the product and makes sense in this case because they plan to produce large quantities. Population testing tests every product that would result in prohibitive cost. [Crosswind Manual 8.10.2; PMBOK® Guide 8.3.2]

6. You are the project manager on a project that will improve the manufacturing process at your company. Quality has been a big issue because there has been an excessive amount spent on inventory with a lot of waste in the building process and return of product after it has been sold. Presently, the company has a 1 sigma quality standard with its manufacturing process. There is a general belief that there are process issues behind this problem. Which of the following options appears to make the most sense in terms of making the process more consistent?

Correct Answer: (B) Making a greater use of checklists
Explanation: When followed, checklists help the employee attain consistent process execution. Assuming the checklist is sufficient and that the employee follows it, the process should possess a greater degree of stability. Fishbone diagrams work with problem isolation. Increasing the quality level makes a process more consistent, but it takes tools to do that. The checklist is a good quick fix that can have standard long-term benefits, especially if the sigma level is increased and higher quality expectations are put in place. [Crosswind Manual 8.11.1; PMBOK® Guide 8.3.2.1]

7. The project team is ordering a server after discovering that it was missed in the original scope discovery of the project. There is an urgency to have it delivered quickly to minimize schedule slippage, but the project team does not want to spend money from dwindling reserves to pay for the additional shipping charges. Which of the following is the most accurate description of this situation?

Correct Answer: (C) There is a mutual exclusivity issue since shipping fast and low cost do not correlate to each other
Explanation: Mutual exclusivity, in this instance, requires that only one choice can be selected. Since delivering quickly and minimizing shipping charges do not correlate to each other this creates the issue. The team must make that determination on which choices to select regarding delivery. [Crosswind Manual 8.10.6; No *PMBOK® Guide* Reference]

8. The finance department is building a call center for its new auto finance division. The project manager and his team completed a model project management plan. What component of the plan will they most likely reference during the project's control quality process?

Correct Answer: (B) Clearly defined standards of acceptable completion criteria
Explanation: A complete project management plan contains clearly defined standards of acceptable completion criteria that is the primary reason the project management plan is helpful during the Control Quality process. [Crosswind Manual 8.10; *PMBOK® Guide* 8.3]

9. The project is going through the manage quality process. Which of the following is a key tool that will be utilized in this process?

Correct Answer: (B) Quality audits which help verify process and output compliance
Explanation: The quality audit is used in Manage Quality to verify that process and output comply with organizational and project policies and procedures. The goals of quality audits are to identify best practices, identify gaps, and share best practices with all appropriate stakeholders. The other answers are distracters. [Crosswind Manual 8.9; *PMBOK® Guide* 8.2]

10. You are performing the plan quality management process on a project. The sponsor puts into the project charter that the quality standard wanted on the project is +/- 2 sigma. This translates to what percentage?

Correct Answer: (B) 95.46%
Explanation: The percentage for 1 sigma is 68.26%, for 2 sigma is 95.46%, and for 3 sigma is 99.73%. 50% is a distracter. [Crosswind Manual 8.8.10; No *PMBOK® Guide* Reference]

11. There is a variance in the manufacturing process that is causing concern among the team. Some results have been above the specification limits, and some within the control tolerances. You want to learn more about the output of the process over the last month. Which of the following items is the most useful for this purpose?

Correct Answer: (A) Run chart because it indicates output over time and provides the opportunity to determine trends and variances

Explanation: The run chart's main purpose is to show output over time. This provides an opportunity to catch any trends and variance with the process. The Pareto diagram shows defect by count. A control chart is similar to a run chart, but the reason given is not accurate. A scatter diagram indicates dependencies between variables. [Crosswind Manual 8.11.6; *PMBOK® Guide* 8.3.2.5]

12. You are the project manager on a project that will improve the manufacturing process at your company that has a 1 sigma quality standard with its manufacturing process. Quality has been a major issue because there has been an excessive amount spent on inventory with a lot of waste in the building process and product returns. There is talk of utilizing quality tools at the company to help minimize these problems. Which of the following options looks like the best example of a quality tool for problem isolation?

Correct Answer: (A) Utilizing a fishbone diagram

Explanation: The fishbone diagram is a quality tool that can be used to look for the source or root cause of other symptoms you might be experiencing in an area. The seven run rule can occur on a control chart when looking at output over time. Increasing the quality level is not a tool nor will it isolate a problem. A checklist could be used as a tool but won't help isolate problems. [Crosswind Manual 8.11.7; *PMBOK® Guide* 8.3.2.5]

13. The sum of all probabilities equals what?

Correct Answer: (C) 1.0 or 100%

Explanation: The sum of all probabilities is equal to 1.0 or 100%. 100% is the maximum sum of all potential outcomes of a situation. [Crosswind Manual 8.8.11; No *PMBOK® Guide* Reference]

14. The project manager of the On-line Loan Application Interface project instructs his team to ensure that the manage quality process is performed thoroughly. What is involved in this process?

Correct Answer: (A) Auditing the quality processes to ensure that appropriate standards are used

Explanation: This is the generally-accepted definition of the manage quality process. All other answers are distracters. [Crosswind Manual 8.9; *PMBOK® Guide* 8.2]

15. The project is going through the control quality process. Which of the following is a key tool that will be utilized in this process and why?

Correct Answer: (B) A cause-and-effect diagram (also known as Ishikawa and fishbone) helps to isolate any potential problems that relate to quality on a project

Explanation: A cause-and-effect diagram (also known as Ishikawa and fishbone) helps to isolate any potential problems that relate to quality on a project. The other answers are distracters because their descriptions are inaccurate. [Crosswind Manual 8.11.7; PMBOK® Guide 8.3.2.5]

16. The project to improve the insurance section of the customer service division is very complex in terms of updating organizational process assets. Which of the following best describes the appropriate time to update these assets?

Correct Answer: (B) Updates should occur as validation data is available from the manage quality process

Explanation: Updating organizational process assets should occur as validation data is available from the manage quality process. [Crosswind Manual 8.9; PMBOK® Guide 8.2]

17. While establishing an overall picture of process output over time, the team plots a chart based on the data available. The plotted chart has seven consecutive data points on one side of the mean. What can be determined from the plotted chart?

Correct Answer: (D) A seven run rule violation has occurred

Explanation: The seven run rule has been violated. This doesn't necessarily mean there is a problem, but at a minimum a situation that warrants investigation to see if there is a problem and the specific details. [Crosswind Manual 8.11.6; PMBOK® Guide 8.3.2.5]

18. Of the following, which is the best description of the relationship between quality control measurements and the manage quality process?

Correct Answer: (B) They can be fed into the manage quality process to validate the efficiency and cost effectiveness of control quality

Explanation: They can be fed into the manage quality process to validate the efficiency and cost effectiveness of the Control Quality process. They are an output of the Control Quality process, but that does not describe the relationship. The other answers are distracters. [Crosswind Manual 8.9; PMBOK® Guide 8.2]

19. The company is implementing a stricter and more proactive quality standard for projects in an attempt to improve the quality culture. Once implemented, which of the following impacts on the product support department is most likely to occur?

Correct Answer: (B) Decreased warranty support

Explanation: Typically, the result of implementing more proactive quality standards decreases the need for warranty support. The other answers are distracters. [Crosswind Manual 8.8.7; No PMBOK® Guide Reference]

20. The computer manufacturer is putting a policy in place to use Just-in-Time manufacturing. It feels this policy will help minimize excess inventory cost and improve efficiency. The amount of inventory needed for this type of process is what?

Correct Answer: (D) Ideally, zero with supplies obtained only when the product is being built

Explanation: The amount of inventory needed for Just-in-Time (JIT) inventory is optimally zero with supplies being obtained only when product is being built. [Crosswind Manual 8.8.9; No *PMBOK® Guide* Reference]

21. To counteract a perception in the marketplace that RM Manufacturing designs products with defects, the company hires a new project manager to head the key design project in its new initiative. The project manager's commitment to quality has earned her industry-wide respect. One of the techniques she utilizes to ensure quality results is flowcharting. Of the following, which is the best description of this technique and in what process is it typically used?

Correct Answer: (A) A technique used during the plan quality management process to define the components of a process and the order in which they should be performed

Explanation: Flowcharting is a technique used during the Plan Quality Management process to define the components of a process and the order in which they should be performed. The other answers are distracters. [Crosswind Manual 8.8; *PMBOK® Guide* 8.1]

22. Crews Manufacturing is known for producing products with consistently high quality. The project manager prefers prevention over inspection for design projects. Which of the following is the best description of this approach to quality?

Correct Answer: (D) A proactive approach to eliminate defects and potential defects from the process

Explanation: Prevention versus inspection is a proactive approach to eliminate defects and potential defects from the process. Flowcharting is a proactive approach to increase the stability and repeatability of a process. The other answers are distracters. [Crosswind Manual 8.8.4; *PMBOK® Guide* 8.1.2.3]

23. The project team is about to begin testing the engine it is creating. The project manager and his team have decided to use sample testing rather than population testing. Of the following reasons, which is not valid in regard to sample testing?

Correct Answer: (C) Sample testing is more thorough

Explanation: Testing the population is thorough because it tests everything; whereas, sample testing tests only a portion of the population. [Crosswind Manual 8.10.2; *PMBOK® Guide* 8.3.2]

24. The company that won the procurement contract is providing additional functionality and reporting in an effort to win more business from the customer. Which of the following best describes this situation?

   Correct Answer: (D) The company is gold plating, which is not a good practice because it violates the standard of delivering the exact product, service, or result that is finalized in the project charter
   Explanation: The company is gold plating, which is not a good practice because it violates the standard of delivering the exact product, service, or result that is finalized in the project charter. Gold plating is a form of scope creep. The other answers are distracters. [Crosswind Manual 8.7; *PMBOK® Guide* Chapter 8 Introduction]

25. You are the project manager on a project that will improve the manufacturing process at your company, which has a 1 sigma quality standard with its manufacturing process. Quality has been a major issue because there has been an excessive amount spent on inventory with a lot of waste in the building process and product returns. Which of the following is the best approach to increasing the quality standard?

   Correct Answer: (C) Changing the quality to a sigma level greater than 1
   Explanation: Increasing the quality standard from 1 sigma to 2 (or greater) sigma will increase the quality standard. The other answers will improve quality rather than the quality standard. [Crosswind Manual 8.8.11; No *PMBOK® Guide* Reference]

26. In testing, special cause variations should be eliminated in a timely manner. How should common cause variations be addressed?

   Correct Answer: (B) Common cause variations should be addressed through long-term process improvements
   Explanation: Common cause variations, also caused normal process variations or random causes, should be addressed through long-term process improvements. [Crosswind Manual 8.10.8; No *PMBOK® Guide* Reference]

27. The company is in the testing phase of its project. It is tracking defects discovered by customers who are testing the project. Given the nature of a new project, a variety of defects are being discovered. Organizing and prioritizing the defects is becoming a challenge. What tool helps organize this type of information and why?

   Correct Answer: (A) The Pareto diagram is a cumulative history of issues prioritized by frequency
   Explanation: The Pareto diagram shows frequency of defects in a graphical format. The flowchart shows process flow. The run chart shows process output over time. The scatter diagram shows a pattern between two variables associated with a process. [Crosswind Manual 8.11.4; *PMBOK® Guide* 8.3.2.5]

28. In preparing his team for the quality improvement initiative, the project manager is holding a quality meeting. He intends to open the meeting with a brief slide show. Slide one contains the definition of quality by the Project Management Institute, Inc. Which of the following definitions corresponds to the one used by the Project Management Institute, Inc.?

Correct Answer: (C) The degree to which a set of inherent characteristics fulfill requirements

Explanation: The Project Management Institute, Inc. defines quality as the degree to which a set of inherent characteristics fulfill requirements, implying that you build what the requirements say should be built, and that the product built will perform and function as defined and needed. [Crosswind Manual 8.1; *PMBOK® Guide* Chapter 8 Introduction]

29. The company has established a control chart that has an upper control limit of five and a lower control limit of two. The customer, however, does not require such a high standard. What is the upper specification limit?

Correct Answer: (B) Greater than five

Explanation: The upper specification limit (USL) is typically greater in value than the upper control limit (UCL); therefore, with an upper control limit of five, the upper specification limit is greater than five. [Crosswind Manual 8.11.6; *PMBOK® Guide* 8.3.2.5]

30. In preparing his team for the quality improvement initiative, the project manager is holding a quality meeting. He intends to open the meeting with a brief slide show, which will include highlighting several quality concepts. Before he discusses the concepts, he asks the team to match the concept with its creator. Which of the following contains the correct matches?

Correct Answer: (B) TQM and W. Edwards Deming, Fitness for Use and Joseph Juran, Zero Defects and Philip Crosby

Explanation: TQM was conceived by W. Edwards Deming, Fitness for Use was conceived by Joseph Juran, and Zero Defects was conceived by Philip Crosby. [Crosswind Manual 8.3, 8.4, and 8.5; *PMBOK® Guide* Chapter 8 Introduction]

PMI, CAPM, and PMBOK are registered marks of the Project Management Institute, Inc.

338 © 2008-2018 Crosswind Learning, www.crosswindpm.com

Chapter 9

Project Resource Management

The purpose of performing the Project Resource Management processes is to ensure that both human and physical resources are available when needed and where needed during the project.

Human resources in this chapter refer to the project team, which is made up of individuals with assigned roles and responsibilities who work together to attain the goals of the project. Members of the project team may:

- Have varied skills
- Have part-time or full-time assignments
- Be added or removed from the team as the project evolves.

The project manager should:

- Lead and manage the project team
- Consider the impact of team environment, geographical location of team members, cultural and organizational considerations, politics, stakeholder communications on the team
- Form the project team into an effective unit
- Take care to expend sufficient effort to acquire, manage, motivate, and empower the team
- Include team members in planning and decision-making to deepen their commitment to the project and to ensure that those processes are informed by the team's experience and skills
- Evolve the skills and competencies of team members
- Improve team motivation and satisfaction
- Subscribe to professional and ethical behavior and ensure that team members do likewise

Physical resources include **infrastructure**, **facilities**, **materials**, and **equipment**. The project manager should ensure that these resources are allocated and used in a manner that results in successful completion of the project. To do so, the project manager should rely on organizational data regarding current and forecasted resource demands, the resource configuration needed to meet those demands, and access to an adequate supply of those resources. Failure to manage and control physical resources can result in: schedule delays if equipment or infrastructure cannot be secured on time; high rate of recall or rework if material ordered does not meet the quality needs of a product; and high operational costs if too much inventory is maintained.

Note that scheduling and monetary resources are addressed in Chapters 6 and 7 respectively.

Trends

Project management is trending toward a cooperative and supportive management approach that enables the team by authorizing team members to participate in decision-making. It is also trending toward optimizing the use of resources. Both trends emphasize the importance of:

- **Resource management methods**
  Methods include Just-in-Time manufacturing, Kaisen, total productive maintenance (TPM), and theory of constraints (TOC) among others.
- **Emotional intelligence (EI)**
  Emotional intelligence encompasses the improvement of inbound (self-management and self-awareness) and outbound (relationship management) team capabilities.
- **Self-organizing teams**
  Self-organizing teams are teams that function without centralized control, such as Agile teams, with the project manager acting primarily as a coach and the team members acting as generalized specialists and continuously adjusting to the changing environment and embracing change and constructive feedback.
- **Virtual/distributed teams** in response to the globalization of projects
  Virtual/distributed teams allow the project to acquire team members with specialized expertise even if they are located at diverse sites. The use of such teams is made possible by the diversity of communication technology available (audio and video conferencing, email, web-based meetings, and social media).

Tailoring

Project tailoring, the manner in which processes of a knowledge area are exercised, is employed to address the distinctive nature of each project. Successful project tailoring is predicated on a careful consideration of:

- Team diversity
- The physical location of team members
- Industry-specific resources
- Acquisition of team members
- Team management
- Life cycle approaches

Agile/Adaptive Environment

Agile methods employ collaboration to increase productivity and facilitate original approaches to problem solving. Collaborative teams may merge distinct work activities, improve communication, provide flexible work assignments, and increase knowledge sharing.

The source for the above text is the Project Management Institute, *A Guide to the Project Management Body of Knowledge, (PMBOK® Guide) – Sixth Edition,* Project Management Institute Inc., 2017, Pages 285-289

Chapter 9 Resource

PMI, CAPM, and PMBOK are registered marks of the Project Management Institute, Inc.

340   © 2008-2018 Crosswind Learning, www.crosswindpm.com

In this chapter, we discuss the following:

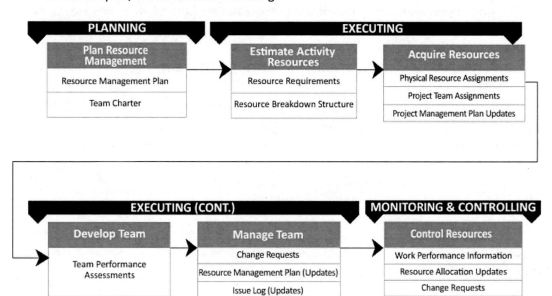

Figure 9-1: Resource Processes

The source for the above figure is the Project Management Institute, *A Guide to the Project Management Body of Knowledge, (PMBOK® Guide)* – Sixth Edition, Project Management Institute Inc., 2017, Figure 9.1, Page 286

Crosswind "Must Knows" for Project Resource Management

☐	Key Inputs, Tools & Techniques, and Outputs for Plan Resource Management
☐	Key Inputs, Tools & Techniques, and Outputs for Estimate Activity Resources
☐	Key Inputs, Tools & Techniques, and Outputs for Acquire Resources
☐	Key Inputs, Tools & Techniques, and Outputs for Develop Team
☐	Key Inputs, Tools & Techniques, and Outputs for Manage Team
☐	Key Inputs, Tools & Techniques, and Outputs for Control Resources
☐	Characteristics of an organizational breakdown structure
☐	Each level of Maslow's Hierarchy of Needs, their order and description
☐	Principles of McGregor's Theory X and Y for management and labor
☐	Leadership and management styles that evolve at each stage of the project
☐	Delegation as a tool to appoint roles, assign responsibilities, and empower team members with the authority to undertake their responsibilities
☐	Roles of the project manager, project management team, sponsor, senior management, functional manager, stakeholder, team member, and other roles as they relate to project management
☐	Characteristics of and differences between formal, reward, penalty, expert, and referent power
☐	Halo Theory
☐	Team development life cycle (form, storm, norm, perform, adjourn)
☐	Characteristics and names of various types of conflict resolution

Although helpful, this list is not all-inclusive in regard to information needed for the exam. It is only suggested material that, if understood and memorized, may increase your exam score.

9.1. Plan Resource Management (Planning Process Group)

During the Plan Resource Management process, project staffing is addressed, including the **roles**, **reporting structure**, **relationships**, and **quantity of project participants** (which can change as the project evolves). After the WBS is established, it is not uncommon to discover that more team members are needed. Depending upon the skill level of added team members, changes in staffing could impact the project in areas such as schedule, budget, and risk.

Know the Key Inputs, Tools & Techniques, and Outputs for Plan Resource Management.

Planning is typically done as early as possible and includes a team charter within the resource management plan. The team charter elaborates on the manner in which the staffing needs for the project will be realized.

Plan Resource Management

Inputs

Project Charter
Project Management Plan
- Quality Management Plan
- **Scope Baseline**

Project Documents
- Project Schedule
- Requirements Documentation
- Risk Register
- Stakeholder Register

Enterprise Environmental Factors
Organizational Process Assets

Outputs

Resource Management Plan
Team Charter
Project Documents Updates
- Assumption Log
- Risk Register

Tools and Techniques

Expert judgment
Data Representation
- Hierarchical Charts
- Responsibility Assignment Matrix
- Text-oriented Formats

Organizational Theory
Meetings

Figure 9-2: Plan Resource Management Data Flow Diagram
The source for the above figure is the Project Management Institute, *A Guide to the Project Management Body of Knowledge*, (*PMBOK® Guide*) – Sixth Edition, Project Management Institute Inc., 2017, Figure 9-2, Page 290

Plan Resource Management (Planning)		
Key Inputs	Project Charter	The project charter is the document that provides authorization for the existence of the project and gives the project manager the power to use organizational resources to execute the project. The project charter typically lists the key deliverables, the milestones, the roles and responsibilities of each person involved in the project, the key stakeholders list, and preapproved resources for financing that may impact resource management.
	Scope Baseline	The scope baseline is the authorized version of project scope. It contains the project scope statement, the work breakdown statement (WBS), the work package, one or more planning packages, and the WBS dictionary. It is referenced for its itemized deliverables in order to determine the types and quantities of resources subject to resource management.
Key Tools & Techniques	Expert Judgment	Expert judgment is judgment based on expertise acquired in a specific area. It is important to consider expertise related to acquiring the best resources available; managing contractors and logistics; managing and developing personnel; identifying the degree of preliminary effort necessary to meet project goals; determining risks related to plans for resource acquisition, retention, and release; regulation compliance; estimation of lead time necessary for acquiring resources; and identifying reporting requirements that accord with the culture of the organization.
	Organizational Theory	Organizational theory describes the manner in which personnel, teams, and organizational units behave. The theory also delineates techniques that can enhance resource planning efforts and reduce the time, cost, and exertion required to create process outputs. To effectively apply organizational theory techniques, the structure and culture of the organization must be considered.
Key Outputs	Resource Management Plan	The resource management plan is a component of the project management plan that documents: identification of resources; the manner in which the team and physical resources are determined, quantified, and acquired; resource roles, responsibilities, authorities, and competence (skill and capacity); project organizational charts; team resource management (definition, management, control, and release); team training; team development; and control of physical resources (availability and acquisition).

Plan Resource Management (Continued)		
Key Outputs (Cont.)	Team Charter _New for 6th edition_	The team charter establishes team values, agreements, and operating guidelines. It typically addresses: the conflict resolution process, meeting and communications guidelines, and the process and criteria related to decision-making.

Situational Question and Real World Application
If the Plan Resource Management process is not effectively executed, the project could be negatively impacted by resources without the proper skill sets, resources that are not brought into the project at the optimal time, and/or an improperly defined reporting hierarchy.

9.1.1. Resource Management Plan

The resource management plan is a component of the project management plan that outlines the methods for classifying, assigning, managing, and releasing resources.

At a minimum, the plan should include:

- Methods for the identification and quantification of the team and required physical resources
- Plans for acquisition of the project team and required physical resources
- Documentation of roles and responsibilities of team members with an emphasis on role definition, role authorities, role responsibilities, and role competencies
- Project organization charts that define team members and their reporting hierarchy
- Plans for project team resource management, including details regarding the definition, staffing, management, control, and release of team members
- A training road map for members of the team
- A development road map for members of the team
- Strategies for management of required physical resources during the project

The resource management plan may be divided between the team management plan and the physical resource management plan in accordance with the specifics of the project.

9.1.2. Team Charter

The team charter is a document that **details team values, agreements, and operational guidelines.** It typically includes guidelines for communication and meetings, processes for decision-making and conflict resolution, team values, and team agreements.

The charter emphasizes acceptable behavior by team members, especially as it pertains to codes of conduct, communication, decision-making, and meeting etiquette.

All team members share a responsibility for ensuring that team charter rules are followed.

9.1.3. Responsibility Assignment Matrix (RAM) Charts

Responsibility Assignment Matrix Charts (RAM Charts) graphically detail the responsibility level of each team member for a specific item.

RAM charts are used in a variety of areas during the project (the risk register is a RAM chart), but those associated with resource management typically detail the responsibility level of each team member with a specific activity.

The most common RAM chart used during the Plan Resource Management process is the **RACI chart**. The RACI chart indicates the type of involvement (Responsible, Accountable, Consult, Inform) that each team member has in a specific activity.

- multiple people can be responsible but only one person can be accountable

Activity/Resource	Tony	Jake	Nikki	Duane	Patty
Planning	R	A	C	C	I
Design	I	R	A	I	C
Development	I	A	R	C	I
Testing	I	A	C	R	C
Closure	I	R	A	C	I
Legend: Responsible = R, Accountable = A, Consult = C, Inform = I					

Figure 9-3: RACI Chart

The source for the above figure is the Project Management Institute, *A Guide to the Project Management Body of Knowledge*, (*PMBOK® Guide*) – Sixth Edition, Project Management Institute Inc., 2017, Figure 9-4, Page 294

9.1.4. Organization Charts (Organizational Breakdown Structure)

Organization charts can have a variety of formats. An organization chart, sometimes called an organizational breakdown structure (OBS), depicts the reporting relationships of the organization's human resources. The chart is typically categorized by divisions, departments, and groups and rarely includes details related to project organization and work.

Know the characteristics of an organizational breakdown structure.

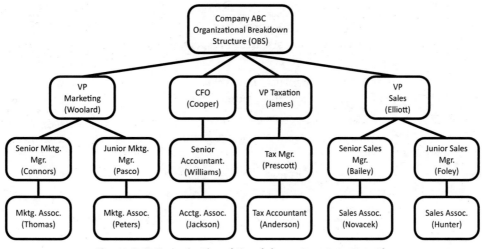

Figure 9-4: Organizational Breakdown Structure Sample

9.1.5. Organizational Theory

Organizational theory involves strategies for motivating employees and creating a productive work environment. The following are some popular theories often used in project management.

Maslow's Hierarchy of Needs

Maslow's Hierarchy of Needs can be used to determine what will motivate a person.

Know each level of Maslow's Hierarchy of Needs.

Needs are listed in hierarchical order, with physiological needs at the bottom level of the pyramid and the need for self-actualization at the topmost level. The table below the pyramid expands the hierarchy by including each need's related motivators.

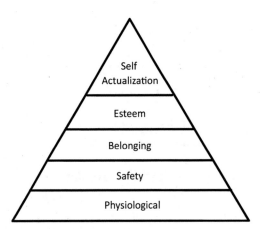

Figure 9-5: Maslow's Hierarchy of Needs

Need Level	Related Motivators
Self Actualization	Opportunities to realize personal potential, achieve personal growth or self-fulfillment, and/or participate in peak experiences
Esteem	Opportunities to experience achievement, mastery, independence, status, self-respect, and/or respect from others
Belonging	Opportunities to experience friendship, trust and acceptance, and/or affiliation with a group
Safety	Opportunities that will achieve or increase security, stability, order, and/or freedom from fear
Physiological	Opportunities to fulfill survival basics, such as air, potable water, food, and shelter

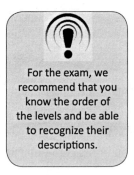

For the exam, we recommend that you know the order of the levels and be able to recognize their descriptions.

Herzberg's Motivational Theory

Herzberg determined that workplace success is predicated on hygiene and motivating agents.

Hygiene is related to factors whose absence create job dissatisfaction. Examples include a safe and clean work environment, organizational policies that are flexible and clear, reasonable pay, and a stable job.

Motivating agents is related to factors whose presence creates job satisfaction. Examples include a sense of achievement, growth opportunities, responsibility, recognition, and meaningful work.

McClelland's Achievement Theory

McClelland's Achievement Theory is based on Maslow's Hierarchy of Needs, but considers only three needs: achievement, power, and affiliation. Those motivated by **achievement** want to meet goals that are challenging and receive regular feedback regarding their progress. Those motivated by **power** want to influence others and are motivated by recognition and status. Those motivated by **affiliation** want to be well-liked members of a group and are motivated by participating in collaborative efforts with little uncertainty.

McGregor's Theory X and Y

McGregor determined that managers' beliefs regarding team motivation impact their management style. He developed Theory X and Theory Y to describe them.

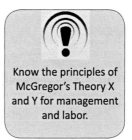

Know the principles of McGregor's Theory X and Y for management and labor.

McGregor's Theory X

Theory X describes an **authoritarian management style.** Managers that employ this style typically use both punishment and reward on a regular basis to motivate employees.

Theory X Labor and Management Characteristics
Labor wants to be told what to do.
Management feels the need to supervise.
Labor is not necessarily motivated to work.
Labor does not want to work.

McGregor's Theory Y

Theory Y describes a **participative management style**. Managers that employ this style motivate employees by providing opportunities for them to grow through responsibility, develop their skills, and contribute their ideas.

Theory Y Labor and Management Characteristics
Labor can work with an end goal in mind.
Management can minimize supervision.
Labor is motivated to do what is necessary for work.
Labor wants to work and enjoys it.

Theory Z
- People are loyal to their organization both on and off the job.

9.1.6. Leadership and Management Styles with the Project Management Life Cycle

Know the leadership and management styles that evolve at each stage of the project.

As the project evolves, so should the project manager's leadership and management approach. **Early** in the project, the project manager employs a **directing** approach. As the **project begins to evolve**, the project management employs a **coaching** approach. As the project realizes **major accomplishments**, the project management employs a **facilitating approach**. During project closure, the project management employs a **supporting** approach.

The table that follows summarizes the project stages and the concurring management approach to each.

Stage of Project	Management Approach
Early	Directing
Gaining momentum	Coaching
Significant work completed	Facilitating
Closure	Supporting

9.1.7. Delegation

Be familiar with delegation as a tool to appoint roles, assign responsibilities, and empower team members with the authority to undertake their responsibilities.

Delegation is a key tool a project manager can use to assign **work** (and the respective **authority** and **responsibility**) to team members for conducting activities on the project.

When used effectively, delegation evolves beyond merely assigning work to giving team members the **responsibility and authority to complete assigned work** accurately and in a timely manner. In return, the project manager expects accountability and reliability from those team members. Effective delegation typically results in a cooperative and engaged team.

Effective delegation requires effective communication. Delegated work must be clearly defined in terms of the work description, the expected results, and the evaluation of progress. The team is expected to provide feedback regarding delegated work.

A productive project manager distinguishes between work that can be delegated and work that should not be delegated.

May Be Delegated	Should Not Be Delegated
Technical activities	Evaluating or ranking team members
Cross-training-related work	Long term (strategic) planning
Routine activities	Monitoring extremely important activities
Enjoyable activities	Rewarding team members
Work to alleviate the stress or routine of assigned work	Determining policies
Work that can be better performed by others	Personnel selection

PMI, CAPM, and PMBOK are registered marks of the Project Management Institute, Inc.

348   © 2008-2018 Crosswind Learning, www.crosswindpm.com

A **traditional role** of the project manager has been to focus on **planning, directing, organizing**, and related activities. Given the **evolving project environment**, these activities should be considered for delegation where applicable so that the **project manager can focus on coaching, motivating, evolving team performance**, and **managing expectations** of key stakeholders.

The **project manager, team, and/or organization can create obstacles to effective delegation**. For a variety of reasons, the project manager may not wish to delegate certain activities to team members; team members might not be willing to accept the delegated work; and the organization might not support the project manager's delegation of certain work.

Delegation can be the basis for highlighting team members' capabilities so they can be promoted.

9.1.8.   Management Styles

For the exam situational questions, a familiarity with management styles is important. Note that a project manager may employ more than one style to successfully realize the project result.

Style	Definition
Autocratic	The autocratic manager has strong or unlimited power and authority.
Charismatic	The charismatic manager has an appealing persona that makes working as a team member enjoyable.
Coach	The coach brings out the best in the team/team members.
Director	The director drives the direction of the team/team members to accomplish specific activities and goals.
Facilitator	The facilitator keeps the project work progressing. Note that this style is not extremely proactive and does not have ownership.
Mediator	The mediator tries to find common ground when there is disagreement. This style is ideal when there are varying technical opinions or disagreements among resource managers.
Mentor	The mentor is similar to the coach, but focuses more on providing a roadmap for individual improvement and helping team members take on new skills and roles.
Visionary	The visionary focuses on where the team or organization needs to be in the future. The visionary focusing on the big picture rather than day-to-day events.

9.1.9.   Team Roles

Team roles can be constructive or destructive to the team and/or the project. For the exam, familiarity with this information is important.

Understand the roles as they relate to project management.

Constructive Team Roles	
Initiator	A proactive role that takes initiative and contributes insights and ideas that improve the project
Information Seeker	A role that works to increase information and knowledge associated with the project
Information Giver	A role that shares information, which results in improved project communication
Encourager	A role that encourages team members to focus on project results rather than project challenges
Clarifier	A role that focuses on ensuring team members understand project details
Harmonizer	A role that focuses on smoothing over any conflicts
Summarizer	A role that relates back to the overall picture of the project's focus
Gate Keeper	A role that helps bring people into the project; note that in business, the gate keeper is often the role that prevents access
Devil's Advocate	A role that contradicts popular views or opinions about the work of the project

Destructive Team Roles	
Aggressor	A role with a negative attitude toward the project
Blocker	A role that interrupts the project's information flow
Withdrawer	A role that is non-participatory regarding project information and issues
Recognition Seeker	A role that expects recognition or other reward in exchange for participation in the project
Topic Jumper	A role that doesn't stay focused on the primary topic
Dominator	A role that promotes its own views without considering the views of others

9.1.10.   Power

One of the keys to successful project management is the ability to use the power of the project manager to meet the challenges of the job. For the exam, a familiarity with the five power types is important.

The following table lists, then describes, the five types of power and includes examples of statements that illustrate the related power.

Understand the characteristics of and differences between formal, reward, penalty, expert, and referent power.

Power	Definition	Example
Formal	Formal power is **legitimate** power. It is the type of power that comes from senior management at a company authorizing you to be the project manager.	As you saw at the kickoff meeting, the sponsor said that I am the manager of this project and the team takes direction from me on matters related to the project.
Reward	A reward is usually the **best** form of power to use. With a reward, someone receives a benefit (reward) for doing something that is needed.	If you complete your work on the project ahead of schedule, we will send you to that training class you want to attend.
Penalty	A penalty is the **worst** form of power to use. With a penalty, people experience negative impact if they don't do what is desired.	If you don't complete the work as planned, I will make sure that you don't get your bonus.
Expert	This form of power is one that project managers must **earn on their own**. With expert power, the project manager is perceived as an expert on the subject by those on the team or at the company.	We must listen to what he says regarding project management. He created the Crosswind Success Series of products.
Referent	This type of power comes from an **attitude or "presence"** that a person has and the corresponding type of influence this person has on the team. It could also come from someone who **aligns** with other people **in a powerful position** at the company or on the team.	**Example #1:** I want to stay late and finish this like I promised the project manager. Because he has always been good to me and the rest of the team, I don't want to let him down. **Example #2:** We must do what the project manager asks. She has lunch with our vice president every week and they play golf together a lot. If we let her down, he will definitely hear about it.

Chapter 9
Resource

Project Manager Power Types

The table below lists, then defines, the power types. For the exam, a familiarity with the power types is important.

Power Type	Definition
Attitude Power	Attitude power typically involves the use of a third party acting as the negotiator for the project manager. This arrangement can minimize the possibility of taking things personally during negotiations.
Commitment Power	Commitment power uses **commitment via alliances and partnerships** to tackle challenges to the project as they arise. It has a potential connection with referent power.
Competition Power	Competition power **maximizes involvement** in the project **in the form of competition** to increase the level of commitment on the part of those involved in the project.
Investment Power	Investment power involves delaying key decisions so that enough time elapses for stakeholders/other appropriate parties to make a **significant time investment in the project.** After such a time investment is made, stakeholders/other appropriate parties are typically more flexible in their negotiations with project management.
Knowledge of Needs Power	Knowledge of needs power attempts to realize **the stated results expected by the other party during negotiations and the actual results expected by the other party during negotiations.** Knowledge of these two items allows the project manager to focus on a solution instead of a moving target.
Moral or Ethical Power	Moral or ethical power **uses a moral or ethical perspective related to personal values during the negotiation process.** This approach typically results in a win-win negotiation result rather than a win-lose negotiation result.
Persistence Power	Persistence power has the negotiator **adhering to the negotiation objective,** rather than giving up in the face of rejection. Persistence involves holding on and working toward the target.
Persuasion Power	Persuasion power **discounts logic**, which technical people can often use to sell ideas. Persuasion is used instead of focusing on comparisons that relate to the experience of the negotiating parties, **creating evidence that can't be overlooked**, and demonstrating how a solution will meet the needs of the other party.
Planning Power	Planning power uses **preparation** followed by **negotiation.**
Precedent Power	Precedent power **is based on an idea or solution that has achieved desired results in the past**. If the idea or solution was used outside the organization, precedent power can be used to challenge the way things have always been done at the organization.
Professionalism Power	Professionalism power involves **working with others in a professional and practical manner.** It helps foster a win/win relationship by allowing the project manager to consider the needs of the other parties.

Power Type	Definition
Risk Power	Risk power employs **calculated risks in negotiations** to achieve project goals. Refusal to move from a negotiating position can limit success during negotiations. It is also important to know as much about the negotiation environment as possible.

The source for the above text is the Project Management Institute, *A Guide to the Project Management Body of Knowledge*, (*PMBOK® Guide*) – Sixth Edition, Project Management Institute Inc., 2017, Pages 289-296

9.2. Estimate Activity Resources (Planning Process Group)

During the Estimate Activity Resources process, **all of the resources required for the project are determined. The amount and type of personnel, material, and equipment** should be carefully examined so the results of this process are as accurate as possible.

Know the Key Inputs, Tools & Techniques, and Outputs for Estimate Activity Resources.

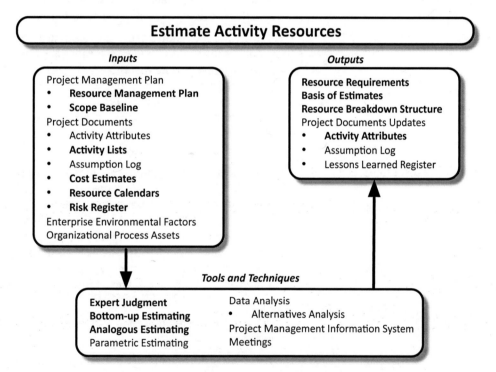

Figure 9-6: Estimate Activity Resources Data Flow Diagram

The source for the above figure is the Project Management Institute, *A Guide to the Project Management Body of Knowledge*, (*PMBOK® Guide*) – Sixth Edition, Project Management Institute Inc., 2017, Figure 9-5, Page 297

Chapter 9 Resource

Estimate Activity Resources (Planning)		
Key Inputs	Resource Management Plan	The resource management plan is a component of the project management plan that documents: the manner in which the team and physical resources are determined, quantified, and acquired; resource roles, responsibilities, authorities, and competence (skill and capacity); project organizational charts; team resource management (definition, management, control, and release); team training; team development; and control of physical resources (availability and acquisition).
	Scope Baseline	The scope baseline is the authorized version of project scope. It contains the project scope statement, the work breakdown statement (WBS), the work package, one or more planning packages, and the WBS dictionary. It describes the work the project is trying to complete and is subject to change management and is a component of the project management plan. The scope baseline necessitates the need for team and physical resources.
	Activity List	The activity list enumerates each schedule activity stipulated for the project. It identifies those activities that need resources. Note that project managers commonly call activities "tasks," but the term "activities" is generally more appropriate according to Project Management Institute, Inc. standards. If rolling wave planning or agile is used the list must be reviewed regularly and updated as necessary.
	Cost Estimates	Cost estimates include quantitative estimates of work completion costs, contingency reserves for identified risks, and management reserves for unidentified work. The estimates consider all resources involved including direct labor, equipment, material, facilities, exchange rates, information technology, financing costs, inflation allowance, and/or a cost contingency reserve. Costs associated with resources may impact resource selection.
	Resource Calendars	Resource calendars delineate project resource accessibility and are referenced to estimate resource utilization.
	Risk Register	The risk register documents identified project risks and should be referenced to determine the risks that impact the selection and availability of resources. The volume of documentation varies in accordance with the size and complexity of the project. Typically the risk register includes the list of risks sufficiently described to ensure clear-cut understanding, the risk owner for each risk, and the response(s) for each risk.

Estimate Activity Resources (Continued)		
Key Tools & Techniques	Expert Judgment	Expert judgment is judgment based on expertise acquired in a specific area. It is important to consider expertise in planning and estimating teams and physical resources.
	Bottom-up Estimating	Bottom-up estimating is an estimation technique in which duration or cost is determined by rolling up estimates of each WBS component of the item being estimated. The size and complexity of the item being estimated impacts the cost and accuracy of the estimation. Team and physical resources are estimated at the activity level and aggregated to the work package level, the control accounts level, and the summary project levels.
	Analogous Estimating	Analogous estimating is a high-level estimation technique based on historical resource data from a similar activity or project. The technique adjusts for known variances in complexity from the current activity or project under consideration and the historical activity or project. Analogous estimating is typically used to estimate a value or values in projects where there is a limited amount of detailed data and can be used to estimate the entire project or a portion of the project. While this technique costs less and is not as time consuming as more detailed techniques, it is typically not as accurate.
Key Outputs	Resource Requirements	Resource requirements define the types and quantities of team and physical resources needed for a work package or for each activity in a work package. This can then be aggregated to calculate the estimated resources for each work package (if the basis for aggregation is the activity), work breakdown structure (WBS) branch, and the project. Exhibits typically include the basis of estimate for each resource and the assumptions made as to the resource type, availability, and required quantities.
	Basis of Estimates	The basis of estimates for resources includes documentation that delineates the manner in which the estimates were determined, assumptions and constraints, resources used to evolve the estimate, range of estimates, risks that impacted the estimate, and degree of certainty in the estimate.

Estimate Activity Resources (Continued)		
Key Outputs (Cont.)	Resource Breakdown Structure	The resource breakdown structure (RBS) is a graphical representation of resources by category and type displayed in hierarchical order. Categories may include, but are not limited to labor, equipment, supplies, and material. Types may include, but are not limited to skill level, grade level, and required certification.
	Activity Attributes	Activity attributes clarify an activity by identifying multiple components related to the activity. The components evolve during the project: during the initial stage, they include a singular activity identifier, a WBS identifier, and an activity label; when completed they typically include a description of the activity, predecessor and successor activities, logical relationships, leads and lags, resource requirements, constraints, assumptions, and exact dates. They are used to clarify reporting.

Situational Question and Real World Application
Failure to effectively perform the Estimate Activity Resources process can result in serious schedule slippage. Reasons for slippage can include a lack of sufficient personnel, a lack of personnel with the appropriate skills sets, and a lack of access to material or equipment appropriate to the project.

9.2.1. Resource Breakdown Structure

The resource breakdown structure displays the breakdown by resource type across an organization. This breakdown makes it possible to distinguish where resources are being used regardless of their organizational group or division.

PMI, CAPM, and PMBOK are registered marks of the Project Management Institute, Inc.

356 © 2008-2018 Crosswind Learning, www.crosswindpm.com

The example in Figure 9-7: Resource Breakdown Structure Sample depicts classrooms and teachers during the fall semester. The fall semester represents the common criteria.

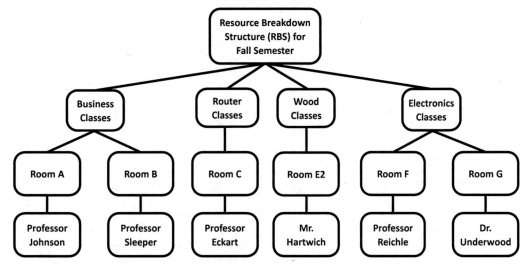

Figure 9-7: Resource Breakdown Structure Sample

The source for the above figure is the Project Management Institute, *A Guide to the Project Management Body of Knowledge*, (*PMBOK® Guide*) – Sixth Edition, Project Management Institute Inc., 2017, Figure 9-7, Page 302

Because this information can include non-HR resources, as well as personnel, there is the potential to track project cost especially if the RBS aligns with the organization's accounting system.

The source for the above text is the Project Management Institute, *A Guide to the Project Management Body of Knowledge*, (*PMBOK® Guide*) – Sixth Edition, Project Management Institute Inc., 2017, Pages 296-302

9.3. Acquire Resources (Executing Process Group)

Project staffing and physical resource needs are satisfied during the Acquire Resources process. **The actual resources that will be working on the project are assigned to the project.**

Factors to consider include cost, ability, experience, availability, and interest of resources.

Know the Key Inputs, Tools & Techniques, and Outputs for Acquire Resources.

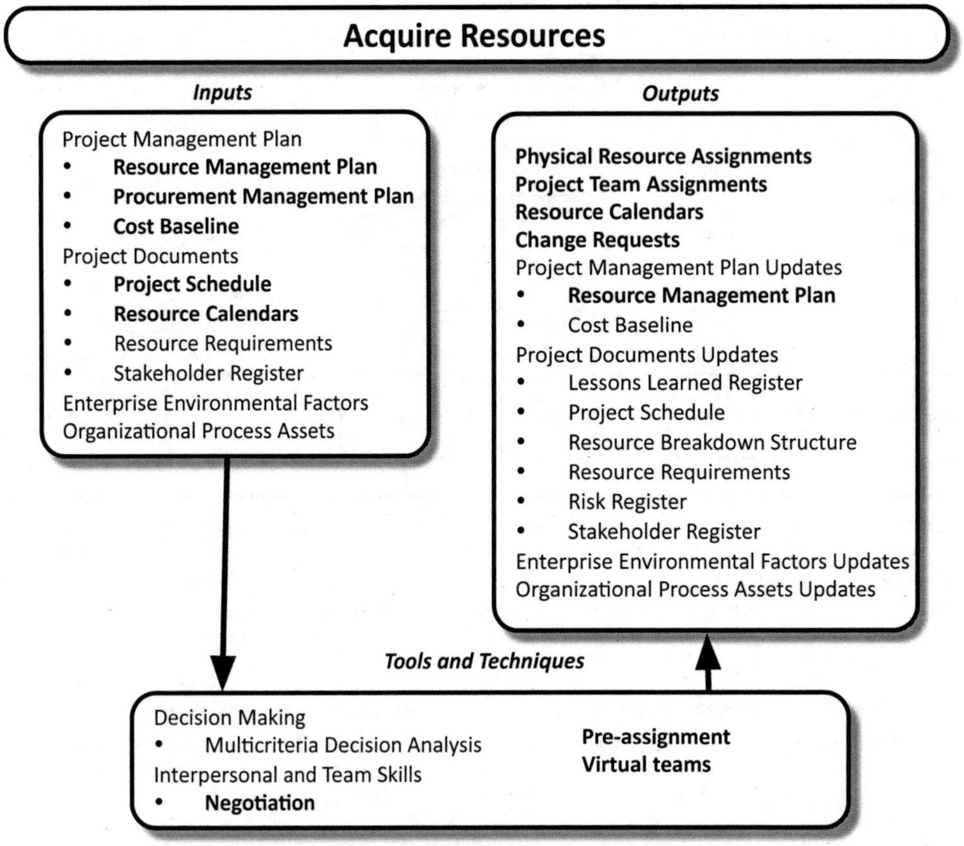

Acquire Resources

Inputs

Project Management Plan
- **Resource Management Plan**
- **Procurement Management Plan**
- **Cost Baseline**

Project Documents
- **Project Schedule**
- **Resource Calendars**
- Resource Requirements
- Stakeholder Register

Enterprise Environmental Factors
Organizational Process Assets

Outputs

Physical Resource Assignments
Project Team Assignments
Resource Calendars
Change Requests
Project Management Plan Updates
- **Resource Management Plan**
- Cost Baseline

Project Documents Updates
- Lessons Learned Register
- Project Schedule
- Resource Breakdown Structure
- Resource Requirements
- Risk Register
- Stakeholder Register

Enterprise Environmental Factors Updates
Organizational Process Assets Updates

Tools and Techniques

Decision Making
- Multicriteria Decision Analysis

Interpersonal and Team Skills
- **Negotiation**

Pre-assignment
Virtual teams

Figure 9-8: Acquire Resources Data Flow Diagram

The source for the above figure is the Project Management Institute, *A Guide to the Project Management Body of Knowledge*, (*PMBOK® Guide*) – Sixth Edition, Project Management Institute Inc., 2017, Figure 9-8, Page 304

Chapter 9
Resource

Acquire Resources (Executing)		
Key Inputs	Resource Management Plan	The resource management plan is a component of the project management plan that documents: the manner in which the team and physical resources are determined, quantified, and acquired; resource roles, responsibilities, authorities, and competence (skill and capacity); project organizational charts; team resource management (definition, management, control, and release); team training; team development; and control of physical resources (availability and acquisition).

Acquire Resources (Continued)		
Key Inputs (Cont.)	Procurement Management Plan	The procurement management plan is a component of the project management plan that documents the manner in which bidding is done and the sources and availability of funding are established if financed externally. The plan can include guidance for: the procurement related roles and responsibilities of stakeholders; constraints and assumptions; the need for independent estimates; the coordination of procurement with project processes; the management of risks; the legal jurisdiction and currency type for making payments; prequalified sellers, if applicable; metrics for contract management; and a timetable of key activities.
	Cost Baseline	The cost baseline is the authorized version of the time-phased budget for the project, excluding management reserves, and subject to change control. It is evolved from a summation of approved budgets for specific schedule activities. Cost estimates are aggregated by work packages, then into higher components of the work breakdown structure (WBS), and then for the entire project. Because the cost estimates included in the cost baseline are linked to schedule activities, a time-phased view of the cost baseline is enabled. It is usually depicted as an S-curve. If the project uses earned value management (EVM), the cost baseline is known as the performance measurement baseline. Changes to the scope, resources, or cost estimates, if severe, can result in a revised cost baseline.
	Project Schedule	The project schedule is the product of a schedule model containing linked activities and their planned dates, durations, milestones, and resources. The schedule is utilized to identify when resources need to be available and acquired based on the start and finish dates of applicable activities.
	Resource Calendars	Resource calendars delineate project resource accessibility and are referenced to ensure a reliable schedule. Both the availability of each resource and schedule constraints, such as holidays, time zones, vacations, and work hours, must be considered.

Acquire Resources (Continued)		
Key Tools & Techniques	Negotiation	Negotiation is the art of reaching a mutual agreement and is a very important skill in relation to resource management. Not only do many projects rely on negotiation for resource acquisition, the team may need to negotiate with functional managers regarding the availability of a resource, with other project teams to assign or share a specialized or scant resource, and with external entities (organizations, vendors, suppliers, contractors) to provide team and/or physical resources.
	Pre-assignment	Pre-assignment occurs when physical or team resources are identified in advance. This typically transpires if the project is dependent on the specialized knowledge or skill of a particular person or if resources are determined as part of a competitive proposal.
	Virtual Teams	Virtual teams, those who work toward the same purpose with little or no face-to-face meetings, communicate using e-mail, conferencing (video and/or audio), web-based meetings, and/or social media. The use of virtual teams often requires additional communication planning so that conflict resolution protocols are adequately developed, expectations are clear, cultural differences are understood, the appropriate people are included in the decision-making process, and credit for achievements is shared. The model for virtual teams enables: forming teams that are geographically diverse, working with geographically diverse experts, working with people who have mobility limitations, working with people subject to different shifts, and/or circumventing cancellation or delay of projects due to travel expenses.
Key Outputs	Physical Resource Assignments	Physical resources include infrastructure, facilities, equipment, and other non-personnel items required to complete the project. Documentation for physical resource assignments typically include the resource breakdown structure and the project schedule.
	Project Team Assignments	Project team resources are project related personnel. Documentation for project team assignments typically include a project team directory, project organizational charts, and project schedules.

PMI, CAPM, and PMBOK are registered marks of the Project Management Institute, Inc.

360   © 2008-2018 Crosswind Learning, www.crosswindpm.com

Acquire Resources (Continued)		
Key Outputs (Cont.)	Resource Calendars	Resource calendars delineate project resource accessibility and are referenced to ensure a reliable schedule. Both the availability of each resource and schedule constraints, such as holidays, time zones, vacations, and work hours, must be considered. Resource calendars are updated to reflect acquired resources.
	Change Requests	Change requests are requests for modification that have not been formally approved through the change control process. Modifications to the schedule, resource breakdown structure, or other impacted components of the project management plan may be requested.
	Resource Management Plan	The resource management plan is a component of the project management plan that documents: the manner in which the team and physical resources are determined, quantified, and acquired; resource roles, responsibilities, authorities, and competence (skill and capacity); project organizational charts; team resource management (definition, management, control, and release); team training; team development; and control of physical resources (availability and acquisition).

Situational Question and Real World Application

If the Acquire Resources process is not executed effectively, staff and other resources could be improperly assigned and the schedule could be incorrect, resulting in work that is inadequate and untimely. Additionally, related documentation could be incorrect resulting in ineffective communication and confusion regarding work hand-offs.

9.3.1. Halo Theory

According to the Halo Theory, people make good project managers regardless of background training in project management, simply because they are good in their fields. The theory also implies that people who do not excel in their fields would not make good project managers.

Know the Halo Theory.

This theory is put into practice when someone is promoted to a project manager from a technical or hands-on position and hasn't had the opportunity to receive any project management training. The results are typically negative.

The source for the above text is the Project Management Institute, *A Guide to the Project Management Body of Knowledge*, (*PMBOK® Guide*) – Sixth Edition, Project Management Institute Inc., 2017, Pages 307-312

9.4. Develop Team (Executing Process Group)

The Develop Team process (team-building) continues throughout the project although the **majority of the process occurs during execution.**

The key to team cohesion is following the resource and project management plans. Key areas of focus should be increasing trust and interactivity between team members and improving the skill levels of team members.

Know the Key Inputs, Tools & Techniques, and Outputs for Develop Team.

Develop Team

Inputs

Project Management Plan
- **Resource Management Plan**

Project Documents
- Lessons Learned Register
- Project Schedule
- **Project Team Assignments**
- **Resource Calendars**
- **Team Charter**

Enterprise Environmental Factors
Organizational Process Assets

Outputs

Team Performance Assessments
Change Requests
Project Management Plan Updates
- Resource Management Plan

Project Documents Updates
- Lessons Learned Register
- Project Schedule
- **Project Team Assignments**
- **Resource Calendars**
- Team Charter

Enterprise Environmental Factors Updates
Organizational Process Assets Updates

Tools and Techniques

Colocation
Virtual Teams
Communication Technology
Interpersonal and Team Skills
- **Conflict Management**
- **Influencing**
- **Motivation**
- **Negotiation**
- **Team Building**

Recognition and Rewards
Training
Individual and Team Assessments
Meetings

Figure 9-9: Develop Team Data Flow Diagram
The source for the above figure is the Project Management Institute, *A Guide to the Project Management Body of Knowledge*, (*PMBOK® Guide*) – Sixth Edition, Project Management Institute Inc., 2017, Figure 9-10, Page 310

© 2008-2018 Crosswind Learning, www.crosswindpm.com

Develop Team (Executing)		
Key Inputs	Resource Management Plan	The resource management plan is a component of the project management plan that documents: the manner in which the team and physical resources are determined, quantified, and acquired; resource roles, responsibilities, authorities, and competence (skill and capacity); project organizational charts; team resource management (definition, management, control, and release); team training; team development; and control of physical resources (availability and acquisition).
	Project Team Assignments	Project team assignments reference the assignment of team members to the project and identify the roles and responsibilities of the team and its members. Documentation for team members typically includes a project team directory, project organizational charts, and project schedules.
	Resource Calendars	Resource calendars delineate project resource accessibility and are referenced to ensure a reliable schedule. Both the availability of each resource and schedule constraints, such as holidays, time zones, vacations, and work hours, must be considered. The calendars also distinguish the availability of teams throughout the project so participation in team development activities can be determined.
	Team Charter	The team charter establishes team values, agreements, and operating guidelines. The framework describing the manner in which team members cooperate is determined by the team values and operating guidelines contained in the charter.
Key Tools & Techniques	Colocation	Colocation describes the placement of most or all of the most active members in one location to enhance team performance. Sometimes referenced as a tight matrix, colocation can occur temporarily or throughout the duration of the project. Typical colocation strategies include communication enhancements (designated areas for team meetings and team schedule postings), osmotic communication (information absorbed from background conversations), and interpersonal communication.
	Virtual Teams	Virtual teams, those who work toward the same goals with little/no face-to-face meetings, bring benefits such as more skilled resources, proximity of team to suppliers, customers, and/or key stakeholders, and travel/relocation expense reduction. Communication issues for virtual teams can be solved technologically through team calendars, on-line file storage, e-mail, video/audio conferencing, and web-based meetings.

**Chapter 9
Resource**

Develop Team (Continued)		
Key Tools & Techniques (Cont.)	Conflict Management	Conflict management addresses the contention over scarce resources, personal approaches to work, scheduling priorities, and other sources of conflict. The project manager is responsible for resolving conflict in a timely and constructive manner to ensure team cohesion and optimum performance.
	Influencing	Influencing skills are useful in promoting performance, especially when there is a lack of direct authority. A key skill used during team development is gathering information that addresses important issues and using that information to reach mutual agreements while maintaining mutual trust.
	Motivation	Team motivation inspires teams to share in the decision-making process and work in a self-sufficient manner.
	Negotiation	Negotiation is the art of reaching a mutual agreement and is a very important skill in relation to team development, since it is used to reach consensus regarding the needs of the project.
	Team Building	Team building is the art of unifying individuals into a cohesive, committed team. Team building activities vary in time and intensity and should continue throughout the project. They are especially important when the project environment changes and with virtual teams.
	Individual and Team Assessments	Individual and team assessments evaluate the strengths and weaknesses of a team and its members in order to increase team productivity. They reveal the preferences, aspirations, and decision-making abilities of team members as well as the manner in which they interact with others and organize/process information. Assessment tools can include structured interviews, ability tests, focus groups, specific assessments, and attitudinal surveys.
Key Outputs	Team Performance Assessments	Team performance assessments evaluate the strength and weaknesses of a team's performances in order to craft the specific training, coaching, mentoring, and assistance required for the performance improvement. Indicators used in the evaluation include: improvements in the skills of team members, improvements in the competency of team members, a reduction in staff turnover, and an increase in team cohesiveness as evidenced by the sharing of information and experience.

Develop Team (Continued)		
Key Outputs (Cont.)	Change Requests	Change requests are requests for modification that have not been formally approved through the change control process. Modifications to the schedule, resource breakdown structure, or other impacted components of the project management plan may be requested.
	Project Team Assignments	Changes to team assignments that result from team development activities are chronicled in the team assignment documentation.
	Resource Calendars	Changes to resource availability are documented in resource calendars.

Situational Question and Real World Application

Failure to effectively execute the Develop Team process can result in a lack of cohesiveness among team members. Such a lack could lead to disharmony or conflict, which could disrupt the work of the project.

9.4.1. Form, Storm, Norm, Perform, Adjourn (Team Development Life Cycle)

Team development involves the convergence of a group of people into a performing organization. A common evolutionary life cycle is characteristic of team development. The team development process includes the **Tuckman ladder (form, storm, norm, perform, and adjourn)** and is typical when a team is put in place.

Understand the team development life cycle (form, storm, norm, perform, adjourn).

Stage	Description
Form	Form refers to the creation of the team, when people on the team are put together per the project organizational planning needs.
Storm	Storm refers to the chaos that occurs as people start to get accustomed to working together.
Norm	Norm refers to the point in time when team behavior starts to normalize and team members are accustomed to each other. .
Perform	Perform refers to the activity that transpires as members work as a team instead of individuals. The group should be working at an optimal level in this phase.
Adjourn	As the team work is completed, the team is disbanded and team members move to new work or assignments.

Instructor's Rock Climbing Story →

9.4.2. Recognition and Rewards

A recognition and rewards system is needed for team development and for performance optimization. Such a system needs to be defined, but also needs to be adaptable in response to personal motivator preferences. A reward and recognition system can provide compensatory time for overtime hours worked or payment for a certification test or training. A successful reward and recognition system is possible when management follows through on its promises. A lack of follow through not only hurts the reward system, it also hurts the project manager's credibility.

The source for the above text is the Project Management Institute, *A Guide to the Project Management Body of Knowledge*, (*PMBOK® Guide*) – Sixth Edition, Project Management Institute Inc., 2017, Pages 309-317

9.5. Manage Team (Executing Process Group)

During the Manage Team process, team performance is analyzed and feedback provided. The process also involves coordination of project-related issues and optimization of project performance.

Know the Key Inputs, Tools & Techniques, and Outputs for Manage Team.

Manage Team

Inputs

Project Management Plan
- **Resource Management Plan**

Project Documents
- Issue Log
- Lessons Learned Register
- Project Team Assignments
- **Team Charter**

Work Performance Reports
Team Performance Assessments
Enterprise Environmental Factors
Organizational Process Assets

Outputs

Change Requests
Project Management Plan Updates
- Resource Management Plan
- Schedule Baseline
- Cost Baseline

Project Documents Updates
- **Issue Log**
- Lessons Learned Register
- Project Team Assignments

Enterprise Environmental Factors Updates

Tools and Techniques

Interpersonal and Team Skills
- **Conflict Management**
- Decision Making
- **Emotional Intelligence**
- Influencing
- **Leadership**

Project Management Information System

Figure 9-10: Manage Team Data Flow Diagram

The source for the above figure is the Project Management Institute, *A Guide to the Project Management Body of Knowledge*, (*PMBOK® Guide*) – Sixth Edition, Project Management Institute Inc., 2017, Figure 9-12, Page 319

PMI, CAPM, and PMBOK are registered marks of the Project Management Institute, Inc.

366 © 2008-2018 Crosswind Learning, www.crosswindpm.com

Manage Team (Executing)		
Key Inputs	Resource Management Plan	The resource management plan is a component of the project management plan that documents: the manner in which the team and physical resources should be managed and released.
	Team Charter	The team charter establishes team values, agreements, and operating guidelines. It specifically addresses the manner in which the team will conduct meetings, resolve conflict, and participate in the decision-making process.
	Work Performance Reports	Work performance reports are representations, either physical or electronic, of work performance information and are used as the basis for decisions and/or actions. With related forecasts, they engender the identification of necessary resource requirements, the determination of recognition and rewards, and updates to the resource management plan.
Key Tools & Techniques	Conflict Management	Conflict management addresses the contention over scarce resources, personal approaches to work, scheduling priorities, and other sources of conflict. To reduce conflict, management applies **team ground rules**, **group standards**, and conventions such as **role definition** and **communication planning**. Conflict reduction methods are influenced by the importance and intensity of the conflict, the immediacy required for resolution, the motivation for resolution, the importance of maintaining good relationships with those involved in the conflict, and the power wielded by those involved in the conflict.
	Emotional Intelligence	Emotional intelligence is the ability to identify, evaluate, and manage emotion in others. Emotional intelligence is used to envisage the actions of team members and to effectively acknowledge their concerns and address their issues.
	Leadership	Leaders must have strong leadership skills including the ability to inspire others, the ability to delegate, the ability to communicate effectively, integrity, and competence. These skills are integral to effecting a successful project.

Chapter 9
Resource

Manage Team (Continued)		
Key Outputs	Change Requests	Change requests are requests for modification that have not been formally approved through the change control process. Modifications to the schedule, resource breakdown structure, or other impacted components of the project management plan may be requested.
	Issue Log	The issue log must be modified to reflect team related issues.
	Enterprise Environmental Factors Updates	Enterprise environmental factors must be modified to reflect the skills of personnel and input to organizational performance evaluations.

Situational Question and Real World Application

Failure to effectively perform the Manage Team process has the same result as a failure to effectively execute the Develop Team process: a lack of cohesiveness among team members. Such a lack could lead to disharmony or conflict, which could disrupt the work of the project.

9.5.1. Sources of Conflict

Conflict is best understood when the sources of conflict are understood. If the project manager is aware of the variables that can cause conflict, a proactive approach can be taken and the conflict repercussions decreased.

If conflict is managed correctly, relationships between team members are often strengthened, resulting in greater productivity on the part of the team.

Traditionally, conflict occurs during planning. Items such as scheduling priorities and resource utilization are the most likely sources of conflict. To minimize conflict, a **project manager can utilize team ground rules, group norms, and project management practices**.

In spite of popular opinion, personality clashes are rarely a source of conflict.

Scheduling Priorities	Scarce Resources	Personal Workstyle	Methodology Details	Cost	Personality
↑ Greatest Source of Conflict					↑ Least Source of Conflict

PMI, CAPM, and PMBOK are registered marks of the Project Management Institute, Inc.

368 © 2008-2018 Crosswind Learning, www.crosswindpm.com

9.5.2. Conflict Resolution

Given the complexity of projects today, conflict is bound to occur. The days of eliminating conflict before it occurs are gone. The process of resolving conflict is a key tool of the project manager.

Conflict Resolution Technique	Description	Example
Collaborating/ Problem Solving	Collaborating/problem solving is an effort in which attempts are made to **work out the actual problem**. It is the **best** type of conflict resolution.	If you can't do what is needed with your current computer, get an upgrade that lets you accomplish what's needed for your job.
Compromising/ Reconciling	Compromising/reconciling is a negotiation attempt to get everyone involved **to give (concede) a little to find common ground and a resolution.** It is sometimes viewed as undesirable because when everyone gives something up, there is a potential that the solution will fail to meet anyone's needs.	If we can get labor to give in on benefits a little, and management to increase their raise increase a little, I think we can find agreement that both sides can live with.
Forcing/ Directing	Forcing/directing is an action in which a **direct order** to resolve something is given. It is typically the **worst** type of conflict resolution.	You will stop using that software and switch to the authorized version or you will not be around here for long.
Smoothing/ Accommodating	Smoothing/accommodating is an attempt to **focus** on the **positive** and **distract** attention from the **negative**.	Look at how well the requirements on the project went. We just have to apply that same view to this phase of the project as well.
Withdrawing/ Avoiding	Withdrawing/avoiding is the **refusal to address** a **problem,** hoping that it either fixes itself or disappears. Typically, withdrawal is not considered a conflict resolution technique because it's not a proactive approach to resolving conflict.	I know he is a pain to work with and takes longer to do his work than we like, but maybe if we let him be, he will just quit and take a new job.

9.5.3.   Interpersonal Skills

Interpersonal skills are utilized by project managers to take advantage of each team member's strengths. Those most commonly used by project managers are:

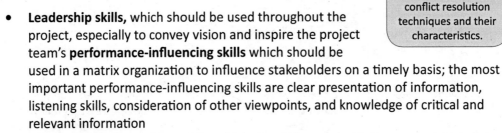

Be familiar with the various conflict resolution techniques and their characteristics.

- **Leadership skills,** which should be used throughout the project, especially to convey vision and inspire the project team's **performance-influencing skills** which should be used in a matrix organization to influence stakeholders on a timely basis; the most important performance-influencing skills are clear presentation of information, listening skills, consideration of other viewpoints, and knowledge of critical and relevant information
- **Effective decision-making skills,** which should be used to influence and negotiate with members of the project team and the organization; effective decision-making skills include focusing on goals, utilizing a decision-making process, knowledge of the environment and its impact on the project, managing opportunities and threats, and stimulating team creativity

9.5.4.   Problem Solving and Situational Questions

For the exam's situational questions, a knowledge of the role responsible for solving various types of problems is very important.

The source for the above text is the Project Management Institute, *A Guide to the Project Management Body of Knowledge*, *(PMBOK® Guide)* – Sixth Edition, Project Management Institute Inc., 2017, Pages 317-324

9.6.   Control Resources (Monitoring and Controlling Process Group)

During the Control Resources process, the team ensures that the physical resources, which have been assigned and allocated to the project, are available as planned. Also, during this process, the team performs any corrective action required as a result of monitoring actual utilization of resources versus planned utilization of resources and ensures that resources are available at the right time, in the right place, and are released when no longer required.

Know the Key Inputs, Tools & Techniques, and Outputs for Control Resources.

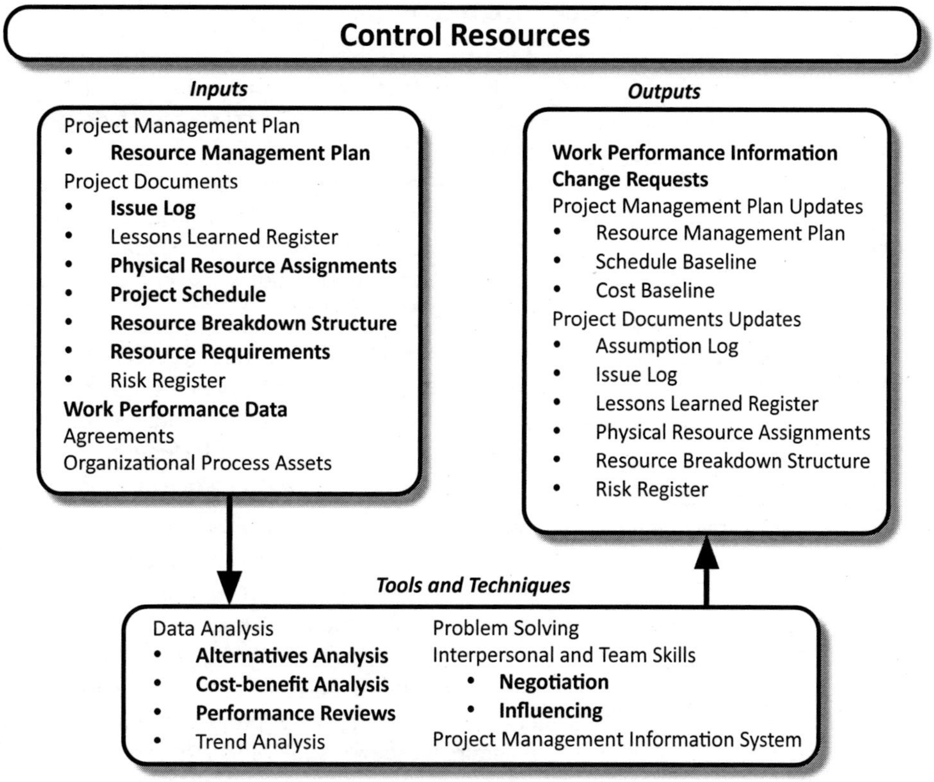

Control Resources

Inputs

Project Management Plan
- **Resource Management Plan**

Project Documents
- **Issue Log**
- Lessons Learned Register
- **Physical Resource Assignments**
- **Project Schedule**
- **Resource Breakdown Structure**
- **Resource Requirements**
- Risk Register

Work Performance Data

Agreements

Organizational Process Assets

Outputs

Work Performance Information
Change Requests
Project Management Plan Updates
- Resource Management Plan
- Schedule Baseline
- Cost Baseline
Project Documents Updates
- Assumption Log
- Issue Log
- Lessons Learned Register
- Physical Resource Assignments
- Resource Breakdown Structure
- Risk Register

Tools and Techniques

Data Analysis
- **Alternatives Analysis**
- **Cost-benefit Analysis**
- **Performance Reviews**
- Trend Analysis

Problem Solving
Interpersonal and Team Skills
- **Negotiation**
- **Influencing**
Project Management Information System

Figure 9-11: Control Resources Data Flow Diagram
The source for the above figure is the Project Management Institute, *A Guide to the Project Management Body of Knowledge*, (*PMBOK® Guide*) – Sixth Edition, Project Management Institute Inc., 2017, Figure 9-14, Page 325

Control Resources (Monitoring and Controlling)		
Key Inputs	Resource Management Plan	The resource management plan is a component of the project management plan that documents: the manner in which the team and physical resources are determined, quantified, and acquired; resource roles, responsibilities, authorities, and competence (skill and capacity); project organizational charts; team resource management (definition, management, control, and release); team training; team development; and control of physical resources (availability and acquisition). It provides direction for the use, control, and release of resources.

Control Resources (Continued)		
Key Inputs (Cont.)	Issue Log	The issue log is used to record and track any project challenges that cannot be immediately resolved. Issues may include a lack of resources, a delay in obtaining necessary resources, or resources that are ineffective or below grade. The project team uses the log to ensure issues are resolved during the execution of the project management plan. Updates occur during activities performed while monitoring and controlling the project.
	Physical Resource Assignments	Physical resources include infrastructure, facilities, equipment, and other non-personnel items required to complete the project. Documentation for physical resource assignments typically include the resource breakdown structure and the project schedule.
	Project Schedule	The project schedule is the product of a schedule model containing linked activities and their planned dates, durations, milestones, and resources. Specifically, the schedule shows what resources are required, when they are required, and where they are required. It is usually formatted as a bar chart, milestone chart, or project schedule network diagram, although tabular formatting may occur. Until resources have been allocated and start and finish dates substantiated, the project schedule is preliminary. A master schedule or milestone schedule is a summary form of the project schedule.
	Resource Breakdown Structure	The resource breakdown structure is a graphical representation of resources by category and type displayed in hierarchical order. Categories may include, but are not limited to labor, equipment, supplies, and material. Types may include, but are not limited to **skill level**, **grade level**, and **required certification**. It is referenced whenever a replacement or reacquisition is required.
	Resource Requirements	Resource requirements define the types and quantities of team and physical resources needed for a work package or for each activity in a work package. This can then be aggregated to calculate the estimated resources for each work package (if the basis for aggregation is the activity), work breakdown structure (WBS) branch, and the project. Exhibits typically include the basis of estimate for each resource and assumptions made as to resource type, availability, and required quantities.

PMI, CAPM, and PMBOK are registered marks of the Project Management Institute, Inc.

372 © 2008-2018 Crosswind Learning, www.crosswindpm.com

Control Resources (Continued)		
Key Inputs (Cont.)	Work Performance Data	Work performance data represents the raw metrics and observations identified during the performance of project work activities. It includes facts related to the number and types of resources used during the project.
Key Tools & Techniques	Alternatives Analysis	Alternatives analysis is a technique utilized to assess the most appropriate options to execute the work of the project. Examples are evaluating alternatives to optimize resource utilization and to determine if using additional resources/paying overtime is better than late delivery or phased deliveries.
	Cost-benefit Analysis	Cost-benefit analysis is a financial tool that determines the scenario that best fits the needs of the project by comparing the cost of each scenario to its expected benefits. During resource control, it is typically used to determine the best corrective action for project deviations.
	Performance Reviews	Performance reviews use metrics, comparison, and analysis to determine the differences between planned resource utilization and actual resource utilization. Cost and schedule related work performance information can be used to identify issues that impact resource utilization.
	Negotiation	Negotiation is the art of reaching a mutual agreement and is a very important skill in relation to resource control. It can be used to obtain additional resources, change resources, or lower resource related costs.
	Influencing	Influencing skills are useful in promoting performance, especially when there is a lack of direct authority. A key skill used during resource control, it can be used to resolve issues and obtain needed resources in a timely manner.
Key Outputs	Work Performance Information	Work performance information includes supplemental and contextualized information regarding the performance of the project scope in comparison to the scope baseline. The information can contain important facets of resource control such as actual resource allocation, which can then be compared to resource requirements.

Chapter 9 Resource

Control Resources (Continued)		
Key Outputs (Cont.)	Change Requests	Change requests are requests for modification that have not been formally approved through the change control process. Modifications to the schedule, resource breakdown structure, or other impacted components of the project management plan may be requested.

The source for the above text is the Project Management Institute, *A Guide to the Project Management Body of Knowledge*, (*PMBOK® Guide*) – Sixth Edition, Project Management Institute Inc., 2017, Pages 324-329

Situational Question and Real World Application

Failure to effectively control resources can result in a project that is over schedule and/or budget due to resources that are not in place at the correct time and/or required corrective actions that are not performed.

9.7. Project Resource Management Formulas and Variables

There are no formulas for this chapter.

9.8. Project Resource Management Terminology

Term	Description
Acquire Resources	The process of establishing the availability of resources, internal and/or external to the organization
Aggressors	A role with a negative attitude toward the project
Attitude Power	A type of power that can involve using a middle person to negotiate for the project manager
Authority	The power to assign resources, disburse funds, make or authorize decisions for the project
Blockers	A role that interrupts information flow on the project
Clarifiers	A role that helps focus on making sure people on the project understand what the details of the project entail
Coercive/Penalty Power	A type of power that uses negative approaches including threatening and punishment to get people to do things they don't want to do
Colocation	A technique for improving team effectiveness, as well as communication and collaboration among team members, by placing them in close proximity to each other
Commitment Power	A type of power that uses commitment via alliances and partnerships on the project team to tackle challenges to the project as they arise; has a potential connection with referent power

PMI, CAPM, and PMBOK are registered marks of the Project Management Institute, Inc.

374   © 2008-2018 Crosswind Learning, www.crosswindpm.com

Term	Description
Competition Power	A type of power that maximizes involvement in the project or idea in the form of competition to help enhance the commitment of those involved to work toward a more successful outcome of the project or idea
Compromise	A conflict resolution technique in which a solution involves (typically) a little of what everyone is proposing for a solution
Conflict Management	The management of conflict within the project by applying such techniques as problem solving, collaboration, forcing, compromising, accommodation, and avoidance
Confrontation	Directly dealing with a conflict via problem-solving techniques so that the parties can work through any disagreement
Control Resources	The process of ensuring that the physical resources assigned and allocated to the project are available as planned and monitored throughout the project to determine that actual utilization conforms to planned utilization; non-conformance to the plan may require corrective action
Develop Team	The process of enhancing the capabilities, interaction and environment of the project team in order to refine project execution
Devil's Advocate	A role that contradicts popular views or opinions about the work of the project
Dictatorship	A decision-making technique involving one person making the decision for the group
Dominators	A role that consumes project communication and focus with their own views without considering others
Emotional Intelligence	The ability to determine, assess, and manage the emotions of individuals or groups
Empathetic Listening	Listening with the goal of understanding what the sender is trying to communicate
Encouragers	A role that helps the project and team by focusing on what the project is creating, not the challenges of the project
Expectancy Theory	The premise that the reward for work achieved will be relative to the amount of effort or perceived effort
Expert Power	A capacity in which one uses personal knowledge and expert opinion to get others to do what is desired
Forcing	Applying an all or nothing (win/lose) to get the desired result
Fringe benefits	An extra, typically not used as a motivator, that is given to everyone in the company or on the project; examples are paid holidays and health insurance
Gate Keeper	The role that regulates the flow of communication between groups, such as between the customer and the project team; in business school, it is more generally referenced as the role that prevents unauthorized users from accessing information, a process, or an application
Ground Rules	Statements that describe the expected behavior of the project team
Harmonizer	A role that helps evolve information and understanding on the project above the team members
Hierarchy of Needs	A pyramid representation of Maslow's Theory that a person's motivation is based on needs (and where the person fits in this pyramid)
Information Giver	A role that shares information and thus helps enhance communication on the project
Information Seeker	A role that works to enhance information and knowledge associated with the project
Interpersonal Skills	The abilities that maximize the establishment and maintenance of relationships with project stakeholders; examples include the ability to communicate clearly, to motivate others, and to effectively negotiate; also known as soft skills

Term	Description
Investment Power	A type of power that involves delaying key decision(s) so enough time passes that stakeholders or other such parties can make a significant time investment in the project
Knowledge of Needs Power	A type of power that attempts to realize the two things that are negotiated for: what the other party says they are after, and what they are after that hasn't been made public
Legitimate Power	Getting people to do what you desire based on your authority
Majority	The votes of more than half of the members of a group, typically used to denote agreement with a decision
Management Skills	The ability to plan, organize, direct, and control in order to achieve project goals
Manage Team	The process of monitoring the performance of team members, providing feedback, resolving issues, and administering team changes to enhance project performance
Mirroring	Matching behavior characteristics of another person or group
Moral or Ethical Power	A type of power that uses a moral or ethical perspective tied to one's values in the negotiation process
Networking	Creating supportive connections and relationships with individuals or groups
Observations	To view individuals performing the tasks required by their positions
Organizational Breakdown Structure (OBS)	A ranked representation of the project organization that illustrates the relationship between activities and their performing organization unit
Organizational Planning	Determining, assigning, and documenting responsibilities, roles, and reporting relationships on a project
Over-allocation	A situation in which a resource is applied to too many activities at the same time to accomplish them all within the acceptable timeframe
Performance Review	A technique that measures, compares, and analyzes actual project data against the baseline
Perks	An extra, typically used as a motivator, that is not given to everyone in the company or on the project; examples are being sent to a special training class or seminar
Persistence Power	Continuing on a course to achieve an objective or goal
Persuasion Power	Discounting logic, which technical people can often use to sell ideas instead of focusing on comparisons that relate to the experience of the negotiating parties, creating evidence that can't be overlooked, and showing how a solution will meet their needs
Plan Resource Management	The process of creating a staffing management plan after identifying and documenting project roles, responsibilities, skills, and a reporting structure
Planning Power	Using preparation followed by negotiation to effectively plan the project
Position Description	A description of the roles and responsibilities of a team member
Power	The possible ability to influence behavior or performance of others
Precedent Power	A type of power that uses something which has achieved desired results in the past regardless if it was on the current project environment or elsewhere
Professional Power	Being professional and practical when working with others; helps to foster a win/win relationship with those that work with the project manager by allowing the project manager to look at the people and their needs
Project Management Staff	Members of the project management team including the project manager and the scheduling, budgeting, and risk management staff

Term	Description
Project Organization Chart	The graphic representation that illustrates the interrelationships between team members assigned to a specific project
Project Resource Management	Project resource management encompasses the processes utilized for the identification, acquisition, and management of the resources required for the successful conclusion of the project
Project Team	The individuals responsible for reinforcing the project manager in the work of the project in order to realize project objectives
Project Team Directory	The listing of project team members which includes their project-related roles and communication needs
RACI Chart	A type of responsibility assignment matrix that designates the status of stakeholder involvement in project activities as responsible, accountable, consult, or inform
Rapport	Possessing comfort or a harmonious relationship with someone
Recognition Seeker	A role that looks at the project first to see what they can get out of it
Referent Power	Using personal charisma to attain desired results from others or using existing relationships to help get things done (who you know)
Resource	Skilled individual/team, equipment, material, supplies, goods, services, budgets, or funds
Resource Loading	The process of applying resources to a schedule and its activities
Resource Management Plan	A component of the project management plan that defines the manner in which project resources are acquired, allocated, monitored, and controlled
Resource Requirements	The types and quantities of resources needed for each activity that makes up a work package
Responsibility	Accountability for the project or for specific project processes or tasks
Responsibility Assignment Matrix (RAM)	A graphical representation of the project resources committed to a monitored area of the project, such as a work package; typically applies RACI (responsible, accountable, consult, inform) indicators to depict the form of commitment
Reward Power	A type of power that uses positive actions or consequences to attain desired results from other people
Risk Power	A type of power that uses calculated risks in negotiations to achieve project goals
Role	A specific function performed by the member of the project team; some examples are testing, analyzing, and coding
Staff Acquisition	The hiring and applying of the needed resources to the project
Summarizers	A role that relates back to the overall picture of what the project is focusing on
Tacit Knowledge	Individual knowledge (such as beliefs, experience, and insights) that can be difficult to express and share
Team Charter	A document that delineates team values, agreements, and operating guidelines and establishes clear expectations regarding acceptable behavior by project team members.
Team Development	The creation of individual and team skills to maximize project output
Team Management Plan	A component of the resource management plan that delineates the manner and timing in which team members are acquired and released
Topic Jumpers	A role that doesn't stay focused on the primary topics of focus and conversation
Withdrawal	A conflict resolution technique in which you withdraw from the disagreement (or source of conflict)
Withdrawers	A role that is non-participatory on the project regarding information and project issues

The source for the above definitions is the Glossary of the Project Management Institute,
A Guide to the Project Management Body of Knowledge, (*PMBOK® Guide*) – Sixth Edition, Project Management Institute Inc., 2017

9.9. Project Resource Management Tests and Exercises

9.9.1. Project Resource Management Practice Test

Answers are in section 9.10.1.

1. Of the following statements, which is correct?

    (A) The key output of the plan resource management process is the resource management plan
    (B) The key output of the plan resource management process is the staffing management plan
    (C) The key output of the acquire project team process is the resource management plan
    (D) The key output of the acquire project team process is the staffing management plan

2. In reference to planning for the resource knowledge area, which of the following is the most accurate statement?

    (A) The resource management plan is used to create the resource breakdown structure
    (B) The project management plan is part of the resource management plan
    (C) The resource management plan contains only non-personnel resource related details
    (D) The resource management plan contains only personnel resource related details

3. The project manager has created the resource management plan and is getting ready to start the project soon. Résumés are being reviewed and some people have been interviewed. The lead candidate for the technical architecture position has been offered a position. In what process is the project manager involved?

    (A) Hiring and interviewing
    (B) Develop team
    (C) Estimate activity resources
    (D) Acquire resources

4. During the plan resource management process of a critical project, the project management team is creating a responsibility assignment matrix. What benefit does this provide for the team?

    (A) The team will know who is responsible for what work
    (B) The team will know who does what work and when they are to do it
    (C) The team will know the location in which the work is performed
    (D) The team will know the sequence in which the resources are to perform the activities

5. The project manager is in the executing phase of a financial regulatory project. Which of the following is the project manager most likely to use to stay updated on the project?

   (A) Personnel management
   (B) Interpersonal and team skills
   (C) Organizational process assets
   (D) Change requests

6. The project manager of the systems upgrade project uses a variety of power types. Which of the following is an example of reward power?

   (A) The project manager instructs the team leaders to prepare status reports for the weekly meeting
   (B) The project manager takes the most productive team member to lunch at an expensive restaurant
   (C) The project manager announces that those who do not complete their tasks in a timely manner without sacrificing quality will be ineligible for a bonus
   (D) The project manager's degree and prior work experience were in systems engineering

7. The project is experiencing conflict as the planning evolves. Of the following, which is the most common set of tools the project manager can utilize to minimize conflict?

   (A) Ground rules, interpersonal skills, and project management practices
   (B) Ground rules, group norms, and project management practices
   (C) Ground rules, group norms, networking and project management practices
   (D) Ground rules, interpersonal skills, networking, and project management practices

8. The project manager of the systems upgrade project uses a variety of power types. Which of the following is an example of penalty power?

   (A) The project manager instructs the team leaders to prepare status reports for the weekly meeting
   (B) The project manager takes the most productive team member to lunch at an expensive restaurant
   (C) The project manager announces that those who do not complete their tasks in a timely manner without sacrificing quality will be ineligible for a bonus
   (D) The project manager's degree and prior work experience were in systems engineering

9. The project manager needs to motivate his team and reviews Maslow's Hierarchy of Needs as a basis for his motivational strategy. Which of the following are the components of Maslow's Hierarchy of Needs?

(A) Physiological, achievement, esteem, psychological, safety, and self-actualization
(B) Physiological, belonging, esteem, safety, and self-actualization
(C) Physiological, achievement, esteem, safety, and self-actualization
(D) Physiological, belonging, esteem, psychological safety, and self-actualization

10. The project manager of the systems upgrade project uses a variety of power types. Which of the following is an example of formal power?

(A) The project manager instructs the team leaders to prepare status reports for the weekly meeting
(B) The project manager takes the most productive team member to lunch at an expensive restaurant
(C) The project manager announces that bonuses will not be awarded to those who do not complete their tasks in a timely manner without sacrificing quality
(D) The project manager's degree and prior work experience were in systems engineering

11. Prescott University is putting together its fall schedule. It is currently trying to align classes, instructors, and classrooms to ensure that every class offering has a room and an instructor. Which of the following is the best basis for this alignment?

(A) Resource list
(B) Resource breakdown structure
(C) Resource sheet
(D) Resource breakdown list

12. The project manager is a major advocate of team development. What is the main benefit of team development?

(A) Increased employee satisfaction
(B) Increased team performance
(C) A more concise and accurate project plan
(D) Reduced employee turnover

13. What can a responsibility assignment matrix eliminate?

(A) Confusion about the order of the activities
(B) Confusion about who is responsible for what
(C) Confusion about the durations of the activities
(D) Confusion about who is on the team

14. The project has had some challenges. Members of the team have needed constant supervision to perform the activities for which they are responsible, they do not seem to trust management, and often appear unmotivated. This is an example of what?

(A) Insufficient team building
(B) Theory X environment
(C) Insufficient project team training
(D) Theory Y environment

15. Senior management has promoted their best electrical engineer to the position of engineering project manager. The promotion was based on the Halo Theory. Of the following, what is the best definition of the Halo Theory?

(A) An effective employee in a discipline will become an effective employee in another discipline
(B) An effective employee in a discipline will become an effective manager in that discipline
(C) An effective employee in a discipline will become an effective employee in another discipline with training
(D) An effective employee in a discipline will become an effective manager in that discipline with training

16. Of the following, which are the key tools and techniques of the acquire resources process?

(A) Multicriteria decision analysis, negotiation, interpersonal skills, pre-assignment, and virtual teams
(B) Multicriteria decision analysis, negotiation, pre-assignment, and virtual teams
(C) Multicriteria decision analysis, negotiation, networking, pre-assignment, and virtual teams
(D) Multicriteria decision analysis, negotiation, interpersonal skills, networking, pre-assignment, and virtual teams

17. The project manager is taking a leave of absence and the company has just designated his replacement. The new project manager is known as a director. Of the following, which best describes negative characteristics of this type of manager?

(A) This style of management is not proactive and may fail to avert issues in a timely manner
(B) This style of management is focused more on the big picture than the details and may let details slip that impact the timeliness of the project
(C) This style of management is focused on specific activities and goals and may fail to see opportunities that arise in the project
(D) This style of management is focused on helping employees take on new skills and roles, which may create quality issues

18. Which of the following are the processes in the resource knowledge area?

(A) Identify stakeholders, plan resource management, acquire resources, develop team, manage team, control resources
(B) Plan resource management, acquire resources, develop team, monitor project team
(C) Plan resource management, estimate activity resources, acquire resources, develop team, manage team, control resources
(D) Plan resource management, acquire resources, train project team, manage project team

19. Leadership and managerial style evolve within the project management life cycle. Of the following, which is the best description of the evolution of leadership and managerial style?

(A) Directing, coaching, delegation, facilitation, and support
(B) Directing, mentoring, facilitation, and support
(C) Directing, mentoring, delegation, facilitation, and support
(D) Directing, coaching, facilitation, and support

20. The project manager is taking a leave of absence and the company has just designated his replacement. The new project manager is known as a visionary. Of the following, which best describes negative characteristics of this type of manager?

(A) This style of management is not proactive and may fail to avert issues in a timely manner
(B) This style of management is focused more on the big picture than the details and may let details slip that impact the timeliness of the project
(C) This style of management is focused on specific activities and goals and may fail to see opportunities that arise in the project
(D) This style of management is focused on helping employees take on new skills and roles, which may create quality issues

21. All of the following are techniques a project manager or organization can use to acquire resources except?

(A) Negotiation
(B) Pre-assignment
(C) Co-location
(D) Virtual teams

22. You are a project manager for the Mr. Understood concert tour. Your project consists of people, equipment, transportation and in each city contractors at the concert venue. Resource management is a large part of the project. When looking at trends and emerging practices in resource management, which of the following best describes what you will consider?

(A) Human resource management methods, emotional intelligence, self-organizing teams, virtual and distributed teams

(B) Resource management methods, emotional intelligence, self-organizing teams, virtual and distributed teams

(C) Resource management methods, emotional intelligence, self-organizing teams, co-located teams

(D) Resource management methods, soft skills, self-organizing teams, virtual and distributed teams

23. The project manager on the systems alignment project is characterized by his penchant for delegation. Effective delegation is a very positive managerial tool. Of the following, which best describes effective delegation?

(A) Effective delegation involves effective communication: a clear definition of the work to be done, the time frame in which the work is to be done, and descriptions of the evaluation process, the milestones, and expected results are all necessary

(B) Effective delegation involves effective communication: a clear definition of the work to be done, the steps needed to accomplish the work, the time frame in which the work is to be done, and descriptions of the evaluation process, the milestones, and expected results are all necessary

(C) Effective delegation involves effective communication: a clear definition of the work to be done, the steps needed to accomplish the work, the time frame in which the work is to be done, and descriptions of the evaluation process and expected results are all necessary

(D) Effective delegation involves effective communication: a clear definition of the work to be done, the time frame in which the work is to be done, and descriptions of the evaluation process and expected results are all necessary

24. The project manager is taking a leave of absence and the company has just designated his replacement. The new project manager is known as a facilitator. Of the following, which best describes negative characteristics of this type of manager?

(A) This style of management is not proactive and may fail to avert issues in a timely manner

(B) This style of management is focused more on the big picture than the details and may let details slip that impact the timeliness of the project

(C) This style of management is focused on specific activities and goals and may fail to see opportunities that arise in the project

(D) This style of management is focused on helping employees take on new skills and roles, which may create quality issues

25. Of the following, which is the most complete definition of the team development life cycle?

(A) Form, storm, inform, perform, adjourn
(B) Form, storm, norm, perform, adjourn
(C) Form, storm, norm, reform, adjourn
(D) Form, storm, inform, reform, adjourn

26. The project manager role is evolving from its focus on planning, directing, and organizing to...

(A) Evolving team performance, managing key stakeholder expectations, cross-training, coaching, and motivating
(B) Evolving team performance, managing key stakeholder expectations, coaching, mentoring, and motivating
(C) Evolving team performance, managing key stakeholder expectations, coaching, and motivating
(D) Evolving team performance, managing key stakeholder expectations, cross-training, coaching, mentoring, and motivating

27. A highly visible IT project has attracted some of the brightest developers in the company. Unfortunately, the potential for conflict is also high. The project manager will rely on all her skill sets to complete the project successfully. She is very aware that her interpersonal skills can influence the project's outcome. What are the specific interpersonal skills she is most likely to utilize?

(A) Active listening, negotiation skills, accommodating, and influencing
(B) Leadership, negotiation, and influencing
(C) Active listening, cultural awareness, leadership, networking, political awareness
(D) Leadership, effective decision-making, active listening, and influencing

28. Motivational theories are useful for motivating employees and creating a productive work environment. A popular theory is McGregor's Theory Y. Of the following, which best explains this theory?

(A) If labor can and wants to see the ultimate reason for doing the work (big picture), management can set the expectation and lead rather than manage
(B) Labor is unmotivated and needs to be told what to do; therefore, management must supervise
(C) Labor will work if given a sense of achievement, power, and affiliation
(D) Labor's prime motivation to work is to meet basic needs, but will work responsibly to meet higher needs such as esteem

29. The project manager is taking a leave of absence and the company has just designated his replacement. The new project manager is known as a mentor. Of the following, which best describes negative characteristics of this type of manager?

(A) This style of management is not proactive and may fail to avert issues in a timely manner
(B) This style of management is focused more on the big picture than the details and may let details slip that impact the timeliness of the project
(C) This style of management is focused on specific activities and goals and may fail to see opportunities that arise in the project
(D) This style of management is focused on helping employees take on new skills and roles that may create quality issues

30. The project manager of the systems upgrade project uses a variety of power types. Which of the following is an example of expert power?

(A) The project manager instructs the team leaders to prepare status reports for the weekly meeting
(B) The project manager takes the most productive team member to lunch at an expensive restaurant
(C) The project manager announces that those who do not complete their tasks in a timely manner without sacrificing quality will be ineligible for a bonus
(D) The project manager's degree and prior work experience were in systems engineering

9.10. Project Resource Management Answers for Tests and Exercises

9.10.1. Project Resource Management Practice Test Answers

We recommend that you download answer sheets from the Crosswind website, so you can practice the test as many times as you like.

1. Of the following statements, which is correct?

   Correct Answer: (A) The key output of the plan resource management process is the resource management plan
   Explanation: The key output of the Plan Resource Management process is the resource management plan. [Crosswind Manual 9.1.1; *PMBOK® Guide* 9.1.3.1]

2. In reference to planning for the resource knowledge area, which of the following is the most accurate statement?

   Correct Answer: (A) The resource management plan is used to create the resource breakdown structure
   Explanation: The resource breakdown structure can be created based on approaches detailed in the resource management plan. The resource management plan is part of the project management plan. The resource management plan includes approaches for personnel and non-personnel resources. [Crosswind Manual 9.1; *PMBOK® Guide* 9.1]

3. The project manager has created the resource management plan and is getting ready to start the project soon. Résumés are being reviewed and some people have been interviewed. The lead candidate for the technical architecture position has been offered a position. In what process is the project manager involved?

   Correct Answer: (D) Acquire resources
   Explanation: Acquire resources involves among other things, getting people on the project. The estimate activity resources process occurs before interviewing starts. Develop team occurs after staff acquisition is complete. Hiring and interviewing is a distracter. [Crosswind Manual 9.3; *PMBOK® Guide* 9.4]

4. During the plan resource management process of a critical project, the project management team is creating a responsibility assignment matrix. What benefit does this provide for the team?

   Correct Answer: (A) The team will know who is responsible for what work
   Explanation: The responsibility assignment matrix shows who is responsible for what work on the project. The Gantt chart shows who does what work and when they are to do it. The network diagram provides the sequence that the resources are to perform the activities in. At what location the work is done is a distracter. [Crosswind Manual 9.1.3; *PMBOK® Guide* 9.1.3.2]

PMI, CAPM, and PMBOK are registered marks of the Project Management Institute, Inc.

386   © 2008-2018 Crosswind Learning, www.crosswindpm.com

5.   The project manager is in the executing phase of a financial regulatory project. Which of the following is the project manager most likely to use to stay updated on the project?

Correct Answer: (B) Interpersonal and team skills
Explanation: Interpersonal and team skills can be used by the project manager in the forms of conflict management, decision making, emotional intelligence, influencing, and leadership. Personnel management is a distracter. Organizational process assets are not specific to the project. Change requests are not necessarily valid since they are not approved and they do not reflect important project information such as task status and team interaction among other items. [Crosswind Manual 9.4; *PMBOK® Guide* 9.5]

6.   The project manager of the systems upgrade project uses a variety of power types. Which of the following is an example of reward power?

Correct Answer: (B) The project manager takes the most productive team member to lunch at an expensive restaurant
Explanation: Reward power comes from the project manager's ability to reward an employee for good work. Formal power is derived from the project charter for the project manager. Penalty power comes from the project manager's ability to penalize an employee when his work is inadequate. Expert power derives from expertise in a discipline. [Crosswind Manual 9.1.10; No *PMBOK® Guide* Reference]

7.   The project is experiencing conflict as the planning evolves. Of the following, which is the most common set of tools the project manager can utilize to minimize conflict?

Correct Answer: (B) Ground rules, group norms, and project management practices
Explanation: The common set of tools the project manager can utilize to minimize conflict are ground rules, group norms, and project management practices. [Crosswind Manual 9.5.1; *PMBOK® Guide* 9.4.2]

8.   The project manager of the systems upgrade project uses a variety of power types. Which of the following is an example of penalty power?

Correct Answer: (C) The project manager announces that those who do not complete their tasks in a timely manner without sacrificing quality will be ineligible for a bonus
Explanation: Penalty power comes from the project manager's ability to penalize an employee when his work is inadequate. Formal power is derived from the project charter for the project manager. Reward power comes from the project manager's ability to reward an employee for good work. Expert power derives from expertise in a discipline. [Crosswind Manual 9.1.10; No *PMBOK® Guide* Reference]

9. The project manager needs to motivate his team and reviews Maslow's Hierarchy of Needs as a basis for his motivational strategy. Which of the following are the components of Maslow's Hierarchy of Needs?

Correct Answer: (B) Physiological, belonging, esteem, safety, and self-actualization
Explanation: The levels of Maslow's Hierarchy of Needs are physiological, belonging, safety, esteem, and self-actualization. [Crosswind Manual 9.1.5; *PMBOK® Guide* 9.1.2.2]

10. The project manager of the systems upgrade project uses a variety of power types. Which of the following is an example of formal power?

Correct Answer: (A) The project manager instructs the team leaders to prepare status reports for the weekly meeting
Explanation: Formal power is derived from the project charter for the project manager. Reward power comes from the project manager's ability to reward an employee for good work. Penalty power comes from the project manager's ability to penalize an employee when his work is inadequate. Expert power derives from expertise in a discipline. [Crosswind Manual 9.1.10; No *PMBOK® Guide* Reference]

11. Prescott University is putting together its fall schedule. It is currently trying to align classes, instructors, and classrooms to ensure that every class offering has a room and an instructor. Which of the following is the best basis for this alignment?

Correct Answer: (B) Resource breakdown structure
Explanation: The resource breakdown structure is used to show where resources (in this case, the rooms and instructors) are being used. The resource list simply shows what resources are available. The resource sheet is similar to a resource list. The resource breakdown list is a distracter. [Crosswind Manual 9.1.4; *PMBOK® Guide* 9.1.2.2]

12. The project manager is a major advocate of team development. What is the main benefit of team development?

Correct Answer: (B) Increased team performance
Explanation: Team development activities are investments with an expected return of improved performance. All other answers, though possible and desirable, are slightly less beneficial than the all-encompassing increased team performance. [Crosswind Manual 9.4; *PMBOK® Guide* 9.1.2.2]

13. What can a responsibility assignment matrix eliminate?

Correct Answer: (B) Confusion about who is responsible for what
Explanation: The responsibility assignment matrix shows who is responsible for what areas on the project. The network diagram provides guidance on what order the activities occur. The organizational structure confirms who is on the team, and what the reporting structure is. The Gantt chart or schedule shows how long the activities are. [Crosswind Manual 9.1.3; *PMBOK® Guide* 9.1.3.2]

14. The project has had some challenges. Members of the team have needed constant supervision to perform the activities for which they are responsible, they do not seem to trust management, and often appear unmotivated. This is an example of what?

Correct Answer: (B) Theory X environment
Explanation: Typically in a Theory X environment, employees must be told what to do, have distrust for management, and lack motivation. Theory Y is the opposite. The other answers are distracters. [Crosswind Manual 9.1.5; *PMBOK® Guide* 9.1.2.2]

15. Senior management has promoted their best electrical engineer to the position of engineering project manager. The promotion was based on the Halo Theory. Of the following, what is the best definition of the Halo Theory?

Correct Answer: (B) An effective employee in a discipline will become an effective manager in that discipline
Explanation: The Halo Theory implies that supervisors often rate employees as having wholly desirable traits, or wholly undesirable traits. Making the assumption that an effective technical employee (a single favorable characteristic) WILL transfer to an effective project manager is an example of this bias. The other answers are distracters. [Crosswind Manual 9.3.1; *PMBOK® Guide* 9.4]

16. Of the following, which are the key tools and techniques of the acquire resources process?

Correct Answer: (B) Multicriteria decision analysis, negotiation, pre-assignment, and virtual teams
Explanation: The tools and techniques of the Acquire Resources process are: decision-making, interpersonal and team skills, multicriteria decision analysis, negotiations, pre-assignment, and virtual teams. [Crosswind Manual 9.3; *PMBOK® Guide* 9.3]

17. The project manager is taking a leave of absence and the company has just designated his replacement. The new project manager is known as a director. Of the following, which best describes negative characteristics of this type of manager?

Correct Answer: (C) This style of management is focused on specific activities and goals and may fail to see opportunities that arise in the project
Explanation: The director is focused on specific activities and goals and may fail to see opportunities that arise. The facilitator is not proactive and may fail to avert issues in a timely manner. The visionary is focused more on the big picture than the details and may let details slip that impact the timeliness of the project. The mentor is focused on helping employees take on new skills and roles that may create quality issues. [Crosswind Manual 9.1.8; No *PMBOK® Guide* Reference]

18. Which of the following are the processes in the resource knowledge area?

Correct Answer: (C) Plan resource management, estimate activity resources, acquire resources, develop team, manage team, control resources
Explanation: The six processes in the Resource knowledge area are Plan Resource Management, Estimate Activity Resources, Acquire Resources, Develop Team, Manage Team, and Control Resources. Identify Stakeholders comes from the Stakeholder knowledge area. Monitor project team and train project team are distracters. [Crosswind Manual Chapter 9 Introduction; *PMBOK® Guide* Chapter 9 Introduction]

19. Leadership and managerial style evolve within the project management life cycle. Of the following, which is the best description of the evolution of leadership and managerial style?

Correct Answer: (D) Directing, coaching, facilitation, and support
Explanation: The evolution of leadership and managerial style starts with directing. As the project gains momentum, coaching is applied. When significant work is completed facilitation comes into play. Support is applied as the project is closing. [Crosswind Manual 9.1.6; *PMBOK® Guide* 9.1.2.3]

20. The project manager is taking a leave of absence and the company has just designated his replacement. The new project manager is known as a visionary. Of the following, which best describes negative characteristics of this type of manager?

Correct Answer: (B) This style of management is focused more on the big picture than the details and may let details slip that impact the timeliness of the project
Explanation: The visionary is focused more on the big picture than the details and may let details slip that impact the timeliness of the project. The facilitator is not proactive and may fail to avert issues in a timely manner. The director is focused on specific activities and goals and may fail to see opportunities that arise. The mentor is focused on helping employees take on new skills and roles that may create quality issues. [Crosswind Manual 9.1.8; No *PMBOK® Guide* Reference]

21. All of the following are techniques a project manager or organization can use to acquire resources except?

Correct Answer: (C) Colocation
Explanation: The tools and techniques of the Acquire Resources process are: decision-making, interpersonal and team skills, multicriteria decision analysis, negotiations, pre-assignment, and virtual teams. [Crosswind Manual 9.3; *PMBOK® Guide* 9.3]

22. You are a project manager for the Mr. Understood concert tour. Your project consists of people, equipment, transportation and in each city contractors at the concert venue. Resource management is a large part of the project. When looking at trends and emerging practices in resource management, which of the following best describes what you will consider?

Correct Answer: (B) Resource management methods, emotional intelligence, self-organizing teams, virtual and distributed teams
Explanation: Trends and emerging practices in resource management are resource management methods such as lean, just in time (JIT), Kaizen, total productive maintenance (TPM), theory of constraints (TOC), emotional intelligence (EI), self-organizing teams, and virtual and distributed teams. [Crosswind Manual Chapter 9 Introduction; *PMBOK® Guide* Chapter 9 Introduction]

23. The project manager on the systems alignment project is characterized by his penchant for delegation. Effective delegation is a very positive managerial tool. Of the following, which best describes effective delegation?

Correct Answer: (D) Effective delegation involves effective communication: a clear definition of the work to be done, the time frame in which the work is to be done, and descriptions of the evaluation process and expected results are all necessary
Explanation: Effective delegation involves effective communication: a clear definition of the work to be done, the time frame in which the work is to be done, and descriptions of the evaluation process and expected results are all necessary. [Crosswind Manual 9.1.7; No *PMBOK® Guide* Reference]

24. The project manager is taking a leave of absence and the company has just designated his replacement. The new project manager is known as a facilitator. Of the following, which best describes negative characteristics of this type of manager?

Correct Answer: (A) This style of management is not proactive and may fail to avert issues in a timely manner

Explanation: The facilitator is not proactive and may fail to avert issues in a timely manner. The visionary is focused more on the big picture than the details and may let details slip that impact the timeliness of the project. The director is focused on specific activities and goals and may fail to see opportunities that arise. The mentor is focused on helping employees take on new skills and roles that may create quality issues. [Crosswind Manual 9.1.8; No *PMBOK® Guide* Reference]

25. Of the following, which is the most complete definition of the team development life cycle?

Correct Answer: (B) Form, storm, norm, perform, adjourn

Explanation: The team development life cycle consists of form, storm, norm, perform, and adjourn. [Crosswind Manual 9.4.1; *PMBOK® Guide* 9.5.2.1]

26. The project manager role is evolving from its focus on planning, directing, and organizing to...

Correct Answer: (C) Evolving team performance, managing key stakeholder expectations, coaching, and motivating

Explanation: The project manager role is evolving from its focus on planning, directing, and organizing to evolving team performance, managing key stakeholder expectations, coaching, and motivating. [Crosswind Manual 9.1.7; No *PMBOK® Guide* Reference]

27. A highly visible IT project has attracted some of the brightest developers in the company. Unfortunately, the potential for conflict is also high. The project manager will rely on all her skill sets to complete the project successfully. She is very aware that her interpersonal skills can influence the project's outcome. What are the specific interpersonal skills she is most likely to utilize?

Correct Answer: (C) Active listening, cultural awareness, leadership, networking, political awareness

Explanation: Interpersonal and team skills used in project management can include active listening, cultural awareness, leadership, networking, and political awareness. [Crosswind Manual 9.4; *PMBOK® Guide* 9.5]

28. Motivational theories are useful for motivating employees and creating a productive work environment. A popular theory is McGregor's Theory Y. Of the following, which best explains this theory?

Correct Answer: (A) If labor can and wants to see the ultimate reason for doing the work (big picture), management can set the expectation and lead rather than manage

Explanation: McGregor's Theory Y states, in essence, that if labor can and wants to see the ultimate reason for doing the work (big picture), management can set the expectation and lead rather than manage. The theory is a modernization of McGregor's Theory X, which states that labor is not motivated, needs to be told what to do, and management must supervise. McClelland's achievement theory loosely states that labor will work if given a sense of achievement, power, and affiliation. Maslow's Hierarchy of Needs simply lists five needs and management's job is to use upward mobility within the hierarchy as motivation. [Crosswind Manual 9.1.5; *PMBOK® Guide* 9.1.2.2]

29. The project manager is taking a leave of absence and the company has just designated his replacement. The new project manager is known as a mentor. Of the following, which best describes negative characteristics of this type of manager?

Correct Answer: (D) This style of management is focused on helping employees take on new skills and roles that may create quality issues

Explanation: The mentor is focused on helping employees take on new skills and roles, which may create quality issues. The facilitator is not proactive and may fail to avert issues in a timely manner. The visionary is focused more on the big picture than the details and may let details slip that impact the timeliness of the project. The director is focused on specific activities and goals and may fail to see opportunities that arise. [Crosswind Manual 9.1.8; No *PMBOK® Guide* Reference]

30. The project manager of the systems upgrade project uses a variety of power types. Which of the following is an example of expert power?

Correct Answer: (D) The project manager's degree and prior work experience were in systems engineering

Explanation: Expert power derives from expertise in a discipline. Formal power is derived from the project charter for the project manager. Reward power comes from the project manager's ability to reward an employee for good work. Penalty power comes from the project manager's ability to penalize an employee when his work is inadequate. [Crosswind Manual 9.1.10; No *PMBOK® Guide* Reference]

Chapter 10

Project Communications Management

The purpose of Project Communications Management is to ensure an efficient and effective flow of information throughout the project. This is accomplished by devising and executing a communication strategy that targets and engages each stakeholder and team member in accordance with project needs and the available organizational assets.

Trends

There are a number of trends used to ensure the efficient and effective flow of information:

- The inclusion of stakeholders in project reviews including frequent reviews of the stakeholder group to update changes in membership and attitudes
- The inclusion of stakeholders in project meetings where appropriate (as an example, the adoption of Agile's practice of including key stakeholders in its daily standup meeting which delineates yesterday's accomplishments and issues the current day's work)
- The increased use of social media to exchange information and build relationships
- The use of a multifaceted communications approach to engage and exchange information with stakeholders, taking into consideration their preferences for language, content, and medium

Tailoring

Project tailoring, the manner in which the processes of a knowledge area are exercised, is employed to address the distinctive nature of each project. Successful project tailoring for communications management is predicated on a careful consideration of:

- The relationship of stakeholders to the organization (internal vs. external)
- The physical location of the team members (colocated vs. dispersed) and time zone variances
- The appropriate technology needed to communicate with stakeholders and to develop, chronicle, disseminate, retrieve, and cache communications
- The use of knowledge management repositories

Agile/Adaptive Environment

For projects where requirements are not stable, it is vital that new and developing details are communicated promptly to the appropriate parties. Daily stand-up meetings, regular stakeholder reviews, and easily accessible information are all used to promote meaningful communication between the team and appropriate stakeholders.

The source for the above text is the Project Management Institute, *A Guide to the Project Management Body of Knowledge*, (*PMBOK® Guide*) – Sixth Edition, Project Management Institute Inc., 2017, Pages 330-335

In this chapter, we discuss the following:

Figure 10-1: Communications Processes

The source for the above figure is the Project Management Institute, *A Guide to the Project Management Body of Knowledge*, (*PMBOK® Guide*) – Sixth Edition, Project Management Institute Inc., 2017, Figure 10-1, Page 331

☑ **Crosswind "Must Knows" for Project Communications Management**

	Key Inputs, Tools & Techniques, and Outputs for Plan Communications Management
	Key Inputs, Tools & Techniques, and Outputs for Manage Communications
	Key Inputs, Tools & Techniques, and Outputs for Monitor Communications
	The dimensions of communication and communication skills
	What a communications management plan is and what it is used for
	The percentage of a project managers job that involves communications
	Communication Model (sender, message, receiver)
	Communication channel calculations

Although helpful, this list is not all-inclusive in regard to information needed for the exam. It is only suggested material that, if understood and memorized, may increase your exam score.

10.1. Communication Skills

Communication skills are vital to successful project integration as the key pieces of the project come together per the project management plan.

Components of communication skills can include the sender-receiver model (reference section 10.3.3), media format, writing styles, management and presentation techniques, encoding, decoding, message, medium, and noise.

Be familiar with the dimensions of communication and communication skills.

Communication Skills Commonly Used by Management
Active and effective listening
Questioning to enhance understanding
Educating to increase the project team's knowledge, leading to increased effectiveness
Fact-finding as a means of identification or confirmation of information
Setting and continuously managing expectations
Using persuasion to elicit desired action
Using negotiation to achieve agreement acceptable to all parties
Using conflict resolution to prevent negative impact
Using summarization, recap, and identification of subsequent steps to ensure adequate understanding of information

The source for the above text is the Project Management Institute, *A Guide to the Project Management Body of Knowledge*, (*PMBOK® Guide*) – Sixth Edition, Project Management Institute Inc., 2017, Pages 335-345

10.2. Dimensions of Communication Activity

The exam addresses dimensions of communication activity. It is important to understand the logic behind the classification, as well as the type of communication.

Dimensions of Communication Activity	
Type	**Description**
Formal	Formal communication should be used for the following: • Legal communication and project documents (written) • Communication involving extreme distance or complexity (written) • Official situations (verbal) • Presentations (written and verbal) • Communication that is primarily one-directional (verbal)
Internal	Communication within the project
External	Communication with the customer, other projects, the media, and the public
Vertical	Communication up and down the organization
Horizontal	Communication with peers
Official	Communication that is on the record, such as newsletters and annual reports
Unofficial	Communication that is not on the record
Written and Oral	Communication that is in writing and/or verbal
Verbal and Non-Verbal	Communication that conveys signals other than words (inflection of voice, body language)

The source for the above text is the Project Management Institute, *A Guide to the Project Management Body of Knowledge*, (*PMBOK® Guide*) – Sixth Edition, Project Management Institute Inc., 2017, Pages 335-345

10.3. Plan Communications Management (Planning Process Group)

Know the Key Inputs, Tools & Techniques, and Outputs for Plan Communications Management.

During Plan Communication Management, the project manager **determines the communication needs of all the stakeholders.** Key criteria is the information required by each stakeholder, when it is required, and the format in which it is required. The criteria is then entered into the communications management plan to show the communication requirements of the project stakeholders.

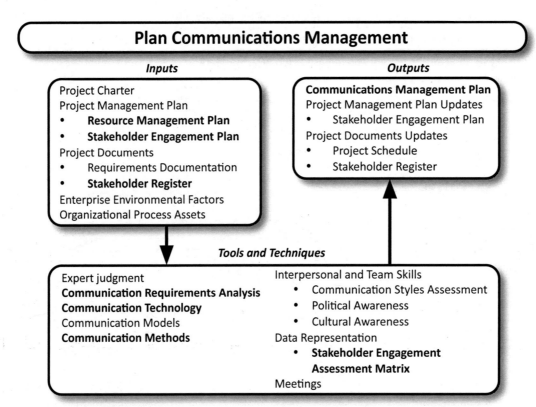

Figure 10-2: Plan Communications Management Data Flow Diagram

The source for the above figure is the Project Management Institute, *A Guide to the Project Management Body of Knowledge*, (*PMBOK® Guide*) – Sixth Edition, Project Management Institute Inc., 2017, Figure 10-2, Page 336

Plan Communications Management (Planning)		
Key Inputs	Resource Management Plan	The resource management plan is a component of the project management plan that documents: the manner in which the team and physical resources are determined, quantified, and acquired; resource roles, responsibilities, authorities, and competence (skill and capacity); project organizational charts; team resource management (definition, management, control, and release); team training; team development; and control of physical resources (availability and acquisition).

Plan Communications Management (Continued)		
Key Inputs (Cont.)	Stakeholder Engagement Plan	The stakeholder engagement plan is a component of the project management plan that documents the plans and activities required to engage stakeholders in an effective manner.
	Stakeholder Register	The stakeholder register contains information related to identified stakeholders. It includes identification information (name, position, location, project role, and contact information), assessment information (key requirements, potential impact on project results, the phase in which the stakeholder wields the greatest influence, and stakeholder expectations), and stakeholder classification (**internal/external**, **impact/ influence/power/interest**, or other classification model).
Key Tools & Techniques	Communication Requirement Analysis	Communication requirement analysis is used to determine stakeholder informational needs. It typically includes a consideration of information and communication requirements from the stakeholder register, the stakeholder engagement plan, organizational charts, responsibility assignment matrixes (RAM), logistics of involved personnel, legal requirements, the development approach, logistics of participants, and internal/external information requirements. The requirements are defined by combining the type and format of the required information with an evaluation of that information's value. Consideration should also be given to the number of communication channels in order to determine the intricacy of project communications. A channel is a physical or electronic connection between a sender and receiver that allows the exchange of information. To determine the number of communication channels multiply the number of stakeholders multiplied by that number minus one and then divide the result by two or, as a formula, $c = n \times (n-1) / 2$.

Plan Communications Management (Continued)		
Key Tools & Techniques (Cont.)	Communication Technology	Communication technology encompasses the methods used to transfer information among project stakeholders, which can include conversations, meetings, databases, documents, social media, email, and websites. The choice of a communication technology is predicated on the sensitivity and confidentiality of the information, the project environment, the availability and ease of use of a technology, and the urgency of the information.
	Communication Methods	Communication methods are used to transfer information among project stakeholders. Methods include: interactive communication (communication between two or more parties exchanging information in real time), push communication (communication sent directly to specific recipients), pull communication (communication used for a large number of recipients that must access content from web portals, intranet sites, e-learning, lessons learned databases, or knowledge repositories), interpersonal communication (communication between individuals, typically face to face), network and social computing communication (communication obtainable from notice boards, newsletters, press releases, email, web portals, phone conversations, and presentations), **small group communication** (communication between groups of **three to six people**), public communication (communication from a speaker addressing a group), and mass communication (communication from a sender to a large, sometimes anonymous, targeted group).
	Stakeholder Engagement Assessment Matrix	The stakeholder engagement assessment matrix is utilized to evaluate the current engagement levels of stakeholders by comparing them to the expected engagement levels of those stakeholders. This comparison can be used to evaluate the need for any additional communication.

PMI, CAPM, and PMBOK are registered marks of the Project Management Institute, Inc.

398   © 2008-2018 Crosswind Learning, www.crosswindpm.com

Plan Communications Management (Continued)		
Key Outputs	Communications Management Plan	The communications management plan is a component of the project management plan that documents the planning, structure, implementation, and monitoring/control of communications. It contains: stakeholder communication requirements; the information to be communicated, including language, format, content, and degree of detail; the case for conveyance of the information; the timeframe for and frequency of the distribution, including the manner in which any acknowledgment or response will be effected; the person responsible for communication of the information; the person responsible for authorizing the release of confidential information; the recipients of the information and their needs, requirements, and expectations; the resources allocated for communication related activities, along with a calendar and budget; the technological methods used for conveyance of the information, including memos, email, press releases, and social media; the methods for updating the communications management plan; a glossary of common terms; flow charts regarding the project's information flow, workflows, meeting plans, and a list of reports; constraints imposed by legislation, regulation, and/or technology; and the guidelines and templates for project status meetings, project team meetings, and email.

Situational Question and Real World Application

The failure to effectively execute the Plan Communications Management process can result in communication breakdowns. Issues such as failure to send appropriate information to appropriate people at the appropriate time can arise from this failure.

10.3.1. Communications Management Plan

The communications management plan defines the communication needs of the stakeholders, the format and frequency of communications, and the person responsible for delivery.

The plan can include communication rules, project expectations, reporting and meeting schedules, change processes, and contact information for the team.

Know what a communications management plan is and what it is used for.

The plan helps the project manager and team do the following:

- Determine communication needs for the project stakeholders
- Establish and utilize communication infrastructure for distributing project information
- Report project performance to the appropriate stakeholders
- Address communication issues that arise on the project

10.3.2. Communication Control

Controlling communication is vital to project management success. The project manager must stay current regarding communication activity and be kept in the project communication loop. **Remember, approximately 90% of a project manager's job involves communication.**

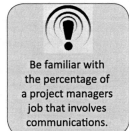

Be familiar with the percentage of a project managers job that involves communications.

10.3.3. Communication Model

The basics of communication are covered in the Communication Model. The three main components are:

- Sender
- Message
- Receiver

Be familiar with the Communication Model (sender, message, and receiver).

The medium is another component to consider because it sets the format of the message and can impact communications positively or negatively.

Given the global nature of projects and diversity of people involved in projects today, breaks in the model are not uncommon.

The key responsibility of the communication sender is to correctly encode (communicate) the message to the communication receiver(s) so that they can correctly decode (understand) it.

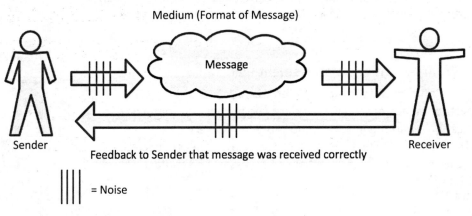

Figure 10-3: Sender/Receiver Interaction

The source for the above figure is the Project Management Institute, *A Guide to the Project Management Body of Knowledge*, (*PMBOK® Guide*) – Sixth Edition, Project Management Institute Inc., 2017, Figure 10-4, Page 361

PMI, CAPM, and PMBOK are registered marks of the Project Management Institute, Inc.

400   © 2008-2018 Crosswind Learning, www.crosswindpm.com

10.3.4. Communication Channels Formula

Communications are a complex part of any project. The greater the number of people involved in a project, the greater the number of communications that will be sent and received.

Know the communication channels calculations.

The formula for this relationship is **N x (N - 1) / 2** with N being the number of people on the project.

Figure 10-4: Communication Channels shows how communications grow as people are added to the project.

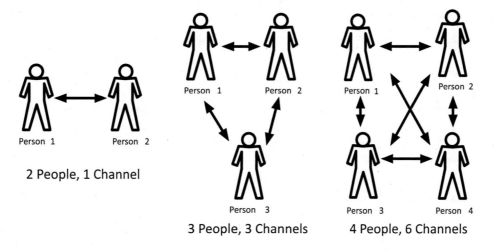

2 People, 1 Channel

3 People, 3 Channels

4 People, 6 Channels

Figure 10-4: Communication Channels

It is very important to know how to calculate the total number of communication channels, the total communication channels if team members are added or removed, and the number of channels added/subtracted if team members are added or removed.

Total number of channels	Total number of channels when team members are added/removed	Number of channels added/removed when team members are added/removed
Use the standard formula.	Use the standard formula for new total number of people.	Use the standard formulas for original number of people and for new total number of people then subtract the difference.
$N^{original}$ x ($N^{original}$ - 1) / 2	N^{new} x (N^{new} - 1) / 2	(N^{new} x (N^{new} -1) / 2) - ($N^{original}$ x ($N^{original}$ -1) / 2)
Sample for team of four: 4 x (4 - 1) / 2 = 6	Sample for two members added to team of four: (4 + 2) x ((4 + 2 - 1) / 2) = 15 Or 6 x ((6 - 1) / 2) = 15	Sample for two members added to team of four: 15 - 6 = 9

Note that a reference to team members may include or exclude the project manager, depending on the wording used. Reference the chart below for examples.

| PM has a team of six (count seven people) | The PM is described as "outside" the team, and the total count must be adjusted to include the PM in the communications channels. |
| The team has six people (count six people) | The PM is described as within the team. No adjustment to the total count is necessary. |

10.3.5. Communication Methods

The methods utilized to share information among stakeholders are:

- **Interactive**, which enables an **exchange of information** between multiple parties and fosters a common understanding between participants
- **Push**, which **distributes information** but does not ensure that the information was received or understood
- **Pull**, which **provides information** in a centrally accessible location such as the Internet

10.3.6. Communication Blockers

Communication blockers are factors that disrupt the message that the receiver is trying to interpret from the sender.

10.3.7. Meeting Rules

Meeting rules are commonly abused. As a result, perception of how to effectively conduct meetings is often inaccurate.

Some basic rules for conducting meetings are:

- When a meeting is scheduled, an agenda should be created and distributed beforehand to give people a chance to review and prepare; this agenda should allocate a portion of time for each topic
- All relevant documents should be distributed prior to the meeting
- Everyone should review the agenda and prepare for the meeting
- During (or before) the meeting, the leader (facilitator) should be established to conduct the meeting and ensure adherence to the agenda; the leader (facilitator) does not always need to be the project manager
- If the leader/facilitator decides to honor a request to add a non-agenda item to the meeting, the item should be added at the end of the meeting or moved to a future meeting
- From an exam readiness perspective, if the project is a priority and a meeting has been scheduled, functional issues (generally speaking) should not delay the meeting

The source for the above text is the Project Management Institute, *A Guide to the Project Management Body of Knowledge*, (*PMBOK® Guide*) – Sixth Edition, Project Management Institute Inc., 2017, Pages 366-378

10.4. Manage Communications (Executing Process Group)

The primary focus of the Manage Communications process is to gather information relevant to the creation, distribution, storage, and retrieval, as well as the conclusive disposition, of communications in accordance with the communications management plan. The process is designed to enable timely and productive communications between project stakeholders.

Know the Key Inputs, Tools & Techniques, and Outputs for Manage Communications.

Manage Communications

Inputs

Project Management Plan
- Resource Management Plan
- **Communications Management Plan**
- Stakeholder Engagement Plan

Project Documents
- Change Log
- **Issue Log**
- Lessons Learned Register
- Quality Report
- Risk Report
- Stakeholder Register

Work Performance Reports
Enterprise Environmental Factors
Organizational Process Assets

Outputs

Project Communications
Project Management Plan Updates
- **Communications Management Plan**
- **Stakeholder Engagement Plan**

Project Documents Updates
- Issue Log
- Lessons Learned Register
- Project Schedule
- Risk Register
- Stakeholder Register

Organizational Process Assets Updates

Tools and Techniques

Communication Technology
Communications Methods
Communication Skills
- Communication Competence
- Feedback
- Nonverbal
- Presentations

Project Management Information Systems
Project Reporting

Interpersonal and Team Skills
- Active Listening
- Conflict Management
- Cultural Awareness
- Meeting Management
- Networking
- Political Awareness

Meetings

Figure 10-5: Manage Communications Data Flow Diagram
The source for the above figure is the Project Management Institute, *A Guide to the Project Management Body of Knowledge*, (*PMBOK® Guide*) – Sixth Edition,

Project Management Institute Inc., 2017, Figure 10-5, Page 379

Manage Communications (Executing)		
Key Inputs	Communications Management Plan	The communications management plan is a component of the project management plan that documents the planning, structure, implementation, and monitoring/control of communications.
	Issue Log	The issue log is used to record and track any project challenges that cannot be immediately resolved. Issue-related information is communicated to affected stakeholders.
	Work Performance Reports	Work performance reports are representations, either physical or electronic, of work performance information and are used as the basis for decisions and/or actions. The reports are distributed to project stakeholders in accordance with the communication plan and can include earned value graphs and data, defect histograms, contract performance data, and risk surveys. The report presentations can include heat reports, dashboards, and stop light charts.
Key Tools & Techniques	Communication Technology	Communication technology encompasses the methods used to transfer information among project stakeholders, which can include conversations, meetings, databases, documents, social media, email, and websites. The choice of a communication technology is predicated on the sensitivity and confidentiality of the information, the project environment, the project culture, team logistics, resources available to the team, the availability and ease of use of a technology, and the urgency of the information.
	Communication Skills	Communication skills include communication competence (with consideration of transparency of purpose in significant messages, leadership behaviors, and effective relationship and data sharing), feedback (in consideration of interactive communication), nonverbal communication (communication that establishes meaning through gestures, voice tonality, and facial expression), and presentations (transparent and meaningful communication through presentations to stakeholders that considers their expectations and needs as well as the needs of the project. Presentations typically address progress reports and informational updates, background information that supports decision-making, general information about the project to elevate its profile, and specific information to garner understanding and support of the project.

Manage Communications (Continued)		
Key Tools & Techniques (Cont.)	Project Management Information System	The project management information system (PMIS) is an enterprise environmental factor. It can be a portal to automated tools, a system that gathers and distributes information, a configuration management system, and/or an interface to online automated systems that are used to direct and manage project work. Project information can be administered through a variety of tools, including electronic management tools, electronic communication management application, and social media management applications.
Key Outputs	Project Communications	Project communications documentation may include performance reports, schedule progress, presentations, the status of deliverables, costs incurred, and other information expected by stakeholders.
	Communications Management Plan	The communications management plan is a component of the project management plan that documents the planning, structure, implementation, and monitoring/control of communications. Any changes to the communications methodology must be reflected in the communications management plan.
	Stakeholder Engagement Plan	The stakeholder engagement plan is updated to reflect changes to the requirements and strategies. Those changes must also be reflected in the communications management plan.

Situational Question and Real World Application
Failure to effectively execute the Manage Communications process could result in ineffective decisions due to the communication of incomplete or untimely information.

Chapter 10
Communications

10.4.1. Communication Types

The communication types are:

Communication Types	Definition
Active Listening	The receiver verifies with the sender that the message was interpreted correctly by asking for clarification or by providing feedback to the sender.
Effective Listening	The receiver observes visual and vocal cues, as well as asking for feedback from the sender.
Feedback	The sender receives feedback from the receiver (the feedback can be in the form of an acknowledgment, a simple interpretation of the message, or questions designed to clarify the message).
Nonverbal	**Nonverbal exchanges,** including body language and facial expression, **can account for 55% of a communication.**
Paralingual	Voice characteristics are particularly important when the sender conveys the message.

10.4.2. Performance Reports

Reporting formats can vary, as can interpretations of the formats. The following definitions clarify the subtle differences between the types of performance reports.

Progress = **P**oint in Time

Status = **S**um of All Progress

Forecast = **F**uture Work

Variance = **V**ary from Plan

Earned **V**alue =

Scope

Schedule   Cost

Progress Reports

Progress reports provide information regarding what has been accomplished during a specific time frame. For example, a weekly progress report contains data regarding the most recent week's accomplishments.

Status Reports

Status reports provide information on the present overall state of the project. For example, the status report contains data on the project since inception to convey the overall state of the project.

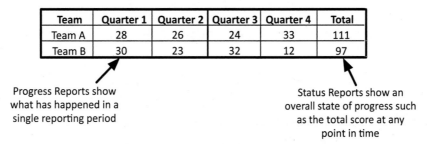

Team	Quarter 1	Quarter 2	Quarter 3	Quarter 4	Total
Team A	28	26	24	33	111
Team B	30	23	32	12	97

Progress Reports show what has happened in a single reporting period

Status Reports show an overall state of progress such as the total score at any point in time

Figure 10-6: Progress/Status Report Data

To clarify the difference between progress and status, review the above example of a four-quarter game between two teams. A **progress report** shows how many points have been scored during a specific period. A **status report** shows the overall score at any point in time. To apply these examples to a project, a **progress report shows what has been accomplished within a given time frame and a status report shows the overall state of the project.** Remember: **The Status Report is the sum of ALL Progress Reports.** For example, in a project with progress reporting weekly at the end of three weeks, the Status Report is the sum of information reported in Progress Reports for weeks 1, 2, and 3.

Forecast Reports

Forecast reporting methods include:

- Time series, which base future outcome estimates on historical information
- Causal/econometric, which base outcome estimates on underlying factors (weather impacts outer-wear sales)
- Judgment, which base outcome estimates on opinion, probability, and intuitive judgment (scenario building, surveys, Delphi method)
- Other methods, such as ensemble forecasting, probabilistic forecasting, and simulation

Forecast reports provide information about what is expected to occur during the project. Forecast reporting associated with cost can include:

- Estimate at completion (EAC): The funds needed to totally finish the project based on current spending efficiency
- Estimate to complete (ETC): Additional funds needed as of this point in time to finish the project
- Variance at completion (VAC): The amount forecasted to be over/under budget based on budget at completion (BAC) versus estimate at completion (EAC)

For more information about the above, refer to Project Cost Management.

Variance Reports

Variance reports show the difference between what was planned and what actually occurred. For example, a variance report would show any variance between what was done and what should have been done.

Earned Value Reports

Earned value reports show the state of the schedule, budget, and scope of the project at specific points in time.

The source for the above text is the Project Management Institute, *A Guide to the Project Management Body of Knowledge*, (*PMBOK® Guide*) – Sixth Edition, Project Management Institute Inc., 2017, Pages 345-353

10.5. Monitor Communications (Monitoring and Controlling Process Group)

Monitoring communications involves monitoring and controlling project communications to make certain that stakeholder communication requirements are achieved. A focus of this process is information flow to determine if information bottlenecks can be either limited or eliminated throughout the life of the project.

Know the Key Inputs, Tools & Techniques, and Outputs for Monitor Communications.

Monitor Communications

Inputs

Project Management Plan
- Resource Management Plan
- **Communications Management Plan**
- **Stakeholder Engagement Plan**

Project Documents
- Issue Log
- Lessons Learned Register
- **Project Communications**

Work Performance Data
Enterprise Environmental Factors
Organizational Process Assets

Outputs

Work Performance Information
Change Requests
Project Management Plan Updates
- **Communications Management Plan**
- Stakeholder Engagement Plan

Project Documents Updates
- **Issue Log**
- **Lessons Learned Register**
- Stakeholder Register

Tools and Techniques

Expert Judgment
Project Management Information Systems
Data Analysis
- **Stakeholder Engagement Assessment Matrix**

Interpersonal and Team Skills
- **Observation/Conversation**
Meetings

Figure 10-7: Monitor Communications Data Flow Diagram

The source for the above figure is the Project Management Institute, *A Guide to the Project Management Body of Knowledge*, (*PMBOK® Guide*) – Sixth Edition, Project Management Institute Inc., 2017, Figure 10-7, Page 353

PMI, CAPM, and PMBOK are registered marks of the Project Management Institute, Inc.

408 © 2008-2018 Crosswind Learning, www.crosswindpm.com

Chapter 10
Communications

Monitor Communications (Monitoring and Controlling)		
Key Inputs	Communications Management Plan	The communications management plan is a component of the project management plan that documents the planning, structure, implementation, and monitoring/control of communications. Specifically it contains the most recent plan for the timely gathering, generating, and dispensing of information.
	Stakeholder Engagement Plan	The stakeholder engagement plan is a component of the project management plan that documents the plans and activities required to engage stakeholders in an effective manner. It indicates planned communication requirements.
	Project Communications	Project communications documentation may delineate distributed communications.
	Work Performance Data	Work performance data represents the raw metrics and observations identified during the performance of project work activities. It also includes data regarding the descriptions and amounts of distributed communications.
Key Tools & Techniques	Expert Judgment	Expert judgment is judgment based on expertise acquired in a specific area. It is often more significant and accurate than the best modeling tools available and can be provided by stakeholders, company personnel external to the project, professional organizations or groups, and consultants. It is important to consider expertise related to communication management systems, project management systems, and both national and international communication with the public, community, and media, as well as communication between virtual groups.
	Project Management Information System	The project management information system (PMIS) is an enterprise environmental factor. It can be a portal to automated tools and is a system that gathers, stores, and dispenses information to internal and external stakeholders in accordance with the communication plan. The information in the system is subject to monitoring to determine its accuracy and effectiveness.
	Stakeholder Engagement Assessment Matrix	The stakeholder engagement assessment matrix is utilized to evaluate the current engagement levels of stakeholders by comparing them to the expected engagement levels of stakeholders. This comparison can be used to evaluate the need for any additional communication.

Monitor Communications (Continued)		
Key Tools & Techniques (Cont.)	Observation/ Conversation	Observation (shadowing) and conversation deliver a firsthand method for determining how people perform activities in their environment. Applying this method with the project team delineates the most suitable approach to updating/communicating project performance information and to responding to stakeholder requests for information.
Key Outputs	Work Performance Information	Work performance information includes supplemental and contextualized information regarding the actual performance of project communication in comparison to planned project communication.
	Change Requests	Change requests are requests for modification that have not been formally approved through the change control process. Modifications may be requested to the communication plan, stakeholder communication requirements (including information distribution, distribution methodology, content, and format), new procedures to improve the communication process and exclude congestion, or other impacted components of the project management plan.
	Communications Management Plan	The communications management plan is a component of the project management plan that documents the planning, structure, implementation, and monitoring/control of communications. The plan is modified to reflect any new information that improves communication.
	Issue Log	The issue log is used to record and track any project challenges that cannot be immediately resolved. The issue log is modified to reflect any new information impacting an issue, including its progress and resolution.
	Lessons Learned Register	The lessons learned register is a record of the challenges, problems, and successes of the project (what worked and didn't). The register contains detailed and important project knowledge and can be modified to include the reason an issue occurred and the reason a corrective action was selected.

PMI, CAPM, and PMBOK are registered marks of the Project Management Institute, Inc.

410 © 2008-2018 Crosswind Learning, www.crosswindpm.com

The source for the above text is the Project Management Institute, *A Guide to the Project Management Body of Knowledge*, (*PMBOK® Guide*) – Sixth Edition, Project Management Institute Inc., 2017, Pages 353-358

10.6. Project Communications Management Formulas and Variables

Description	Formula	Variable (Components)	Example
Communication Channels Formula This formula shows the number of communication channels on a project.	N x (N - 1) / 2 = Number of Communication Channels	N = Number of people	6 x (6 - 1) / 2 = 15
N = the number of people on the project	Provided on the exam	6	15 channels on the project

Chapter 10 Communications

10.7.   Project Communications Management Terminology

Term	Description
Communication Blockers	Factors that disrupt the message
Communication Constraints	Limitations imposed by legislation, regulation, technology, or policy on message content, timing, audience, or delivery vehicle (person or mechanism)
Communication Methods	Procedures, techniques, and processes that are employed to disseminate information to project stakeholders
Communication Model	A facsimile that demonstrates the manner in which project communications will be performed
Communication Requirements Analysis	An approach to the determination of stakeholder communication requirements, which can include interviews, lessons learned, and analysis of previous projects
Communication Styles Assessment	A technique utilized to identify the approach, format, and content preferred by each stakeholder for planned communication activities
Communication Technology	The tools, systems, and computer applications utilized in the dissemination of information to project stakeholders
Communications Infrastructure	Tools and techniques used to create the foundation for information transfer on a project
Communications Management Plan	The document, part of the project or program management plan, that addresses the communication flow of the project and contains a detailed description of the transmittal process, the transmittal schedule, and the administration process
Control	The process of contrasting actual performance to planned performance, assessing the resulting variances, and determining the actions that will improve performance levels
Distribute Information	Deliver needed project information to stakeholders in an appropriate timeframe
Exception Report	A report that includes significant variations from the planned activities
Forecast	The estimation of a future state of a project based on the performance levels of the organization or a previous project; typically includes measurements associated with estimate at completion (EAC) or estimate to complete (ETC)
Information Gathering Techniques	Processes used to obtain and organize data from a variety of sources
Kickoff Meeting	A meeting used to initiate the start of the project; typically attended by all the key stakeholders; can be done when initiating or planning is complete depending upon the organization
Log	Documentation of selected items that occur during a project, typically modified to reflect the condition of the item (issue, quality control item, action, or defect)
Manage Communications	The gathering of meaningful project data to create communications that will be disseminated, placed in a repository for future access, and disposed of per the communications management plan.
Manage Stakeholder Expectations	The process of communicating with the stakeholders to determine their expectations and addressing issues in a timely manner
Monitor Communications	The process of fulfilling the informational needs of the project and its stakeholders
Performance Reporting	The collection and interpretation of performance data; can include status, progress, and forecast reports

PMI, CAPM, and PMBOK are registered marks of the Project Management Institute, Inc.

412   © 2008-2018 Crosswind Learning, www.crosswindpm.com

Term	Description
Plan Communications Management	The process of identifying and evaluating stakeholder information and requirements for the purpose of developing a suitable project communications approach
Progress Report	A report that states what has been accomplished in a specific amount of time on the project (but not the entire project)
Project Communications Management	The processes required to gather, produce, allocate, deposit, retrieve, administer, regulate, track, and ultimately dispose of project information so that the appropriate parties receive the appropriate information at the appropriate time
Project Forecasting	A reporting method in which future performance is estimated based on past performance of the project
Report Performance	The process of amassing project performance data and disseminating it in a clear and meaningful format to the intended audience
Reporting Systems	Processes and procedures utilized to generate or consolidate reports from information management systems and distribute those reports to project stakeholders
Status Report	A report that states the current shape or state of the project to date
Threshold	Any value (typically applied to cost, schedule, quality, technical, or resource) that is used as a parameter; typically crossing the threshold results in a triggered action
Trend Analysis	An analytical technique that uses mathematical paradigms to predict future outcomes based on historical data
Variance	Any difference between a planned value or baseline and an actual result
Variance Analysis	The assessment of the level and reasons for a variance from planned value or baseline
Work Performance Reports	Project status and performance data utilized to produce communications and advance discussion

The source for the above definitions is the Glossary of the Project Management Institute,
A Guide to the Project Management Body of Knowledge, (*PMBOK® Guide*) – Sixth Edition, Project Management Institute Inc., 2017

10.8. Project Communications Management Tests and Exercises

10.8.1. Project Communications Management Practice Test

Answers are in section 10.9.1.

1. There are 45 communication channels on the project. How many people are on the project team?

   (A) 9
   (B) 10
   (C) 5
   (D) 15

2. The project manager and his team spend a great deal of time in meetings. Which of the following is not a good reason to cancel a meeting?

   (A) The agenda wasn't published until right before the meeting
   (B) A key team member had to attend a different meeting
   (C) A functional manager wanted to meet with the project manager at the same time
   (D) The topic partially changed and the presentation material wasn't complete yet

3. There are five basic performance reports. Of the following, which best describes the contents of a forecast report?

   (A) Information related to the state of the schedule, budget, and scope of the project at various parts of time
   (B) Information related to the present overall state of the project
   (C) Information related to future project occurrences
   (D) Information related to recent project occurrences

4. Conflict resolution is an example of, or component of, which of the following?

   (A) Dimensions of communication activity
   (B) Communication skills commonly used by management
   (C) Stakeholder management strategy
   (D) Communication process types

5. Sam and Tracy are running their string theory project. They are in the process of monitoring project communications with the various stakeholders. This has been a challenge given it is a global project with many virtual employees. Which of the following is a tool and technique they will use with the monitor communications process?

(A) Communications management plan
(B) Change requests
(C) Work performance information
(D) Project management Information system

6. The project is approximately 50% complete. The project manager is communicating with stakeholders regarding the status of the project. Which will he likely use to determine what to communicate to whom?

(A) Communications technology, models, and methods
(B) Communications management plan
(C) Communications requirements analysis
(D) Stakeholder management strategy

7. A major manufacturing company has initiated a project to determine the best course of action to take in response to the new "green laws" recently passed by congress. The company has many plants located in the U.S. and overseas, some of which have been in place for decades and will likely not be cost effective to modernize. The CEO has warned that this project will rise or fall based on effective communications. During the plan communications management process, the project manager and his team will rely on potentially five key inputs. Which of the following is a key input of the process?

(A) Project management plan
(B) Communications technology
(C) Meetings
(D) Lessons learned register

8. You are the project manager for a global point of sale upgrade project that is utilizing an offshore development company. There have been a number of communication challenges with misinterpretation of requirements and failure to follow through with things associated with the store roll-out that the project manager felt needed attention. What type of communication would help improve these problems?

(A) Verbal
(B) Informal verbal
(C) Formal written
(D) Formal

9. There are five basic performance reports. Of the following, which best describes the content of a variance report?

   (A) Information related to the state of the schedule, budget, and scope of the project at various parts of time
   (B) Information related to the difference between planned and actual occurrences
   (C) Information related to future project occurrences
   (D) Information related to recent project occurrences

10. Sam and Tracy are in the planning stage of their wedding. Communication is a big issue with all the stakeholders and their geographical locations. Of the following, which is an input they will use in the manage communications process?

    (A) Project management plan
    (B) Communications management plan
    (C) Power interest grid
    (D) Feedback

11. Six full time and one part time person report to the project manager. Three more people are added to the project. How many communication channels were added to the project?

    (A) 56 channels
    (B) 28 channels
    (C) 55 channels
    (D) 27 channels

12. There are five basic performance reports. Of the following, which best describes the contents of an earned value report?

    (A) Information related to the state of the schedule, budget, and scope of the project at various points of time
    (B) Information related to the present overall state of the project
    (C) Information related to future project occurrences
    (D) Information related to recent project occurrences

13. Nicole is in pharmaceutical sales. As she is mapping out details for a new marketing campaign, she is sensitive to communication with key stakeholders. Communication is key to campaign success. As she focuses on monitoring communications, which is an input she will use during this process?

(A) Risk register
(B) Reporting systems
(C) Change requests
(D) Issue log

14. All of the following are examples of communication requirements on a project except...

(A) Project status, meeting time, and location
(B) The product functionality required by the primary customer
(C) Steps to take regarding a project change request
(D) Names and contact information for the members of the project change control board

15. Michelle is in pharmaceutical research. As she is mapping out details for a new compound, she is sensitive to communication with key stakeholders. Communication is key to campaign success. As she focuses on monitoring communications, which is a tool or technique she will use during this process?

(A) Organizational process assets
(B) Expert judgment
(C) Change requests
(D) Stakeholder management strategy

16. The project manager has scheduled several meetings to facilitate information sharing with the project management team and the customer. The meetings have been unorganized, chaotic, and lacking direction. Which of the following would improve the meetings?

(A) Determine who is in charge of the meeting
(B) Send the team to communication training
(C) Create and publish an agenda, and establish the leader of the meeting
(D) Create and publish an agenda

17. All the following could be considered mediums for communication by a project team member except...

(A) Staff meetings
(B) Email
(C) Message
(D) Video conference

18. One of the activities a project manager performs on a day-to-day basis is communicating with individual team members, the team, company personnel, vendors, and customers. Approximately how much of a project manager's job is spent communicating?

    (A) At least 30%
    (B) Not more than 50%
    (C) Approximately 90%
    (D) 100%

19. What is the most effective use of feedback on a project?

    (A) To give the sender of the message a chance to ensure their message is delivered
    (B) To ensure that the receiver of a message understands the message
    (C) To give the receiver of the message a chance to get status updates from the sender
    (D) To ensure that the sender of the message understands the message

20. The project has eight people on it. Two more are added. What is the total number of communication channels added to the project?

    (A) 45 channels
    (B) 17 channels
    (C) 28 channels
    (D) 10 channels

21. There are five basic performance reports. Of the following, which best describes the contents of a status report?

    (A) Information related to the state of the schedule, budget, and scope of the project at various points in time
    (B) Information related to the present overall state of the project
    (C) Information related to future project occurrences
    (D) Information related to recent project occurrences

22. Ronnie is planning Comicfest for the fall. It will include over 200 vendors, over 60 celebrities and approximately 10,000 attendees. Which of the following is not a tool or technique available during the plan communications management process?

    (A) Communications methods
    (B) Communications technology
    (C) Communications requirements analysis
    (D) Communications management plan

23. Although the communications model only contains three components, there is another facet of communications that must be considered. Of the following, which best describes that other facet?

(A) Language, specifically the special usages of a professional group
(B) Medium, specifically the technique that dictates the format of a message
(C) Feedback, specifically in regard to message interpretation
(D) Confirmation, specifically tracking communication receipt

24. Project communications lead to a number of concerns on the part of the project manager. Which of the following best describe those concerns?

(A) Sender, receiver, message, medium, and feedback
(B) Sender, receiver, message, and feedback
(C) Sender, receiver, message, and medium
(D) Sender, receiver, medium, and feedback

25. The project manager sent a letter to the company's legal director regarding the legal system project and enclosed a copy of the communications management plan for the project. He also enclosed a handwritten note congratulating the director on the excellent privacy overview article the director wrote for the company's monthly newsletter. Of the following, which best describes the communication types sent by the project manager?

(A) Informal, internal, unofficial communication and internal, unofficial communication
(B) Informal, internal, official communication and internal, unofficial communication
(C) Formal, internal communication and unofficial, internal communication
(D) Formal, internal, official communication and informal, internal, unofficial communication

26. There are five basic performance reports that are utilized during the project. One of these is a progress report. Of the following, which best describes the contents of a progress report?

(A) Information related to the state of the schedule, budget, and scope of the project at various parts of time
(B) Information related to the difference between planned and actual occurrences
(C) Information related to future project occurrences
(D) Information related to recent project occurrences

27. The project manager sent a communication to the project manager of a related project requesting a copy of the communications management plan used on the related project. Of the following, which best describes the communication type sent by the project manager?

(A) Formal, official, internal, vertical communication
(B) Informal, unofficial, internal, horizontal communication
(C) Formal, official, internal, horizontal communication
(D) Formal, unofficial, internal, horizontal communication

28. The project manager and his team are about to begin the monitor communications process. Which is an output of the process they will create?

(A) Reporting systems
(B) Work performance information
(C) Scope statement
(D) Enterprise environmental factors

29. The network infrastructure project is having problems. People are unaware of meetings and not involved in approval of project deliverables. The project is being audited for health. Of the following, which document is likely to show information that could fix this problem?

(A) Communications management plan
(B) Project management plan
(C) Performance reporting plan
(D) Information distribution plan

30. Walton publishing is executing the curriculum update project. They are currently in the final process of communications. There are a number of key tools and techniques available for use. Which of the following is the best description of the tools and techniques with this process?

(A) Forecasting methods, variance analysis, communication management plan, and reporting systems
(B) Communication methods, forecasting methods, and approved changes
(C) Work performance measurements, forecasting methods, communication methods, and the project management plan
(D) Project management information system, expert judgment, and meetings

10.9. Project Communications Management Answers for Tests and Exercises

10.9.1. Project Communications Management Practice Test Answers

We recommend that you download answer sheets from the Crosswind website, so you can practice the test as many times as you like.

1. There are 45 communication channels on the project. How many people are on the project team?

   Correct Answer: (B) 10
   Explanation: Ten is the number of team members on the project. This is established by applying the formula, N x (N - 1) / 2 to the answers and seeing that 10 people produces 45 channels. 10 x (10 - 1) / 2 = 45. [Crosswind Manual 10.3.4; No *PMBOK® Guide* Reference]

2. The project manager and his team spend a great deal of time in meetings. Which of the following is not a good reason to cancel a meeting?

   Correct Answer: (C) A functional manager wanted to meet with the project manager at the same time
   Explanation: The functional manager's decision to meet with the project manager at the same time as an existing team meeting is not a good reason to cancel a meeting. The project manager should offer to schedule a meeting for a different time with the functional manager because project-related work has a higher priority. [Crosswind Manual 10.3.7; No *PMBOK® Guide* Reference]

3. There are five basic performance reports. Of the following, which best describes the contents of a forecast report?

   Correct Answer: (C) Information related to future project occurrences
   Explanation: The forecast report shows what is expected to occur on the project. The progress report shows what has been completed since the last reporting period. The status report shows where the project is to date. The variance report shows the difference between planned and unplanned occurrences. The earned valued report shows the state of the schedule, budget, and scope of the project at various points in time. [Crosswind Manual 10.4.2; *PMBOK® Guide* 10.2.1.3]

4. Conflict resolution is an example of, or component of, which of the following?

   Correct Answer: (B) Communication skills commonly used by management
   Explanation: Conflict resolution is a communication skill commonly used by management. The other answers are distracters. [Crosswind Manual 10.1; *PMBOK® Guide* Chapter 10 Introduction]

5. Sam and Tracy are running their string theory project. They are in the process of monitoring project communications with the various stakeholders. This has been a challenge given it is a global project with many virtual employees. Which of the following is a tool and technique they will use with the monitor communications process?

Correct Answer: (D) Project management information system
Explanation: The tools and techniques for the Monitor Communications process are: expert judgment, project management information systems, data analysis, stakeholder engagement assessment matrix, interpersonal and team skills, observation/conversation, and meetings. [Crosswind Manual 10.5; *PMBOK® Guide* 10.3]

6. The project is approximately 50% complete. The project manager is communicating with stakeholders regarding the status of the project. Which will he likely use to determine what to communicate to whom?

Correct Answer: (B) Communications management plan
Explanation: The communications management plan helps determine the stakeholders' communication needs. The other answers are distracters. [Crosswind Manual 10.3.1; *PMBOK® Guide* 10.1.3.1]

7. A major manufacturing company has initiated a project to determine the best course of action to take in response to the new "green laws" recently passed by congress. The company has many plants located in the U.S. and overseas, some of which have been in place for decades and will likely not be cost effective to modernize. The CEO has warned that this project will rise or fall based on effective communications. During the plan communications management process, the project manager and his team will rely on potentially five key inputs. Which of the following is a key input of the process?

Correct Answer: (A) Project management plan
Explanation: The project management plan is an input to the plan communications management process. The other answers are tools and techniques or distracters. [Crosswind Manual 10.3; *PMBOK® Guide* 10.1]

8. You are the project manager for a global point of sale upgrade project that is utilizing an offshore development company. There have been a number of communication challenges with misinterpretation of requirements and failure to follow through with things associated with the store roll-out that the project manager felt needed attention. What type of communication would help improve these problems?

Correct Answer: (C) Formal written
Explanation: Formal written communication is appropriate for communications where the message must be specific or the message is being sent over a long distance. Formal is a good answer but not as good as formal written. Both verbal answers would expose the project to problems. [Crosswind Manual 10.2; *PMBOK® Guide* Chapter 10 Introduction]

9. There are five basic performance reports. Of the following, which best describes the content of a variance report?

Correct Answer: (B) Information related to the difference between planned and actual occurrences

Explanation: The variance report shows the difference between planned and unplanned occurrences. The forecast report shows what is expected to occur on the project. The progress report shows what has been completed since the last reporting period. The status report shows where the project is to date. The earned valued report shows the state of the schedule, budget, and scope of the project at various points in time. [Crosswind Manual 10.4.2; *PMBOK® Guide* 10.2.1.3]

10. Sam and Tracy are in the planning stage of their wedding. Communication is a big issue with all the stakeholders and their geographical locations. Of the following, which is an input they will use in the manage communications process?

Correct Answer: (B) Communications management plan

Explanation: The inputs for the Manage Communications process are: project management plan, resource management plan, communications management plan, stakeholder engagement plan, project documents, change log, issue log, lessons learned register, quality report, risk report, stakeholder register, work performance reports, enterprise environmental factors, and organizational process assets. [Crosswind Manual 10.4; *PMBOK® Guide* 10.2]

11. Six full time and one part time person report to the project manager. Three more people are added to the project. How many communication channels were added to the project?

Correct Answer: (D) 27 channels

Explanation: The formula for communication channels is N x (N - 1) / 2. First, calculate the number of communication channels based on the existing team 6.5 people (rounds up to a full person) 7 AND the project manager=8). That is 28 communication channels. Next, calculate the number of communication channels with the new people added. This is 55 communication channels. Finally, subtract the difference (55-28=27) to establish that 27 communication channels were added. [Crosswind Manual 10.3.4; No *PMBOK® Guide* Reference]

12. There are five basic performance reports. Of the following, which best describes the contents of an earned value report?

Correct Answer: (A) Information related to the state of the schedule, budget, and scope of the project at various points of time

Explanation: The earned valued report shows the state of the schedule, budget, and scope of the project at various points in time. The forecast report shows what is expected to occur on the project. The progress report shows what has been completed since the last reporting period. The status report shows where the project is to date. The variance report shows the difference between planned and unplanned occurrences. [Crosswind Manual 10.4.2; *PMBOK® Guide* 10.2.1.3]

13. Nicole is in pharmaceutical sales. As she is mapping out details for a new marketing campaign, she is sensitive to communication with key stakeholders. Communication is key to campaign success. As she focuses on monitoring communications which is an input she will use during this process?

Correct Answer: (D) Issue log
Explanation: The inputs for the Monitor Communications process are: project management plan, communications management plan, stakeholder engagement plan, project documents, issue log, lessons learned register, project communications, work performance data, enterprise environmental factors, and organizational process assets. [Crosswind Manual 10.5; *PMBOK® Guide* 10.3]

14. All of the following are examples of communication requirements on a project except...

Correct Answer: (B) The product functionality required by the primary customer.
Explanation: Project status meeting, time and location, steps to take regarding a project change request, and contact information for the members of the CCB are all communication requirements on a project. Product functionality is communicated using some type of requirements documentation. Notice that this answer does not indicate **how** or **when** or **how often** the product requirements will or should be communicated. [Crosswind Manual 10.3; *PMBOK® Guide* 10.1]

15. Michelle is in pharmaceutical research. As she is mapping out details for a new compound, she is sensitive to communication with key stakeholders. Communication is key to campaign success. As she focuses on monitoring communications, which is a tool or technique she will use during this process?

Correct Answer: (B) Expert judgment
Explanation: The tools or techniques for Monitor Communications include expert judgment, project management information system, data analysis, stakeholder engagement assessment matrix, interpersonal and team skills, observation/conversation, and meetings. [Crosswind Manual 10.5; *PMBOK® Guide* 10.3]

16. The project manager has scheduled several meetings to facilitate information sharing with the project management team and the customer. The meetings have been unorganized, chaotic, and lacking direction. Which of the following would improve the meetings?

Correct Answer: (C) Create and publish an agenda, and establish the leader of the meeting
Explanation: Creating and publishing an agenda and knowing who is in charge of a meeting are two ways to have a highly organized, effective meeting. Though the project manager may organize a meeting, he or she may not necessarily be in charge of the meeting, as is sometimes the case with highly technical subject matter. [Crosswind Manual 10.3.7; No *PMBOK® Guide* Reference]

17. All the following could be considered mediums for communication by a project team member except...

Correct Answer: (C) Message
Explanation: The message is what is actually conveyed in the communication. The other three answers are formats for conveying information. [Crosswind Manual 10.3.3; *PMBOK® Guide* 10.1.2.4]

18. One of the activities a project manager performs on a day-to-day basis is communicating with individual team members, the team, company personnel, vendors, and customers. Approximately how much of a project manager's job is spent communicating?

Correct Answer: (C) Approximately 90%
Explanation: Approximately 90% of a project manager's time is spent communicating. This could be via email, meetings, listening, speaking, web conference, etc. [Crosswind Manual 10.3.2; No *PMBOK® Guide* Reference]

19. What is the most effective use of feedback on a project?

Correct Answer: (B) To ensure that the receiver of a message understands the message
Explanation: It is vital that the receiver correctly interprets the message sent, so the sender requests feedback. The request is typically in the form of asking additional questions to clarify the recipients understanding of the message. [Crosswind Manual 10.3.3; *PMBOK® Guide* 10.1.2.4]

20. The project has eight people on it. Two more are added. What is the total number of communication channels added to the project?

Correct Answer: (B) 17 channels
Explanation: To calculate this result, you need to calculate the number of communication channels with eight people. The formula is N x (N - 1) / 2. This means that with eight people, there are 28 channels of communication. Next, add the two additional people for a total of ten people and use the communication channel formula. This shows that there are 45 communication channels with ten people on the project. Subtract 28 from 45 for a difference, and the answer of 17 communication channels. [Crosswind Manual 10.3.4; No *PMBOK® Guide* Reference]

21. There are five basic performance reports. Of the following, which best describes the contents of a status report?

Correct Answer: (B) Information related to the present overall state of the project
Explanation: The status report shows where the project is to date. The forecast report shows what is expected to occur on the project. The earned valued report shows the state of the schedule, budget, and scope of the project at various points in time. The progress report shows what has been completed since the last reporting period. [Crosswind Manual 10.4.2; *PMBOK® Guide* 10.2.1.3]

22. Ronnie is planning Comicfest for the fall. It will include over 200 vendors, over 60 celebrities and approximately 10,000 attendees. Which of the following is not a tool or technique available during the plan communications management process?

Correct Answer: (D) Communications management plan
Explanation: The tools and techniques for the Plan Communications Management process are: expert judgment, communications requirements analysis, communication technology, communication models, communication methods, interpersonal and team skills, communication styles assessment, political awareness, cultural awareness, data analysis, stakeholder engagement assessment matrix, and meetings. [Crosswind Manual 10.3; *PMBOK® Guide* 10.1]

23. Although the communications model only contains three components, there is another facet of communications that must be considered. Of the following, which best describes that other facet?

Correct Answer: (B) Medium, specifically the technique that dictates the format of a message

Explanation: The communications model includes the sender, the receiver, and the message. The medium should also be considered in that it sets the format of the message. [Crosswind Manual 10.3.3; *PMBOK® Guide* 10.1.2.4]

24. Project communications lead to a number of concerns on the part of the project manager. Which of the following best describe those concerns?

Correct Answer: (A) Sender, receiver, message, medium, and feedback

Explanation: Communication involves a sender who encodes the message and delivers it via the medium to the receiver to decode. The receiver then should have a chance to provide feedback to the sender to verify correct understanding of the message. [Crosswind Manual 10.3.3; *PMBOK® Guide* 10.1.2.4]

25. The project manager sent a letter to the company's legal director regarding the legal system project and enclosed a copy of the communications management plan for the project. He also enclosed a handwritten note congratulating the director on the excellent privacy overview article the director wrote for the company's monthly newsletter. Of the following, which best describes the communication types sent by the project manager?

Correct Answer: (D) Formal, internal, official communication and informal, internal, unofficial communication

Explanation: The letter that accompanied the communications plan was a formal, internal, official communication and the hand written note was an informal, internal, unofficial communication. [Crosswind Manual 10.2; *PMBOK® Guide* Chapter 10 Introduction]

26. There are five basic performance reports that are utilized during the project. One of these is a progress report. Of the following, which best describes the contents of a progress report?

Correct Answer: (D) Information related to recent project occurrences

Explanation: The progress report shows what has been completed since the last reporting period. The forecast report shows what is expected to occur on the project. The status report shows where the project is to date. The variance report shows the difference between planned and unplanned occurrences. The earned valued report shows the state of the schedule, budget, and scope of the project at various points in time. [Crosswind Manual 10.4.2; *PMBOK® Guide* 10.2.1.3]

27. The project manager sent a communication to the project manager of a related project requesting a copy of the communications management plan used on the related project. Of the following, which best describes the communication type sent by the project manager?

Correct Answer: (B) Informal, unofficial, internal, horizontal communication

Explanation: The communication is a simple request to a peer; therefore it is an informal, unofficial, internal, horizontal communication. [Crosswind Manual 10.2; *PMBOK® Guide* Chapter 10 Introduction]

28. The project manager and his team are about to begin the monitor communications process. Which is an output of the process they will create?

Correct Answer: (B) Work performance information
Explanation: The outputs of monitor communications are work performance information, change requests, project management plan updates, communications management plan, stakeholder engagement plan, project documents updates, issue log, lessons learned register, and stakeholder register. [Crosswind Manual 10.5; *PMBOK® Guide* 10.3]

29. The network infrastructure project is having problems. People are unaware of meetings and not involved in approval of project deliverables. The project is being audited for health. Of the following, which document is likely to show information that could fix this problem?

Correct Answer: (A) Communications management plan
Explanation: The communications management plan should show what meetings are planned, who should be involved in the deliverables, sign-off, and other communication needs of the project. This plan is in the project management plan. The other answers are distracters. [Crosswind Manual 10.3.1; *PMBOK® Guide* 10.1.3.1]

30. Walton publishing is executing the curriculum update project. They are currently in the final process of communications. There are a number of key tools and techniques available for use. Which of the following is the best description of the tools and techniques with this process?

Correct Answer: (D) Project management information system, expert judgment, and meetings
Explanation: The tools and techniques of the Monitor Communications process are: expert judgment, project management information system, data analysis, stakeholder engagement assessment matrix, interpersonal and team skills, observation/conversation, and meetings. [Crosswind Manual 10.5; *PMBOK® Guide* 10.3]

Chapter 11

Project Risk Management

During Project Risk Management, the project team strives to decrease the probability and impact of individual negative risks (threats), increase the probability and impact of individual positive risks (opportunities), and keep overall project risk within an acceptable range.

Individual risk is the negative or positive effect of a random event or condition on one or more project goals. Management of individual risk seeks to minimize threats and enhance opportunities. Unmanaged threats typically result in issues that negatively impact the schedule, the budget, and/or performance. Unmanaged opportunities typically result in failure to accrue additional project benefits for stakeholders.

Overall project risk is the negative or positive effect of individual risks and other sources of uncertainty on the project as a whole. Management of overall project risk seeks to keep risk within an acceptable range. Unmanaged overall project risk typically results in decreasing the chances of attaining project goals.

Note that risks continue to emerge throughout the life of the project, so the Project Risk Management processes should be conducted iteratively. As the project evolves, identified risks should be monitored and managed and emergent risks should be identified and addressed.

Effective risk management for the project requires that the project team knows the acceptable amount of risk exposure that is informed by measurable risk thresholds that reflect organizational and stakeholder risk tolerance. Risk thresholds specify the degree of acceptable variation around a project goal and are included in the definitions of project risk impact levels.

Trends
There are a number of trends emerging in project risk management:

There is a growing focus on the two types of **non-event risks**: variability and ambiguity.

- **Variability** is represented by an event where key characteristics are uncertain
  An example of variability that could occur during a construction project is unseasonable weather. Variability risk can be addressed with the use of Monte Carlo simulation followed by activities designed to minimize the range of possible outcomes.
- **Ambiguity** is represented by a lack of certainty regarding the future
  An example of ambiguity that could occur on a mortgage lending system project is future regulations. Ambiguity risk can be addressed by obtaining expert external input, benchmarking against best practices, incremental development, prototyping, and/or simulation.

The **management of emergent risks** (unknowable unknowns) is receiving increased notice. Emergent risks are risks that are recognized only after they occur. The only way to manage these risks is through project resilience. To achieve project resilience, the project must have the right level of budget and schedule contingency for emergent risks (in addition to the contingency for known risks), flexible project processes with an emphasis on change management, an empowered project team with clear-cut goals, frequent review of early signs of emergent risk, immediate response to an identified emergent risk, and clear input from key stakeholders regarding areas of allowable scope or strategy adjustment as a response to identified emergent risk.

Another trend is **integrated risk management**. A coordinated approach to risk across the organization insures balance and consistency in the management of risks. If a project is part of a program or portfolio, risks should be owned and managed at the appropriate level. That said, **some risks identified at higher levels may be delegated to the project team and some project risks may be escalated to higher levels.**

Tailoring

Project tailoring, the manner in which the processes of a knowledge area are exercised, is employed to address the distinctive nature of each project. Successful project tailoring for project risk management is predicated on a careful consideration of:

- Project size
- Project complexity
- Project importance
- The development approach to the project (predictive or adaptive)

Agile/Adaptive Environment

For high-variability projects:

- Incremental products are frequently reviewed
- Cross-functional teams are utilized to escalate knowledge sharing
- Project requirements are maintained as a living document and updated frequently
- Based on improved understanding of risks over the progression of the project, work may be reprioritized.

The source for the above text is the Project Management Institute, *A Guide to the Project Management Body of Knowledge*, (*PMBOK® Guide*) – Sixth Edition, Project Management Institute Inc., 2017, Pages 359-364

In this chapter, we discuss the following:

Figure 11-1: Risk Processes

The source for the above figure is the Project Management Institute, *A Guide to the Project Management Body of Knowledge, (PMBOK® Guide)* – Sixth Edition, Project Management Institute Inc., 2017, Figure 11-1, Page 360

☑	**Crosswind "Must Knows" for Project Risk Management**
	Key Inputs, Tools & Techniques, and Outputs for Plan Risk Management
	Key Inputs, Tools & Techniques, and Outputs for Identify Risks
	Key Inputs, Tools & Techniques, and Outputs for Perform Qualitative Risk Analysis
	Key Inputs, Tools & Techniques, and Outputs for Perform Quantitative Risk Analysis
	Key Inputs, Tools & Techniques, and Outputs for Plan Risk Responses
	Key Inputs, Tools & Techniques, and Outputs for Implement Risk Responses
	Key Inputs, Tools & Techniques, and Outputs for Monitor Risks
	The definition of a risk, an opportunity, and a threat
	The risk breakdown structure (RBS) and risk categorization (internal, external, technological, and organizational)
	Know the definition of uncertainty
	Be familiar with the concepts and differences of pure risk and business risk
	Benefits and risks of contracting
	Characteristics of a risk seeker, a risk-neutral person, and risk-averse person and how they relate to risk tolerance
	What a risk register contains and its purpose
	Risk reviews and risk triggers
	Probability as it relates to risk management
	Impact as it relates to risk management
	How to calculate expected monetary value (EMV) and make a project selection decision based on the outcome
	Monte Carlo simulation
	Characteristics of management reserves (unknown unknowns) and contingency reserves (known unknowns)
	What residual and secondary risks are and how they are created

	Risk owners and their responsibility
	Characteristics of a risk response plan including recognition of the strategies (avoid, transfer, mitigate, escalate, exploit, share, enhance, acceptance, and contingent response strategy)
	What a work-around is in relation to Plan Risk Responses

Although helpful, this list is not all-inclusive in regard to information needed for the exam. It is only suggested material that, if understood and memorized, may increase your exam score.

11.1. What is Risk?

A risk is an event that can impact the project positively or negatively and has some degree of uncertainty. The risk event may or may not occur.

Know the definition of a risk, an opportunity, and a threat.

The objective of assessing risk is to determine its impact. Once determined, the team works to offset any negative impact and enhance any positive impact.

An example of a negative risk (threat) is a reliance on a piece of software that does not work as planned, forcing the team to come up with an alternative.

An example of a positive risk (opportunity) is sales of a new product exceeding expectations.

11.2. Plan Risk Management (Planning Process Group)

During the Plan Risk Management process, the risk management plan is created. The project manager and the team proactively plan the manner in which risks will be identified, ranked, and addressed.

Know the Key Inputs, Tools & Techniques, and Outputs for Plan Risk Management.

The project team uses the organization's risk management policies and procedures as a guide when creating the risk management plan.

PMI, CAPM, and PMBOK are registered marks of the Project Management Institute, Inc.

432 © 2008-2018 Crosswind Learning, www.crosswindpm.com

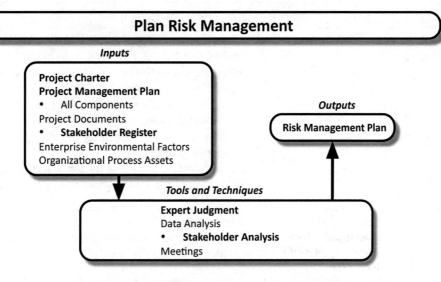

Plan Risk Management

Inputs

Project Charter
Project Management Plan
• All Components
Project Documents
• **Stakeholder Register**
Enterprise Environmental Factors
Organizational Process Assets

Tools and Techniques

Expert Judgment
Data Analysis
• **Stakeholder Analysis**
Meetings

Outputs

Risk Management Plan

Figure 11-2: Plan Risk Management Data Flow Diagram
The source for the above figure is the Project Management Institute, *A Guide to the Project Management Body of Knowledge*, (*PMBOK® Guide*) – Sixth Edition, Project Management Institute Inc., 2017, Figure 11-2, Page 365

Plan Risk Management (Planning)		
Key Inputs	Project Charter	The project charter is the document that provides authorization for the existence of the project and gives the project manager the power to use organizational resources to execute the project. The project charter typically lists the key deliverables, the milestones, and the roles and responsibilities of each person involved in the project. It also contains high-level requirements and risks, as well as a high-level description of the project and its assumptions and constraints.
	Project Management Plan	To ensure consistency, the approved components of the project management plan should be considered when creating the risk management plan. The procedures outlined in the approved components may influence risk management planning.
	Stakeholder Register	The stakeholder register delineates stakeholder information that includes, but is not limited to, identification data (name, position, location, contact information, and project role), assessment information (important requirements, expectations, attitudes toward risk, and level of influence), and classification (internal or external, influence, or other classification model). It is utilized to identify roles and responsibilities for managing project risks and to establish risk thresholds.

Chapter 11
Risk

Key Tools & Techniques	Expert Judgment	Expert judgment is judgment based on expertise acquired in a specific area. It is often more significant and accurate than the best modeling tools available and can be provided by stakeholders, company personnel external to the project, professional organizations or groups, and consultants. It is important to consider expertise related to customizing risk management to a specific project. It is also important to consider familiarity with types of risk for similar projects and with organizational and, if applicable, enterprise risk management.
	Stakeholder Analysis *understand their power & appetite for risk*	Stakeholder analysis is performed to assess the positions of stakeholders toward risk since those positions influence the tenor of the risk management plan.
Key Outputs	Risk Management Plan	The risk management plan is a component of the project management plan that details the manner in which risk management activities are configured and implemented. Typically it addresses risk strategy, risk methodology, roles and responsibilities, financing (the budget for risk-related activities, contingent reserves, and management reserves), timing of risk processes, risk classification for grouping individual risks (typically, a risk breakdown structure provides the framework for classification), the probability and impact of individual risks (often supported by a probability and impact matrix), reporting formats, and tracking. It may also include a determination of the manner in which risk thresholds are established and risks are tracked, reported, scored, and interpreted.

Situational Question and Real World Application

If Plan Risk Management is ignored, it is likely that the project risk environment will become reactive. A reactive project risk environment typically has no predetermined responses for risks that do occur and/or no process for addressing those risks.

11.2.1. Risk Management Plan

An effective risk management plan addresses the methodologies that will be used to manage risk, as well as the risk-related roles and responsibilities, budget estimates for the activities of risk-related resources, guidelines for using contingency and management reserves, and the impact of risk activities on the project schedule.

The plan is used by the project manager and team to:

- Create the risk register
- Identify risks (positive and negative) and triggers
- Define the probability and impact matrix, as well as its thresholds
- Determine when and how to perform quantitative risk analysis, expected monetary value (EMV), and decision tree analysis
- Establish risk responses
- Establish risk owners and detail the responsibilities of each risk owner
- Implement risk responses
- Monitor and respond to risks

Reference Figure 11-3: Risk Processes Interaction for an overview of how the processes of risk work together as a result of the risk management plan.

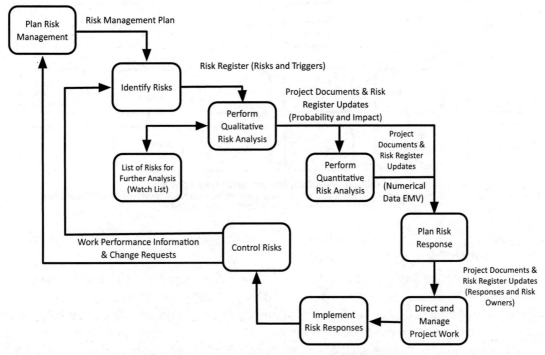

Figure 11-3: Risk Processes Interaction

The source for the above figure is the Project Management Institute, *A Guide to the Project Management Body of Knowledge*, (*PMBOK® Guide*) – Sixth Edition, Project Management Institute Inc., 2017, Figure 11-1, Page 360

The risk breakdown structure and risk probabilities and impact rating matrix are two examples of documents that can be created within the risk management plan. The risk breakdown structure is typically used during the Identify Risks process and the probabilities and impact matrix is used during the Perform Qualitative Risk Analysis process.

11.2.2. Risk Breakdown Structure (RBS)

The risk breakdown structure (RBS) can be utilized to **break down project risks**. A brainstorming environment can be created if the **risks** are **categorized**, so the team can identify and categorize additional risks. This approach is similar to decomposition of the work on a project to create a WBS. Typical risk categories can include **internal**, **external**, **technological**, and **organizational**.

Be familiar with risk breakdown structure (RBS) and risk categorization such as internal, external, technology, and organizational.

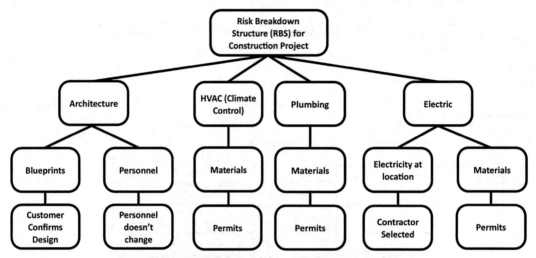

Figure 11-4: Risk Breakdown Structure Sample

The source for the above figure is the Project Management Institute, *A Guide to the Project Management Body of Knowledge*, (*PMBOK® Guide*) – Sixth Edition, Project Management Institute Inc., 2017, Figure 11-4, Page 368

11.2.3. Probability and Impact Matrix

The probability and impact matrix is part of the risk management plan and can be used as the basis for the evaluation of risks in terms of their probability and impact. It is typically used during the Perform Qualitative Risk Analysis process. Its criteria are established by those associated with the project, including the sponsors, the project manager, and/or team members.

The following table displays the probability (a value between 0 and 1.0), followed by the probability range (low, medium, and high), followed by the impact to scope, schedule, cost, and quality for the occurrence of a specific event.

PMI, CAPM, and PMBOK are registered marks of the Project Management Institute, Inc.

436 © 2008-2018 Crosswind Learning, www.crosswindpm.com

The threshold information in the table that follows is an example only. Specific thresholds are determined by the appropriate project party.

	Low	Medium	High
Probability	0 to 0.33	0.34 to 0.66	0.67 to 1.00
Project Objective (Impact)	Low	Medium	High
Scope	Minimal changes	Significant changes for functionality	Potentially flawed product
Schedule	5% or less delay	6% to 15% delay	16% or greater delay
Cost	5% or less increase	6% to 15% increase	16% or greater increase
Quality	Quality slippage minimal	Slippage requires sponsor sign-off	Product is basically useless

11.2.4. Uncertainty

Uncertainty is a component of risk that denotes the amount of information known (or unknown) about the outcome. The range regarding the possible outcome starts with no knowledge and ends with a high degree of knowledge.

Know the definition of uncertainty.

11.2.5. Types of Risk

There are two types of risk – pure risk and business risk.

Pure risk	Pure risk is a risk for which **insurance can be purchased,** thereby transferring the risk for financial benefit to the party accepting the risk.
Business risk	Business risk is **typically uninsurable.** It is an event that can occur during the process of doing business. An example of business risk is **the forecast of sales over the next six months.**

Be familiar with the concepts and differences of pure risk and business risk.

11.2.6. Risk and Contracting

There is a belief that if a company out-sources a piece of work, the provider assumes the risk and the purchaser has no risk exposure. This is NOT THE CASE. When outsourcing, a **buyer can minimize risk exposure (some risk remains) and there is a new risk exposure.** An example of a new risk is the failure of the seller to provide the services as promised. Reference the Procurement chapter for more information about risk as it relates to the buyer, seller, and contracting.

Know the benefits and risk of contracting.

11.2.7. Risk Tolerance and Perspective

The risk tolerance of a person or organization can influence the project environment. There are three types of risk tolerance: Risk-Averse, Risk Seeker, and Risk-Neutral. The risk tolerance of the customer/sponsor, project manager, and the organization greatly impacts the project environment.

Type	Description
Risk-averse	Those that are risk-averse practice **risk avoidance**. They invariably select the low risk option or the sure thing.
Risk seeker	Those that are risk seekers **do not fear risk** and may embrace it. They are typically early adopters of new products and often take an all or nothing approach to an initiative.
Risk-neutral	Those that are risk-neutral have a measured attitude toward risk; however, depending on specific circumstance, that attitude can become risk-averse or risk seeking.

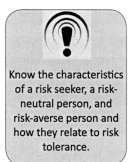

Know the characteristics of a risk seeker, a risk-neutral person, and risk-averse person and how they relate to risk tolerance.

The source for the above text is the Project Management Institute, *A Guide to the Project Management Body of Knowledge*, (PMBOK® Guide) – Sixth Edition, Project Management Institute Inc., 2017, Pages 364-370

11.3. Identify Risks (Planning Process Group)

During the Identify Risks process, the project manager, team, key stakeholders, and/or subject matter experts identify possible project risks. A predefined list from previous projects may be utilized as a starting point for the identification.

When the Identify Risks process is complete, the identified risks are subject to the Perform Qualitative Risk Analysis process.

Know the Key Inputs, Tools & Techniques, and Outputs for Identify Risks.

Identify Risks

Inputs

Project Management Plan
- **Requirements Management Plan**
- **Schedule Management Plan**
- **Cost Management Plan**
- **Quality Management Plan**
- **Resource Management Plan**
- **Risk Management Plan**
- **Scope Baseline**
- **Schedule Baseline**
- **Cost Baseline**

Project Documents
- **Assumption Log**
- Cost Estimates
- **Duration Estimates**
- **Issue Log**
- Lessons Learned Register
- **Requirements Documentation**
- Resource Requirements
- **Stakeholder Register**

Agreements
Procurement Documentation
Enterprise Environmental Factors
Organizational Process Assets

Outputs

Risk Register
Risk Report
Project Documents Updates
- **Assumption Log**
- Issue Log
- Lessons Learned Register

Tools and Techniques

Expert Judgment
Data Gathering
- Brainstorming
- **Checklists**
- **Interviews**

Data Analysis
- **Root Cause Analysis**
- **Assumption and Constraint Analysis**
- **SWOT Analysis**
- **Document Analysis**

Interpersonal and Team Skills
- Facilitation

Prompt lists
Meetings

Figure 11-5: Identify Risks Data Flow Diagram
The source for the above figure is the Project Management Institute, *A Guide to the Project Management Body of Knowledge*, (*PMBOK® Guide*) – Sixth Edition, Project Management Institute Inc., 2017, Figure 11-6, Page 371

Identify Risks (Planning)		
Key Inputs	Requirements Management Plan	The requirements management plan is a component of the project management plan that details the evaluation, documentation, and administration of project requirements. It includes the methods for designing, monitoring, and reporting requirement activities and configuration activities; prioritizing requirements; determining requirement metrics; and capturing attributes for the requirements traceability matrix. The plan may indicate project goals that are especially at risk.
	Schedule Management Plan	The schedule management plan is a component of the project management plan that details the delineation, evolution, monitoring, and control of the schedule. The plan may indicate areas of concern, such as those that are uncertain/unclear or those relying on assumptions that could foster risk.
	Cost Management Plan	The cost management plan is a component of the project management plan that details the manner in which project costs are planned, configured, and controlled. The plan may indicate areas of concern, such as those that are uncertain/unclear or those relying on assumptions that could foster risk.
	Quality Management Plan	The quality management plan is a component of the project management plan that details the manner in which the policies, methods, and criteria of the organization are executed. It details activities and necessary resources to accomplish quality goals. The plan may indicate areas of concern, such as those that are uncertain/unclear or those relying on assumptions that could foster risk.
	Resource Management Plan	The resource management plan is a component of the project management plan that documents the manner in which the team and physical resources are determined, quantified, and acquired. The plan may indicate areas of concern, such as those that are uncertain/unclear or those relying on assumptions that could foster risk.
	Risk Management Plan	The risk management plan is a component of the project management plan that details the manner in which risk management activities are configured and implemented. It may also include a determination of the manner in which risk thresholds are established and risks are tracked, reported, scored, and interpreted.

PMI, CAPM, and PMBOK are registered marks of the Project Management Institute, Inc.

440　　© 2008-2018 Crosswind Learning, www.crosswindpm.com

Identify Risks (Continued)		
Key Inputs (Cont.)	Scope Baseline	The scope baseline is the authorized version of the project scope statement, WBS (to the level of work package with individual identification codes) and WBS dictionary. It includes deliverables and their acceptance criteria that could foster risk. Note that the WBS can be used as the basis for constructing risk identification techniques.
	Schedule Baseline	The schedule baseline is the authorized version of the schedule model. It contains baseline start and baseline finish dates, is subject to change control, and is used as the basis of comparison to actual results. It can be used to determine milestones and deliverable due dates. The baseline may lead to risk discovery if the milestones and deliverable due dates are uncertain/unclear or reliant on assumptions that could foster risk.
	Cost Baseline	The cost baseline is the authorized version of the time-phased budget for the project, excluding management reserves, and subject to change control. It is evolved from a summation of approved budgets for specific schedule activities. It can be used to determine costs or funding requirements, which may be of concern if they are uncertain/unclear or those relying on assumptions that could foster risk. Note that the budget consists of the cost baseline plus the management reserves.
	Assumption Log	The assumption log is a document that lists the assumptions and constraints identified during the creation of the project charter. An assumption is an idea or statement taken to be true. An example of an assumption is the statement "there will be a robust market for the product created as a result of this project once it is available to the public." Examples of constraints are the project completion deadline, the budget threshold, or the limit on the number of employees that can be dedicated to the project. It's important to identify assumptions and constraints as early as possible and to update them as the project evolves. Due to the risks inherent in assumptions and constraints, they may impact the overall project risk level.

Identify Risks (Continued)		
Key Inputs (Cont.)	Duration Estimates	Duration estimates provide quantitative assessments of activity durations in which lags are not considered. They are often expressed as a range of time with the extent of the range indicating the measure of risk. Further analysis is typically undertaken to ensure that allocated time is sufficient to complete project activities. Inadequate time denotes a risk to the project.
	Issue Log	The issue log is used to record and track any project challenges that cannot be immediately resolved. An issue may foster a project risk and impact the overall project risk level.
	Requirements Documentation	Requirements documentation lists the requirements and delineates how requirements fulfill the business needs of the project. The requirements evaluated by the project team to determine those that are at risk.
	Stakeholder Register	The stakeholder register contains information related to identified stakeholders. It includes identification information (name, position, location, project role, and contact information), assessment information (key requirements, potential impact on project results, phase in which stakeholder wields the greatest influence, and expectations), and stakeholder classification (internal/external, impact/influence/ power/interest, or other classification model). It is used to determine which stakeholders could best identify risks and/or have the availability to act as risk owners.
	Agreements	Agreements define project intentions and can be written (such as **letters of agreements**, **contracts**, **memorandums of understanding**, **service level agreements**, and **email**) or verbal. For work to be performed by an external source, a contract between buyer and seller is typically used. The contract is identified by type and contains information such as milestone dates, acceptance criteria, awards, and penalties that can present risks (threats or opportunities).
	Procurement Documentation	For work or materials from an external source, related project documentation should be reviewed to ascertain possible project risks (threats or opportunities).

Key Tools & Techniques	Expert Judgment	Expert judgment is judgment based on expertise acquired in a specific area. It is often more significant and accurate than the best modeling tools available and can be provided by stakeholders, company personnel external to the project, professional organizations or groups, and consultants. It is important to consider expertise related to similar projects or business areas. Those possessing this expertise should be invited to provide carefully considered feedback regarding individual project risks as well as overall project risk.
	Checklists *check to see if you have identified all the risks*	The risk checklist itemizes the risks that are likely to occur on the project. It is important that the project team conducts robust risk identification to develop the risk checklist, even if the team references a risk checklist, evolved from historic information and knowledge from comparable projects, provided by the organization or a generic risk checklist available through the industry. It is also important that the team reviews the checklist from time to time to add new information and delete outdated information.
	Interviews	Interviews are direct elicitations of information and can be formal or informal. Typically, the interviewer asks questions of the interviewee and records the responses. Specific project risks and the origins of overall project risk can be determined through interviews with knowledgeable project stakeholders, participants, and subject matter experts.
	Root Cause Analysis *Fishbone/ Ishakowa*	Root cause analysis (RCA) is used to ascertain the underlying cause of a variance, defect, or risk. It is an analytical technique that may also be used to ascertain risk by starting with a problem or benefit statement and investigating the threats or opportunities that might result in the occurrence of the risk.

Identify Risks (Continued)		
Key Tools & Techniques (Cont.)	Assumption and Constraint Analysis	An assumption and constraint analysis involves validating the assumptions and constraints upon which the project is based. An assumption is an idea or statement taken to be true. An example of an assumption is the statement "there will be a robust market for the product created as a result of this project once it is available to the public." Examples of constraints are the project completion deadline, the budget threshold, or the limit on the number of employees that can be dedicated to the project. Assumptions that are fragmentary, inexact, unsound, or inconsistent are considered threats to the project. Constraints that can be eased or withdrawn are considered opportunities.
	SWOT Analysis	SWOT analysis identifies the **strengths**, **weaknesses**, **opportunities**, and **threats** related to the organization, business, and project. During risk identification, the SWOT analysis can be used to identify the threats that can arise from the identified weaknesses and the opportunities that can arise from the identified strengths. It can also be used to determine if the weaknesses can negatively impact the strengths.
	Document Analysis	Document analysis is the review of project documents to identify risks that may arise from discrepancies within a document or between documents.
Key Outputs	Risk Register	Each identified risk is recorded in the risk register. It typically includes the potential owner of and potential response(s) to each identified risk and may include a title, category, status, cause(s), trigger(s), impacted activity(ies), date of identification, date range for probable occurrence, and response deadline.
	Risk Report	The risk report details the origins of overall project risk and recaps key data about unique project risks (typically the number of threats and opportunities and other summary metrics).
	Assumption Log	The assumption log is a document that lists the assumptions and constraints identified during the creation of the project charter. The assumption log is updated with the addition, modification, or removal of any assumptions and constraints determined during risk identification.

11.3.1. Risk Register

The risk register is a project document created during the risk planning processes. It evolves as the risk management processes and the project evolve, and it contains the following:

Know what the risk register contains and its purpose.

- Risks
- Triggers
- Probability (Likelihood) and Impact ($) from risk analysis
- Planned Responses
- Risk owners

Figure 11-6: Risk Register illustrates that something as basic as a spreadsheet can be used to track risk related information for a project or program.

Risk #	Risk Name	Trigger(s)	Probability	($) Impact	Response(s)	Risk Owner	Reserve Amount

Figure 11-6: Risk Register

11.3.2. Diagramming Techniques

Diagramming techniques may be used to help decompose or categorize risk. This activity could involve a number of techniques such as cause-and-effect (Ishikawa) diagrams, system or process flow charts, and influence diagrams. Influence diagrams show graphical relationships associated with process timing and interactions.

11.3.3. Risk Triggers

Risk triggers are risk event indicators that are typically identified in conjunction with identification of the risk. The occurrence of a risk trigger is an indication that a risk event **could occur in the near future**.

Know risk triggers and risk reviews.

11.3.4. Risk Reviews

During risk reviews, **the state of each identified risk is assessed and any new risks are identified.** Identified risks are assessed for occurrence and any change to ranking, characteristics, probabilities, and impact.

The source for the above text is the Project Management Institute, *A Guide to the Project Management Body of Knowledge*, (PMBOK® Guide) – Sixth Edition, Project Management Institute Inc., 2017, Pages 370-379

11.4. Perform Qualitative Risk Analysis (Planning Process Group)

Know the Key Inputs, Tools & Techniques, and Outputs for Perform Qualitative Risk Analysis.

During the Perform Qualitative Risk Analysis process, **risks are analyzed for probability and impact**. Such analysis provides an overall risk ranking for the project based on the evaluation of each identified risk (both probability of occurrence and impact are rated as high, medium, or low).

A numeric value can be assigned to specific project parameters to ascertain a total score. Parameters may include the duration of the project and the number of people on the project team. Historical information can provide past experience the team and/or organization has had on similar projects.

When the risk analysis is complete, depending upon the score of the project, the risk range can be determined (for example, 0-5 low risk, 6-10 medium risk, 11-15 high risk), based upon the combined score of all evaluated risks. Reference Figure 11-8: Probability and Impact Matrix in section 11.4.1 for a sample matrix.

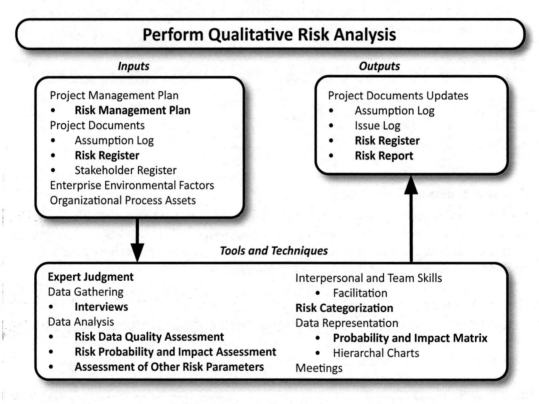

Figure 11-7: Perform Qualitative Risk Analysis Data Flow Diagram

The source for the above figure is the Project Management Institute, *A Guide to the Project Management Body of Knowledge*, (*PMBOK® Guide*) – Sixth Edition, Project Management Institute Inc., 2017, Figure 11-8, Page 380

PMI, CAPM, and PMBOK are registered marks of the Project Management Institute, Inc.

446   © 2008-2018 Crosswind Learning, www.crosswindpm.com

Perform Qualitative Risk Analysis (Planning)		
Key Inputs	Risk Management Plan	The risk management plan is a component of the project management plan that details the manner in which risk management activities are configured and implemented. It addresses roles and responsibilities, financing (the budget for risk-related activities, contingent reserves, and management reserves), timing of risk processes, risk classification for grouping individual risks (typically, this is accomplished by using a risk breakdown structure), the probability and impact of individual risks (often supported by a probability and impact matrix), and the risk thresholds of individual stakeholders.
	Risk Register	Each identified risk is recorded in the risk register. It typically includes the potential owner of and potential response(s) to each identified risk and may include a title, category, status, cause(s), trigger(s), impacted activity(ies), date(s) of identification, date range for probable occurrence, and response deadline(s).
Key Tools & Techniques	Expert Judgment	Expert judgment is judgment based on expertise acquired in a specific area. It is often more significant and accurate than the best modeling tools available and can be provided by stakeholders, company personnel external to the project, professional organizations or groups, and consultants. It is important to consider expertise related to prior, comparable projects, and qualitative risk analysis.
	Interviews	Interviews are direct elicitations of information and can be formal or informal. Typically, the interviewer asks questions of the interviewee and records the responses. If the interview is structured or semi-structured, the responses can be utilized to estimate the probability and impact of individual risks on the project. Note that the interviewer should nurture an accepting and confidential environment so that the responses are candid and impartial.
	Risk Data Quality Assessment	The risk data quality assessment determines the extent to which individual project risk data is correct and trustworthy. One method of assessing the risk data is to have stakeholders complete questionnaires regarding their perceptions of individual risk characteristics, including relevance, pertinence, and comprehensiveness.

Perform Qualitative Risk Analysis (Continued)		
Key Tools & Techniques (Cont.)	Risk Probability and Impact Assessment	The risk probability and impact assessment is utilized to determine the probability that each identified risk will occur. The possible effect on one or more project objectives (schedule, budget, performance, and/or quality) is considered during the assessment. Typically, the assessment also indicates if each risk is an opportunity or threat. Probabilities and impacts are often assessed in accordance with the risk management plan during a meeting or interviews with knowledgeable participants. The level of probability, along with any assumptions that justify the assigned level, are recorded. Risks with low probability and impact may be added to the risk register for future tracking. Risks can be grouped by priority based on probability, then impact.
	Assessment of Other Risk Parameters	In addition to probability and impact, other parameters may be assessed during the prioritization of risks for further action and assessment. Factors such as **criticality**, **immediacy**, **latency**, **manageability**, **governance**, **discovery**, **connection to other risks**, **strategic impact**, and **importance** are considered.
	Risk Categorization	Risk categories are assigned to individual risks in accordance with the categories detailed in the risk management plan. Categorizing risks can lead to more effective responses, since generic responses can be devised for groups of related risks. If risks are grouped by probability and impact using the risk breakdown structure (RBS) or other device (budget, roles and responsibilities, or phase), the team can concentrate on devising responses for risks that subject the project to the highest risk exposure.
	Probability and Impact Matrix	The probability and impact matrix is a grid utilized to delineate the probability of each risk occurrence and the effect on project priorities (in terms of time, cost, and performance) should the risk occur. Risks can be grouped by priority based on probability, then impact (the risk score is derived by assigning numeric values to probability and to impact, then combing those values). Typically, the matrix also indicates if each risk is an opportunity or threat.

Perform Qualitative Risk Analysis (Continued)		
Key Outputs	Risk Register	Each identified risk is recorded in the risk register. The register typically includes the potential owner of and potential response(s) to each identified risk and may include a title, category, status, cause(s), trigger(s), impacted activity(ies), date(s) of identification, date range for probable occurrence, and response deadline(s). It is updated with new information related to each risk, including the probability and impact evaluation, priority level, score, owner, urgency, and category.
	Risk Report	The risk report details the origins of overall project risk and recaps key data about unique project risks (typically the number of threats and opportunities and other summary metrics). It is updated with information related to risks with the highest risk scores. The risk report also includes a prioritized catalogue of all identified risks and a brief overview of project risk.

Situational Question and Real World Application

Failure to effectively address the Perform Qualitative Risk Analysis process may lead to an inability to appreciate the impact of a risk and/or a failure to execute risk responses effectively or in a timely manner.

11.4.1. Probability and Impact Matrix

Figure 11-8: Probability and Impact Matrix can be used to evaluate the impact of a risk and the probability of its occurrence. The probability scale is on the left, and the impact is shown in the bottom-most row. The result of multiplying the impact by the probability is displayed in the intersecting cell. For example, .09 in row 2, column 3 represents the multiplication of the impact (0.1 in the final row, column 3) by the probability (0.9 in row 2, column 2). Depending upon the scoring, the risk could be viewed as low, medium, or high.

		Opportunities					Threats						
Probability	0.9	0.09	0.225	0.45	0.675	0.81	0.81	0.675	0.45	0.225	0.09	0.9	**Probability**
	0.75	0.075	0.1875	0.375	0.5625	0.675	0.675	0.5625	0.375	0.1875	0.075	0.75	
	0.5	0.05	0.125	0.25	0.375	0.45	0.45	0.375	0.25	0.125	0.05	0.5	
	0.25	0.025	0.0625	0.125	0.1875	0.225	0.225	0.1875	0.125	0.0625	0.025	0.25	
	0.1	0.01	0.025	0.05	0.075	0.09	0.09	0.075	0.05	0.025	0.01	0.1	
	Impact>	0.1	0.25	0.5	0.75	0.9	0.9	0.75	0.5	0.25	0.1		

Figure 11-8: Probability and Impact Matrix

The source for the above figure is the Project Management Institute, *A Guide to the Project Management Body of Knowledge*, (*PMBOK® Guide*) – Sixth Edition, Project Management Institute Inc., 2017, Figure 11-5, Page 370

A matrix such as this can be used to analyze each risk, and then create an overall risk ranking for the project. An accurate score is predicated on unbiased and accurate matrix data.

The source for the above text is the Project Management Institute, *A Guide to the Project Management Body of Knowledge*, (*PMBOK® Guide*) – Sixth Edition, Project Management Institute Inc., 2017, Pages 379-386

11.5. Perform Quantitative Risk Analysis (Planning Process Group)

The Perform Quantitative Risk Analysis process is evolved as a result of the Identify Risks and Perform Qualitative Risk Analysis processes. Perform Quantitative Risk Analysis breaks down risks from a high, medium, and low ranking based on actual numerical values and probabilities of occurrence. **Risks that are higher in probability and impact are more likely to be evaluated during the Perform Quantitative Risk Analysis process. Techniques used include decision tree analysis and Monte Carlo simulation**, which yield realistic schedule and cost targets for the project in accordance with the documented risk.

Perform Quantitative Risk Analysis provides the details necessary to recognize such impacts, whereas Perform Qualitative Risk Analysis often does not.

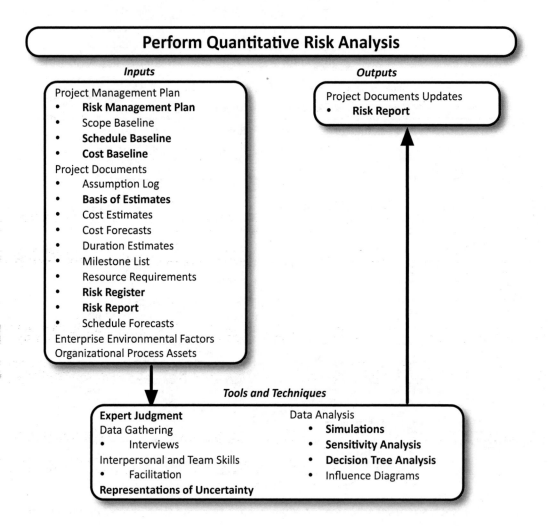

Know the Inputs, Tools & Techniques, and Outputs for Perform Quantitative Risk Analysis.

Figure 11-9: Perform Quantitative Risk Analysis Data Flow Diagram

The source for the above figure is the Project Management Institute, *A Guide to the Project Management Body of Knowledge, (PMBOK® Guide)* – Sixth Edition, Project Management Institute Inc., 2017, Figure 11-11, Page 387

PMI, CAPM, and PMBOK are registered marks of the Project Management Institute, Inc.

450   © 2008-2018 Crosswind Learning, www.crosswindpm.com

Perform Quantitative Risk Analysis (Planning)		
Key Inputs	Risk Management Plan	The risk management plan is a component of the project management plan that details the manner in which risk management activities are configured and implemented. Typically it addresses risk strategy, risk methodology, roles and responsibilities, financing (the budget for risk-related activities, contingent reserves, and management reserves), timing of risk processes, risk classification for grouping individual risks (typically, this is accomplished by using a risk breakdown structure), the probability and impact of individual risks (often supported by a probability and impact matrix), reporting formats, and tracking. It also indicates if qualitative risk analysis is required, the frequency at which the analysis will be performed, and the resources available to conduct the analysis.
	Schedule Baseline	The schedule baseline is the authorized version of the schedule model. It contains baseline start and baseline finish dates, is subject to change control, and is used as the basis of comparison to actual results. In addition, it delineates the point in time at which individual project risks and other sources of unpredictability can be assessed.
	Cost Baseline	The cost baseline is the authorized version of the time-phased budget for the project, excluding management reserves, and subject to change control. It is evolved from a summation of approved budgets for specific schedule activities. Cost estimates are aggregated by work packages, then into higher components (typically control accounts) of the work breakdown structure (WBS), and then for the entire project. In addition, it delineates the point in time at which individual project risks and other sources of unpredictability can be assessed.
	Basis of Estimates	The basis of estimates includes documentation that delineates the manner in which the estimates are determined, lists all assumptions and constraints, identifies the resources used to evolve the estimates, the range of estimates, and the degree of certainty in the estimates, and details the risks that impact the estimates. It may be reflected in the variability modeled during a quantitative risk analysis. This may include consideration of the category, accuracy, intention, genesis, and strategy.

Perform Quantitative Risk Analysis (Continued)		
Key Inputs (Cont.)	Risk Register	Each identified risk is recorded in the risk register records. It typically includes the potential owner of and potential response(s) to each identified risk and may include a title, category, status, cause(s), trigger(s), impacted activity(ies), date(s) of identification, date range for probable occurrence, and response deadline(s). It is used to reference details about individual risks that are inputs for quantitative analysis.
	Risk Report	The risk report details the origins of overall project risk and recaps key data about unique project risks (typically the number of threats and opportunities and other summary metrics). It is updated with information related to risks with the highest risk scores. The risk report also includes a prioritized catalogue of all identified risks and their sources as well as the degree of overall project risk.
Key Tools & Techniques	Expert Judgment	Expert judgment is judgment based on expertise acquired in a specific area. It is often more significant and accurate than the best modeling tools available and can be provided by stakeholders, company personnel external to the project, professional organizations or groups, and consultants. It is important to consider expertise related to knowledge or experience in assigning numeric values to individual and overall project risk for use as inputs to quantitative risk analysis, determining the most consequential representation of uncertainty, selecting the most appropriate tools for modeling, and decoding quantitative risk analysis outputs.
	Representations of Uncertainty	Quantitative risk analysis requires the entry of inputs that represent individual risks and other sources of uncertainty into the quantitative risk analysis model. In instances where the duration, resource, or cost requirement is not clear, a range of values in the form of a probability distribution can be used. If a risk is not related to a specific activity, a probabilistic branch can be used instead. If risks are related through a dependency or by a common cause, correlation is used in the model.
	Simulations	The quantitative risk analysis model is used to simulate the likely affect of risk on the project. A common approach to the simulation is the Monte Carlo method. Note that for a quantitative cost risk analysis model, cost estimates are used and for a quantitative schedule risk analysis model, duration estimates are used.

Perform Quantitative Risk Analysis (Continued)		
Key Tools & Techniques (Cont.)	Sensitivity Analysis	Sensitivity analysis is a comparison of the relative importance of variables. When applied to risks, a tornado diagram (a type of bar chart) is typically used. The diagram displays individual risks ordered by impact on project outcomes (highest to lowest).
	Decision Tree Analysis	A decision tree analysis is a method employed to choose between possible decisions. The decision tree consists of branches and nodes. Each branch depicts a discreet decision with costs and risks delineated. For each branch, there is a node containing the expected value of the decision.
Key Outputs	Risk Report	The risk report details the origins of overall project risk and recaps key data about unique project risks (typically the number of threats and opportunities and other summary metrics). It is updated with information related to risks with the highest risk scores. The risk report also includes a prioritized catalogue of all identified risks and recommended responses, as well as a brief overview of project risk.

Situational Question and Real World Application

Failure to effectively address the Perform Quantitative Risk Analysis process may lead to an inability to maximize opportunities and minimize threats. It could also result in not knowing the overall risk exposure of the project.

11.5.1. Probability

Probability is the likelihood that an event will occur. It is usually measured in percentages (0 to 100%) or real numbers (0.0 to 1.0). The **sum of all probabilities is equal to 100% or 1.0**, which denotes that all possible outcomes (100%) have been considered. Probability can also be measured as low, medium, and high (or another non-numerical method can be used).

Understand probability as it relates to risk management.

11.5.2. Impact

Impact is the consequence to the project if the risk event occurs. The impact can be positive or negative. An example of impact is a large number of sales resulting from the launch of a website for a start-up company. If the company can fulfill the orders, the impact is positive; if not, the impact is typically negative.

Understand impact as it relates to risk management.

11.5.3. Probability Distributions

Continuous probability distributions graphically represent uncertainty in schedule and cost values and are used extensively in modeling and simulation.

The three most common types of probability distribution functions are normal distribution, beta distribution, and triangular distribution.

Normal distribution is typically used for statistical or scientific computing.

Beta distribution is used to model events that must take place within an interval that has a minimum and maximum value. Beta distribution, along with triangular distribution, is commonly used with PERT and CPM.

Triangular distribution is the most common distribution used in business modeling because its parameters (minimum, most likely, and maximum) are understood even by those unfamiliar with risk analysis.

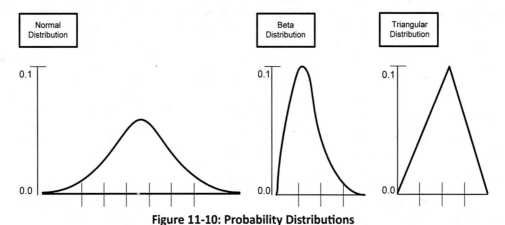

Figure 11-10: Probability Distributions

11.5.4. Decision Trees and Expected Monetary Value (EMV)

Decision tree analysis is based on an analysis of the probability and impact of all potential decisions to determine the potential expected monetary value (EMV), or expected risk value, of the opportunity as a whole.

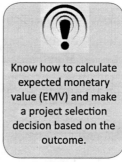

Know how to calculate expected monetary value (EMV) and make a project selection decision based on the outcome.

This is accomplished by multiplying the probabilities and the impact (minus any costs), then totaling the results for each project or opportunity. Note that the sum of all probabilities must equal 1.0 (or 100%).

For example, an organization wishes to create a specific product and currently does not have the capacity to do so. The organization must decide if it will purchase a new company that currently has the capability of creating the product or if it will retool a current company so that it will have the capacity to create the product. The organization uses a decision tree to compare the EMV of purchasing against the EMV of retooling. Reference Figure 11-11: Decision Tree.

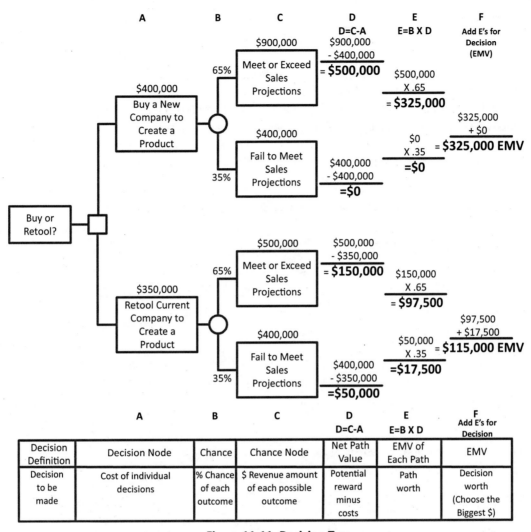

	A	B	C	D	E	F
				D=C-A	E=B X D	Add E's for Decision
Decision Definition	Decision Node	Chance	Chance Node	Net Path Value	EMV of Each Path	EMV
Decision to be made	Cost of individual decisions	% Chance of each outcome	$ Revenue amount of each possible outcome	Potential reward minus costs	Path worth	Decision worth (Choose the Biggest $)

Figure 11-11: Decision Tree

The source for the above figure is the Project Management Institute, *A Guide to the Project Management Body of Knowledge*, (*PMBOK® Guide*) – Sixth Edition, Project Management Institute Inc., 2017, Figure 11-15, Page 394

Figure 11-11: Decision Tree shows that purchasing a new company makes more sense than retooling, since the EMV for retooling is $115,000 compared to the EMV of $325,000 for purchasing a new company.

Note that in the exam, if only one percentage value is referenced in a question, the other value can be determined by subtracting the referenced value from 100%. For example: if a value of 70% is the only value referenced in the question, the other value is 30% (100% - 70%).

11.5.5. Monte Carlo

Monte Carlo is a mock-up technique that uses software to simulate project characteristics in order to determine the possible outcome. While the simulation is typically applied to scheduling in order to determine the necessary schedule reserve, it can be used in other areas of the project.

Know what a Monte Carlo simulation does.

11.5.6. Probabilities Tables

The following tables display the probabilities associated with a project's cost and schedule parameters.

Tables like this can be helpful. If management wanted to know if a project could be completed for no more than $41,000, the budget table prepared by the Monte Carlo software indicates an 80% confidence level that the project will be completed for that cost. The confidence level (as a percentage) typically increases as costs and durations increase because the likelihood of realizing those targets becomes more realistic.

The Monte Carlo software considers many project variables to generate the data.

Quantitative Analysis For Total Budget Table			
Confidence Level	Total Cost	Confidence Level	Total Cost
100%	$ 43,564	60%	$30,000
95%	$42,500	55%	$27,500
90%	$42,000	50%	$ 25,000
85%	$ 41,500	45%	$22,500
80%	$ 41,000	40%	$ 20,000
75%	$ 40,500	35%	$ 17,500
70%	$40,000	30%	$ 15,000
65%	$35,000	25%	$14,500

Quantitative Analysis For Completion Date Table			
Confidence Level	Date Complete	Confidence Level	Date Complete
100%	12/15/xx	60%	08/15/xx
95%	12/01/xx	55%	08/01/xx
90%	11/15/xx	50%	07/15/xx
85%	11/01/xx	45%	07/01/xx
80%	10/15/xx	40%	06/15/xx
75%	10/01/xx	35%	06/01/xx
70%	09/15/xx	30%	05/15/xx
65%	09/01/xx	25%	05/01/xx

11.5.7. Tornado Diagram

The tornado diagram is a graphical representation of project risks and their potential impact as determined by a sensitivity analysis. The risk with the highest potential impact is represented by the top bar in the diagram, the risk with the next highest potential impact is represented by the bar directly underneath the top bar, etc. When completed, the chart typically resembles a funnel or tornado.

Project Value (Baseline $0K is on Track)

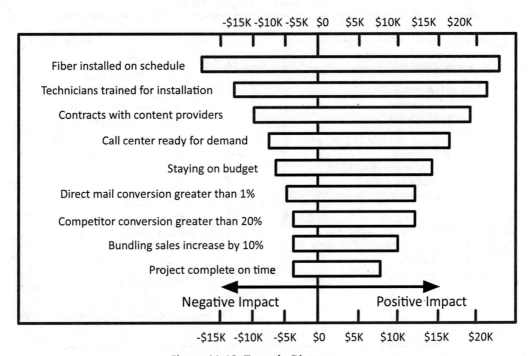

Figure 11-12: Tornado Diagram

The source for the above figure is the Project Management Institute, *A Guide to the Project Management Body of Knowledge*, (*PMBOK® Guide*) – Sixth Edition, Project Management Institute Inc., 2017, Figure 11-14, Page 393

Sensitivity analysis determines risk impact by considering how much the uncertainty of each project element impacts a particular project objective when the other elements remain at their baseline values.

The source for the above text is the Project Management Institute, *A Guide to the Project Management Body of Knowledge*, (*PMBOK® Guide*) – Sixth Edition, Project Management Institute Inc., 2017, Pages 386-395

11.6. Plan Risk Responses (Planning Process Group)

During the Plan Risk Responses process, responses for risks are developed, strategies for addressing risks are determined, and actions for addressing risk exposure are decided for both individual risks and overall project risk.

Know the Key Inputs, Tools & Techniques, and Outputs for Plan Risk Responses.

Chapter 11
Risk

Plan Risk Responses

Inputs

Project Management Plan
- **Resource Management Plan**
- **Risk Management Plan**
- **Cost Baseline**

Project Documents
- Lessons Learned Register
- Project Schedule
- Project Team Assignment
- **Resource Calendars**
- **Risk Register**
- **Risk Report**
- Stakeholder Register

Enterprise Environmental Factors
Organizational Process Assets

Outputs

Change Requests
Project Management Plan Updates
- Schedule Management Plan
- Cost Management Plan
- Quality Management Plan
- **Resource Management Plan**
- Procurement Management Plan
- **Scope Baseline**
- **Schedule Baseline**
- **Cost Baseline**

Project Documents Updates
- **Assumption Log**
- Cost Forecasts
- Lessons Learned Register
- Project Schedule
- Risk Register

Tools and Techniques

Expert Judgment
Data Gathering
- Interviews

Interpersonal and Team Skills
- Facilitation

Strategies for Threats
Strategies for Opportunities

Contingent Response Strategies
Strategies for Overall Project Risk
Data Analysis
- **Alternatives Analysis**
- **Cost-benefit Analysis**

Decision Making
- Multicriteria Decision Analysis

Figure 11-13: Plan Risk Responses Data Flow Diagram

The source for the above figure is the Project Management Institute, *A Guide to the Project Management Body of Knowledge, (PMBOK® Guide) – Sixth Edition*, Project Management Institute Inc., 2017, Figure 11-16, Page 396

Plan Risk Responses (Planning)		
Key Inputs	Resource Management Plan	The resource management plan is a component of the project management plan that documents the manner in which the team and physical resources are determined, quantified, and acquired. It is referenced to coordinate resources assigned to risk responses with other resources.

Plan Risk Responses (Continued)		
Key Inputs (Cont.)	Risk Management Plan *How to manage risk*	The risk management plan is a component of the project management plan that details the manner in which risk management activities are configured and implemented. Typically it addresses risk strategy, risk methodology, roles and responsibilities, financing (the budget for risk-related activities, contingent reserves, and management reserves), timing of risk processes, risk classification for grouping individual risks (typically, this is accomplished by using a risk breakdown structure), the probability and impact of individual risks (often supported by a probability and impact matrix), reporting formats, and tracking. It may also include a determination of the manner in which risk thresholds are established and applied.
	Cost Baseline *Every risk has cost*	The cost baseline is the authorized version of the time-phased budget for the project, excluding management reserves, and subject to change control. It contains details related to contingency reserves allocated for risk responses.
	Resource Calendars *Need to know if we have skill set to address risk*	Resource calendars delineate project resource availability and are referenced to allocating resources for risk responses.
	Risk Register	The risk register records each identified risk. It typically includes the potential owner of and potential response(s) to each identified risk and may include a title, category, status, cause(s), trigger(s), impacted activity(ies), date of identification, date range for probable occurrence, and response deadline. It may contain data useful for planning risks responses (root cause, triggers, immediacy, need for analysis) and/or recommended responses.
	Risk Report	The risk report details the origins of overall project risk and recaps key data about unique project risks (typically the number of threats and opportunities and other summary metrics). It includes a prioritized catalogue of all identified risks and a brief overview of project risk and may include an analysis of individual risk distribution. It is referenced since the overall level of project risk and the distribution of individual risks can impact the selection of risk responses.

Plan Risk Responses (Continued)		
Key Tools & Techniques	Expert Judgment	Expert judgment is judgment based on expertise acquired in a specific area. It is often more significant and accurate than the best modeling tools available and can be provided by stakeholders, company personnel external to the project, professional organizations or groups, and consultants. It is important to consider expertise related to risk response strategies (both threat and opportunity), contingent response strategies, and overall project risk strategies.
	Strategies for Threats	Strategies for threats include escalation, avoidance, transference, mitigation, and acceptance.
	Strategies for Opportunities	Strategies for opportunities include escalation, exploitation, sharing, enhancement, and acceptance.
	Contingent Response Strategies	Strategies for contingent risks are defined by the team and are only executed if triggered by predefined events. An example of a contingent risk is failure to meet an intermediate milestone in accordance with the schedule.
	Strategies for Overall Project Risk	Strategies for overall project risk include avoidance, exploitation, transference/sharing, mitigation/ enhancement, and acceptance.
	Alternatives Analysis	Alternatives analysis can be used to compare alternative risk responses to determine the most appropriate response.
	Cost-benefit Analysis	Cost-benefit analysis is a financial tool that determines the scenario that best fits the needs of the project by comparing the cost of each scenario to its expected benefits. If the impact of an individual risk can be quantified, the cost effectiveness of alternative responses can be determined.
Key Outputs	Change Requests	Change requests are requests for modification that have not been formally approved through the change control process. Modifications to the cost and schedule baselines or to other impacted components of the project management plan may be requested.
	Resource Management Plan	The resource management plan is a component of the project management plan that documents the manner in which the team and physical resources are determined, quantified, and acquired. The resource management plan is updated with approved modifications to resource allocation and updates to resource strategy.

Plan Risk Responses (Continued)		
Key Outputs (Cont.)	Scope Baseline	The scope baseline is the authorized version of the scope statement, WBS (to the level of work package with individual identification codes), and WBS dictionary. The scope baseline is subject to change control. The scope baseline is approved with approved changes arising from agreed-upon risk responses.
	Schedule Baseline	The schedule baseline is the authorized version of the schedule model. It contains baseline start and baseline finish dates, is subject to change control, and is used as the basis of comparison to actual results. Approved changes to schedule estimates arising from agreed-upon risk responses update the schedule baseline.
	Cost Baseline	The cost baseline is the authorized version of the time-phased budget for the project, excluding management reserves, and subject to change control. It is evolved from a summation of approved budgets for specific schedule activities. Cost estimates are aggregated by work packages, then into higher components of the work breakdown structure (WBS), and then for the entire project. The cost baseline is updated with approved changes to cost estimates arising from agreed-upon risk responses.
	Assumption Log	The assumption log is a document that lists the assumptions and constraints identified during the creation of the project charter. The assumption log is updated with the addition, modification, or removal of any assumptions and constraints determined during plan risk responses.

Situational Question and Real World Application

Failure to effectively address the Plan Risk Responses process could result in a failure to develop responses and strategies for identified project risks, which could negatively impact the schedule and budget.

Risk Management Known and Unknown Table			
Name	**Created For**	**Description**	**Example**
Contingency Reserves	Known Unknowns	Schedule and budget reserves for risk events whose occurrence can be forecasted.	An event whose occurrence increases the cost of production (a cost increase for materials) and/or increases the project duration (the software architect was ill for two weeks during a critical stage in planning), or scope creep
Management Reserves	Unknown Unknowns	Reserves for risk events whose occurrence cannot be forecasted, but which may occur.	An event such as a natural disaster or terrorist attack.

Know the characteristics of management reserves (unknown unknowns) and contingency reserves (known unknowns).

11.6.1. Risk Owner

The risk owner is the person responsible for implementing the response if a risk event occurs.

Know who risk owners are and what they are responsible for.

11.6.2. Risk Response Strategies

The following strategies are recommended for use in planning risk responses. For the exam, each response type should be recognizable in a situational question (memorization of the types and their characteristics is recommended). A mnemonic device (aid for memorization) is **SEEE** the **ATM**, which contains the initial letters of the response types (share, exploit, enhance, escalate, avoid, transfer, mitigate).

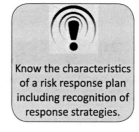

Know the characteristics of a risk response plan including recognition of response strategies.

PMI, CAPM, and PMBOK are registered marks of the Project Management Institute, Inc.

462   © 2008-2018 Crosswind Learning, www.crosswindpm.com

Risk Response Strategies for Positive Risks or Opportunities		
Risk Response Tool	**Description**	**Example**
Share	The share strategy involves **splitting the benefit (and responsibility)** of the risk with a third party to maximize an opportunity (or minimize a threat).	The technology company formed a partnership with a marketing company to launch a sales campaign supporting the product under development.
Exploit	The exploit strategy involves **ensuring the success** of the opportunity or project.	The new project had the best resources assigned to maximize the probability of success.
Enhance	The enhance strategy takes steps to **improve the size or capacity of the risk event** (opportunity) by determining the key components of the risk and maximizing those components.	With sales exceeding projections, the organization hired more sales people to ensure that as many customers as possible knew of their products.
Escalate	The escalation strategy involves **entrusting the opportunity**, which is outside the project scope, to program management, portfolio management, or another relevant area of the organization.	The manager of the project to build a revolutionary new habitat for the zoo's big cats escalated the affiliated funding campaign to the program manager.

Risk Response Strategies for Negative Risks or Threats		
Risk Response Tool	**Description**	**Example**
Avoid	The avoid strategy involves modifying the plan so that risk doesn't have to be considered.	Selecting alternative potential vendors to ensure the organization has sufficient inventory.
Transfer	The transfer strategy **reassigns risk** exposure **to another party.** Note that all risk is not necessarily eliminated and that additional risk might be created.	**Example #1:** Hiring an outside organization to produce a product component rather than building the component **Example #2:** Buying insurance against the risk
Mitigate	The mitigate strategy involves minimizing the negative characteristics of the risk.	Eliminating outside sources and doing work internally mitigates the risk of the vendor failing to produce project deliverables in a timely manner.

Risk Response Strategies for both Positive and Negative Risks		
Risk Response Tool	**Description**	**Example**
Acceptance	The acceptance strategy involves **tolerating the risk**. It is a valid option if there are no other options available.	Determining that, if a union goes on strike, the project will have to be delayed until the strike is settled.

Note that there is active acceptance, which involves a risk response, and passive, which does not involve a risk response.

Contingent Response Strategy		
Risk Response Tool	**Description**	**Example**
Contingent Response Strategy	The contingent response strategy involves defining responses that will only be enacted if triggered by predefined events, such as a change in project conditions or the need to accommodate worst-case situations.	The team developed a contingency plan to add staff to the project if the important development milestone was missed.

The source for the above text is the Project Management Institute, *A Guide to the Project Management Body of Knowledge*, (*PMBOK® Guide*) – Sixth Edition, Project Management Institute Inc., 2017, Pages 395-406

11.7. Implement Risk Responses (Executing Process Group)

Know the Key Inputs, Tools & Techniques, and Outputs for Implement Risk Responses.

During the Implement Risk Responses process, risk response plans are implemented.

Note that implementation of a specific risk response may result in residual risk (risk remaining after implementation of a risk response) and/or secondary risk (risk resulting from implementation of a risk response).

Also note that if the risk response is not effective, a work-around may be necessary.

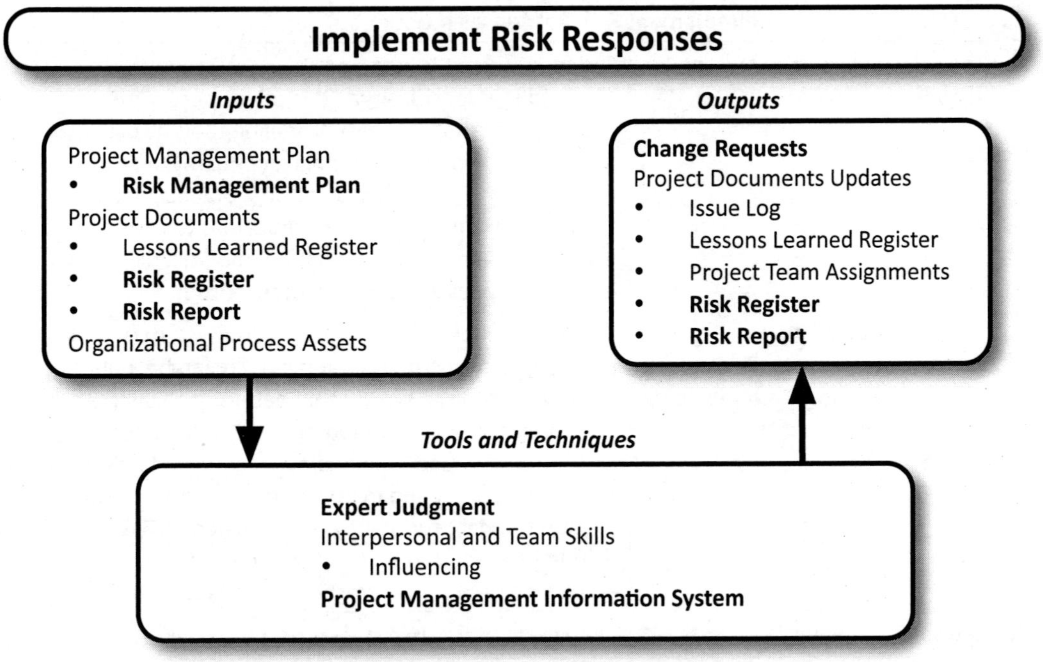

Implement Risk Responses

Inputs

Project Management Plan
- **Risk Management Plan**

Project Documents
- Lessons Learned Register
- **Risk Register**
- **Risk Report**

Organizational Process Assets

Outputs

Change Requests
Project Documents Updates
- Issue Log
- Lessons Learned Register
- Project Team Assignments
- **Risk Register**
- **Risk Report**

Tools and Techniques

Expert Judgment
Interpersonal and Team Skills
- Influencing

Project Management Information System

Figure 11-14: Implement Risk Responses Data Flow Diagram
The source for the above figure is the Project Management Institute, *A Guide to the Project Management Body of Knowledge*, (*PMBOK® Guide*) – Sixth Edition, Project Management Institute Inc., 2017, Figure 11-18, Page 406

Implement Risk Responses (Executing)		
Key Inputs	Risk Management Plan	The risk management plan is a component of the project management plan that details the manner in which risk management activities are configured and implemented. Because it addresses risk thresholds and roles and responsibilities, the plan is referenced during the assignment of risk response ownership and during the identification of acceptable risk response outcomes.
	Risk Register	The risk register records each identified risk. It typically includes the potential owner of and potential response(s) to each identified risk and may include a title, category, status, cause(s), trigger(s), impacted activity(ies), date(s) of identification, date range for probable occurrence, and response deadline(s).
	Risk Report	The risk report details the origins of overall project risk and risk response strategy. It recaps key data about unique project risks (typically the number of threats and opportunities and other summary metrics) and is updated with information related to risks with the highest risk scores. The risk report also includes a prioritized catalogue of all identified risks and a brief overview of project risk.

	Implement Risk Responses (Continued)	
Key Tools & Techniques	Expert Judgment	Expert judgment is judgment based on expertise acquired in a specific area. It is often more significant and accurate than the best modeling tools available and can be provided by stakeholders, company personnel external to the project, professional organizations or groups, and consultants. It is important to consider expertise related to the validation, modification, and effective implementation of risk responses.
	Project Management Information System	The project management information system (PMIS) is an enterprise environmental factor. It can be a portal to automated tools, a system that gathers and distributes information, a configuration management system, and/or an interface to online automated systems that are used to direct and manage project work. It can include software for managing the schedule, costs, and resources which can be utilized to integrate activities associated with the risk response plan into the project.
Key Outputs	Change Requests	Change requests are requests for modification that have not been formally approved through the change control process. Modifications to the budget and schedule baselines or other impacted components of the project management may be requested
	Risk Register	The risk register is updated with individual project risk information updated during Monitor Risks.
	Risk Report	The risk report is updated to show the current status of major individual risks and the current level of overall project risk. If the report contains details of the top individual risks, agreed-upon responses, and owners, that information is also updated if applicable.

Situational Question and Real World Application

Failure to effectively address the Implement Risk Responses process could result in a failure to avert or minimize negative project risks or in a failure to take advantage of positive project risks.

11.7.1. Residual Risk

Residual risk is the **amount of risk remaining after a risk response (from the risk response plan) has been implemented.** For example, in a medical situation, residual risk is the risk that remains after the treatment.

11.7.2. Secondary Risk

Secondary risk is risk that **results from the implementation of a risk response.** In the medical situation, secondary risk is a side effect that occurs as a result of the treatment.

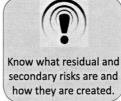

Know what residual and secondary risks are and how they are created.

11.7.3. Work-around

A work-around is an action taken when the risk response(s) and any backup plans don't work.

Know what a workaround is in relation to Plan Risk Responses.

The source for the above text is the Project Management Institute, *A Guide to the Project Management Body of Knowledge, (PMBOK® Guide) – Sixth Edition,* Project Management Institute Inc., 2017, Pages 406-409

11.8. Monitor Risks (Monitoring and Controlling Process Group)

During the Monitor Risks process, the project manager and team focus on **observing the project activities for risks, risk triggers, and appropriate risk responses.**

It can also include verifying that project assumptions are still applicable, the occurrence of any trends, and a determination of contingency reserves for the schedule and budget.

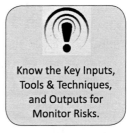

Know the Key Inputs, Tools & Techniques, and Outputs for Monitor Risks.

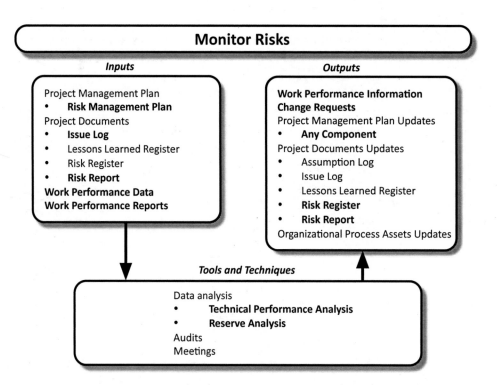

Figure 11-15: Monitor Risks Data Flow Diagram

The source for the above figure is the Project Management Institute, *A Guide to the Project Management Body of Knowledge*, (*PMBOK® Guide*) – Sixth Edition, Project Management Institute Inc., 2017, Figure 11-20, Page 410

Monitor Risks (Monitoring and Controlling)		
Key Inputs	Risk Management Plan	The risk management plan is a component of the project management plan that details the manner in which risk management activities are configured and implemented. Typically it addresses risk strategy, risk methodology, roles and responsibilities, financing (the budget for risk-related activities, contingent reserves, and management reserves), timing of risk processes, risk classification for grouping individual risks (typically, this is accomplished by using a risk breakdown structure), the probability and impact of individual risks (often supported by a probability and impact matrix), reporting formats, and tracking. It delineates the timing and manner in which risks are reviewed and addresses the review procedures, roles and responsibilities, and format for review-related reporting.
	Issue Log	The issue log is used to record and track any project challenges that cannot be immediately resolved. Issue-related information is communicated to affected stakeholders. The log is periodically reviewed for updates that may impact the risk register

PMI, CAPM, and PMBOK are registered marks of the Project Management Institute, Inc.

468   © 2008-2018 Crosswind Learning, www.crosswindpm.com

Monitor Risks (Continued)		
Key Inputs (Cont.)	Risk Report	The risk report details the origins of overall project risk and recaps key data about unique project risks (typically the number of threats and opportunities and other summary metrics). It is updated with information related to risks with the highest risk scores. The risk report also includes a prioritized catalogue of all identified risks and their owner, as well as a brief overview of project risk.
	Work Performance Data	Work performance data represents the raw metrics and observations identified during the performance of project work activities. It also includes data regarding risks that occurred, risks that are active, risks that have been closed out, and risk responses that have been executed.
	Work Performance Reports	Work performance reports are representations, either physical or electronic, of work performance information and are used as the basis for decisions and/or actions. The reports can include **variance analysis**, **earned value data**, and **forecasting data**. This information may be pertinent to performance-related risk.
Key Tools & Techniques	Technical Performance Analysis	Technical performance analysis is the comparison of actual technical performance to targeted technical performance. An anomaly may signify risk. Note that technical performance measurements may include **velocity**, **capacity**, and **accuracy.**
	Reserve Analysis	Reserve analysis is used to determine the amount of contingency reserves required for the project. If a risk does occur that impacts the budget or schedule contingency reserve, reserve analysis can be used to compare the remaining contingency to the remaining project risk. A burndown chart may be used to depict the comparison.
Key Outputs	Work Performance Information	Work performance information includes information regarding the performance of risk management, specifically the effectiveness of planning and implementing risk responses.
	Change Requests	Change requests are requests for modification that have not been formally approved through the change control process. They can include actions that would prevent or correct the impact of individual risks or overall project risk. Modifications to the cost and schedule baselines or other impacted components of the project management plan may be requested.

Monitor Risks (Continued)		
Key Outputs (Cont.)	Any Component of the Project Management Plan	Changes to the project management plan are subject to the change control process. Authorized changes are used to update the plan so that it reflects the current approach to, and state of, the project.
	Risk Register	Each identified risk is recorded in the risk register. It typically includes the potential owner of and potential response(s) to each identified risk and may include a title, category, status, cause(s), trigger(s), impacted activity(ies), date of identification, date range for probable occurrence, and response deadline. It is updated with new information related to each risk, including the probability and impact evaluation, priority level, score, owner, urgency, and category.
	Risk Report	The risk report details the origins of overall project risk and recaps key data about unique project risks (typically the number of threats and opportunities and other summary metrics). The risk report also includes a prioritized catalogue of all identified risks and a brief overview of project risk. It is updated with information related to risks with the highest risk scores and the current status of major risks and overall project risk.

Situational Question and Real World Application
Failure to effectively perform the Monitor Risk process can result in a reactive environment. Instead of prioritizing risks by impact and probability, determining cogent risk responses, and anticipating risk occurrences based on triggers, each risk would be addressed as it occurred without any planning and with no regard for the urgency or impact of the risk.

The source for the above text is the Project Management Institute, *A Guide to the Project Management Body of Knowledge*, (*PMBOK® Guide*) – Sixth Edition, Project Management Institute Inc., 2017, Pages 409-414

11.9.   Project Risk Management Formulas and Variables

Description	Formula	Variable (Components)	Example
The sum of all probabilities for outcome of an event must equal 1.0.	Total Probabilities = Sum of all probabilities	N/A	Outcome A = 0.5 Outcome B = 0.3 Outcome C = 0.2 Totals equal 1.0
EMV is expected monetary value. Here, the probability of the outcome is multiplied by the impact, and then the products of the outcome are summed for a total EMV of the decision.	Probability x Impact (summed)	Probability = P Impact = I Expected Monetary Value = EMV	Outcome A = 0.5 x $100 Outcome B = 0.3 x $300 Outcome C = 0.2 x $300 Total probabilities equal 1.0 and EMV equals $200

11.10.   Project Risk Management Terminology

Term	Description
Analytical Techniques	Techniques used to evaluate, analyze or forecast potential outcomes based on project variables and relationships among those variables
Contingency	A possible event that could negatively impact the project and is typically neutralized by accessing the time or cost reserve established for that purpose
Contingency Allowance	An allowance or reserve, typically related to the budget or schedule, set aside to compensate for unanticipated events
Contingency Reserve	Funds set aside for unforeseen events that can negatively effect the project
Contingent Response Strategies	The tactics that will be employed if a specific risk trigger occurs
Data Gathering and Representation Techniques	The collection, organization, and presentation of data and information
Decision Tree Analysis	A technique used to assess possible responses to a threat or opportunity in order to make the best decision; it involves diagramming the options and noting the expected monetary value (EMV) potential of each option
Document Analysis	The evaluation of current documentation related to project risk
Expected Monetary Value	A statistical technique, typically applied in decision tree analysis, used to determine the average outcome when contingent scenarios for future project risks must be considered
Fallback Plan	The plan that will supersede the original plan if it is not effective

Term	Description
Identify Risks	The process of identifying the risks that can impact the project and documenting their attributes
Implement Risk Responses	The process of determining the actions that will be taken should a threat or opportunity arise within the project
Management Reserve	Funds set aside for unanticipated project work and excluded from the performance measurement baseline
Modeling	The process of evaluating counterfeit situations to determine their impact on the project
Monitor Risks	The process of monitoring the implementation of risk response plans, tracking identified risks, identifying and analyzing new risks, and evaluating risk process effectiveness
Monte Carlo Simulation	A process that simulates possible project schedule or cost outcomes; often used to estimate required reserves based on the scatter diagram or probability table that is typically the output of the process
Multicriteria Decision Analysis	A process that utilizes a decision matrix to systematically analyze project information such as risk levels, uncertainty, value, and prioritization
Opportunity	A risk whose occurrence will result in a positive impact on the project
Overall Project Risk	The impact that uncertainty, including the cumulative effect of individual risks, has on the project; the exposure of stakeholders to the implications of variations in project outcome, both positive and negative
Perform Qualitative Risk Analysis	The process of ranking risks for additional evaluation based on the probability of each risk and the impact on the project if the risk occurs
Perform Quantitative Risk Analysis	The process of numerically evaluating the impact of identified risks on the project
Plan Risk Management	The process of determining the methods that will be used to execute project risk management activities
Plan Risk Responses	The process of determining the actions that will be taken should a threat or opportunity arise within the project
Probability and Impact Matrix	An array used in qualitative risk management to prioritize risk, typically based on each risk's probability of occurrence and potential impact
Project Risk Management	The process required to plan for, determine, evaluate, respond to, and control potential or actual project threats and opportunities
Quantitative Risk Analysis and Modeling Techniques	Common approaches to producing a more detailed evaluation of project risk; techniques include expected monetary value (EMV) and decision tree analysis
Reserve	Funds set aside for risks to the budget or schedule, for example management reserves or contingency reserves, as provided for in the project management plan
Reserve Analysis	An analysis technique used to identify the critical features and relationships of components in order to determine the amount of reserves realistically needed for the project with consideration of schedule duration, budget, and cost estimation
Residual Risk	The remaining risk following the implementation of risk responses
Risk	An unscheduled, but possible, event that may have a positive or negative impact on the project if it occurs
Risk Acceptance	A risk response strategy that involves acknowledgment only of the risk; no planned response is formulated unless the risk occurs

Term	Description
Risk Appetite	The amount of uncertainty an organization or individual is willing to accept in anticipation of a reward
Risk Audits	The evaluation of project risk responses to determine the effectiveness of the utilized approach to risk
Risk Avoidance	A risk response strategy that involves the elimination of the threat or protection of the project from the impact of the threat
Risk Breakdown Structure (RBS)	A representation of risks ranked by category
Risk Categorization	The organization of risks by source or other criteria to increase understanding of overall project risk
Risk Category	A class of risks, such as organizational risks or market risks, defined by its potential cause
Risk Data Quality Assessment	An evaluation of risk-associated data to determine its quality
Risk Database	A data repository that stores and manipulates information associated with the risk management processes
Risk Enhancement	A risk response strategy that increases the probability of occurrence or impact of an opportunity as a result of deliberate team action
Risk Escalation	A risk response strategy that transfers ownership of the risk from the project team to a higher organizational level for more effective management
Risk Events	Events that may impact the project (either negative or positive)
Risk Exploiting	A risk response strategy that ensures the occurrence of an opportunity as a result of deliberate team action
Risk Exposure	A quantified potential for loss or gain at any given time during the project
Risk Factors	Numbers representing the risk of certain events, the likelihood of their occurring, plus the impact on the project (if the event does occur)
Risk Management Plan	The document, part of the project or program management plan, used to describe the manner in which risk management activities will be framed and executed
Risk Mitigation	A risk response strategy that involves the reduction of the threat or the probability that the risk will occur
Risk Owner	The person responsible for the monitoring of a risk and for the determination and implementation of an appropriate risk response strategy
Risk Register	A document that lists each risk along with the results of its analysis and risk response planning
Risk Reassessment	The process of identifying new risks, reassessing risks that have already been identified, and closing of expired risks
Risk Report	A project document that establishes the progressive development of risk management processes throughout the project, summarizes individual project risk information, and delineates the degree of overall project risk
Risk Review	A meeting used to examine and document the effectiveness of risk responses in relation to identified, individual project risks and to overall project risk
Risk Seeking	Possessing a higher tolerance than most for risk
Risk Sharing	A risk responses strategy that allocates ownership of an opportunity from the project team to a third party who is best able to capture the benefits of that opportunity
Risk Symptoms	Characteristics which indicate that a risk event is possibly starting to occur; could also be called risk triggers

Term	Description
Risk Threshold	The degree of risk exposure that defines the upper limit of risk acceptance; risks whose level exceed the threshold must be addressed
Risk Tolerance	The level of risk that an individual or organization is willing to permit; also known as risk utility
Risk Transference	A risk response strategy that involves shifting the impact of a threat, as well as accountability for the response, to a third party
Risk Urgency Assessment	The evaluation of risk responses to determine priority in order of timing
Risk-averse	Possessing a low desire or tolerance for risk
Risk-neutral	A middle ground between the risk taken and the benefit received
Root Cause Analysis	An analytical technique used to ascertain the fundamental reason a variance, defect, or risk exists
Secondary Risk	A risk that results from a risk response implementation
Sensitivity Analysis	A quantitative risk analysis and modeling technique used to identify those risks that have the greatest effect on the project
Simulation	A project computer model that can counterfeit the project outcome when there is uncertainty associated with schedule, cost or resources
Strengths, Weaknesses, Opportunities, and Threats (SWOT) Analysis	A risk analysis technique which considers the strengths, weaknesses, opportunities, and threats of the project to facilitate a more knowledgeable risk management analysis
Threat	A risk whose occurrence will result in a negative impact on the project
Trigger Condition	An indicator that a risk event could occur
Workaround	A response to a risk that was unplanned or that had an ineffective planned response

The source for the above definitions is the Glossary of the Project Management Institute,
A Guide to the Project Management Body of Knowledge, (*PMBOK® Guide*) – Sixth Edition, Project Management Institute Inc., 2017

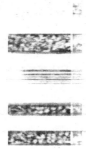

11.11. Project Risk Management Tests and Exercises

11.11.1. Project Risk Management Practice Test

Answers are in section 11.12.1.

1. Calculate EMV from the following: 0.4 probability of $6,500, 0.3 probability of -$3,200, 0.2 probability of $2,000, 0.1 probability of $1,000.

   (A) $10,500
   (B) $2,700
   (C) $2,140
   (D) $2,500

2. In defining a risk trigger, which of the following is most accurate?

   (A) A trigger is an indication that a risk event could occur in the near future
   (B) A trigger is the same as a risk
   (C) A trigger is an indicator that a risk event has definitely occurred
   (D) A trigger is an indicator that a risk event will definitely occur

3. The telecom project is scheduled to run until year's end. There is a strong possibility that the union collective bargaining agreement will not be renewed immediately upon its expiration next month. Union negotiation is outside the control of senior management and the project, so senior management has decided to reassign the job responsibilities of union personnel to non-union personnel to minimize project schedule slippage. Of the following, what best describes the type of risk response represented by this decision?

   (A) Risk avoidance, which avoids negative risk by taking actions to prevent it
   (B) Risk transference, which avoids negative risk by transferring or reassigning responsibilities
   (C) Risk mitigation, which mitigates negative risk by taking actions to lessen its impact
   (D) Risk acceptance, which accepts negative risk and has a plan to deal with it if it occurs

4. The company is concerned about its position during the economic downturn. Its CEO is a risk taker. Of several strategies on the table for consideration, which is he most likely to pursue?

   (A) Mandating that senior management lay the ground work for a reduction in force in the event it is necessary
   (B) Entering a relatively untested market in the hope of significant reward
   (C) Trying new markets that do not require significant investment while mandating traditional "belt-tightening" procedures
   (D) None of the answers

5. In discussing risk with his project team, the project manager begins the conversation by defining risk. Which of the following is the most accurate definition of risk?

(A) A possible negative event that can impact the project
(B) A possible positive event that can impact the project
(C) Answers (A) and (B)
(D) A negative issue that occurs as a result of uncertain factors

6. A film distribution company involved in global expansion has a chief marketing officer who is familiar with cutting edge marketing techniques and strategies. The marketing project for the expansion is set to rollout in 10 countries via the Internet and cable television. It's discovered that the chief marketing officer has been embezzling from the company for the last 90 days to help a terminally ill relative. Senior management is extremely concerned because this person knows more about this type of campaign than anyone in the industry and it doesn't want to impact the company negatively. Which of the following best represents a risk acceptance strategy based on the discovery of the embezzling?

(A) Allow him to remain at the company because the embezzlement was not done for personal gain
(B) Allow him to remain in his position and reimburse the company for the amount embezzled plus all incidental expenses
(C) Terminate him, file felony theft charges, and have someone different run the campaign
(D) Terminate him and outsource the marketing function to an ad agency

7. The project manager and the team have made risk-related contract decisions and updated the risk register and project management plan. Which of the following best describes the process they have just completed?

(A) Identify risks, which entails determining what risks and triggers could occur on the project
(B) Plan risk responses, which entails determining what will be done if risk events occur and who will be responsible for executing those actions
(C) Control risks management, which entails observing project activities for risks and risk triggers and implementing the means to control them
(D) Perform qualitative risk analysis, which entails assigning probability and impact ratings to each risk

8. In response to economic and market changes, the company is moving from a conservative strategy to a more market-driven strategy. As a result of this change, the company has just approved a project that aligns with the new strategy. A number of the stakeholders, however, are still risk-averse. The project manager is meeting with them to explain his risk management plan. The stakeholders are very interested in the concept of a risk review. Which of the following best describes a risk review?

(A) The process of determining the project risks
(B) The process of determining the characteristics of the project risks
(C) The process of determining the validity of the documented risks and looking for new risks that could occur
(D) The process of determining who will implement a risk response plan

9. The project manager and the team created change requests as a result of unforeseen occurrences. Which of the following best describes the process they have just completed?

(A) Identify risks, which entails determining what risks and triggers could occur on the project
(B) Plan risk responses, which entails determining what will be done if risk events occur and who will be responsible for executing those actions
(C) Monitor risks, which entails observing project activities for risks and risk triggers and implementing the means to control them
(D) Perform qualitative risk analysis, which entails assigning probability and impact ratings to each risk

10. The reservation system has been working well. Today, the main database engine crashed, preventing the airline from creating reservations for its flights. The risk response didn't fix the problem, so the airline must respond. Which of the following should it perform first?

(A) Fix the problem with a work-around
(B) Determine why the risk response plan failed
(C) Adjust the risk response plan
(D) Determine why the problem occurred

11. Perform qualitative risk analysis uses a variety of tools for analysis. Which of the following is most closely associated with this process?

(A) A probability and impact matrix
(B) The expected monetary value (EMV) formula
(C) Templates for work-around documentation
(D) Risk trigger determination

12. The makers of the video game are making a new version. It's key to have it released in time for the holiday shopping season. The project manager is monitoring the schedule and has noticed that an event has been triggered showing there is a high probability the schedule will slip. The project manager follows the plan and brings in 4 new contract programmers to help get it back on track. What process is she doing?

(A) Planning risk responses
(B) Updating the risk management plan
(C) Monitoring risks
(D) Implementing risk responses

13. Perform quantitative risk analysis uses a variety of tools for analysis. Which of the following is most closely associated with this process?

(A) A probability and impact matrix
(B) The expected monetary value (EMV) formula
(C) Templates for work-around documentation
(D) Risk trigger recognition reporting

14. Of the following, which best describes a secondary risk?

(A) A vendor was unable to fulfill a contract commitment by the due date in the contract
(B) A vendor was unable to fulfill a contract commitment by the due date in the contract due to a strike
(C) A vendor was unable to fulfill a contract commitment by the due date in the contract because a sub-contractor delivered a defective product
(D) A vendor was unable to fulfill a contract commitment by the due date in the contract, so the team chose another vendor that also could not meet the due date because of the late start

15. If a risk on the project has a high probability of occurring and a high-impact if it does occur, the project team will more than likely do what?

(A) Determine the insurable risk amount
(B) Perform qualitative risk analysis
(C) Determine the pure risk amount
(D) Perform quantitative risk analysis

16. The construction company has been awarded a $40M contract to build an upscale community shopping center. Of the following, which is the best example of an exploit type of risk response strategy?

   (A) The company hires inexperienced workers and pays them only 25% of the salary received by union workers
   (B) The company realizes the adjoining land will increase in value upon completion of the project, so it purchases the adjoining land at current prices
   (C) The company purchases materials below the grade specified in the contract, although satisfying local building standards
   (D) The company hires inexperienced workers and pays them scale, but does not provide the benefits given to the union workers

17. The project manager is discussing risk with a risk-averse stakeholder regarding the market expansion project. The stakeholder has been exposed to project management concepts, but wants to know more about management reserves. The project manager explains that management reserves are created specifically for…

   (A) Risk events you know can occur on the project
   (B) Risk events you cannot logically forecast for the project
   (C) Risk events that do occur with a cumulative cost greater than the amount set aside in management reserves
   (D) Risk events that do occur with a cumulative cost greater than the amount set aside in contingency reserves

18. The mobile application transition project is going basically as planned, but a market related risk has occurred: two competitors have merged. While a possible merger was anticipated, there was a great deal of uncertainty as to which competitors would be involved. The team has identified the potential impact. Which of the following will graphically demonstrate the impact to the project and company?

   (A) Probability and impact matrix
   (B) Tornado diagram
   (C) Expected monetary value
   (D) Risk register

19. The project management team has just completed the process of identifying risks on the project. They have broken the information into categories and displayed this information in a graphical format. What have they created?

   (A) Prioritized list of quantified risks
   (B) Risk breakdown structure
   (C) Risk probabilities and impact matrix
   (D) Risk checklist analysis chart

20. The project manager is discussing risk with a risk-averse stakeholder on the market expansion project. The stakeholder has been exposed to project management concepts, but wants to know more about contingency reserves. The project manager explains that contingency reserves are created specifically for...

(A) Risk events you know can occur on the project
(B) Risk events you cannot logically forecast for the project
(C) Risk events that do occur with a cumulative cost greater than the amount set aside in management reserves
(D) Risk events that do occur with a cumulative cost greater than the amount set aside in contingency reserves

21. The risk management plan is created to help the team identify risks and triggers, establish risk responses, establish risk owners and their responsibilities, and plan the control and monitoring of risk and risk responses. Two documents are typically created within the plan and used within separate risk processes. Select the two documents and the associated processes.

(A) The risk breakdown structure used in the identify risks process and the risk probabilities and impact-rating matrix used in the perform quantitative risk analysis process
(B) The risk breakdown structure used in the identify risks process and the probabilities table used in the perform quantitative risk analysis process
(C) The risk breakdown structure used in the identify risks process and the probabilities table used in the perform qualitative risk analysis process
(D) The risk breakdown structure used in the identify risks process and the risk probabilities and impact rating matrix used in the perform qualitative risk analysis process

22. The construction company has been awarded a $20M contract to build a shopping community center. The company is relatively small, and this contract is bigger than anything it has been awarded to date. To ensure that it can effectively complete the contract and not jeopardize other work, it has chosen to pursue a share strategy. Of the following, which is the best example of the share strategy?

(A) The company subcontracts the finishing work to a company with large cash reserves
(B) The company partners with a company that specializes in foundation and concrete work
(C) The company assigns its best employees to the shopping center contract and uses the remaining employees and day workers from Employee Share, Inc. for its other projects
(D) None of the answers

23. Your company is evaluating two projects for consideration. Project A has a 40% probability of $69,000 and a 60% probability of -$10,000. Project B has a 60% probability of $56,000 and a 40% probability of -$15,000. Which of the projects do you select based on the greatest expected monetary value?

(A) Project A
(B) Project B
(C) Project A and B are of even value
(D) The expected monetary value is not high enough on either to make a selection

24. The database project team members are planning the project. They are involved in planning risk responses and assigning risk owners. What will the risk owner potentially do next?

(A) Watch for additional risks on the project
(B) Watch for risk triggers and tell the project manager when they occur
(C) Let the project manager know that the risk has occurred
(D) Implement a risk response if the risk event occurs

25. The company is concerned about its position during the economic downturn. Its CEO is risk-averse. Of several strategies on the table for consideration, which is he most likely to pursue?

(A) Mandating that senior management lay the ground work for a reduction in force in the event it is necessary
(B) Entering a relatively untested market in the hope of significant reward
(C) Trying new markets that do not require significant investment while mandating traditional "belt-tightening" procedures
(D) None of the answers

26. A film distribution company involved in global expansion has a chief marketing officer who is familiar with cutting edge marketing techniques and strategies. The marketing project for the expansion is set to rollout in 10 countries via the Internet and cable television. An account manager discovers that the chief marketing officer has been embezzling from the company for the last 90 days to help a terminally ill relative. During risk management execution, which of the following best represents an escalation strategy?

(A) Confront the senior marketing manager about his actions
(B) Allow him to remain in his position and reimburse the company for the amount embezzled plus all incidental expenses
(C) Terminate him, file felony theft charges, and have someone different run the campaign
(D) Update the CEO with the details of what you have discovered

27. Sheldon is doing quantitative risk analysis on his project. He has gotten resistance from his sponsor about doing this. Which of the following best describes why he would want to do this type of risk analysis?

(A) On higher probability, higher impact risks
(B) On new types of projects where there is a greater degree of uncertainty
(C) On higher probability, higher impact risks, or new types of projects where there is a great degree of uncertainty
(D) Any risk that has financial impact

28. The project manager and the team are performing the identify risks process. They have learned recently that risk categorization will help organize risks better and potentially allow them to see risks that might have been missed otherwise. Which of the following is the best example of risk categories?

(A) Initiating, planning, executing, monitoring and controlling, closing
(B) Scope, time, cost
(C) Quality, schedule, budget
(D) External, internal, technology, personnel

29. A film distribution company involved in global expansion has a chief marketing officer who is familiar with cutting edge marketing techniques and strategies. The marketing project for the expansion is set to rollout in 10 countries via the Internet and cable television. It's discovered that the chief marketing officer has been embezzling from the company for the last 90 days to help a terminally ill relative. Senior management is extremely concerned because this person knows more about this type of campaign than anyone in the industry and it doesn't want to impact the company negatively. During risk management execution, which of the following best represents an avoidance strategy associated with the embezzlement?

(A) Allow him to remain at the company because the embezzlement was not done for personal gain
(B) Allow him to remain in his position and reimburse the company for the amount embezzled plus all incidental expenses
(C) Terminate him, file felony theft charges, and have someone different run the campaign
(D) Terminate him and outsource the marketing function to an ad agency

30. The project manager and the team created the risk register. Which of the following best describes the process they have just completed?

   (A) Identify risks, which entails determining what risks and triggers could occur on the project
   (B) Plan risk responses, which entails determining what will be done if risk events occur and who will be responsible for executing those actions
   (C) Monitor risks, which entails observing project activities for risks and risk triggers and implementing the means to control them
   (D) Perform qualitative risk analysis, which entails assigning probability and impact ratings to each risk

11.12. Project Risk Management Answers for Tests and Exercises

11.12.1. Project Risk Management Practice Test Answers

We recommend that you download answer sheets from the Crosswind website, so you can practice the test as many times as you like.

1. Calculate EMV from the following: 0.4 probability of $6,500, 0.3 probability of -$3,200, 0.2 probability of $2,000, 0.1 probability of $1,000.

Correct Answer: (C) $2,140
Explanation: To calculate the expected monetary value (EMV), multiply each probability by its dollar amount and add the products of all multiplication. The result is a value of $2,140. [Crosswind Manual 11.5.4; *PMBOK® Guide* 11.4.2.5]

2. In defining a risk trigger, which of the following is most accurate?

Correct Answer: (A) A trigger is an indication that a risk event could occur in the near future
Explanation: A trigger is an indication that a risk event could occur in the near future. Just because a trigger occurs, don't automatically assume that the risk will occur. [Crosswind Manual 11.3.3; No *PMBOK® Guide* Reference]

3. The telecom project is scheduled to run until year's end. There is a strong possibility that the union collective bargaining agreement will not be renewed immediately upon its expiration next month. Union negotiation is outside the control of senior management and the project, so senior management has decided to reassign the job responsibilities of union personnel to non-union personnel to minimize project schedule slippage. Of the following, what best describes the type of risk response represented by this decision?

Correct Answer: (C) Risk mitigation, which mitigates negative risk by taking actions to lessen its impact
Explanation: Risk mitigation attempts to minimize the bad risk or maximize the good risk. In this case, management is attempting to minimize the impact of a labor strike. Risk acceptance simply deals with the risk if it occurs. Risk avoidance involves doing what can be done to eliminate the risk. Transference assigns or transfers the risk to some external party. [Crosswind Manual 11.6.2; *PMBOK® Guide* 11.5.5.3]

4. The company is concerned about its position during the economic downturn. Its CEO is a risk taker. Of several strategies on the table for consideration, which is he most likely to pursue?

Correct Answer: (B) Entering a relatively untested market in the hope of significant reward
Explanation: A risk seeker mentality is that of looking for the big reward and being prepared to pay significantly if it is missed. The risk-averse mentality is a very conservative approach to risk. A risk-neutral mentality is somewhere between that of a risk seeker and risk-averse mentality. [Crosswind Manual 11.2.7; No *PMBOK® Guide* Reference]

5.	In discussing risk with his project team, the project manager begins the conversation by defining risk. Which of the following is the most accurate definition of risk?

Correct Answer: (C) Answers (A) and (B)
(A) A possible negative event that can impact the project
(B) A possible positive event that can impact the project

Explanation: Risk can be of negative or positive consequence on a project. It is something that can occur but hasn't yet. Risk involves uncertainty with regard to what could occur, not what has occurred. [Crosswind Manual 11.1; *PMBOK® Guide* Chapter 11 Introduction]

6.	A film distribution company involved in global expansion has a chief marketing officer who is familiar with cutting edge marketing techniques and strategies. The marketing project for the expansion is set to rollout in 10 countries via the Internet and cable television. It's discovered that the chief marketing officer has been embezzling from the company for the last 90 days to help a terminally ill relative. Senior management is extremely concerned because this person knows more about this type of campaign than anyone in the industry and it doesn't want to impact the company negatively. Which of the following best represents a risk acceptance strategy based on the discovery of the embezzling?

Correct Answer: (A) Allow him to remain at the company because the embezzlement was not done for personal gain
Explanation: Allowing him to stay because he did not use the money for personal gain would be to accept (or tolerate) the risk. Allowing him to stay at the company and pay back the amount represents an attempt to mitigate (or minimize) risk, but it could still occur again. An avoidance strategy is the strategy that eliminates the risk, i.e. terminating him to eliminate further exposure and having someone else run the campaign is the best answer in terms of an avoidance strategy. Outsourcing the work is a transference strategy. [Crosswind Manual 11.6.2; *PMBOK® Guide* 11.5.5.3]

7.	The project manager and the team have made risk-related contract decisions and updated the risk register and project management plan. Which of the following best describes the process they have just completed?

Correct Answer: (B) Plan risk responses, which entails determining what will be done if risk events occur and who will be responsible for executing those actions
Explanation: Plan Risk Responses documents who should do what if risk events occur. Identify Risks is the process of determining what risks and triggers could occur on the project. Monitor Risks focuses on observing project activities for risk triggers and risks and implementing the means to control them. Perform Qualitative Risk Analysis assigns probability and impact ratings to the risk. [Crosswind Manual 11.7; *PMBOK® Guide* 11.6]

8.   In response to economic and market changes, the company is moving from a conservative strategy to a more market-driven strategy. As a result of this change, the company has just approved a project that aligns with the new strategy. A number of the stakeholders, however, are still risk-averse. The project manager is meeting with them to explain his risk management plan. The stakeholders are very interested in the concept of a risk review. Which of the following best describes a risk review?

Correct Answer: (C) The process of determining the validity of the documented risks and looking for any new risks that could occur

Explanation: Risk reviews verify that the risks are still valid and that no new risks have appeared on the project. The other answers come before or after risk reviews. [Crosswind Manual 11.3.4; *PMBOK® Guide* 11.2.3.1]

9.   The project manager and the team created change requests as a result of unforeseen occurrences. Which of the following best describes the process they have just completed?

Correct Answer: (C) Monitor risks, which entails observing project activities for risks and risk triggers and implementing the means to control them

Explanation: Monitor Risks focuses on observing project activities for risk triggers and risks and implementing the means to control them. Plan Risk Responses documents who should do what if risk events occur. Identify Risks is the process of determining what risks and triggers could occur on the project. Perform Qualitative Risk Analysis assigns probability and impact ratings to the risk. [Crosswind Manual 11.8; *PMBOK® Guide* 11.7]

10.   The reservation system has been working well. Today, the main database engine crashed, preventing the airline from creating reservations for its flights. The risk response didn't fix the problem, so the airline must respond. Which of the following should it perform first?

Correct Answer: (A) Fix the problem with a work-around

Explanation: This is a chicken or the egg question in that you more than likely will do all the answers, but what comes first? Fixing the problem, then determining why the risk response plan failed, and why the problem occurred, then adjusting the risk response plan is the sequence for the other answers. [Crosswind Manual 11.7.3; No *PMBOK® Guide* Reference]

11.   Perform qualitative risk analysis uses a variety of tools for analysis. Which of the following is most closely associated with this process?

Correct Answer: (A) A probability and impact matrix

Explanation: Perform Qualitative Risk Analysis uses a risk rating matrix to rank risks and create an overall risk rating for the project. Expected monetary value (EMV) is used in Perform Quantitative Risk Analysis. The other answers are distracters. [Crosswind Manual 11.4; *PMBOK® Guide* 11.3]

12. The makers of the video game are making a new version. It's key to have it released in time for the holiday shopping season. The project manager is monitoring the schedule and has noticed that an event has been triggered showing there is a high probability the schedule will slip. The project manager follows the plan and brings in 4 new contract programmers to help get it back on track. What process is she doing?

Correct Answer: (D) Implementing risk responses
Explanation: The process being described is implementing risk responses. Planning risk responses is where they establish what will be done if needed. Updating the risk management plan is not a process, but can come from a variety of processes as applicable. Monitoring risks would lead to the implementing of risk responses. [Crosswind Manual 11.7; *PMBOK® Guide* 11.6]

13. Perform quantitative risk analysis uses a variety of tools for analysis. Which of the following is most closely associated with this process?

Correct Answer: (B) The expected monetary value (EMV) formula
Explanation: Expected monetary value (EMV) is used in Perform Quantitative Risk Analysis. Perform Qualitative Risk Analysis uses a risk rating matrix to rank risks and create an overall risk rating for the project. The other answers are distracters. [Crosswind Manual 11.5.4; *PMBOK® Guide* 11.4.2.5]

14. Of the following, which best describes a secondary risk?

Correct Answer: (D) A vendor was unable to fulfill a contract commitment by the due date in the contract, so the team chose another vendor that also could not meet the due date because of the late start
Explanation: Secondary risk is what occurs when a risk event occurs and its response creates new risk. [Crosswind Manual 11.7.2; *PMBOK® Guide* 11.5.5.3]

15. If a risk on the project has a high probability of occurring and a high-impact if it does occur, the project team will more than likely do what?

Correct Answer: (D) Perform quantitative risk analysis
Explanation: The team will undertake the Perform Quantitative Risk Analysis process if the Perform Qualitative Risk Analysis process shows that the risk has a high probability of occurring and high-impact if it does. Perform Qualitative Risk Analysis helps determine the probability and impact of a risk; therefore, you must complete this analysis before you can evaluate the probability and impact of the risk. Determination of insurable risk and determination of pure risk are distracters. [Crosswind Manual 11.5; *PMBOK® Guide* 11.4]

16. The construction company has been awarded a $40M contract to build an upscale community shopping center. Of the following, which is the best example of an exploit type of risk response strategy?

Correct Answer: (B) The company realizes the adjoining land will increase in value upon completion of the project, so it purchases the adjoining land at current prices
Explanation: Exploiting the risk is to undertake activity that grows or expands the positive aspects of the risk. Sharing the risk is to work with someone else to maximize the risk. Mitigate attempts to minimize the negative impact of the risk. Accepting the risk is to tolerate whatever occurred. [Crosswind Manual 11.6.2; *PMBOK® Guide* 11.5.5.3]

17. The project manager is discussing risk with a risk-averse stakeholder regarding the market expansion project. The stakeholder has been exposed to project management concepts, but wants to know more about management reserves. The project manager explains that management reserves are created specifically for...

Correct Answer: (B) Risk events you cannot logically forecast for the project
Explanation: Management reserves are created for unknown unknowns: risk events you cannot forecast for the project. Contingency reserves are created for known unknowns: risk events you know can occur during the project. The other answers are distracters. [Crosswind Manual 11.6; *PMBOK® Guide* 11.5]

18. The mobile application transition project is going basically as planned, but a market related risk has occurred: two competitors have merged. While a possible merger was anticipated, there was a great deal of uncertainty as to which competitors would be involved. The team has identified the potential impact. Which of the following will graphically demonstrate the impact to the project and company?

Correct Answer: (B) Tornado diagram
Explanation: The tornado diagram graphically demonstrates the potential impact of the event to the project and the company via sensitivity analysis. The probability and impact matrix demonstrates the probability and impact of the risk. Expected monetary value (EMV) demonstrates what the opportunity is worth, but doesn't necessarily show it graphically. The risk register contains all the information about the project risks. [Crosswind Manual 11.5.7; *PMBOK® Guide* 11.4.2.5]

19. The project management team has just completed the process of identifying risks on the project. They have broken the information into categories and displayed this information in a graphical format. What have they created?

Correct Answer: (B) Risk breakdown structure
Explanation: The risk breakdown structure (RBS) is a graphical representation of the risk categorization and risks within those categories of the project. The prioritized list of quantified risks comes in the risk register and involves risk ranking, not identification categorization. The risk probabilities and impact matrix is part of the risk management plan and is used in qualitative risk analysis. The risk checklist analysis chart is a distracter. [Crosswind Manual 11.2.2; *PMBOK® Guide* 11.1.3.1]

20. The project manager is discussing risk with a risk-averse stakeholder on the market expansion project. The stakeholder has been exposed to project management concepts, but wants to know more about contingency reserves. The project manager explains that contingency reserves are created specifically for...

Correct Answer: (A) Risk events you know can occur on the project
Explanation: Contingency reserves are created for known unknowns: risk events you know can occur during the project. Management reserves are created for unknown unknowns: risk events you cannot forecast for the project. The other answers are distracters. [Crosswind Manual 11.6; *PMBOK® Guide* 11.5]

21. The risk management plan is created to help the team identify risks and triggers, establish risk responses, establish risk owners and their responsibilities, and plan the control and monitoring of risk and risk responses. Two documents are typically created within the plan and used within separate risk processes. Select the two documents and the associated processes.

Correct Answer: (D) The risk breakdown structure used in the identify risks process and the risk probabilities and impact-rating matrix used in the perform qualitative risk analysis process
Explanation: The risk breakdown structure is typically used in the Identify Risks process and the risk probabilities and impact-rating matrix is typically used in the Perform Qualitative Risk Analysis process. The other answers were distracters. [Crosswind Manual 11.3, 11.4; *PMBOK® Guide* 11.2, 11.3]

22. The construction company has been awarded a $20M contract to build a shopping community center. The company is relatively small, and this contract is bigger than anything it has been awarded to date. To ensure that it can effectively complete the contract and not jeopardize other work, it has chosen to pursue a share strategy. Of the following, which is the best example of the share strategy?

Correct Answer: (B) The company partners with a company that specializes in foundation and concrete work
Explanation: Sharing the risk with another company is the basis of a share strategy. Subcontracting is not risk sharing. [Crosswind Manual 11.6.2; *PMBOK® Guide* 11.5.5.3]

23. Your company is evaluating two projects for consideration. Project A has a 40% probability of $69,000 and a 60% probability of -$10,000. Project B has a 60% probability of $56,000 and a 40% probability of -$15,000. Which of the projects do you select based on the greatest expected monetary value?

Correct Answer: (B) Project B
Explanation: To calculate the expected monetary value (EMV), multiply the probabilities by their dollar amounts and add the products of the multiplication for each project. This results in a value of $21,600 for Project A and $27,600 for Project B. With the highest expected monetary value, Project B is the one to select. [Crosswind Manual 11.5.4; *PMBOK® Guide* 11.4.2.5]

24. The database project team members are planning the project. They are involved in planning risk responses and assigning risk owners. What will the risk owner potentially do next?

Correct Answer: (D) Implement a risk response if the risk event occurs
Explanation: Risk owners are responsible for implementing the risk response assigned to them. Watching for additional risks on the project could fall under the responsibility of a risk owner, but isn't the main responsibility. Letting the project manager know that a risk event has occurred isn't the main responsibility of the risk owner. Watching for risk triggers and telling the project manager if they occur isn't taking a proactive approach to risk or project management. [Crosswind Manual 11.7; *PMBOK® Guide* 11.6]

25. The company is concerned about its position during the economic downturn. Its CEO is risk-averse. Of several strategies on the table for consideration, which is he most likely to pursue?

Correct Answer: (A) Mandating that senior management lay the ground work for a reduction in force in the event it is necessary
Explanation: The risk-averse mentality is a very conservative approach to risk and often takes a wait-and-see approach. A risk seeker mentality is that of looking for the big reward and being prepared to pay significantly if they miss it. A risk-neutral mentality is somewhere between that of a risk seeker and risk-averse mentality. [Crosswind Manual 11.2.7; No *PMBOK® Guide* Reference]

26. A film distribution company involved in global expansion has a chief marketing officer who is familiar with cutting edge marketing techniques and strategies. The marketing project for the expansion is set to rollout in 10 countries via the Internet and cable television. An account manager discovers that the chief marketing officer has been embezzling from the company for the last 90 days to help a terminally ill relative. During risk management execution, which of the following best represents an escalation strategy?

Correct Answer: (D) Update the CEO with the details of what you have discovered
Explanation: Updating the CEO would be an example of an escalation strategy. Outsourcing the work is a transference strategy. Allowing him to stay at the company and pay back the amount represents an attempt to mitigate (or minimize) risk, but it could still occur. Terminating him and having someone different run the campaign would be a combination of avoid and mitigate. Confronting the manager doesn't fit any option. [Crosswind Manual 11.6.2; *PMBOK® Guide* 11.5.5.3]

27. Sheldon is doing quantitative risk analysis on his project. He has gotten resistance from his sponsor about doing this. Which of the following best describes why he would want to do this type of risk analysis?

Correct Answer: (C) On higher probability, higher impact risks, or new types of projects where there is a great degree of uncertainty
Explanation: Quantitative risk analysis is typically done on higher probability, higher impact risks, or to establish the overall risk of a project compared to other projects. New projects often fit this criteria because of the uncertainty. There is usually some threshold that is used to establish the justification for the additional effort with the quantitative risk analysis. [Crosswind Manual 11.5; *PMBOK® Guide* 11.4]

28. The project manager and the team are performing the identify risks process. They have learned recently that risk categorization will help organize risks better and potentially allow them to see risks that might have been missed otherwise. Which of the following is the best example of risk categories?

Correct Answer: (D) External, internal, technology, personnel
Explanation: Risk categorization is the grouping of risks into similar categories for better organization and control. The other answers are distracters because they relate to project management process groups or interpretations of the triple constraint. [Crosswind Manual 11.2.2; *PMBOK® Guide* 11.1.3.1]

29. A film distribution company involved in global expansion has a chief marketing officer who is familiar with cutting edge marketing techniques and strategies. The marketing project for the expansion is set to rollout in 10 countries via the Internet and cable television. It's discovered that the chief marketing officer has been embezzling from the company for the last 90 days to help a terminally ill relative. Senior management is extremely concerned because this person knows more about this type of campaign than anyone in the industry and it doesn't want to impact the company negatively. During risk management execution, which of the following best represents an avoidance strategy associated with the embezzlement?

Correct Answer: (C) Terminate him, file felony theft charges, and have someone different run the campaign
Explanation: An avoidance strategy is the strategy that eliminates the risk, i.e. terminating him to eliminate further exposure and having someone else run the campaign is the best answer in terms of an avoidance strategy. Allowing him to stay at the company and pay back the amount represents an attempt to mitigate (or minimize) risk, but it could still occur. Allowing him to stay because he did not use the money for personal gain would be to accept (or tolerate) the risk. Outsourcing the work is a transference strategy. [Crosswind Manual 11.6.2; *PMBOK® Guide* 11.5.5.3]

30. The project manager and the team created the risk register. Which of the following best describes the process they have just completed?

Correct Answer: (A) Identify risks, which entails determining what risks and triggers could occur on the project
Explanation: Identify Risks is the process of determining what risks and triggers could occur on the project. Plan Risk Responses documents who should do what if risk events occur. Monitor Risks focuses on observing project activities for risks and their triggers and implementing the means to control them. Perform Qualitative Risk Analysis assigns probability and impact ratings to the risk. [Crosswind Manual 11.3; *PMBOK® Guide* 11.2]

Chapter 12

Project Procurement Management

Project Procurement Management is the process of obtaining products, services, or results from a person or entity that is not part of the project team. The process can be very complex and mistakes can have legal consequences.

There are a variety of documents that may be used during the process. It is very important to know what each document is intended to accomplish and when it should be used.

An agreement, whether it is a simple hourly staffing agreement or a multinational contract, describes the relationship between the buyer and the seller. It must be very clear regarding results expected, including any knowledge transfer, and be in compliance with local, national, and, if applicable, international laws.

The seller (contractor, subcontractor, vendor, service provider, or supplier) typically applies project management to the work unless the acquisition is for shelf material, goods, or common products. When the seller manages the work as a project:

- The buyer is the customer and key stakeholder in the seller's project
- The seller's project management team will apply all project management processes to the work
- The contract terms and conditions are key inputs to the seller's management processes

Unless stated otherwise, **the exam references procurement from a buyer's perspective**.

Trends
There are a number of procurement trends designed to ensure project success:

- Advances in tools utilized to manage the procurement and implementation phases of the project (specifically online tools that can provide buyers with a single point to advertise procurements and can provide sellers with a single source for accessing and completing online procurement documents)
- Advanced risk management tools that allow risk allocation to both buyers and sellers
- Alterations in contracting processes to accommodate mega projects and projects using contractors from other countries (such projects typically require the use of internationally recognized standard contract forms)
- Logistics and supply chain management
- Technology and stakeholder relations
- Paid trial engagements for several vendors before commitment to one vendor

Tailoring

Project tailoring, the manner in which the processes of a knowledge area are exercised, is employed to address the distinctive nature of each project. Successful project tailoring is predicated on a careful consideration of:

- The intricacy of the procurement
- The physical location of the buyer and seller
- The governance and regulatory climate
- The availability of those who will perform the work

Agile/Adaptive Environment

In Agile environments, the team may be extended by utilizing vendors. This approach allows for risk and reward sharing.

Mega-projects may utilize both an adaptive approach for some deliverables and a more stable approach for others. To accommodate this situation, a master services agreement is typically used for the overall engagement and a supplement contains the details of the adaptive work.

The source for the above text is the Project Management Institute, *A Guide to the Project Management Body of Knowledge*, (*PMBOK® Guide*) – Sixth Edition, Project Management Institute Inc., 2017, Pages 415-420

In this chapter, we discuss the following:

Figure 12-1: Procurement Processes

The source for the above figure is the Project Management Institute, *A Guide to the Project Management Body of Knowledge*, (*PMBOK® Guide*) – Sixth Edition, Project Management Institute Inc., 2017, Figure 12-1, Page 416

✓ Crosswind "Must Knows" for Project Procurement Management

	Key Inputs, Tools & Techniques, and Outputs for Plan Procurement Management
	Key Inputs, Tools & Techniques, and Outputs for Conduct Procurements
	Key Inputs, Tools & Techniques, and Outputs for Control Procurements
	Make-or-buy process and how to calculate it
	What a contract is and the components that make a contract
	Various names for a buyer and seller
	How to recognize and calculate, as well as know the advantages and disadvantages of, the different contract types

	Different types of scope of work
	Characteristics of procurement documents and the environment in which they should be used
	What a qualified sellers list is and how it's used
	Purpose of and the activities that occur at a bidder conference
	When to use a noncompetitive form of procurement
	Incentive fees
	Negotiating goals and options for a win-win result
	Characteristics of procurement agreements (formerly known as contract awards)
	Differences between standard terms and conditions and special provisions
	Difference between the project manager and contract administrator in relation to the contract
	Differences between centralized and decentralized contracting environments
	What formal acceptance is and what can occur once its been issued

Although helpful, this list is not all-inclusive in regard to information needed for the exam. It is only suggested material that, if understood and memorized, may increase your exam score.

12.1. Plan Procurement Management (Planning Process Group)

During the Plan Procurement Management process, a company analyzes its procurement or outsourcing needs.

Know the Key Inputs, Tools & Techniques, and Outputs for Plan Procurement Management.

The procurement typically relates to a product, result, or service that the organization is unable to produce or undertake due to a lack of expertise, a lack of access (a patented product), or a lack of capacity.

During this process, the organization may involve people specialized in law, purchasing, or contracts.

The organization then completes the solicitation needs for the project, which include creation of documents such as:

- Request for Information (RFI)
- Request for Quote (RFQ)
- Request for Proposal (RFP)
- Evaluation criteria for comparison with the proposal

Chapter 12
Procurement

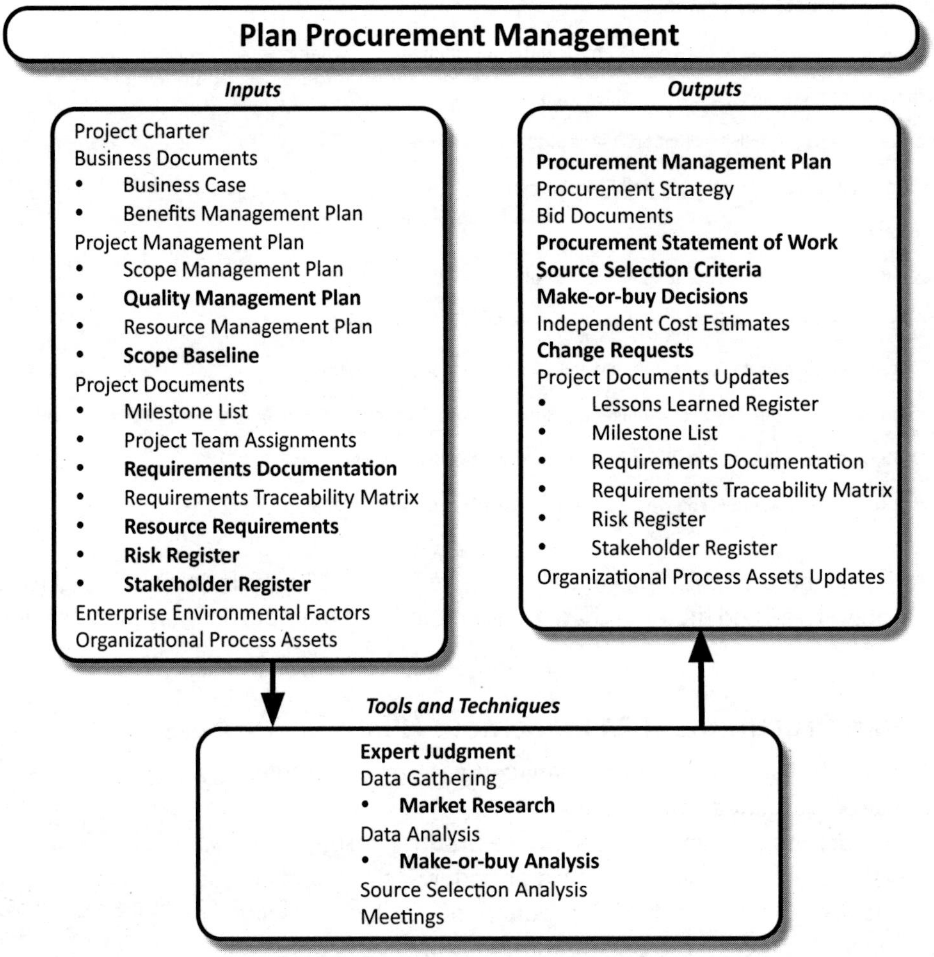

Plan Procurement Management

Inputs	Outputs
Project Charter	**Procurement Management Plan**
Business Documents	Procurement Strategy
• Business Case	Bid Documents
• Benefits Management Plan	**Procurement Statement of Work**
Project Management Plan	**Source Selection Criteria**
• Scope Management Plan	**Make-or-buy Decisions**
• **Quality Management Plan**	Independent Cost Estimates
• Resource Management Plan	**Change Requests**
• **Scope Baseline**	Project Documents Updates
Project Documents	• Lessons Learned Register
• Milestone List	• Milestone List
• Project Team Assignments	• Requirements Documentation
• **Requirements Documentation**	• Requirements Traceability Matrix
• Requirements Traceability Matrix	• Risk Register
• **Resource Requirements**	• Stakeholder Register
• **Risk Register**	Organizational Process Assets Updates
• **Stakeholder Register**	
Enterprise Environmental Factors	
Organizational Process Assets	

Tools and Techniques

Expert Judgment
Data Gathering
• **Market Research**
Data Analysis
• **Make-or-buy Analysis**
Source Selection Analysis
Meetings

Figure 12-2: Plan Procurement Management Data Flow Diagram
The source for the above figure is the Project Management Institute, *A Guide to the Project Management Body of Knowledge*, (*PMBOK® Guide*) – Sixth Edition, Project Management Institute Inc., 2017, Figure 12-2, Page 421

Plan Procurement Management (Planning)		
Key Inputs	Quality Management Plan	The quality management plan is a component of the project management plan that details the manner in which the policies, methods, and criteria of the organization are executed. It defines the activities and resources necessary to accomplish quality goals. The plan also enumerates the industry standards and codes applicable to the project, information that is used to create bidding documents such as the Request for Proposal.

Plan Procurement Management (Continued)		
Key Inputs (Cont.)	Scope Baseline	The scope baseline is the authorized version of the scope statement, WBS (to the level of work package with individual identification codes), and WBS dictionary. The scope baseline is subject to change control. Note that if the scope is still evolving, the known scope constituents are used to create the Statement of Work (SOW) and the Terms of Reference (TOR).
	Requirements Documentation	Requirements documentation includes the requirements management plan, technical requirements that must be met by a seller, and requirements that appertain to contractual and legal considerations (such as requirements related to safety, health, intellectual property rights, licenses, security, permits, environmental factors, and equal employment opportunity). Requirements documentation delineates how requirements fulfill the business needs of the project. In order to baseline requirements, they must be measurable, testable, traceable, complete, consistent, and acceptable to appropriate stakeholders. Requirements may be categorized as **business** requirements, **stakeholder** requirements, **solution** (both **functional** and **non-functional**) requirements, **transition** requirements, **project** requirements, and **quality** requirements.
	Resource Requirements	Resource requirements delineate the classes and numbers of resources that are needed for individual activities utilized in the schedule model. Note that resources are not limited to people, but include items such as equipment and office space.
	Risk Register	The risk register records each identified risk. It typically includes the potential owner of and potential response(s) to each identified risk. It may include a title, category, status, cause(s), trigger(s), impacted activity(ies), date of identification, date range for probable occurrence, and response deadline. Note that some risks may be transferred through the use of a procurement agreement.

	Plan Procurement Management (Continued)	
Key Inputs (Cont.)	Stakeholder Register	The stakeholder register contains information related to identified stakeholders. It includes identification information (name, position, location, project role, and contact information), assessment information (key requirements, potential impact on project results, phase in which stakeholder wields the greatest influence, and expectations), and stakeholder classification (internal/external, impact/influence/power/interest, or other classification model).
Key Tools & Techniques	Expert Judgment	Expert judgment is judgment based on expertise acquired in a specific area. It is often more significant and accurate than the best modeling tools available and can be provided by stakeholders, company personnel external to the project, professional organizations or groups, and consultants. It is important to consider expertise related to procurement, purchasing, contract types, contract documents, pertinent regulatory information, and pertinent compliance information.
	Market Research	Market research is a data-gathering method that entails analyzing the capabilities of suppliers. Procurement teams may also use information gained at conferences, online reviews, and other sources to determine market capabilities.
	Make-or-buy Analysis	A make-or-buy analysis is utilized to determine if it is more advantageous for the project team to perform work/create a deliverable or to contract the work/purchase the deliverable from an outside source. The analysis considers a variety of factors, including the current availability of resources and their proficiency/experience, the need for specialized expertise, control of intellectual property, and receptivity to resource expansion.

Plan Procurement Management (Continued)		
Key Outputs	Procurement Management Plan	The procurement management plan is a component of the project management plan that addresses procurement activities. It details the need for international competitive bidding, national competitive bidding, and/or local bidding and delineates the manner in which external financing is aligned with the plan and the project schedule. It often contains guidelines for coordinating procurement with other project processes (project schedule development and control processes), contract management metrics, activity timetables, constraints and assumptions related to procurement, risk issues related to procurement, and stakeholder roles and responsibilities.
	Procurement Statement of Work	The procurement statement of work for each procurement item depicts the item in sufficient detail for aspiring sellers to determine if they have the ability to provide the expected service, product, or result. It typically includes specifications, quantity, quality level, required performance data, and other requirements. The SOW is elaborated from the scope baseline and is limited to the part of the project scope that is addressed by the related contract.
	Source Selection Criteria	Source selection criteria are the standards by which the buyer judges the quality of each aspiring seller's proposal to provide the expected service, product, or result. Criteria typically include product cost; life cycle cost; delivery dates; the knowledge transfer program; intellectual property rights; and the seller's capability, capacity, management experience, technical proficiency, technical approach, relevant experience, references, and financial soundness. The criteria is scored and considered when selecting the seller.
	Make-or-buy Decisions	Make-or-buy decisions are reached as a result of a make-or-buy analysis. The analysis is utilized to determine if it is more advantageous for the project team to perform work/create a deliverable or to contract the work/purchase the deliverable from an outside source.
	Change Requests	Change requests are requests for modification that have not been formally approved through the change control process. Modifications to the cost and schedule baselines or to other impacted components of the project management plan may be requested as the result of procurement decisions.

12.1.1. Procurement Management Plan

The procurement management plan:

- Formalizes the types of contracts and procurement documents that will be used
- Details procurement metrics, assumptions, constraints, and risk management issues
- Indicates if, and when, independent estimates will be used
- Designates any prequalified sellers
- Describes the manner in which multiple suppliers are managed
- Describes the manner in which make-or-buy decisions are conducted
- Describes the manner in which the project management team will work with the procurement department of the performing organization
- Describes the manner in which procurement is coordinated with other project processes, such as scheduling and reporting

The procurement management plan helps the project manager and team do the following:

- Determine make vs. buy for the various needs of the project
- Establish what procurement documents (RFP, RFI, RFQ) are needed for the project
- Create the procurement documents for the project
- Run bidder conferences
- Address single source and sole source procurement
- Select vendors to do work
- Establish contract(s) with vendors

12.1.2. Make-or-buy Decisions

One of the basics of procurement is the make-or-buy decision. There are a number of considerations a company can use in making this decision.

Be familiar with the make-or-buy process and how to calculate it.

Make Decision Qualities	The buyer owns intellectual property associated with the work and considers doing the work internally in order to maintain control of the information.
	The buyer has excessive qualified capacity.
Buy Decision Qualities	The buyer doesn't possess the skills needed for the work.
	The buyer doesn't possess the capacity to do the work.

PMI, CAPM, and PMBOK are registered marks of the Project Management Institute, Inc.

500   © 2008-2018 Crosswind Learning, www.crosswindpm.com

12.1.3. Procurement Strategy

The procurement strategy is created after the make-or-buy analysis is complete and the decision to acquire the product, service, or result from outside of the project has been made.

The strategy addresses delivery methods, contract payment types, and the advancement of the procurement through its phases.

Delivery methods for professional services include buyer/services provider with no subcontracting allowed, buyer/services provider with subcontracting allowed, joint venture between buyer and services provider, and buyer/services provider acting as the representative.

Delivery methods for industrial projects or construction projects include, but are not limited to, turnkey, design build (DB), design bid build (DBB), design build operate (DBO), and build own operate transfer (BOOT).

Contract payment types are coordinated with the buying organization's internal financial systems. They include, but are not limited to, lump sum, firm fixed-price, cost plus award fees, cost plus incentive fees, time and materials, and target cost. Note that fixed-price contract payment types are used with projects that have stable and well defined requirements, as well as predictable work. Also note that cost plus contracts are used with projects where the work is evolving, is likely to change, or is not well defined and incentives/awards may be utilized as a means of aligning the objectives of the buyer and seller.

Procurement phase information typically includes phasing/sequencing of the procurement with phase descriptions and objectives, procurement performance indicators and milestones, criteria for the movement from phase to phase, a monitoring and evaluation plan for tracking progress, and a knowledge transfer process that will be used in subsequent phases.

12.1.4. Rent or Buy Calculation

It is very important to know the rent or buy calculation for the exam. The components are typically as follows:

- Purchase cost and daily maintenance with the purchase option
- Daily (or weekly, monthly) rental fee, which usually includes maintenance fees for the rent option

Typically, related exam questions focus on calculating the point where it makes sense to either rent or buy the product.

You are the project manager for a housing developer. The development requires a skid loader to clean out the lots where the houses will be built. You can rent the skid loader for $100 per day (including maintenance) or you can purchase one for $750, with a $50 per day maintenance cost. What is the maximum time you would want to rent this tool before considering purchasing it?

To determine the answer, first convert the information to a formula. The options from the above sample question show rental at $100 per day or purchase at $750 with $50 per day maintenance.

The formula is ($ per day) x (number of days) = purchase price + (maintenance fee per day x number of days) or, in algebraic terms, $100x = $750 + $50x, where x is the number of days.

Step 1. (-$50x + $100x) = $750 or $50x = $750 (Move any item with the variable x to one side of the equation, changing the operator of the item moved, in this case change positive $50x to negative $50x.)
Step 2. $750 / $50 = x (Divide to determine the value of x.)
Step 3. $750 / $50 = 15
Step 4. x = 15 (the maximum number of days renting the tool makes more sense than purchasing it.)

12.1.5. Contract

When awarding a contract, the buyer establishes a relationship with the seller to obtain sufficient information to determine that the seller is able to provide the needed product, results, or services at terms acceptable to the buyer.

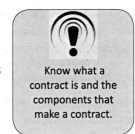

Know what a contract is and the components that make a contract.

A contract is a mutually binding legal agreement between buyer and seller. Other names for a contract could be a **purchase order** (PO), **subcontract**, or **agreement**.

For the exam, it is important to know the requirements for a contract.

- **Capacity** (individual legal entities who are competent and are of legal age)
- **Offer** (the proposition that the seller will provide a product, service, or result for remuneration)
- **Consideration** (the remuneration given to the seller by the buyer)
- **Legal purpose**
- **Acceptance** (the buyer's willingness to accept the offer from the seller)

A memory tool for the contract is CCOLA—**C**apacity, **C**onsideration, **O**ffer, **L**egal, **A**cceptance.

Additional Components That May Be Included in Contracts		
Statement of Work (SOW)	Deliverables Description	Performance Reporting
Period of Performance	Roles and Responsibilities	Sellers Place of Performance
Pricing	Payment Terms	Place of Delivery
Inspection and Acceptance Criteria	Warranty	Product Support
Limitation of Liability	Fees and Retainage	Penalties and Incentives
Insurance and Performance Bonds	Subordinate Subcontractor Approvals	Change Control Procedures
Termination and Alternative Dispute Resolution	Service Level Agreements	---

12.1.6. Buyer and Seller Names

The table below delineates a number of terms that can be used to describe the buyer and seller.

Know the various names for a buyer and a seller.

Buyer	Seller
Client	Contractor
Customer	Subcontractor
Prime Contractor	Vendor
Contractor	Service Provider
Acquiring Organization	Supplier
Government Agency	---
Service Requester	---
Purchaser	---

Note that, depending on circumstances, the terms for the buyer and seller can change during the project.

If the outsourced work is not just for materials or products, the seller usually manages the project. In this case, the buyer becomes the customer.

The seller's team is concerned with all the details of the project, not just procurement, and has a greater degree of input into the overall project planning than if it is merely providing an existing product.

The seller's title can also change during the project. For example, typically, the seller starts as a bidder, then becomes a selected source, and then a vendor.

Note that this is a case for a greatly customized scope of work.

12.1.7. Contract Type Selection

Knowledge of contract type selection is very important for the exam.

There are four main types of contracts available for use on a project: purchase order (PO), fixed-price (FP), cost reimbursable (CR), and time and materials (T&M).

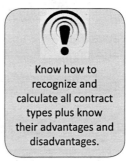

Know how to recognize and calculate all contract types plus know their advantages and disadvantages.

Each of these contracts can involve variations including incentives, fees, and more.

It is very important to know the types of contracts and, for each type, the outstanding features, when it should (and should not) be used, and the risks to the buyer and seller.

The following figure shows buyer and seller risk relevant to contract type.

Figure 12-3: Contract Type Selection

Contract Type	Risk for Buyer	Risk for Seller	Description	Example
Purchase Order (PO)	Neutral	Neutral	A **unilateral** agreement that requires approval by only one party because the other party has offered the product for the predefined price *Typically, a PO is used for commodity items. Some consultants mentioned that the workplace typically gets a contract type signed off and then gets a PO. For the exam, a PO is considered a separate contract type.*	27" computer monitors for $99.00 each
Firm Fixed-Price (FFP) also known as Lump Sum	Minimal	Significant	One of the most common contracts in business today, popular because a company can budget for a fixed price *Because it **requires detail for the seller to estimate accurately**, a firm fixed price contract is typically used when there is a **detailed scope of work**. For the seller, profit is everything after cost is covered and the downside is cost*	Purchases the company-wide implementation of a computer network from an outside vendor for $2,000,000 after providing the vendor a detailed scope of work

PMI, CAPM, and PMBOK are registered marks of the Project Management Institute, Inc.

504   © 2008-2018 Crosswind Learning, www.crosswindpm.com

Contract Type	Risk for Buyer	Risk for Seller	Description	Example
Fixed-Price Incentive Fee (FPIF)	Minimal	Significant	A contract type with the fixed-price component plus **incentive fees** to motivate the seller to produce at a rate greater than the minimum required *An FPIF is usually used to help accelerate a buyer's need, such as a market opportunity. It provides an opportunity for the seller to determine what is needed to make additional profit via the incentive fee.*	A city buys services from a company to construct a new freeway for $4,000,000 and agrees to pay an additional $65,000 for each week the construction is completed prior to the target completion date
Fixed-Price Economic Price Adjustment (FP-EPA)	Minimal	Significant	A fixed-price contract with similar components listed previously that is typically associated with a multi-year contract ***To compensate for economic changes from year to year***, *the economic price adjustment is factored in. The item determining the amount of change from year to year is usually some national economic metric not directly tied to the buyer or seller.*	A city buys services from a construction company to build a new freeway for $4M over three years; at the start of each year, the amount varies relative to the national cost of living or some other negotiated standard
Cost Plus Fixed Fee (CPFF)	Medium	Minimal	Typically used when the buyer knows generally what is needed but lacks details *The CPFF covers the cost of the seller and includes a predefined fee for the work.*	A buyer hires a vendor to produce a video training series before finalizing all the details for the video and agrees to pay the vendor for cost plus a $37,000 fee

Contract Type	Risk for Buyer	Risk for Seller	Description	Example
Cost Plus Incentive Fee (CPIF)	Medium	Minimal	Typically used when the buyer knows generally what is needed but lacks the details *Generally, the buyer has some sort of need that requires that something be created as soon as reasonably possible. The incentive fee gives the buyer an opportunity to motivate the seller to complete the project more quickly, to higher quality standards, or other criteria.*	A buyer hires a vendor to write a manual for publication and sale and agrees to pay cost plus an incentive fee of $7,500 for each week the project is completed prior to the target completion date
Cost Plus Award Fee (CPAF)	Minimal	Significant	Covers the seller for legitimate costs, but the fee is only awarded if the buyer is satisfied with broad subjective criteria detailed in the contract	A buyer agrees to pay for costs incurred to construct a freeway bridge; if the seller meets the agreed on date and completes the bridge with minimal negative impact to the environment, the buyer will award the seller an additional $500,000
Cost Plus Percentage of Cost (CPPC) or Cost Plus Fee (CPF)	Significant	Minimal	Covers the seller for legitimate costs and pays a percentage of total costs as a fee *The more the seller spends, the higher the fees. Most companies will not enter into this type of contract because it can negatively impact the buyer if the seller is not ethical.*	A buyer hires a company to install a computer network for 500 users and agrees to pay for the costs incurred by the seller plus a 17% fee of all costs

Contract Type	Risk for Buyer	Risk for Seller	Description	Example
Time and Materials (T&M)	Minimal	Minimal	Typically used **for smaller initiatives, staff supplementation,** the initial piece of a project where discovery occurs before the full details of the project are known, or for materials on an initiative to complement the labor	A buyer hires a technical writer at $75 per hour to supplement its staff or a buyer has a bathroom added to her house at $50 per hour plus the cost of materials

12.1.8. Share

A share is a contract component that divides any remaining money (typically the difference between the total price and actual seller's costs) between the buyer and the seller. It is normally a negotiated split between the two parties. It is typically different from a traditional incentive fee in that an incentive fee pays compensation based on certain measurable performance metrics that have been established and agreed upon.

It is very important to understand and be able to calculate the total share and the amounts that will be allotted to the buyer and to the seller.

Example: The buyer and seller have contracted for the seller to provide a debit card add-on system in all 50 of the buyer's retail stores. The total price is to be $50,000. The need for implementation is great because the old systems are being leased and must be returned by a particular date. Both parties negotiate and agree that if the project's actual cost is below the baseline (target) cost, the buyer and seller split the difference 60%/40%. The project accrues an actual cost of $45,000 when complete. Calculate the share total amount and the share for the buyer and seller.

The project has a $5,000 share amount ($50,000 - $45,000). Of that $5,000, 60% goes to the buyer and 40% to the seller. The buyer keeps $3,000 and the seller gets $2,000. With the actual cost of $45,000 and the share amount of $2,000, the seller is paid $47,000 on the contract.

[handwritten margin note: Always Buyer over Seller]

12.1.9. Point of Total Assumption

The calculation for the point of total assumption establishes the point at which the seller is responsible for all cost overruns associated with a fixed-price incentive fee (FPIF) contract. Contrary to what fixed-price may imply, a contract of this sort can be negotiated so that the buyer agrees to share in cost overruns or under-runs. This calculation is typically used in government or defense-type contracts.

Chapter 12 Procurement

Point of Total Assumption Variables and Calculation	
Purpose	To calculate the maximum that a buyer pays in a fixed-price incentive fee (FPIF) contract when taking into consideration the share ratio on cost overruns
Target Cost (TC)	The expected cost of the work in the contract (Ex: $1,000,000)
Target Profit (TP)	The expected profit of the work in the contract (Ex: $200,000)
Profit Rate at Target Cost	The profit margin of the target profit compared to the target cost (target profit/target cost) (Ex: 20%)
Target Price	The total of the target cost and target profit; i.e. the total target value of the contract work barring any cost savings or overruns (Ex: $1,200,000)
Ceiling Price	A percentage of the target cost (TC) that is equal to the maximum total amount the work is expected to cost with any cost overruns being considered (Ex: 140% of cost or $1,400,000)
Share Ratio (SR)	The ratio that establishes the percentage of cost savings or cost overruns that will be assigned to the buyer and to the seller. Note that cost savings or overruns impact the total contract amount and profit. (Ex: 70/30)
Point of Total Assumption (PTA)	The total amount the buyer will pay regardless of cost overruns. Reference the formula in the subsequent cell. (Ex: $1,285,714.29)
Point of Total Assumption Formula	$$PTA = \left[\frac{Ceiling\ Price - Target\ Price}{Buyer\ Share} \right] + Target\ Cost$$ $$\$1,285,714.29 = \left[\frac{\$1,400,000 - \$1,200,000}{0.70} \right] + \$1,000,000$$ NOTE: The difference between ceiling price and target price is divided by the **buyer's** share.

12.1.10. Scope of Work

Scope of work is typically the part of the contract that describes what the seller will do for the buyer. When the scope of work is complete, the main work of the contract is complete and closing can begin. Because the level of detail and planning in a contract may vary, there are two main approaches available to develop the scope of work in the contract.

Know the different types of scope of work.

Scope of Work	Description	Example
Design	A scope of work type in which the buyer provides the seller with the **exact details of what is required** *Design is typically used when buyers know exactly what they want and want no variance from specifications. It typically works with fixed-price contracts.*	A company hires a vendor to build a prototype cabinet to house telecom equipment and provides the vendor with specifications for the cabinet, which must hold a number of devices already created.
Functionality	A scope of work type in which the buyer details to the seller the **functionality needed in the new system or development** *Functionality allows sellers to propose their own solutions as long as the end-results are achieved.* **It typically works with cost plus (CP) contracts.**	A company hires a vendor to implement a phone system and provides only functional requirements; as long as the those requirements are met, the vendor can build the solution at its discretion.

12.1.11. Procurement Documents

The documents associated with the procurement process lay the foundation for vendor relationships. They apply to the selected vendors and those who are considering the work.

An ideal procurement document answers the questions of the potential vendors and allows them to make a well-planned bid, creating a win/win relationship with the vendor.

Be familiar with all types of procurement documents and know the environments in which to use them.

Document Type	Typical Purpose	Description	Example
Request for Information (RFI)	Typically used to solicit information to learn more about a company that could provide service for a buyer	A document requesting information about a service provider's qualifications	A request from a state government to determine if a consulting company has the appropriate experience to bid for the project
Request for Quote (RFQ)	Typically used to solicit proposals for a small dollar amount or used for commodity type of products that do not require a great degree of customization	A document that requests a price for a standard item *There is a general assumption that negotiation is not associated with this type of procurement document.*	A request for prospective sellers wishing to provide pricing for customer-established server criteria: Quantity 50 XYZ Servers with 64G RAM, 4TB hard drive to be purchased within 90 days of submittal

Chapter 12 Procurement

Document Type	Typical Purpose	Description	Example
Request for Proposal (RFP) sometimes called **Request for Tender (RFT)**	Typically used to solicit proposals for larger, higher priced customized services or products *The seller describes the detailed solution approach it proposes to take and includes a list of related experiences.*	A document that requests an approach, price, and significant detail about how the seller proposes to do the requested work *The general assumption is that negotiations occur based on the scope, schedule, and cost of the buyer's request and in consideration of the seller's suggestions.*	A request for a proposal to prospective sellers for design, implementation, and training for a data warehouse to consolidate five different enterprise databases at a fortune 500 company named Widgets, Inc.
Invitation for Bid (IFB) sometimes called **Request for Bid (RFB)**	Used for government sealed bidding processes with characteristics similar to those for an RFP (request for proposal)	A document that requests an approach, price, and significant detail about how the seller proposes to do the requested work *The general assumption is that negotiations occur based on the scope, schedule, and cost of the buyer's request and in consideration of the seller suggestions.*	A request from a branch of the U.S. government to sellers regarding the design, implementation, and training of an enterprise reporting system; the selection process is sealed bid and the contract is awarded on March 25th

The source for the above text is the Project Management Institute, *A Guide to the Project Management Body of Knowledge, (PMBOK® Guide)* – Sixth Edition, Project Management Institute Inc., 2017, Pages 421-434

12.2. Conduct Procurements (Executing Process Group)

Know the Key Inputs, Tools & Techniques, and Outputs for Conduct Procurements.

Conduct Procurements incorporates soliciting responses from the sellers, selecting a seller, and awarding the contract. The team will request bids or proposals from potential sellers, apply the defined selection criteria to the bids or proposals received to determine the selected seller, and award the contract to the selected seller.

Major procurements may require iterations of this process and include negotiation.

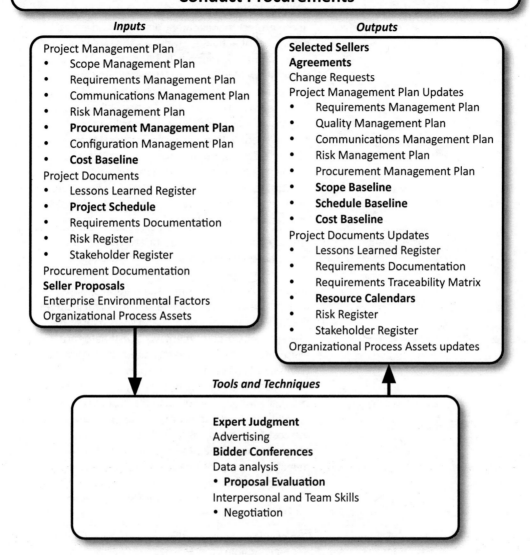

Figure 12-4: Conduct Procurements Data Flow Diagram

The source for the above figure is the Project Management Institute, *A Guide to the Project Management Body of Knowledge, (PMBOK® Guide) – Sixth Edition,* Project Management Institute Inc., 2017, Figure 12-4, Page 435

Conduct Procurements (Executing)		
Key Inputs	Procurement Management Plan	The procurement management plan is a component of the project management plan that addresses procurement activities. It details the need for international competitive bidding, national competitive bidding, and/or local bidding and delineates the manner in which external financing is aligned with the plan and the project schedule. It often contains guidelines for coordinating procurement with other project processes (project schedule development and control processes), contract management metrics, activity timetables, constraints and assumptions related to procurement, risk issues related to procurement, and stakeholder roles and responsibilities.
	Cost Baseline	The cost baseline is the authorized version of the time-phased budget for the project, excluding management reserves, and subject to change control. It is evolved from a summation of approved budgets for specific schedule activities and includes the budget for procurement and costs related to managing the procurement. Cost estimates are aggregated by work packages, then into higher components of the work breakdown structure (WBS), and then for the entire project. Because the cost estimates included in the cost baseline are linked to schedule activities, a time-phased view of the cost baseline is enabled. It is usually depicted as an S-curve. If the project uses earned value management (EVM), the cost baseline is known as the performance measurement baseline. The budget consists of the cost baseline plus the management reserves.
	Project Schedule	The project schedule is the product of a schedule model containing linked activities, including those related to procurement. The schedule also contains planned dates, durations, milestones, and resources for each activity. It is usually formatted as a bar chart, milestone chart, or project schedule network diagram, although tabular formatting may occur. Until resources have been allocated and start and finish dates substantiated, the project schedule is preliminary. A master schedule or milestone schedule is a summary form of the project schedule.

Chapter 12
Procurement

Conduct Procurements (Continued)		
Key Inputs (Cont.)	Seller Proposals	Seller proposals are submitted in response to a procurement document package and contain the information that will be assessed against the source selection criteria to determine the bid(s) that satisfy the criteria. Typically, a seller proposal is separate from a price proposal.
Key Tools & Techniques	Expert Judgment	Expert judgment is judgment based on expertise acquired in a specific area. It is important to consider expertise related to proposal evolution, knowledge about the procurement item and applicable functionality (finance, engineering, design, etc.), negotiation, and pertinent industry regulations and compliance requisites.
	Bidder Conferences	Bidder conferences are meetings between the buyer and aspiring sellers that are conducted prior to proposal submission for the purpose of providing all aspiring sellers with an explicit and common interpretation of the procurement. The meetings must be conducted in a manner that eliminates preferential treatment of any bidder.
	Proposal Evaluation	Proposal evaluation is a data analysis technique utilized to assess proposals in terms of completeness and alignment with procurement documents, the statement of work (SOW), source selection criteria, and any additional documents contained in the bid package.
Key Outputs	Selected Sellers	Selected sellers are aspiring sellers who have been deemed competitive based on the results of the proposal/bid assessment. For more sophisticated, high-value, and/or high-risk procurements, approval by senior management is typically required prior to awarding the contract.

Key Outputs (Cont.)	Agreements	For work to be performed by an external source, a contract between buyer and seller is the type of agreement that is typically utilized. The contract is a mutually binding agreement that commits the seller to provide specified products, services, or results and commits the buyer to pay the seller. It represents a legal relationship subject to remedy through the court system. It contains information such as a schedule with milestone dates, performance reporting criteria, pricing/payment terms, inspection/quality/acceptance criteria, warranties, future support requirements, awards and penalties, insurance/performance bonds, subcontractor approval terms, general terms and conditions, change request procedures, termination clause, and processes for alternative dispute resolution.
	Scope Baseline	The scope baseline is the authorized version of the scope statement, WBS (to the level of work package with individual identification codes), and WBS dictionary. The scope baseline is subject to change control and is compared to actual results to ascertain if any changes, corrective actions, or precautionary actions are required. The WBS, deliverables, assumptions, and constraints contained in the scope baseline must be considered during the performance of procurement activities.
	Schedule Baseline	The schedule baseline is the authorized version of the schedule model. It contains baseline start and baseline finish dates, is subject to change control, and is used as the basis of comparison to actual results. Procurement delivery changes that impact the overall schedule require approval and an update of the schedule baseline.
	Cost Baseline	The cost baseline is the authorized version of the time-phased budget for the project, excluding management reserves, and is subject to change control. It is evolved from a summation of approved budgets for specific schedule activities. Procurement cost changes (labor and/or material) must be incorporated into the cost baseline.

Conduct Procurements (Continued)		
Key Outputs (Cont.)	Resource Calendars	Resource calendars delineate project resource accessibility and are referenced to ensure a reliable schedule. Both the availability of each resource and schedule constraints, such as holidays, time zones, vacations, and work hours, must be considered. Resource calendars must be updated to reflect the availability of sellers.

Situational Question and Real World Application

Failure to effectively perform the Conduct Procurements process can result in selected sellers that are not awarded a contract, selected sellers that are inferior to other bidders, and agreements that are unenforceable or heavily favor the buyer or the seller.

The source for the above text is the Project Management Institute, *A Guide to the Project Management Body of Knowledge*, (*PMBOK® Guide*) – Sixth Edition, Project Management Institute Inc., 2017, Pages 421-434

12.2.1. Qualified Sellers List

Know what a qualified sellers list is and how it's used.

The qualified sellers list is a **list that a buyer can use as a screening mechanism in the procurement process.** It allows a buyer to consider only sellers of services that have met predefined conditions.

This list can save time by eliminating the preliminary screening process and allowing buyers to make their selection from vendors that have already met the predefined qualifications.

12.2.2. Bidder Conferences

Know the purpose of and the activities that occur at a bidder conference.

Bidder conferences are meetings that provide potential sellers a forum to ask a buyer questions and obtain clarification about potential issues before creating a proposal. Such conferences can also include a formal presentation by the buyer.

The conferences should let potential sellers ask questions and should make the questions and answers available to anyone considering bidding on the project. Buyer representatives need to be sure that all questions and answers are available to all potential sellers and they must take all reasonable steps to ensure that potential sellers do not collude to inflate pricing.

12.2.3. Noncompetitive Form of Procurement

Know when to use a noncompetitive form of procurement.

Typically, noncompetitive procurement is done when there is **only one source for the products** or when the **buyer has an established relationship with the seller** and there are mechanisms in place to ensure that the buyer of the products or services attains a fair price.

If a vendor is selected without competition, there is a chance for inappropriate selection and unreasonable pricing. There should be a mechanism in place to assure that appropriate actions are taken in this area. The two noncompetitive forms of Procurement are defined in the following table.

Sole Source	Single Source
Sole source involves using a company that has no competition. Typically the sole source owns a patent or some other type of intellectual right.	Single source involves choosing a preferred vendor rather than accepting bids from competing vendors. The purchasing organization typically uses a single source if it has a preferred vendor or does not have time to go through the full selection process.

12.2.4. Incentive Fees

An incentive fee is a fee that the **buyer can use to impose a specified standard of productivity on the seller.**

The fee is typically an amount paid to the seller in addition to the base price of the contract.

Know what incentive fees are.

12.2.5. Negotiations

Negotiations may occur between the buyer and the seller when the buyer is outsourcing work to another company. **Negotiations should result in a win/win situation for both parties.** Although some people believe that one party must win and the other must lose in order to have successful negotiations, the better position is to accept a reasonable price for reasonable work.

There are a number of negotiation strategies that are used in everyday business, some unethically. It is important to recognize these strategies for the exam's situational questions.

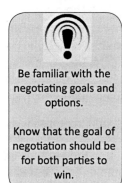

Be familiar with the negotiating goals and options.

Know that the goal of negotiation should be for both parties to win.

Common Negotiation Strategies	
Competition	Using one seller against another to attain the best price or other terms the buyer desires
Deadline	Using a deadline to attempt to get a party to sign the contract
The Boss is Missing	Explaining that a person who is key to the approval is not available

12.2.6. Agreements (Previously called contract awards)

Each selected seller is awarded a procurement contract or agreement.

The contract is a legally binding agreement obligating the seller to provide one or more specified products, services, or results and obligating the buyer to compensate the seller.

Know the characteristics of procurement agreements.

The agreement is subject to remedy in the courts. The agreement (contract) may be simple or complex and components vary. Components may include a statement of work or deliverables, performance reporting, period of performance, schedule baseline, roles and responsibilities, seller's place of performance, place of delivery, pricing, payment terms, inspection criteria, acceptance criteria, warranty, product support, liability limits, fees and retainage, penalties, incentives, insurance/performance bonding, approval terms for subordinate subcontractors, handling of change requests, and termination and alternative dispute resolution (ADR) mechanisms.

12.2.7. Standard Terms and Conditions

Standard terms and conditions are typically common (non-negotiable) contract items.

They can be subject to negotiation, but generally the company's legal department imposes a tight range of parameters. The range can cover payment options, intellectual property rights, and the ability to subcontract among other parameters.

Know the difference between standard terms and conditions and special provisions.

12.2.8. Special Provisions

Special provisions are items typically **added to a contract to account for any standard terms and conditions that will not meet the needs of the work involved.** The buyer and seller negotiate these provisions, which complement any workable standard terms and conditions that have already been defined in the contract as acceptable.

12.2.9. Contract Interpretation

Contract interpretation is important in that it can keep the organization out of court or put it in court.

Generally, the contract administrator (reference the Control Procurements process in the subsequent section) should understand what is defined in the contract and interpret that in alignment with general legal opinion.

The following are sensitive areas in contract interpretation:

- The contract replaces anything that was agreed to before it was signed; if it is not in the contract, it is not a requirement
- All the items of the contract should be completed, including reports, quality control, inspections, etc.
- It's better to spell out numbers than use only the numerical symbols
- Any agreement to modify the contract should be created and signed as an attachment to the contract
- If any changes are made to the contract before it has been signed, the changes should be handwritten and initialed by all parties
- Specific details associated with qualification criteria for the work should be defined at an appropriate level of detail; using verbiage such as "system will work" falls short of "system will perform requirements A through Z listed in the scope of work requirements"

The source for the above text is the Project Management Institute, *A Guide to the Project Management Body of Knowledge*, (*PMBOK® Guide*) – Sixth Edition, Project Management Institute Inc., 2017, Pages 421-434

12.3. Control Procurements (Monitoring and Controlling Process Group)

Know the Key Inputs, Tools & Techniques, and Outputs for Control Procurements.

Control Procurements is the process of administering procurement affiliations, tracking buyer and seller performance, making any necessary adjustments to the contract, and closing the contract, if applicable.

The designated contract administrator verifies the product, service, or result that will be provided by the seller as they fulfill the terms and conditions of the agreement. If there are multiple sellers, the contract administrator is also responsible for **managing interface points** between the providers.

There are a number of project processes that can influence, or be influenced by, this process. They include Direct and Manage Project Work (Project Integration Management), Monitor Communications (Project Communication Management), Control Quality (Project Quality Management), Perform Integrated Change Control (Project Integration Management), and Monitor Risks (Project Risk Management).

The cost aspect of this process involves managing payments due to the seller with a focus on paying only for completed work.

The performance aspect of this process involves a review of each seller's performance against the corresponding agreement. If there are any deficiencies, corrective actions must be established.

PMI, CAPM, and PMBOK are registered marks of the Project Management Institute, Inc.

518   © 2008-2018 Crosswind Learning, www.crosswindpm.com

Control Procurements

Inputs

Project Management Plan
- Requirements Management Plan
- Risk Management Plan
- **Procurement Management Plan**
- Change Management Plan
- Schedule Baseline

Project Documents
- Assumption Log
- Lessons Learned Register
- Milestone List
- **Quality Reports**
- Requirements Documentation
- **Requirements Traceability Matrix**
- **Risk Register**
- Stakeholder Register

Agreements
Procurement Documentation
Approved Change Requests
Work Performance Data
Enterprise Environmental Factors
Organizational Process Assets

Outputs

Closed Procurements
Work Performance Information
Procurement Documentation Updates
Change Requests
Project Management Plan Updates
- Risk Management Plan
- Procurement Management Plan
- Schedule Baseline
- Cost Baseline

Project Documents Updates
- Lessons Learned Register
- Resource Requirements
- Requirements Traceability Matrix
- Risk Register
- Stakeholder Register

Organizational Process Assets Updates

Tools and Techniques

Expert Judgment
Claims Administration
Data Analysis
- **Performance Reviews**
- Earned Value Analysis
- Trend Analysis

Inspection
Audits

Figure 12-5: Control Procurements Data Flow Diagram

The source for the above figure is the Project Management Institute, *A Guide to the Project Management Body of Knowledge*, (*PMBOK® Guide*) – Sixth Edition, Project Management Institute Inc., 2017, Figure 12-5, Page 443

Control Procurements (Monitoring and Controlling)		
Key Inputs	Procurement Management Plan	The procurement management plan is a component of the project management plan that addresses procurement activities. It details the need for international competitive bidding, national competitive bidding, and/or local bidding and delineates the manner in which external financing is aligned with the plan and the project schedule. It often contains guidelines for coordinating procurement with other project processes (project schedule development and control processes), contract management metrics, activity timetables, constraints and assumptions related to procurement, risk issues related to procurement, and stakeholder roles and responsibilities.
	Quality Reports	Quality reports, which can be presented in graphical, numeric, or qualitative form, can be used as the basis for the performance of corrective action(s) in order to meet project quality expectations. Information included in the reports can include any quality issues promoted by the team, corrective action recommendations, and improvements to a process, project, or product. The reports can also distinguish vendor processes, procedures, or products that do not meet quality expectations.
	Requirements Traceability Matrix	The requirements traceability matrix is a grid used to align requirements to the deliverables that satisfy them in order to ensure that each requirement adds value. The matrix allows the requirements to be monitored throughout the project life cycle and provides a framework for managing scope changes. Requirements can be traced to business needs, project aims, project scope and WBS deliverables, product design and development, testing, and high-level requirements at a minimum. The matrix associates product requirements with deliverables in an effort to insure that each requirement is tested and that tested requirements increase the overall project quality.

PMI, CAPM, and PMBOK are registered marks of the Project Management Institute, Inc.

520

		Control Procurements (Continued)	
Key Inputs (Cont.)	Risk Register	The risk register records each identified risk including those linked to sellers. A determination of seller-related risks is based on the seller's organization, the type of contract, the duration of the contract, the project delivery approach, the external environment, and the contract price. The register typically includes the potential owner of and potential response(s) to each identified risk and may include a title, category, status, cause(s), trigger(s), impacted activity(ies), date(s) of identification, date range(s) for probable occurrence(s), and response deadline(s).
	Agreements	For work to be performed by an external source, a contract between buyer and seller is the type of agreement that is typically utilized. The contract is a mutually binding agreement that commits the seller to provide specified products, services, or results and commits the buyer to pay the seller. It represents a legal relationship subject to remedy through the court system. It contains information such as a schedule with milestone dates, performance reporting criteria, pricing/payment terms, inspection/quality/acceptance criteria, warranties, future support requirements, awards and penalties, insurance/performance bonds, subcontractor approval terms, general terms and conditions, change request procedures, termination clause, and processes for alternative dispute resolution. Review of all pertinent agreements is required to determine that their terms and conditions are satisfied.
	Procurement Documentation	Procurement documentation includes comprehensive supporting records for procurement process management, specifically the statement of work (SOW), payment information, contractor work performance detail, plans, drawings, and relevant correspondence.

Control Procurements (Continued)		
Key Inputs (Cont.)	Approved Change Requests	Approved change requests are requests for modification that have been approved by authorized personnel during the formal change control process. The changes can expand or contract the scope of the project and modify policies, procedures, the project management plan, budgets, and schedules. Approved change requests include such items as changes to a contract's terms and conditions, specifically the statement of work, pricing, and depictions of the products, services, or results that will be provided. An approved change implementation should be verified, its completeness confirmed, retested, and then certified for correctness. Any change to the status of a change request must be updated in the change request log.
Key Tools & Techniques	Claims Administration	A claim is a change where the buyer and seller are unable to agree on the cost or that a change has occurred. If a resolution of the claim cannot be reached, the contested change becomes a dispute that is addressed in accordance with alternative dispute resolution (ADR) per the terms of the contract. If the dispute cannot be resolved, it is considered an appeal, which is addressed through the court system. Claims are recorded, processed, monitored, and administered throughout the contract life cycle.
	Performance Reviews	Performance reviews for contracts use metrics, comparison, and analysis to determine any variances in quality, resource, schedule, and cost performance from the terms and conditions set forth in the contract.
	Inspection	An inspection is performed to measure, examine, and validate that the work and deliverables produced by the contractor fulfill the requirements and product acceptance criteria as documented in the contract.

PMI, CAPM, and PMBOK are registered marks of the Project Management Institute, Inc.

522   © 2008-2018 Crosswind Learning, www.crosswindpm.com

Control Procurements (Continued)		
Key Tools & Techniques (Cont.)	Audits	A procurement audit is a process, performed in accordance with the procurement contract, to determine that procurement activities and deliverables comply with the terms and conditions set forth in the procurement contract. Audit observations should be submitted to the buyer's product manager and the seller's project manager.
Key Outputs	Closed Procurements	Requirements for formal procurement closure are usually delineated in the procurement contract and contained in the procurement management plan. As a rule, the buyer provides a formal, written notice of completion to the seller when all deliverables meet quality and technical requirements and were submitted on time, any claims have been satisfied, and all payments have been made.
	Work Performance Information	Work performance information includes information regarding the performance of the vendor. The vendor's performance is evaluated through a comparison of submitted deliverables, technical performance, and accepted costs to the statement of work (SOW) budget for the work completed.
	Change Requests	Change requests are requests for modification that have not been formally approved through the change control process. Modifications to the cost and schedule baselines or to other impacted components of the project management plan may be requested as the result of procurement decisions.
	Organizational Process Assets Updates	Organizational process assets that can be modified as a result of the control procurements process include payment schedules and requests, the prequalified sellers list, lessons learned, and the procurement file (indexed contract documentation).

12.3.1. Contract Administrator

The contract administrator is the manager of the contract. The main responsibility of the contract administrator is **to protect the integrity and purpose of the contract**.

Know the difference between the project manager and contract administrator on a project in relation to the contract.

12.3.2. Project Manager in the Control Procurements Area

The role of the project manager during Control Procurements is to help ensure successful execution of the contract. Project managers typically work with the contract administrator to accomplish a successful execution as the scope, terms, and conditions of the contract are defined and as work results become complete. Remember that even though project managers are responsible for delivery of the project deliverables, they cannot change the contract. **Only the contract administrator is authorized to change the contract**.

12.3.3. Centralized and Decentralized Contracting

In a **centralized** environment, contract administrators **support each other**. They have **career paths** and likely have a great degree of **shared expertise**.

In a **decentralized** environment, the project **has only one contract administrator who does not have support** from other contract administrators. The position is viewed more as a need instead of a career type position; the person **likely works on only one project**, or is the only contract administrator working on a specific project.

Understand and know the differences between centralized and decentralized contracting environments.

12.3.4. Formal Acceptance

Formal acceptance is a major component of the contract because it represents the buyer's agreement that the outsourced work is acceptably complete.

Know what formal acceptance is and what can occur once its been issued.

The source for the above text is the Project Management Institute, *A Guide to the Project Management Body of Knowledge*, (*PMBOK® Guide*) – Sixth Edition, Project Management Institute Inc., 2017, Pages 443-452

12.4. Project Procurement Management Formulas and Variables

Description	Formula	Variable (Component)	Example
The **expected cost** of the work in the contract for an FPIF contract	Sum of the costs of the work of the contract for the seller	(TC) Target Cost	TC = $1M
The **expected profit** of the work in the contract for an FPIF contract	Can be calculated in a variety of ways, depending on contract environment	(TP) Target Profit	TP = $200,000
The **profit margin** compared to the target cost for an FPIF contract	Typically established by industry and company	Profit Rate at Target Cost	20%
The **total of the target cost and target profit**; should be the total target value of the contract work barring any overruns or underruns for an FPIF contract	Target Cost + Target Profit Target Price = TC + TP	Target Price	$1,200,000
A **percentage of the target cost (TC)** for an FPIF contract This is the maximum total amount the buyer expects to pay for the work. Anything above this amount is covered by the seller.	Typically established by industry and company	Ceiling Price	140% of Cost or $1,400,000

Description	Formula	Variable (Component)	Example
The **ratio between the buyer and seller for any cost savings or overruns** that impact the total contract amount and profit for an FPIF contract or other applicable contract	Negotiated between buyer and seller	Share Ratio (SR)	70%/30%
The total **amount of money the buyer will pay** regardless of cost overrun on the contract for an FPIF contract	PTA=(Ceiling Price - Target Price) / Buyer Share + Target Cost $1,285,714.29 = ($1,400,000 - $1,200,000) / 0.70 + $1,000,000	Point of Total Assumption (PTA)	$1,285,714.29
Calculation that determines the point at which it makes more sense **to make-or-buy** (rent) something needed for a project	($ per day) x (number of days) = purchase price + (maintenance fee per day x number of days)	Make-or-Buy Analysis	$100x = $5,000 + $50x. Solve for x as the number of days

12.5. Project Procurement Management Terminology

Term	Description
Acquisition	Obtaining human and material resources for project activities
Advertising	Any activity that results in positive attention to the project
Agreements	A document or communication that defines the intentions of a project; examples include a contract, a memorandum of understanding (MOU), and letters of agreement
Bid Documents	The documentation utilized to request information, quotations, or proposals from prospective sellers
Bidder Conference	Meetings with potential sellers that occur before bids or proposals are prepared and which are used to ensure that all sellers have an unambiguous and common comprehension of the procurement; also known as a contractor conference, vendor conference, or pre-bid conference
Bill of Materials (BOM)	A formal document showing the hierarchy of the components and subcomponents that make up the product
Buyer	The person, group, or entity that obtains the products, services, or results of the project
Claim	A demand, under the terms of the contract, for consideration by the buyer from the seller or the seller from the buyer
Claims Administration	The process of managing a project's contract claims
Closed Procurements	The written formal notification, from the buyer to the seller, that the contract has been completed; typically completion is dependent on the seller meeting the terms and conditions of the contract
Conduct Procurements	The process of receiving the seller response(s) to the request(s) for quote(s), information, proposal(s), or bid(s), then determining the seller(s), and awarding the contract(s)
Contract	A mutually binding agreement that requires, in accordance with the terms of the agreement, the seller to deliver goods or services to the purchaser and the purchaser to compensate the seller for those goods or services
Contract Change Control System	System that manages contract amendments
Control Procurements	The process of managing contract performance
Cost Plus Award Fee Contract (CPAF)	A contract in which the seller receives payments for actual costs related to completed work plus an award that is at the discretion of the buyer; the award that typically represents seller profit
Cost Plus Fixed Fee (CPFF) Contract	A contract in which the supplier receives payment for allowable costs plus a fixed fee typically based on estimated cost
Cost Plus Incentive Fee (CPIF) Contract	A contract in which the supplier receives payment for allowable costs, as well as a pre-negotiated fee and an incentive fee (if incentives are met)
Cost Plus Percentage of Cost (CPPC) Contract	A contract that reimburses the seller for cost, plus a negotiated percentage of the total costs

Term	Description
Cost Reimbursable (CR) Contract	A mutually binding agreement that compensates the seller for goods or services on the basis of actual costs plus a fee that represents the seller's profit and typically includes an incentive if specific objectives, such as budget or schedule targets, are met
Fee	Profit realized by the seller upon completion of a procurement contract
Fixed Price Contract	A mutually binding agreement that compensates the seller for goods or services on the basis of a fixed amount identified in the agreement, notwithstanding the seller's costs; also known as a Firm Fixed-Price Contract (FFP)
Fixed-Price Incentive Fee Contract (FPIF)	A contract in which the seller provides products or services based on a well defined scope of work for a set price, but which allow for additional payments to the seller if predefined performance objectives are met; the seller assumes the majority of the risk
Fixed-Price with Economic Price Adjustment Contract (FP-EPA)	A contract that requires the seller to provide products or services for a set price based on a well defined scope of work and allows a price adjustment over time in response to a specific indicator, typically a change in the cost of labor or materials; the seller assumes the majority of the risk
Incentive Fee	An amount paid, in addition to the contract amount, for exceeding expectations, particularly in the areas of cost, schedule, or technical performance
Invitation for Bid (IFB)	A procurement document, typically used when requirements are complete, clear, and accurate or with governmental sealed bids, issued by the seller to request a proposal from the seller; in addition to detailed requirements, it often includes acceptability criteria
Make-or-Buy Analysis	The process of determining whether specific work should be created by the project team or purchased from an external source
Make-or-Buy Decision	The result of the process of determining whether specific work should be created by the project team or purchased from an external source
Negotiated Settlement	The resolution and finalization of any contract related issues, claims, and disputes
Negotiation	The process of bringing about a final, objective settlement of all outstanding issues, claims, and disputes
Payment Systems	A system that creates invoices and tracks payments for project products and services
Plan Procurement Management	The process of documenting purchasing decisions and approaches, as well as identifying potential vendors for contract work
Point of Total Assumption (PTA)	The total amount of money the buyer will pay regardless of cost overrun on the contract
Procurement	The acquisition of goods or services from an outside source (vendor)
Procurement Audits	Examinations of contracts and contract processes for legality, completeness, accuracy, and effectiveness
Procurement Documents	The instruments used with bid and proposal activities that include the Invitation for Bid (IFB), the Request for Information (RFI), the Request for Quotation (RFQ), and the Request for Proposal (RFP)
Procurement Management Plan	The document, part of the project or program management plan, used to describe the methods that will be employed by the project team to obtain goods and services from outside the organization

Term	Description
Procurement Performance Reviews	An examination of the seller's execution of the contract, particularly as it relates to the on schedule and within budget delivery and overall quality of the product or service
Procurement Statement of Work	A description of a procurement item that is broken down to the appropriate level of detail that will allow potential sellers to determine if they are capable of providing the products or services associated with the contract scope
Procurement Strategy	The buyer's approach to determining the project delivery method and the class of legally binding agreement(s) that will be used to deliver the desired results
Project Procurement Management	The processes required to purchase or acquire any products, services, or results from a source outside of the project team
Proposal Evaluation Techniques	A formal seller review process used with complex procurements and carried out in accordance with the buyer's procurement policies
Prospective Sellers of Products or Services	The list of vendors the company has determined to be capable of providing goods or services
Records Management System	The processes, controls, and tools used to record and maintain project information
Request for Information (RFI)	A buyer issued procurement document requesting a potential seller to provide information related to the seller's ability to deliver a product, service, or capability
Request for Proposal (RFP)	A procurement document issued by the buyer to request a proposal from the seller; typically describes acceptability criteria and a description of the product, service, or capability the buyer wishes to procure
Request for Quote (RFQ)	A document used to get bids or quotes from possible suppliers, usually for commodity type items, with minimal customization
Retainage	A part of the payment per the terms of the contract that the buyer retains until the project is complete; used to ensure that the seller completes the work per terms of the contract
Selected Sellers	Vendors chosen to provide products or services
Seller	An individual or entity that provides goods or services to a buyer
Seller Proposals	An offer from a vendor who is being considered as a provider of a product or service
Service Level Agreement (SLA)	A contract between an internal or external service provider and the end user that delineates the level of service expected from the service provider
Source Selection Criteria	Seller attributes that will be considered by the buyer; typically includes capacity to deliver, costs, delivery dates, expertise, and contract approach
Termination Clause	A clause in the contract that allows both the buyer and the seller to end the contract
Time and Material Contract (T&M)	A mutually binding agreement that compensates the seller for goods or services on the basis of fixed hourly rates for labor and the actual costs of materials; represents a composite of a cost-reimbursable contract (cost of materials can rise) and a fixed-price contract (labor cost are agreed on by buyer and seller before the start of the contract)

The source for the above definitions is the Glossary of the Project Management Institute, *A Guide to the Project Management Body of Knowledge*, (*PMBOK® Guide*) – Sixth Edition, Project Management Institute Inc., 2017

Chapter 12 Procurement

12.6.   Project Procurement Management Tests and Exercises

12.6.1.   Project Procurement Management Practice Test

Answers are in section 12.7.1.

1.   The project is using a company to provide the technicians for a national network upgrade project. Presently, the buyer is having issues with the seller accomplishing the work of the project according to the contract schedule. The buyer lets the seller know that it is in default for failure to execute per terms of the contract. The buyer also decides to stop payment for work already accomplished until the issue is resolved. What most accurately describes this situation?

(A) The buyer is right in stopping payment until the issue is resolved
(B) The buyer is wrong in stopping payment until the issue is resolved
(C) Both sides appear to be in default of the contract
(D) The seller is wrong and needs to correct the situation

2.   The contract is expected to cost $560K. Actual cost is $510K. There is a 50%/50% share of any cost savings. What is the total value of the contract?

(A) $535K
(B) $510K
(C) $560K
(D) $610K

3.   You are the project manager working with the customer on a call center implementation. Your company is responsible for the call center infrastructure. The customer needs some modifications to the scope of the project due to the availability of new functionality. This modification requires that the scope of work to the contract be modified. Who can modify the contract?

(A) The project manager for the buyer
(B) The contract administrator for the company
(C) The project managers for the buyer and seller
(D) The project manager for the seller

4.   What type of contract exposes the seller to the most risk when entering into a contract?

(A) Time and materials because there is no provision for an increase in the workers salary
(B) Cost plus percentage of cost because the seller's net can decrease if the cost decreases
(C) Purchase order because there is no provision for an increase in material costs
(D) Fixed-price because there is no provision for increases in the seller's costs

5. Your company is involved in a new project in which the information and intellectual property associated with it are highly sensitive. Given this, which of the following makes the most sense when planning the project?

(A) Outsourcing and having the partner sign a nondisclosure agreement
(B) Having only the creators of the idea work on the project to control who knows about the intellectual property
(C) Outsourcing to an offshore development facility so your local competitors won't know your intellectual property details
(D) Making the product internally

6. The project will be using a vendor to purchase network equipment for a national network upgrade project. The buyer of the equipment is providing the list of models and quantity of each piece of equipment that she wants to purchase. What type of document is being provided to the sellers?

(A) Request for information (RFI)
(B) Invitation for bid (IFB)
(C) Request for quote (RFQ)
(D) Request for proposal (RFP)

7. You are purchasing 67 desktop computers, monitors, and a standard desktop software package for an upcoming project. What type of contract will you likely use?

(A) Net 30 because interest charges are avoided if you pay the entire cost within 30 days
(B) Fixed-price because the price will be locked in
(C) Net 90 because interest charges are avoided if you pay the entire cost within 90 days
(D) Purchase order because it is a general purchase vehicle for commodity purchases

8. All the following are reasons for outsourcing work except...

(A) Your company doesn't possess the skills needed for the work
(B) Your company doesn't have excessive capacity for the work
(C) Your company isn't concerned about protecting the information associated with the work
(D) Your company has excessive capacity for the work

9. What is the primary mechanism that needs to be in place for a single source noncompetitive procurement?

(A) A mechanism that insures there are no kickbacks
(B) A mechanism that insures that there is no impropriety or unreasonable pricing
(C) A mechanism that insures there is no price gouging
(D) A mechanism that insures there is no inappropriate relationship between the procurer and the source

10. A city is buying services from a construction company to build a new freeway for $4M over three years. At the start of each year, the amount fluctuates relative to the national cost of living. This is an example of what type of contract?

(A) Cost plus economic price adjust
(B) Cost plus incentive fee
(C) Fixed-price cost of living adjust
(D) Fixed-price economic price adjust

11. The project will be using a company to provide the technicians for a national network upgrade project. Presently, the team is in the process of conducting a make-or-buy analysis. What is the primary factor that will influence the team's decision?

(A) The comparison of skill sets between alternatives
(B) The comparison of resource availability between alternatives
(C) The comparison of costs between alternatives
(D) The comparison of experience between alternatives

12. The project is utilizing a vendor to purchase and install a network solution for a national network upgrade project. The buyer of the solution is providing a functionality scope of work to the seller. Of the following, which is the most logical reason this scope was selected?

(A) The buyer knows exactly what is needed and wants no variance from the specifications
(B) The buyer's only concern is that the vendor achieves the required goals
(C) The buyer must have the solution in place within a tight timeframe and needs the vendor to conform to a rigid schedule
(D) The buyer does not have the personnel to ensure that each step in the process is completed according to specifications

13. Your company just completed a make-or-buy decision regarding a new area of development. The project manager and the team will refer to the procurement management plan for guidance in connection with a number of ensuing activities. Which of the following best describes those activities?

(A) Establishing which procurement documents are needed, running bidder conferences or addressing noncompetitive forms of procurement, selecting vendors, and establishing contracts
(B) Running bidder conferences or addressing noncompetitive forms of procurement, selecting vendors, establishing contracts, executing contracts, and closing contracts
(C) Establishing which procurement documents are needed, creating the procurement documents, running bidder conferences or addressing noncompetitive forms of procurement, selecting vendors, and establishing contracts
(D) Running bidder conferences or addressing noncompetitive forms of procurement, selecting vendors, establishing contracts, administering contracts, and closing contracts

14. The project utilizes a vendor to provide the technicians for a national network upgrade project. The buyer agrees to pay the vendor an incentive fee. Of the following, which is the most logical reason the buyer would pay the fee?

(A) The buyer wants to ensure that the vendor will be responsive to any issues that arise during the upgrade
(B) The buyer wants to ensure that the vendor's standard of productivity is aligned to that of the buyer
(C) The buyer wants to ensure that the vendor will work well with the buyer's employees
(D) None of the answers

15. You are the project manager on a defense project. The buyer wants to get an idea of how much he will pay for cost overruns. With the following variables, calculate the point of total assumption: Expected Cost=$125,000; Expected Profit=$25,000; Target Price=$150,000; Buyer/Seller Share Ratio=60%/40%; Ceiling Price=$180,000; Maximum Overrun=130%.

(A) $175,000.00
(B) $137,019.23
(C) $151,442.31
(D) $129,807.69

16. The project will be using a company to provide the technicians for a national network upgrade project. The buyer of the solution is providing a design scope of work to the seller. Of the following, which is the most logical reason this scope was selected?

(A) The buyer knows exactly what is needed and wants no variance from the specifications
(B) The buyer's only concern is that the vendor achieves the required goals
(C) The buyer must have the solution in place within a tight timeframe and needs the vendor to conform to a rigid schedule
(D) The buyer does not have the personnel to ensure that each step in the process is completed according to specifications

17. Of the following, what best represents a contract component and the reason for including it in a contract between a buyer and vendor in connection with the purchase of a debit card add-on system?

(A) Share because the buyer needs the work done in a timely manner
(B) Incentive because the buyer needs the costs to come in as low as possible
(C) Incentive because the buyer needs the work done with minimal resources
(D) Share because the buyer needs the costs to come in as low as possible

18. The project will be using a company to provide the technicians for a national network upgrade project. The buyer is providing to the prospective seller a greatly detailed description of what the buyer wants the seller to do on the project. What type of document is being provided to the seller?

(A) Request for information (RFI)
(B) Request for proposal (RFP)
(C) Invitation for bid (IFB)
(D) Request for quote (RFQ)

19. A contract is being negotiated with a single source provider that will contain special provisions since the work is being performed at a loss so the provider can gain experience in the market. Of the following, which best represents a special provision?

(A) Payment terms, including arbitration remedies
(B) Intellectual property rights and required nondisclosure documentation
(C) Ability to subcontract
(D) Criteria around which the provider of services can refer to the work

20. You are the project manager on a defense project. The buyer wants to get an idea of how much he will pay for cost overruns. With the following variables, calculate the point of total assumption: Expected Cost=$120,000; Expected Profit=$30,000; Target Price=$150,000; Buyer/Seller Share Ratio=75%/25%; Ceiling Price=$156,000; Maximum Overrun=125%.

(A) $106,400.00
(B) $128,000.00
(C) $117,600.00
(D) $100,800.00

21. All the following items are requirements of a legal contract except...

(A) A proposition to exchange something of value for something of value
(B) A purpose for the contract
(C) A buyer willingness to accept a seller's offer
(D) A buyer and seller with the capacity to enter into a contract

22. You are the owner of a house painting company. You occasionally have the need for an automated paint sprayer. This tool sells for $1,250 and costs $20 a day to maintain. You can rent one for $150 a day with maintenance included. How many days would you need to use this tool before it makes sense to buy instead of rent?

(A) Twelve days
(B) Six days
(C) Ten days
(D) Eight days

23. The customer is doing a national network upgrade program. The customer has issues with the vendor accomplishing the work in accordance with the schedule set out in the contract. The customer informs the vendor that it is in default for failure to execute per the terms of the contract. A senior manager for the customer suggests stopping payment for work already accomplished, but the procurement department rejects this idea. What most accurately describes this situation?

(A) The senior manager's suggestion to stop payment until the issue is resolved is the best course of action
(B) The procurement department's rejection of the senior manager's idea is the best course of action
(C) Both sides appear to be in default of the contract
(D) The vendor appears to be wrong and needs to accept lack of payment until it corrects the situation

24. Why is a cost plus percentage of cost contract bad for the buyer?

(A) It provides no reason for the seller to control cost
(B) It provides no reason for the buyer to control cost
(C) It requires the seller to audit all costs incurred
(D) It requires use of a more detailed request for proposal (RFP)

25. All the following are advantages of centralized contracting except...

(A) Lack of career path for contract administrators
(B) Career path for contract administrators
(C) Contract administrators have teammates for contract-related support
(D) Expertise in the contracting area

26. Of the following, which is a procurement document?

(A) Management plan contract
(B) Procurement management plan
(C) Proposal management plan
(D) Solicitation management plan

27. Your company is working with a staffing company to provide a technical writer for your newest project. The cost is $75 per hour. The technical writer will work on the project until it is complete, then the contract will end. Which of the following best describes the type of contract typically used in this situation?

(A) Fixed-price because it lends itself to small initiatives and staff supplementation
(B) Time and materials because it ensures that the cost of the writer does not increase during the term of the contract
(C) Time and materials because it lends itself to small initiatives and staff supplementation
(D) Fixed-price because it ensures that the cost of the writer does not increase during the term of the contract

28. A single-phase medical software project is in the process of closing. There are a number of processes coming together as things finish up. Which of the following is correct?

(A) Control procurements comes before close project or phase
(B) Close project or phase occurs only if the project is completed as planned
(C) Close project or phase and control procurements occur at the same time
(D) Close project or phase comes before control procurements

29. You are the project manager on a defense project. The buyer wants to get an idea of how much he will pay for cost overruns. With the following variables, calculate the point of total assumption: Expected Cost=$150,000; Expected Profit=$37,500; Target Price=$187,500; Buyer/Seller Share Ratio=60%/40%; Ceiling Price=$225,000; Maximum Overrun=150%.

(A) $201,875.00
(B) $223,125.00
(C) $212,500.00
(D) $191,250.00

30. Which of the following best describes a unilateral contract?

(A) The seller establishes a price, and the buyer simply has to purchase the item
(B) The buyer and seller establish contract parameters during a single negotiation session
(C) The buyer establishes a not-to-exceed price for the seller to accept or reject
(D) The seller establishes a not-to-exceed price for the buyer to accept or reject

12.7.   Project Procurement Management Answers for Tests and Exercises

12.7.1.   Project Procurement Management Practice Test Answers

We recommend that you download answer sheets from the Crosswind website, so you can practice the test as many times as you like.

1.   The project is using a company to provide the technicians for a national network upgrade project. Presently, the buyer is having issues with the seller accomplishing the work of the project according to the contract schedule. The buyer lets the seller know that it is in default for failure to execute per terms of the contract. The buyer also decides to stop payment for work already accomplished until the issue is resolved. What most accurately describes this situation?

Correct Answer: (C) Both sides appear to be in default of the contract
Explanation: A seller who fails to perform as defined in the contract is in default of the contract. The buyer choosing to stop payment creates a default situation as well. Two wrongs do not make a right in this case. The buyer is not right in stopping payment just because the other side is in default. The other answers are both accurate, but they are not the best answer. [Crosswind Manual 12.1.5; *PMBOK® Guide* 12.1.1.6]

2.   The contract is expected to cost $560K. Actual cost is $510K. There is a 50%/50% share of any cost savings. What is the total value of the contract?

Correct Answer: (A) $535K
Explanation: The $560K is the expected value of the contract and the actual cost of the contract is $510K, resulting in a savings of $50K. $25K of the savings goes to the seller and the other $25K goes to the buyer. The actual cost of $510K and $25K savings share makes the total value of the contract worth $535K. [Crosswind Manual 12.1.8; No *PMBOK® Guide* Reference]

3.   You are the project manager working with the customer on a call center implementation. Your company is responsible for the call center infrastructure. The customer needs some modifications to the scope of the project due to the availability of new functionality. This modification requires that the scope of work to the contract be modified. Who can modify the contract?

Correct Answer: (B) The contract administrator for the company
Explanation: The contract administrator for the company is the only person with the authority to change the contract. The project managers from the buyer and the seller will likely have input to the changes, but the contract administrator is the person making those changes to the contract. [Crosswind Manual 12.3.2; No *PMBOK® Guide* Reference]

4. What type of contract exposes the seller to the most risk when entering into a contract?

Correct Answer: (D) Fixed-price because there is no provision for increases in the seller's costs

Explanation: The fixed-price contract has the most risk for the seller because the contract limits the amount that the buyer will pay for the project. The seller must have a detailed understanding of exactly what is needed on the project so it can control cost. Cost plus percentage of cost provides the least risk to the seller. A purchase order provides the seller with no risk because the price for a commodity type item has been established. Time and materials contracts are typically used for smaller amounts of work and staff augmentation. [Crosswind Manual 12.1.7; *PMBOK® Guide* 12.1.1.6]

5. Your company is involved in a new project in which the information and intellectual property associated with it are highly sensitive. Given this, which of the following makes the most sense when planning the project?

Correct Answer: (D) Making the product internally

Explanation: When intellectual property and proprietary information are involved, it makes sense for a company to keep the work internal. Having an outsourcing partner sign a nondisclosure agreement is not the best answer. The other answers are distracters. [Crosswind Manual 12.1.2; *PMBOK® Guide* 12.1.3.2]

6. The project will be using a vendor to purchase network equipment for a national network upgrade project. The buyer of the equipment is providing the list of models and quantity of each piece of equipment that she wants to purchase. What type of document is being provided to the sellers?

Correct Answer: (C) Request for quote (RFQ)

Explanation: A request for quote (RFQ) obtains prices from a company for goods or services. A request for proposal (RFP) is a detailed, very specific approach to a customized solution. A request for information (RFI) is associated with finding potential vendors for consideration for proposals or quotes. An invitation for bid (IFB) is similar to the RFP but is typically used in government contracting. [Crosswind Manual 12.1.11; *PMBOK® Guide* 12.1.3.3]

7. You are purchasing 67 desktop computers, monitors, and a standard desktop software package for an upcoming project. What type of contract will you likely use?

Correct Answer: (D) Purchase order because it is a general purchase vehicle for commodity purchases

Explanation: The purchase order is a general purchase vehicle for commodity type purchases. Typically, it is for items that are standard, non-customized, and non-negotiable in price. Fixed-price is typically for a detailed, customized, negotiated solution. Net 30 and Net 90 are distracters. [Crosswind Manual 12.1.7; *PMBOK® Guide* 12.1.1.6]

8. All the following are reasons for outsourcing work except...

Correct Answer: (D) Your company has excessive capacity for the work

Explanation: Excessive capacity to do work is a good reason not to outsource the work. The other answers are good reasons to outsource the work. [Crosswind Manual 12.1.2; *PMBOK® Guide* 12.1.3.2]

9. What is the primary mechanism that needs to be in place for a single source noncompetitive procurement?

Correct Answer: (B) A mechanism that insures that there is no impropriety or unreasonable pricing
Explanation: One type of noncompetitive form of procurement is single source, in which a single company is chosen even though others are available. There must be a mechanism in place to insure there is no impropriety or unreasonable pricing. [Crosswind Manual 12.2.3; No *PMBOK® Guide* Reference]

10. A city is buying services from a construction company to build a new freeway for $4M over three years. At the start of each year, the amount fluctuates relative to the national cost of living. This is an example of what type of contract?

Correct Answer: (D) Fixed-price economic price adjust
Explanation: A fixed-price economic price adjust contract is a contract that generally has a fixed price, but because of contract length, will adjust year-by-year as a neutral economic indicator moves upward or downward. The other answers are distracters. [Crosswind Manual 12.1.7; *PMBOK® Guide* 12.1.1.6]

11. The project will be using a company to provide the technicians for a national network upgrade project. Presently, the team is in the process of conducting a make-or-buy analysis. What is the primary factor that will influence the team's decision?

Correct Answer: (C) The comparison of costs between alternatives
Explanation: Assume, for the exam, that cost comparison is the only factor considered during a make-or-buy analysis. In reality, skill sets, experience, and resource availability are also considered. [Crosswind Manual 12.1.2; *PMBOK® Guide* 12.1.3.2]

12. The project is utilizing a vendor to purchase and install a network solution for a national network upgrade project. The buyer of the solution is providing a functionality scope of work to the seller. Of the following, which is the most logical reason this scope was selected?

Correct Answer: (B) The buyer's only concern is that the vendor achieves the required goals
Explanation: The functionality scope of work shows the general functional specifications that the outcome of the project needs to have when complete. A design scope of work shows specifically what is to be created. The other answers are distracters. [Crosswind Manual 12.1.10; No *PMBOK® Guide* Reference]

13. Your company just completed a make-or-buy decision regarding a new area of development. The project manager and the team will refer to the procurement management plan for guidance in connection with a number of ensuing activities. Which of the following best describes those activities?

Correct Answer: (C) Establishing which procurement documents are needed, creating the procurement documents, running bidder conferences or addressing noncompetitive forms of procurement, selecting vendors, and establishing contracts
Explanation: Once the buy decision has been made, the procurement management plan is the guidance source for establishing which procurement documents are needed, creating the procurement documents, running bidder conferences or addressing noncompetitive forms of procurement, selecting vendors, and establishing contracts. All the other answers are distracters. [Crosswind Manual 12.2; *PMBOK® Guide* 12.2.2.3]

14. The project utilizes a vendor to provide the technicians for a national network upgrade project. The buyer agrees to pay the vendor an incentive fee. Of the following, which is the most logical reason the buyer would pay the fee?

Correct Answer: (B) The buyer wants to ensure that the vendor's standard of productivity is aligned to that of the buyer
Explanation: Incentive fees are used by the buyer to get the seller aligned to a standard of productivity similar to the buyer's. All the other answers are distracters. [Crosswind Manual 12.1.7; *PMBOK® Guide* 12.1.1.6]

15. You are the project manager on a defense project. The buyer wants to get an idea of how much he will pay for cost overruns. With the following variables, calculate the point of total assumption: Expected Cost=$125,000; Expected Profit=$25,000; Target Price=$150,000; Buyer/Seller Share Ratio=60%/40%; Ceiling Price=$180,000; Maximum Overrun=130%.

Correct Answer: (A) $175,000
Explanation: The formula for point of total assumption (PTA) is as follows:
((Ceiling Price - Target Price) / Buyer Share) + Expected Cost
$175,000 = ($180,000 - $150,000) / 0.60) + $125,000
[Crosswind Manual 12.1.9; No *PMBOK® Guide* Reference]

16. The project will be using a company to provide the technicians for a national network upgrade project. The buyer of the solution is providing a design scope of work to the seller. Of the following, which is the most logical reason this scope was selected?

Correct Answer: (A) The buyer knows exactly what is needed and wants no variance from the specifications
Explanation: A design scope of work shows specifically what is to be created. The functionality scope of work shows the general functional specifications that the outcome of the project needs to have when complete. The other answers are distracters. [Crosswind Manual 12.1.10; No *PMBOK® Guide* Reference]

17. Of the following, what best represents a contract component and the reason for including it in a contract between a buyer and vendor in connection with the purchase of a debit card add-on system?

Correct Answer: (D) Share because the buyer needs the costs to come in as low as possible

Explanation: A share is a contract component that divides any remaining money between the buyer and the seller. It is normally a negotiated split between the two parties. It is typically different from a traditional incentive fee in that an incentive fee pays compensation based on certain measurable performance metrics that have been established and agreed upon. [Crosswind Manual 12.1.8; No *PMBOK® Guide* Reference]

18. The project will be using a company to provide the technicians for a national network upgrade project. The buyer is providing to the prospective seller a greatly detailed description of what the buyer wants the seller to do on the project. What type of document is being provided to the seller?

Correct Answer: (B) Request for proposal (RFP)

Explanation: A request for proposal (RFP) deals with a detailed, very specific approach to a customized solution. A request for information (RFI) deals with finding potential vendors for consideration for proposals or quotes. A request for quote (RFQ) obtains prices from a company for goods or services. An invitation for bid (IFB) is similar to the RFP but typically used in government contracting. [Crosswind Manual 12.1.11; *PMBOK® Guide* 12.1.3.3]

19. A contract is being negotiated with a single source provider that will contain special provisions since the work is being performed at a loss so the provider can gain experience in the market. Of the following, which best represents a special provision?

Correct Answer: (D) Criteria around which the provider of services can refer to the work

Explanation: Special provisions are extra items that are added to a contract after negotiations have occurred. Standard terms and conditions are typically part of a template the company will use in a contract and often address payment options, intellectual property rights, and subcontracting. [Crosswind Manual 12.2.8; No *PMBOK® Guide* Reference]

20. You are the project manager on a defense project. The buyer wants to get an idea of how much he will pay for cost overruns. With the following variables, calculate the point of total assumption: Expected Cost=$120,000; Expected Profit=$30,000; Target Price=$150,000; Buyer/Seller Share Ratio=75%/25%; Ceiling Price=$156,000; Maximum Overrun=125%.

Correct Answer: (B) $128,000.00

Explanation: The formula for point of total assumption (PTA) is as follows:
((Ceiling Price - Target Price) / Buyer Share) + Target Cost.
$128,000.00 = (($156,000 - $150,000) / 0.75) + $120,000
[Crosswind Manual 12.1.9; No *PMBOK® Guide* Reference]

21. All the following items are requirements of a legal contract except...

Correct Answer: (B) A purpose for the contract
Explanation: A contract must have a <u>legal</u> purpose. The other answers are components of a contract. [Crosswind Manual 12.1.5; *PMBOK® Guide* 12.1.1.6]

22. You are the owner of a house painting company. You occasionally have the need for an automated paint sprayer. This tool sells for $1,250 and costs $20 a day to maintain. You can rent one for $150 a day with maintenance included. How many days would you need to use this tool before it makes sense to buy instead of rent?

Correct Answer: (C) Ten days
Explanation: To complete this question, solve for the number of days. The number of days is the variable D in the formula. $1,250+20D=$150D is the formula. First, move D to one side of the equation. Subtracting $20D from both sides gives $1,250=$130D. Next, divide both sides by 130, which isolates D. That equals 9.6 (rounded up), which means you would need to use the tool for ten full days before it makes sense to buy the tool.
[Crosswind Manual 12.1.4; No *PMBOK® Guide* Reference]

23. The customer is doing a national network upgrade program. The customer has issues with the vendor accomplishing the work in accordance with the schedule set out in the contract. The customer informs the vendor that it is in default for failure to execute per the terms of the contract. A senior manager for the customer suggests stopping payment for work already accomplished, but the procurement department rejects this idea. What most accurately describes this situation?

Correct Answer: (B) The procurement department's rejection of the senior manager's idea is the best course of action
Explanation: A company who fails to perform as defined in the contract is in default of the contract. That the vendor is in default is obvious; the customer will only be in default if it stops payment for work already accomplished. [Crosswind Manual 12.1.5; *PMBOK® Guide* 12.1.1.6]

24. Why is a cost plus percentage of cost contract bad for the buyer?

Correct Answer: (A) It provides no reason for the seller to control cost
Explanation: In a cost plus percentage of cost contract, the seller is paid a fee that is a percentage of the total cost. As a result of this characteristic of the contract, there is no incentive for the seller to control cost. The other answers are distracters. [Crosswind Manual 12.1.7; *PMBOK® Guide* 12.1.1.6]

25. All the following are advantages of centralized contracting except...

Correct Answer: (A) Lack of career path for contract administrators
Explanation: Centralized contracting provides a functional type of environment for the role, meaning that there is a career path for the person, instead of a lack of career path. The other answers fit the description of advantages for centralized contracting. [Crosswind Manual 12.3.3; No *PMBOK® Guide* Reference]

26. Of the following, which is a procurement document?

   Correct Answer: (B) Procurement management plan
   Explanation: The procurement management plan describes how the project team will obtain goods and services from outside the organization. [Crosswind Manual 12.1; *PMBOK® Guide* 12.1]

27. Your company is working with a staffing company for supplementing a technical writer for your newest project. The cost is $75 per hour. The technical writer will work on the project until it is complete, then the contract will end. Which of the following best describes the type of contract typically used in this situation?

   Correct Answer: (C) Time and materials because it lends itself to small initiatives and staff supplementation
   Explanation: A time and materials contract is typically used for smaller projects or staff augmentation, such as this example. The fixed-price contract has a seller doing work for a set price. The cost plus contract pays a seller costs plus a negotiated fee. The cost plus incentive fee pays a seller costs plus an incentive fee for meeting performance goals. [Crosswind Manual 12.1.7; *PMBOK® Guide* 12.1.1.6]

28. A single-phase medical software project is in the process of closing. There are a number of processes coming together as things finish up. Which of the following is correct?

   Correct Answer: (A) Control procurements comes before close project or phase
   Explanation: In a single-phase project, controlling procurements will occur before the phase (or project) is closed out. Close Project or Phase occurs regardless of how the project ends. [Crosswind Manual 12.3; *PMBOK® Guide* 12.1.3.6]

29. You are the project manager on a defense project. The buyer wants to get an idea of how much he will pay for cost overruns. With the following variables, calculate the point of total assumption: Expected Cost=$150,000; Expected Profit=$37,500; Target Price=$187,500; Buyer/Seller Share Ratio=60%/40%; Ceiling Price=$225,000; Maximum Overrun=150%.

   Correct Answer: (C) $212,500.00
   Explanation: The formula for point of total assumption (PTA) is as follows:
   ((Ceiling Price - Target Price) / Buyer Share) + Target Cost.
   $212,500.00 = (($225,000 - $187,500) / 0.6) + $150,000
   [Crosswind Manual 12.1.9; No *PMBOK® Guide* Reference]

30. Which of the following best describes a unilateral contract?

   Correct Answer: (A) The seller establishes a price, and the buyer simply has to purchase the item.
   Explanation: In a unilateral contract, the seller establishes a price and the buyer has the option to purchase at that price. Thus, *uni* means one-sided on the negotiations. The other answers are distracters. [Crosswind Manual 12.1.7; *PMBOK® Guide* 12.1.1.6]

Chapter 13

Project Stakeholder Management

Project Stakeholder Management entails identifying stakeholders and planning, managing, and monitoring their engagement.

Stakeholders are the people, groups, or entities that may impact, be impacted by, or perceive to be impacted by, the work of the project.

The project team is responsible for evaluating the stakeholders' expectations and their impact on the project. The team is also responsible for involving stakeholders in the project and, if at all possible, persuading them to support the decisions and strategies developed for the work of the project and their implementation. Stakeholder involvement, or engagement, relies heavily on continuous and effective communication.

It's important to remember that stakeholder management is ongoing as new stakeholders are identified and as the expectations and impact of existing stakeholders evolve during the project.

Trends

New stakeholder trends designed to ensure project success are:

- The increased effort required during stakeholder identification due to the expanded definition of stakeholders
    - The traditional definition included employees, suppliers, and shareholders who may impact or be impacted by the project, as well as anyone who feels they may be impacted by the project
    - The expanded definition now includes regulatory, lobbying, and environmental groups that may impact or be impacted by the project, in addition to employees, suppliers, and shareholders who may impact or be impacted by the project, as well as anyone who feels they may be impacted by the project
- An increased emphasis on stakeholder engagement
    - The participation of all team members in stakeholder engagement
    - Regular review of stakeholders (which should be at the same rate as reviews of individual project risks)
    - Working with major stakeholders through the concept co-creation, i.e. including them as partners/part of the team
    - Tracking the value of effective stakeholder engagement: positive (benefits of active stakeholder support) and negative (true costs of not engaging stakeholders, typically product recall and/or loss of organization reputation)

Tailoring

Project tailoring, the manner in which the processes of a knowledge area are exercised, is employed to address the distinctive nature of each project.

Successful project tailoring is predicated on a careful consideration of:

- The diversity of stakeholders
- The complexity of stakeholder relationships (the more networks in which stakeholders participate, the greater the chances of their receiving both information and disinformation)
- The communication technology (not only availability, but effectiveness)

Agile/Adaptive Environment

In Agile/adaptive environments (environments where a high degree of change is expected) active and direct engagement of, and robust participation by, the stakeholders is crucial to the success of the project.

These environments advance aggressive transparency, including inviting stakeholders to attend meetings and reviews and publishing artifacts publicly, so that issues can be quickly discovered and addressed. Aggressive transparency is designed to facilitate a dynamic exchange of information between the customer, users, and developers through a co-creative process, which results in increased stakeholder involvement and satisfaction

The source for the above text is the Project Management Institute, *A Guide to the Project Management Body of Knowledge*, (*PMBOK® Guide*) – Sixth Edition, Project Management Institute Inc., 2017, Pages 453-456

In this chapter, we discuss the following:

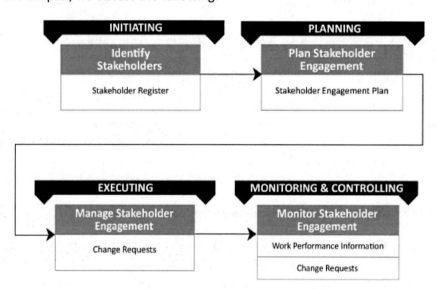

Figure 13-1: Stakeholder Processes

The source for the above figure is the Project Management Institute, *A Guide to the Project Management Body of Knowledge*, (*PMBOK® Guide*) – Sixth Edition, Project Management Institute Inc., 2017, Figure 13-1, Page 454

Although helpful, this list is not all-inclusive in regard to information needed for the exam. It is only suggested material that, if understood and memorized, may increase your exam score.

13.1. Stakeholder Management

Stakeholder management is a complex subject due to the number of people involved in the project, their individual agendas, and the varied situations that can be encountered.

Understand how to balance stakeholder interests.

Some project management training discusses "negotiation" instead of stakeholder management. It is fair to say that negotiation can often resolve issues encountered during the project, but management encompasses much more than negotiation.

A key characteristic of stakeholder management is that, early in the project, an individual stakeholder can have a great degree of influence, but that influence often decreases as the project evolves.

A key area of stakeholder management that needs to be considered is the **identification and analysis of each stakeholder.** It is vital that key stakeholders are engaged, as appropriate, throughout the project.

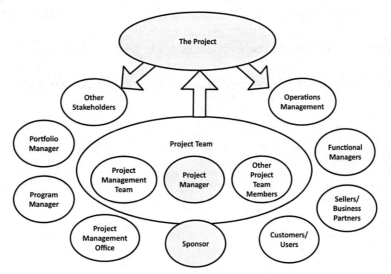

Figure 13-2: Project Stakeholders

Chapter 13
Stakeholder

Typical Stakeholders	
Customers/Users	Project Managers
Sponsor	Project Team
Portfolio Managers	Functional Managers
Portfolio Review Board	Operations Management
Program Managers	Sellers/Business Partners
Project Management Office	Regulatory/Governmental Entities

13.1.1. Balancing Conflicting Stakeholder Interests

There are three considerations, ordered by precedence, for approaching the conflicting stakeholder interests that may arise in the exam's situational questions:

Understand how to balance stakeholder interests.

1. The reasons for undertaking the project with a focus on the market conditions or business needs and the priority of the project compared to other projects
2. The requirements defined in the project charter
3. The project management plan

Sample question: You are the manager of a project where two stakeholders have conflicting ideas about the reporting application that will be used. Stakeholder one wants to use the existing application (a proprietary software) because he is familiar with it. Stakeholder two wants to use an alternate application (a cloud based software), because it is new and has good reviews. The project management plan references the proprietary software. The project charter references the cloud based software. The circumstances surrounding the project do not impact the reporting software choice. Which application should you choose?

To decide on the application, the project manager must first consider the reason for the project, the market conditions or business needs, and the project priority. Since none of those impact the decision, the project manager then considers the project charter. In this case, the project charter indicates the alternate application is to be used, so the correct answer is the alternate application. Even though the project management plan references the existing proprietary application, the application cited in the project charter takes precedence.

13.1.2. Managing Project Change Requests

With regard to addressing project-specific change requests by the customer/sponsor, the following order should help ensure success:

1. Never tell the customer/sponsor "no" when asked about a request. If the customer/sponsor is willing to encounter a delay or pay more to implement the change, it is the decision of the customer/sponsor.
2. Listen to the customer/sponsor regarding their request.
3. Involve the appropriate team members to determine the options associated with the request and their impact.
4. Communicate the options to the customer/sponsor.
5. Let the customer/sponsor make the final decision based on the options you have provided them.
6. If applicable, create a change request to accommodate the option decided upon by the customer/sponsor.

13.2. Identify Stakeholders (Initiating Process Group)

During the Identify Stakeholders process, a determination is made regarding which people and organizations impact and/or are impacted by the project.

Know the Key Inputs, Tools & Techniques, and Outputs for Identify Stakeholders.

Stakeholders may include sponsors, the customer, and those who impact, or perceive themselves to be impacted by, the project.

To manage a successful project, the project manager must ensure that all stakeholders are identified early and that their expectations, influence, importance, and levels of interest are analyzed and periodically reviewed in case adjustments are necessary.

An effective analysis enables the project manager to focus on the expectations of the stakeholders.

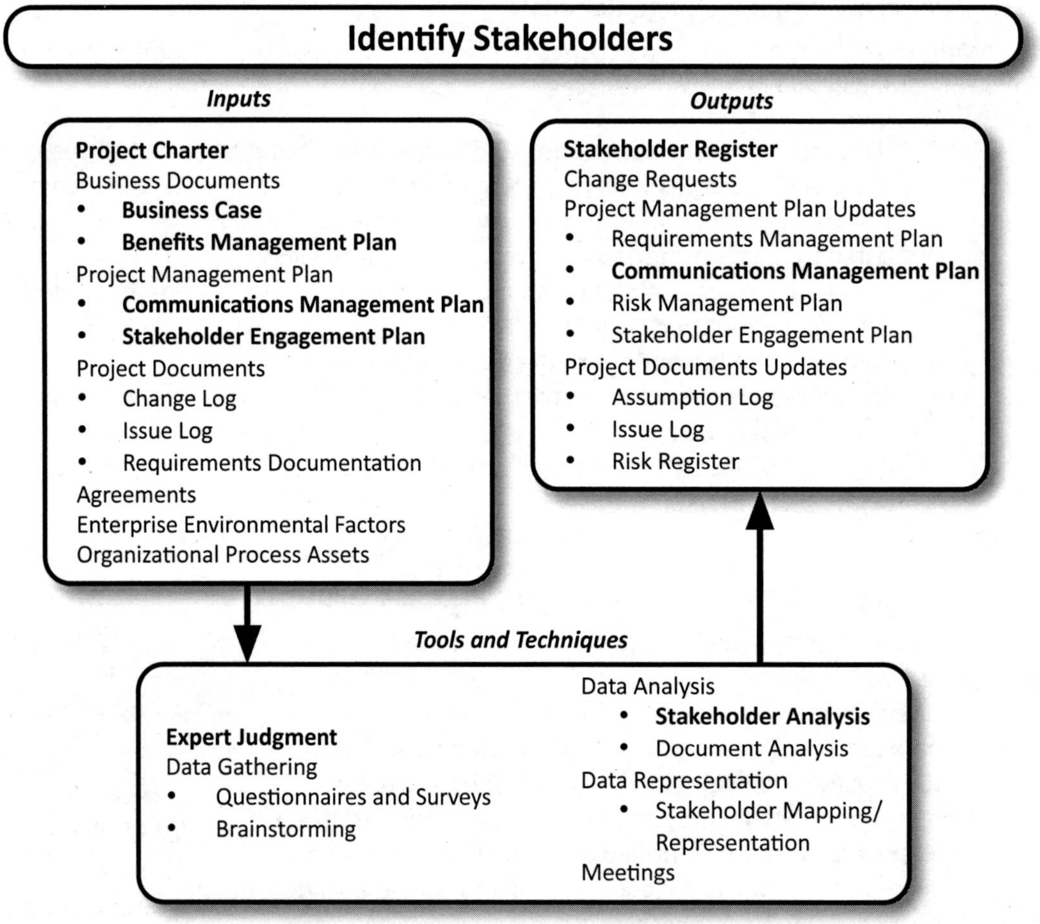

Identify Stakeholders

Inputs

Project Charter
Business Documents
- **Business Case**
- **Benefits Management Plan**
Project Management Plan
- **Communications Management Plan**
- **Stakeholder Engagement Plan**
Project Documents
- Change Log
- Issue Log
- Requirements Documentation
Agreements
Enterprise Environmental Factors
Organizational Process Assets

Outputs

Stakeholder Register
Change Requests
Project Management Plan Updates
- Requirements Management Plan
- **Communications Management Plan**
- Risk Management Plan
- Stakeholder Engagement Plan
Project Documents Updates
- Assumption Log
- Issue Log
- Risk Register

Tools and Techniques

Expert Judgment
Data Gathering
- Questionnaires and Surveys
- Brainstorming

Data Analysis
- **Stakeholder Analysis**
- Document Analysis
Data Representation
- Stakeholder Mapping/ Representation
Meetings

Figure 13-3: Identify Stakeholders Data Flow Diagram
The source for the above figure is the Project Management Institute, *A Guide to the Project Management Body of Knowledge, (PMBOK® Guide) – Sixth Edition,* Project Management Institute Inc., 2017, Figure 13-2, Page 457

Identify Stakeholders (Initiating)		
Key Inputs	Project Charter	The project charter is the document that provides authorization for the existence of the project and gives the project manager the power to use organizational resources to execute the project. The project charter typically lists the key deliverables, the milestones, and the roles and responsibilities of each person involved in the project.
	Business Case	A business case, which usually describes the business need and contains a cost-benefit analysis, is used to justify the creation of the project and is the basis for the project charter. In addition to distinguishing the objectives of the project, it provides an initial catalog of stakeholders.

Draft proj. Charter
- Because it only has one stakeholder right now

Identify Stakeholders (Continued)		
Key Inputs (Cont.)	Benefits Management Plan	The benefits management plan describes the alignment of the project with organizational business goals, the targeted benefits, and the manner in which the benefits are transitioned and measured. Note that the project manager is not responsible for updating or modifying the benefits management plan since it is a business document.
	Communications Management Plan	The communications management plan is a component of the project management plan that documents the planning, structure, implementation, and monitoring/control of communications. It contains: stakeholder communication requirements; the information to be communicated, including language, format, content, and degree of detail; the case for conveyance of the information; the timeframe for and frequency of the distribution, including the manner in which any acknowledgment or response will be effected; the person responsible for communication of the information; the person responsible for authoring release of confidential information; the recipients of the information and their needs, requirements, and expectations; the resources allocated for communication related activities, along with a calendar and budget; the technological methods used for conveyance of the information, including memos, email, press releases, and social media; the methods for updating the communications management plan; a glossary of common terms; flow charts regarding the project's information flow, workflows, meeting plans, and a list of reports; constraints imposed by legislation, regulation, and/or technology; guidelines and templates for project status meetings, project team meetings, and email.
	Stakeholder Engagement Plan	The stakeholder engagement plan is a component of the project management plan that documents the management approach and activities utilized to competently engage stakeholders.

Identify Stakeholders (Continued)		
Key Tools & Techniques	Expert Judgment	Expert judgment is judgment based on expertise acquired in a specific area. It is often more significant and accurate than the best modeling tools available and can be provided by stakeholders, company personnel external to the project, professional organizations or groups, and consultants. It is important to consider expertise related to the organizational politics and power structures, organizational culture, the relevant industry, and a knowledge of the expertise and contributions of individual team members.
	Stakeholder Analysis	Stakeholder analysis is performed to determine the positions and roles of stakeholders, as well as their expectations, interest in the project, level of support for the project, and "stake." Stakes can include one or more of the following: interest (the effect of the project on the stakeholder); legal rights (such as occupational health and safety); moral rights (such as environmental impact); ownership; knowledge; contribution; results of the power/influence grid or power/interest grid or stakeholder cube (three-dimensional model depicting the stakeholder community); results of the salience model (model describing stakeholders in terms of power, urgency, and legitimacy); and results of the directions of influence model, which classifies stakeholders as upward (senior management, sponsor, and steering committee), downward (team members or specialists), outward (stakeholder groups outside the project), or sideward (project manager peers such as middle managers or other project managers).
Key Outputs	Stakeholder Register	The stakeholder register contains information related to identified stakeholders. It includes identification information (name, position, location, project role, and contact information), assessment information (key requirements, potential impact on project results, phase in which the stakeholder wields the greatest influence, and expectations), and stakeholder classification (impact/influence/power/interest, internal/external, or other classification model). It is used to determine which stakeholders could best identify risks and/or have the availability to act as risk owners.

[handwritten margin notes:] Sponsor is 1st stakeholder on register

5 classification of stakeholder
supporter
resister
neutral
unaware
leading

[handwritten bottom note:] Key stakeholder is considered decision makers

Identify Stakeholders (Continued)		
Key Outputs (Cont.)	Communications Management Plan	The communications management plan is a component of the project management plan that documents the planning, structure, implementation, and monitoring/control of communications. It contains: stakeholder communication requirements; the information to be communicated, including language, format, content, and degree of detail; the case for conveyance of the information; the timeframe for and frequency of the distribution, including the manner in which any acknowledgment or response will be effected; the person responsible for communication of the information; the person responsible for authoring release of confidential information; the recipients of the information and their needs, requirements, and expectations; the resources allocated for communication related activities, along with a calendar and budget; the technological methods used for conveyance of the information, including memos, email, press releases, and social media; the methods for updating the communications management plan; a glossary of common terms; flow charts regarding the project's information flow, workflows, meeting plans, and a list of reports; constraints imposed by legislation, regulation, and/or technology; guidelines and templates for project status meetings, project team meetings, and email.

Situational Question and Real World Application
Failure to effectively perform the Identify Stakeholder process can result in a deficient stakeholder register and a project outcome that doesn't align with the needs of the stakeholders.

13.2.1. Stakeholder Analysis Methods

There are a number of analysis methods that can be used to determine whose interests it is most important to consider during the project. The methods include power/interest grid, power/influence grid, influence impact grid, and salient models.

The power/interest grid graphically illustrates which stakeholders need to be kept satisfied, managed closely, monitored, or kept informed based on the level of their power and their interest in the outcome of the project.

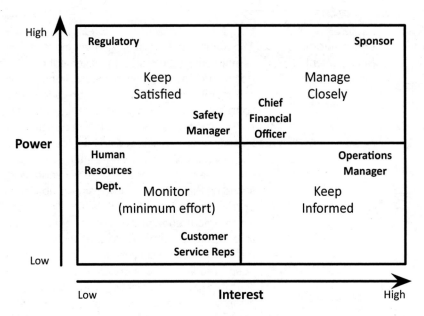

High

Power

Low

| Regulatory | Sponsor |

Keep Satisfied

Manage Closely

Safety Manager

Chief Financial Officer

Human Resources Dept.

Operations Manager

Monitor (minimum effort)

Keep Informed

Customer Service Reps

Low   Interest   High

Figure 13-4: Power/Interest Grid

13.2.2. Stakeholder Register

The stakeholder register is used to manage an increase in the positive impact, and a decrease in the negative impact, of stakeholders.

Project managers typically create a stakeholder register, which may or may not be shared based on the sensitivity of the information contained.

A typical register includes the stakeholder name, level of interest in the project, level of impact on the project, and strategies to gain support or minimize negative impact.

Stakeholder	Level of Interest	Impact Assessment	Strategies

Figure 13-5: Stakeholder Register

The source for the above text is the Project Management Institute, *A Guide to the Project Management Body of Knowledge*, (PMBOK® Guide) – Sixth Edition, Project Management Institute Inc., 2017, Pages 464-471

13.3. Plan Stakeholder Engagement (Planning Process Group)

The purpose of the Plan Stakeholder Engagement process is to create a stakeholder engagement plan that details the strategies that will be used to engage stakeholders with the project in alignment with their desires, stake, and potential influence on the success of the project.

Know the Key Inputs, Tools & Techniques, and Outputs for Plan Stakeholder Engagement.

PMI, CAPM, and PMBOK are registered marks of the Project Management Institute, Inc.

554   © 2008-2018 Crosswind Learning, www.crosswindpm.com

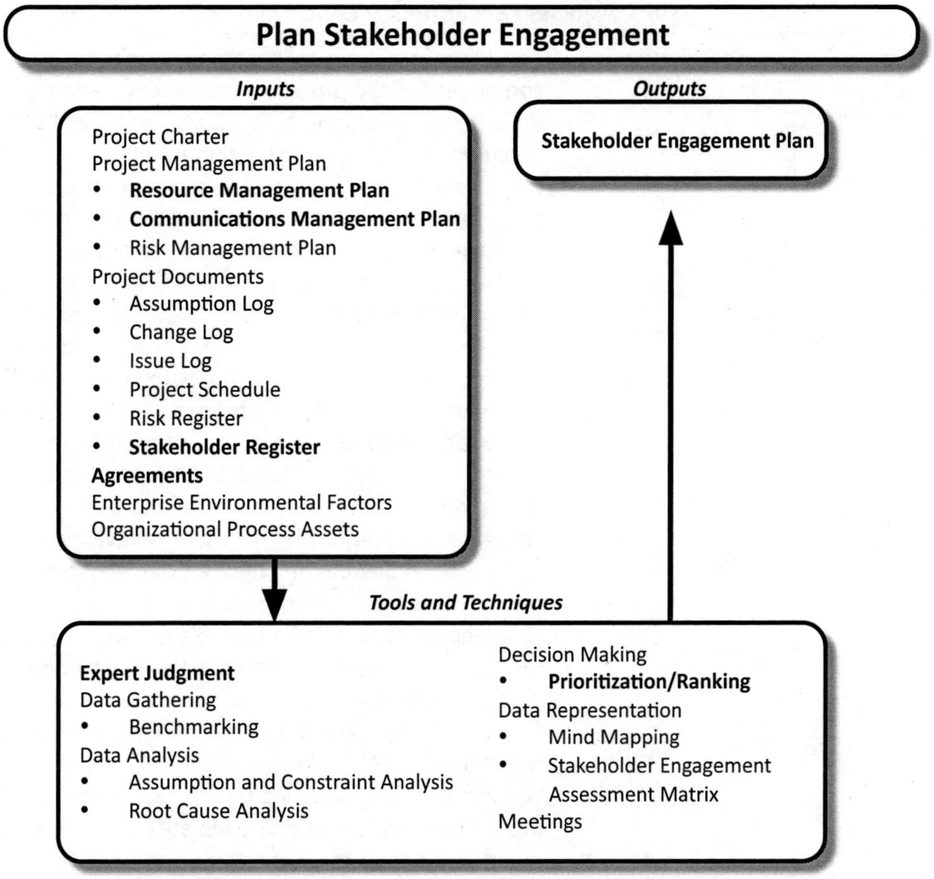

Plan Stakeholder Engagement

Inputs

Project Charter
Project Management Plan
- **Resource Management Plan**
- **Communications Management Plan**
- Risk Management Plan

Project Documents
- Assumption Log
- Change Log
- Issue Log
- Project Schedule
- Risk Register
- **Stakeholder Register**

Agreements
Enterprise Environmental Factors
Organizational Process Assets

Outputs

Stakeholder Engagement Plan

Tools and Techniques

Expert Judgment
Data Gathering
- Benchmarking

Data Analysis
- Assumption and Constraint Analysis
- Root Cause Analysis

Decision Making
- **Prioritization/Ranking**

Data Representation
- Mind Mapping
- Stakeholder Engagement Assessment Matrix

Meetings

Figure 13-6: Plan Stakeholder Engagement Data Flow Diagram

The source for the above figure is the Project Management Institute, *A Guide to the Project Management Body of Knowledge*, (*PMBOK® Guide*) – Sixth Edition, Project Management Institute Inc., 2017, Figure 13-4 Page 466

Plan Stakeholder Engagement (Planning)		
Key Inputs	Resource Management Plan	The resource management plan is a component of the project management plan that documents: the manner in which the team and physical resources are determined, quantified, and acquired; resource roles, responsibilities, authorities, and competence (skill and capacity); project organizational charts; team resource management (definition, management, control, and release); team training; team development; and control of physical resources (availability and acquisition).

		Plan Stakeholder Engagement (Continued)	
Key Inputs (Cont.)	Communications Management Plan	The communications management plan is a component of the project management plan that documents the planning, structure, implementation, and monitoring/control of communications. It contains: stakeholder communication requirements; the information to be communicated, including language, format, content, and degree of detail; the case for conveyance of the information; the timeframe for and frequency of the distribution, including the manner in which any acknowledgment or response will be effected; the person responsible for communication of the information; the person responsible for authoring release of confidential information; the recipients of the information and their needs, requirements, and expectations; the resources allocated for communication related activities, along with a calendar and budget; the technological methods used for conveyance of the information, including memos, email, press releases, and social media; the methods for updating the communications management plan; a glossary of common terms; flow charts regarding the project's information flow, workflows, meeting plans, and a list of reports; constraints imposed by legislation, regulation, and/or technology; guidelines and templates for project status meetings, project team meetings, and email.
	Stakeholder Register	The stakeholder register contains information related to identified stakeholders. It includes identification information (name, position, location, project role, and contact information), assessment information (key requirements, potential impact on project results, phase in which stakeholder wields the greatest influence, and expectations), and stakeholder classification (impact/influence/power/interest, internal/external, or other classification model).
	Agreements	Agreements define project intentions and can be written (such as **letters of agreement**, **contracts**, **memorandums of understanding**, **service level agreements**, and email) or verbal. For work to be performed by an external source, a contract between buyer and seller is typically used and coordination with the procurement/contracting group is involved to guarantee the competent management of contractors and suppliers.

PMI, CAPM, and PMBOK are registered marks of the Project Management Institute, Inc.

556   © 2008-2018 Crosswind Learning, www.crosswindpm.com

Plan Stakeholder Engagement (Continued)		
Key Tools & Techniques	Expert Judgment	Expert judgment is judgment based on expertise acquired in a specific area. It is often more significant and accurate than the best modeling tools available and can be provided by stakeholders, company personnel external to the project, professional organizations or groups, and consultants. It is important to consider expertise related to the organizational politics and power structures, organizational culture, the relevant industry, and a knowledge of the expertise and contributions of individual team members.
	Prioritization/ Ranking	A decision making technique used to prioritize and rank stakeholders based on interest and influence.
Key Outputs	Stakeholder Engagement Plan	The stakeholder engagement plan is a component of the project management plan that documents the management approach and activities utilized to competently engage stakeholders.

Situational Question and Real World Application
Failure to effectively perform the Plan Stakeholder Engagement process may result in stakeholder communication issues, such as failure to inform a stakeholder of status updates to issue logs or change requests and approvals.

13.3.1. Stakeholder Engagement Plan

Know what a stakeholder engagement plan is and its purpose.

The stakeholder engagement plan can be formal and structured or informal and unstructured. The purpose of the document is to establish guidelines for the engagement, management, and control of stakeholders and their expectations.

The plan helps the project manager and team:

- Compare the current and desired level of key stakeholder engagement
- Identify interrelationships between stakeholders
- Identify stakeholder communications requirements
- Update the stakeholder engagement plan when needed

13.3.2. Stakeholder Engagement Assessment Matrix

The stakeholder engagement assessment matrix is used to compare the current and desired level of stakeholder engagement.

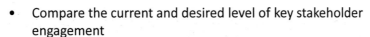

Chapter 13
Stakeholder

Stakeholder	Unaware	Resistant	Neutral	Supportive	Leading
Tony					D,C
Jake			C	D	
Patty		C		D	
Duane		C			D
Nikki				D,C	

C = Current, D = Desired (Level of Engagement)

Figure 13-7: Stakeholder Engagement Assessment Matrix

The source for the above figure is the Project Management Institute, *A Guide to the Project Management Body of Knowledge*, (*PMBOK® Guide*) – Sixth Edition, Project Management Institute Inc., 2017, Figure 13-6, Page 470

The matrix helps focus the team on stakeholder interaction. As the project evolves, the objective is to have the C (current) and D (desired) in the same cell for each stakeholder.

The source for the above text is the Project Management Institute, *A Guide to the Project Management Body of Knowledge*, (*PMBOK® Guide*) – Sixth Edition, Project Management Institute Inc., 2017, Pages 467-471

13.4. Manage Stakeholder Engagement (Executing Process Group)

The Manage Stakeholder Engagement process focuses on communicating with stakeholders, meeting their expectations, addressing their problems in a timely manner, and encouraging their commitment to the project.

This process enables an increased probability of success by ensuring that stakeholders are aware of project benefits and risks.

Know the Key Inputs, Tools & Techniques, and Outputs for Manage Stakeholder Engagement.

Chapter 13
Stakeholder

PMI, CAPM, and PMBOK are registered marks of the Project Management Institute, Inc.

558   © 2008-2018 Crosswind Learning, www.crosswindpm.com

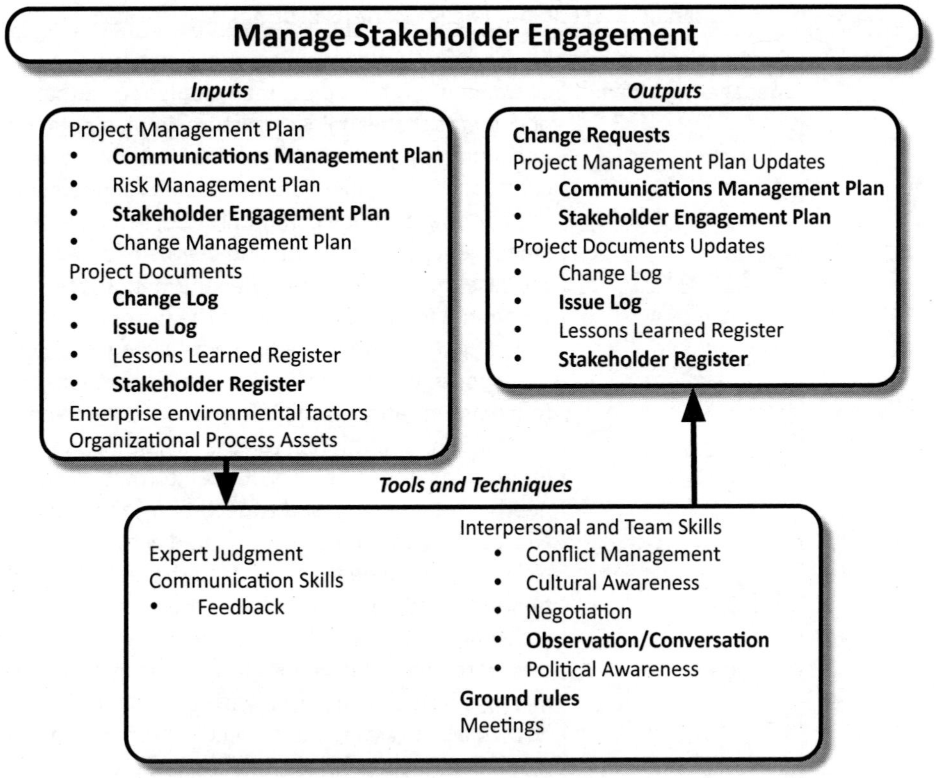

Manage Stakeholder Engagement

Inputs

Project Management Plan
- **Communications Management Plan**
- Risk Management Plan
- **Stakeholder Engagement Plan**
- Change Management Plan

Project Documents
- **Change Log**
- **Issue Log**
- Lessons Learned Register
- **Stakeholder Register**

Enterprise environmental factors
Organizational Process Assets

Outputs

Change Requests
Project Management Plan Updates
- **Communications Management Plan**
- **Stakeholder Engagement Plan**

Project Documents Updates
- Change Log
- **Issue Log**
- Lessons Learned Register
- **Stakeholder Register**

Tools and Techniques

Expert Judgment
Communication Skills
- Feedback

Interpersonal and Team Skills
- Conflict Management
- Cultural Awareness
- Negotiation
- **Observation/Conversation**
- Political Awareness

Ground rules
Meetings

Figure 13-8: Manage Stakeholder Engagement Data Flow Diagram

The source for the above figure is the Project Management Institute, *A Guide to the Project Management Body of Knowledge*, (*PMBOK® Guide*) – Sixth Edition, Project Management Institute Inc., 2017, Figure 13-7, Page 471

Manage Stakeholder Engagement (Executing)		
Key Inputs	Communications Management Plan	The communications management plan is a component of the project management plan that documents the planning, structure, implementation, and monitoring/control of communications. It contains: stakeholder communication requirements; the information to be communicated, including language, format, content, and degree of detail; the case for conveyance of the information; the timeframe for and frequency of the distribution, including the manner in which any acknowledgment or response will be effected; the person responsible for communication of the information; the person responsible for authoring release of confidential information; the recipients of the information and their needs, requirements, and expectations; the resources allocated for communication related activities, along with a calendar and budget; the technological methods used for conveyance of the information, including memos, email, press releases, and social media; the methods for updating the communications management plan; a glossary of common terms; flow charts regarding the project's information flow, workflows, meeting plans, and a list of reports; constraints imposed by legislation, regulation, and/or technology; guidelines and templates for project status meetings, project team meetings, and email.
	Stakeholder Engagement Plan	The stakeholder engagement plan is a component of the project management plan that documents the plans and activities required to engage stakeholders in an effective manner.
	Change Log	The change log is used to record change requests and their statuses. Updates occur during activities performed while monitoring and controlling the project. New and updated information is then conveyed to pertinent stakeholders.
	Issue Log	The issue log is used to record and track any project challenges that cannot be immediately resolved. The project team uses the log to ensure issues are resolved during the execution of the project management plan. Updates occur during activities performed while monitoring and controlling the project.

Manage Stakeholder Engagement (Continued)		
Key Inputs (Cont.)	Stakeholder Register	The stakeholder register contains information related to identified stakeholders. It includes identification information (name, position, location, project role, and contact information), assessment information (key requirements, potential impact on project results, phase in which stakeholder wields the greatest influence, and expectations), and stakeholder classification (impact/influence/power/interest, internal/external, or other classification model). It is used to determine which stakeholders could best identify risks and/or have the availability to act as risk owners.
Tools & Techniques	Observation/ Conversation	Observation/conversation is a technique used to ensure awareness of any changes in the work and attitudes of team members and stakeholders.
	Ground Rules	Ground rules, the governing principles of conduct, are put into place to set behavioral expectations for team members and other stakeholders.
Key Outputs	Change Requests	Change requests are requests for modification that have not been formally approved through the change control process. Modifications to the project scope or product scope, as well as other impacted components of the project management plan, may be requested as a result of this process.
	Communications Management Plan	The communications management plan is a component of the project management plan that documents the planning, structure, implementation, and monitoring/control of communications. New or changed stakeholder requirements may effect a change to the communications management plan.
	Stakeholder Engagement Plan	The stakeholder engagement plan is a component of the project management plan that documents the plans and activities required to engage stakeholders in an effective manner.

Manage Stakeholder Engagement (Continued)		
Key Outputs (Cont.)	Issue Log	The issue log is used to record and track any project challenges that cannot be immediately resolved. The project team uses the log to ensure issues are resolved during the execution of the project management plan. Updates occur during activities performed while monitoring and controlling the project.
	Stakeholder Register	The stakeholder register contains information related to identified stakeholders. Updates occur based on new information regarding settled issues, authorized changes, and project status updates.

Situational Question and Real World Application
Failure to effectively perform the Manage Stakeholder Engagement process may result in failure to meet stakeholders' expectations and addressing their issues in a timely manner, which negatively impacts stakeholder engagement.

The source for the above text is the Project Management Institute, *A Guide to the Project Management Body of Knowledge*, (*PMBOK® Guide*) – Sixth Edition, Project Management Institute Inc., 2017, Pages 471-477

© 2008-2018 Crosswind Learning, www.crosswindpm.com

13.5. Monitor Stakeholder Engagement (Monitoring and Controlling Process Group)

The Monitor Stakeholder Engagement process focuses on stakeholder relationships and modifies stakeholder engagement strategies and plans as appropriate.

The benefit of effectively performing this process is that stakeholder engagement will be maintained or increased throughout the project.

Know the Key Inputs, Tools & Techniques, and Outputs for Monitor Stakeholder Engagement.

Monitor Stakeholder Engagement

Inputs

Project Management Plan
- Resource Management Plan
- **Communications Management Plan**
- **Stakeholder Engagement Plan**

Project Documents
- **Issue Log**
- **Lessons Learned Register**
- Project Communications
- Risk Register
- Stakeholder Register

Work Performance Data
Enterprise Environmental Factors
Organizational Process Assets

Outputs

Work Performance Information
Change Requests
Project Management Plan Updates
- Resource Management Plan
- Communications Management Plan
- **Stakeholder Engagement Plan**

Project Documents Updates
- Issue Log
- Lessons Learned Register
- Risk Register
- Stakeholder Register

Tools and Techniques

Data Analysis
- Alternatives Analysis
- Root Cause Analysis
- **Stakeholder Analysis**

Decision Making
- Multicriteria Decision Analysis
- Voting

Data Representation
- **Stakeholder Engagement Assessment Matrix**

Communications
- Feedback
- Presentations

Interpersonal and Team Skills
- **Active Listening**
- Cultural Awareness
- Leadership
- Networking
- Political Awareness

Meetings

Figure 13-9: Monitor Stakeholder Engagement Data Flow Diagram

The source for the above figure is the Project Management Institute, *A Guide to the Project Management Body of Knowledge, (PMBOK® Guide) – Sixth Edition,* Project Management Institute Inc., 2017, Figure 13-9, Page 477

Monitor Stakeholder Engagement (Monitoring and Controlling)		
Key Inputs	Communications Management Plan	The communications management plan is a component of the project management plan that documents the planning, structure, implementation, and monitoring/control of communications. It contains: stakeholder communication requirements; the information to be communicated, including language, format, content, and degree of detail; the case for conveyance of the information; the timeframe for and frequency of the distribution, including the manner in which any acknowledgment or response will be effected; the person responsible for communication of the information; the person responsible for authoring release of confidential information; the recipients of the information and their needs, requirements, and expectations; the resources allocated for communication related activities, along with a calendar and budget; the technological methods used for conveyance of the information, including memos, email, press releases, and social media; the methods for updating the communications management plan; a glossary of common terms; flowcharts regarding the project's information flow, workflows, meeting plans, and a list of reports; constraints imposed by legislation, regulation, and/or technology; guidelines and templates for project status meetings, project team meetings, and email.
	Stakeholder Engagement Plan	The stakeholder engagement plan is a component of the project management plan that documents the plans and activities required to engage stakeholders in an effective manner.
	Issue Log	The issue log is used to record and track any project challenges that cannot be immediately resolved. Issue-related information is communicated to affected stakeholders.
	Lessons Learned Register	The lessons learned register is a record of the challenges, problems, and successes of the project (what worked and didn't). The register contains detailed and important project knowledge and can be modified to include the reason an issue occurred and the reason a corrective action was selected.
Key Tools & Techniques	Stakeholder Analysis	Stakeholder analysis is performed to assess the positions of stakeholders at a particular point in the project.

Monitor Stakeholder Engagement (Continued)		
Key Tools & Techniques (Cont.)	Stakeholder Engagement Assessment Matrix	The stakeholder engagement assessment matrix is utilized to evaluate the current engagement levels of stakeholders by comparing them to expected engagement levels of stakeholders. Stakeholder engagement levels can be classified as **unaware**, **resistant**, **neutral**, **supportive**, or **leading**. A SWOT analysis (a technique used to assess **strengths**, **weaknesses**, **opportunities**, and **threats**) can be adapted to indicate the current level (C) and desired level (D) of each stakeholder by creating a grid that lists each classification horizontally and each stakeholder vertically. To indicate the current level of engagement, place a C in the cell located in the considered stakeholder row and the appropriate classification column. To indicate the desired level of engagement, place a D in the cell located in the considered stakeholder row and the appropriate classification column.
	Active Listening	Active listening is a technique that requires the listener to concentrate on the message conveyed by the speaker, then to repeat or paraphrase the message to confirm understanding.
Key Outputs	Work Performance Information	Work performance information includes information regarding the current status of stakeholder engagement. The information can include such data as a comparison of the current level of project support to the desired level of engagement.
	Change Requests	Change requests are requests for modification that have not been formally approved through the change control process. Modifications to the project scope or product scope, as well as other impacted components of the project management plan, may be requested as a result of this process.
	Stakeholder Engagement Plan	The stakeholder engagement plan is a component of the project management plan that documents the plans and activities required to engage stakeholders in an effective manner. Modifications to the plan may be requested as a result of this process.

Situational Question and Real World Application
Failure to effectively perform the Monitor Stakeholder Management process may result in failure to distribute work performance information and requested changes to the appropriate stakeholders. Such a situation can decrease stakeholder engagement.

The source for the above text is the Project Management Institute, *A Guide to the Project Management Body of Knowledge*, (*PMBOK® Guide*) – Sixth Edition, Project Management Institute Inc., 2017, Pages 477-482

13.6. Project Stakeholder Management Formulas and Variables

There are no formulas for this chapter.

13.7. Project Stakeholder Management Terminology

Term	Description
Identify Stakeholders	The process of determining all people and entities affected by the project, evaluating and recording any information appropriate to their concerns, involvement, interdependencies, and possible affect on the success of the project
Issue	A disputed or unsettled condition
Issue Log	A project document that tracks elements that cause stakeholder concern or dissension
Manage Stakeholder Engagement	Work and communicate with stakeholders to ensure satisfaction of their legitimate needs and expectations, to resolve their issues, and to include them in appropriate decision-making
Monitor Stakeholder Engagement	The process of monitoring stakeholder relationships and optimizing the approach to stakeholder engagement through the modification of related strategies and plans.
Plan Stakeholder Engagement	The process of establishing management strategies that will engage stakeholders in project related decisions; the strategies are based on the needs, interest levels, and impact levels of the stakeholders
Project Stakeholder Management	The knowledge area that identifies stakeholders, as well as analyzes and manages their expectations and engagement in the project during its lifetime
Stakeholder	Any person or entity that may impact, be impacted by, or perceive itself to be impacted by any decision, activity, or outcome of the project
Stakeholder Analysis	A technique by which quantitative and qualitative information is amassed and evaluated to determine whose interests should be considered throughout the project
Stakeholder Engagement Assessment Matrix	A matrix in which current and desired stakeholder engagement levels are listed for comparison
Stakeholder Engagement Plan	The document, part of the project or program management plan, used to depict all processes, procedures, tools, and techniques that will be used to effectively involve stakeholders in project determinations and performance based on the stakeholders' requirements, concerns, and potential impact
Stakeholder Register	A project document that lists stakeholder information including name, role, assessment, and classification

The source for the above definitions is the Glossary of the Project Management Institute,
A Guide to the Project Management Body of Knowledge, (PMBOK® Guide) – Sixth Edition, Project Management Institute Inc., 2017

13.8. Project Stakeholder Management Tests and Exercises

13.8.1. Project Stakeholder Management Practice Test

Answers are in section 13.9.1.

1. During which process is the project manager most likely to increase support and minimize resistance from stakeholders?

   (A) Identify stakeholders
   (B) Plan stakeholder management
   (C) Manage stakeholder engagement
   (D) Control stakeholder engagement

2. Maxron electrical has won the contract to install wireless networking in Lincoln stadium in Darlington Hills. This is a very complex contract because there are a number of stakeholders involved: the owner of Lincoln stadium, various companies associated with the owner, and the city of Darlington Hills. What documentation will be most effective for organizing the stakeholders?

   (A) Stakeholder register
   (B) Stakeholder engagement plan
   (C) Issue log
   (D) Charter

3. All of the following are descriptions derived from analytical techniques used in stakeholder management except...

   (A) Nonresistant
   (B) Neutral
   (C) Supportive
   (D) Leading

4. The marketing brochure redesign project is entering the manage stakeholder engagement process. To effectively manage stakeholder engagement, the project manager has a variety of tools and techniques available during this process. What are they?

   (A) Interpersonal and team skills, communication feedback, and ground rules
   (B) Communications methods, alternatives analysis, and management skills
   (C) Communications skills, communications management plan, and management skills
   (D) Product analysis, communications methods, and management skills

5. Sam is running a project to upgrade a client's website to a new framework. Expectation management has been very challenging on this project. Sam has had challenges keeping the main sponsor involved as the project has evolved. Currently Sam is managing stakeholder engagement. Which of the following best describes what he will expect to create?

(A) Updates to the stakeholder engagement plan, change log and issue log
(B) Approved change requests and updated stakeholder registry
(C) Resolved issues and approved change requests
(D) Updated stakeholder registry, resolved issues, and change requests

6. The project to update the retail store to accommodate the new video game platform is ready for initial planning. Stakeholders have been identified. What documentation will be created as a result of the identification?

(A) Stakeholder register
(B) Stakeholder management plan
(C) Issue log
(D) Charter

7. All of the following interpersonal or soft skills are applicable to managing stakeholder engagement except...

(A) Building trust
(B) Resolving conflict
(C) Passive listening
(D) Overcoming resistance to change

8. During the plan stakeholder engagement process for the accounting system upgrade project, what tools and techniques are available to the project manager?

(A) Issue Logs, stakeholder analysis, reporting systems, and approved change requests
(B) Expert judgment, meetings, and mind mapping
(C) Management skills, communication methods, stakeholder analysis, and interpersonal skills
(D) Stakeholder analysis, issue logs, and approved change requests

9. Which processes does the project manager use to manage the project stakeholders?

(A) Plan stakeholder engagement, manage stakeholder engagement, monitor stakeholder engagement
(B) Identify stakeholders, plan stakeholder engagement, manage stakeholder engagement, monitor stakeholder engagement
(C) Identify stakeholders, plan stakeholder engagement, monitor stakeholder engagement
(D) Identify stakeholders, plan stakeholder engagement, manage stakeholder engagement

10. During the identify stakeholders process, the project manager of the security project has what key tools and techniques at his disposal?

(A) Stakeholder analysis, stakeholder management strategy chart, and expert judgment
(B) Power/interest grid, stakeholder analysis, and expert judgment
(C) Stakeholder management strategy chart, stakeholder analysis, power/interest grid, and expert judgment
(D) Expert judgment and stakeholder analysis

11. To effectively manage stakeholders to increase support for and minimize negative impact to a project, project managers often rely on strategy tools during the identify stakeholders process. A key tool is the analysis matrix. Of the following, which best represents typical matrix entries?

(A) Level of impact on the project, strategies to gain support or minimize negative impact, stakeholder name, level of interest in the project, requirements for level of communication
(B) Level of interest in the project, stakeholder name, political influence within the organization, strategies to gain support or minimize negative impact
(C) Strategies to gain support or minimize negative impact, level of interest in the project, stakeholder name, level of impact on the project
(D) Requirements for level of communication, stakeholder name, level of interest in the project, political influence within the organization, strategies to gain support or minimize negative impact

12. The chief financial officer of the mortgage banking company has been reassigned to the IT department and will have no further involvement in the financial department. Which of the following documents should be updated for the Tax Laws Accounting Upgrade project?

(A) Stakeholder register
(B) Power/interest grid
(C) Stakeholder register and power/interest grid
(D) Issue log

13. Which of the following is the best description of stakeholders?

(A) All persons and groups that are impacted by the project and have a job because of the project
(B) All persons who are members of the project team and their job changes because of the project
(C) All persons that are impacted by the project, have a job because of the project, and/or consider themselves stakeholders
(D) All persons who consider themselves stakeholders and have a job because of the project

Chapter 13
Stakeholder

14. Maxron electrical has won the contract to install wireless networking in Lincoln stadium in Darlington Hills. This is a very complex contract because there are a number of stakeholders involved: the owner of Lincoln world, various companies associated with the owner, and the city of Darlington Hills. What is the best approach for managing stakeholders?

(A) Identify all the stakeholders early and establish their needs
(B) Identify all the stakeholders as situations come up on the project
(C) Identify all the stakeholders early, establish their needs, and communicate with them throughout the duration of the project
(D) Inform the stakeholders that the project will be executed in accordance with the scope of work and that their feedback will not be required

15. Which of the processes can update the issue log?

(A) Identify stakeholders, plan stakeholder engagement, manage stakeholder engagement, monitor stakeholder engagement
(B) Identify stakeholders, manage stakeholder engagement, monitor stakeholder engagement
(C) Plan stakeholder engagement, manage stakeholder engagement, monitor stakeholder engagement
(D) Identify stakeholders, plan stakeholder engagement, manage stakeholder engagement

16. During which process is the stakeholder register created?

(A) Identify stakeholders
(B) Plan stakeholder engagement
(C) Manage stakeholder engagement
(D) Control stakeholder engagement

17. During which process is the stakeholder engagement plan created?

(A) Identify stakeholders
(B) Plan stakeholder engagement
(C) Manage stakeholder engagement
(D) Control stakeholder engagement

18. Given the complex nature of projects, which area of change generally has the highest impact?

(A) A change in the company that is creating the project
(B) A change in the market for which the work of the project is intended
(C) A change in the team on the project
(D) A change in the project

19. Your company is doing market analysis to see about creating a next generation thermostat that will increase the efficiency of home energy use and can be controlled by a smartphone. While the company is evaluating the market potential for this product and determining its target audience, which of the following stakeholder groups will they likely engage?

(A) Distribution customers
(B) End users
(C) Regulatory agencies
(D) Advertising agencies

20. Which of the following is an input to the manage stakeholder engagement process?

(A) Communication
(B) Communications management plan
(C) Meetings
(D) Negotiations

21. You are the project manager on a restaurant POS system project for Hamburger Prince Restaurants. You are fortunate in having the top technical architect in the company on your project. In your monthly meeting with the CEO, you are informed that the architect will be reassigned to a higher priority enterprise reporting system project. You inform the CEO that the resource's involvement on your project is critical to the project's success, but the CEO will not reconsider. What is the best action to take next?

(A) Evaluate the impact of the person's absence on the project and communicate to senior management
(B) Continue to lobby for the person to be returned to your project
(C) Change the scope of the project to accommodate for the loss of the resource
(D) Continue as the original plan, but without the resource

22. The project team is creating a power/interest grid to use for the rental renovation project. Which of the following best describes the purpose of this grid?

(A) Effective management of stakeholder engagement can be the result of identifying the levels of power and interest of stakeholders
(B) Effective management of stakeholder engagement can be the result of organizing the reporting structure of stakeholders
(C) Effective management of stakeholder engagement can be the result of identifying the stakeholder reporting structure
(D) Effective management of stakeholder engagement can be the result of graphically depicting the relationship between team member roles and authority levels

Chapter 13
Stakeholder

23. The project to update the retail store to accommodate the new video game platform is ready for initial planning. Stakeholders have been identified and a stakeholder register created. What documentation will be created next?

(A) Stakeholder register
(B) Stakeholder engagement plan
(C) Issue log
(D) Charter

24. The project manager is engaged in a project that will result in an Internet-driven thermostat to save electricity and cut energy costs. Since this is an innovative project, which of the following stakeholder groups is most likely to have the most influence early in the project?

(A) Distribution customers
(B) End users
(C) Regulatory agencies
(D) Manufacturing partners

25. Which of the following is least likely to be in a high power, high interest position on a power/interest grid?

(A) Persons who are impacted by the project
(B) Persons who are on the project team
(C) Persons who consider themselves to be stakeholders
(D) All of the answers

26. The project to upgrade the accounting software in consideration of upcoming tax law changes is underway. The project manager is working with the chief information officer (CIO) and chief financial officer (CFO) to ensure regulatory compliance and requirements alignment. Where will these two stakeholders most likely fit in a power/interest grid?

(A) High power/low interest
(B) Low power/low interest
(C) High power/high interest
(D) Low power/high interest

27. Which of the following stakeholders is most likely to be viewed as a low power/low interest stakeholder on a project to update tax code software?

(A) The chief financial officer (CFO)
(B) The department administrator
(C) The chief information officer (CIO)
(D) The software architect

28. Which of the following is the most accurate statement about a power/interest grid?

   (A) Stakeholders cannot be added once the document is created
   (B) Stakeholders cannot be repositioned in the document once they are positioned
   (C) Stakeholders should let the project manager know if their power/interest levels change
   (D) Stakeholder power and interest levels can change throughout the project and it's incumbent on the project manager to proactively monitor these changes

29. All of the following are descriptions derived from analytical techniques used in stakeholder engagement except...

   (A) Aware
   (B) Resistant
   (C) Neutral
   (D) Supportive

30. All of the following interpersonal or soft skills are applicable to managing stakeholder engagement except...

   (A) Conflict management
   (B) Minimizing conflict
   (C) Cultural awareness
   (D) Political awareness

13.9. Project Stakeholder Management Answers for Tests and Exercises

13.9.1. Project Stakeholder Management Practice Test Answers

We recommend that you download answer sheets from the Crosswind website, so you can practice the test as many times as you like.

1. During which process is the project manager most likely to increase support and minimize resistance from stakeholders?

    Correct Answer: (C) Manage stakeholder engagement
    Explanation: The Manage Stakeholder Engagement process is the execution of the stakeholder engagement plan. Some of the key goals of the stakeholder engagement plan are to maximize stakeholder engagement, minimize stakeholder resistance and adjust expectations as applicable. The Identify Stakeholders process creates the stakeholder register and identifies stakeholders. The Plan Stakeholder Engagement process creates, among other documentation, the stakeholder engagement plan. The Monitor Stakeholder Engagement process creates, among other documentation, work performance information. [Crosswind Manual 13.4; *PMBOK® Guide* 13.3]

2. Maxron electrical has won the contract to install wireless networking in Lincoln stadium in Darlington Hills. This is a very complex contract because there are a number of stakeholders involved: the owner of Lincoln stadium, various companies associated with the owner, and the city of Darlington Hills. What documentation will be most effective for organizing the stakeholders?

    Correct Answer: (A) Stakeholder register
    Explanation: The stakeholder register is used to identify stakeholders and provide key information about them. The stakeholder engagement plan is used to provide direction for managing stakeholder engagement. The issue log is used to track issues and provide key information about them. The charter is the basis of the project and provides initial high-level information about the project. [Crosswind Manual 13.2; *PMBOK® Guide* 13.1]

3. All of the following are descriptions derived from analytical techniques used in stakeholder management except...

    Correct Answer: (A) Nonresistant
    Explanation: Stakeholder engagement levels are typically described as unaware, resistant, neutral, supportive and leading. [Crosswind Manual 13.3.2; *PMBOK® Guide* 13.2.2.5]

4.   The marketing brochure redesign project is entering the manage stakeholder engagement process. To effectively manage stakeholder engagement, the project manager has a variety of tools and techniques available during this process. What are they?

Correct Answer: (A) Interpersonal and team skills, communication feedback, and ground rules
Explanation: The tools and techniques for the Manage Stakeholder Engagement process are: expert judgment, inspection, communication, feedback, interpersonal and team skills, conflict management, cultural awareness, negotiation, observation/conversation, political awareness, ground rules, and meetings. [Crosswind Manual 13.4; *PMBOK® Guide* 13.3]

5.   Sam is running a project to upgrade a client's website to a new framework. Expectation management has been very challenging on this project. Sam has had challenges keeping the main sponsor involved as the project has evolved. Currently Sam is managing stakeholder engagement. Which of the following best describes what he will expect to create?

Correct Answer: (A) Updates to the stakeholder engagement plan, change log and issue log
Explanation: The outputs for the Manage Stakeholder Engagement process are change requests, project management plan updates, communication management plan updates, stakeholder engagement plan updates, project documents updates, change log updates issue log updates, lessons learned register updates and stakeholder register updates. [Crosswind Manual 13.4; *PMBOK® Guide* 13.3]

6.   The project to update the retail store to accommodate the new video game platform is ready for initial planning. Stakeholders have been identified. What documentation will be created as a result of the identification?

Correct Answer: (A) Stakeholder register
Explanation: The stakeholder register is used to identify stakeholders and provide key information about them. This is the main output of the identify stakeholders process. The stakeholder engagement plan is used to provide direction for managing stakeholder engagement. The issue log is used to track issues and provide key information about them. The charter is the basis of the project and provides initial high-level information about the project. [Crosswind Manual 13.2; *PMBOK® Guide* 13.1]

7.   All of the following interpersonal or soft skills are applicable to managing stakeholder engagement except...

Correct Answer: (C) Passive listening
Explanation: Interpersonal or soft skills applicable to managing stakeholder engagement are building trust, resolving conflict, active listening, and overcoming resistance to change. [Crosswind Manual 13.4; *PMBOK® Guide* 13.3]

8. During the plan stakeholder engagement process for the accounting system upgrade project, what tools and techniques are available to the project manager?

   Correct Answer: (B) Expert judgment, meetings, and mind mapping
   Explanation: The tools and techniques for the plan stakeholder management process are expert judgment, data gathering, benchmarking, data analysis, assumption and constraint analysis, mind mapping, root cause analysis, stakeholder engagement assessment matrix, SWOT analysis, decision-making, prioritization/ranking, and meetings. [Crosswind Manual 13.3; *PMBOK® Guide* 13.2]

9. Which processes does the project manager use to manage the project stakeholders?

   Correct Answer: (B) Identify stakeholders, plan stakeholder engagement, manage stakeholder engagement, monitor stakeholder engagement
   Explanation: The processes associated with the stakeholder knowledge area are Identify Stakeholders, Plan Stakeholder Engagement, Manage Stakeholder Engagement, and Monitor Stakeholder Engagement. [Crosswind Manual Chapter 13 Introduction; *PMBOK® Guide* Chapter 13 Introduction]

10. During the identify stakeholders process, the project manager of the security project has what key tools and techniques at his disposal?

    Correct Answer: (D) Expert judgment and stakeholder analysis
    Explanation: The tools and techniques for the Identify Stakeholder process are expert judgment, data gathering, questionnaires and surveys, brainstorming, data analysis, stakeholder analysis, document analysis, and meetings. [Crosswind Manual 13.2; *PMBOK® Guide* 13.1]

11. To effectively manage stakeholders to increase support for and minimize negative impact to a project, project managers often rely on strategy tools during the identify stakeholders process. A key tool is the analysis matrix. Of the following, which best represents typical matrix entries?

    Correct Answer: (C) Strategies to gain support or minimize negative impact, level of interest in the project, stakeholder name, level of impact on the project
    Explanation: The stakeholder analysis matrix typically contains the stakeholder name, level of interest in the project, strategies to gain support or minimize negative impact, and level of impact on the project. The other answers are noise. [Crosswind Manual 13.2; *PMBOK® Guide* 13.1]

12. The chief financial officer of the mortgage banking company has been reassigned to the IT department and will have no further involvement in the financial department. Which of the following documents should be updated for the Tax Laws Accounting Upgrade project?

    Correct Answer: (C) Stakeholder register and power/interest grid
    Explanation: The stakeholder register and the power/interest grid for the project should be updated to reflect the appropriate information for the CFO and his replacement. [Crosswind Manual 13.2; *PMBOK® Guide* 13.1]

13. Which of the following is the best description of stakeholders?

Correct Answer: (C) All persons that are impacted by the project, have a job because of the project, and/or consider themselves stakeholders
Explanation: Stakeholders can be team members or any persons or groups that are impacted by the project, have a job because of the project, or consider themselves stakeholders. [Crosswind Manual 13.2; *PMBOK® Guide* 13.1]

14. Maxron electrical has won the contract to install wireless networking in Lincoln stadium in Darlington Hills. This is a very complex contract because there are a number of stakeholders involved: the owner of Lincoln stadium, various companies associated with the owner, and the city of Darlington Hills. What is the best approach for managing stakeholders?

Correct Answer: (C) Identify all the stakeholders early, establish their needs, and communicate with them throughout the duration of the project
Explanation: In this complex situation, it is very important to identify all stakeholders as early as possible, establish their needs (imperative for effective engagement management), and communicate with them throughout the duration of the project (imperative to effectively manage their ongoing engagement). Identifying stakeholders as situations arise will likely cause you to revert to the planning stage and delay the project. Refusal to obtain stakeholder feedback will likely result in a lack of buy-in from the stakeholders. [Crosswind Manual 13.1; *PMBOK® Guide* Chapter 13 Introduction]

15. Which of the processes can update the issue log?

Correct Answer: (B) Identify stakeholders, manage stakeholder engagement, monitor stakeholder engagement
Explanation: Three of the four stakeholder processes can result in the issue log being updated. They are identify stakeholder, manage stakeholder engagement, and monitor stakeholder engagement. [Crosswind Manual 13.2, 13.4, and 13.5; *PMBOK® Guide* 13.1, 13.3, and 13.4]

16. During which process is the stakeholder register created?

Correct Answer: (A) Identify stakeholders
Explanation: The Identify Stakeholders process creates the stakeholder register. The Plan Stakeholder Engagement process creates, among other documentation, the stakeholder management plan. The Manage Stakeholder Engagement process creates, among other documentation, change requests, project management plan updates, and project documents updates. The Monitor Stakeholder Engagement process creates, among other documentation, work performance information. [Crosswind Manual 13.2; *PMBOK® Guide* 13.1]

17. During which process is the stakeholder engagement plan created?

Correct Answer: (B) Plan stakeholder engagement
Explanation: The Plan Stakeholder Engagement process creates, among other documentation, the stakeholder engagement plan. The Identify Stakeholders process creates the stakeholder register. The Manage Stakeholder Engagement process creates, among other documentation, change requests and project management plan updates. [Crosswind Manual 13.3; *PMBOK® Guide* 13.2]

18. Given the complex nature of projects, which area of change generally has the highest impact?

Correct Answer: (B) A change in the market for which the work of the project is intended

Explanation: The highest impact is a change in the market for which the work of the project is intended. A negative change could result in a radically altered or eliminated market. A positive change could result in a totally reinvented market. [Crosswind Manual 13.1.1; No *PMBOK® Guide* Reference]

19. Your company is doing market analysis to see about creating a next generation thermostat that will increase the efficiency of home energy use and can be controlled by a smartphone. While the company is evaluating the market potential for this product and determining its target audience, which of the following stakeholder groups will they likely engage?

Correct Answer: (B) End users

Explanation: Your company will engage the end users, probably selected as a focus group, since they can provide feedback on their interest in purchasing the product. Other stakeholder groups would have a lesser influence or their influence would be greatest at another point in the project. Distribution customers would influence the product's deployment. Regulatory agencies would influence product requirements. Advertising agencies would influence the marketing of the product. [Crosswind Manual 13.2; *PMBOK® Guide* 13.1]

20. Which of the following is an input to the manage stakeholder engagement process?

Correct Answer: (B) Communications management plan

Explanation: The inputs for the Manage Stakeholder Engagement process are the project management plan, communications management plan, risk management plan, stakeholder engagement plan, project documents, change log, issue log, lessons learned register, stakeholder register, enterprise environmental factors, and organizational process assets. [Crosswind Manual 13.4; *PMBOK® Guide* 13.3]

21. You are the project manager on a Restaurant POS System project for Hamburger Prince Restaurants. You are fortunate in having the top technical architect in the company on your project. In your monthly meeting with the CEO, you are informed that the architect will be reassigned to a higher priority enterprise reporting system project. You inform the CEO that the resource's involvement on your project is critical to the project's success, but the CEO will not reconsider. What is the best action to take next?

Correct Answer: (A) Evaluate the impact of the person's absence on the project and communicate to senior management

Explanation: Letting senior management know the impact of not having the resource on the project is the best action to take next. You don't change the scope of the project because that isn't the call of the project manager. If you encounter a significant change such as the loss of a resource, you are expected to revise the plan to accommodate the change. [Crosswind Manual 13.1.2; No *PMBOK® Guide* Reference]

22. The project team is creating a power/interest grid to use for the rental renovation project. Which of the following best describes the purpose of this grid?

Correct Answer: (A) Effective management of stakeholder engagement can be the result of identifying the levels of power and interest of stakeholders
Explanation: The power/interest grid depicts the levels of power and project interest of the stakeholders. The more power and interest a stakeholder has, the more closely project management should monitor and manage that stakeholder's engagement. The other answers are distracters. [Crosswind Manual 13.2.1; PMBOK® Guide 13.1.2.4]

23. The project to update the retail store to accommodate the new video game platform is ready for initial planning. Stakeholders have been identified and a stakeholder register created. What documentation will be created next?

Correct Answer: (B) Stakeholder engagement plan
Explanation: The stakeholder engagement plan is used to provide direction for managing stakeholder engagement. The stakeholder register is used to identify stakeholders and provide key information about them. The issue log is used to track issues and provide key information about them. The charter is the basis of the project and provides initial high-level information about the project. [Crosswind Manual 13.2; PMBOK® Guide 13.1]

24. The project manager is engaged in a project that will result in an Internet-driven thermostat to save electricity and cut energy costs. Since this is an innovative project, which of the following stakeholder groups is most likely to have the most influence early in the project?

Correct Answer: (C) Regulatory agencies
Explanation: Since this is such an innovative project, and it involves energy, it is very likely to come under the scope of a regulatory authority that would have significant influence over product requirements which are established early in the project. Other stakeholder groups would have a lesser influence or their influence would be greatest at another point in the project: End users would influence the company's positioning of the product. Distribution customers would influence the product's deployment. Manufacturing partners would influence the assembly of the product. [Crosswind Manual 13.2; PMBOK® Guide 13.1]

25. Which of the following is least likely to be in a high power, high interest position on a power/interest grid?

Correct Answer: (C) Persons who consider themselves to be stakeholders
Explanation: Of the possible answers, persons who consider themselves stakeholders are the most unlikely to be in a high power, high interest position on the power grid. Typically, persons in the power grid are very aware of their power and interests and know they are stakeholders. Additionally, those who create the power grid are aware of those who have power and can determine if they might have an interest in the project. [Crosswind Manual 13.2; PMBOK® Guide 13.1]

26. The project to upgrade the accounting software in consideration of upcoming tax law changes is underway. The project manager is working with the chief information officer (CIO) and chief financial officer (CFO) to ensure regulatory compliance and requirements alignment. Where will these two stakeholders most likely fit in a power/interest grid?

Correct Answer: (C) High power/high interest
Explanation: The positions of CIO and CFO imply a high degree of power. Their involvement in ensuring regulatory compliance and the alignment of requirements imply a very high degree of interest. [Crosswind Manual 13.2.1; *PMBOK® Guide* 13.1.2.4]

27. Which of the following stakeholders is most likely to be viewed as a low power/low interest stakeholder on a project to update tax code software?

Correct Answer: (B) The department administrator
Explanation: Of the roles lists, the administrator for the department is likely the least powerful position. Although interest is not specifically addressed in the question, it is likely that the CFO, CIO, and software architect would have the most interest in the project. [Crosswind Manual 13.2.1; *PMBOK® Guide* 13.1.2.4]

28. Which of the following is the most accurate statement about a power/interest grid?

Correct Answer: (D) Stakeholder power and interest levels can change throughout the project and it's incumbent on the project manager to proactively monitor these changes
Explanation: The power and interest of stakeholders can change during a project. Typically, the project manager is responsible for monitoring these changes. Stakeholders can be added as needed to the grid and their power/interest levels changed as appropriate. [Crosswind Manual 13.2.1; *PMBOK® Guide* 13.1.2.4]

29. All of the following are descriptions derived from analytical techniques used in stakeholder engagement except...

Correct Answer: (A) Aware
Explanation: Stakeholder engagement levels are typically described as unaware, resistant, neutral, supportive and leading. [Crosswind Manual 13.3.2; *PMBOK® Guide* 13.2.2.5]

30. All of the following interpersonal or soft skills are applicable to managing stakeholder engagement except...

Correct Answer: (B) Minimizing conflict
Explanation: Interpersonal or soft skills applicable to managing stakeholder engagement are building trust, resolving conflict, active listening, and overcoming resistance to change. While resolving conflict and minimizing conflict might appear to be similar, resolving eliminates the conflict and minimizing conflict merely makes the conflict less acute. [Crosswind Manual 13.4; *PMBOK® Guide* 13.3]

Index

Symbols

100% rule 132

A

Accepted deliverables 96
Accuracy vs. precision 296
Active listening 406, 565
Activity attributes 163, 356
Activity list 163, 354
Actual cost (AC) 261
Adaptive life cycles 34
Administrative closure 94
Agile release planning 182, 194
Agreements 74, 181, 244, 514, 517, 556
Alternatives analysis 127, 239, 302, 373, 460
Analogous estimating 175, 176, 238, 355
Approved change requests 83, 307, 522
Arrow diagramming method (ADM) 169
Assessments (individual and team) 364
Assumption log 75, 128, 174, 461
Assumptions 80
Attribute sampling 310
Attribute vs. variable sampling 296
Audits 303, 304, 523

B

Backward pass 188
Baseline 81
Basis of estimates 91, 176, 240, 355
Benchmarking 123, 294
Benefits management 96
Benefits management plan 71, 74, 551
Bidder conferences 513, 515
Bill of materials (BOM) 132
Bottom-up estimating 175, 177, 239, 355
Brainstorming 123
Budget at completion (BAC) 261
Business case 71, 73, 96, 123, 550
Business documents 71
Business risk 437
Buyer and seller names 503

C

Cause-and-effect diagram 303, 308, 315
Change control board 92, 93
Change control system 93
Change control tools 92
Change log 82, 560
Change management plan 90
Change requests 83, 137, 198, 250, 303, 361, 410, 460, 499, 549
Chart of accounts 245
Checklists 79, 308, 311
Check sheets 308, 311
Claim administration 522
Closed procurements 523
Closing 32
Closure
  Sequence 98
Code of accounts 246
Colocation 363
Communication blockers 402
Communication channels formula 401
Communication control 400
Communication methods 398, 402
Communication requirements analysis 397
Communication skills 394
Communication technology 398
Communication types 406
Communications documentation 405
Communications management plan 399, 551
Composite organization 51
Computerized/Monte Carlo estimating 177
Conduct procurements process 510
Configuration management 93
Configuration management activities 94
Configuration management plan 90
Configuration management system 94
Conflicting stakeholder interests 548
Conflict management 364
Conflict resolution 369
Constraints 81
Contingency reserves 462
Contingent response strategies 460
Continuous improvement (Kaizen) 290
Contract administrator 524
Contract awards 517
Contract file 97
Contracting 437
  Centralized 524
  Decentralized 524
Contract interpretation 517